France and Algeria

Florida A&M University, Tallahassee
Florida Atlantic University, Boca Raton
Florida Gulf Coast University, Ft. Myers
Florida International University, Miami
Florida State University, Tallahassee
University of Central Florida, Orlando
University of Florida, Gainesville
University of North Florida, Jacksonville
University of South Florida, Tampa
University of West Florida, Pensacola

France and Algeria

A History of Decolonization
and Transformation

Phillip C. Naylor

University Press of Florida

Gainesville · Tallahassee · Tampa · Boca Raton
Pensacola · Orlando · Miami · Jacksonville · Ft. Myers

Copyright 2000 by the Board of Regents of the State of Florida
Printed in the United States of America on acid-free paper
All rights reserved

05   04   03   02   01   00   6   5   4   3   2   1

Excerpts from *Songs of the F.L.N.*, copyright Folkways Records,
   Album No. FD 5441, copyright 1962. Reprinted with permission.
Excerpt from "Some Kinda Love" by Lou Reed, copyright 1991
   Metal Machine Music, Inc., appeared in *Between Thought and
   Expression: Selected Lyrics of Lou Reed,* published by Hyperion.
   For information contact Hyperion, 114 Fifth Avenue, New York,
   N.Y. 10011. Reprinted with permission.

ISBN 0-8130-1801-3
Library of Congress Cataloging-in-Publication Data are available.

The University Press of Florida is the scholarly publishing agency for
the State University System of Florida, comprising Florida A&M
University, Florida Atlantic University, Florida Gulf Coast University,
Florida International University, Florida State University, University
of Central Florida, University of Florida, University of North Florida,
University of South Florida, and University of West Florida.

University Press of Florida
15 Northwest 15th Street
Gainesville, FL 32611-2079
http://www.upf.com

To my parents,
Alexander Chiviges
and
Sappho Dereby

Relations between France and Algeria
cannot be so simple or indifferent.
Michel Jobert

Relations between Algeria and France are always important.
When they are bad, they are important. When they are good,
they are also important.
Abdelaziz Bouteflika

Contents

Maps and Tables

Maps

Tables

Preface

The relationship between France and Algeria did not end in 1962. Yet it seemed that way, given the relative lack of scholarly attention devoted to the relationship's postcolonial history as compared with the colonial experience. I felt that there was a need to continue the inquiry, the story. As I researched the postcolonial relationship, my mentor, David E. Gardinier, advised that I study it comprehensively. Having already introduced me to Frantz Fanon's work when I was a graduate student, Professor Gardinier insisted that the complexities of the relationship needed a survey in breadth and depth. This has resulted in a sweeping study ranging from *beur* novels to Saharan hydrocarbon condensates. Though the book should interest a variety of specialized audiences, my chief purpose was to write a detailed historical narrative. My hope is that it will inspire other inquiries concerning the postcolonial histories of former metropolitan powers and their ex-colonies.

I tried to live this history. My research has taken me from the corporate headquarters of French and Algerian hydrocarbons enterprises to the refugee tents of proud Sahrawis displaced by the war in Western Sahara. I traveled with Algerian emigrant workers across the Mediterranean and shared meals with *pieds-noirs, harkis,* and Polisario cadres. I also discussed the relationship or conducted formal interviews with a variety of people. I thank them for their kindness and consideration. They included Maurice Couve de Murville, Olivier Wormser, Louis Joxe, Bernard Tricot, Georges Gorse, François Scheer, Jean Basdevant, Marcel Crozatier, Georges Jasseron, Stéphane Hessel, Vincent Labouret, Michel Schneider-Manoury, Marcelle Routier, Jean-Pierre Gonon, Nicole Grimaud, Jean Déjeux, Alain Gillette, Mohamed Sahnoun, Mihoubi el-Mihoub, Abdelhak Belghit, Messafeur Abbas, Kamal Nefti, Ali Khamis, Madjid Abdallah, Mohamed Salem Ould Salek, the Bachaga Said, and Ali Boualam. The Association France-Algérie (Michèle Moreau) provided research facilities and contacts. The United States embassy in Algiers provided gracious hospitality under Ambassadors Ulric Haynes Jr. and Michael Newlin and their respective staffs. I was also very well received by the Algerian United Nations delegation and the Algerian embassy in Washington, D.C.

Librarians at the following institutions provided invaluable assistance: in Aix-en-Provence, the Archives d'outre-mer and the Centre de recher-

ches et d'études sur les sociétés méditerranéennes; in Paris, the Bibliothèque de la Documentation française and the Institut d'études politiques;
in Algiers, the Bibliothèque nationale, the Centre national d'études historiques, and the Université d'Alger; and in the United States, Marquette
University (Dennis Higgins and Rose Trupiano), Northwestern University
(Mette Shayne and Hans Panofsky), Boston University (Gretchen Walsh),
Merrimack College (Sandy Thomas), Harvard University, and the University of Wisconsin-Milwaukee.

I appreciated the collegial and departmental support at Marquette
University and Merrimack College. The book also benefited from my affiliations at the African Studies Center at Boston University and the Center
for Middle Eastern Studies at Harvard University. Special thanks for the
contributions and encouragement of David E. Gardinier, John P. Entelis,
Robert A. Mortimer, Alf Andrew Heggoy, Lewis Livesay, Yahia Zoubir,
Susan G. Miller, Peter Ford, Edward G. Roddy, David Knepper, Muhammad Bakr Alwan, Abd al-Hamid Alwan, Brigitte Coste, Sylvia Pressman,
Paula Dicks, Carl Schwartz, Thomas C. Anderson, Donna Schenstrom,
and Kevin Lacey. Many others provided encouragement and support
over the years. Among them were Jim Jablonowski, John J. Steinberger,
OSA, Dan Schmidt, Pete deRosa, Don Tubman, Ivan Peterlin, Nick Top-
ping, Jerome Hardt, Gary Giesemann, Helen Bistis, Thomas E. Hachey, F.
Paul Prucha, SJ, Robert W. Reichert, Ronald and Olive Johnson, Mike
Gregory, Elsie D. Mack, Moody Prior, Constance Cryer Ecklund, Esther
Masters, and Thelma and Andy Hamilton. Chris Hofgren of the University Press of Florida conscientiously and constantly pursued this manuscript; I appreciate the particular attention to the manuscript and its production by Jacqueline Kinghorn Brown of the University Press of Florida
and by copy editor Ann Marlowe.

My parents instilled a deep interest in travel and scholarship. This book
is dedicated to them. My brother has profoundly influenced the development of my historical consciousness and transcultural interests. My family
has been exceptionally understanding and considerate. Thank you all.

A note on transliterations: I used familiar spellings for Arabic persons
and places, for example, the transliterated French Ahmed Tewfiq for
Ahmad Tawfiq. While Ali Ben (Bin) Hajj or Ben Hadj is now common, it
was initially Belhadj in the Arabic and French press and is still often
spelled that way in English publications. Where a standard English form
exists (Algiers, Muslim, the prophet Muhammad), this is used, although
diverse persons may spell their names Mohamed, Mohammed, or M'ham-

med. I kept Pouvoir in French and *fitna* in Arabic since these words appear in popular as well as scholarly print.

During a photographic exploration of Algiers's labyrinthine Casbah, I came across a little girl who was playing alone. She saw me, smiled, and began to dance. To me she symbolized Algeria, and I hope that, twenty years later, as her country emerges from a violent decade, she dances again.

Abbreviations

AAN—*Annuaire de l'Afrique du Nord*
AD—*Articles et documents* (Documentation française)
AFP—Agence France-Presse
AI—*Algérie informations* (Association France-Algérie)
APS—Algérie Presse Service
AUFS:NAS—*American Universities Field Staff: North African Series*
BG—*Boston Globe*
CCCE—Caisse centrale de coopération économique
CNRS—Editions du Centre national de la recherche scientifique
CR—*Country Report* (EIU)
CRESM—Centre de recherches et d'études sur les sociétés
 méditerranéennes
CSM—*Christian Science Monitor*
CT—*Coopération technique*
DA—dinars algériens
EIU—Economist Intelligence Unit
E-M—*El-Moudjahid*
ENAL—Entreprise nationale du livre
F-A—*France-Algérie* (Association France-Algérie)
FBIS—Foreign Broadcast Information Services
FF—French francs
FT—*Financial Times*
LM—*Le Monde*
LMdipl—*Le Monde diplomatique*
MEED—*Middle East Economic Digest*
MEJ—*Middle East Journal*
MERIP—*Middle East Research & Information Project*
MMBtu—million British thermal units
MTM—*Marchés tropicaux du monde* (to 1958), then *Marchés
 tropicaux et méditerranéens*
ND—*Notes et études documentaires* (Documentation française)
NES—*Near East South Asia Series* (FBIS)
NYT—*New York Times*
OECD—Organization for Economic Cooperation and Development
PE—*Petroleum Economist*

PEF—Politique étrangère de la France (Documentation française)
PPS—Petroleum Press Service (after 1 January 1974 *PE*)
PUF—Presses Universitaires de France
QER—Quarterly Economic Report (EIU)
RA—Révolution africaine
*RASJEP—Revue algérienne de sciences juridiques, économiques, et
    politiques*
*RASJPES—Revue algérienne de sciences juridiques, politiques,
    économiques et sociales* (to 1968, then *RASJEP*)
RDN—Revue de défense nationale
RFEPA—Revue française d'études politiques africaines
SNED—Société nationale d'édition et de diffusion
SONATRACH—Société nationale pour la recherche, la production, la
    transport, transformation et la commercialisation des hydrocarbons
TN—Textes et Notes (Documentation française)
WEU—Western Europe Series (FBIS)
WSJ—Wall Street Journal

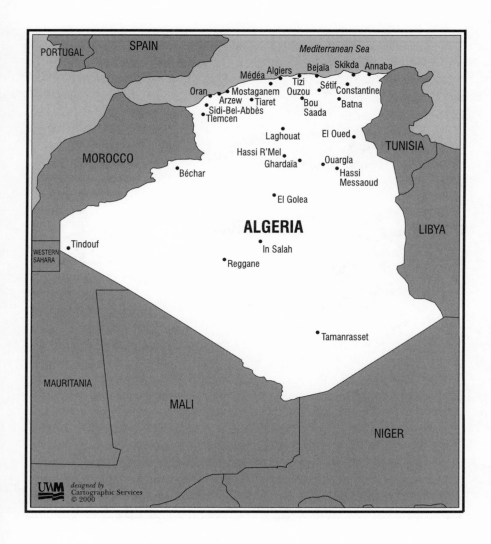

PORTUGAL

SPAIN

Mediterranean Sea

Médéa   Algiers   Bejaïa   Skikda   Annaba
                              Tizi
Oran   Mostaganem   Ouzou   Sétif   Constantine
        Arzew   Tiaret   Bou   Batna
    Sidi-Bel-Abbès   Saada
    Tlemcen

                Laghouat   El Oued

        Hassi R'Mel   Ouargla
            Ghardaïa   Hassi
                                    Messaoud
    Béchar

                El Golea

            ALGERIA

MOROCCO   TUNISIA

                                            LIBYA

WESTERN
SAHARA   Tindouf   In Salah

            Reggane

                        Tamanrasset

MAURITANIA

        MALI

                            NIGER

UWM   designed by
       Cartographic Services
       © 2000

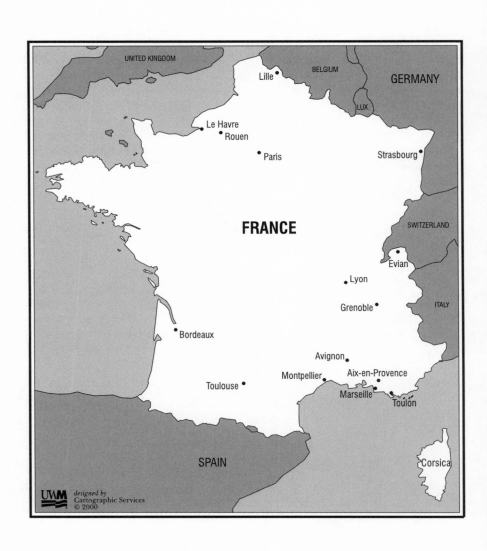

Prologue

On 1 July 1962, Algerians massively voted for independence not "from France" but "in cooperation with France." The referendum marked a reformulation rather than a repudiation of the relationship between the metropolitan power and the ex-colony.[1] Colonialism had ended, but a French presence persisted and in many ways still predominated. This resulted in a complex, protracted transformation for both countries rather than a simpler transfer of power and identity.

France's transformation relied upon its enduring essentialism. With a glorious history of *grandeur* (i.e., political, cultural, moral greatness) and independence, its unique spirit or essence had been expressed for centuries as a powerful imperial identity, a gratifying atavism. During the late 1950s and early 1960s, Charles de Gaulle masterly reworked the imperial discourse by presenting the ideal of a "renovated" France "wedded to new realities" operating independently between the monolithic superpowers. To de Gaulle, the end of empire marked the beginning of a new enterprise offering opportunities to influence the world again, as only "eternal France" could, as a great contributor of culture and civilization. He opened his *Memoirs of Hope* with this characteristic essentialist observation: "France has emerged from the depths of the past. She is a living entity. She responds to the call of the centuries. Yet she remains herself through time."[2] This "timeless" heroic perception, a powerful idealization of France as a great and independent power, expedited the transition from colonialism to "cooperation." De Gaulle's essentialist vision, which also ascribed a strategic importance to postcolonial Algeria, appealed to his successors in the Elysée Palace.

Algeria's transformation, on the other hand, projected an existentialism. The new nation found itself dislocated by the multiple disorientations and deprivations caused by 132 years of colonialism compounded by its War of Independence (1954–62). Though the Front de Libération Nationale (FLN) succeeded in producing a polity, it had deferred defining specific economic, social, and cultural programs. Consequently, the FLN's primary postcolonial objective was to conceive and construct a state. According to one official publication: "Real independence remains incomplete if it does not liberate both the land and the soul of the people. Algeria recovered by the Algerians does not suffice. The Algerians must re-become and remain themselves."[3] This constituted existential engagement. The

FLN posited that by freeing Algeria from its perpetuated postcolonial dependence upon France, it would finally experience an authentic liberation. The Revolution continued to serve as a unifying matrix, and Algerian governments sustained a revolutionary discourse after independence, though in practice this meant delicate and pragmatic compromises with the neocolonial contradictions inherent in French cooperation.

Therefore, in many ways decolonization was not over in 1962. Instead there was an ongoing transformation of bilateral power, perception, and identity. The strong French economic and cultural presence in Algeria necessitated a number of postcolonial decolonizations. To borrow from David Prochaska's important work on colonial history, Algeria engaged in the postcolonial task of "making Algeria Algerian." Concurrently, France endeavored to redefine itself as a postimperial power while evoking its traditional essentialist ideals of independence and occasionally grandeur.

Beginning with the October 1988 riots, the bilateral relationship entered a convulsive period of discontinuity and displacement. In Foucauldian terms, it represented an epistemic shift where the relationship's familiar discourse and practice, even its recurrent psychodramas, dispersed. This was primarily because Algeria's "second revolution" discredited the FLN's legacy and legitimacy. It repudiated the power apparatus that had dictated the country's destiny since 1962. The subsequent democratization, destabilization, and, after President Chadli Benjedid's deposal in January 1992, the fierce *fitna*, or "trial" of itself as a nation, collectively confirmed Algeria's persistent existential predicament: an inability to define and develop a consensual national identity. France's ambivalent response to these events indicated that it, too, had difficulty adapting to and accepting the rapidly changing conditions in Algeria. French governments on the right and left considered Algeria "the door to the Third World," a bilateral means to multilateral ends. The objective was to establish or perpetuate positive and occasionally privileged relations with Algeria to enhance France's image among developing nations and to extend its influence as a great and independent power. Algeria's fall from Third World exemplar to embarrassment had profound ramifications for France: it marked the end of a strategic political equation. Compounded by post–Cold War geopolitics, France's self-perceived importance — long regarded as anachronistic by many critical specialists, given the country's real power and influence — now needed reformulation. Above all, the crisis ushered in a new period that tragically recalled an old one, the colonial past. As in 1962, France again faced refashioning its essentialist identity as Algeria, once more a profoundly strife-torn country, pursued its existential project to restore self and state.

This study surveys the multiplicity of histories composing their complex bilateral relationship. It invokes the French essentialist perspective and the Algerian existentialist praxis not as thematic reductions or totalizing metahistorical typologies but as active "ordering frameworks," providing coherence and intelligibility to a complicated network of political, economic, social, and cultural relations. The frameworks present dispositions as well as discourses. Historically, they have subjectified and then often objectified the reception and perception of the other. They have created or mediated knowledge, power, and identity.[4] The frameworks serve, too, as interpretive grids that help explain how juxtaposed historical continuities and discontinuities, reconstituted legitimacies, and imagined national identities produced paradoxes such as independence with dependence and conflict yet cooperation. The French-Algerian relationship, an unparalleled case study in postcolonial history, not only invites a sweeping yet syncretic historical methodology and inquiry, but insists upon such an approach.

There have been several specific works concerning the postcolonial relationship.[5] Bilateral ideological and economic differences producing a multitude of political and social contentions and crises are considered by Inga Brandell in *Les Rapports franco-algériens depuis 1962* (1981) and especially detailed by Salah Mouhoubi in *La Politique de coopération algéro-française* (1986). In the brief *Algérie: Avec ou sans la France* (1973), Jean Offredo contends that France's inability to accept Algeria's independence was the primary cause of postcolonial problems. Ahmad Nazali's *Relations between Algeria and France* (in Arabic, 1978) emphasizes the overriding political nature of the relationship during the immediate postcolonial period. Nicole Grimaud's numerous articles and her first three chapters in *La Politique extérieure de l'Algérie* (1984) underscore the fundamental political and psychological nature of this relationship. Benjamin Stora in *La Gangrène et l'oubli* (1992) examines the War of Independence's influence upon the national memories of both countries and has inspired a variety of similar works.[6] Given its intricacies and intimacies, the study of French-Algerian relations demands pluralist approaches that take into account cultural representations alongside material realities, qualitative and quantitative analyses, epistemological as well as economic explanations, and, of course, both contesting and collaborating voices. For example, statistics and novels complement each other to disclose the dilemmas confronted by the Algerian immigrant community in France. The strategic value of hydrocarbons equates with independence and identity as well as with viscosity and volume.

This book begins by briefly examining the colonial period leading to decolonization and the Evian Accords, which formalized an unavoidably incomplete transfer of power. The subsequent historical narrative of the postcolonial relationship, plotted along the essentialist-existentialist interpretive grids, charts chronologically the continuing transformation of a constellation of relations up to the intersection of tragic contemporary events. The book concludes with an evaluation of the relationship through a variety of perspectives, including recent postcolonial theory.

Since 1962, both France and Algeria have understood the special importance of the other and have even mirrored broad objectives. Each nation has also targeted the other in pursuit of its own strategic interests. This has resulted in a complicated recent history characterized by unique tangible and intangible influences. The postcolonial French-Algerian relationship, like its colonial predecessor, possesses an exceptional character and significance.

|

French-Algerian Colonial Relations, 1830–1958

The coming age is none other than that of turmoils.
That state of living man is no longer anything but a state;
Those who are dead are at ease.
Shaykh Si Abd al-Qadir

Colonization will not stop with the conquest: in time,
it will invade everything.
Marshal Thomas-Robert Bugeaud, *De la colonisation de l'Algérie*

A consideration of the colonial period is indispensable for understanding the postcolonial relationship. French colonialism imposed itself throughout Algerian life, transforming matter and mind while instituting a coercive system that ultimately impelled violent revolution. It offered protective myths and mentalities to the colonialists while obliterating the collective properties as well as personalities of the colonized. Above all, it framed the modern relationship by ordering and regulating knowledge, power, and, especially, identity. It regulated binary subjectification and subsequently objectification, the "othering" of the French and the Algerian communities.

Algeria's Existential Predicament

Besides announcing the beginning of the revolution against French colonialism, the FLN's Proclamation of 1 November 1954 listed grievances and goals, including the extraordinary demand for the abrogation of "all edicts, decrees, and laws . . . denying the history, geography, language, religion, and customs of the Algerian people."[1] By calling for the "restoration of the . . . Algerian State within the framework of Islamic principles" and the "recognition of Algerian nationality," the FLN targeted colonialism's denial of the idea of a historical Algerian past. France would have to acknowledge not only Algeria's independence but also, implicitly, its extant historical and national identities. What made this existential objective problematic, however, was the FLN's own inherent difficulty in defining those identities, i.e., an authentic national consciousness, an inclusive ideology, and a consensual imagination of an Algerian nation. The fundamental reason for this dilemma was that the FLN itself was a product of the system that it aimed to destroy.

Precolonial Polities

An established Algerian "nation," in the modern sense of the word, was nonexistent when the French invaded in 1830, but there was a distinct sense of community. Indeed, the geopolitical trilateralism of the Maghrib today dates from the thirteenth-century disintegration of the Almohad Empire with the emergence of the Hafsids in Tunisia, the Abd al-Wadids in Algeria at Tlemcen, and the Marinids in Morocco. During the Ottoman period, the demarcations were redrawn as the Tunisian Husaynid beylik, the Algerian deylik (known as the Regency), and the Moroccan sharifian Saadian and Alawi sultanates. The Algiers Regency acted as a sovereign state and concluded treaties with many nations. The distinguished historian and nationalist Ahmed Tewfiq al-Madani referred to it as the "first Algerian state" and as the "Algerian Ottoman Republic." He lauded it as a defender of Islam.[2] After the fall of Algiers and Dey Husayn's capitulation to Marshal Louis de Bourmont on 5 July 1830, the bey of Constantine, Ahmad Hajj, sought to perpetuate the Ottoman presence. From 1836 to 1837, he stoutly defended his city against the French. The tribes in the interior also viewed the French as political and cultural threats. Alf Andrew Heggoy believed the assistance provided to the Regency by usually non-cooperative tribes "indicated that an Algerian state or, at the very least, an embryonic Algerian nationalism existed."[3]

The emir Abd al-Qadir became an inspiration and paradigm for independent Algeria by creating, through military prowess and astute diplomacy, a veritable state in western Algeria in the 1830s, seriously rivaling French territorial ambitions. In the Treaty of Tafna (1837), the French acknowledged his political authority.[4] Conflicting ambitions between the Algerian emirate and France eventually provoked war leading finally to Abd al-Qadir's surrender in 1847. The subsequent serious rebellions of the Awlad Sidi Shaykh in 1864 and of Muqrani and the (Berber) Kabyles in 1871 had less to do with specific oppressive colonial policies than with the French refusal to recognize tribal procedure, prestige, and dignity.[5] The establishment of the Third Republic, compounded by the exhaustion of the indigenous population after the Revolt of 1871, entrenched the colonial system by disinheriting and disorienting the colonized.

An Existential Economic and Social Dislocation

The colonized's military subjugation ineluctably led to the massive expropriation of their land and properties and to their supplantation by colonial settlers (*colons/pieds-noirs*).[6] Pierre Bourdieu explained that expropriations "were conceived . . . as measures that would lead to the destruction of the fundamental structure of the economy and of the traditional society."[7] When France took over Algiers, it immediately claimed all beylik/ crown and religiously endowed lands (*habous/habus*). The Ordinances of the mid-1840s, the Sénatus-Consulte of 1863, the failure of the Revolt of 1871, and the Warnier Law of 1873 offered Europeans and wealthy Muslims vast opportunities for land speculation.[8] From 1830–1940 the colonized lost 3,445,000 hectares.[9] The introduction of intensive viticulture, particularly as a result of the European phylloxera blight of the 1870s and 1880s, reflected an economic dimension to the existential disposition of this relationship. It was a stark repudiation of the colonized's identity, given the Muslim proscription of alcohol. Vineyards replaced wheat fields to maximize profits as hunger haunted the colonized masses. The territorial investment devoted to viticulture expanded from 40,000 hectares in 1880 to 400,000 in 1940.[10]

Dispossession reduced the colonized to destitution (Germaine Tillion's coined *clochardisation*). The land left to them was usually poor and cultivable only by traditional methods that hastened erosion, diminishing returns, and, ultimately, the grim consequence of soil exhaustion, starvation. Without a dynamic second sector to absorb its rising "subproletarian" numbers, the desperate colonized (and colonial authorities) confronted a Malthusian nightmare.[11] Many Muslims, especially Kabyles, risked social dishonor and sought subsistence in France, rather than joining the hundreds of thousands unemployed or underemployed in Algeria. The European settlers regretted this loss of labor but generally ignored the harsh reality of a colonialism that inexorably excluded native economic participation.

Emigration began in the late nineteenth century. During World War I, 119,000 Algerian workers arrived in France to labor in factories.[12] By 1948 there were 180,000 emigrant workers in the *métropole;* their numbers rose to 280,000 four years later.[13] The Algerian emigrant workers accepted the lowliest jobs to support family in Algeria and France. They became familiar reminders of colonial victimization. They confronted physical abuse and cultural discrimination. Their children, known as "the second generation," anguished during the postcolonial period over an identity suspended between Algerian and French cultures—yet another dimension of the existential quandary.

French education, given its restricted accessibility and its assimilationist nature, further fragmented the colonized. Students discovered that even their Muslim instructors believed that French values and institutions ensured genuine progress.[14] Colonial curricula taught Arabic, the sacred language of the Qur'an, as a foreign language. Though there were some important educational initiatives after World War II, by 1954 more than 90 percent of the colonized were illiterate and only one out of ten Muslim children attended primary school.[15]

The economic and social consequences of colonialism were physical, psychological, and profoundly personal. Mostefa Lacheraf viewed it as an "obscurantist" system that "decultured" the indigenous society.[16] Frantz Fanon observed that the colonized's culture "becomes closed, fixed in the colonial status, caught in the yoke of oppression. Both present and mummified, it testifies against its members. . . . The cultural mummification leads to a mummification of individual thinking."[17] In an earlier work, Fanon defined the trauma of French colonialism on the colonized as a "massive psychoexistential complex."[18] This involved philosophical and historical questions concerning identity, compounded by psychological inferiorities derived chiefly from economic inequality, racism, and cultural prejudice. It was more than an inferiority complex: it was "a feeling of non-existence."[19] The imposition of foreign social values confronted and confused traditions, thereby exacerbating the colonized's condition.[20] A deep individual and collective alienation resulted in distorted social and spatial structures. Dualisms appeared, sometimes described by analysts as "Manichaean" or "binary," such as colonialist and colonized urban quarters[21] and modern and traditional sectors in the agricultural economy. These convulsive conditions generated defiant but divided elites.

Imaginings of a Nation: Literary Elites

Algerian literary elites disclosed other dimensions of the colonized's existential predicament. At first, Algerian francophone literature illustrated the intrusion of French cultural chauvinism. Native novels (1900–50) produced in French were often efforts to prove to the colonialists that the colonized could compose in the settlers' language using proper syntax, style, and vocabulary. France was regarded as the *mère patrie*.[22] Jean Amrouche, a Christian Kabyle, emerged as the greatest figure during this period. Unlike his contemporaries, however, Amrouche began a quest to discover a pure, precolonial Algerian personality as he realized the contradictions of his own. During the War of Independence, he revealed poignantly how colonialism had afflicted his spiritual self: "France is the spirit of my soul, Algeria is the soul of my spirit."[23] His great essay "L'Eternel Jugurtha" (1946), on the enduring ideal of an Algerian nation, illuminated both the predicament and the promise of a hybrid identity.[24]

In the 1950s a group of remarkable young francophone writers, imbued with the tensions of Algerian nationalism, strove to create a national consciousness and liberate it, too, from colonialism. They included Mouloud Feraoun, Mouloud Mammeri, Malek Haddad, Mohammed Dib, and Kateb Yacine. Their common theme was the cultural alienation (to Haddad an "asphyxia") caused by colonialism. Their novels collectively described the dilemmas of francophone native elites accepted neither at home nor in the *métropole*, the differences between generations, the social dualisms such as traditionalism/modernism that characterized Algerian society, and eventually the hostilities provoked by the War of Liberation. Malek Haddad resented the "depersonalization" caused by colonialism as painfully demonstrated by his inability to express himself adequately in Arabic. He lamented that "the French language is my exile."[25] They shared an "existential trope." Kateb Yacine particularly layered existential themes in his internationally acclaimed Faulkneresque novel *Nedjma* and his play *Le Cadavre encerclé*. These works examined the actions and imaginations of a group of characters searching individual daemons while exploring personal links with an ancient, unstained Algerian heritage.

The young writers also reacted to the portrayals of Algeria by "others," meaning Europeans. For example, Mouloud Feraoun, a good friend of Nobel literary laureate Albert Camus, criticized the noted *pied-noir* for ignoring Muslims in his description of Oran in *The Plague*.[26] Kateb Yacine criticized also Camus's "surface" portrayals of Algeria and his "exoticism" in *The Stranger* and other works.[27]

Arabophone literature, especially historiography, predated the published national consciousness of the francophone writers. Muhammad al-Mili in his history of Algeria (1931) especially targeted the circumscribed historical consciousness of Algerian intellectuals (*mut'alimin*, or the "learned"). He criticized how "they severed the link with their past," which resulted ultimately in their "alienation from their fellow citizens" (*bani jinsihi*).[28] A member of the Association of Reformist Ulama founded by Abd al-Hamid Ben Badis in 1931, al-Mili viewed history as a means for illustrating how the past can serve the present and future. Shaykh Ben Badis was deeply impressed with al-Mili's work and suggested the book be titled "Algeria's Life."[29] In the complementary *Kitab al-Jaza'ir* (Book of

Algeria) (1931), Ahmed Tewfiq al-Madani, another Ulama brother, urged the youth of Algeria, "the spirit of this noble nation," to discover the reality of an Algerian state. He indicted the older generation who "are ignorant of everything about the Algerian nation." Al-Madani appealed to the youth to embrace the Ulama's "precepts, in life and deed, these words: Islam is my religion; Arabic is my language; Algeria is my nation."[30] Though few of the colonized could read Arabic, these histories represented a call to Algerians to examine themselves in order to develop both a historical and a national consciousness.

The Political Elite: Diversity and Division

In many ways, the revolutionary FLN was a historical recapitulation as well as a culmination of nationalist elite development. It defined itself as a unified front of different political persuasions though it was, as the venerable but disaffected nationalist Messali Hadj claimed, "a movement full of contradictions and confusions."[31] Its young leadership that splintered from Messali was tempered by the Sétif-Guelma atrocities of May 1945, the "Berberist crisis" of the late 1940s, the suppression of the paramilitary OS (*Organisation Spéciale;* many had been members), and the MTLD (*Mouvement du Triomphe des Libertés Démocratiques*) split of 1953. Nevertheless, they shared Messali's populist objectives, the foremost being the establishment of an independent Algerian state.[32] The liberal *évolués,* personified by Ferhat Abbas, who reluctantly joined the Front in 1956, evolved from initially earnest assimilationists, who questioned the possibility of a national polity, to nationalists who still wished to preserve a special relationship with France.[33] The Ulama, with their commitment to cultural affirmation, representing the third major nationalist component of the FLN, also joined well after the conflict began. In January 1956, Ahmed Tewfiq al-Madani, their secretary-general, called for "the free existence of an Algerian nation along with its specific personality."[34]

Given its educational, social, and political differences that were further compounded by internal/external, Arab/Berber, and civilian/military rivalries, it was impossible for the FLN to embrace a common ideology save for the eradication of French colonialism, the restoration of an authentic identity, and the inauguration of an independent nation. The inability to develop institutions as well as programs prevented compromise or political pluralism, thus in effect repudiating Algeria's nationalist legacy. It meant that the dominating group's exercise of power would have to produce truth or myth and its own legitimacy—an exclusive rather than inclusive imagination of nation. Eventually, this was disclosed by the continued postcolonial articulation of a revolutionary discourse, a "metanarrative," as a means for providing a semblance of what was in reality a lost unity rather than a genuine national identity. The consequences of the irreconcilable nationalist movement contributed significantly to the tragic political and cultural traditions in contemporary Algeria.[35]

The Revolution as an Existential Project

Albert Camus moralized that "one can rebel against lies as against oppression."[36] Ironically, the Algerian revolutionaries fulfilled Camusian conditions for "metaphysical revolt" or "the movement by which man protests against his condition and against the whole of creation. . . . The metaphysical rebel protests against the condition in which he finds himself as a man."[37] The FLN asserted: "We do not only want to liberate ourselves from colonialism. We also want to construct a new society."[38] Fanon believed that the struggle for independence would eliminate the psychoexistential affliction and transform the values and structures of Algerian society.[39] "At the level of individuals, violence is a cleansing force," the dying theorist wrote. "It frees the native from his inferiority complex and from his despair and inaction; it makes him fearless and restores his self-respect."[40] Slimane Chikh complemented these ideas: "The colonized in taking arms creates himself, because he creates his own history and forges his own destiny and becomes a *historical subject.*"[41] Simply, the violence, such as the bloody assaults at Philippeville (1955) and the Battle of Algiers (1956–57), finally forced the colonialist to recognize the colonized. Therefore, liberation to the Algerian revolutionaries was also an existential praxis. *El-Moudjahid,* the official organ of the FLN, underscored that "the misery, the material privations, were not the most painful. It is on the moral plane, in its personality, in its dignity, where the Algerian people felt French domination's most profound blow."[42]

Nevertheless, when Messali asked: "What exactly is your political program?" the FLN could not respond decisively.[43] In 1956, Mohammed Larbi Ben M'hidi expected "a Democratic and Social Republic"[44] as declared by the Proclamation of 1 November and anticipated by the Soummam Conference Platform, constructed in August–September 1956. Four years later, however, Lakhdar Ben Tobbal, eventually an Evian negotiator, illustrated elite uncertainty when he reflected: "We are not saying that Algeria will be socialist. . . . The political, economic, social, and diplomatic future can only be precisely defined by an elected assembly."[45]

The FLN's economic positions mirrored the political uncertainty. Ben M'hidi projected a "socialist system" that would initiate "profound and revolutionary agrarian reforms."[46] The Soummam Conference (August–September 1956) enunciated the need for agrarian reform after the "destruction of colonialism," and this was often repeated in *El-Moudjahid*.[47] The FLN seemed attracted to Maoist mobilization of the peasantry, yet the Proclamation of 1 November stipulated respect for private property. Consider another example of ambiguity: "[Economic development strategy] must be both destructive and constructive. Destructive, in that it will have to break the ties of dependency linking the nation to the dominant country. . . . Constructive at the same time because it must correspondingly organize an economic system oriented towards the satisfaction of internal needs and . . . development."[48] Could France be excluded? A more precise economic direction was qualified, too, by the future status of the settler establishment in an independent Algeria; a significant settler presence was anticipated in postcolonial Algeria.[49] Saad Dahlab, who would play such an important role in negotiating with the French, stated that Algeria's colonial economy needed to be transformed into a national economy. Nevertheless, he asserted that this "is not incompatible with the interests of France."[50]

The FLN certainly understood that decolonization would not be completed with political independence; a social and economic task remained and with it an insistent, if paradoxical, postcolonial liberation struggle. As the nationalists prepared to negotiate with Gaullist France, the identity of the future Algerian state still remained undetermined and, most important, undefined. What was clear especially during the negotiation of the Evian Accords was that Algeria's future relations would be inevitably configured against and with France.

France's Essentialist Perspective

Since the conquest of Algiers on 5 July 1830, France often identified its power and potential, its grandeur and independence, in relation to Algeria. This profoundly differentiated Algeria, even with its obvious strategic geopolitical significance, from the *métropole*'s other overseas territories. Algeria particularly appealed to France's imagination of itself as a great power, an acutely sensitized national identity. Therefore, the irrepressible arguments which inspired French imperialism in Algeria remained compelling during decolonization, and later, too, in the postcolonial era, which produced recodified discourses and practices founded on familiar essentialist dispositions. An imperative emerged and endured: a perpetuation of a French presence in Algeria.

Algeria and the Imperial Impulsion

Initially, Paris's imperialist ambitions toward Algiers were incidental to France's internal affairs. Exploiting old commercial and political disputes with the dey of Algiers, Charles X, the last Bourbon monarch, ordered an expedient attack to shift the attention of his subjects, restless with his ultraconservative policies at home, toward exciting foreign adventures. Algeria became a means to serve Bourbon internal and external interests. Not surprisingly, Charles explained his decision with an essentialist rationale: "To take Algiers, I considered only the dignity of France, to keep or yield it, I will consider only its interest."[51] Marshal Louis de Bourmont, the commander of the expedition, asserted the self-appointed civilizing mission when he addressed his troops: "The cause of France is that of humanity."[52] Ironically, several days after the successful seizure of Algiers, liberal revolutionaries deposed Charles. His successor and Orleanist cousin, Louis-Philippe, desired to disassociate himself from Charles's policies, including the troubling Algiers affair. He feared that pursuing a military campaign in Algeria would alienate the French bourgeoisie who had placed him on the throne. Nevertheless, members of that class entertained ideas of colonial enterprise.[53] In 1833 Louis-Philippe dispatched a consultative Special Commission to Algeria to assist him in deciding upon the future French role in North Africa.

Using such discourse as *"grande"* and *"vaste entreprise"* — reiterated by Charles de Gaulle more than a century later — the commission contended that France, because of her strength, could undertake such a demanding project as the colonization of Algeria.[54] It was "a question of national self-respect."[55] "To abandon [it]," the report warned, "would be to expose France to derision." It would be viewed as an "act of weakness" or a "concession made to foreign influences."[56] The commission examined strategic considerations and claimed that Algeria would be "a possession both military and maritime . . . fortifying [French] influence."[57] It predicted that "a new population will consume the products of our manufacturers"[58] and projected "the development of a new people beneficial to the civilized world."[59] Sensitive to public satisfaction and pressure, the commission concluded that the "manifest expression of the national will" necessitated colonization.[60] This decisive argument persuaded Louis-Philippe to colonize Algeria.

The commission's argumentation clearly illustrated essentialist principles and perceptions. Grandeur and independence, complemented by the self-obligated mission of expanding the genius of French culture, related directly to an unchanging idealization of France. Economic concerns were secondary, though providing persuasive rationales inflating political prestige. Algeria was destined to be a mirror reflecting France's vision of itself as a world power.

Algeria and the Imperial Imagination: The *Pieds-noirs*

The "legalization" of Algeria as a French possession in July 1834 opened the territory to European settlers, who became known as *pieds-noirs*.[61] Though the *métropole* dispatched many social and political misfits to Algeria, *pieds-noirs* were also victims of European political upheaval and economic distress. Immigrants included Alsatians after the Franco-Prussian War (1870–71) and continental winegrowers withered by the phylloxera blight of 1880. Algeria became a "melting pot" of European nationalities. The settlers often related their experience to the much admired American model. By 1954, approximately half of the *pieds-noirs* were not of French origin.[62] Albert Camus wrote: "The French of Algeria are a bastard race, made up of unexpected mixtures."[63] In spite of their ethnopluralism or "hybridity," the settlers shared a profound love for the land and received a particular French identity from colonialism. This social and cultural legacy led to ruinous obsessions and ultimately tumultuous and traumatic consequences during decolonization.

Ian Clegg contended that the *pieds-noirs'* different backgrounds created a "desperate need for identity." They discovered "their basic unity in defence of the privileges accorded them by the French administration and their hostility to the Muslims. This appeared in an assertion of their basic Frenchness, in a fervour for things that far surpassed its equivalent in the metropolis. In this vision they . . . became the true guardians of French civilization."[64] Jean Plumyène and Raymond Lasierra perceived that there was a *pied-noir* "idealization of the *métropole*."[65] Fanon observed that the *pieds-noirs* considered themselves an "extension" of France.[66] Their political power was based on that presumption and, as events proved during decolonization, it was infectious. Fanon witnessed during the War of Independence that the *métropole's* "national consciousness has been conditioned by one simple principle—Algeria is France."[67] Political integration, however, was impossible.[68] Though the settlers were legally French citizens, they understood that they differed socially and culturally.[69] These differences, created by colonialism, led to misunderstandings with the *métropole*, political presumptions, and later, from the *pieds-noirs'* perspective, betrayal and abandonment.

Colonial literature illustrated settler conviction and culture. Louis

Bertrand, a stylist of the Mouvement Algérianiste, viewed the *pieds-noirs* as the inheritors of Latin Africa. In the preface of his *Les Villes d'or* (1921), he wrote: "French Africa today is Roman Africa, which continues to live, and has never ceased to live."[70] Albert Camus exemplified the romanticist Sensibilité Méditerranéenne group.[71] His works portrayed a unique Mediterranean temperament invoking Nature, especially the sun, sky, and sea.

As colonialism entrenched itself in Algeria, the *pieds-noirs* became consumed by illusions that distorted their historical perspective.[72] This explained their garrison mentality and opposition to change or reform. Colonialism produced the *pieds-noirs'* identity at the expense of the colonized. The European settlers' identity became inventive; it not only subordinated the native Muslims but also "inferiorized" them. Pierre Bourdieu observed that "the European gradually created an environment that reflected his own image . . . , a world in which he no longer felt himself to be a stranger and in which, by a natural reversal, the Algerian was finally considered to be the stranger."[73] Even in the works of Camus, a man with extraordinary sensitivities, Meursault thinks nothing of killing an Arab in *The Stranger* and Oran's epidemic seems to have remarkably spared the missing, omitted Muslim population in *The Plague*.[74] Camus's posthumous autobiographical novel *The First Man* centered on a *pied-noir's* obsessive search for a past, an identity;[75] the inclusion of Muslims was incidental and the idea of a Muslim identity not explored. Camus recognized, however, that the "first man" could possibly be a "last man," given the imminent end of colonial Algeria.[76]

Algeria and the Metropolitan Imagination

In general, the works of pamphleteers, historians, military men, and travelers fortified dominant colonialist rationales by ignoring or "forgetting" native realities, thereby reinforcing a numbing collective amnesia.[77] An array of literature extolled the civilizing mission while directly and indirectly repudiating the idea of a precolonial Muslim history or the very existence of a cultured and sophisticated people. Signaling the existential obliteration faced by the native population, metropolitan literature often presented Algeria as a virgin, even vacant, territory offering spectacular opportunities for France. An anonymous author spoke of "bringing civilization to barbarous regions, culture to lands practically abandoned."[78] Another conjectured that mineral wealth in the Atlas "must exist" and disparaged "the ignorance of the inhabitants" who had failed to mine it.[79]

France's ideal self-appointed charge was to create a modern, progressive identity for Algeria. To refuse to accept this national responsibility would be dishonorable. In 1832 the question was asked that would be repeated again (and answered) during decolonization: "Will France desert this especially noble mission that destiny appears to have confided to her?" The author believed that if France did not accept the mission it would be not only "cowardice" but also simply "impolitic" since even at this early time there was "growing national identification" (plus nationale en France) with the conquest.[80] This discourse constantly echoed throughout the colonial period. M. H. Fisquet proclaimed: "Today France has as its mission to preside over the formation of a new civilized nation."[81] Victor Hugo told a skeptical Marshal Thomas-Robert Bugeaud that the Algerian "conquest . . . is civilization marching against barbarousness. It is an enlightened people finding a people in the night. We are the Greeks of the world; it is up to us to illuminate the world."[82] Another author reiterated in essentialist terms that "to raise an empire, to create a society, to give birth (mettre au monde) to a new people, to increase the wealth, the grandeur, the strength of one's country, or simply to aid, even if from afar, in all of that, this is the supreme honor."[83] The centenary celebrations of French Algeria amplified this discourse, as demonstrated by the words of Léon Baréty, colonial undersecretary of state for the budget of Algeria: "To promote the evolution of backward people after uprooting them from a static state where they lay: there is not a more noble mission for a colonizing nation or a more ideal way to intend colonization."[84] It is no wonder that many equated decolonization with national decline and decadence. To their imaginations, Algeria mirrored France's political, cultural, and moral power and potential, its grandeur and independence.

Besides a civilizing mission linked to France's prestige, there was a corresponding Christianizing one.[85] During the celebration of the first Mass after the conquest of Algiers, the comte de Bourmont declared that the French had come "to reopen . . . the door of Christianity in Africa."[86] Edouard d'Ault-Dumesnil, a staff officer of de Bourmont, wrote a generation later that "the Christian conversion of Algerian Muslims is a duty that Providence has bestowed upon France."[87] After receiving an appointment to Algeria, Bishop (later Archbishop and Cardinal) Charles Lavigerie wrote to Governor-General MacMahon: "Algeria is the only door opened by Providence on a barbaric continent of two hundred million souls. It is especially there that we must bring the Catholic apostolate."[88] The metaphor of Algeria as a "door" would be applied, too, by the de Gaulle government when it spoke of extending French influence in Africa and the Third World. Lavigerie quickly established his mission-

ary *"pères blancs"* (White Fathers, officially called the Society of Mission-
aries of Africa) and pursued proselytism in Kabylia and the Sahara but
with limited success. The White Fathers also campaigned against slavery
and the slave trade. The ascetic mystical priest Charles de Foucauld
(1858–1916) moved into the deep Sahara, built a hermitage on Mount
Assekrem in the Ahaggar Mountains, and earned the respect of the
Tuareg. Though he failed to convert them, his presence still symbolized
France in the Sahara. Indeed, he often reported on tribal conditions and
attitudes in the Sahara. De Foucauld, like Cardinal Lavigerie, believed that
France had a Christian colonial mission. In December 1914 he wrote: "At
the moment we have fifty million infidels in our colonies: God has given us
charge over their souls in putting them under our dominion. Now, when
they are dying so as to defend us, now is surely the moment to remember
our duties towards them, of which the first is to try to win their salvation."[89] During the War of Independence, Robert Martel, a charismatic
"mystic-farmer" of the Mitijda and a political ultra, denounced
decolonization since he associated a Christian mission with the preservation of French Algeria.[90]

Barthélemy Prosper (Père) Enfantin, Marshal Thomas-Robert Bugeaud, and Ismaël Urbain imagined Algeria as a social laboratory for their
utopian plans of colonization. Urbain, a Saint-Simonian, influenced Napoleon III's fanciful and romantic view of Algeria as an "Arab kingdom,"
which particularly rankled the settlers. Honoré de Balzac supported the
colonization of Algeria while Alphonse Daudet satirized it. Théophile
Gautier was awed by the country's fabulous beauty. Victor Hugo lionized
Abd al-Qadir as a vehicle to vent his hostility toward Napoleon III. The
canvasses of Eugène Delacroix, Théodore Chassériau, Jules Meunier,
Pierre Renoir, and Henri Matisse romanticized Algerian subjects and land-
scapes.[91] Even a young Charles de Gaulle imagined the life of a lovelorn
spahi officer in southern Algeria.[92] Postcards and travel posters advertised
images of an exotic colonialism which were reinforced, too, by occasional
spectacular colonial exhibitions such as that in Paris in 1931.

The correlative political power produced by these conscious and un-
conscious fabrications or "knowledge" of Algeria deflected infrequent
metropolitan reform initiatives, e.g., the critical Senate investigations during the 1890s, the Clemenceau-Jonnart post–World War I legislation, and
the Blum-Viollette Bill of 1936 which aimed to establish and extend full
French citizenship rights to select Muslims. The *métropole* dismissed
Charles-André Julien's efforts to restore a sense of historicism with his
brilliant *Histoire de L'Afrique du Nord* (1931), which refuted the impres-

sion that Algeria had no significant history before the French colonization. In *L'Algérie, vivra-t-elle?* (1931), former governor-general Maurice Viollette called for a reassessment of French colonialism and an opening to Algerian *évolués*. He asked: "Are we going to make revolutionaries or Frenchmen?"[93] The simultaneous appearance of these works along with those of al-Mili and al-Madani, right during the centenary celebration of French colonialism in Algeria, indicated an intellectual discontinuity and an incipient transformation of knowledge, power, and identity.[94] Furthermore, Germaine Tillion's sociological research and Camus's investigative reporting in Kabylia in the 1930s disclosed the social and economic disasters produced by colonialism. Yet even with the remarkable convergence of these critical, contestable discourses, colonial Algeria was not stirred from its oblivion.

The Algerian War and French Essentialism

France identified itself as an imperial power and the thought of changing that identity, especially concerning Algeria, meant rejecting the "hegemonic conception" of a unified Republic.[95] The prolonged, brutal repression after the Sétif uprising in 1945 demonstrated the extent of this attachment. Those who subscribed to the wistful and fallacious interpretation of the "lost opportunities" and the "almosts" of reforms misperceived not only the intensity of entrenched colonialism but also the power of its imagination. For example, the Blum-Viollette legislation never left committee. Though enacted as a reform measure, the Statute of 1947 safely secured colonialist privileges and advantages through corruption and through electoral manipulation, as in 1948 and 1951. In October 1954 the minister of the interior, François Mitterrand, completed a tour of Algeria and reported to Premier Pierre Mendès-France that "the climate is getting worse over there." Mitterrand recognized the urgent need to apply honestly the Algerian Statute and to integrate more Algerians into the colonial administration.[96] Several weeks later, however, after the outbreak of the Revolution, Mitterrand stood before the National Assembly uttering the appropriate political platitudes asserting that "Algeria is France, because Algerian departments are departments of the French Republic."[97]

The outbreak of the Algerian War, especially after the Dien Bien Phu disaster in Indochina, profoundly affected the essentialist perspective. Georges Le Beau, a former governor-general, underscored the popular notion that "the future of Algeria is also that of France."[98] Officially, the Fourth Republic declared that success in the Algerian War would condition "the destiny of France."[99] This conflict was more than a question of secession from the Republic; it increasingly represented despair that France was in decline. Jacques Soustelle argued that "to abandon Algeria is to condemn France to decadence."[100] Tony Smith judged that during decolonization "the major stake the French had in Algeria was . . . intangible: their sense of national identity."[101] Algeria represented, as Hanson W. Baldwin reflected, a "battle for the French soul."[102] The battle had to be won—or thought to be won.

France and Algeria's Economic and Social Development, 1955–1958

As the war escalated, newly appointed governor-general Jacques Soustelle delivered an impassioned speech before the Algerian Assembly in 1955. Calling Algeria an "exceptional situation," he declared his intention to initiate "exceptional methods." He outlined plans for education and *formation* (job training), adding that "cultural missions" would "assault ignorance . . . not only by knowledge but by empathy."[103] The Fourth Republic articulated its "sole, exclusive objective to guarantee systematically and to accelerate the advance, in all developments, of the native population."[104] At the Brussels World's Fair in 1958, France publicized its vision of Algeria as an "economic and social liberation" naturally leading to "a psychological and sociological liberation, a veritable conversion of spirits."[105] It seemed that France finally recognized a genuine responsibility for Algeria; thus, the civilizing mission returned, expediently refashioned, taking into account transforming French modalities of power. Though the Fourth Republic floundered in its political attempts to remedy the Algerian situation, it did identify and address social and economic problems by the Maspétiol, Frappart, Pellenc, and Delavignette Reports. It also provided the *Plan d'Industrialisation* (December 1956) and the *Perspectives décennales* (February 1958), which de Gaulle's Constantine Plan (October 1958) and independent Algerian governments recognized and respected.[106]

Development in the first sector featured the Caisse d'Accession à la Propriété et l'Exploitation Rurale (CAPER) in 1956 to stimulate land redistribution from the European *colons* to the native *fellahin*. This was done by purchasing and even expropriating (a form of "nationalization") farmland, and by the transfer of public lands. In 1958, CAPER possessed 610,000 hectares with the land divided into thirty-hectare lots.[107] The Constantine Plan called for a continuation of land transfers (250,000 hectares), a "renaissance of the *bled*" (i.e., *bilad* or countryside), and the Sections Coopératives Agricoles du Plan de Constantine (SCAPCO) promised increased support to the native farmers. The number of monitors to assist the *fellahin* was to increase from 400 to 2,950, averaging out to one monitor for two hundred farmers.[108] Governor-General Soustelle's Sections Administratives Spécialisées (SAS) provided added technical and educational assistance.[109] Ideas for agricultural reform even included one promoting communalism which predated Ahmed Ben Bella's vaunted *autogestion* (self-management).[110] The construction, and reconstruction, of rural housing and infrastructure as well as the idea of a "thousand villages" (600 under construction in 1960) to transform the *bled* also anticipated the postcolonial Agrarian Revolution.[111]

In the second sector, the *Perspectives décennales* reflected the dramatic change toward Algeria's traditional economic development. The agricultural sector, so selfishly guarded by the colonial *colonat* (large landowners), was to be relatively ignored. Instead, nonagricultural activities would receive critical attention. The objectives of the *Perspectives* were to provide jobs, raise the standard of living, and exploit natural resources.[112] The last objective referred to the recent (1954–56) sensational discoveries of natural gas and petroleum that stimulated not only economic enterprise but also the national imagination.[113] According to French planners, their goals could be attained through the rapid industrialization of Algeria and by continued extraction of its hydrocarbon wealth in the Sahara. The expected need of 50,000 technicians also ensured a French presence. The *Perspectives* projected 875,000 new jobs, 552,000 in the industrial sector alone.[114] The Constantine Plan projected 400,000 new jobs and large-scale industrial projects including the construction of a steel complex at Bône (Annaba), petrochemical works at Arzew, and a refinery in Algiers.[115] Clearly, the postcolonial policy of "industrializing industries" featuring hydrocarbons as the multiplier had its origins with these plans. De Gaulle's government provided attractive incentives to private industry for capital investment in Algeria.[116] In spite of the hesitation of French companies to contribute to the capitalization of Algeria, Paris persuaded a substantial participation.[117]

The third sector received particular attention. The Le Gorgeu Commission designed an educational plan (*Plan d'Equipement scolaire*) in 1955 that targeted the enrollment of 850,000 Muslim children or 35.2 percent of the projected student population during the 1963–64 school year.[118] As the Revolution spread throughout Algeria, education was reorganized (Decree of 13 September 1956) with an increased effort to enroll the rapidly multiplying Muslim student population and to construct school buildings to serve them (Decree of 18 May 1957). Twelve hundred classrooms were built in 1956, and a year later 3,300 classrooms and teaching units were added.[119] In 1957, Muslim children attending classes numbered 345,533. In 1960 there were 714,774 in school.[120] Only by devoting the entire Algerian budget to education could learning opportunities be provided for all. Nevertheless, the education allocation rose and accounted for 16.8 percent of the budget.[121] More children attended Algerian schools from 1958 to 1962 than between 1830 and 1958.[122] The Constantine Plan projected full attendance by the end of the 1960s. Without Algerian teachers available, French educators arrived from the *métropole*.

The Fourth and Fifth Republics extended social services, such as social security and medical care, to include greater numbers of Muslims. With the alarming growth of Algeria's population, approximately 3 percent per year, chronic housing shortages became very serious. Increased interest in housing began before the Revolution, especially because of an earthquake in western Algeria in September 1954. In 1955 there were 2,500 housing units under construction. This figure more than doubled in 1956.[123] The Constantine Plan aimed for housing to accommodate one million persons. Nevertheless, the demographic situation worsened with the growing migration to the cities to escape the Malthusian conditions of the *bled* and the devastation wrought by revolutionary war.[124] This also swelled emigration of Algerian unskilled labor to France.

In 1956 the Fourth Republic established the Office Algérien de la Main-d'Oeuvre (OFAMO) to supervise and study emigrant labor. During this time, Algerian workers sent back to their families 35 billion *anciens francs* annually in family allowances.[125] Economists claimed that the 400,000 emigrants in France supported about 2,000,000 people in Algeria.[126] De Gaulle's government established the Fonds d'Action Sociale (FAS) in December 1958 to promote the social welfare of the emigrant worker community in France.[127]

De Gaulle Shifts Discourse and Objectives

Collectively, these projects and programs illustrated Paris's perception that the "primary shortcoming of French rule was not its *domination* but its *neglect* of the Muslim population."[128] Nevertheless, there was an important shift in intention, strategy, and the exercise of French power after de Gaulle took over. Unlike the Fourth Republic, which initiated reforms to reinforce a political presence, de Gaulle hoped that French financial, technical, and cultural (educational) assistance would secure associative ties protecting and preserving strategic interest and influence. In April 1961, de Gaulle spoke of the Constantine Plan as a means "to preserve and develop ties which exist between the Algerian and French communities . . . in spite of griefs that both sides have unfortunately experienced."[129] The Plan itself reached two conclusions: "The Algerians cannot solve their problems by themselves, except at the cost of one or two generations, and then with uncertain results. . . . Secondly[,] only France can provide them with the timely amount of necessary support that is indispensable."[130] The Constantine Plan mirrored de Gaulle's translucent political positions at this time "as evidence that France meant to stay permanently in the country (thereby meeting military expectations), or as an attempt to divide the rebellion, or as an indication to the GPRA [Gouvernement Provisoire de la République Algérienne, the FLN's provisional government] that it should not ignore the practical benefits to be obtained from cooperation with France."[131] Fulfillment of all the Constantine Plan's goals mattered less to de Gaulle than the perpetuation of a French strategic position in Algeria whatever the political conclusion of the war. Indeed, the Plan continued to be implemented in the postcolonial period. As its General Report stated, "The ambition of the Constantine Plan, it is necessary to recall, is not to ensure the revenues of an assisted Algeria, but to make Algeria a modern country, modern for all its inhabitants living in every part, from the coast to the Sahara, in symbiosis with France."[132] It was this symbiotic relationship, rather than a politically integrationist one, that de Gaulle wanted to secure—and he did.

Consumed throughout his life by the idealization of France as a great and independent power, the general often seemed to incarnate this identity. The crucial difference between the protagonists of French Algeria and de Gaulle at this time was his conviction that French grandeur and independence no longer equated with a tenacious hold on an increasingly anachronistic empire including Algeria. His discourse during Algerian decolonization, often termed "unctuous" and "delphic" by detractors, endeavored to convince his formidable colonialist opposition that France's prestige or, fundamentally, its essential nature was not at mortal risk. He agreed, however, "that the best thing to do—and even the only thing to do—would be to prevent Algeria from drawing away from France."[133] Algeria should be "associated" with France in some way, though de Gaulle recognized that "France's task with regard to Algeria must change in nature and form."[134] By 1962 the "association which safeguards our interests"[135] would be defined as "cooperation" and would be stipulated in the Evian Accords.

2

The Political Decolonization of Algeria and the Evian Accords, 1958–1962

We rebel for life and death,
and we promised to vivify Algeria:
be witnesses of it!
We are rebel soldiers, and we fight
for right and independence;
'cause France doesn't listen to our voices . . .
"Hymn of the Underground"

Oh De Gaulle, stop barking:
certainly we will not leave the weapons.
War lasts, and fight spreads everywhere.
If you, instead of barking,
want to speak,
here is F.L.N.
ready to listen.
Djaafer Beck, "Oh! De Gaulle"

Louis Joxe sat across from me smoking Chesterfields in his stately
apartment on the quai de l'Horloge. I asked him what was the greatest
problem of the Evian negotiation. He answered: "Everything."
Author, interview of 22 May 1978

It took three years for Charles de Gaulle to prepare France and himself for
the decolonization of Algeria, and then about a year of intermittent but
intensive negotiations. The subsequent Evian Accords' stipulations disclosed inevitable continuities as well as discontinuities, as relations were
reformulated to accommodate new historical realities and national identities. Algeria would gain its independence, yet France's presence would be
preserved too, inaugurating the postcolonial paradoxes of dependence
with independence and conflict yet cooperation, and with them a prolonged postcolonial transformation rather than just a transfer of power.

De Gaulle's Political Policy, 1958–1961

Charles de Gaulle came to power as a result of the Fourth Republic's political immobility and inability to control events.[1] The general did not have a plan of decolonization, but by May 1958 he believed that the French-Algerian colonial relationship had to evolve into a refashioned associateship.[2] At first de Gaulle's approach toward Algeria seemed a recapitulation of Fourth Republic policy. On 4 June 1958 he reassured the integrationist masses in Algiers with "I have understood you," though in the same speech he called for a single electoral college. Then in October he offered a "peace of the brave" that was reminiscent of Premier Guy Mollet's efforts from 1955 to 1957. And, as shown in the last chapter, he extended social reform and economic enterprises. Still, de Gaulle kept the idea of "association" before the French public. In his inaugural speech as first president of the Fifth Republic, he spoke of a "special place" for Algeria within the French community but, more important, he imagined in essentialist-existential terms "an Algeria that will be pacified and transformed, developing its personality itself and closely associated with France."[3] De Gaulle's government reworked the Fourth Republic's *loi-cadre* federal plan and increased the number of Algerian departments. Elections were eventually held from a single electoral college. These featured the political aspect of integration most feared by settlers, greater Algerian representation. De Gaulle's implementation of Fourth Republic initiatives seemed designed, nevertheless, to cool the political passions of the army and the *pieds-noirs*. By demonstrating that past policy was politically bankrupt, as he contended while he was out of office, he hoped to coopt his dangerous colonial opposition while constructing a decisive metropolitan consensus.[4]

De Gaulle's task was political and pedagogical.[5] He carefully deflected the identification of Algeria with France's ultimate fate and oriented the crisis to himself and his government. Using his "mystic stature and his regime-centered analysis," he convinced and "reassured the deeply troubled French masses" that "the Algerian debacle . . . was not a reflection of deep flaws in themselves, in France, or in their conception of France's role in the world."[6] De Gaulle understood completely that Algerian decolonization had to be addressed by redirecting French essentialism, reconstructing the ordering framework.

On 16 September 1959 de Gaulle offered Algeria several types of "self-determination." The preferred choice to de Gaulle was "a government of Algerians by Algerians, backed by French help and in close relationship

with her, as regards the economy, education, defense and foreign relations."[7] De Gaulle's vision of an associated Algeria would be impaired—
by the increasingly desperate resistance of the *pieds-noirs* evidenced during the January 1960 Barricades Week, by the premature and brief
discussions with the FLN in Melun in June, and by the Muslim demonstrations in December—but by November de Gaulle already had uttered the
words "Algerian republic." During his 11 April 1961 press conference, de
Gaulle clearly defined his policy as "decolonization," but its significance
went beyond an Algeria that "costs us much more that it is worth to us."
De Gaulle spoke of a redefinition of French power, saying that
decolonization was imperative since "it seemed to me contrary to France's
present interests and new ambition to remain bound by obligations and
burdens which are no longer in keeping with the requirements of her
strength and influence."[8] Later that month, the president's moral and political authority crushed military rebels led by four generals in Algiers.

When the French government finally faced the FLN in negotiations
with a degree of political confidence (especially after the 8 January 1961
referendum), de Gaulle found himself at a distinct disadvantage.[9] Unlike
the fundamental diplomatic objectives of the Algerian revolutionaries, his
own had not been precisely articulated from the beginning (that would
have been disastrous), but evolved, contingent on events and on the development of a political consensus. He wanted to preserve a postcolonial
French presence, "an effective association between the new state and
France."[10] Menacing any political solution was the increasingly insurrectionary nature of the military-*pied-noir* complex, then being channeled
toward the nihilistic terrorism of the OAS (Organisation de l'Armée
Secrète).

The FLN: Torn yet Tenacious

The FLN hoped to harness the Algerian people's energies and unleash
them against colonialism, but the revolutionary elite's endemic dissension
and division (Arab/Kabyle, internal/external, "easterner"/"westerner";
civilian/military) as well as French military power prevented the articulation and implementation of a coherent ideology and a comprehensive program. Further, without a concurrent social revolution to promote and
project a genuine, inclusive national consciousness, the Algerian identity
remained suspended, until defined or invented by a fractious and exclusive
FLN elite. The nationalists also suffered severe blows in losing important
revolutionary cadres through capture (Rabah Bitat; the skyjacked Ben

Bella and associates: see below; and Ben M'hidi, captured, probably tortured to death), battlefield deaths (Mourad Didouche, Mostefa Ben Boulaid), and elite fratricide (Ramdane Abane). Yet the quest for national independence and a common opposition to the Messalist MNA (Mouvement Nationaliste Algérien) compelled real, if at times reluctant, intra-FLN unity. For example, the elite consistently pursued negotiating positions first presented in the Proclamation of 1 November (reaffirmed by the Soummam Platform of August 1956). The FLN declared then that (1) "French cultural and economic interests, honestly acquired, will be respected"; (2) French nationals desiring to stay in Algeria might become Algerian citizens or remain French (no dual citizenship); and (3) relations between France and Algeria would be defined by "an accord between both states founded on equality and respect for the other."[11] As Alistair Horne remarked: "The truly remarkable feature of the FLN proclamation as a document was that its basic principles were to be adhered to with absolute fidelity during seven and a half years of war, right through the final settlement."[12]

The Beginning of Dialogue

Secret exploratory contacts between FLN external members and Guy Mollet's government began in Cairo in March 1956; meetings were also convened in Belgrade and Rome.[13] Proposals included a cease-fire, an autonomous Algeria closely tied to France, elections from a single college with FLN participation in a provisional government, and legal protection for the *pieds-noirs*. Ben Bella was particularly enthusiastic about the proposals, claiming "peace was within reach." Mollet apparently offered Ben Bella safe passage to Algeria for negotiations.[14] How significant were these initial conversations? Jérôme Hélie contended the Mollet government was not that serious about these sessions, given that participating officials were low-level, unlike de Gaulle's later team. Redha Malek viewed the dialogue as one between the FLN and Mollet's SFIO (Section Française de l'Internationale Ouvrière) delegates, rather than one with the French government.[15] These talks terminated in October with the skyjacking of an Air Maroc flight carrying Ahmed Ben Bella, Mohamed Khider, Mohamed Boudiaf, Hocine Ait Ahmed, and Mostefa Lacheraf, compounded by France's intervention in the Suez Canal adventure.

The seizure of Ben Bella and his high-level FLN associates seemed to contradict a promising dialogue, perhaps first illustrating, as Alistair Horne suggested, the ascendancy of the French military over the civilian government.[16] Finally, "external" negotiations were bound to receive a hostile response by the "internal" elite fighting within Algeria. Indeed, the "externals" were not invited to the FLN's Soummam Conference in August. There was another less concrete but more convincing argument. France could not at that time imagine Algeria rent from it; that was contrary to its essentialism.

Though popular support ebbed and flowed, the FLN presented a persistent and sometimes a spectacular security threat, as in the Battle of Algiers, 1956–57. In addition, France's political immobility and then instability exaggerated the effectiveness of the nationalists. The FLN's growing visibility and consideration in international forums such as the Bandung Conference and Algeria's emergence as an international issue in the United Nations General Assembly and the United States Senate menaced the *métropole* with diplomatic alienation and isolation, especially among Arab and emerging Third World nations. De Gaulle may have viewed negotiating with the FLN, as Redha Malek contended, as a "last resort," but without viable (and pliable) interlocutors (*interlocuteurs valables*), there would be no other choice.[17] Indeed, in September 1958 the FLN had proclaimed the Gouvernement Provisoire de la République Algérienne (GPRA), an audacious assertion of its own legitimacy.

Toward Full Negotiations

Serious secret discussions began in February 1961 in Switzerland where de Gaulle confidant and adviser Georges Pompidou, Bruno de Leusse, and Claude Chayet (who had spoken with FLN officials in December 1960) met Ahmed Boumendjel, who had negotiated briefly at Melun,[18] and Tayeb Boulahrouf;[19] conversations resumed in March. Paris conceded during these sessions that a cease-fire was no longer a precondition for negotiations. The French even informed the FLN that they would conduct a unilateral cease-fire (limiting operations to defensive activities) to demonstrate good faith. The hoped-for reciprocation was an Algerian assent to start negotiating a settlement. The GPRA must have felt that there was an urgency, because the French were particularly interested in discovering, even at this preliminary stage, the Algerian vision of the postcolonial relationship.[20] Full negotiations were scheduled to begin in April at the resort city of Evian.

Unfortunately, the talks were postponed (31 March 1961) when Louis Joxe angered the FLN by mentioning that he would be willing to talk to any nationalist group, even the MNA.[21] De Gaulle intensified the pressure on the FLN to reconsider during his 11 April press conference. Reviving the old self-determination option of "secession" from his 16 September 1959 address, he reviewed its dire consequences for nationalist interests, including the cessation of French investments, the deportation of emigrant workers, and the relocation into protected enclaves of the *pieds-noirs* who "too have the right to self-determination." De Gaulle also invoked the existential onus that "an Algerian sovereignty has never existed."[22] Thereby de Gaulle tabled his diplomatic trumps: the offer of French aid and, most important, the fact that France was still in control in Algeria with an ability to dismember the Sahara or partition off the *pied-noir* population.

At Soummam the FLN clearly disclosed its interest in postcolonial French aid and assistance, as long as it was not neocolonialist in nature.[23] Belkacem Krim, who was to lead the GPRA delegation, projected that independent Algeria would aspire to have "peaceful and fruitful relations with all countries and even with France."[24] M'hammed Yazid wrote in 1959, "We envisage friendly cooperation with France."[25] The FLN understood that an expulsion of emigrant workers was belied by the expanding need of the French economy for cheap labor. This threat would be taken more seriously during the postcolonial period. The FLN's position on national integrity dated from the Proclamation of 1 November 1954; it persistently assailed partition. It denounced the *loi-cadre* and de Gaulle's elections within Algeria as Balkanization.[26] Before the first negotiation at Evian, *El-Moudjahid* reasserted: "This principle of territorial integrity is for us fundamental: there exists in Algeria between the regions of the north and territories of the south incontestable human, economic and historical links."[27] Belkacem Krim declared: "The essential point is to restore to the Algerian people its personality and sovereignty."[28]

With diplomatic positions aired before negotiations began, it was obvious that there would be no immediate solution. Krim's gall bladder operation and the generals' putsch of April 1961 headed by General Maurice Challe postponed the opening of formal negotiations. The delays allowed each delegation a longer opportunity to size up the other's negotiating positions and strategies. Finally, negotiations were rescheduled for 20 May.

Evian I

The conversations between the delegations began cordially. Led by Belkacem Krim, the GPRA delegation included Saad Dahlab, Boumendjel, Boulahrouf, Ahmed Francis, Mohammed Benyahia, Redha Malek, and

Majors Slimane (Kaid Ahmed) and Ali Mendjli. Louis Joxe informed the Algerians that he was there to consider "everything."[29] He and his associates (Bernard Tricot, de Leusse, Roland Cadet, Yves Roland-Billecart, Chayet, and Generals Jean Simon and Hubert de Seguins Pazzis) learned quickly that dual citizenship for the Europeans was out of the question, as well as specific guarantees protecting their particular political and property rights. The GPRA negotiators argued that if the settlers chose to remain in independent Algeria, they would have to become Algerian nationals. A modern form of French "capitulations" or extralegal rights was intolerable.[30] To Tricot, the *pieds-noirs'* opposition to the negotiation constrained the government even when backed by metropolitan consensus ("an entente between State and Nation").[31]

Changing the subject to the Sahara in an attempt to use it as a diplomatic lever, Joxe contended that it was not realistically or historically a part of Algeria.[32] This provoked the charged existential question of an Algerian nationhood and generated a "Jacobin" Algerian reaction, an ironic "assimilation of French law." Reminiscent of the Ulama's credo of cultural unity, the GPRA negotiators insisted that the state was indivisible.[33] The Sahara's hydrocarbon wealth had captured the imagination of the French, but its attraction was fundamentally economic even with its weighty political significance. On the other hand, the Algerians equated the Sahara with their imagination of a postcolonial polity. It was primarily a political question relating to the definition of their nation, though it had correlative economic consequence. This would eventually be understood by both sides, especially by Saad Dahlab, who astutely proposed separating French interests in the Sahara from a political settlement.[34] The Algerians resisted any type of compromise over the general principles that had bound the centrifugal FLN elite together, while the French remained adamant over the Sahara. On 13 June the talks broke down, primarily over the Sahara, though other issues such as dual nationality for the *pieds-noirs* remained unresolved. Contacts continued, but an attempt from 20 to 28 July to revitalize full negotiations at the nearby Château de Lugrin failed.[35]

During these "Evian I" negotiations, the Algerians displayed a stubborn stance matched by an exasperating patience. They also applied broad principles encompassing the totality of the questions under discussion. On the other hand, the French wanted specific clarification on particulars. These differing tactical and philosophical approaches to diplomacy were crucial during the first formal meetings and were also emblematic of French-Algerian negotiations after independence.

Assessments of Evian I and Aftermath

El-Moudjahid's analysis of the Evian discussions included repudiation of the "Gaullist plan toward the dismemberment of Algeria while according it an ersatz independence."[36] Though critical of "the unreal intransigence of the French government," the article ended on a positive note, stating that Evian "permitted the establishment of a beginning dialogue."[37] Abdelkader Chanderli, reporting to the Afro-Asian UN representatives, called the negotiations a "first phase." Though recognizing that "the divergence of views is considerable," he pointed out that "the major success to date would seem to be the fact . . . that the two delegations have actually met and talked about basic questions."[38]

According to Chanderli, the major contention was over the sovereign territorial integrity of the nation. While recognizing the "special characteristics of the European minority, in particular as concerns the cultural, linguistic and religious areas," the FLN opposed special "undemocratic" guarantees, such as permanent political representation for the "European community" in the future Algerian state.[39] Chanderli reaffirmed that "the Sahara is an integral part of Algeria," but he also distinguished "between the question of sovereignty over the Sahara and the exploitation of its mineral wealth." He perceived that an economic "cooperative effort" in the hydrocarbons sector with France was needed.[40] Finally, the FLN representative attacked the French demand for "military enclaves" in Algeria by which France "would hold complete sovereignty."[41]

After the Evian discussions, it soon became apparent that the nature of the FLN's future diplomatic dialogue with Paris would be conditioned not only by French positions but also by its own often vituperative and occasionally violent intra-elite conflicts. The FLN delegation adjourned to Tripoli where the Conseil National de la Révolution (CNRA) of the GPRA held a congress in August. Houari Boumedienne and his hostile external military elite accused Krim of weakness, but the Kabyle leader defended himself effectively and remained head of the negotiating team.[42] The military did succeed, however, in altering the leadership of the GPRA by purging the authority and influence of the "politicians," a coded term for the civilian elite. This included the replacement of the internationally respected Ferhat Abbas by Ben Youssef Ben Khedda whose ideological affinities were closer to Boumedienne's. To Redha Malek, the new government was "homogenized" and this strengthened the negotiating team.[43] On the other hand, the military elite began to champion the incarcerated Ben Bella. A die was cast that had bloody repercussions in Algeria's immediate postcolonial history.

On the French side, Joxe found himself in a political and existential quandary. The FLN's legitimacy was a serious consideration for him.[44] With whom was he negotiating? A delegation from a sovereign state? How binding could an agreement be with the FLN revolutionaries? What defined Algeria as a nation? He had brought on the impasse, but that had helped disclose the FLN's staunch commitment to its principles and objectives. During this time, the French unsuccessfully tried to intimidate and isolate the FLN. Paris continued to assert that the Sahara was an inland French sea, but found strategic littoral states unsympathetic. The Bizerte assault in July alienated Tunisian president Habib Bourguiba, who had styled himself a mediator (while desiring a change in border demarcation in order to exploit Saharan hydrocarbon riches). Mali's Modibo Keita enjoyed very cordial relations with the GPRA. Furthermore, Ferhat Abbas had shored up the regional diplomatic front by negotiating an agreement with Morocco in July promising a resolution of the disputed frontier after independence.[45]

De Gaulle Changes Position

During his press conference of 5 September de Gaulle reminded the FLN: "Cooperation, as desirable as it may appear to us, and especially so sentimentally—this cooperation is by no means necessary to us; we hold on to it only insofar as it implies exchange and understanding."[46] Nevertheless, he also aimed to stimulate a resumption of negotiations by modifying the French position on the Sahara: "The question of the sovereignty of the Sahara does not need to be considered. . . . But what concerns us is that there emerge from this agreement—should it come about—an association which safeguards our interests."[47] Those strategic interests included "free exploitation of the oil and gas which we have discovered or would discover, disposal of airfields and traffic rights for our communications with Black Africa."[48] He questioned, however, the FLN's political legitimacy by mentioning that France would like to renew negotiations with "the FLN or . . . with another representative body."[49] By this time the issue was moot, as was demonstrated in October when the FLN's political power was paraded in the streets of Paris.

Emigrant Workers to the Streets

From the beginning of the Revolution, a "fifth column" nightmare stalked the French subconscious. It concerned the growing Algerian emigrant worker population living in France—approximately 400,000 in 1962; an increase of some 25 percent since 1954. The FLN's efforts to influence and to raise the political consciousness of the workers eventually overcame the strong Messalist tradition dating from the days of the Etoile Nord-Africaine in the mid-1920s.[50] The emigrants' politicization menaced the *métropole*'s internal security and precipitated systematic police repression. With terrorism increasing in the autumn of 1961, police harassment intensified with a stifling curfew in the Algerian quarters of Paris. This finally forced the workers to rally. A dramatic march of twenty to thirty thousand emigrants through the heart of Paris on 17 October publicized their protest over their repression while proclaiming their support of Algerian independence. A brutal suppression left scores of nameless dead and unaccounted (now estimated in the hundreds).[51] This protest and subsequent demonstrations illustrated that the independence movement had acquired a convincing momentum.

Found: An *Interlocuteur Valable*—the OAS

Though de Gaulle considered the Organisation de l'Armée Secrète a "vicissitude, both foreseeable and undoubtedly inevitable," he minimized its significance. "It makes no change in the problem which remains that of the future—to insure close cooperation between both countries."[52] Nevertheless, the OAS emerged ironically as a menacing kind of *interlocuteur valable* (*absent*), which imposed pressures on both the French and the Algerian sides, quickened the negotiations, and hastened the end of colonial Algeria.[53] Led by Generals Raoul Salan and Edmond Jouhaud, both of whom fled underground after the military coup collapsed in April 1961, the OAS cadre and corps represented the final desperate attempt of the military-*pied-noir* complex to impose its will.

The OAS aimed to perpetuate French national integrity, to reconstruct France "morally and materially," and to reestablish "traditional friendship with the Muslim world."[54] (These objectives mirrored de Gaulle's goals, but his essentialist vision no longer identified with colonial Algeria.) It equated decolonization with communism and contended that the FLN and the French government were in collusion.[55] The OAS's operations began in the spring of 1961 with a sheer terror that rocked Paris's authority in Algeria, fomented anarchy, and starkly symbolized the "nihilistic rebellion" described by the late Albert Camus (d. January 1960).[56] They were spearheaded by Roger Degueldre's dreaded Delta group, who made assassination a favorite tactic, but OAS killings were often arbitrary and indiscriminate, as in the murder of the brilliant author Mouloud Feraoun. Police could not handle the situation and the army often openly sympathized with the OAS, in part because of personal friendships with its members and those in command. To challenge the OAS, Paris imported a group of misfits known as *barbouzes*.[57] Degueldre and other OAS agents annihilated them. On the other hand, a counter-OAS team known as Force C was markedly successful. Nevertheless, the OAS operated freely, protected by a desperate and often coerced *pied-noir* population fearful for its future, its very existence.

The appalling violence of the OAS and its affiliated groups reached the *métropole*. De Gaulle was targeted and he and his wife narrowly survived an assassination attempt in August 1962. The mayor of Evian, Camille Blanc, was an early victim. A bombing attempt on André Malraux blinded a little girl and enraged Paris. A rally and march protesting OAS atrocities incited violence resulting in the death of eight people on 8 February. As the savagery climaxed in February 1962, deepening divisions between the communities in both Algeria and France, negotiations resumed and progressed decisively toward a cease-fire and a general settlement.

The Resumption of Negotiations at Les Rousses and Evian II

The GPRA decided to return to full negotiations for three reasons. First, it feared that the disintegration of civilian authority marked especially by the indiscriminate murders of Muslims, would force the French to augment their military deployment.[58] Second, as the war extended, the FLN intra-elite power struggle intensified; the growing power of Boumedienne and his restless military cadre alarmed the civilian elites.[59] Third, promising diplomatic conversations in Basel, Switzerland, on 28 October and 9 November had led to a positive meeting between Saad Dahlab and Louis Joxe one month later.[60] Enough progress occurred for the GPRA to justify resumption, with a proviso: the approval of Ben Bella and his incarcerated "brothers" interned at the Château d'Aulnoy near Melun. De Gaulle facilitated the fulfillment of that precondition. Full negotiations resumed secretly in mid-February at the Les Rousses hideaway high in the Jura Mountains.

Speaking to the nation on 5 February 1962, de Gaulle articulated France's diplomatic objectives. He anticipated cooperation in many fields, even if it would be "more numerous and burdensome for us." Cooperation would be accorded, however, "on condition that our essential interests, particularly in the Sahara, are respected and that at the same time the participation of the minority of European origin in Algerian activities is guaranteed."[61] In *Memoirs of Hope,* de Gaulle wrote that "the object of the negotiations . . . was to persuade the FLN to accept the provisions which were essential." He also hoped to attain "an effective association between the new state and France."[62] According to Robert Buron, who along with Jean de Broglie now joined Joxe,[63] de Gaulle instructed his chief negotiator: "Do not let the negotiations prolong themselves indefinitely. . . . Besides that, do not attach yourselves to details. There is the possible and the impossible."[64] After his recent experience with the Algerians, Joxe did not have to be reminded.

El-Moudjahid reiterated the GPRA's objectives before Les Rousses: total independence (thus rejecting an association or Community-like situation); a cease-fire subordinated to a comprehensive political accord; and territorial integrity (prohibiting a "cramped corner" European enclave) including the Sahara with control of its riches and resources.[65] Les Rousses revealed, however, that there would be compromises. During these secret "preliminaries" the GPRA conceded that a French presence was inevitable. The FLN understood the urgent need for French aid after independence; therefore, cooperation was accepted despite its neocolonial implications.[66] The FLN also recognized the perpetuation of French privileged interests in the Sahara (its partition no longer mooted by this time). Contentious issues centered on the European community's postcolonial rights and the continued French use of military bases.

Buron wrote that the entire negotiation would be judged by the guarantees the French could secure for the European population.[67] The French presented meticulous arguments founded on the premise that most of the *pied-noir* population would remain in Algeria. The FLN accepted numerous guarantees for the European community, including political and property rights. As for the French military presence, disagreements reached the point where Joxe exhausted his preplanned options. After communicating with de Gaulle, he received enough latitude on 18 February to prevent an impasse. Illustrating his appreciation of intangibles, Joxe reflected that the spirit of the accord with the FLN transcended its stipulations. As for its provisions, who knew how history would affect their validity?[68] By 19 February, both sides believed that they had reached a general settlement. They agreed to resume formal and final negotiations on 7 March at Evian.

Evian II and the Conclusion of the Negotiation

Returning to Tripoli and another hostile CNRA deliberation, Krim and Dahlab confronted the aggressive military elite, increasingly influenced by Nasserism, who claimed that they had been duped over the proposed postcolonial French military and petroleum presences as well as the particular privileges reserved for Europeans in future "Algerian" institutions. Krim reputedly demanded: "And you who are at the head of the army, explain to us how you plan to chase the French out. By arms?" Dahlab was accused of giving Algerian petroleum away to the French. He retorted: "You have given me the impression that we are here in an opium den. . . . The French are giving us the oil." Dahlab asked for a "reality check" and reminded the Conseil that the French still controlled Algeria. After bitter discussion, the CNRA voted in favor of the Les Rousses agreements, implicitly supporting Krim's diplomatic conduct.[69] The grim antagonisms among the elites, fundamentally over power and the imagination of the future nation, however, portended tragic political and ideological divisiveness that would plague postwar Algeria.

As for the French, Joxe worried that the arduously attained Les Rousses agreements were in danger of becoming merely academic. Escalating OAS terrorism (Salan's "Instruction No. 29" ordered a "general offensive" on 23 February) menaced the dream of a fraternal symbiosis founded on both communities' love of the land. His apprehension was well founded. When both teams reconvened at Evian, the French discovered that, for the Algerians, the European minority no longer posed such a great problem. It was clear that many of the *pieds-noirs,* if not most of them, could not bear to live in the inevitable independent Algerian state. Instead, discussion centered on the immediate composition of the transitional government that would arrange for self-determination.

Buron described how at one point another impasse seemed imminent over the nature of French participation during the transitional period. Then suddenly an accord was reached.[70] The impetus to surmount any obstruction had to come from the Algerian delegation. According to what Buron observed at Les Rousses, Krim appeared to feel more pressure from his "brothers" than from the French. Perhaps the Kabyle wanted to achieve an accord in order to relieve the intra-elite rivalry or weaken the military's political potential.[71]

Dahlab did not disclose "fraternal" pressures on the GPRA team, but they must have been felt. He recalled these final negotiations as being tedious, marked by a meticulous French review of the agreements. He witnessed Joxe's unease as he liquidated France's empire. At one point Joxe complained, "I have never seen such a negotiation." Dahlab politely responded, "But . . . it is the first time you are negotiating with Algerians."[72] A cease-fire was proclaimed to begin at noon on 19 March. De Gaulle wrote in his memoirs that the Evian agreements "contained everything we had wanted them to contain."[73]

The Evian Accords

The Evian Accords offered Algeria political independence while preserving France's presence through cooperation (and the stipulated protection of bases and investments). They began with a cease-fire "agreement," followed by introductory governmental declarations containing five chapters complemented and elaborated by detailed declarations of guarantees and principles.[74]

Chapter I discussed the transition period and described the nature of the interim government in which roles were reserved for Europeans as well as Muslims. This government's task was to organize the referendum on self-determination that would be conducted within six months. This chapter recognized the existence of the FLN as "a legal political body," thus assuring its legitimacy as well as the legality of the Accords. A general amnesty was also announced.

Chapter II addressed Algerian internal and external sovereignty, including introduction of those crucial stipulations concerning the Europeans' future role in independent Algeria, expounded in the Declaration of Guarantees. After proving Algerian residence, Europeans could become Algerian citizens after three years. They could participate in government, but their representation would reflect their numbers (ending *pied-noir* political domination). The European concentration in Algiers and Oran would be "the subject of special provisions." The Accords respected Europeans' property rights and assured that any dispossessions would not be undertaken unless "fair compensation" had been agreed upon. The Europeans received "guarantees appropriate to their cultural, linguistic, and religious particuliarities." The *rayonnement* (propagation) of the French language seemed secured by this chapter stipulating its continued use in public discourse. Finally, in order to guarantee Europeans' rights, the Accords included provisions for a "safeguarding association" and a Court of Guarantees.[75]

Chapter II also established the framework for French-Algerian cooperation, detailed in several Declarations of Principles. The two countries would have "mutual respect" for each other's independence. Algeria would guarantee French interests and would receive in return French technical and cultural assistance. France promised privileged financial aid for social and economic development, in the short term (for the next three years) "fixed in conditions comparable to and at a level equivalent to those of the programs now under way." This perpetuated the programs initiated by the Constantine Plan. There would be privileged commercial exchanges, including Algeria's membership in the franc zone. Freedom of transfer was allowed as long as it was "compatible with the economic and social development of Algeria."

The discovery of Algeria's hydrocarbon wealth during the War of Independence was a vital consideration. France wanted to secure its investments in the desert. Both sides concurred that a technical body, the Organisation Technique de Coopération Saharienne, would be established to develop Saharan riches. Algeria had the right to distribute mining titles and had full sovereignty in enacting mining legislation. The perpetuated Code Pétrolier Saharien protected French interests, and French companies would receive preferential consideration in the granting of concessions. The Accords consolidated France's position in the Sahara.

France and Algeria agreed to develop their cultural relations. Besides sharing cultural exchanges, France would assist in the *formation* of Algerian technicians. A key stipulation was that "French personnel, in particular teachers and technicians, will be placed at the disposal of the Algerian Government." The stipulations on cooperation were especially significant since they indicated that both sides anticipated a closely configured and initially symbiotic bilateral relationship.

Chapter III concerned military questions. Overall, there would be a gradual disengagement from Algeria. French forces would be reduced to 80,000 one year after the vote for self-determination. France was granted a fifteen-year lease of its Mers-el-Kébir naval base. Crucial to de Gaulle's desire to develop an independent nuclear force (*force de frappe*), Algeria allowed France "the use of a number of military airfields, . . . terrains, sites, and installations." This postcolonial military deployment conspicuously called into question the idea of Algerian sovereignty.

Chapter IV stipulated that any dispute be approached by negotiation. If the two countries did not reach agreement, each would have recourse "directly to the International Court of Justice."

Chapter V provided that, if Algerian independence with cooperation should be adopted, France would immediately recognize the new nation.

The Immediate Reaction to the Accords

The Accords, and especially the historical circumstances in which they were negotiated and presented, incited heated debates in France's parliament. These debates were extraordinary: they represented a discursive historical survey of decolonization. After Robert Buron presented the Accords before the Senate, Senator Bernard Lafay condemned them as a "capitulation" and an "abandonment."[76] Edgar Faure found the debates an appropriate time to review his own political conduct during those recent years. In a speech that reads as a political expiation, he reiterated his support for the controversial idea of integration. To Faure, integration had actually meant a kind of "internal independence." That was in the past, however; now France could be proud of its colonial achievement as well as become a "moral power."[77] François Mitterrand followed Faure. Though this future president of the Fifth Republic resigned himself to Evian, there was a tone of bitterness as he recalled the lost opportunities during the Fourth Republic.[78] In the National Assembly, Prime Minister Michel Debré had the unenviable task of explaining the government's position on the Accords. Jean-Baptiste Biaggi railed against the "pseudoaccords," indicting them as "illegal, illegitimate, and repulsive."[79] Alain Peyrefitte countered by arguing that the FLN had moderated its positions, citing El-Moudjahid excerpts as authoritative proof.[80]

Analysts also offered various interpretations of the Accords. Marcel Torti considered them "conceived as an exchange" with "reciprocities," e.g., a French military presence for financial and educational aid.[81] Maurice Allais contended that the communities could not coexist politically as stipulated by the Evian agreements. Only by amending the Accords, by including provisions for a federal system, a minority veto, and the establishment of international guarantees, could the Europeans and pro-French Muslims be protected. A Cassandra of the immediate postcolonial period, Allais predicted that if these changes were not made, the politically beleaguered minorities would be forced to leave, consequently engendering a totalitarian regime with pro-Communist affinities.[82] Alfred Grosser noted that "there was scant provision for coordination; there was no provision at all for harmonizing foreign policies, and independent Algeria was empowered, from the very beginning, to pursue whatever policies it desired,"[83] impugning the idea of an Algeria "associated" with France. To Jean-Pierre Gonon, the Accords represented a remarkable negotiation by granting Algeria the freedom to choose an economic and political direction that went beyond "traditional relations between developed and underdeveloped countries."[84] Jean Daniel offered a guarded appraisal: "The manner in which the Algerian drama has unrolled has not laid a promising basis for Franco-Algerian cooperation."[85]

The Dénouement of Political Decolonization

The conclusion of the Evian Accords failed to temper the turmoil raging in Algeria. Camus had feared that revolution without restraint would lead to nihilism. In his terms, the virulent violence at this time produced a fatal fury, a pestilence, as manifested by the execution by the OAS of Camus's friend Mouloud Feraoun (15 March), the shocking rue d'Isly firefight where Frenchmen shot Frenchmen (26 March), the burning of the University of Algiers's library (7 June), and ultimately the pathetic sight of hundreds of thousands of *pied-noir* refugees. Though Camus did not live to witness these convulsive events, his writings anticipated them as well as the revolutionary elite's bloody strife.[86]

The transitional administration, headed by Abderrahmane Farès, former president of the Algerian Assembly, tried unsuccessfully to reconcile the settler and native communities. Its influence, however, was moral rather than military.[87] Though vitiated by the arrests of General Jouhaud in March and Roger Degueldre in April and the capture of General Salan in May, the OAS continued such terror tactics as nihilistic scorched-earth operations and murderous "*ratonnades*" (rat hunts) against Muslims. Finally on 17 June it negotiated an agreement with the FLN that mirrored the guarantees of Evian, but it was anticlimactic and anachronistic.[88]

The referendum of 8 April, designed to determine support for the Evian Accords, gave de Gaulle a huge 90-percent approval with 75 percent of the registered voters participating.[89] As Paris prepared for the 1 July vote for self-determination (i.e., independence), the FLN's wartime CNRA met in May–June for the last time in Tripoli and produced a document that, like the Proclamation of 1 November, would be faithfully adhered to during the postcolonial period.

The Tripoli Program and the FLN's Disarray

Rapidly changing political, social, and economic situations, compounded by the fractured FLN's indeterminate national program, quickly contradicted the clauses of the Evian Accords. For example, the European community, which had pathologically opposed Algerian independence, was now supposed to receive special protection; the reality was that it was in widespread panic and flight (see below). Ben Khedda considered the Evian Accords a "revolutionary compromise" which secured "key positions" while being "flexible on secondary positions" that he believed were "susceptible of being revised."[90] He characterized the Accords as "the victory of Evian" since they affirmed Algeria's territorial integrity, national unity, and sovereignty and recognized the FLN as a legitimate interlocutor. In spite of its successes, the GPRA remained, however, under attack by the military elite, the recently released Ben Bella, and other "historic chiefs" for its acceptance of stipulations compromising national sovereignty. Ben

Khedda reflected that there was no "irreversible concession" or "insurmountable obstacle" in the Accords.[91] Nevertheless, as William Quandt and others have emphasized, there was no political process in place to reconcile the recalcitrant factions.[92] Under these conditions and crises the CNRA convened at Tripoli.

This meeting had decisive and long-lasting significance. First, the FLN articulated an ideology that clearly refuted the recently agreed settlement. The Tripoli Program of June 1962 viewed the Evian Accords as "neocolonialist," and cooperation as a French means to "maintain the links of dependence in economic and cultural domains." For example, it considered the "pseudoliberal" Constantine Plan a subtle strategy providing "economic bases" for a postcolonial French presence. Furthermore, the French community and the OAS endangered "the fundamental perspectives of the Revolution." Repeatedly, the discourse underscored that the Revolution was not over: "The immediate task of the FLN is to liquidate, by all means, colonialism such as manifests itself still after the cease-fire." This applied to the immediate menace of the OAS and to the perpetuated "neocolonialist enterprises." The Tripoli Program's recourse to a socialist option threatened conflict rather than cooperation, given the ex-*métropole*'s "new form of domination."[93]

The Tripoli Program also disclosed a healthy dose of self-criticism of the FLN's underestimation of the consequences of the War of Liberation, implicitly meaning its failure to provide a social program during the Revolution. It used Marxist terminology warning of a variety of dangers such as a "feudal mentality" and the "petty bourgeoisie" within the party. It also projected a "popular democratic republic" featuring a planned economy, agrarian reform, Arabization, and an independent foreign policy. It called for "a new definition of culture" as "national, revolutionary, and scientific." This "revolutionary transformation of society," however, would have to be reconciled with Islam, and that proved to be problematic (and calamitous in the 1990s), as David C. Gordon predicted in his contemporary observations.[94] Responding to the FLN's Marxist rhetoric, the Ulama of Islam and the Arabic Language wondered in a public appeal "what sense one can give to independence if our personality is not independent."[95] This group equated the Algerian personality with Islamic traditions and values, the Arabic language, and history. In other words, the fundamentally existential cultural question needed to be genuinely and decisively addressed. Nevertheless, the CNRA insisted that the Revolution catalyzed and "consolidated [the Algerian people's] national unity." The Revolution would be the existential matrix of the new state, the source of its identity, its legitimacy, and its rationality.

The ideals of the Tripoli Program received unanimous endorsement. Ironically, the FLN's show of unity actually marked its disintegration and with it the repudiation of political inclusion. Abbas and his liberal faction were already targeted within the document. In a telling illustration of elite dynamics, the Program perceived a collusion between France and "moderate nationalists." Mohamed Boudiaf, stubbornly independent and soon alienated, founded the opposition Parti de la Révolution Socialiste in September and began a long self-imposed exile in Morocco before his dramatic return to Algeria in 1992. Hocine Ait Ahmed retired to foment revolution in Kabylia. The FLN would perceive itself as the genuine representative of the Algerian people but would neglect, ignore, and finally become insensitive to the historical reality of Algeria's political and social pluralism. According to one observer, Algeria at this time was in "existential dislocation," suspended between its colonial past and independent future.[96] Even after the institutionalization of the state, this dislocation would endure in different ways and at deeper levels. The practice of the politics of exclusion rather than inclusion portended an ominous future for the new nation.

The GPRA moved to Algiers on 3 July 1962, two days after the overwhelming vote for national independence "cooperating with France," but it found itself inexorably confronted by Ben Bella and Boumedienne, headquartered at Tlemcen. On 11 July they established their Political Bureau in hostile opposition to the GPRA. Efforts to negotiate a power accommodation failed; the "summer of shame" began.[97] Internal ALN (Armée de Libération Nationale) units, especially those of Wilaya 4, supported the GPRA and resented the well-armed and well-fed externals who had enjoyed the haven of frontier sanctuaries during the War of Liberation. When Ben Bella ordered Boumedienne to march on Algiers, internals put up a brief but bitter resistance. Power gravitated to the Political Bureau ostensibly but actually to Boumedienne and the military. This tragic culmination after years of courageous struggle against colonialism tainted the FLN's heroic revolutionary image and cast a shadow of illegitimacy over postcolonial Algerian governments.

The Human Dimension: Decolonization and Repatriation

On 31 December 1960, Charles de Gaulle addressed his nation: "Needless to say, no matter what happens, France will protect her children, whatever their origin, in their persons and in their property, just as she will safeguard her own interests."[98] In many respects France's efforts on behalf of repatriated or "expatriated" communities fell far short of expectations.

Indeed, the victims of expatriation/repatriation as well as the growing Algerian emigrant worker community in France added a unique human dimension, another intangible to haunt the postcolonial period and the bilateral relationship.

The *Pieds-Noirs*

The despair of decolonization caused the great *"exode"* (exodus) after the signing of the Evian Accords and the rue d'Isly massacre a week later. Fanned by indiscriminate individual and organized intercommunity and fratricidal violence (perpetrated especially by the OAS) and compounded by the French army's noninterference after the signing of the Accords, the specter of abandonment materialized and panicked the *pieds-noirs*.[99] One *pied-noir* equated this murderous milieu with a hypothetical situation where all Israelis would be disarmed, leaving only the Palestinians with weapons.[100] Another bitterly recounted how she was forced out of her estate in the Oranais by the army—the *French* Army.[101]

Suffering from their own "psychoexistential" mentality that projected a superiority complex, most *pieds-noirs* found the idea of an "Arab" Algerian independence unbearable.[102] From their perspective, they had constructed Algeria for France; it belonged to themselves and France. *Pieds-noirs* were portrayed by the French press as OAS supporters, while actually the vast majority who entered France were confused, disoriented victims of its terror.[103] Some *pieds-noirs* who openly supported the cause of *Algérie française* were threatened and even imprisoned. One *pied-noir* confided that he was sent to an internment camp for seven months "all for holding a political opinion."[104] Ironically, the *pieds-noirs* were now stereotyped as they had done to Algerians. Pierre Bourdieu observed at the time: "There is a good deal of unfairness in the attitude of those Frenchmen who make the *pieds-noirs* their scapegoats and blame all the tragic happenings in Algeria on their racism. . . . it is the colonial Algeria that has produced the *pied-noir* and not the reverse."[105] There were also *pieds-noirs* who expected and accepted eventual independence in some form; some even supported and collaborated with the FLN.

An interviewed *pied-noir* couple who remained in Algeria declared that they had anticipated independence after Morocco and Tunisia had gained theirs. They contended, however, that what angered the Europeans was not so much de Gaulle's decision on independence as the "betrayal" and perfidy of the French president who misled them through his calculated ambiguities.[106] With his eyes filled with tears, another *pied-noir* declared that if he had known what the future of French Algeria was to be, he would have shot de Gaulle dead when he passed in front of him in Oran on the day (6 June 1958) the general declared: "Yes, France is here, with her vocation. She is here forever."[107]

The influx of *pieds-noirs* in France was unexpected. Official repatriation plans of the French government proved grossly inadequate.[108] Most *pieds-noirs* were very dissatisfied with their "welcome." It was "zero," according to one *pied-noir* woman.[109] Despite the slowdown of the repatriation in the fall of 1962, problems of finding employment and housing and of contending with the official bureaucracy continued to aggravate the anxious repatriates.[110] Fortunately, within several years the expanding French economy managed to absorb this industrious population. The demographic data underscored the *pied-noir* community's traumatic displacement. There were slightly more than one million Europeans in French Algeria in 1961. By the signing of the Algiers Accords in July 1965, their number had dropped to about seventy thousand.[111]

From a strictly political perspective, the terrible and traumatic unanticipated mass repatriation of the *pieds-noirs* was highly significant. Their repatriation removed an anticipated problematic variable in the postcolonial bilateral relationship. Furthermore, with the enormous loss of settler cadres, cooperation now was imperative and Algeria's continued need for France was underscored.

The Jews

The word *exode* especially applied to the Jewish community of Algeria, most of whom also fled, ending a long and significant historical presence. Jews had arrived in Algeria as early as the period of Phoenician exploration and enterprise. Their numbers increased with the spread of the Diaspora under the Romans and again, in the fourteenth and fifteenth centuries, in the wake of Andalusian persecutions during the *reconquista*. The dispute over a French debt to a Jewish merchant firm in Algiers was a cause of the invasion of Algeria in 1830.[112]

During the colonial period, settlers steeped in anti-Semitism repeatedly targeted the Jews. Settlers also attempted to incite rivalries between Jews and Muslims.[113] The Crémieux Law gave Jews French citizenship in 1870, but this did not stop prejudice or particularly serious assaults in 1897–98. The resistance to the Blum-Viollette initiative in the 1930s stemmed in part from the fact that Blum was a Jew. In 1941, Vichy fulfilled the wish of many *pieds-noirs* by abrogating the Crémieux Law until de Gaulle's Free French movement restored Jewish rights. Mendès-France's decolonizing policies in Indochina, Tunisia, and Morocco were the more suspect because of his Jewish background. Despite this discriminatory climate, the Algerian Jews assimilated very well. Many abandoned their Judeo-Arabic language (written in Hebrew) and adopted French. Their economic and political success in colonial Algeria contributed significantly toward producing *pied-noir* prejudice.

The FLN regarded the Jews as natural allies, given the anti-Semitic sentiments of the *pieds-noirs*. Nevertheless, as the War of Independence continued, the community was placed in a difficult position. Resented by the *pieds-noirs*, even though the Jews shared their assimilated values, they were also confronted by an Arab nationalism intensified by the defeats of Arab armed forces by Israel in 1948 and in 1956. This was tragically symbolized by the well-publicized killings of William Lévy, the Socialist Party's secretary-general for Algiers, by the OAS, and of his son by the FLN. Other incidents during the war included the desecration of a Jewish cemetery in Oran and, on 12 December 1960, the attack on the Great Synagogue of Algiers by Muslims. As late as 1961, the FLN still declared: "The homeland of the Jews of Algeria is Algeria." Further, it proclaimed: *"For the first time in History the Jews have been claimed—and by a government composed of followers of another religion—as the sons of one and the same country."*[114] Yet insecurity for political and cultural reasons nevertheless forced another Jewish diaspora. This time they had somewhere to go. Out of 140,000 Algerian Jews in 1954, some 110,000 opted to settle in France[115] and 8,500 chose Israel; Marseille became a staging point for further emigration.[116] A small number remained in Algeria.[117]

Algerian Jews benefited from official repatriation programs and especially from the well organized and mobilized Fonds Social Juif Unifié (FSJU).[118] This organization succeeded in "humanizing" the welcome, which was often lacking in governmental efforts. Though there were fewer Jews to repatriate, the FSJU relieved the hard-pressed French government. The arrival of Algerian Jews in France introduced cultural differences into French Judaism. The major difference was that they were Sephardic, but this was less a cultural conflict than an enrichment of French Jewry.[119] Like other repatriated populations, the Algerian Jews encountered relocation problems. Often they were sent to areas where there were no synagogues. Again this community displayed great initiative by instituting itinerant rabbinical missions. In Marseille the Jewish population rose from 10,000 to 70,000 and twenty new synagogues were constructed.[120] Out of all the repatriates from Algeria, the Jewish community's reinsertion (actually a first insertion in most cases) was most successful.[121]

The *Harkis*

The most pathetic displaced population remains the *harkis*. The term refers to Algerians who served in some military capacity for France during the war.[122] Their loyal service impressed French military cadres and particularly General Challe. Indeed, many of the officers who served with *harkis* tried personally to repatriate them, with mixed success.[123] In Algeria's anarchic dislocation after the signing of the Evian Accords, savage retribution caused the disappearance of many thousands.[124] Efforts by the Red Cross to locate the missing were frustrated.[125] Left behind after the war, they were all but forgotten.[126] Those subjected to internment often faced horrific tortures in concentration camps.[127] Despite the executions and other violent acts that ravaged the Muslim population already afflicted by years of atrocities on both sides, some *harkis* managed to escape to France, leaving families and friends behind only to face isolation and racial discrimination within the *métropole,* their country.[128] Their impoverished rural backgrounds inhibited their insertion into the modern French economy. In the postcolonial period the Bachaga Said Boualam (1906–82), with his son Ali (d. 1991), particularly publicized and championed the *harki* cause through his activism and his books *Mon pays . . .la France!* (1962), *Les Harkis au service de la France* (1963), and *Les Harkis sans la France* (1964).

Political Decolonization: An Appraisal

The Evian Accords did not simply terminate French Algeria. As will be seen, they marked in Foucauldian terms the surface "displacement" rather than the disappearance of colonial discourses and practices. On a deeper level, the ordering frameworks continued to serve as familiar interpretive grids during this transition. De Gaulle's Herculean effort successfully persuaded the French public that decolonization corresponded to France's grandeur and independence. Historic realities had changed, but not the immutability of essential France. The FLN attained independence, but the French legacy and presence qualified the new state's sovereignty. Above all, the nation needed a compelling and convincing definition of itself. Independence was a mighty step in this continuing existential quest. As power and both reception and perception of the other were transformed, relations between the two peoples and polities were recodified and identities redefined.

The Accords symbolized a diplomatic conjecture as well as a historic conjuncture of the colonial and postcolonial periods. They presented a new and unique historical relationship, imaginative and inventive, between an imperial nation and its most intimate former colonial possession. According to I. William Zartman, the Accords created "a delicate system of counterbalancing obligations between Algeria and France. In a sense, either the Accords left Algeria with a conditional independence, or the obligations were not absolutes at all but were merely subjects of continuing negotiations."[129] Given the impossibility of a clean transfer of power and the generally unforeseen vast upheavals in Algeria, the inconclusive nature of the Accords actually served both sides well. They provided a workable flexibility permitting the gradual transformation of relations during the postcolonial period. In 1962 history shifted, and with it the techniques of exercising power and imagining identity.

3

Independence with Interdependence, 1962–1965

We must take into account . . . the sequels of colonial domination. . . .
We must take into account the numerous implications of the Evian Accords. . . . This cooperation must not hinder the realization of our economic and social imperatives.
Ahmed Ben Bella, 28 September 1962

What France and Algeria are beginning to do in common is an example
for the whole world.
Charles de Gaulle, 21 March 1962

The Evian Accords and Algeria's subsequent independence marked a historic discontinuity, dramatically ending France's colonial domination and
imperial age. Nevertheless, there was also continuity, the perpetuation of
bilateral interdependence, as particularly illustrated by the first three years
of the postcolonial relationship. For France, the interdependence was primarily political, as Algeria retained a crucial strategic importance, especially concerning Third World relations, complementing French foreign
policy pursuits of grandeur and independence. For Algeria, its inevitable
reliance upon France for its social and economic needs, as exemplified by
a prodigious cooperation program, restricted its assertion of sovereignty
and its revolutionary identity. Ahmed Ben Bella delicately balanced confrontation and cooperation with the ex-*métropole* when dealing with a
variety of crises that repeatedly threatened the new national government.
Algeria's chronic instability magnified the already daunting existential
task of achieving definition and genuine deliverance and led to the coup of
19 June 1965.

De Gaulle's Foreign Policy Principles

In the opening pages of his *War Memoirs,* Charles de Gaulle equated
France with greatness: "France cannot be France without grandeur."[1] De
Gaulle perceived France as possessing a natural genius, a unique *élan* that
necessitated a world role. In 1963 he proclaimed: "France, because she
can do so, because everything invites her to do so, because she is France,

should conduct amidst the world a world power."[2] De Gaulle had an intuitive, mystical attachment to the notion that he was a symbolic incarnation of France's essentialism, and his powerful presence idealized a uniquely French spirit.[3]

Under de Gaulle, foreign policy became an act of international didacticism with France defining and regulating "the economic and diplomatic process by which relations are to be conducted."[4] To set the example and to attain the goal of greatness, there was this precondition, itself an objective: France had to be independent.[5] De Gaulle desired freedom of action, which meant no outside interference in the determination of French policy.[6] France had to be independent in order to help other nations acquire or reinforce their own independence.[7] Maurice Couve de Murville reasoned that by being independent itself, France could "from then on champion all independences."[8] By liberating itself from its colonial predicament, France ended its diplomatic dislocation caused by the Algerian War.[9] De Gaulle achieved his cherished opportunity to initiate a foreign policy predicated on grandeur and independence.

Superpower bipolarization, however, threatened French international objectives. The hegemonic pretensions of the Soviet Union and particularly the United States's political and military domination endangered France's "independence, her personality, her soul, and even her *raison d'être*."[10] France could not belong to either hegemony. Détente with the East emerged as a means to reinforce France's freedom from the West (as well as mapping a way of securing general peace). France advocated a "concerted" European policy in which Europe would coordinate political and economic policies and free itself from superpower dependence. De Gaulle directed this initiative more at the Americans than the Soviets, where the general hoped for a liberalization of Eastern Europe. The symbolic affirmation of French leadership would be the development and deployment of de Gaulle's vaunted atomic deterrent weapon system, the *force de frappe,* as the guarantor of European security.[11]

Gaullist foreign policy accepted political and ideological pluralism. It easily identified itself with the nonaligned Third World and supported its positions with the attractive offer of generous cooperation. Gaullism saw an amplified need for a strong and independent France: the need to offer the developing world a "third way," an alternative to the superpowers, in conducting foreign affairs. France could point the way as an exemplar toward creating the conditions of world peace.[12]

Frequently, de Gaulle recollected past glories when there was no questioning France's world power status. This was not political romance: it reflected his firm belief that France's national essence had a substance of grandeur and independence. This nature was eternal and should be reasserted throughout the world.[13] De Gaulle respected history and perceived the importance of understanding its changing realities. Stanley Hoffmann explained: "His *mystique* is not a quest for anachronism, a vain nostalgia for past greatness. . . . When he talks to the French about their greatness, then and now, it is in order to get them to adapt to, and to act in, the world as it is, not in order to keep them in a museum of past glories. It is flattery for reform."[14] His essence (a Bergsonian *élan vital*), which he equated with that of France, demanded that France's natural grandeur be "renovated" and "transformed," and "wedded to its times." His foreign policy aimed to project a dynamic identity that "could claim to be both revolutionary (opposed to big-power rule) and revisionist (possessed of a special right, founded on nuclear weapons and traditional and legal precedents, to global leadership and an elevated status among nations). It could be selfless and self-interested without fear of logical inconsistency or political hypocrisy."[15] The policy of cooperation with the Third World and especially Algeria was viewed as a vehicle to propel France's global resurgence.

Cooperation as Essentialism

Not surprisingly, the new policy of cooperation stemmed from earlier discourses and practices. It shared with colonialism "élans" including "the same presumptions and vanities."[16] For example, perpetuated ideas like the glory and greatness of France, coupled with the self-imposed duty to spread the genius of its culture, affected colonial and postcolonial mentalities and especially "official minds."[17] Henri Brunschwig's analysis of colonial policy distinguished economic "myths" from political and psychological "realities" and concluded that the French regarded their imperialism as an "ideal." He wrote: "The pride of standing in the front rank of nations which were shaping the world of the future, the delight in ruling and the excitement of competing with foreign rivals: this is what gripped the public imagination."[18] Compare those ideas with Stéphane Hessel's analysis of a poll published in 1967 surveying French attitudes toward cooperation with the Third World. Its popularity (75 percent in favor) was attributed in part to "the French fear, conscious or not, that their country [was] becoming a second rate power" and that France was no longer pursuing its "universal, civilizing mission" or its "veritable grandeur." Consistent with the Orleanist commissions and Brunschwig's interpretation, postcolonial French public opinion considered cooperation "the means to assure for France, today and in the future, a respected place in the world [and] to permit France to remain a great power politically, economically, and culturally."[19]

Charles F. Gallagher observed: "Co-operation seems to be becoming an integral part of the French national personality of the 1960's and of its projection abroad—a new form of cultural universalism which has always marked this country in the past."[20] Gallagher referred to the "complex motivations" involved with postcolonial assistance programs, which included a "vestigial chauvinism and a retained sense of imperial missions, with territorial and physical sublimated into the cultural."[21] I. William Zartman considered cooperation a "habitude,"[22] while Alfred Grosser viewed it as fundamentally an institutional, structural continuity. "This explanation may appear to be little enlightening or logical," Grosser wrote, "but it appears to me to be the essential explanation behind the continuing of aid both to Algeria and to Africa. . . . Things are in place, the structures, the forms of financial aid, of technical assistance."[23]

France flaunted cooperation as a means of reconciliation, and certainly many *coopérants* viewed themselves as symbols of a changed mentality. Stéphane Hessel, a leading theorist of cooperation, reflected:

> Equating independence with cooperation for Algeria was a formidable challenge for both partners and resulted in a major step forward in French development thinking. Many of the experimental procedures developed in sub-Saharan Africa had to be reshaped to meet Algerian requirements. Thousands of young Frenchmen, allowed to fulfill their military obligations as technical assistants overseas [beginning in 1963], acquired feeling for the problems and tasks of the developing world during their year in Algeria.[24]

The French have portrayed themselves traditionally "as a people in some sense exemplary for the rest of the world, that allowed them to pretend to a certain intangible hegemony over less richly endowed countries."[25] Maurice Couve de Murville recognized a "missionary aspect" present in cooperation "to teach, to spread, if not to preach, the language and the culture of France." France favored francophone states since a French cultural presence gave the former *métropole* great advantages over other nations when competing for interests.[26] Couve de Murville described cooperation as "the means to pursue the civilizing work and development conducted by the colonial power."[27] Consider this updated essentialist reflection by Charles Flotte, a French *coopérant* serving in independent Algeria: "We shall have had the privilege in the course of our professional life to be able to assist a people to develop. We shall have done it in the name of human equality and in the name of fraternity between peoples[,] and this will be our sole title of glory."[28] The civilizing mission was recodified now as the *rayonnement* (a "radiant" diffusion of influence) of France but was still fundamentally expressed in a deontological discourse. When listing his first term's accomplishments, de Gaulle naturally included "cooperation replacing colonialism."[29]

There was also a compensatory, expiatory dimension to cooperation. It served as a "substitution" to "'fill a void,' and prevent a disastrous rupture between the new states and the former colonizer."[30] Nicole Grimaud perceived cooperation as palliating a "bad conscience," fulfilling a "moral obligation," and "perpetuating a presence under a modern and generous form, in harmony with the transformation of international relations." Finally, it was a means "to compensate the . . . painful loss of Algeria."[31] Robert Buron regretted how the OAS undercut Evian guarantees to the dwindling European minority, but he also admired how cooperation created a vital "new French presence" in Algeria.[32]

Algerians recognized the ideological contradictions inherent in cooperation, since it perpetuated that French presence and underscored the "liberated" nation's embarrassing postcolonial dependence upon the ex-*métropole*. Yet it was also necessary. Abdelaziz Bouteflika, who served as foreign minister under Presidents Ahmed Ben Bella and Houari Boumedienne, credited cooperation with expediting "a spectacularly rapid decolonization."[33] Later he reflected that cooperation itself was difficult to define. Nevertheless, he claimed that it prevented a "divorce" between the two countries. From his perspective, cooperation suggested that "Algeria had the right to material, moral, and political reparations, and that France was disposed to fulfill its obligations in these domains."[34] According to Redha Malek, cooperation was accepted because of enduring "friendly ties . . . between the French and Algerian peoples" and, significantly, a consequence of "French culture learned by Algeria's generations." To Malek, cooperation represented "all that France undertook in participating in modern Algeria's development."[35] During President Valéry Giscard d'Estaing's visit to Algeria in 1975, President Boumedienne stated that cooperation was more than a "framework of formal and bilateral accords," it was an "ethic."[36]

In an article in *Révolution africaine*, Mustapha Sehimi perceived the essentialist nature of cooperation. It was ideologically compatible with Christian morality and the humanitarian ideals of the Enlightenment. It ensured the continuation of French strategic interests while projecting a new model for relations between developed and developing nations. Above all, it underscored that "a French presence must be maintained. Why? Because her presence is the best of any other."[37] Algerians understood France's political and cultural egoism and the reality that its presence in Algeria was transformed rather than terminated.

Raymond Aron wrote that during the imperial period the national "dream was to transform the empire into an overseas France."[38] D. Bruce Marshall described "the dream" as a French "colonial myth" which idealized "a worldwide community of peoples bound together into a single nation by common ties of economic and political interest, embodied in republican governmental institutions, and sharing a common cultural base."[39] The myth incorporated "the idea that France had a special mission to initiate the colonial peoples into the responsibilities of modern political life."[40] The colonial myth may have been "decolonized," but not necessarily "demythified." The establishment of the French Community and the conclusion of a constellation of cooperation agreements with new francophone states disclosed the perpetuation of essentialist principles and the reformulation of the colonial myth. This also applied to Algeria. When de Gaulle promoted the Constantine Plan he declared that "a vast physical and spiritual transformation is under way in Algeria. France, because it is her duty and because she alone is capable of doing it—France is bringing about this transformation."[41] He equated Algerian "transformation" with French "renovation" as a great and independent world power, and viewed cooperation with Algeria as a global model: "International life may be transformed by this, in the direction of our spirit, which is that of liberty, of equality and fraternity. By adopting this vast and generous plan, the French people are going to contribute, once more in their history, to the enlightenment of the world."[42] To de Gaulle, it finally became a question of adapting discourse and practice semantically and syntactically in order to protect and promote French influence and interests. Cooperation with Algeria and other francophone states represented a recalibrated instrument of power and a reformulated essentialism.

French Opposition to Cooperation

The great assistance Algeria would receive, and the liberal policy of global cooperation pursued by France in the immediate postcolonial era, provoked great controversy and threatened to become a serious political issue. In a series of articles (1963–64) in the popular magazine *Paris-Match*, editor-in-chief Raymond Cartier urged that the financial assistance accorded to the Third World be invested instead within France, itself underdeveloped and needing aid. Cartier especially ridiculed French aid to Algeria after nationalizations were not followed by indemnities.[43] France's commitment of *coopérants* was inherently foolish, given the Algerian objective of Arabization.[44] Cartier characterized the material investment and achievement in the latter days of colonial Algeria as an "apotheosis of folly." He wrote: "It is impossible to speak of it without infuriation."[45] He repeatedly criticized Algerian policy during the early postcolonial period.[46]

The Jeanneney Report of June 1963 complemented Cartier's fundamental criticisms. This unofficial report analyzed French aid policy and recommended changes to make it more effective (e.g., less attention to the franc zone).[47] The commission faulted the administration of French aid and proposed restructuring the system and exploring multilateral channels.[48] While recognizing an intangible cultural (or essentialist) imperative to accord aid, it saw the amplitude threatening France's own economic growth. The Jeanneney Report advised that aid be limited to a still impressive 1.5 percent of the GNP.[49]

Naturally, the Jeanneney Report fueled the Gaullist opposition. Cartier called those who drew it up *ironistes* for suggesting that there were "contingent and long-term advantages" to French programs.[50] Less satirical, Guy de Carmoy cited Jeanneney Report evidence and concluded that "the policy of cooperation has been more disadvantageous to the French economy than to its principal industrial competitors, whose direct costs are lower and who have neither indirect costs to contend with nor loss of assets."[51] Yves Fuchs, a Marxist and former *coopérant,* maintained that cooperation was a means of safeguarding "colonial links" and of securing "a sphere of influence particularly in Africa." He accused the Jeanneney Report of "masking this imperialist power under the cover of certain moral justifications."[52] Alfred Grosser agreed that "as the Jeanneney Report implied, there are scarcely any economic arguments to justify our form of technical assistance and aid."[53] He realized, however, that cooperation was popular even among anti-Gaullists, who diverged "more on the means than on the purpose of cooperation, which is the presence of France in the world."[54] Citing the numbers of engaged *coopérants* in Algeria, Robert Buron simply stated: "The young are not 'Cartiéristes'."[55]

De Gaulle Responds

The Gaullists' opposition attacked cooperation by using economic arguments; de Gaulle defended on political grounds. During his 31 January 1964 press conference, he admitted that aid was "costly for us" and even cited statistics from the Jeanneney Report. Expressing, however, his politics of prestige, he declared: "There is not a single nation in the world that dedicates to the progress of others a similar proportion of what it is doing for its own." De Gaulle asserted that "the importance of cooperation relates less to figures and immediate results than to the advantages of a general nature which it can ensure in the future for ourselves and our partners."[56] These advantages were political, though de Gaulle had mentioned earlier that "the concessions granted us with regard to certain raw materials, particularly a share of the Algerian oil, are not without value to us."[57] As during the colonial period, economics played a secondary role in French policy. De Gaulle viewed cooperation as a means of establishing new multilateral political relationships within the new historical realities and opportunities resulting from *France's* liberation from the Algerian War.

In general, French essentialism facilitated the remarkably smooth transition from colonialism to cooperation, especially under the stewardship of de Gaulle. Its successful implementation in Algeria was crucial to France's own political, and moral, transformation from an imperialist to a *tiersmondiste* (Third-Worldist) nation and to the credibility and legitimacy of the Fifth Republic. Edward Kolodziej summarized: "De Gaulle could hardly let Algeria go. Vindication of his personal leadership and France's global mission significantly depended upon the success of the postwar relations."[58] Thus a paradox arose: though freed from Algeria, France still needed Algeria. There was another critical consideration, as Alfred Grosser perceived: "The FLN assumed responsibility for the future Algerian state. . . . It was in France's best interest to see the leaders of the FLN become the government of Algeria."[59]

Ben Bella and the Revision of the Evian Accords

Though a tenet of Gaullist foreign policy was noninterference in the internal affairs of another country, France feared a "congolization" of Algeria and consequently cooperated with the Political Bureau of Ahmed Ben Bella during the tragic postindependence civil war. Arslan Humbaraci contended that French intelligence informed Paris that the Political Bureau was politically more viable. Thus, the French opened the Tunisian border barricades for Houari Boumedienne's external ALN as well as supporting columns.[60] Nicole Grimaud reported the "public rumor" that the French government had "promised" Ben Bella that it would not interfere as long as the Evian Accords were not contested. Louis Joxe told the

Council of Ministers that neither elite faction contested Evian.[61] By the time Ben Bella assumed power, cooperation was substantially in place because of agreements signed with the Algerian Provisional Executive. Therefore, Evian stipulations were implemented despite the ideological opposition to them enunciated by the Tripoli Program and particularly the Political Bureau.

The new National Constituent Assembly met on 25 September 1962 and elected Ferhat Abbas its president. Ben Bella became premier the following day and the ambitious Boumedienne became defense minister. In September 1963, Ben Bella was elected president after the first constitution had been approved. From the beginning, the strength of the political bond between Ben Bella and Boumedienne (and what was left of the politically active nationalist elite) lay in their opposition to the Evian Accords and France.

The Evian Accords Challenged

Before Canadian television in October 1962, Ben Bella announced that "the Evian Accords constituted a compromise in certain regards incompatible with the socialist perspectives of Algeria."[62] On 8 November 1962, the Algerian leader criticized their "stranglehold on our development" and declared that "they had to be adapted to reality."[63] Then on 20 March 1963, ten days after a French nuclear test in the Sahara, Ben Bella called for the revision of the Accords. To Ben Bella, the Accords represented a political solution to a political problem, and should be followed more in spirit than by the letter.[64] Jean de Broglie, secretary of state for Algerian affairs, retorted: "Adaptation does not mean revision. It is not in question to open negotiations . . . to review the Evian Accords and to replace them by others."[65] Nevertheless, both sides understood that historical conditions had changed dramatically since March 1962.

There was no longer a sizable European minority, as a result of the traumatic events after Evian, especially the OAS scorched-earth campaign of terror. The anarchic settler departure vitiated the meticulous articles designed to protect the *pieds-noirs*. Though Evian declared a general amnesty and prohibited acts of revenge, there were thousands of European and especially *harki* casualties (including "disappearances"). The Algerian government curtailed the remaining European community's civil, economic, and political "guarantees."[66] Concurrently, the principle of "freedom of movement" between Algeria and France was limited—notably by the emigrant labor accord of April 1964—and capital transfers were frozen.

Political, social, economic, and ideological pressures, such as the imperative to apply the Tripoli Program's principles, prodded the Ben Bella government. Nationalization became an attractive alternative and earned popular support. The tobacco industry and the media were soon under the control of the government. The dramatic decision to expropriate vacated settler land and property was a risk, but it was one Ben Bella was compelled to take.

Autogestion and the Decrees

During the Revolution the FLN projected agrarian reform as an immediate objective of an independent Algeria. It was a plank of the Soummam Platform (1956) and eventually stipulated within the Evian Accords.[67] French negotiators had perceived the inevitability of the continuation of reform (possibly radical reform) in that sector and wanted Paris's participation in order to protect the remaining *colons*. Nevertheless, settler flight left *pied-noir* property and particularly *colon* farms vacant. *Fellahin* spontaneously moved in and began to manage farms and factories themselves.[68] This process evolved into a remarkable form of socialism, resembling the Yugoslav system, called *autogestion* (self-management). Ben Bella characterized *autogestion* as the "most precious achievement of the Revolution."[69] An official publication regarded the spontaneity of *autogestion* as "the result of a natural collectivist mentality" and "the original Algerian way toward socialism."[70] Ben Bella told Robert Merle: "He who attacks *autogestion* . . . violates the elementary rights of the masses, hoodwinks and betrays them, and stabs them in the back."[71] Nevertheless, *autogestion* needed direction. Furthermore, the emergence of privileged self-managed socialist farms contrasting with undercapitalized private plots recast the prejudicial modern/traditional colonial duality within the sector.

Richard Brace asked Ben Bella "what his most important and first work inside Algeria would be." Ben Bella answered, "Agricultural reform."[72] During his reflections with Robert Merle, Ben Bella later described the paradox of dependence in spite of independence as it related to this sector: "As long as Algerian soil was still in the hands of the big landowners, whether French or Algerian, the words 'Independence' and 'Revolution' made no sense, and the Tripoli programme remained a dead letter."[73] A joint commission established in the fall of 1962 aimed to resolve anticipated indemnification problems in the first sector. Concurrently, the Algerian government expected French agricultural assistance, especially in the development of trained cadres.[74] Continuing upheavals in this sector, however, ended the discussions.

A series of decrees beginning in October 1962 instituted the legal framework for the *autogestion* system and finally led to the nationalization of all European property in October 1963.[75] The five thousand farms nationalized were considered as reparations for the eight thousand Algerian villages destroyed during the War.[76] According to Algeria's interpretation of the Evian Accords, France was responsible for indemnification.

Paris Reacts

These decrees represented a unilateral Algerian repudiation of Evian guarantees, but they also allowed France to loosen its interpretation of the Accords on other points. Conforming to Evian stipulations, the French planned to participate in Algerian agricultural reform, e.g., through conversations in Paris in late January 1963, which also provided an opportunity to protect and possibly preserve the remaining *colons'* property. After the March Decrees, which defined and dealt with vacated property to expedite expropriation, a communiqué issued by Jean de Broglie conveyed France's irritation over Algerian actions; however, it also signaled a liberal French interpretation of the Evian Accords. While recognizing Algeria's political, social, and economic problems, France stated that its objective was "to aid Algeria to overcome these difficulties," asserting that "cooperation . . . is the basis of the Evian Accords."[77] The Europeans in Algeria were no longer as decisively important as a year earlier.

France conceded Algeria's right of nationalization but condemned the lack of proper indemnification.[78] Though official French reaction was remarkably mild, public outrage pressured de Gaulle's government. Paris informed Algiers that financial aid would be cut slightly to indemnify some of the *colons* affected by the agricultural nationalizations. Though this was a French violation of the Evian Accords, de Broglie attempted to mollify the Algerian government by assuring them of early French withdrawal from military bases.[79] The October 1963 nationalizations removed the possibility of an immediate French commitment toward Algerian agrarian reform.[80] While Algerian unilateral initiatives angered French policymakers, generous financial, commercial, technical, and cultural cooperation continued. France's strategic political and economic interests and investments necessitated continuing a positive relationship despite repeated humiliations. De Gaulle said: "Fundamentally, now that almost all the *pieds-noirs* have left, it's only petroleum and the [atomic] tests that count."[81]

Edward Kolodziej contended that President de Gaulle understood and even respected the Algerian government's refusal to recognize Evian safeguards. There was a Gaullist sympathy for "the Algerian claim that it had a sovereign right to deal with its nationals as it wished and that treaty obligations were subject to reinterpretation when they conflicted with state interests. De Gaulle was to display the same logic for entirely different purposes in his unilateral revision of French commitments within NATO in 1966."[82] De Broglie admitted that "adjustments [to the Accords] are conceivable," though he added ambiguously that "they do not denature at all the previous commitments."[83]

A Privileged Cooperation

Cooperation can be defined as the totality of relations between France and a developing nation. What made cooperation with Algeria so important was Paris's perception of its strategic geopolitical position. Poised between the Arab and African worlds, Algeria also enjoyed popularity and prestige among the developing nations. A privileged relationship with Algeria would open that "narrow door," as articulated by Jean de Broglie, extending a penitent France's influence into the Third World.[84] Generous aid through a variety of programs asserted France's "third way" and promoted Paris's image of independence from the superpowers. Another consideration was that vast aid to Algeria prevented a humiliating Cuba-like situation in North Africa, since there was already the Guinean embarrassment.[85] Finally, it was in the Algerian Sahara that France first tested the *force de frappe,* the paramount symbol of grandeur and independence.

Algeria's economic potential excited France, especially as it complemented French political and foreign policy objectives.[86] The Evian Accords reaffirmed the organic economic relationship, safeguarded major colonial development enterprises, and ensured French participation and predominance in Algeria's development. Underscoring Algeria's strategic importance, Paris inaugurated a special secretariat of state for Algerian affairs immediately after independence. Attached to the prime minister's office, the secretary of state was responsible for all aspects of cooperation. Louis Joxe was secretary from July 1962 to January 1963, followed by Jean de Broglie, who viewed the "cooperation that links the two countries [as] an example in the relations of a country with a liberal economy with one that has opted socialist, an industrial country with an underdeveloped one, a former *métropole* with an emancipated country; it constitutes a pilot experience in which its success will contribute at the same time to the peace of the world and to the prestige of the power that conceived it."[87] Paris viewed cooperation as the vehicle to propel France's global resurgence; it was in France's definite interest to see Algeria succeed.

Ben Bella's government inaugurated an Algerian position that was both pragmatic and principled. Though the superpowers expressed an interest in the new state, their real support was minimal compared with what France could offer.[88] Yet the Tripoli Program saw cooperation as neocolonialism, seemingly incompatible with the socialist option—a "conversion, by which neocolonialism tries to substitute itself for classic colonialism."[89] This view was reinforced two years later in the Algiers Charter of April 1964, the product of an FLN congress and another illustration of Algeria's existential praxis.[90] The charter legitimized the FLN as "the avant-garde of the Algerian people" and their *"moteur principal,"* emphasized the socialist option, and perceived Algeria as enduring a "period of transition" from capitalism to socialism. Evian was a "compromise peace" which needed to be "rearranged to Algeria's national interest." Still, until Algeria could fend for itself, dependence on the willing ex-*métropole* was inevitable and in many ways even desirable, though it also meant that Algiers risked embarrassment.

Military Cooperation

On the first anniversary of the Evian Accords, France symbolically challenged Algerian sovereignty by detonating a nuclear device in the Sahara. Ben Bella vociferously demanded the end of nuclear testing and the revision of military clauses of the Accords. While acknowledging France's right to test, Ben Bella asserted that the "veritable spirit" of cooperation rested with the stipulated phrases of "mutual respect" and "reciprocity of benefit and interest."[91] The timing of the settler expropriation decrees later in the month probably reflected Algeria's disapproval of France's military presence.[92]

In order to improve relations, de Gaulle's government accommodated Ben Bella's most desired objective, a revision of the Evian Accords' military clauses. By an agreement of 2 May 1963, the French promised to accelerate the evacuation of French troops. According to David and Marina Ottaway, Algeria "backed down over the issue of French bases in order to safeguard cooperation."[93] Troop withdrawals, other than those at leased bases, were implemented about eight months ahead of schedule; they left by June 1964. This pleased Ben Bella since it presented "a new dimension" promoting "a fruitful and stable cooperation."[94] When France completed its atomic testing sites in the South Pacific, it vacated its Saharan bases in 1965.

Financial Cooperation

The Evian Accords stipulated the continuation of massive French financial assistance toward Algerian development. An accord concluded on 26 June 1963 provided an annual aid package of FF 800 million, divided between *aide libre* (free aid) and *aide liée* (linked, or tied, aid). Free aid was transferred to the development fund of the Algerian treasury called the Caisse Algérienne de Développement (CAD). This aid could be allocated as Algeria wished. Linked aid—made, like free aid, in the form of grants—was directed toward realizing the projects of the Constantine Plan. This aid was allotted by the perpetuated Caisse d'Equipement pour le Développement de l'Algérie (CEDA).[95] French loans at this time were long-term—more than ten years, with one-third exceeding twenty years—at interest rates of only 1 to 3 percent.[96] France permitted "treasury advances," which funneled francs to Algeria in order to stabilize the deteriorating financial situation. Until 12 November 1962, the French and Algerian treasuries remained integrated, with Algiers receiving unlimited drawing rights. A debt estimated at one billion francs was accumulated.[97]

Financial cooperation provided, on the one hand, stark evidence of Algeria's dependence upon France. From the Algerian perspective, the Evian financial aid package protected French interests and inhibited the exercise of the "socialist option." *Révolution africaine* reported that 45 percent of linked aid allocations "without Algerian control directly profited French enterprises." Another 28 percent continued the financing of Constantine Plan projects that "presented enormous inconveniences and involved serious constraints for Algeria." New enterprises to be realized with French capital received the remaining 27 percent of linked aid. Algiers viewed free aid, the other half of the financial aid program, as insufficient "reparations." This dependence hampered diversification.[98]

On the other hand, the aid package staved off not only financial failure but also political bankruptcy. French generosity permitted Algeria to pursue a highly visible and ideological foreign policy in spite of embarrassing financial contradictions. Transfers did protect the investments of the Fourth and Fifth Republics, but Algerian economic planners fundamentally endorsed the French direction of development long after this "period of organization" (the phrase used by Algerian minister of national economy Bachir Boumaza).

Table 3.1. French Aid, 1963–1965 (in millions of French francs)

	1963	1964	1965
Public aid			
Grants and loans	612	462	218
Cultural/technical cooperation	160	186	204
Economic/financial support	425	266	253
Subtotal	1,197	914	675
Private aid	927	862	599
Total	2,124	1,776	1,274

Source: *MTM*, no. 1625 (1976): 3653, citing OECD statistics.

In spite of France's qualified help, Algeria's loss of settler cadres and capital—often called the "hemorrhage" of the Algerian economy—meant a decrease in the tax base and, with it, purchasing power and financial freedom. This necessitated the development of national financial institutions.[99] Algeria took its first steps toward financial liberation with the introduction of the Algerian dinar (DA) in 1963. The creation of a currency disclosed Algeria's intention to leave the franc zone and assert its independent monetary and economic identity.[100]

Commercial Cooperation

The Evian Accords' promise of privileged commercial relations implied that France would maintain its domination and offer opportunities to the *patronat*. This was achieved by several commercial accords (30 November 1963, 18 December 1964). Paris recognized, however, Algiers's imperative to secure the French market for Algerian wine, the most crucial export of the new nation's fledgling economy, even if this meant angering French producers in the Midi. On 18 January 1964 the two countries concluded a commercial agreement that preset, for the period 1964–68, French importation at 33.8 million hectoliters of Algerian wine.

Algeria's situation with regard to commercial cooperation mirrored the financial predicament, since its commercial network remained integrated with France's. During the colonial period, Algeria's extroverted agricultural economy complemented the *métropole*'s, making it dependent upon French markets. Efforts to make Algeria more self-reliant through eleventh-hour development programs were ineffective and actually tightened dependence. Bachir Boumaza, Ben Bella's powerful economic minister, simply stated the obvious when he said that "the Algerian economy is dependent upon the French economy."[101] However, in the short term, both

Table 3.2. French Trade with Algeria, 1962–1965 (in millions of French francs)

	1962	1963	1964	1965
French exports	2,758.8	2,736.9	2,444.6	2,525.8
French imports	2,442.7	2,816.8	3,011.3	2,811.5
Balance	316.1	-79.9	-566.7	-285.7

Source: EIU, QER (Algeria, Morocco, Tunisia).

sides continued to need exclusive accessibility to their established markets. The commercial treaty concluded in June 1963 satisfied these Evian stipulations. Anxious to protect its infant industries and manufacturing, Algeria delineated customs zones in October, with France receiving preferential status, but the application of commercial restrictions to African francophone countries and the introduction of the dinar effectively removed Algeria from the franc zone.

By imposing some exchange controls, Algeria took substantial steps toward commercial liberation. The Algerian government had already endeavored to control agricultural marketing with its Office National de Commercialisation (ONACO) in December 1962, but with limited success.[102] Though Algeria considered the legacy of viticulture an "agricultural crime," the demand for a long-term French commitment was seemingly fulfilled with the January 1964 accord. It promised to preserve an export market while assisting state planning by the anticipated revenues. Boumaza rationalized that wine exportation was beneficial to France since the monies received led to orders for French equipment (and also toward remunerating nationalized settler growers).[103]

Nevertheless, there was a need for diversification. In 1964, France received 73 percent of Algeria's exports, while 70 percent of Algeria's total imports arrived from France.[104] With France increasingly importing hydrocarbons and Algeria still relying on a wide array of French commodities and durable goods, trade in the short term remained interdependent and remarkably balanced.

Cultural and Technical Cooperation

The multiple dislocations at independence necessitated the commitment of thousands of French *coopérants* (specialists and teachers) to Algeria. Cultural *coopérants* assumed academic positions ranging from primary to university levels; technical *coopérants* applied their expertise, especially in *formation* (training), in every sector.[105] The official "primary objective" was "the maintenance of essential services." By the spring of 1963, "essential results were obtained."[106] This was the brief period of "substitution." A particularly significant protocol toward providing *coopérants* was signed on 23 October 1963 to permit the recruitment of *coopérants militaires* or the Volontaires de Service National Actif (VSNA).[107] The VSNA opted to serve their military obligation in the service of cooperation. There were approximately 25,000 French cultural and technical specialists in Algeria in 1962. This figure dropped to about 12,000 in 1965.[108]

During the autumn of 1964, French and Algerian authorities defined a new direction for cultural and technical cooperation. First, Algerian cadres would be developed to ensure "Algerianization" of all sectors; education and technical training would become priorities. Second, recruitment and retention of *coopérants* would be actively pursued. Third, there would be evolution from direct assistance, in which *coopérants* actually assumed the vacant positions, to an indirect role in which *coopérants* would act as counselors/consultants to the newly formed Algerian cadres. Finally, cooperation would be applied to selected sectors according to their needs.[109]

Cultural and technical cooperation involved a deeper, existential question concerning language. As in other sectors, there would be a paradox. The Ben Bella government quickly posited Arabization as a way to (re)discover an Algerian identity, but it also perceived French as crucial for acquiring modern technology. The elite itself was francophone. Ben Bella recalled a speech before the Arab League in 1953 where his audience cringed at his speaking French.[110] As president, he said that it was difficult to express himself in Arabic but that Algerians "feel Arab from the bottom of our hearts."[111]

While the French linguistic presence in Algeria could be understood, in light of cultural chauvinism and the "foreign" status accorded Arabic during the colonial era, the continued use of French reflected the perpetuation of a postcolonial "psychoexistential" or "psycho-cultural" problem.[112] Cultural *coopérants* were surprised to see their students' preference for French literature over Algerian.[113] The Jeanneney Report viewed the French language as "a mode of expression and a method of thought."[114] This discursive "method of thought" threatened the assertion of an authentic Algerian identity. Marie-Odile Bouveresse affirmed correctly in her dissertation that "in effect, language like culture cannot be neutral."[115] Ben Bella understood that "when the colonial learns a foreign language, he more or less adopts the mental attitudes which that language interprets."[116]

The government initiated the Arabization of the primary schools, but there were inherent problems in this linguistic policy. Arabic is a complex language where words' meanings are often determined through velarizings, syllabic emphases, and glottal stops. While "classical" Arabic is widespread in the Mashriq, Berber languages and French have influenced the Maghrib. Therefore, Arabization itself was in certain ways an introduction or imposition of a foreign language and created further linguistic confusion. For example, the language in the media is primarily "classicist," contrasting markedly with dialectical spoken Arabic. Moreover, Kabyles evinced a distinct preference for their own Berber languages rather than Arabic. They also had a particular penchant for French, owing in part to colonial policy that promoted cultural divisions by favoring the Berbers. In 1963 Ahmed Taleb Ibrahimi called for a "rapprochement" between classical Arabic and the Maghribi dialect.[117] Indeed, there needed to be one between Arabic and French.[118] The arrival of Arabic teachers from Egypt and other countries would be portentous, as many of the instructors were influenced by a variety of Islamist political movements.

Ben Bella recognized an existential aspect to the linguistic dilemma, "the deep disquiet" of Algerians "when they try to give expression to their ideas in French, while at the same time they 'feel' in Arabic." Yet he realized that "it would certainly be folly to declare war on the French language in the name of ill-conceived nationalism, because it provides a most necessary bridge between the Algerian intelligentsia and Western expert knowledge," and he appreciated "the breadth of mind which the French language has given us," even while appealing to Algerians to "recover" Arabic.[119] Though Ben Bella gratefully credited *coopérants* for maintaining education in Algeria during the immediate postcolonial period,[120] technical and cultural cooperation displayed all the paradoxes of the bilateral relationship. Algerian identity, as posited by the FLN, would be both assisted and negated by it; cooperation was both collaboration and contradiction, benefit and betrayal.

Emigrant Labor

During the postcolonial period, the emigrant workers' presence in France was not only a painful legacy of French colonialism but also a consequence of the ironically convergent interests of French capitalism and Algerian socialism.[121] With France's economy still expanding in the 1960s, there was a continued demand for cheap unskilled labor. Algerian workers met this demand but were often victims of discrimination and violent assaults. Algerian governments officially aspired to "reinsertion" of the emigrant population, but the economic choices made during the postcolonial period perpetuated their exile. The paramount example was the decision to develop an ultramodern industrial sector that was not labor-intensive. Through it all, the workers have endured. As Malek Haddad wrote of these "orphans of the *mère-patrie*" in *La Dernière impression,* "there is something heroic in their presence."[122]

France benefited in many ways from the Algerian emigrant workers' presence. Though the money sent back to family in Algeria was a debit to the French balance of payments, the financial transfers provided an anti-inflationary service too. Algerians also contributed to French social security programs. The workers' remittances were invaluable across the Mediterranean. Germaine Tillion related during decolonization that the workers "support, directly or indirectly, a third of the rural Moslem population in Algeria."[123] Michel Massenet believed at independence that their monies directly enabled 1.25 million Algerians to subsist. Other economists claim that the number was as high as 2 million. In certain areas of the Constantinois and Kabylia, 80 percent of the population's revenues came from these workers.[124]

In 1962 the Evian Accords had reaffirmed the principle of "freedom of movement" between the countries.[125] But the escalating arrival of Algerians seeking security and employment, concurrent with the *pied-noir exode,* indicated the need for regulation.[126] An accord on 10 April 1964 tied workers' access to the passing of a French-monitored medical examination but also, more important, to job availability in France (reviewed trimestrially). France agreed to provide vocational training. A joint commission was supposed to supervise the accord, under which about twelve thousand emigrants could enter France each year, but many Algerians entered illegally or remained as "false tourists"—a practice that had prompted the 1964 accord in the first place. Mark J. Miller contended that Algerian compliance with French quota demands "probably contributed to the downfall of the Ben Bella government."[127]

Hydrocarbons

The most important economic correlative of Gaullist foreign policy objectives was to protect the concessions of the French petroleum companies whose discoveries and subsequent production freed France from an embarrassing overdependence on Anglo-American hydrocarbon purchases. The Evian Accords secured French interests by assuring (1) the perpetuation of the Code Pétrolier (with its eleventh-hour modifications giving the

Table 3.3. Algerian Petroleum and Natural Gas Production, 1962–1965

	1962	1963	1964	1965
Petroleum*	20,452	23,568	26,670	26,365
Natural gas**			809	1,839

*Petroleum production measured in thousands of metric tons.
**Natural gas production measured in millions of cubic meters. Its production was not begun until 1964.

Source: Gérard Destanne de Bernis, "L'Economie algérienne depuis l'indépendance," in CRESM, *Les Economies maghrébines*, 15.

companies full freedom in their transfer flows while preserving their property rights and their preferential treatment in concession granting) and (2) the promotion of the use of French francs in all hydrocarbon financial matters, to fortify the international value of that currency. The *franc pétrole* became another important political symbol. French companies, with their position entrenched, continued to expand production.[128] The Organisme Technique pour la Mise en Valeur du Sahara also disbursed official aid for energy exploration and exploitation. The French government forced importers to buy Saharan crude at an elevated price ($2.30/barrel) which increased the companies' profit, rate of amortization, and monies available for investment in the Sahara or other international areas. Paris's de facto control of the Saharan fields improved France's overall balance of payments, enhanced its competitive position, provided economic security, promoted modernization, and above all projected grandeur and independence.

The significance of the hydrocarbons (oil and natural gas) sector transcended economic matters of prices, metric tons, and cubic volumes; this sector's strategic implications often dictated the political temper and direction of French-Algerian relations.[129] It provided occasions for conflict as well as opportunities for cooperation. In spite of both countries' efforts to isolate this sector, the whole complex network of bilateral relations often hinged upon the hydrocarbons situation. Finally, the evolution of the hydrocarbons relationship had a multifaceted effect on France's and Algeria's assertions of their postcolonial national identities.

Algeria's existential perspective and discourse demanded liberation from the legacies of colonialism, which were best exemplified by the blatant neocolonial presence of French hydrocarbon concessions. The French position constrained Algeria's ambitious development plans and contradicted its revolutionary discourse and political image. Algeria's response to the French Saharan hydrocarbons establishment complemented its policy of economic independence, which aimed at the national recovery of all natural resources.

The FLN's Position during the War

Dating from its War of Liberation, the FLN displayed economic realism when referring to the hydrocarbons sector. The Algerian nationalists understood that Saharan hydrocarbon wealth could be exploited only with international capital's assistance. Nevertheless, the FLN regarded all contracts signed between France and the companies prospecting and producing in the Sahara as having a "provisional character."[130] Though eventual nationalization was intimated during the War, there was no outright declaration of that intention. By choice and necessity, the FLN had to defer all economic and social questions until the realization of political independence.

The FLN's immediate concern during the War was how the Saharan natural gas and particularly petroleum discoveries of 1954–56 would affect France's determination to keep Algeria in its colonial status. The FLN recognized that the Sahara had "very great psychological value" for France.[131] The French-controlled fields seeped not only oil and natural gas but also prestige. For the French companies, it was a first great find which could be flaunted before the fabulously successful Anglo-American Cartel.[132] Therefore, French hydrocarbons assets had both tangible and especially intangible aspects. After assuming power in 1958, de Gaulle perceived that France's position as a major oil and natural gas producer correlated with essentialist ideas of grandeur and independence, and he promoted an ambitious hydrocarbons policy that could advance French foreign policy objectives.

Algeria's Hydrocarbons Policy

The extensive French privileges acquired through the Evian Accords and subsequent agreements in August 1962 and June 1963 were challenged by the elaboration and evolution of an Algerian hydrocarbons policy. The Tripoli Program proclaimed Algeria's long-term objective in June 1962 as the "nationalization of mineral and energy riches."[133] But in the hydrocarbons sector as elsewhere, principled pragmatism dictated immediate policy. Algeria welcomed the importation of capital and cadres as long as it could increase its participation in production and profit. Yet the "Algerianization" goal of the Algiers Charter of April 1964 called for the training of national technicians.[134] In spite of its willingness to cooperate with concessionaires, the Algerian government was also willing to have conflict.

In October 1963, Algiers demanded that the companies reinvest their receipts within Algeria in order to stimulate development. The companies resisted, since this demand repudiated their rights under the Code Pétrolier. Algerian diplomatic determination forced their reconsideration, however, and in July 1964 the companies agreed to retain 50 percent of their receipts in Algeria.[135] The Algerian government also criticized the companies' declining commitment to exploration. Though there were registered strikes in 1963, in 1964 there were no major discoveries. The number of geophysical surveys and exploratory drillings dropped. Algeria conducted its first independent study in 1965.[136] Compounding Algeria's dissatisfaction over the companies' transfers and explorations was its minority capital participation in the sector. With the expanding volume of petroleum production, however, the Algerian government seized an opportunity to "capitalize."

The lack of a third pipeline prevented the expansion of Saharan production and commercialization. With the Code Pétrolier protecting their right of free transport, the companies organized a consortium to construct a new trunkline. The companies presumed automatic Algerian consent, since another pipeline would increase revenues. Astounding the companies, the Algerian government demanded a share of the pipeline's capital. The companies initially refused, invoking their legal rights. Nevertheless, the prospect of delayed construction or Algiers's refusal of new titles led to the consortium's offer of a fragmented participation with an assured dividend.[137]

Algeria's reaction was extraordinary for its time. On 31 December 1963, Algiers inaugurated a national enterprise called SONATRACH (Société Nationale pour la Recherche, la Production, le Transport, la Transformation et la Commercialisation des Hydrocarbures) to manage the pipeline's construction. Then in January 1964 the Algerian government announced that it would build the pipeline without the companies' participation. This marked the first time that a major oil-producing nation had taken such an initiative, and it complemented Algeria's progressive, if not revolutionary, image.

In September 1964, President Ahmed Ben Bella articulated Algeria's hydrocarbons policy.[138] First, Algeria was not content merely to collect royalties but wanted to play a more active role and participate in all aspects of production "from the wellheads to the gasoline pumps." Second, in exercising its legitimate sovereign rights in the Sahara, Algeria wanted the exploiting companies to understand that their operations must benefit Algeria's development as well as their own. A modus vivendi was desirable, for the moment, in order to preclude nationalization. Third, Algeria wanted all hydrocarbons questions discussed at the state-to-state level because of their national and international importance. Ben Bella's speeches on these matters can be viewed less as a definition than as a recapitulation of a policy in progress.[139]

Paris by now had perceived that conflicts between Algiers and the companies were inevitable, given the Algerian socialist option. After the Algerian government asked in October and November 1963 for state-level negotiations to redefine hydrocarbons relations, the French government agreed in December to open full negotiations and to represent the interests of the French companies.[140] The ensuing talks were cordial but tedious.

The Quai d'Orsay gave its economics chief, Olivier Wormser, considerable latitude. By early 1965, France had a negotiating advantage. An innovative Iranian contract, achieved despite determined Cartel competition, ensured a diversification of sources. In addition, French oil companies were very active in two promising regions, the North Sea and Nigeria. A French firm struck natural gas in the Netherlands, and a hydrocarbons agreement with the Soviet Union gave France another source of energy.

Meanwhile, Algeria's momentum had slowed, as efforts to attract foreign capital failed. An imaginative agreement with Italy's Ente Nazionale Idrocarburi (ENI) had stagnated. And the British, despite investing in the third pipeline, generally evinced a diminished interest in Algerian hydrocarbons that would last until the 1990s. The imminent end of French financial aid provided under the Evian Accords also pressured Algeria. By June 1965, the framework of a remarkable accord began to take definite shape.

The De Gaulle–Ben Bella Summit

In order to shore up relations, especially after the nuclear testing controversies and the agricultural nationalizations, de Gaulle secretly invited Ben Bella to Paris. On 13 March 1964, at the Elysée Palace, they discussed the bilateral relationship as well as world affairs privately and then with Foreign Minister Bouteflika, Ambassador Gorse, and Secretary of State de Broglie. The summit lasted from 3:30 to 5:00 P.M. Recounting the meeting to Alain Peyrefitte, de Gaulle said he found it ironic how Ben Bella had wanted the *pieds-noirs* to leave carrying their suitcases but now welcomed the arrival of *coopérants* with their luggage. He also strongly expressed to Ben Bella his concern about the flow of emigrant workers to France.[141] The French communiqué stated that the two presidents "indicated their common wish to maintain and to develop, in the interest of both countries, the policy of cooperation."[142] Algiers's *Le Peuple* reported that the presidents discussed the bilateral relationship and considered "large perspectives founded on our reciprocal interests."[143] After returning to Algiers, Ben Bella described his meeting as "fruitful and positive. I was able to have very open and very frank conversations with President de Gaulle. . . . The exchanges of views that we had . . . will also permit our countries to play a positive role . . . above all to consolidate the links between newly independent countries."[144] Ben Bella and de Gaulle perceived that their political objectives were closely linked to the bilateral relationship.

The two men shared certain personal characteristics. They were romantic politicians and egotists who attempted to personify their states and to pursue international prestige. According to Ben Bella, both presidents spoke during the summit of their ambition to lead strong, dynamic nations.[145] After the visit de Gaulle commented, "I have the impression that this man wishes us no harm."[146] Why should he? Ben Bella was a bit like himself, as would be his successor, Houari Boumedienne. This would be the last visit of an Algerian president to France until Chadli Benjedid's state visit in November 1983.

Ben Bella's Balancing Act

Ben Bella delicately and astutely balanced conflict with cooperation. After the Algerian government confiscated the wealthy *pied-noir* Henri Borgeaud's vast properties in March 1963, Ben Bella declared on 3 April: "We want no more Borgeauds in this country. Out with him, and good riddance. . . . If that's contrary to the Evian Accords, I don't care two hoots."[147] A month later, when he personified the image of revolutionary Algeria at the May 1963 Organization of African Unity meeting at Addis Ababa, he praised France's cooperation.[148] In June, before the Algerian National Assembly, Ben Bella presented cooperation as a model for relations between developed and developing nations, and said it "enlarges . . . our present possibilities."[149] A year later, Algiers hosted a denuclearization conference—but cautioned all participants not to criticize France.[150]

Algiers's reliance and dependence upon cooperation led to other contradictory political behavior. Though Algiers projected itself as the capital of revolutionary Africa and a bastion against imperialism, it was remarkably reserved, on the one hand, when de Gaulle dispatched *"paras"* to Gabon to reinstate Léon Mba in February 1964.[151] On the other hand, secure in its French financial cooperation agreements, Algiers could afford to affirm Arab solidarity by breaking relations with the Federal Republic of Germany after Bonn recognized Israel, even if this risked an important source of foreign aid.[152] Ben Bella's close ties with Moscow (which bestowed the Lenin Peace Prize upon him), the People's Republic of China, Cuba, Egypt, and even initially the United States were also strategic parries against Paris's advances. Algiers demonstrated its radical political potential while enduring its contradictory but necessary neocolonial link to France.

Economically, Algerian planners generally pursued French development plans protected by the Evian Accords. The Algerian difficulties with the Accords were fundamentally political, such as questions of sovereignty, rather than economic. As noted, the FLN had not blueprinted a national economy, its chief error according to some observers. Apart from *autogestion* and the nationalization of settler property, Algeria's development policy under Ben Bella was "in effect a continuation of the French effort."[153] This was determined, too, by the arrangement of financial aid programs provided by France. French projects like the Annaba (Bône) steel complex and the Algiers refinery were continued. Nevertheless, it was Ben Bella's government that founded SONATRACH, the national enterprise that would champion sovereignty by confronting the French and foreign hydrocarbon concessions in the Sahara.

In three years of personal rule, Ben Bella constantly confronted internal political opposition: vestigial Messalist factions, remnants of the Algerian Communist Party, Ait Ahmed's insurrectionary Front des Forces Socialistes (FFS) in Kabylia, the Union Générale des Travailleurs Algériens (UGTA), the Union Nationale des Etudiants Algériens (UNEA), and eventually members of his own government (Colonels Chaabani and Boumedienne).[154] Morocco's frustrations and ambitions along the western frontier and Algeria's insensitivity to them provoked a brief War of the Sands in October–November 1963 which humiliated Algeria's armed forces. Peace was restored under the auspices of the Organization of African Unity. According to David and Marina Ottaway, "Ben Bella could not stop to plan his course. In order to keep himself in power, he had to respond immediately to every threat, and these political acrobatics could only be accomplished at the expense of a coherent and chartered course of action."[155] Mahfoud Bennoune added that "the Ben Bella regime was largely responsible for anti-democratic practices by resorting, from the outset, to purges, calumnies, blackmail and systematic intolerance of other views, opinions and attitudes even within the single party."[156] Ben Bella's presidential circle of advisers, including the Frenchman Michel Raptis, influenced the articulation of the socialist option, which provoked protest from "proto-Islamists," especially the Jama'a al-Da'wa (Assembly of the Call, a group of Muslim preachers) and al-Qiyam (the Values), highlighted by the participation of the respected and popular academic, Malek Bennabi. Collectively, these Islamists feared that the government's ideological predilections, founded on foreign ideas, menaced Algeria's Muslim identity and cultural life.

Despite the enormous problems he confronted, Ben Bella did "give purpose and direction to independence,"[157] especially in relations with France. Ben Bella exercised a principled pragmatism while pursuing post-colonial liberation, which his successors also followed. The recovery of land and property was a stunning achievement, and policies challenging the French military and hydrocarbon presences represented significant initiatives aiming at securing full Algerian sovereignty. Ben Bella's discourse and practice, while often bombastic, still asserted Algerian independence and dignity.

Ben Bella Toppled from Power

In order to strengthen his political position, Ben Bella decided to remove from his cabinet Ahmed Medeghri and then Abdelaziz Bouteflika. Both were close associates of the powerful leader of the Armée Nationale Populaire (ANP, formerly the ALN), Houari Boumedienne, who was also vice-president and minister of defense. The lack of structured development programs concerned Boumedienne, but above all he feared that Ben Bella would inevitably turn against him.[158] With the coming of the second Afro-Asian Conference to Algiers in June 1965 (the first being the landmark Bandung Conference in 1955) and the expected favorable publicity on the revolutionary hydrocarbons accord, Boumedienne knew that Ben Bella's presidential prestige would increase and, with it, his political power.[159] He decided to act. In the early morning of 19 June 1965, ANP units assumed key posts in Algiers. The conspirators arrested Ben Bella and placed him in secret confinement.[160]

A proclamation from a "revolutionary council" excoriated the overthrown president. It denounced Ben Bella's policies as "narcissistic" and claimed he had a "morbid love of power." The "tyrant" was condemned for political "charlatanism" and "mystification" and accused of "bad

management of the national heritage, the wasting of public funds, instability, demagogy, anarchy, lying and improvisation." These acrimonious attacks also disclosed how the Boumedienne regime planned to rule the
country: "The Revolutionary Council will devote itself to setting in order
and improving our economy." The Revolutionary Council asserted: "In
short, a socialism fitting the country's realities must replace a socialism of
circumstance and publicity." This was "a new phase of the Revolution."[161]

A statement, extraordinary under these circumstances, was made by
the ANP periodical *El-Djeich*, listing the accomplishments of the Ben Bella
period: 1.5 million children attending school, inauguration of training
institutes, literacy initiatives, and some industrial complexes such as the
Algiers refinery. It recognized Ben Bella's "safeguarding the political and
economic independence of the country."[162] Furthermore, Boumedienne
appreciated the "purpose and direction" of the Ben Bellist policy toward
France. Algeria continued to define itself as a state through the articulation of a revolutionary discourse and "postcolonial decolonizations."

Ben Bella was a mercurial and quixotic leader with a puzzling personality.[163] Consider his clothing: Ben Bella began wearing military fatigues à
la Castro, then wore a Maoist tunic, before returning to Western suits.
According to an adjunct of Boumedienne's: "A psychoanalyst would be
able to tell us what that means. He must be searching for his identity."[164]
Ben Bella's political "fashion statement" also mirrored his country's identity when he exercised power. Algeria would become more ideological and
dogmatic under Boumedienne, as state-building became the paramount
priority. Though intending to remove the French neocolonialism in Algeria, the Revolutionary Council reassured Paris and saluted cooperation's
achievements,[165] but power and identity were inevitably transformed.

4

The Decline and Demise of
Privileged Cooperation, 1965–1971

> If I ask myself who has dealt a blow to cooperation, on the moral and
> psychological plane, I have to answer: France.
> **Houari Boumedienne**

> The Algerian authorities do not always understand the subtleties of our
> political life.
> **Jean de Broglie**

These years introduced the leadership of Houari Boumedienne, who fervently aimed to continue postcolonial decolonization by removing the most humiliating stipulations of the Evian Accords: the French military and hydrocarbon presences. Though he shared the ideological ambitions of Ben Bella, he was a man of a different temperament. He was willing, even eager, to confront the ex-*métropole*. Proud, he was also particularly sensitive about earning France's regard and respect as an equal. Indeed, with the innovative Algiers Accords of July 1965, relations changed as each nation considered or imagined the other as a "partner." A refashioned cooperation codified this new relationship. At the same time, Boumedienne faced a changing French strategic attitude toward Algeria. As France achieved multilateral objectives, its political and economic dependence upon Algeria, especially for oil, decreased. Then in 1969 de Gaulle's resignation from the presidency ushered in a new political team eager to step from the general's shadow and make its own mark. Against this background, relations endured a dramatic transformation as the "partnership" dissolved during the hydrocarbons crisis of 1970–71.

Boumedienne's "Revolutionary Readjustment"

Houari Boumedienne announced on 5 July 1965, Independence Day, "Verbal socialism is dead, the construction of a socialist economy is going to begin."[1] Boumedienne's regime projected the disciplined internalization of the Revolution and its consolidation through planned programs, and rejected the spontaneity that had characterized Ben Bella's government.[2] One official publication wrote: "It became urgent to put an end to this process of catastrophic degradation and to put the Algerian Revolution back on its right path[;] this was the task assumed by the revolutionary authorities."[3] Accordingly, the Revolutionary Council aimed at "historical rectification" and "revolutionary readjustment."

Mirroring Ben Bella's policy but not his flamboyance, Boumedienne was a serious and sullen figure, even regarded initially as "mysterious." Early in his regime his power was threatened—by sporadic student protests in 1965–66, a foiled military coup in December 1967, an assassination attempt in April 1968—and he avoided public appearances. The notorious murders of exiled Mohamed Khider in 1967 and Belkacem Krim in 1970 eliminated prominent political opposition. Boumedienne's staunch commitment to socialism drew Islamist protests, exemplified by the founding of Ahl al-Da'wa (the People of the Call) in 1970. Nevertheless, the threat from Islamism was regarded as slight at this time and was tempered, too, by the selection and supervision of imams by the Ministry of Religious Affairs. Boumedienne's policies of Arabization, and his changing the weekend from the Western Saturday-Sunday to the Muslim Thursday-Friday, were well received by Islamists. Unlike Ben Bella, Boumedienne was able, through his command of the military and his paternalism toward the growing Algerian technocracy running national enterprises led by SONATRACH, to amass immense political authority. He kept it by an astute handling of Algerian political factions.

Internal political stability gave Boumedienne the opportunity to engage in international affairs. After the June 1967 War and Gamal Abdel Nasser's sudden death in 1970, his presence began to be felt within the Arab world. His enthusiastic support of the Palestine Liberation Organization (PLO) indicated the continuation of Algeria's "traditional" policy of solidarity with liberation movements. Boumedienne, like Ben Bella, also projected Algeria as a Third World champion, providing leadership to the developing nations that in 1967 organized into the Group of 77. Algeria insisted upon the need for a North-South dialogue and especially a new economic order. Above all, foreign policy continued to be an expression of internal policy; it was clear that the new government aimed to orient its external affairs to fit domestic development plans.[4]

Boumedienne subscribed to the popular socialist (and eleventh-hour French colonial) model of development that projected an expansive industrial multiplier effect ("industrializing industries") especially through intensive hydrocarbons exploitation which would benefit other sectors of the Algerian economy.[5] This economic choice appeared in three-year (1967–69) and four-year (1970–73 and 1974–77) development plans that subordinated agriculture, despite the legacy of *autogestion* and Boumedienne's own Agrarian Revolution of 1971. Concurrently, he inaugurated a Cultural Revolution highlighted by an accelerated program of Arabization.[6]

I. William Zartman astutely noted: "The primary emphasis of Boumedienne is on the state, not the nation."[7] Existentially, Boumedienne posited that the state had to precede the nation. His praxis was state-building and the development of a definition of a nation. This imagination of Algeria, inspired by his idea of the Revolution, ineluctably targeted France's postcolonial presence in the country.

The Algiers Accords Initiate a "Partnership"

The overthrow of Ben Bella's government did not complicate the ongoing hydrocarbons discussions. Foreign Minister Bouteflika, the chief negotiator and probably Boumedienne's closest confidant, undoubtedly had informed him of the projected agreement's favorable terms. It was in Boumedienne's immediate interest to expedite the conclusion of negotiations in order to bolster his position and secure his new government.

The Algiers Accords were signed on 29 July 1965 and went into effect on 30 December 1965.[8] They marked the crowning achievement of this period of privileged cooperation. The French companies kept their concessions and their control, though modified by the new Association Coopérative (ASCOOP), an ingenious partnership between an Algerian state company (SONATRACH) and a French one (eventually ERAP, the Entreprise de Recherches et d'Activités Pétrolières). The two companies would explore and exploit together, with the French state enterprise financing 60 percent of the research costs. Algeria's royalties would be computed at a fixed barrel price increasing annually to $2.08/barrel f.o.b. Bougie, significantly above Middle East crude pricing. This insulated Algeria from caprice in the world petroleum market and gave Algiers an opportunity to plan its revenues. The Algerian government would also be permitted to tax a greater percentage of the profits. France would assist Algeria in marketing its hydrocarbon production, especially natural gas. An imaginative new financial aid arrangement was included in the Accord (see below). And an Organisme de Coopération Industrielle (OCI) was inaugurated to work jointly to stimulate Algeria's industrialization.

To France, the new accords' bilateral consequences counted less than their multilateral implications. They amplified the "French alternative" and illustrated how France was willing to conduct a state-to-state relationship elevating petroleum from a micro- to a macroeconomic scale. The linkage of financial assistance and technical collaboration was also impressive, implicitly underscoring the privileged relationship. The powerful Anglo-American group of oil companies known as the Cartel suspected French motives and modalities, while the developing world commended France as the only advanced country with a serious consciousness and comprehension of Third World development problems.[9] As Couve de Murville related, Olivier Wormser and his team of negotiators (which included Claude Cheysson, Jacques Bonnet de Latour, and Yves Roland-Billecart) succeeded in reaching an agreement that "would be acceptable by Algiers and placed itself in line with our policy regarding the developing countries."[10] The Algiers Accords contributed to the cosmetic make-over of a French world image scarred from wars of decolonization. Algerian foreign minister Abdelaziz Bouteflika affirmed: "The agreements . . . define principles which may be used as a basis for new ties between developed and developing countries."[11]

By the 1965 Accords, France retained its privileged petroleum position, but at a price disturbingly high to some: "at least one estimate placed [it] as high as 65 percent above that paid by Germany for oil."[12] The idea that "de Gaulle gave the house away but saved the furniture" was partially true.[13] The house was given away in 1962. What the Accords prevented was a rummage sale. De Gaulle safeguarded French energy sources, satisfied the Algerians, and, above all, wedded his Algerian/Third World policy to grandeur and independence. Jean de Broglie understated: "The agreement we have just signed is a political one, in every sense of the term."[14]

The Accords realized Algeria's objective of participation/partnership in every aspect of the hydrocarbons sector. Its share of the French state-owned SN REPAL (Société Nationale de Recherche et d'Exploitation du Pétrole en Algérie) increased to 50 percent. The accompanying natural gas package gave Algeria, in return for paying production costs, a marketing monopoly and a half interest in a mixed liquefaction enterprise. Moreover, France offered—and in 1967 formally agreed—to become an LNG (Liquified Natural Gas) purchaser. These stipulations pleased Algerian planners, since they foresaw natural gas fueling Algeria's industrialization. In addition, Algeria's Supreme Court would play a significant, though not final, role in arbitration. Algeria regarded the Accords as another stage toward territorial recovery and economic liberation. They seemed to promise an eventual "naturalization" (as in the natural gas package) rather than a disruptive nationalization of the sector. At the signing ceremonies, Foreign Minister Abdelaziz Bouteflika nonetheless reminded Jean de Broglie that Algeria was "prepared to offer all required guarantees for the safeguard of its partner's interest, as long as these interests do not clash with our economic development, the protection of our patrimony, our sovereignty and territorial integrity as well as our fundamental decisions as stated in the Tripoli Program and in the Algiers Charter."[15] Bouteflika's words portended eventual conflict, given the obvious ideological contradictions.

Algeria's literal interpretation of the Algiers Accords as opposed to France's broad application (a general reversal of their initial stances on the Evian Accords) disclosed a maturity that subsequently presented Paris not only with an economic crisis but also with a political issue, bringing into question the need to preserve a privileged political cooperation with Algiers. The Algerian government perceived the dubious nature of the "partnership" and was already casting a new political perspective before the "little crisis" involving the nationalization of French hydrocarbon interests. Ideally, the Algerian government wanted to separate hydrocarbons from other sectors of cooperation.

Cooperation Redefined

In January 1966 the Algerian Secretariat was assigned to the Foreign Ministry's Secretariat of State for Foreign Affairs in Charge of Cooperation.[16] The Quai d'Orsay became responsible for cooperation with Algeria and collaborated closely with other ministries, notably cooperation, labor, and education. The termination of the Algerian Secretariat symbolized, too, a relegation of Algeria's special importance in spite of impressive cooperation initiatives and allocations.

Though considered neocolonial, cooperation continued to be officially admired by the Algerian government. Bouteflika viewed cooperation as a strategic imperative—an instrument of decolonization.[17] The irony was profound; Algeria needed France's vital assistance to liberate itself from the consequences of the *metropole's* colonial legacy. While serving as ambassador to France, Redha Malek praised French culture and especially recognized the importance of mutual cooperation toward Algeria's development.[18] In 1967, even with official Arabization, Bouteflika noted that "Algeria offers France a large field of cultural cooperation for the diffusion of the French language."[19]

Financial Cooperation

The Algiers Accords' imaginative "aid for industrialization" package called for a billion francs to be distributed in five annual allocations of FF 200 million. Of this sum, FF 40 million were in direct grants and FF 160 million in soft 3-percent loans repayable in twenty years. An additional billion francs would be provided to promote private export credits, backed by the French national credit agency COFACE. The new Organisme de Coopération Industrielle (OCI) would stimulate Algerian industrialization.[20] Though the amount of financial assistance dropped significantly, the tone of the Accords reaffirmed a French desire to continue a generous policy of cooperation with Algeria. The payment in francs for Algerian oil protected and strengthened the French economy. The Algerian treasury's accumulation of francs helped de Gaulle counter the Americans monetarily. During France's financial crisis of 1968–69 Algeria released some of its reserves, but it held FF 600 million to help stabilize the franc.[21]

From 1962 to 1968, Algeria's portion of French aid shrank from 42 percent to 13 percent. The Organization for Economic Cooperation and Development (OECD) reported that "this decrease is the result of France's withdrawal and difficulties which have arisen in applying the industrial co-operation agreements signed in 1965."[22] The diminution also resulted from the Algerianization of the administration (see below). The substituting French *coopérants* were no longer needed. Nevertheless in 1969–71 France still contributed 90 percent of Algeria's official development assis-

Table 4.1. French Public Aid and Loans to Algeria, 1965–1970 (in millions of French francs)

	1965	1966	1967	1968	1969	1970
General aid*	415	262	230	227	139	140
Gross loans**	24	6	11	36	147	108
Total	439	268	241	263	286	248

*General aid includes free and linked (tied) aid (from the June 1963 accord), grants from the Algiers Accords (1965), and contributions from the Organisation Saharien, the Organisation de Coopération Industrielle, and civil aviation.
**These statistics include active loans approved for development prior to 1962 for development and later ones including significantly the "aid for industrialization" loan initiative.
Source: *France-Algérie*, no. 34 (1971): 6–7.

tance (ODA).[23] In 1970–71, Algeria received 8.7 percent of France's total ODA.

After the administrative transfer in 1966, which also underscored Algeria's relative political and economic stability, the well-established Caisse Centrale de Coopération Economique (CCCE) took over from the anachronistic CEDA on 1 January 1968.[24] In addition, the CCCE supervised French participation in the OCI. In 1971, all the funds projected by the 1965 Algiers Accords were allocated. In other financial support programs, the CCCE was affiliated with a financial subsidiary, the Société d'Equipement des Zones d'Industrialisation Décentralisée (SEZID), in regional investment projects, as well as with the Banque Algérien de Développement. By previous agreements from 1963 and 1966, the CCCE also directed reinvestment credits.

Pursuing its commitment to sectoral postcolonial decolonization, the Boumedienne government liquidated two-thirds of the colonial debt by the Accord of December 1966.[25] The nationalization of foreign banks and the creation of an independent Algerian system by the end of 1967 signaled other important stages in Algeria's quest for financial freedom. Taking advantage of France's instability, the Algerian government also took control of foreign insurance companies in May 1968.[26] When France devalued the franc in August 1969, the dinar maintained its value. This indicated Algeria's financial stability and confidence and, by this time, its diversity of international loan and transfer sources—the World Bank, the Soviet Union, the United States, Japan, and West Germany.[27] Most significantly, it symbolized Algeria's continuing effort to liberate itself financially from French dependence.

Commercial Cooperation

The commercial accord of January 1964 notwithstanding, bitter feelings over the War, the infusion of a vocal *pied-noir* winegrower group into the powerful French lobby, and capricious relations between the two countries caused the French government to constrict the Algerian flow of wine and even block it in 1965 and 1967 (coincident with elections). The winegrowers, infected by endemic French fear of competition, saw Algerian exports as a threat to their lower-grade domestic vintages. The economic consequence was an unanticipated elasticity in demand; on the political side, the commercial crisis compounded serious concurrent issues concerning emigrant labor and hydrocarbons.

As a goodwill gesture, France advanced FF 300 million to Algeria in July 1968 to be reimbursed when French imports rose again.[28] Algeria was forced to find other markets. The Soviet Union took advantage of

Table 4.2. French Trade with Algeria, 1966–1970 (in millions of French francs)

	1966	1967	1968	1969	1970
French exports	2,158	1,996	2,326	2,356	3,124
French imports	2,781	2,620	2,751	3,074	3,539
Imports excluding oil	1,074	652	576	794	955
Balance including oil	-623	-624	-425	-718	-415
Balance excluding oil	1084	1344	1750	1562	2169

Source: *France-Algérie*, no. 34 (1971): 8.

Algeria's desperation to diversify its wine exportation by importing millions of hectoliters, but at a price that was far more to its own advantage than to Algeria's.[29] A poor French harvest created, briefly, a very strong demand for Algerian wine which finally fulfilled the wine agreement. After 1970 imports dropped to an insignificant level. The loss of its profitable and privileged position in the French market forced Algeria to hasten the conversion of vineyards to cereal fields for economic as well as cultural reasons.

With Algerian commercial diversification during the late 1960s, the percentage of imports from France decreased from 90 percent to approximately 30 percent. After the hydrocarbon nationalizations, France's role in Algerian commerce dropped to 25 percent of the export market. During the 1960s when France imported wine and hydrocarbons, Algeria showed a positive balance in bilateral trade. After the hydrocarbon nationalization in 1971, France reduced its imports of Algerian products while Algeria increased importation of French goods, tipping the balance of trade in France's favor. This especially contributed to the general deterioration of relations during the 1970s.

The microcosmic perspective disclosed a pattern that matched the political relationship. From 1962 to 1970, French manufacturers and industrialists inherited and exploited a privileged position in the Algerian market, despite restrictive investment codes. With liberal transfers as well as governmental protection and credits, French firms controlled some 40–45 percent of foreign investment. French predominance was challenged in the late 1960s as American interest in Algerian natural gas fields attracted consulting and hydrocarbon firms.

Algeria's nationalization of French hydrocarbon interests caused an economic rupture (a political rupture was out of the question) ending, for the time being, the preferential French situation within the Algerian economy. Political problems poisoned the commercial spirit, and CO-FACE became apprehensive over investment credits and assurances. Algerian diversification in trading partners, as contracts were signed with American, West German, Japanese, and Italian firms, reduced France from predominance to a subordinate position.[30] Much to the chagrin of the French *patronat,* the United States became Algeria's leading trade partner,[31] while the Soviet Union also became more active in the Algerian market.[32]

Technical and Cultural Cooperation

Though both France and Algeria desired a continuation of cooperation, soon after the signing of the Algiers Accords the French Embassy reported an atmosphere of "uncertainty" concerning the future of cultural and technical activities.[33] In order to institutionalize technical and cultural cooperation, the Algerian authorities were anxious to obtain an accord facilitating recruitment and securing a general French commitment to cooperation. An accord would demonstrate Algeria's willingness to welcome *coopérants* to aid in its development. But the *coopérants* needed both accommodation and reassurance. Finally the two sides concluded a convention with a twenty-year duration.

The April 1966 Convention on Technical and Cultural Cooperation reaffirmed the guarantees of the protocols and addressed the troubling question of the *coopérants'* affiliation with the French social security system.[34] Concerning financial transfers, the *coopérant* could relay 50, 70, or 100 percent of his pay to France, according to his family situation. The pay of the civilian *coopérant* (as opposed to the military VSNA) was calculated with complicated allowance increments that could make his salary triple that of his metropolitan counterpart. A cultural *coopérant* could expect about 177 percent more than his counterpart's base salary. Generally, France and Algeria split the cost fifty-fifty. By the 22 August 1970 agreement, Algeria assumed about 60 percent of the remuneration for the civilian *coopérant* and the complete financial support of the military *coopérant* serving in Algeria.[35] Most important, Algeria received a long-term French commitment to cultural and technical cooperation.

Stéphane Hessel, as director of the French embassy's Cultural and Technical Cooperation Mission, discovered disheartening *coopérant* reaction to the April Convention. The greatest complaints were over the rigidity of the stipulations and disappointment with regard to salaries.[36] The tepid reception of the April Convention, the austerity intrinsic to life in Algeria, and the historical relations between the two countries made recruitment Hessel's "essential preoccupation."[37] He understood that though the April Convention facilitated attracting new *coopérants,* quality more than quantity was now needed in Algeria.

A transition occurred after 1965, complementing the political and economic "partnership" by virtue of the Algiers Accords. The number of *coopérants* serving in Algeria dropped, not by directive from Paris, but because Algerian cadres had been trained to replace the French who had occupied positions since independence and, in some cases, before. From approximately 12,000 *coopérants* in service in 1965, the number dropped to about 8,000 during the period of the hydrocarbon nationalization.[38] Moreover, there was a determined desire by Algiers to have cooperation based on *formation* (skills training) as an instrument of Algerianization rather than on substitution. France complied by participating through the CCCE in the establishment of training or technical institutes, beginning with the inauguration of the Institut Algérien du Pétrole in 1965.[39] The CCCE affirmed that "the *formation* of Algerian cadres remains the essential objective of our programs."[40] The deontological position was unchanged. Stéphane Hessel still perceived cooperation as "a task which aims to give Algeria its own character, its individuality as a nation, its true fundamental independence, its personality."[41] France still had a special role to play in Algeria's existential search for national identity.

Through cooperation, the French language continued to be an extraordinary instrument of foreign policy and *rayonnement* (diffusion of French influence).[42] Despite the Algerian government's policy of cultural liberation, Hessel observed that Arabization programs had only "symbolic significance" and could proceed only by "small stages" because of the popularity of French.[43] Besides the *coopérants'* direct and indirect contributions to *rayonnement*, France welcomed young Algerians as scholarship students and military cadres.[44] In addition, cultural centers were opened in Algeria to serve remaining *pieds-noirs, coopérants,* Algerians, and complementary French interests.[45]

In a telling statement concerning this sector of cooperation, Hessel wrote that problems over wine, natural gas, and workers "do not penetrate the [Algerian] opinion, which demands France's cultural and technical resources and products, and places confidence only in the French engineer, doctor, and instructor."[46] France was regarded by Algeria as its "most desired partner in matters of cultural and technical cooperation."[47]

Emigrant Labor

France's economic boom in the 1960s attracted unmonitored emigrant labor, especially from Portugal. As Mark Miller related: "Algerian authorities correctly pointed out that French tolerance . . . amounted to a diminution of the privileged character of the Franco-Algerian program."[48] The continuing administrative problems of Algerian circulation necessitated the negotiation of a comprehensive three-year accord that was signed in December 1968.[49] This agreement permitted the entry of 35,000 Algerians for three years. The new emigrants were to be screened by the Office National Algérien de la Main-d'Oeuvre (ONAMO), examined by a French medical mission, and then presented with a national identity card or a passport. The most significant stipulation was the institution of a certificate of residence for all the workers. This certificate of residence had to be renewed within a preset period determined by the time already spent working in France. Ten-year residence permits replaced the three-year permits. The Algerians' special position in French immigration policy was secured.

Because of these residence cards, the 1968 Accord could confidently reassert the Evian principle of free circulation between Algeria and France for all, but there were qualifications. New emigrant workers were given nine months to find a job. If they did not, they could be repatriated. The French could also apply a quota each year. According to the agreement, France would endeavor especially to improve the workers' cultural and social well-being, such as ameliorating abysmal housing conditions and creating more educational and vocational opportunities.[50] A joint commission was established to supervise the Accord's application.

Military Cooperation

Military cooperation equated with political cooperation. The French withdrew from their Saharan atomic testing sites in 1965, and on 1 February 1968 France pulled out of Mers el-Kébir, a naval base no longer considered strategic. Except for the air base at Bou Sfer, handed over in December 1970, the French postcolonial military presence ended.[51] Boumedienne achieved an important objective that he had striven for since the Evian negotiations: military decolonization. Some officers still received training in France, but an increasing number went to the Soviet Union, the source of most of Algeria's matériel.

De Gaulle and the "Events": Rebellion to Resignation

Answering charges that his global policies such as the nuclear *force de frappe* and cooperation were beyond France's resources, the president chastised the French for not living up to their potential.[52] In spite of France's impressive political momentum and economic expansion under the Fifth Republic, the entire Gaullist establishment quaked when students and workers rebelled in the streets of Paris in May 1968. The so-called Events of May 1968 produced questions concerning President de Gaulle's international ambitions and seriously affected the French-Algerian relationship.

May 1968

While the causes of the Events are still debated, it became clear that France's modernization had far outpaced social and institutional changes.[53] This lack of governmental sensitivity, at a time of rising social expectations, provoked protest and insurrection. De Gaulle survived the immediate crisis, but with his authority and aura diminished. The political destabilization had economic consequences. The franc weakened despite de Gaulle's international efforts to strengthen it. He refused to devalue as a matter of national prestige. Budget allocations were diverted to satisfy domestic needs, affecting cooperation transfers and credits.

International events exacerbated de Gaulle's problems. The United States and the Soviet Union competed more aggressively through their Mideast client states. Militarization of the Mediterranean Sea created a new area of superpower contention. Finally, the Soviet invasion of Czechoslovakia in October 1968 stifled the Gaullist aspiration to broker an East-West détente.

Gaullist tenets, including the global objectives of grandeur and independence, now seemed illusory. France had to adapt to changing conditions, as it had in 1962. This time, however, de Gaulle found it difficult to accept the new circumstances. The man who was so proud of his perspicacity failed to discern the fragility of France's overextended political position and especially its domestic ramifications.

The Events and Algeria

Again, Algeria haunted de Gaulle's destiny. During the crisis, de Gaulle visited General Jacques Massu to secure his support. He also pardoned protagonists of *Algérie française,* including Georges Bidault and former OAS chief Raoul Salan, who ten years earlier had collaborated so significantly in bringing de Gaulle back to power. Bidault "suggested that one reason for the unrest of youth was the loss of opportunity for careers and adventure resulting from General de Gaulle's dissolution of the French Empire in Africa."[54] Meanwhile, repatriated *pieds-noirs* vented pent-up exasperation, especially over the lack of indemnity payments, through protests and civil disobedience.

Algeria exploited the situation by nationalizing a variety of French businesses. In May the Algerian government took over enterprises dealing with hydrocarbon distribution, and in June it expropriated chemical and construction companies. Characteristic of the paradox of conflict and cooperation, the government concurrently supported the failing franc by holding reserves.

De Gaulle could not afford the deterioration of the relationship, since French-Algerian cooperation was a cornerstone of Gaullist foreign policy and a symbol of the general's international prestige. Nevertheless, there were indications that the public popularity of French-Algerian cooperation had dropped. In July 1965, 49 percent of those surveyed believed that France had an interest in Algeria and should pursue a policy of cooperation, with 23 percent disagreeing. By November 1967 the percentages had changed to 38 for and 33 against.[55] Though the French did not settle the major commercial problem over wine importation, the emigrant worker situation was considered and, for the time being, resolved by the aforementioned 1964 Accord.

Seeking to secure and reaffirm privileged French-Algerian cooperation, de Gaulle dispatched Jean Basdevant as the new French ambassador to Algiers.[56] In his presentation of his letters, Basdevant described his diplomatic mission as "one of the most important in French diplomacy." He reviewed how France had assisted Algeria militarily, technically, and culturally. Basdevant observed that both French and Algerian foreign policies were based on the principles of independence and cooperation. He concluded: "France proposes to Algeria a policy of confident and equitable cooperation on a basis of reciprocity." Though recognizing France's efforts at cooperation, Colonel Boumedienne tempered his reply to Basdevant by stating that there were "insufficiencies" concerning wine and hydrocarbons.[57] These two problems were to be inherited by de Gaulle's successor, Georges Pompidou.

De Gaulle Resigns

Threatened by labor union militancy and with the failing franc eroding his political power and personal prestige, de Gaulle announced a referendum for 27 April 1969, ostensibly over regional and legislative reform. Actually, it was a vote of confidence in de Gaulle's leadership. The *non* vote provoked the president's immediate resignation and marked the end of an extraordinary political career and period in French history. A year later he died as the bilateral relationship entered its most tempestuous period in the postcolonial period—a time of another dramatic transformation of power.

Pompidou to Power

Charles de Gaulle's resignation led to elections in June that brought Georges Pompidou to the Elysée Palace. "I will not imitate the style of General de Gaulle," Pompidou declared. "I would not be able to do this anyway; as you can see, I am a different man."[58] After serving as President de Gaulle's prime minister (1962–68), it seemed natural that Pompidou would follow his predecessor's broad foreign policy objectives. There would be, however, changes in designs and dimensions. The second president of the Fifth Republic characterized himself as "a realist committed to giving French policy a solid foundation."[59]

Recognizing France's troubled position, Pompidou decided to reorient French policies. In August 1969, Finance Minister Valéry Giscard d'Estaing devalued the franc 12.5 percent, which restored its stability and international support. Pompidou permitted British entry into the Common Market but continued Gaullist criticisms of the United States while pursuing détente with the USSR. Though he also played the Gaullist role projecting France as an interlocutory, independent, and moral power, he scaled down global foreign policy interests and initiatives by focusing on the immediate periphery of the Mediterranean basin. Observers viewed the Mediterranean Policy as a sign of French weakness, but this circumscribed course reflected realism.[60] France had a significant presence in the Mediterranean as a result of its privileged relationship with Algeria and improving relations with Algeria's Maghribi neighbors. And its historical and cultural influence in the Mashriq was now strengthened by a general rapprochement with the Arab states in the Middle East since Evian and especially since the Six-Day War in June 1967.

While the dimensions of French foreign policy changed, France could still project its essential qualities of grandeur and independence. Though Pompidou knew that he could not personify greatness like de Gaulle, the Mediterranean offered excellent opportunities to assert independence and to counter strategically the deepening superpower penetration and bipolarization of the Middle East.

The Libyan Mirage Deal

France launched its Mediterranean Policy in a sensational way. Pompidou's government announced in late 1969 its intention to sell one hundred Mirage fighter-bombers, including advanced-design Mirage IIIs, to the new Libyan revolutionary government of Colonel Muammar Qadhafi. Qadhafi seemed to have the charismatic and mercurial qualities of Algeria's overthrown Ben Bella, and similar Third World ambitions.[61]

The bold French move trumped any serious Soviet approach toward the Maghrib. It also gave France a competitive edge over the Anglo-Americans, who had enjoyed a privileged status during the rule of King Idris. The arms sale and subsequent close relations with the Libyan Republic demonstrated that France had regained its international initiative and would play an active role in the Mediterranean.[62] The disapproval of the United States, the shock of Israel, and the Soviet Union's surprise heightened French prestige in the Mashriq and Maghrib.

Pompidou's vaunted realism took into account tangible considerations in the Libyan affair. France was importing an increasing volume of oil from Libya, fifteen million metric tons in 1969. It was calculated that one hundred Mirages cost ten million tons of oil. Arms for hydrocarbons became an attractive policy.[63]

Two French aims in cultivating closer ties with Libya were not realized. First, the French hoped that Libya would buffer the Maghrib against Mideast turmoil, but that was dashed by Libya's revolutionary ideology, which complemented Algeria's. Second, the French hoped that Libya would directly or indirectly temper Algeria's attitude in sensitive hydrocarbon negotiations.[64] Unfortunately for Paris, Tripoli and Algiers held common positions in opposition to Western petroleum interests.

Pompidou and Algeria

On assuming the presidency, Pompidou was conscious of Algeria's manifold strategic importance. Indeed, Pompidou had played a significant role during decolonization by representing President de Gaulle's government during secret talks with the GPRA in Switzerland in February 1961. According to Louis Joxe, the Pompidou mission was a "turning point" as Pompidou convinced the Algerians that they heard through him "the very voice of General de Gaulle." It was Pompidou who provided them "the perspective of future French-Algerian relations, which would be those of cooperation."[65] As prime minister, Pompidou stated before the National Assembly that "the entire future of French influence in Africa" depended on successful cooperation with Algeria.[66] The former colony's compelling geographic position and its particular historical relationship with France meant that a generous cooperation would be axiomatic.

Foreign Minister Schumann's Visit to Algeria

In October 1969, Maurice Schumann became the first French foreign minister to visit Algeria since independence. His arrival was greeted with extraordinary cordiality and seemed to signal the importance Paris gave to

its strategic axis with Algiers. Though his counterpart, Abdelaziz Bouteflika, recognized cooperation's "shortcomings," he contended that "it
remains highly promising and many of its promises have already become
a reality." The Algerian foreign minister specifically praised cultural and
technical cooperation and the December 1968 accord on emigrant workers. To Bouteflika, cooperation represented "the fruit of deliberate determination; its profound justification sprang from both Algeria's and
France's attachment to the inalienable principles of national independence
and international cooperation." Given these principles, Bouteflika reasserted his government's position: "Algeria for its part is resolutely determined to pursue its policy commanded by the principle of national independence. Its accession to internal and external sovereignty, and the
sacrifices it has accepted in order to attain that goal impose upon it a
sacred duty of intransigence in that respect."[67] Bouteflika's speech emphasized that Algeria valued cooperation, but within the context of its national ambitions. To Algiers, the visit seemed to suggest that new president
Georges Pompidou wanted to continue the privileged relationship.[68]

The Battle of Petroleum

The postcolonial decolonization of the hydrocarbons sector had more to
do with identity, imagination, and power than with economics. Algeria's
refusal to link a general "transitory" cooperation accord to French petroleum "decapitalization" led to a dramatic nationalization, a coming of
age. This action also effectively terminated privileged relations, with enduring political and economic bilateral consequences. Cooperation would
be preserved but qualified or, as Pompidou put it, "placed in focus." Algeria would be regarded as another Third World country deserving of aid,
but the privileged status was ended, and even the new goal of "normalization" elusive.

The Background to the "Battle of Petroleum"

Schumann's visit to Algeria occurred at the beginning of delicate hydrocarbons negotiations. Algeria was a different country in 1969–70 than in
1962–63.[69] It was politically stable and its economy held exceptional
promise. Hydrocarbons were the decisive sector of Algeria's planned development. The Algerians feared, however, that if the hydrocarbons negotiations with the French failed, the entire framework of cooperation
would collapse. Algeria needed cooperation to realize the social and economic objectives of its first Four-Year Plan (1970–73). Nevertheless, Alge-

ria had long made plain its intention to take over the sector. There had already been nationalizations in agriculture (1963), mining (1966), industries (1963, 1968), banking (1966), and foreign commerce (1966).

In October 1967, Colonel Boumedienne welcomed ministers of the less-developed countries' Group of 77. His speech projected Algeria as playing the exemplary role of a developing country controlling its own political and economic destiny.[70] This ambitious image and Boumedienne's antipathy toward continued dependence upon France demanded an accelerated postcolonial decolonization and a substantial change in the nature of Algeria's most important bilateral relationship. Contentions and crises inevitably arose.

Algeria bought out British Petroleum's remaining interests in January 1967, which gave SONATRACH new commercial conduits and capital including BP's share of the Algiers Refinery.[71] A revolutionary Algerian action—which would be adopted by other oil producers in 1973—followed the disastrous Arab-Israeli Six-Day War of June 1967. Algeria slapped an embargo on the United States and the United Kingdom.[72] A few months later, five American companies were nationalized.[73] Getty Oil negotiated a portentous accord with SONATRACH that gave Algeria 51 percent control of its concessions.[74]

Despite problems with American petroleum companies and a rupture in diplomatic relations with the United States after the Six-Day War, numerous new American investments began to give Algeria an opportunity to accumulate capital and to diversify trading partners. Etienne Mallarde called the "Americanization of Algeria" a "technical colonization" by computer programmers and consultants from firms such as Booz Allen & Hamilton, Xerox Datasystems, and above all Arthur D. Little.[75] The most sensational example of the growing American interest in Algeria's energy potential was the contract signed by El Paso Natural Gas with SONATRACH in 1969 calling for the annual delivery of ten billion cubic meters over a period of twenty-five years. The El Paso contract proved that Algeria's hydrocarbons could attract capital and new markets. Diversification was possible and most desirable.

French Hydrocarbons Policy

Concurrently, French hydrocarbons policy had four basic objectives: (1) diversification of sources (preferably under French control with French companies as operator-concessionaires) to ensure economic and political independence; (2) purchase of hydrocarbons at the least cost, coupled with (3) stimulation of French exports to the energy-producing nation's

Table 4.3. French Participation in Algerian Petroleum Production, 1965–1970
(in millions of metric tons)

	1965	1966	1967	1968	1969	1970
Total production	26.0	33.2	38.3	42.1	43.8	47.9
French production	21.5	26.3	29.8	32.4	31.0	32.9
French percentage of total production	82.7%	79.2%	77.8%	77.0%	70.8%	68.7%

Source: *France-Algérie*, no. 34 (1971): 15.

national company; and (4) development of an efficient French distribution system.[76] From the Algiers Accords to the nationalization of the Saharan concessions in 1971, the French hydrocarbons industry substantially realized these objectives.

ERAP achieved rapid success in diversifying French oil sources by negotiating agreements with Iran in 1966 and Iraq in 1967 (both called *contrats d'entreprise*) and with Libya in 1968 (*contrats d'association,* using the Algiers Accords as a model).[77] ERAP and the CFP provided technical cooperation through the Institut Français du Pétrole which had been established after World War II. (By the Algiers Accords, the French had helped establish the Institut Algérien du Pétrole.) ERAP integrated more state companies and organized an efficient French distribution system of hydrocarbon products marketed under the name Elf.

The Elf group competed with Total, the CFP group of private subsidiaries, and both companies improved France's strategic position in the world oil market. The CFP was closely linked with the Cartel and operated freely in the private sector, while ERAP became an effective public arm of French political and economic policy.[78] Thus, when Algeria confronted France in negotiations over the Algiers Accords' fiscality, both nations' hydrocarbon enterprises were in full expansion with rising expectations.[79]

The Battle Begins

On 26 February 1969, Algeria advised the concessionaires to raise the posted petroleum price to $2.65/barrel. Despite their reluctance and resentment, the French oil companies eventually complied. When negotiations opened in November 1969, Algeria proposed that the posted price become the new reference price. The Algerian government wanted to continue the 55 percent tax rate and to ensure that negotiations would correlate with OPEC fiscal guidelines. (Algeria had joined in July.)[80] These Algerian proposals were aimed at a short-term accord pending a more comprehensive agreement. While willing to let the French concessionaires continue exploitation, Algeria left little doubt that "naturalization" of the sector remained the national goal.

According to Georges Pompidou's confidant and eventual foreign minister, Michel Jobert, the French president was anxious to resolve the hydrocarbons situation: "For him, it was a miracle that the 1965 accords had lasted so long."[81] Pompidou realized that Algeria would inevitably control its own resources. Yet he did not have the political strength to overcome powerful groups within the French government that became embroiled in the negotiations and contributed to their maladroit direction. Jobert intimated that the interests of the Ministries of Foreign Affairs and Industrial Development, as well as the secret dialogue of Prime Minister Jacques Chaban-Delmas through Simon Nora, interfered with the efforts of the appointed negotiator, François-Xavier Ortoli, and his successor, Hervé Alphand. The French government, as it did in the negotiations leading to the Algiers Accords, represented the oil companies but disregarded their counsel, which only soured intra-French relations. The result of all this diplomatic disorder was a muddled nineteen-month negotiation that Jobert appropriately termed *mal engagée*.[82]

After reviewing the short-term proposals, the French agreed to adjust the reference price, but said the calculations must take into account expenditures, such as ASCOOP credits, since not all investments had been amortized. Nor should a comparison between Middle East crude and Algerian crude bear on the price. While Algeria argued the advantages of Saharan petroleum (such as its light density), the French did not want to give Algeria a privileged position over other Third World producers with whom France had new and positive relations. With oil prices falling in this period, the French negotiators demonstrated a most striking ignorance of intangibles of the relationship, proposing a four-cent-a-barrel drop in the reference price (from the $2.08 f.o.b. Bougie price set by the Algiers Accords). The Algerians found the proposal preposterous, and the level of French insensitivity alarming. They prepared themselves for an arduous negotiation.

In June 1970 the French reversed their position and offered an increase to $2.16/barrel, to be raised to $2.31/barrel as a reference price for 1975.[83] This formula, Nicole Grimaud noted, corresponded to one projected by Occidental in Libya.[84] Yet it also indicated that France was willing to coordinate with the Cartel's direction, and that the hydrocarbons initiatives of an independent France would no longer be as innovative as under

President de Gaulle. The hostile reception of this new French position forced an adjournment on 13 June 1970.

Privileged Cooperation Endangered

On 24 June, Algeria's minister of industry and energy, Belaid Abdesselam, announced that the French had to repatriate 90 percent of their earnings to Algeria as long as the new reference price remained unresolved. Pierre Guillaumat, de Gaulle's former minister of defense and now president of ERAP, announced during a press conference on 8 July that, given these new impositions, ERAP would have to consider whether "to stay or not to stay" in Algeria. Then he related the oil crisis to the entire "special relationship" between France and Algeria. He specified the role of the emigrant workers and Algerian external debts.

El-Moudjahid considered Guillaumat's tone neocolonial. In a bitter reproach it stated: "The relation built up between the transfers of oil revenues and the immigrant workers shows that Algerian labour would be used in France as a means of pressure to impose the over-exploitation of our resources." As for the "enormous external debt for which she was in no way responsible . . . the question was settled by the 1966 Financial Agreement."[85] Risking the *pétrolisation* of cooperation, Abdesselam on 20 July declared in a letter addressed to the French companies that they should be prepared to consider their fiscal obligation at a $2.85/barrel reference price. The French Council of Ministers replied with a strict interpretation of Article 27 of the Algiers Accords, which stipulated that a new reference price could be instituted only after an "exchange of notes between the two governments."[86]

With the dispute increasingly vitriolic, President Pompidou suggested that France would be willing to discuss the entire policy of cooperation between the two countries if the 20 July Algerian decision were suspended. In a gesture of goodwill, Algiers agreed. François-Xavier Ortoli received the mission to conclude an accord with Algiers that included a reexamination of the framework of cooperation. The French negotiating team represented the French government and oil companies. There seemed to be, however, little coordination between the negotiators and the companies. Their attitude was far from the imaginativeness of the team that had concluded the revolutionary Algiers Accords. Foreign Minister Bouteflika would negotiate for Algeria.

The signing of an accord in August 1970 defining new modalities of technical and cultural cooperation did not satisfy the Algerians. France seemed reluctant to continue the amplitude of assistance that it had given Algeria in the past.[87] The accord failed to allay Algiers' fear that any hydrocarbons initiative could provoke the French to retaliate by cutting *coopérants*. A natural gas agreement between SONATRACH and Gaz de France (GDF) also failed to stem the relationship's deterioration. A poor French harvest did allow France to meet its wine importation commitment (though at a later date than originally stipulated), but future wine imports were cut mercilessly. Compounding the situation was a growing French hostility toward the Algerian emigrant worker community (see below). There were caustic attacks by the media on both sides of the Mediterranean and sensational espionage trials in Paris and Algiers.[88] Inevitably, this menacing milieu aggravated the negotiations.

A Comprehensive Negotiation

Meanwhile, a comprehensive negotiation ensued endeavoring to maintain some type of special bilateral relationship. The Algerian demands included: the adoption of OPEC fiscality; a price fixing such as those in Libyan, Persian Gulf, and eastern Mediterranean ports; and the purchase of French oil and gas interests to ensure Algerian control. Algiers argued that a unilateral decision could nationalize the fields, but in the "spirit of cooperation" two choices were offered: (1) the total repurchase of French interests so that French companies would only provide services such as the guaranteed provision of petroleum to the French market, and (2) an association between the companies and SONATRACH, on Algerian conditions, that would give Algeria majority control over operations while securing the recovery of its natural resources. The French opted for the second choice, but preferred "increase in participation" to the word "control."[89]

Ortoli offered a transition formula for reorganization of the entire sector whereby Algerian participation in total capital would increase. Indeed, both sides would operate from a "common policy" in production, transport, refining, and marketing. Grimaud wrote that "it was an innovative formula, even revolutionary." But the oil companies "bitterly reproached" Ortoli. The Algerians remained suspicious of French designs and felt that the "common policy" would still favor the French because of their heavy capital investment. Moreover, there were problems in the formula's application concerning transport and taxes. Confronted by the companies and by the Algerians, Ortoli's initiative was wasted. Another

French proposal to regroup the French concessions in only the Hassi Messaoud region met with Algerian opposition.[90]

At the end of the year under these trying conditions, Ortoli made the last French offer: the cession of one-third of French mining rights, which would give SONATRACH 51 percent control of total crude production; the cession of all natural gas production and its transport (marketing was already controlled by Algeria); the renewal of French financial assistance to Algeria; a guarantee of revenue if France did not buy Algerian wine; and an increase in the number of workers admitted to France. Nicole Grimaud contended that this was an "amiable transitory solution."[91]

Still, after propounding the recovery of natural resources and national sovereignty, Algeria could not "lose face." Bouteflika found the "decapitalizing" offer unsatisfactory and seemed particularly adamant. He wanted to end the hydrocarbons question even if it meant risking co-operation.[92] He felt that France would not be able to fulfill the promises on financial aid and emigrant workers. Most important, he did not want to compromise the question of Algeria's national sovereignty by allowing France to preserve petroleum concessions. That would have contradicted the amplified arguments of the Algerian media as well as his efforts and those of Minister Abdesselam to gain international support, especially at the Caracas OPEC Conference that discussed strategy in December 1970. Indeed, with removal of the French from the Sahara, the Four-Year Plan's implementation would be more symbolic and possibly more rewarding.

Addressing the new Algerian ambassador to Paris in December 1970, President Pompidou spoke of maintaining "a climate of reciprocal confidence and comprehension."[93] Yet rising tensions over hydrocarbon negotiations tainted Pompidou's cordial words. In an effort at conciliation, France agreed that the companies should transfer to the Algerian treasury the back taxes they had been hesitant to pay because of the crisis.[94] This aggravated the companies' fear that they were being abandoned by the French government. On 4 February 1971 Ortoli asked for an adjournment in order to await the OPEC-Cartel confrontation in Teheran.

To Algiers, this indicated an indirect collaboration with the Cartel. Algeria was anxious to keep negotiations moving because of Syria's willingness to reopen the Tapline pipeline, speculation about the future of the Suez Canal (and the Suez surcharge since its closing), supertanker construction, and the significant emergence of Nigerian oil on the market.[95] These variables weakened its increasingly worrisome position.

Nationalization

President Boumedienne stated on 3 February 1971 that Algeria wanted to "safeguard" its position toward French cooperation, but he reiterated: "We are ready to co-operate with all those who wish to set up with us a co-operation based on mutual interests, but it must be understood once and for all, that threats and pressure will have no effect on us."[96] Finally, the usual adamant (and effective) demeanor that had characterized Algerian diplomacy gave way to exasperation over the French hydrocarbon position. In these circumstances, OPEC's success in raising prices against the Cartel emboldened Algeria. On 24 February 1971 President Boumedienne issued the order to nationalize natural gas deposits and land infrastructure and to increase Algeria's participation in petroleum production to 51 percent. Boumedienne promised compensation and added that Algeria remained willing to continue supplying France, but only at the prices agreed by the Mediterranean producers at Tripoli.[97]

During an interview with *Le Monde,* Boumedienne said that the turning point in the negotiations was in December when "suddenly . . . the French positions stiffened. We were told we could take it or leave it: the conditions put to us were not couched in the language of negotiation. We could sense at that time that something was about to happen, especially in the light of the violent press campaign which was started against Algeria." According to Boumedienne, what happened was "the 'holy alliance' of the Cartel" with the French companies in anticipation of the Teheran negotiations. This action apparently had a decisive influence on the Algerian position: "The thought that France could turn the Cartel on its supposedly 'privileged' partner disturbed us a great deal. . . . The French negotiators then told us that they were awaiting the results of the Teheran negotiations; then it was the results of the Tripoli meeting that they were waiting for. What does this bilateral cooperation mean, if it is tied to so many variables?" Nevertheless, Boumedienne was conciliatory and suggested that it was up to the French to make a move.[98]

On 9 March, Prime Minister Jacques Chaban-Delmas handed Ambassador Mohammed Bedjaoui a memorandum. The French government recognized "in principle the inherent right of the Algerian Government to nationalize the property of companies operating within specific economic sectors on Algerian soil under certain conditions, the first of which is the solemn statement of indemnification made by the highest Algerian authority." While condemning the unilateral nature of Algerian decisions which contradicted the "spirit of negotiations" of 1962 and 1965, the French submitted legal and economic conditions or "guarantees" that would have limited Algerian control.[99] Though the Algerian government rejected these conditions, it allowed a representative of the French government to meet with Foreign Minister Bouteflika. Hervé Alphand received the unenviable task of revitalizing negotiations between the two countries and, in particular, resolving indemnities.

The Last Chance

Hervé Alphand, a veteran diplomat, was sent to Algeria after the nationalization to seek "an equitable indemnity" and to "define the new cadre of relations between Paris and Algiers."[100] While recognizing Algeria's right to nationalize, Alphand declared: "We are ready to confirm and even extend cooperation in other domains."[101] France appeared willing to maintain a privileged relationship, however, only with fair reciprocation to the French oil companies. The calculations of Alphand and Bouteflika over the nationalized interests were far apart. Compounding the controversy was the past, as the two men argued over debts dating from the time when their countries' treasuries were united and over the lack of complete compensation for the confiscated property of the *pieds-noirs*. Nevertheless, Alphand reiterated Ortoli's initiative concerning financial aid, remuneration for nonimportation of Algerian wines, and an extension of the emigrant worker accord of 1968. Nicole Grimaud judged that Algeria had "everything to gain and nothing to lose" by taking advantage of this French willingness to continue special cooperation.[102] Perhaps Algeria feared that a comprehensive reconciliation or a resumption of the special relationship would compromise the significance of the decision of 24 February, or that President Pompidou would not be politically able to deliver the cooperation package. President Boumedienne's subsequent declaration of a new petroleum code on 12 April terminated the concession system, raised the price of oil to $3.60/barrel, and set a DA 500 million indemnity. It also ruptured the Alphand-Bouteflika dialogue.

Algiers's unilateral decisions concerning price, indemnity, and French participation in the fields alienated Paris. Pompidou directed the oil companies to negotiate directly with the Algerian government and SONATRACH.[103] In a rare instance of collaboration, ERAP and the CFP acted immediately to apply pressure on the Algerian government. Production was stopped and technicians were removed from the field. Further, both groups threatened legal actions against any purchaser of "their" petroleum, which they termed Algerian "red oil."[104] By the end of the year the compensation problem was resolved.[105]

Pompidou's "Focus"

During his 20 April 1971 press conference, President Pompidou remarked that "cooperation with Algeria is only an aspect of French cooperation with the Third World."[106] That measured statement anticipated the "normalization" of the relationship. France seemed willing to continue, but with a more qualified assistance.[107] Nationalization, like the Evian Accords nine years earlier, was in fact a liberation. It freed France from a no longer critical dependence upon Algeria, which had at one time supplied more than 30 percent of its oil needs. The success of French political and economic diversification was illustrated by Algeria's failure to mobilize its political and economic (OPEC) allies to pressure and oppose France. Before and during the concessions crisis, France imported oil from sources including Saudi Arabia, Iraq, Nigeria, and Abu Dhabi. This variety of sources, along with France's friendly Arab relations, enabled France to receive preferential treatment during the oil boycott after the Yom Kippur War of October 1973. In addition, France's balance of payments improved.[108]

The preservation of the Algerian concessions may have been impossible in view of Algeria's determination. Nonetheless, the loss of "its oil" was a blow to France's essentialism and its imagination of itself. France's grandeur and independence needed redefinition, another conversion of power, perception, and identity; the ordering framework needed reformulation.

In June, Pompidou dispelled any remaining Algerian anxiety about *coopérant* retribution by stating: "We are continuing cooperation. . . . We are ready to participate in Algeria's economic development, in proportion to our possibilities, our interests, and in relation to the value of the projects undertaken." He declared, however, France's new Algerian policy of cooperation: "We are not giving Algeria a priority in our cooperation, but we are not at all excluding her from a number of other states in which we cooperate closely." Finally, Pompidou spoke of "normalization" by reflecting that "relations between France and Algeria had need to be placed in focus and that this *mise en point* could not have been made without a little crisis." He hoped that this "little crisis" would clear the way for "more equitable relations."[109] Pompidou sought a more mature relationship.

Reflections on the Nationalization

The nationalization achieved Boumedienne's objective to decolonize postcolonial Algeria. It terminated the privileged relationship and its generous cooperation. Thus Boumedienne declared in May: "If our refusal to perpetuate the colonial pact drawn up at Evian is tantamount to disavowing our commitments, then we are disavowing them."[110] He stated dramatically: "Our determination to free our country from the vestiges of colonialism is unshakable."[111] Algiers viewed the "battle of petroleum" as a great victory, not only because it heightened the prestige of Boumedienne and his country, but also because cooperation continued.

The Pompidou administration perceived nationalization as another stage of decolonization. While serving under de Gaulle, Pompidou had called Evian a "phase" of French decolonization.[112] Pompidou's prime minister, Jacques Chaban-Delmas, told the National Assembly that "France has never considered the Evian Accords as eternally settling" the French-Algerian relationship. Instead, the Accords were by nature "evolutionary."[113] Foreign Minister Schumann perceived Evian as ending the Algerian War, fashioning new rapport between the two countries, safeguarding French interests, and continuing French social and economic commitments under the Constantine Plan. He declared, however, that "privileged cooperation established by the 1962 accords was vitiated little by little of its substance" by Algeria.[114] Of course, to Boumedienne, the Evian Accords' "real objective" was to maintain Algerian subservience to France. They "aimed to make Algeria a dependent country under French neocolonialism."[115]

President Pompidou acknowledged his responsibilities in the affair.[116] At the time, the narrow, nonpolitical views of influential technocrats influenced the Elysée Palace.[117] Pompidou's political behavior also reflected a growing disaffection toward Algeria in the French polls. When asked if it was normal for France to have closer (privileged) relations with Algeria than with other Third World countries, 38 percent said it was normal, 37 percent said it was not, while 25 percent chose not to answer. Moreover, just before nationalization 50 percent asserted that Algeria gained most from cooperation, only 16 percent perceived France as benefiting most, with 34 percent having no opinion.[118] By being neither too tough nor too soft, Pompidou wanted to strengthen his own presidential position. But with criticism from both the left and right, he achieved neither credibility nor consensus.

The crisis was not a question of culpability. Edward Kolodziej contended that France and Algeria realized that "too close a relationship was suffocating; that each had much to gain from a broader set of foreign relations in the Mediterranean."[119] Nicole Grimaud believed that a privileged relation "so personalized" by de Gaulle "could hardly survive the change of political personnel."[120] Nevertheless, to Jean Lacouture, the end of privileged relations was a political contradiction. If France intended to pursue a Mediterranean policy, it seemed to him that a natural condition would be a close relationship ("fundamental entente") with Algeria.[121]

According to Henri Sanson, the nationalizations inaugurated a new, undefined period of "*après-coopération*." The privileged relationship had ended, but a bewildering number of tangible and intangible ties remained, necessitating a new formulation of the relationship.[122] Like Evian and, to a lesser degree, the Algiers Accords of 1965, this was a pivotal period illustrating discontinuity and continuity. On the existential level, Algeria proclaimed itself liberated from the vestiges of French colonialism, which was a great achievement in asserting its own personality and identity. If 1962 marked political decolonization, 1971 marked economic decolonization. Yet at the same time, Algeria lost its privileged position in France's foreign affairs, now strategically outlived. Ironically, within a year, Boumedienne's government signaled that it wanted to restore a special relationship with France. That status would not recur for another decade.

5

Turning the Page, 1972–1980

Algeria and France are predisposed to each other by their history and
their spirituality.
**Houari Boumedienne, during President Valéry Giscard d'Estaing's visit
to Algeria, April 1975**

The Evian Accords do not correspond to the present reality of our relations.
Valéry Giscard d'Estaing, 9 February 1978

Official relations during the immediate post-nationalization period were
methodical but morose. Then a year after the nationalization of French
petroleum concessions, President Boumedienne, while engaged in accelerated state-building, signaled his willingness to upgrade the relationship:
"We are ready to develop our commercial, cultural and economic links
with France in so far as the will to do so exists in equal measure in our
partner."[1] On the tenth anniversary of Algerian independence, he reiterated: "We have now no problems with the former colonial power, France.
We now need only to develop future co-operation on the basis of the
respect of the sovereignty of States, common interests and the respect of
the underlying options of each country."[2] This became a curious obsession
with Boumedienne: the man who sought to champion Algerian independence still wanted a special regard from France.

France soon realized that "normalization" did not depreciate Algeria's
enduring strategic, geopolitical, and economic value, especially as inscribed in the essentialist imagination. The discontinuity provoked by the
petroleum nationalization could not dislocate the continued complex significance of the bilateral relationship. This mandated Paris's reappraisal,
resulting in the *relancement* (relaunching) of a special interest, if not relationship, with Algiers.

Algeria's State-Building

The nationalization of the French hydrocarbons concessions in 1971 underscored Algeria's determination to complete decolonization and, with it,

Table 5.1. Algerian Investment Plans, 1967–1977 (in millions of dinars)

Sector	1967–69	Pecentage	1970–73	Percentage	1974–77	Percentage
Agriculture	1,869	16.87	4,140	14.92	12,005	10.89
Industry	5,400	48.73	12,400	44.70	48,000	43.53
Infrastructure	1,537	13.87	2,307	8.32	15,521	14.08
Education	1,039	9.38	3,310	11.93	9,947	9.02
Other sectors	1,236	11.15	5,583	20.13	24,784	22.48
Total	11,081	100.00	27,740	100.00	110,257	100.00

Source: *AI*, commemorative publication (July 1982), 24.

the assertion of an independent identity. Subscribing to the classic Marxist model of state-building, Algeria attempted to modernize and thereby extricate itself from the economic and social vestiges of French colonialism. Envisioned as the decisive revolutionary enterprise, this engagement aimed at achieving a genuinely independent Algeria with an authentic revolutionary and socialist national identity. Ironically, this ambitious effort, characterized by the simultaneous pursuit of three "revolutions" serving as ideological apparatuses, would also be reminiscent of, and even reliant upon, the initiatives of French colonial and postcolonial planners. The paradox reared its head again: Algeria aimed to free itself from France in economic and social domains, yet needed French assistance, especially cooperation, to achieve this liberation.

The Industrial Revolution

Algerian industrial planning subscribed to the idea proposed by the French colonial *Perspectives décennales* and the Constantine Plan of using hydrocarbons as multipliers, to create complementary industries. In the postcolonial period, Gérard Destanne de Bernis reformulated this concept as "industrializing industries," which was enthusiastically endorsed by Algerian authorities. For example, the production of petrochemicals could be used for plastics and fertilizers. The Algerians emphasized the need to invest intensively in heavy industry, such as the El-Hadjar steel complex at Annaba, a *grande entreprise* of the Constantine Plan.

Industrialization was viewed as the chief means to convert Algeria's extroverted economy to one that was introverted, integrated, and more self-sufficient. It would also attract new trading partners, especially in hydrocarbons, freeing the country from its commercial dependence upon France for durable commodities.[3] Finally, industrialization would provide jobs for a labor pool increasing by approximately 175,000 a year. The

First and Second Four-Year Plans allocated more than 40 percent of their investments in the second (industrial) sector. Adjusted to the 1978 DA, Algerian industrial production doubled from 1967 to 1978 and stimulated a remarkable 7.2 percent annual growth of the Algerian economy.[4] Nevertheless, by the end of the decade, complaints of lopsided growth in the sector provoked calls for a reassessment of industrial and general economic planning.

The Agrarian Revolution

In November 1971 the Algerian government promulgated the Charter of the Agrarian Revolution, which aimed to extend socialism throughout the first sector in phases. The plan featured the formation of cooperatives and the construction of self-contained "socialist villages." The projected thousand villages were designed to stem rural flight to the bulging cities and to provide markets for the anticipated new industrial production. Algerian authorities also announced their aim to appropriate property from large private farms and redistribute the land. These intentions mirrored the eleventh-hour colonial plan of a "renaissance of the *bled*," which had also included land redistribution (see chapter 1).

Rhetorically, the Agrarian Revolution promised a profound transformation of rural Algeria. Actually, two-thirds of the land redistributed came from public holdings, although absentee landlordship was addressed and for the most part eliminated. Only 640,000 hectares were expropriated from private lands. Agricultural production did not benefit significantly from the reform and remained inelastic.[5] With a growing population (more than 3 percent annually), the need to subsidize and import foods became an increasing worry.[6]

Ironically, it was Algeria's ideology of solidarity that prevented real social and economic change in the first sector. The government was assiduously careful not to provoke a confrontation or "class conflict."[7] The Agrarian Revolution was a "political mobilization" rather than a social one. It projected "a revival of the political myth of the peasant revolutionary and the idealization of peasant values."[8] It failed to mobilize and motivate the peasantry. Its chief historical consequence eventually was ideological, even existential: a rhetorical reaffirmation of a revolutionary state.

The Cultural Revolution

Boumedienne also initiated the Cultural Revolution in 1971 and proclaimed it "the crowning of the [Algerian] Revolution."[9] Ahmed Taleb

Ibrahimi elaborated that the Cultural Revolution would (1) promote and provide education (with an emphasis on literacy); (2) democratize culture through "libraries, museums, cinemas, theaters, and cultural tours"; (3) create a "new man within a new society" to help construct the new socialist state; and (4) ensure continuing social mobilization.[10] Concurrently, the Ministry of Culture began publishing the journal *al-Thaqafa* (Culture). In the introduction to the first issue, the Cultural Revolution was presented as another "stage" toward liberation that complemented the political and industrial revolutions. Arabic, the "national language," was Algeria's past, present, and future; it "fashioned its identity." *Al-Thaqafa* linked cultural liberation to the elimination of "every colonial influence whatever its form," an implicit repudiation of neocolonialism.[11]

Sid-Ahmed Boghli echoed the official position: "Algerian cultural policy should be seen within the double context of the people's struggle for independence and the will to overcome underdevelopment."[12] For example, the one thousand socialist villages of the Agrarian Revolution would be matched by construction of a thousand libraries. Though national cultural policy recognized that the replacement of the French language was an important aspect of Algerianization, what was most needed was a change in the nation's mentality as well as discourse.

Historicism became an important instrument for fashioning the new national identity. Often colored and inferiorized by colonial historians (see chapter 1), Algerian history had to be rethought and reinterpreted.[13] On 8 May 1974, Boumedienne spoke of the struggle against colonialism as a struggle also "to liberate our History." It had been "de-natured" by colonialism and was part of the total and violent process to "eliminate the component [parts] of the Nation."[14] The repatriation of "national archives" from France emerged as a contentious bilateral issue, underscoring the growing role of history in Algerian cultural affairs. Yet in the creation of a "national history" there was the inherent risk of being "propagandist." David Gordon astutely perceived that, while "a mythical view of history may be a useful negative weapon against the colonizer, with independence it might become a force of obscurantism and reaction, and a bar to genuine and realistic social progress."[15] Eventually, the manufacture and manipulation of a national history produced serious political and social problems for the FLN and even led to the "de-mystification" of the Revolution.

No other aspect of Algeria's postcolonial history underscored its existential quest better than linguistic policy.[16] Ahmed Taleb Ibrahimi stated in 1962 that "there is a tight correlation between the history of a people and the history of its language." He concluded: "Arabization is thus necessary, since it is one of the essential ways of restoring the Algerian personality."[17] Besides being the sacred language of all Muslims, Arabic was also linked to the socialist option. Ben Bella, who was self-conscious about his own limitations in the language, declared: "Arabization is necessary, for there is no socialism without Arabization."[18] It was another means to mobilize, define, and unify the nation. Boumedienne asserted in 1968: "Without the recovery [of] the national language, our efforts will be in vain, our personality incomplete[,] and our entity a body without a soul."[19] Arabization was a reminder that "the resentment against France was not merely political, but cultural, too."[20] Abdellah Cheriet recognized the continuing postcolonial cultural struggle: "Yesterday we fought against the physical presence of colonialism while today we fight against its spirit and its language."[21] Language had to be decolonized.

Underscoring the paradox in the relationship, the French instituted Arabization in 1961, abrogating the 1938 law that made Arabic a foreign language, and mandating the teaching of the native language in elementary schools.[22] By the time of Ben Bella's deposal in 1965, the first grade had been Arabized. In 1978 all primary education was in Arabic, though French was taught as a foreign language.[23]

Still, Ahmed Taleb Ibrahimi and others, notably Mostefa Lacheraf, also perceived a need for bilingualism. Taleb Ibrahimi contended that "bilingualism . . . is not a doctrine but a stage."[24] He argued that it was the means of securing technical skills "while waiting for the Arabic language to adapt and adopt the modern world. . . . In our scholastic programs, French will have the status of a privileged foreign language."[25] Soon after independence, Lacheraf went so far as to question the practicality of Arabization. He concluded that French would still have to be used and foresaw a bilingual but still revolutionary Algeria.[26] As minister of education in 1977, he slowed Arabization and even reinstituted bilingualism in pedagogical training.[27]

While Arabization targeted the French language, it was accepted in official circles that, to train national cadres in the latest technology, French cultural and technical cooperation had to be accommodated. An article in the new journal published from 1971 to 1981 by the Ministry of Religious Affairs, al-Asala (Authenticity), addressed this contradiction. It complained that Algeria "summons thousands of foreign coopérants," which taxed Algerian resources, and questioned the foreigners' commitment since "they do not wish to see the country develop and progress."[28] Al-Asala's articles stressed Salafiyyi (Ben Badist) themes such as Arabization and recounted Islamist resistances to colonialism; some of its contributors also implicitly (and carefully) challenged the secular nature of the state. This critical discourse would be influential and appealing in the 1980s. Boumedienne, himself an Arabist, felt compelled to attach the country to the Muslim weekend (Thursday and Friday), much to the chagrin of his secular technocrats. Clearly, Arabization was not only a cultural matter, it was also increasingly linked to the assertion of political legitimacy.

Algerian Emigrants Assaulted

Throughout the history of the Algerian presence in France, relentless violence, driven by racial and political motives, besieged the emigrant community. The frequency of attacks and France's response to them often served as a barometer of bilateral relations. For example, emigrant workers were especially targeted after the hydrocarbons nationalization of February 1971. The December 1971 accord could be viewed as a transcendent triumph, given the acute divergences at that time, but its stipulations reduced emigration from 35,000 to 25,000 for 1972–73. Furthermore, the closely monitored emigrant workers had to provide proof of employment. Increasing violence against them led to the passage of an antidiscrimination law in 1972.

The situation worsened in June 1973. A foreign worker strike at Renault pointed up the strategic importance of emigrants to the French economy. Then in August a Marseille bus driver was murdered by a mentally unbalanced Algerian, which provoked numerous retaliatory attacks throughout France.[29] On 19 September 1973 the Algerian government, responding to the assaults, stopped emigration to France by suspending exit visas.[30] President Boumedienne warned: "If the present situation continues, it will be necessary to consider the return of our emigrants."[31] However well meant, presidential solidarity with the emigrant community had little substance: Algeria was in no position for a mass "reinsertion," given its enormous shortages of employment and housing.[32] Boumedienne also equated "the future of Algerian-French relations" with the emigrant labor situation.[33] President Pompidou condemned the attacks, but the terrorism continued.[34] On 14 December 1973 the so-called Charles Martel Club perpetrated the single most violent crime during this horrific period by bombing the Algerian consulate in Marseille with a toll of four dead and twenty-two wounded.

Though the intensity and frequency of assaults lessened slightly after the carnage in Marseille, the emigrant community found itself in economic peril for a variety of reasons. Though France's Sixth Plan (1971–75) projected an annual arrival and integration of 75,000 emigrant workers, it had to be reevaluated in light of the oil crisis and embargo after the Mideast's Yom Kippur War of October 1973, which threatened the French economy along with those of other petroleum-dependent countries.[35] Compounded by "stagflation" (inflation and industrial stagnation), the workers' positions were vulnerable, with many layoffs that burdened the French social welfare system. The emigrants' employment opportunities, so tied to the French economy's expansion, evaporated, leaving a worker often with a wife and children facing an intimidating future. In July 1974, France closed its borders to foreign laborers and emigrant families.[36]

The French-Algerian Relationship's *Relancement*

The particular nature of the relationship, with its unique tangible and intangible historical variables, inevitably necessitated an improvement or *relancement* (relaunching). The *relancement* should be viewed as a shared initiative. Each country appreciated the importance of the other for a variety of reasons.

Algeria's continued importation of large quantities of French commodities and France's diversification of its oil suppliers after the hydrocarbons nationalization led to a significant trade imbalance in the latter's favor. Commercial deficits exacerbated by the emigrant worker crisis disclosed that Algerian economic liberation was still conditioned by the French relationship. Despite the recent rancor, Algeria viewed France as the natural supplier of technology and capital for its Four-Year Plan and future economic development. A special relationship remained an appealing objective. The resolution of the oil companies' grievances over the nationalizations, and the signing of a new accord with the CFP in June 1973, as well as automobile and railway contracts, signaled welcome improvement.[37]

Table 5.2. French Trade with Algeria, 1971–1975 (in millions of French francs)

	1971	1972	1973	1974	1975
French exports	2,771	2,383	3,339	6,178	8,071
French imports	1,294	1,702	2,116	4,806	3,183
Balance	1,477	681	1,223	1,372	4,888

Source: *MTM*, no. 1625 (1976): 3655.

On the French side, there were both economic and political reasons for a *relancement*. Algeria's state-planning, marked by accelerated industrialization, offered French enterprises exceptional market opportunities. France's growing consumption of natural gas made Algeria's vast resources increasingly attractive: the Sixth Plan (1971–75) projected that natural gas would account for 10 percent of France's basic energy needs. Politically, France wanted to take advantage of Algeria's prestige within the Third World, which had been heightened by the nationalization of the French hydrocarbons concessions. Algeria distinguished itself during this period mobilizing and politicizing Third World countries and championing a "new economic order" between the developed North and developing South. Algeria was especially regarded as "an essential key" to French-Arab relations. In other words, the Algerian "door to the Third World" remained a desired way to extend French influence. *Rayonnement,* the diffusion of French culture and language, also remained a valid argument for the *relancement,* with French staffing of multiplying Algerian training institutes. Obviously, the emigrant labor situation necessitated close contact. Finally, both countries shared the idea of the Mediterranean as a "lake of peace."[38] Foreign Minister Michel Jobert understood the manifold strategic importance of Algeria and concluded that the time was at hand to construct a closer relationship. He invited his counterpart to Paris.

Foreign Minister Bouteflika's Visit

Abdelaziz Bouteflika's visit to Paris in July 1973 formally inaugurated the *relancement* of the special bilateral relationship. Bouteflika was very accommodating, and even announced that 5,500 blocked *pied-noir* accounts would be allowed to be repatriated. Acknowledging the new "focused" relationship, Bouteflika said that he did not come to France as a suppliant: "There is no precise negotiation, no precise dossier to settle or not to settle." This was actually a specious stance, since his government wanted and needed a closer French relationship, especially regarding Algerian development projects. He claimed: "For us, France has a place of choice and of quality." He also addressed cooperation. In a remarkable statement, he declared: "Cooperation has never been slackened[;] Algerian-French relations have always been good. They could become excellent." Talks were very cordial, and Bouteflika invited President Pompidou to visit Algeria.[39] His country wanted "to begin a new page" marked by a "renovated vision" and end the "morose" and "banal" conditions that had caused the bilateral relationship to stagnate. Michel Jobert responded that bilateral "consideration" with "sensitivity (*sympathie*) and respect" were particularly important. While specific issues were not addressed in detail, Bouteflika's visit stimulated a renewed French interest in Algeria.[40]

The *Relancement* Gains Momentum

A series of events made the *relancement* even more attractive to the French. The October War of 1973 and the astonishing unity of the Arab oil boycott sensitized Paris to those producers who displayed friendly attitudes. Concurrently, French trade and private investment in Algeria increased markedly. The subsequent visits of French and Algerian governmental officials also raised expectations, especially in Algiers.

The communiqué published after French foreign minister Michel Jobert's visit to Algeria in March 1974 indicated the relationship's positive momentum. Talks were held in "an amicable atmosphere and in a spirit of cooperation and reciprocal comprehension." The situation of the emigrant workers received "particular attention" and was regarded as "the symbol of the quality of French-Algerian relations." Reciprocally, the Algerians expressed their "high appreciation" of the *coopérants* whose "presence in Algeria constitutes also a precious link in the friendship between the Algerian and the French people." Means to improve cultural, technical, and commercial cooperation were studied. Common strategic interests in the Mediterranean were emphasized. The two sides agreed to promote a "fruitful dialogue" between North and South, European and Arab regions, in furtherance of their shared interests concerning energy resources and general economic development. The talks, the communiqué concluded, were distinguished by "concrete results which respond to the legitimate interests of both countries."[41]

Relations had improved to the point of permitting a visit by Pompidou, but the president died on 2 April 1974.[42] The *relancement* would be addressed by a new administration.

Giscard d'Estaing Elected President

Before the election of the new president of the Fifth Republic, former premier Pierre Mendès-France said of the French-Algerian relationship that, whether the right or left won, "there is a fabric of past relations . . . that every government is obligated to take into consideration."[43] This truth was painfully learned by the winner of the presidential election, Valéry Giscard d'Estaing. Soon after Giscard's election, Georges Gorse, the former ambassador who headed the Association France-Algérie, visited Boumedienne and relayed a paradoxical message from the new president. Giscard aspired to have "banal" relations, a suggestion of a relationship with Algeria like that of any other state. This was an early indication of Giscard's insensitivity toward Algeria and the historical intimacies that gave it unique status within the framework of French foreign relations. Boumedienne tersely replied: "The relations between France and Algeria can be good or bad, in no case can they be banal."[44]

Mondialisme

Giscard prided himself on his political independence from Charles de Gaulle and Georges Pompidou, under both of whom he had served as minister of finance, yet he shared many of his predecessors' positions. There were shades of change, the "*oui, mais* (yes, but)"; nevertheless, according to John R. Frears, Giscard's foreign policy interest was "*continuité,* not change."[45]

By imagining a special role for France in global affairs, Giscard effectively refashioned French essentialism. On 24 October 1974, Giscard articulated a foreign policy that would be described as *mondialiste* (globalist). This meant that Giscard, like de Gaulle, believed that an independent France should play an active world role. Frears observed: "*Mondialisme* is just another synonym for *grandeur.*"[46] Like Pompidou, he recognized France's limitations and interdependencies and wished to associate closely with other Western states. Raymond Aron assessed: "Giscard d'Estaing is following a foreign policy which in its essentials does not differ from that of Georges Pompidou or of General de Gaulle, even though the international context has changed."[47] Giscard usually pursued a more multilateral rather than a Gaullist bilateral approach to foreign affairs. According to Alan Clark: "Such a global perspective necessitated . . . a policy of *concertation,* that is of dialogue and harmonious coordination rather than intimidation and conflict (*la confrontation*)."[48]

Giscard intensified France's Third World activism, as he perceived France as the potential interlocutor between the developed and developing worlds. He appeared particularly sensitive to North-South economic problems.[49] Continuing Pompidou's and Jobert's resistance to Henry Kissinger's policy of confrontation with OPEC, Giscard proposed a conciliatory conference between oil producers and major consumers. The Algerian government, anxious to continue the *relancement,* welcomed Giscard's initiative. Belaid Abdesselam, the powerful minister of industry and energy, remarked, "We think that it is a proposition which must succeed."[50] *Mondialisme* presupposed an amicable relationship with Algeria, the Third World's self-appointed leader.[51] Indeed, Algeria and Boumedienne were at the height of their international influence during this time. Giscard accepted an invitation to pay a state visit to Algeria in the spring of 1975.[52]

The *Relancement* Continues

When Abdesselam arrived in Paris in November 1974 for discussions, he invited significant French participation in the Second Four-Year Plan (1974–77).[53] This was reiterated during Interior Minister Michel Poniatowski's preparatory visit to Algiers in December. Abdesselam suggested that French contracts could reach FF 20 billion. Ahmed Medeghri, the minister of the interior, believed that it was imperative "to integrate the different components of cooperation between the two countries within a framework of a total vision of our relations." Smail Mahroug, the finance minister, expected that "long-term cooperation" would be "cemented by Giscard's visit." For his part, Boumedienne recognized the important contribution of the *coopérants* and was willing to improve their conditions, especially housing, in Algeria.[54]

A refashioned cooperation founded on "new bases" was envisioned as a strategic "triangular" axis among France, Algeria, and Black Africa. Besides sharing Algerian positions on the Palestinians and the Israeli-occupied Arab territories, Poniatowski suggested that Giscard's administration understood "the lesson of General de Gaulle" concerning "self-determination and nonalignments." Before leaving Algiers he concluded, "There are no more disagreements between us."[55] Visits by Norbert Ségard, the minister of exterior commerce, and Georges Gorse in March reinforced the *relancement*.

In February 1975 Giscard visited an Algerian emigrant worker quarter in Marseille after that community suffered racist attacks.[56] The renowned sociologist Germaine Tillion was called upon to study the emigrant worker family.[57] (In June 1974, Giscard had created a secretariat of state for emigrant labor.) The French president's presence among the workers and continued official consideration of the emigrants' dilemma received enthusiastic endorsement across the Mediterranean.[58] Paving the way for Giscard's arrival, Algerian authorities loosened restrictions on some colonial financial accounts, allowing their transfer and repatriation.

The Algiers Summit: A Page Unturned

Despite the amelioration of relations between the two countries, serious problems remained. The working and housing conditions of the emigrant laborers and the lack of promised training and development concerned the

Algerian government. The issue of *harki* "free circulation" loomed, after recent agitation by this community in France, including hunger strikes and hostility toward emigrant workers. Algiers desired more *coopérants* and worried over the steep imbalance of trade. There was a genuine feeling in governmental circles, however, that there would be constructive efforts toward resolving these problems as a result of the upcoming summit.[59] Above all, the Algerian president wanted the summit to demonstrate bilateral recognition as equals. This required a symbolic gesture of some type.

When Giscard arrived in Algiers, the French President declared: "La France historique salue l'Algérie indépendante." France with its long history and colonial past greeted independent Algeria, the pride of its old empire. It was thirteen years since Evian; final reconciliation appeared at hand. As Georges Gorse rejoiced: "This time, it is truly the end of the Algerian War."[60] Nevertheless, Giscard's statement more than any other during the postcolonial period disclosed the historical disposition of this relationship. France with its essentialist past greeted a state that was independent and finding itself, implicitly a state with no history. It especially illustrated Giscard's recurrent insensitivity and offended perceptive Algerian sensibilities.

The visit of President Giscard d'Estaing was the most powerful symbolic act in the postcolonial relationship. This was also Boumedienne's political apogee. He wanted to demonstrate that Algeria had its dignity and its prestige, and he wanted France's recognition and respect. Boumedienne announced, "The page is turned." Elaborating, the Algerian president recounted Algeria's political and economic development and achievements. He reviewed past bilateral problems: "These vicissitudes—and the fact that cooperation has survived them—testifies to why we . . . continue to believe in this type of relationship with your country. The best proof of this is that there is no longer any major contention between Algeria and France."[61]

As his speech continued—a remarkably warm, even sentimental address, spoken in French although Boumedienne usually preferred Arabic—it became evident what Boumedienne wanted more than the continuation and enlargement of cooperation from Giscard. Metaphorically, the page should be turned, turned back to the time when Algeria held a privileged position within the framework of French foreign policy. He spoke of the unique character of the relationship, particularly the role of intangibles in the human dimension (emigrant workers, *coopérants*). Boumedienne regarded French cooperation as "inscribed imperatively in the total process of Algerian development." By participating, France would "inevitably . . . benefit in the enterprise as much in the economic domain as in the cultural."[62] Advertising Algeria as "a great client for machine manufacturers," there was no hiding that President Boumedienne preferred France to reassume "its place of choice in our development."[63]

Later at the French embassy, Giscard said that it was time "to write a new page" in the relationship. He declared that the purpose of his visit was the creation of a climate of confidence. Giscard characterized cooperation as a "great fraternal task." The two presidents traveled together and were acclaimed in Skikda and Constantine, as well as during an enthusiastic motorcade in Algiers. Giscard stayed for three days and was impressed with the warmth and hospitality of the Algerian people. The joint communiqué recapitulated many of the basic ideas of the Jobert visit a year before. While claiming the reestablishment of "the conditions for a fruitful dialogue," the future "perspectives" would be based upon "the measure of potentialities and political wills."[64]

Paul Balta believed before the state visit that Giscard intended to "turn a dolorous page; to strengthen ties which had proven their solidarity in resisting all contingencies; and to open new perspectives to cooperation to complete the reconciliation between the two peoples."[65] To attain these objectives, Giscard needed to sustain and exercise his "political will," but he seemed more interested in "normalizing" the relationship than restoring it, as Boumedienne wished, to a privileged position.[66] As Nicole Grimaud related, the warm welcome and promising economic opportunities did not result in reciprocal confidence.[67] The summit produced no substantial, concrete achievement, agreement, or "gesture" (e.g., oil purchases, assistance for an anticipated automobile factory in Oran). Nevertheless, the very presence of the French president seemed to promise closer relations.

The Algerian president recognized that shared multilateral interests should naturally lead to a closer bilateral cooperation if not collaboration. In words evoking the Gaullist French-Algerian axis and the aspirations of Giscardian *mondialisme*, Boumedienne contended that cooperation's "success will contribute incontestably . . . to the Arab-European dialogue, and will enlarge perspectives between the Arab-African world and Europe."[68] Opportunities to purchase oil and natural gas were apparently presented to France in order to correct commercial imbalances. A joint committee to evaluate the relationship was also proposed. Unfortunately, despite Boumedienne's cordial invitation to France to participate decisively in Algeria's development and his genuine desire to establish an ex-

Table 5.3. French Trade with Algeria, 1976–1980 (in millions of French francs)

	1976	1977	1978	1979	1980
French exports	7,034.1	8,786.1	6,913.0	8,215.5	11,077.6
French imports	3,314.9	3,894.3	3,203.6	4,857.8	7,431.4
Balance	3,719.2	4,891.8	3,709.4	3,357.7	3,646.2

Source: EIU, *QERs.*

emplary bilateral relationship, the *relancement* faltered over commercial questions and especially over the regional problem of the decolonization of Spanish (or Western) Sahara. Furthermore, the two men failed to create a close, confident friendship, although Boumedienne's personal efforts were particularly commendable, given his ideological bent. The failure to achieve a lasting *relancement* and, most important, a privileged relationship again with France, after almost two years of anticipation, was a bitter blow for the Algerian government and a personal affront to its leader.

In June 1975 Algiers expressed its disappointment over French oil purchases from Persian Gulf competitors. The French government's explanation that it could not control independent companies clearly indicated that the political will to establish a "renovated" cooperation was not shared in Paris.[69] This exacerbated the commercial imbalance. Algeria had already suspended buying 5,500 French trucks a month after the visit.[70] In the first trimester of 1975, Algeria imported FF 2,267 million against FF 644 million exports.[71] Chronic violence against emigrant workers became especially intense in February 1976 with attacks against Algerians and the bombing of the Algeria's Office National du Tourisme. *El-Moudjahid* questioned Giscard's assertion to *Le Nouvel Observateur* that there was "neither crisis nor tension, nor even a conflictive situation" between the two countries.[72] There would be soon.

The Western Sahara Imbroglio

Continuing to assert France's interest and presence in the Maghrib, Giscard also visited Morocco. Relations with Morocco had suffered initially as a result of the privileged relationship accorded to its rival Algeria, but during the late 1960s the relationship between Paris and Rabat improved significantly.[73] By the time the French president arrived in Morocco, King Hassan II could confidently declare, "There are no contentions between Morocco and France." Indeed, he called President Giscard d'Estaing a "perfect pal (*copain*)."[74] Their friendship contributed to

Paris's accommodation of Rabat's grandiose ambition of a Greater Morocco. Morocco had claimed traditional and historical rights to the northwest corner of the continent including western Algeria, Mauritania, and, at that time most appealing, the Spanish or Western Sahara.[75]

Spain was then in the throes of domestic political crisis caused by Generalísimo Francisco Franco's failing health. Taking advantage of the situation, the Moroccan king targeted the Spanish Sahara and received the French president's assurance of support for an anticipated operation.[76] Among the reasons for Giscard's decision were: Hassan's strategic pro-Western orientation; the need to strengthen the Alawite monarchy, which had faced coup attempts in the early 1970s; the possibility of French economic opportunities; the protection of the large French community living in Morocco; the improbability of serious Sahrawi (Western Saharan) resistance, though the nationalist Polisario—Popular Front for the Liberation of Saguia el Hamra and Rio de Oro—had conducted military operations against the Spanish since 1973; and finally the personal friendship between the two leaders. Morocco assumed the privileged status that Algeria coveted.[77]

A tenet of Algerian foreign policy had always been the support of liberation movements. The Polisario struggle was of particular significance since it involved a contiguous contested territory.[78] Mauritanian and— most disturbing, given the memory of the brief Border War of 1963— Moroccan ambitions rekindled Algerian fears of King Hassan's desire for a Greater Morocco that would encompass Algeria's mineral-rich Tindouf region.

The sudden "decolonization" of the Spanish Sahara surprised and embarrassed Algeria. Though Boumedienne dismissed Rabat's Green March as *"grand cinéma,"*[79] he also knew that he was not playing a major role; worse, he was ignored. King Hassan's bold diplomacy alienated and isolated Algeria. This led to Algiers's massive military aid to Polisario units and humanitarian assistance to tens of thousands of Sahrawi refugees living in Algerian havens. Clearly, Algeria's support of Polisario was ideological and self-interested.[80] In addition, Algiers suspected that Paris played an indirect role in the tripartite Madrid Accords of November 1975 that partitioned the Spanish Sahara between Mauritania and Morocco.[81] Later, French military support and then intervention seemed to confirm this suspicion.

France's abandonment of the *relancement* and embrace of Morocco bristled Boumedienne. In an interview with French journalists in January 1976 he claimed that he had advised Giscard to pursue a policy of "strict neutrality. . . . I thought to have been heard.'" Boumedienne said, "Giscard fooled me. Giscard lied to me."[82] In the following month, Giscard expressed his opposition to "the multiplication of microstates," further tainting France's "neutrality" and tilting toward Morocco. Nevertheless, given Paris's close relations with Morocco and Mauritania coupled with Prime Minister Jacques Chirac's positive statements concerning the Sahrawis, Boumedienne still considered France to be in a position to mediate the conflict as early as April 1976.[83]

Unfortunately, the bilateral relationship worsened as a result of Polisario attacks at Mauritania's Zouerate mines in May and October 1977 which also directly assaulted French *coopérants* (two dead, eight captured). The Algerian Foreign Ministry regretted these casualties but declared that "they are inherent in each war of liberation."[84] Giscard proceeded with plans for military intervention. This decision substantiated an Algerian journalist's observation comparing France's "neutrality" toward the Western Sahara with its "condemnation" of *apartheid*.[85] In November, the largest anti-French demonstrations since the War of Liberation manifested Algeria's disapproval of French policy. According to one journalist, French hostility was aimed at the Algerian Revolution itself.[86] The potential for French military operations targeting the Algerian-supported Sahrawi nationalists was particularly upsetting to Boumedienne. He reminded France that Africa should no longer be regarded as an area of imperialist spheres of influence.[87]

French air strikes commenced against the Sahrawis on 2 December. Polisario released the French hostages by the end of the month to United Nations Secretary-General Kurt Waldheim. From the Algerian perspective, France's support of Mauritanian forces, especially by the deadly use of sophisticated Jaguar aircraft, and the continued arrival of military advisers and matériel to the Moroccans implicated Paris further in the Western Saharan intrigue.[88] Boumedienne ordered his ministries and state enterprises to boycott French commodities—in part also to help correct the commercial imbalance in France's favor. There were other variables contributing to the deterioration of the bilateral relationship.

Anti–Emigrant Labor Legislation

President Giscard d'Estaing's creation of a secretariat of state for emigrant workers and his visit to a worker area in Marseille before the Algiers summit in April 1975 seemed to indicate his government's good intentions. But growing domestic economic problems and unemployment, aggravated by the deteriorating bilateral situation, caused Paris to reevaluate the entire emigrant worker situation. As the Algerian community was 800,000 strong, this reassessment had considerable importance. Familial emigration, which had been provisionally interrupted in 1974, was reinstated only at a reduced rate. Now additional measures were initiated to monitor the workers' activities; these included assigning new work cards and increasing arbitrary identity checks for suspected illegals by the police, especially in the metro.[89] Algiers's concern over these actions deepened when the French government decided to pursue financial persuasion and even to threaten massive deportation.

As economic problems continued, a growing number of French believed that the deportation of emigrant workers and their families (most of the laborers were single men) would be an economic panacea. In 1977, Premier Raymond Barre instituted a ten-thousand-franc incentive to persuade emigrant worker repatriations. A more drastic move came from Interior Minister Christian Bonnet, who introduced a bill that would give the government the power to expel any of the estimated 300,000 illegal foreign residents. Amendments softened the bill slightly.[90]

On 27 September 1977, Lionel Stoléru, a secretary of state in the Ministry of Labor, announced measures that stopped the issuance of work cards to foreigners, extended financial incentives to repatriate unemployed emigrant workers, and suspended for three years all familial emigration. Gone was the automatic renewal of residence permits. Instead, the workers would receive three-year permits to work in France. Renewal would be based on regional unemployment. With only a three-year residence possible, families would be discouraged from joining workers.[91] The objective was to promote the voluntary repatriation of 35,000 emigrant workers a year. Opposition from the left, the unions, the churches, and the Council of State diluted these initiatives. Support groups concerned with workers' welfare, such as the Mouvement contre le Racisme et pour l'Amitié entre les Peuples and the Fédération des Associations de Solidarité avec les Travailleurs Immigrés, were particularly critical of the government's action.[92] Though these measures applied to all emigrant workers, the Algerians seemed most imperiled.

The emigrant worker crisis, coupled with the French-Algerian imbroglio over Western Sahara, triggered violence, including the murder of Laid Sebai, an Algerian employee at the Paris branch of the Amicale des Algériens en Europe, in December 1977. El-Moudjahid proclaimed: "The French Government is responsible."[93]

Meanwhile, another dispute loomed which was critical to Algerian development and French energy demands: the pricing of natural gas.

The Growing Importance of Natural Gas

After independence both French and Algerian planners valued petroleum over natural gas. This was owing in part to existing energy markets and operating systems and the technical problems of natural gas recovery and delivery. In the short term, oil was easier to exploit and more profitable. Natural gas liquefaction processes were just beginning to come on line. Indeed, French liquefaction technology implemented in Algeria was revolutionary. Appreciating the opportunities presented by its proven vast and recoverable volumes (in comparison with limited petroleum reserves), Algerian planners also saw natural gas as an economic multiplier ("industrializing industry") and invested heavily in infrastructure. With the complicated oil question settled, natural gas inevitably received greater attention.[94]

Background to the Gas Pricing Negotiations

When French companies discovered vast reserves of natural gas in the Algerian Sahara in 1954–56, planners immediately perceived its use in accelerated industrialization. A marketing plan, the Lemaire Project, aimed to deliver natural gas to the Maghrib, neighboring African states (the OCRS), and Europe. French planners already posited Eurafrican economic and political interdependence, an idea inherited and subscribed to by their Algerian counterparts.[95]

In 1964 the French-controlled Compagnie Algérienne de Méthane Liquide (CAMEL) liquefaction plant at Arzew began production and marketed gas to France and the United Kingdom. France contracted to import 500 million m³/year for twenty-five years. In the following year, the gas relationship was substantially changed. By the Algiers Accords, natural gas was "nationalized" in the ground. The French kept their status as producing concessionaires and maintained their infrastructure until the February 1971 nationalizations. They were obliged to supply Algeria, however, with all the gas it needed at a fixed price at the wellhead. Algeria would manage and profit from the general commercialization of the gas, though sharing with an anticipated joint Algerian-French company charged specifically with LNG and methane sales to France. France also agreed to assist in marketing natural gas internationally, though Algeria would handle all third markets. By an exchange of letters, France was prepared to receive 1.5 billion m³/year of gas from 1968 on, if possible from French concessions. Thus they were kept on as operators, but their status changed. The French would still lift it but would sell it at cost to the Algerians. The condensates (propane, butane, methane) could be marketed freely by the concessionaires. Though from 1965 to 1971 Algeria's oil relationship with France received critical and concentrated attention, there were also conflicts over natural gas.

As with French oil operations, Algeria wanted to see greater exploration and exploitation of gas. Obviously, infrastructure development was desirable, as the Algerians expected complete national "recovery" of their hydrocarbon resources. The French effort did not satisfy them. Furthermore, gas was burned off, provoking charges that petroleum companies did not take full advantage of the gas condensates.[96] The higher relative price for Algerian gas (and crude), as claimed in "certain [French] circles," was also challenged by Algiers.[97]

In the view of Gérard Destanne de Bernis, France's equivocal attitude toward Algerian gas was caused by (1) the low utilization of natural gas in the French economy, (2) the availability of other gas sources in the North Sea and the Netherlands, (3) GDF's weak financial situation and its inability "to elaborate a proper strategy with regard to the petroleum companies," and (4) the general failure to perceive natural gas as a "great industrial raw material of the future."[98] Withal, France recognized the value of Algeria's natural gas.

Agreements in 1967 and 1970 resulted eventually in a contract concluded in 1972 providing for delivery to France of an additional 3.5 billion m³ annually for twenty years. The 1969 El Paso LNG contract anticipated shipping 10 billion m³ annually to the United States and strengthened Algeria's resolve while bolstering its confidence during the negotiations with the French in 1969–71. The subsequent nationalization of the French concessions and infrastructure provoked more anger in petroleum than in natural gas circles, revealing, too, the independent natures of the French national enterprises.

The 1976 Accord

On 2 April 1976, GDF and SONATRACH signed a new contract which called for the annual delivery of 5 billion m³/year starting in 1980. The fulfillment of the accord was bound to reduce the commercial deficit. For its new contracts SONATRACH set a base of $1.40/MMBtu (up from $0.40), with the price to be linked to collective Algerian gas exports. GDF wanted to link the price to actual sales, a bilateral rather than a multilateral pricing system.[99] The LNG price controversy began its contentious course.

Algeria articulated its pricing policy and rationale in a specially published article in *Le Monde*.[100] It argued that the price paid by GDF ($0.40/MMBtu f.o.b. to a $0.60 c.i.f.) was artificial, well below the international market. To Algeria, this represented a loss of $150 million/year. Algeria asked for price equality with other sources such as the Netherlands and the USSR. It claimed that not only Distrigas-Boston and ENAGAS but British Methane Ltd. were undergoing price revisions. Algeria wanted a fair price. The gist of the argument was political. Algeria felt the "attitude adopted by the French government" was "curious." It criticized France's inconsistency in commercial relations: while professing liberal convictions, the government had not always acted accordingly.

Furthermore, a "renovated France, freed from the demons and myths inherited from a long colonial past [and] engaged in favor of calm negotiation and faithful cooperation with the Third World" was contrasted with one that "hardly distinguishes France from other industrialized countries which intend to exploit systematically, to their profit, all economic relations which are susceptible to play in their favor to the detriment of Third World countries." France's acclaimed sensitivity to Euro-Arab and North-South relations was paradoxical if not contradictory. Algeria, "well placed to know this particular aspect of French economic policy," considered the LNG issue to be "one of numerous illustrations." Simply, the draining of natural resources to the profit of the developed country could be termed neocolonialist. Algeria again complained that Giscard's warm words of April 1975 were repudiated by subsequent acts. Clearly, any price settlement would have political repercussions.

The Battle of Gas: Oil Redux?

Algeria dismissed arguments that GDF should receive preferential treatment because of French investment in Algeria under the Algiers Accords. Those monies had nothing to do with the price of LNG. Besides, the infrastructure also benefited ERAP at that time. Those facilities were settled in the post-nationalization 1971 SONATRACH-ERAP Accord. Indeed, by the Algiers Accords, the price of gas delivered to France was three to four times less than the international price. There were also unanticipated construction problems at Skikda resulting in almost doubled costs for planned liquefaction facilities.

GDF, like ERAP and the CFP in the petroleum sector, had not had an LNG policy except to obtain it as cheaply as possible. This can be excused in part by the minor role of natural gas in French energy needs (10–12 percent). Now France was interested in diversifying its LNG sources. (In 1977, France imported natural gas from four sources: Algeria, the North Sea, the Netherlands, and the USSR. Its internal production at the Lacq fields accounted for about 20 percent of its needs.) LNG relations with Algeria, like petroleum, could not rest merely on economic considerations.

The April 1976 Accord, signed during the deteriorating *relancement,* again demonstrated the paradox of conflict yet cooperation. With a commercial deficit of FF 5 billion, Algiers welcomed the accord. France would be paying a higher price than in the past.[101] Obviously, this was crucial to Algiers. But the worsening political conditions affected French enterprises' ambitions and specifically compromised the French firm Technip's hope to provide the capital for GNL 3, the third liquefaction complex at Arzew.[102] Once again, as with petroleum, American rather than French companies gained important commercial footholds.

Distrigas of Boston signed an accord on 12 April 1976 that took into account rising energy costs.[103] This agreement, along with the anticipated implementation of the El Paso contract of 1969, gave Algeria added impetus to ask for price revisions to fuel its state-building projects. El Paso already contributed to capital expenditures for an ultramodern liquefaction infrastructure. Algeria's Valorisation des Hydrocarbures (VALHYD) development plan of 1978, articulated with the significant assistance of American Bechtel consultants, blueprinted oil and gas production and economic development.[104] It underscored President Boumedienne's accelerated state-building ambitions. The VALHYD plan forecast rapidly accumulated revenue and capital ($22 billion allocated for infrastructure alone) from projected annual export sales of 70 billion m^3 of natural gas. By 2005, known hydrocarbon resources would be exhausted, but Algeria would be by that time a modern economic state. VALHYD presumed an inelastic American demand for LNG. Algeria felt it was not only playing its "America card," it had also trumped the French.

Another *Relancement?*

Despite setbacks over the Western Sahara, emigrant labor, and natural gas, both sides realized that the deterioration of relations had to be stopped. Giscard, ironically assuming a former Ben Bellist position, pronounced in February 1978 that the Evian Accords no longer seemed applicable to the realities existing between France and Algeria. His call for a reevaluation represented a positive initiative.[105] With emigrant labor being targeted and the need for French commercial markets and *coopérants,* Algeria was receptive to a shift in French policy. An official communiqué stated: "For its part, the Algerian Government will approach the dossier of cooperation in a positive and total (*globale*) fashion, economic and political relations being naturally complementary."[106] Boumedienne expressed his willingness to upgrade the relationship by metaphorically referring to the past promise of the *relancement:* "The page is certainly turned but not erased."[107] Foreign Minister Bouteflika signaled moderation by recognizing France's right to provide military cooperation for training, e.g., to Moroccan and Mauritanian armed forces, but he denounced direct intervention.[108] (By the time Mauritania withdrew from the Western Sahara conflict in the summer of 1978, France had already reduced its direct military role.) His brief talk with Giscard on 12 July affirmed the necessity of a "concerted policy" between the two states.[109] Boumedienne's considerate and warm 14 July message called for "confident and effective dialogue."[110]

Fatally ill with a rare blood disease, Boumedienne concentrated on improving the Algerian-French relationship. Returning from treatment in Moscow, he communicated with Giscard while flying in French airspace on 15 November. He urged France to use its influence as a mediating force in the Maghrib, especially concerning the self-determination of the Sahrawi people. In addition he called for a "new page of history, done in justice, progress, and peace."[111] With French doctors among the medical team treating him, President Boumedienne died on 27 December 1978.

Boumedienne and the French Relationship: An Assessment

From 1971 until his death, Boumedienne sought to restore a privileged relationship, albeit on Algerian terms, and suffered bitter personal disappointment especially when the *relancement* collapsed. He envisioned a respectful state-to-state relationship, if not partnership, against superpower pretensions. Giscard's condescending attitude during his visit, together with the lack of concrete achievements, was an embarrassment. Boumedienne was a proud man who wanted to earn recognition both for himself and for the state he was building. Paradoxically, this intractable self-styled revolutionary, who wanted to rid Algeria of every "complex," who himself often pursued a "banal" French policy, still sought special consideration, even admiring approval, from France.

Boumedienne achieved specific decolonizing objectives such as the transfer of military bases and the recovery of hydrocarbons concessions, thereby finally revising "the colonial pact drawn up at Evian." Yet he knew that a special relationship with France was still a necessity. He declared: "Let France get used to the fact of our national sovereignty and all problems, big and small, can be settled. The common interests of the two countries are numerous and evident. They are dictated by history, geography, and the economy."[112] His ardent pursuit of postcolonial decolonization successfully projected an Algeria asserting its sovereign rights and independence, an exemplary nation for the Third World.

The National Charter of 1976, yet another example of an existential definition and reaffirmation of the Algerian state, reiterated the aim "to consolidate national independence" by "liquidating all forms of imperialist or neocolonialist influence."[113] It underscored the familiar theme that "socialism, in Algeria, is an irreversible movement." It linked socialist state-building to the "Islamic values which are a fundamental constitutive element of the personality of the Algerian people" rather than to a "materialist metaphysic" or a "dogmatic foreign conception." The consistent use of a revolutionary discourse also aimed to reinforce an internal consensus. Nevertheless, Boumedienne's technocratic state-building created a wide disparity, socially as well as economically, between the elite and the increasingly youthful masses. The timely Constitution of 1976 complemented the National Charter and created institutions such as the National Popular Assembly and offices that permitted an impressive and orderly presidential succession.[114] When Chadli Benjedid was elected President in 1979, relations with France had ameliorated.

Chadli Benjedid Comes to Power

Unlike Ben Bella and Boumedienne, Chadli Benjedid, a compromise candidate for the presidency, pursued policies that were much more pragmatic than ideological, reconciliatory rather than revolutionary.[115] He stated in November 1981: "In effect, we are living in a new stage of our Revolution."[116] Before Italian television he acknowledged that "the principles are the same" but "the method can be adapted following the evolution of international life."[117] William B. Quandt had written: "There seems to be no a priori reason to exclude the possibility of development toward either a rigid, authoritarian, unresponsive, and bureaucratic state or toward a more pragmatic, relatively tolerant, participant polity."[118] If Boumedienne's regime was the former, Benjedid's government was the latter.

Benjedid inherited several problems from the Boumedienne era: (1) emigrant labor, (2) the Western Sahara conflict, (3) LNG negotiations, and (4) a significant trade imbalance. In his response to Giscard's congratulatory message after his election, Benjedid expressed interest not only in a stronger relationship between the two states but also in a greater role in the western Mediterranean. He also reminded Paris of Algiers's sensitivity toward emigrant worker "dignity" and "security" to which "we attach the highest price."[119] While relations had warmed between Paris and Algiers before Boumedienne's untimely death, there was certainly no indication that there would be a renewed *relancement*.

Benjedid was not as desirous as Boumedienne of a special relationship. His ideas were closer to Michel Jobert's past aspirations for a "confident," realistic, and reliable one. Though improved relations were welcomed, Algiers hoped to solve bilateral problems without injecting the passion of the past or the promise of an idealized privileged relationship. Less ideologically oriented than Ben Bella or Boumedienne, Benjedid simply aimed at resolving issues between the two countries.[120] Giscard seemed willing to cooperate. When the new Algerian ambassador, Mohamed Sahnoun, presented his letters on 25 October 1979, the French president spoke of a "spirit of collaboration (*concertation*)."[121]

Benyahia's Visit to Paris

Almost a month after the death of Boumedienne, Algeria signaled its willingness to continue better relations with France by awarding the building of the third natural gas liquefaction plant to the French firm Technip working in a consortium with a subsidiary of Italy's ENI. COFACE would provide credits. Indeed, the estimated FF 2.5 billion loan was the most given to Algeria by France for a single project.[122] It underscored France's desire to upgrade the relationship. This was reaffirmed by the visit of Foreign Minister Jean François-Poncet to Algiers in June 1979.

François-Poncet's conversations with the new Algerian leaders confirmed that a serious "adult dialogue" was now under way between the two countries. According to Algerian ambassador Mohamed Bedjaoui, "explosive subjects" (especially emigrant labor, given the pending Bonnet and Stoléru legislation) were calmly addressed.[123] *El-Moudjahid* hoped that "the will of both countries to transcend the ephemeral" would result in positive achievements.[124] That aspiration was fulfilled with Mohamed Benyahia's reciprocal mission to Paris in January 1980, which reached an important threshold in the postcolonial relationship.

Benyahia's visit aimed to address such serious problems as emigrant labor, financial questions, and the repatriation of Algerian archives (natural gas being for the most part successfully isolated). Besides those issues, he wanted to impress upon his counterparts that this was a new Algerian government with a sense of political and national maturity. He wanted to dispel *demandeur* images, and he succeeded. Benyahia clearly wished relations to be confident and conventional. Upon his arrival he asserted that in the global context Algeria and France each had its own particular "personality" as well as responsibility.[125] This statement reaffirmed Algeria's independent identity. Benyahia described his 17 January meeting with Giscard as "very friendly, very frank and . . . even very encouraging." They discussed the entire relationship and especially the most pressing bilateral problems. The Algerian foreign minister implied that the objective was more than just "new relations" but "the perspectives of a sound and solid cooperation."[126]

At a dinner in his honor Benyahia rejected the "ephemeral reconciliations" and "transitory conciliations" of the past. Algeria's mission was now *concertation*. This could only occur in a "dialogue" between "equal partners." He acknowledged past problems and related them to Algeria's pursuit of patrimony and equality through recovering resources and reestablishing the "full dignity of its personality's cultural foundations" including the restoration of Arabic-Islamic values. Benyahia quoted President Benjedid's realistic reference to the Boumedienne-Giscard summit: "To consider the past a page turned, not torn."[127] Benyahia wanted to impress upon the French government that Algeria thought itself decolonized. With the existential definition done, it was time to settle pressing problems.

He told *Le Monde* that for "a mutually profitable cooperation" there must be established "political and psychological conditions." Benyahia wanted straightforward relations without "ambiguity." He wanted to convince the French government that this was not only a new Algerian government but also an independent and equal sovereign Algerian state with a foreign policy founded not on a *rayonnement révolutionnaire* but on independence and peace. While acknowledging that "it is not always simple to efface anachronistic reflexes," he discussed the need "to create a new psychological climate . . . to approach problems between Algeria and France with a spiritual state disencumbered of certain inherited historical conceptions."[128] On the personal level, what lent this comment weight was that Benyahia himself was a veteran of French-Algerian diplomacy who had participated significantly at Melun, Les Rousses, and Evian.

The Algerian foreign minister's mission was a success. Besides creating a more confident climate, it brought concrete results. A consular convention was signed to benefit both emigrant workers and *coopérants,* while six committees were organized to study specific bilateral problems. François-Poncet also spoke of a Grand Commission to study the entire relationship, an idea discarded earlier by Giscard.

Benyahia's visit demonstrated Algerian independence much more than Bouteflika's six and half years earlier. The Algeria of July 1973, though not a *demandeur,* still wanted to restore a favored relationship to assist development plans. Benyahia was less concerned with attaining that status than with simply resolving immediate problems. Consider his remarks concerning the consular convention: "It is more than a symbol. It is . . . the product of hard work. It has been established with the political will to develop more cooperation between the two countries."[129]

Boussad Abdiche accurately assessed Benyahia's visit: "It was a historic moment, and the beginning of a great turn in the relations between Algeria and France."[130] Benyahia succeeded in the short term in targeting problems and dispelling images. Mohamed Sahnoun, a key negotiator during this period, reflected that "anachronistic reflexes and attitudes" did not appear.[131] For the next nine months the committees worked on specific issues: social security, financial transfers, citizen problems, archives, emigrant labor. Emigrant labor particularly involved intensive conversations and finally substantial conclusions.

Emigrant Expulsion?

One of the chief reasons for Benyahia's visit to Paris was Algiers's apprehension over the French government's deteriorating attitude toward emigrant workers. Of particular concern was the passage in December 1979 of the Bonnet Law, which strengthened the French government's power to deport emigrant workers. It even provided for the forced repatriation of workers if residence cards were not renewed. Previously, renewals had been practically automatic. New legislation, the Stoléru Proposal, attempted to equate work cards with residence cards, which could expedite a massive expulsion of unemployed, unproductive emigrants.[132] Though the two governments exchanged letters (26–27 December 1978 and 20 December 1979) that renewed the five- and ten-year residence cards scheduled for expiration during these periods, the situation was critical. Indeed, the renewals were only for one year. There was an urgent need for an enduring accommodation.

French action taken against the emigrants elicited domestic political responses and repercussions. Over the years a solidarity had developed between the emigrant workers and France's powerful and syndicalist-natured labor unions, the Confédération Générale du Travail (CGT) and the Confédération Française Démocratique du Travail (CFDT). Both unions denounced expulsion measures and defended the emigrant workers. In addition, the council of the Amicale des Algériens en Europe called for the application of the 1968 accord with its automatic renewal stipulations.[133] The Association France-Algérie condemned the "simplistic affirmations" of those who maintained that repatriation would solve French unemployment. Instead, the organization referred to the Anicet le Pors Report and the drafts of the Seventh Plan, which disputed the contention that the emigrants' presence produced French unemployment. The Association hoped for *concertation* in resolving this situation for the "mutual benefit of both countries."[134]

New and intense negotiations resulted in the 17 September 1980 agreements.[135] The exchange of letters between the governments called for training programs conducted in special centers and within French and Algerian enterprises to train workers in trades, ensuring employment in planned positions after repatriation. The French government would also provide low-interest loans for new enterprises, while the Algerian government would offer tax and customs concessions. New housing would be earmarked for the returning workers. France would pay the travel costs, for workers and for their families as well. Repatriation allocations (for those not receiving financial assistance for their own enterprises) varied according to time at a job and pay rates. For example, a worker who had steady employment during the previous six months would receive four times the net average weekly pay for that period. The two governments projected the resettlement of 12,000 trained workers a year. Certificates of residence would be also renewed for workers electing to stay in France. Cards of emigrants working in France before 1962 would be recertified for ten years. Five- and ten-year certificates issued after July 1962 would be renewed automatically for the next three years and three months. There would be a concerted effort to promote Arabic studies in French primary and secondary schools. Most important from the Algerian perspective, there would be no forced expulsions. Obviously there would be important linkages with financial and cultural and technical cooperation.

The emigrant labor agreement stemmed the decline of French-Algerian relations. Reinsertion would be conditioned upon the capitalization of Algeria's economy, ideally providing hundreds of thousands of jobs; it also offered France an implicit privileged role in future investments. Training emigrant workers in France to fill projected positions in Algeria, as anticipated by French and Algerian planners, promised to be an extraordinary example of cooperation.[136] It also symbolically remunerated the workers' participation in the development of France's modern economy, while sublimating the painful memory of colonial economics which forced thousands to work in the *métropole*.

The emigrant worker agreement, a social security agreement signed on 1 October, and progress on the issue of archives were all received well by the Algerian public. A programmatic method of reinsertion with French help was also viewed favorably in governing circles.[137] Above all, the agreements disclosed the positive possibilities of close coordination (*concertation*).

Natural Gas Price Stalemate

Interest rates, overruns, debts, and the ambitions of the VALHYD Plan forced an Algerian reformulation of gas pricing. The man responsible for the pricing revolution was the talented Nordine Ait Laoussine, described by Jonathan P. Stern as "the intellectual driving force behind gas price policy."[138] In 1977 he began arguing that LNG prices should be equivalent to competing energies. Laoussine also concluded that exporter risk-taking in the construction of export facilities should be shared by consumers.[139] He explained: "The price paid by the consumer must, over the long term, not only be acceptable in absolute terms, but also relative to other energy forms. The need for a harmonious structure of energy prices worldwide makes this imperative. A link between gas and oil prices should therefore be the fundamental objective of any gas-export system."[140] The decision to link gas and oil prices was made with Benjedid's accession to the presidency in 1979, a year earmarked for *rattrapage*, or making up for one's losses. This promised difficult negotiations with consumer nations.

There was an internal political dimension to pricing policy. Belaid Abdesselam and Ahmed Ghozali were blamed for mismanagement of the El Paso relationship and replaced.[141] Though El Paso had provided a psychological trump in Algeria's dealings with the French oil companies in 1969 by proving that Algeria could attract new clients, the American corporation found the new pricing principle uneconomic after Algeria had invested billions in creating the most modern liquefaction facilities in the world and in building tankers to haul the huge anticipated volumes of LNG. Ait Laoussine left in mid-1980. By removing these powerful technocrats, Benjedid could assert his own direction besides securing his presidential position. According to Jonathan Stern: "The men who had taken over gas policy in Algeria had . . . less experience of market conditions than their predecessors, although this may have been less important than the pressure they were under from their political leaders."[142] Belkacem Nabi, the new minister of energy, stated the new policy simply as "A therm is a therm."[143] As president of OPEC, Nabi wanted this position supported internationally. As Saharan Blend crude headed toward $40/barrel, Algerian adherence to the new pricing correlation proved prohibitive to its principal customers. GDF in particular was increasingly concerned with this pricing strategy.

In February 1980 negotiations commenced with GDF. The Algerian insistence on parity, which would have doubled the price to $6.11/MMBtu, was stoutly resisted by the French national enterprise.[144] Originally, the indexing formula agreed to in July 1976 had calculated the price of gas to equate with concurrent heavy and domestic fuels, which raised the price from $0.40 to $1.30/MMBtu. Another agreement in 1979 secured $3.05/MMBtu beginning on 1 January 1980.[145] During the following month SONATRACH crimped its LNG deliveries to GDF, claiming that the liquefaction plant at Arzew (constructed in part by Technip) was having "technical problems." This reduction was linked, however, to the arduous negotiations. Meanwhile, the CFP found its situation uncomfortably compromised by having the negotiation of its own contract linked to a new LNG contract. The French, however, stubbornly resisted the parity question. SONATRACH resumed its exportation.

On 30 October 1980 André Giraud, the minister of the interior, tried to take advantage of the recent emigrant worker and social security accords to stimulate the stalled LNG price negotiations. Apparently, there was movement at this time toward French recognition of the Algerian principle of linking gas to crude. The Algerians had in turn evolved toward a different indexing of Saharan Light crude and seemed more flexible on transportation and regasification costs.[146] Giraud proposed linkage of a natural gas price to a general cooperation agreement on the transfer of nuclear and solar technology.[147] Though some progress occurred, the problem of pricing remained unresolved.

SONATRACH'S relations with El Paso deteriorated further. Deliveries were suspended in early spring 1980 and negotiations on the new pricing formula finally broke off in February 1981.[148] Nevertheless, other clients began to subscribe to the parity pricing. British Gas agreed in December 1980 to an "interim accord" with a nine-month delivery schedule in 1981.

The price would meet the equivalence principle by steps, beginning with a $4.60/MMBtu price and rising to $4.80 in June 1981. The interim accord projected a continuing negotiation for a medium-term (five-year) agreement. At this time, the parity price of oil to gas ranged from $5.70 for Arabian Light to $6.60 for Saharan Light ($37/barrel).[149] For the United Kingdom, a producer from its North Sea fields, to purchase gas at the higher rates was also obviously self-serving.

Belgium's Distrigaz, with no obvious ulterior motive, signed a significant accord with SONATRACH on 8 April 1981. This accord revised their 1975 contract which had called for the importation of 5 billion m³ annually. The new price was calculated at about $4.80/MMBtu and was based not on Algerian crude but on a "basket" of crudes (quoted c.i.f.) that Belgium imported.[150] While it could be argued that linkage to a basket was not the same as to higher-priced Algerian crude, the principle of parity was certainly followed. Algiers regarded this contract as a victory in the continuing "battle of gas," especially since it pressured GDF to come to a similar settlement. But that would have to wait until the next French presidential election and the arrival of François Mitterrand in the Elysée Palace.

The Impossible Normalization and the Human Dimension

The nationalization of the French concessions in the Sahara marked the end of the immediate postcolonial period. With that crisis resolved, an opportunity, if an illusory one, arose for France and Algeria to engage in more normal relations. During the 1970s, however, too many historical intangibles prevented "normalization." On the one hand, Algeria's state-building, distinguished by its economic and social revolutions, was inevitably related to the dislocations caused by French colonialism. On the other hand, France quickly realized that Algeria's geopolitical significance still demanded special attention, and concurred in a *relancement* of relations. Even Giscard was resigned to this reality before the end of the decade, after he rejected in 1975–76 the genuine Algerian offer of favorable, if not privileged, relations.

Normalization was also impossible because of the human dimension. As discussed above, emigrant labor emerged as a recurrent major issue during the decade. Concurrently, the agitation of *pieds-noirs* and *harkis* and the continuing presence of thousands of *coopérants* in Algeria underscored the unique social variables that distinguished the bilateral relationship.

The *Pieds-Noirs*

During the 1960s the French economy's extraordinary expansion expedited the government's employment placement efforts on behalf of the displaced *pieds-noirs*.[151] This permitted them to congregate in the Midi and retain a sense of social cohesion, although many opted to leave France.[152] Since many arrived without possessions, their need for consumer goods helped stimulate the economy.[153] Their industrious nature was also evident, especially in the development of viticulture on Corsica.[154]

Their apparent economic integration masked, however, a social insecurity. The *pieds-noirs* were different from the metropolitan French and they knew it. Their "expatriation" and the cold, reserved "welcome" by the French remained a bitter memory.[155] Many suffered from psychopathological health problems derived from melancholy and depression.[156] The *pieds-noirs* were particularly concerned about perpetuating their identity. This was evidenced by an emerging postcolonial *pied-noir* literature that was nostalgic and often critical of the community's abrupt abandonment during decolonization.[157] In addition, numerous organization were established to promote a cultural consciousness while lobbying the government for indemnification.

The *pieds-noirs* actively sought reparations for their losses in Algeria.[158] On 15 July 1970 an indemnification law was enacted which was considered merely a "contribution."[159] Only 27 percent of the 180,000 dossiers were settled by 1976.[160] For *pied-noir* support in the 1974 election, Giscard raised indemnity payments in 1975 and allowed the consideration of properties valued at one million francs. The new indemnity law of 2 January 1978 increased payments and added interest.[161] Repatriate organizations still regarded the legislation as inadequate. The indemnities would take too long to pay (up to fifteen years) and inflation was not accurately taken into account. *Pied-noir* disappointment in Giscard led Jacques Roseau, the spokesman and cofounder of the Rassemblement et Coordination Unitaire des Rapatriés et Spoliés d'Outre-mer (RECOURS) to declare his intention to vote against Giscard in 1981.[162]

The *Harkis*

The condition of the *harkis* remained disgraceful.[163] They faced many of the same problems and prejudices that confronted the emigrant worker community: unemployment, lack of proper housing, no training, and, particularly distressing, the nonrecognition of their community. Many

Frenchmen considered *harkis* foreigners rather than ultraloyal citizens of France who had risked everything, lost, and ended up exiled in the country they had believed in and defended. An indication of the *harkis'* own psychoexistential problem could be discerned in their hybrid names: Pascal-Said, Nelly-Aisha, Johnny-Mohammed, Christine-Sada.[164] As Mohammed Laradji, the president of the Confédération des Français Musulmans Rapatriés d'Algérie, once remarked: "It is difficult to be French when one is named Mohammed."[165]

Bachaga Said Boualam (d. 1982) was the most celebrated leader of the *harkis*. The Bachaga believed in France, as his forebears had, but that faith was tested sorely during his difficult exile. He hoped for the construction of mosques for French Muslims, the reunification of families, a resolution of pension distribution for the veterans, and indemnity settlements (so difficult to assess because of a lack of records).[166]

The *harkis* began to express their pent-up exasperation through sensational and often spontaneous acts bordering on terrorism. On 19 March 1971, the ninth anniversary of the conclusion of the Evian Accords, a French Muslim set himself on fire on Paris's boulevard Raspail. In October 1974 *harkis* staged a hunger strike in the fashionable Madeleine church. By the end of the month, Prime Minister Jacques Chirac announced these measures: (1) a new housing proposal, (2) a consideration of indemnification, (3) new dispositions toward "reintegration," and (4) free circulation for *harki* children between France and Algeria. *Le Monde* pointed out that these measures did not include job training.[167] The *harkis* remained restive.

In June 1975 four young French Muslims briefly took hostage the director of the Saint-Maurice-l'Ardoise camp to publicize the condition and lack of integration of the *harki* community.[168] When a son of a *harki* was not allowed to return to France after a visit to Algeria because of a legal formality, *harkis* seized four hapless emigrant workers. An official of the Amicale des Algériens was also kidnapped that summer. Though these situations were peacefully resolved, they signaled the *harkis'* desperate discontent.

As a consequence of the "hot summer" of 1975, the French government reexamined the *harki* situation. It announced in August new measures: (1) the destruction of the camps by the end of 1976, (2) a policy of professional training, (3) aid to youth in finding work, (4) reinstallation in better housing, and (5) indemnities for those who lived in the camps.[169] Though these measures were well-intentioned, the critically needed programs to provide training and job-search assistance were impractical in a stagflated and sluggish French economy. Nevertheless, the French government continued its gestures on behalf of the *harkis*. Giscard, in particular, demonstrated greater sympathy and sensitivity toward the French Muslims than he did the *pieds-noirs*. A national committee to resolve the problems of the French Muslims was established in December 1977, and in February 1978 the president visited a *harki* camp. Despite these highly publicized affirmations of support, the *harkis* sadly remained segregated and discriminated against in French society.

The *Coopérants*

Coopérants served in Algeria for many reasons: guilt over the Algerian War, solidarity with a revolutionary society (these *coopérants* were called *pieds-rouges*), substitution for military service, financial rewards, altruism, and opportunity to apply one's education. They faced a variety of problems including inadequate housing, difficulties with Algerian counterparts and bureaucrats, and work environments. There was little or no social life after work. There were also intra-*coopérant* rifts. The VSNA resented the enormous disparity in salaries between themselves and the civilian *coopérants*. Algeria was not a favorite choice among professional civilian *coopérants* and military VSNA. Nevertheless, *coopérants* were popular with their Algerian students/trainees.[170]

The *coopérants* were not supposed to take political positions. Some *pieds-rouges* vociferously protested the deposal of Ben Bella and most of them left Algeria disillusioned with the "reactionary" course of events. Many *coopérants* regarded themselves as pawns in a neocolonial plan that "profited" from their participation.[171] Most felt, however, that their presence was provisional and that their purpose was to create the conditions and cadres to replace themselves.[172] In the 1970s, they protested the political and social conditions of emigrant workers in France and the plans to repatriate them. They also condemned the murder at the Amicale in Paris as an "odious attack" and contrasted how Algerians had accepted them in their country.[173] Generally, they kept their political opinions private.

Though their presence perpetuated a French presence and challenged the objectives of Algeria's Cultural Revolution, their general effectiveness in preparing national cadres led to a chronic demand for more *coopérants*. Algerian governments often complained that the country preference offered by France to *coopérants* discriminated against Algeria. There were not enough qualified *coopérants* to satisfy demand. Mohamed Sahnoun told how 2,210 *coopérants* were requested in 1979; the French government recruited 1,556, but only 829 took up posts in Algeria.[174]

The Shifting Essentialist-Existentialist Dispositions

The essentialist-existentialist dispositions shifted during the 1970s. France still saw itself exercising its independent role in regional and world affairs, through Pompidou's more modest Mediterranean Policy and Giscard's tempered *mondialisme*.

While the grandeur of a policy *à tous azimuts* was restrained by realism and a stagflated economy, Algeria's multilateral and bilateral strategic value continued to be appreciated (even if reluctantly by Giscard) as a means to extend French influence to the Third World as well as to secure energy resources, with the emphasis now on natural gas rather than oil. The deontological and paternalistic emphasis of cooperation also changed. France no longer perceived cooperation as a high moral imperative to provide help and to collaborate in Algeria's definition of its postcolonial identity, but as a practical policy to serve French interests and Algerian wishes, i.e., *rayonnement* and Algerianization of national cadres through education. By the end of the decade, there were still more than five thousand *coopérants* in Algeria.

Concurrently, Algeria aimed to secure the country's independent identity by projecting a national personality that was revolutionary, socialist, secular, yet Islamic. The simultaneous pursuit of the Industrial, Agrarian, and Cultural Revolutions illustrated the continued existential praxis that culminated in the National Charter of 1976. But the late Boumedienne's dream of an independent, decolonized socialist state had dissipated. Criticisms of "intersectoral imbalances" suggested future reorientations in state-planning. In addition, the Cultural Revolution became immersed in controversies over bilingualism and Arabization.

An emerging post-Revolution generation being Arabized—often by foreign instructors influenced by political Islam—began to discover themselves in a dilemma. As Bruno Etienne and Jean Léca put it: "The student who is only an Arabist has perhaps recovered his soul[,] but he has the feeling of having lost his chance of social advancement."[175] This manifested itself in late 1979 and early 1980 with rioting between arabophone and francophone students.[176] The Arabized students protested the employment advantages of their francophone peers. President Benjedid responded by opening new opportunities in the legal establishment for Arabized students and by accelerating Arabization. This in fact widened ethnic divisions by provoking the Kabyles, who concurrently were commemorating and celebrating their unique Berber language and culture.[177] The Kabyles resented the injudicious imposition of Arabization as an existential affront to their own Berber identity. The "Tizi-Ouzou spring" in 1980 saw the most protracted violence since 1963. Benjedid offered cultural concessions to the Kabyles, especially in the media.

These events underscored that Algeria's existential quest remained incomplete. In carefully worded articles, a new cultural discourse began to appear. *El-Moudjahid*'s 28 March 1981 edition included a supplement titled "Réflexions sur la personnalité nationale." Though a pseudonym was used, the actual author was Taleb Ibrahimi. He called for a more realistic assessment of Algerian social realities and the recognition of its pluralistic character.[178] These ideas were reinforced in a series of articles on culture by Wadi Bouzar that appeared in *Révolution africaine* (May–June 1981). Bouzar appealed for more freedom in cultural exchange. He argued that a culture is a social "sum of syntheses" in constant transition and transformation."[179] There was a need for cultural consensus.

Indeed, Algeria's new leaders were more concerned with pragmatism than revolutionary mobilization. Their realism contrasted with the idealism of France's new government driven by its socialist ideology, as well as its president's perception of French essentialism which would restore the privileged bilateral relationship.

6

Redressing the Relationship, 1981–1988

It is a new page that the Algerian people inaugurate with the French
people, in all sincerity, in all honesty, far from rancors and far from
complexes.
Chadli Benjedid, November 1983

We recognize it well, this past, your past, our past, its good and bad
moments, its passions and its torments. But there is no reason to reject
this past that we have lived.
François Mitterrand, November 1983

The election of François Mitterrand ushered in a new period in the French-
Algerian relationship that would be highlighted initially by a new formulation of cooperation called codevelopment. Conjured memories of the
War of Independence, however, undercut Mitterrand's ambitions to "redress" the relationship and, with it, his own troubled personal history
with Algeria. The end of this period of *redressement* found Algeria distressed by deteriorating economic fortunes. Worse—though indiscernible
or perhaps unimaginable to most specialists—Algeria's vaunted political
stability tottered as the FLN lost its credibility, especially among the
nation's estranged and restive youth, in October 1988.

President Mitterrand and Algeria

François Mitterrand's victory in the 1981 presidential election surprised
Algiers. In his congratulatory message Benjedid said, "The strengthening
of trust and understanding between Algeria and France will contribute to
the establishment of a climate of peace and security for all peoples of the
region."[1] Benjedid felt the relationship was already at a good level and
wanted it reaffirmed or attached, if possible, to multilateral (e.g., Western
Sahara) as well as bilateral concerns.

From an Algerian perspective, Giscard had been quite "complex."
Here was a man who showed an anti-Algerian bias, provided arms to

Morocco, and bought little petroleum, but who surprisingly wanted to resume a *relancement* that would feature a visit by Benjedid to France. Though Giscard pressed Benjedid to accept his invitation, the Algerian president politely and wisely waited to respond until after the election.[2] Ironically, before he left office in 1981, Giscard had quietly achieved the relationship's *relancement* (perhaps too quietly to benefit the French president politically). His *concertation* with Algeria would eventually be conceived as "codevelopment" under President Mitterrand. Compared with Giscard and Boumedienne, Mitterrand and Benjedid were ideologically and personally more compatible. Mitterrand was also determined to do something for Algeria for political and personal reasons.

During the presidential election, Proposal 109 of the Socialist Party's (PS) "110 Proposals" called for "privileged links with the nonaligned countries of the Mediterranean zone and of the African continent, especially Algeria."[3] The PS also proposed (no. 105) "support for the right of self-determination . . . of Western Sahara."[4] Proposals 79–81 demanded the protection of emigrant workers from forced expulsion and the guarantee of their rights, including voting privileges in municipal elections. Once in power, Mitterrand, like Giscard, demonstrated his goodwill with initiatives in favor of emigrant labor, beginning with "regularization" of the status of thousands of workers. Algerian officials became convinced that they were heading toward a renewal of a privileged relationship.

Algiers welcomed Mitterrand's ministerial choices.[5] Claude Cheysson, the new foreign minister, had a history of impressive empathy toward the Third World. He had led in the construction of the Lomé Convention giving developing nations preferential commercial relations with the EEC and had earlier participated in the initiation of cooperation with Algeria as director of the Organisme Saharien and played an important role in negotiating the Algiers Accords of 1965. The young and charismatic Jean-Pierre Cot headed the Ministry of Cooperation and intended to pursue different directions, eventually termed codevelopment, which shifted aid from programs that reinforced dependency toward those specifically tailored to development needs. Michel Jobert, though ideologically opposed to Mitterrand, possessed admirable acumen and agreed to take the portfolio of external trade. Pierre Mauroy (prime minister), Michel Rocard (minister of planning), Lionel Jospin (secretary-general of the PS), and Jean-Pierre Chevènement (minister of equipment and research) were also respected by the Algerian government for their *tiersmondisme* or Third World sensibilities.

Mitterrand's Algerian Past

Unlike Giscard and Pompidou, Mitterrand was profoundly identified with Algeria. Among the presidents of the Fifth Republic, only Charles de Gaulle had a deeper historical and personal relationship with Africa, and particularly Algeria, than François Mitterrand. In spite of their ideological differences, the two men pursued remarkably similar policies which aimed at establishing innovative and privileged relations with Africa and especially Algeria.

While serving as minister of Overseas France in the Georges Bidault administration (1949–50), Mitterrand toured Africa and advocated greater metropolitan assistance. Sensitive to incipient African nationalism, Mitterrand claimed that he had thought of a Franco-African federation before de Gaulle implemented his Community policy in 1958–59.[6] Observing Africa's exploitation by the *métropole,* he yet perceived that France was admired by its colonies.[7] His visits to North Africa convinced him that Algeria particularly needed decisive reforms, but this meant confronting the powerful *pieds-noirs.*

On coming to power in June 1954, Mendès-France appointed Mitterrand minister of the interior. It was Mitterrand who warned Mendès-France of the possibility of "unhealthy" conditions in Algeria.[8] During a visit there in October 1954, Mitterrand attempted to balance reform and reinforcement by stating that there was a need to increase the native participation in "the management of public affairs," though this would require "taking into account the experience of the Algerian administration."[9] Like de Gaulle, Mitterrand understood that the failure to implement decisively the Statute of 1947 would lead to serious problems. Before flying back to Paris he told journalists: "I have found the three French departments of Algeria in a state of calm and prosperity. I am leaving filled with optimism." To Mendès-France he confided: "The climate is getting worse over there. It is necessary to act very quickly."[10]

Mendès-France recalled that Mitterrand "alerted me several times with much lucidity. He judged that the situation over there was dangerous."[11] Four days after war broke out, on 5 November, Mitterrand reputedly declared, "The only possible negotiation is war." He then delivered one of the most important speeches of his political career. Before the National Assembly he declaimed, "Algeria is France," but this was interpreted in many ways. He was sensitive to the fragility of Mendès-France's coalition. Denis MacShane believed that Mitterrand's war "rhetoric was aimed at reassuring the Algerian deputies whose votes were so vital."[12] Almost twenty years later in an interview with Franz-Olivier Giesbert, Mendès-France interpreted Mitterrand's speech as a message that the French government, and nothing or no one else, would decide matters in Algeria.[13] Mitterrand's position was popularly acclaimed in November 1954. His oratory would not be forgotten, however, in postcolonial Algeria.

Mitterrand did not abandon plans for reform. He angered the colonial "ultras" by proposing and initiating substantial social and economic reforms (the Mitterrand Plan). Later, as minister of justice in Guy Mollet's administration, he was aware of the infamous torture and tried to curb it. According to Gaston Defferre, Mitterrand's actions prevented the executions of several Algerian nationalists.[14] In October 1956 he saw as "the only outlet possible" a policy that would lead to "a veritable Franco-Algerian community."[15] Mitterrand opposed de Gaulle's deliberate and, from the left's perspective, "dictatorial" policies toward Algeria. He was elected to the Senate in April 1959, but in October was "duped" in the bizarre Pesquet affair which discredited and tainted his political image.[16]

After the War, Mitterrand continued his opposition to de Gaulle. Indeed, he surprised observers by his remarkable showing in the 1965 presidential election. In 1971 he resuscitated the Socialist Party and collaborated a year later with the French Communist Party to produce the Common Program. Though he won the first round of the presidential election of 1974, Gaullists swung their votes to elect Giscard. After the right's success in the 1978 elections, Mitterrand's political future seemed to be in jeopardy. Like de Gaulle, Mitterrand experienced an "exile."

By 1981 the ineffectiveness of Premier Raymond Barre's economic program revived political opportunities for the left. Calling for limited nationalizations, job creation, a thirty-five-hour week, and other social programs, Mitterrand struck a responsive public chord. With unemployment at 1.7 million, compounded by double digit inflation, Mitterrand appeared as an attractive political alternative. Furthermore, Giscard's political hauteur alienated traditional supporters.[17] On 10 May, François Mitterrand, a "politician" of the Fourth Republic (and an eleven-time minister) became the fourth president of the Fifth Republic.

Mitterrand's Gaullism

Though of the left, Mitterrand remained faithful to Gaullist foreign policy tenets and de Gaulle's brand of French essentialism. He favored international interdependence and integration, but believed, too, in France's grandeur and independence. His assertion of these latter essentialist principles would be, however, more subtle.[18]

Like de Gaulle, Mitterrand perceived himself as an incarnation of France: "I do not need an 'idea' of France. I live France. . . . There is no need for me to seek the soul of France—it lives in me."[19] William Styron wrote: "This comes as close to de Gaulle as anyone concerning the incorporation of France in one's own person."[20] Mitterrand confessed concerning de Gaulle: "His acts created him, and his conviction that he *was* France, that he was the manifest expression of her truth, that he incarnated a moment in some eternal destiny, moved me more than it annoyed me. I have never found this conviction laughable or ridiculous."[21] While claiming he was never a Gaullist, Mitterrand insisted that he "always refused to be an anti-Gaullist."[22] According to Thierry Desjardins: "Mitterrand is a fierce nationalist who dreams again of a strong and respected France, which would have a mission." Desjardins considered Mitterrand's desire for a "strong government" with a "'style'" to be Gaullist.[23] Dominique Moïsi concluded: "In his style, in his historical and literary approach to politics, in his duration in power, Mitterrand has proven to be the most Gaullist of de Gaulle's successors."[24]

F. Roy Willis correctly pointed out that "the election had not been a plebiscite on the Gaullist legacy in foreign policy."[25] Alex Rondos observed: "Mitterrand, like de Gaulle, perceives an autonomous strategic role for France. . . . The former African colonies play a key role in giving France its autonomous clout among its Western allies."[26] Differences with the right arose over foreign policy practice rather than discourse and objectives. For example, Giscard's interventionism in Africa was opposed ideologically by the Common Program, which asserted strict noninterference while implementing new forms of cooperation.[27] A month before the presidential election, the Socialist Party published an "Africa plan" which attacked Giscard's government for contributing to the conditions eventually forcing intervention. The Socialists repudiated the failing policy rather than the principle of intervention.[28] Willis perceived: "In relations with the Third World, Mitterrand, too, seemed to be modifying rather than completely reworking the principles of Gaullist policy."[29] Mitterrand supported the North-South dialogue, especially concerning debts, prices of raw materials, and reform of the international monetary system. He argued that "the best way to aid the Third World is to modify our model of development so that our abundance is founded no longer on their misery."[30] This new cooperation would be called "codevelopment."[31] Mitterrand earmarked Algeria for particular attention.

After the War, Mitterrand attempted to reconcile with Algeria. Yet in March 1972 *El-Moudjahid* remembered him as the man who conducted "all-out war" and considered him a "social zionist" because of his support of Israel.[32] Four years later, twenty years after his last visit to Algeria, Mitterrand arrived in Algiers. Interested in initiating "personal relations" with Algerian leaders, Mitterrand in his position as secretary-general of the Socialist Party responded to the deterioration of Giscard's *relancement* by calling for a *redressement* of the relationship.[33] The FLN-PS communiqué rehearsed important issues that influenced Mitterrand's future presidency such as commercial balance, security for emigrant workers, "a new economic world order," and the Mediterranean as a "lake of peace." The communiqué also attacked Morocco's "aggression . . . against the Sahrawi people."[34]

Algeria had a special meaning for Mitterrand; it had scarred his political career and his personal sensibilities.[35] His election as president in 1981 promised a redressing of policy and of personal responsibility for past actions.

Codevelopment Initiated

Mitterrand's government quickly, even urgently, engaged Algiers in its effort to restore an exemplary bilateral relationship. A visit by Mitterrand to Algeria began to be prepared.[36] Foreign Minister Claude Cheysson arrived there in August and spoke of a *"coup de passion"* occurring in the relationship. Addressing the contentious LNG price negotiations, he stated: "We must go beyond the technicians' arguments in order to find solutions which respect Algerian policy and satisfy France."[37] The idea of a codevelopment through more accommodating cooperation became thematic in discussions. Michel Rocard hosted his counterpart, Abdelhamid Brahimi, and surveyed sectors for cooperation in October.[38] The traditional Algerian preference for a total perspective on cooperation rather than a sector-by-sector approach apparently was satisfied. Brahimi remarked that he found "a new attitude."[39] When the two presidents met during the North-South meeting at Cancún, Mexico, in October 1981, *El-Moudjahid* regarded French pro-South positions as "a message of hope."[40]

There were other signals of France's intention to recast a privileged relationship. Prime Minister Pierre Mauroy and Interior Minister Gaston Defferre restored automatic renewals of certificates of residence for emigrant labor, though ironically this ended the meticulous program prescribed by the September 1980 agreement. The French government recognized the emigrant workers' right to organize, stopped arbitrary expulsions of young Algerians, and promised to provide security, to address the administration of SONACOTRA (the emigrant worker housing authority), and to establish a policy on "clandestine" emigrant labor.[41] The repatriation of archives remained a thorny issue. While this had obvious "existential" significance for Algeria, it was also a delicate question for France. Before the summit, documents pertaining to the Ottoman period and technical aspects of French colonization were dispatched to Algiers.[42]

Summit in Algiers

Before Mitterrand's visit Benjedid had told *Paris-Match:* "I believe that both parties have arrived at a simple conclusion: they are condemned to cooperate."[43] Mitterrand wanted, however, to go beyond traditional cooperation and to construct a model North-South relationship. To Mitterrand, his visit was "an essential political act."[44]

The theme of Mitterrand's visit (30 November–1 December) was "a new given: trust."[45] Before the Algerian Popular Assembly the French president declared: "The past is the past. Let's look now, resolutely, toward the future." He asserted: "All demand that an exemplary cooperation finally establish itself between our countries." He reaffirmed France's commitment to Third World development and underscored with regard to Western Sahara that "each people has the right to self-determination."[46] The summit's communiqué stated that both countries "intend to open the way to original and exemplary forms of international economic cooperation."[47]

Mitterrand received, like Giscard six years earlier, a very warm welcome from the Algerian leadership and people.[48] Unlike Giscard, Mitterrand aimed not only to gain Algiers's political confidence but to sustain it by concrete achievement. He provided the requisite political will. Where Giscard had ignored the symbolism of a petroleum importation agreement, Mitterrand addressed the contentious LNG negotiation and accepted a higher price. In return, Algeria would offer French companies privileged consideration in awarding development contracts in order to offset anticipated large commercial imbalances. In many respects, the projected accord reformulated the "generous" cooperation surrounding the Algiers Accords of 1965. Both Mitterrand and Benjedid, exhibiting a political bonhomie, entrusted the details of the LNG agreement to their foreign ministers. The agreement signaled the reemergence of political rather than economic and technocratic determinants in French policymaking.

Gas Accord

Even before the summit, the election of Mitterrand had already changed the tone of the negotiations. According to *Le Monde*, "the dossier passed from the hands of technicians to those of 'politicians'."[49] On 26 August, Mitterrand tapped Jean-Marcel Jeanneney, the first ambassador to Algeria, as his personal representative to study the gas problem. In talks with Hadj Yala, the Algerian minister of finance, Jeanneney addressed the linking of gas deliveries and, implicitly, price to other "common interests in the industrial domain."[50] Jeanneney and Yala significantly prepared the groundwork for the "political accord" of Mitterrand and Benjedid. During his visit to the International Fair of Algiers in September, Michel Jobert, the minister of external commerce, remarked that "the problem . . . is to find a price permitting at the same time the development of Algeria and of France."[51] But in spite of these efforts, Algeria contended that GDF's "inamicable attitude" prevented a resolution of the problem.[52]

Several days after Mitterrand took the matter into his own hands, *Le Monde* linked the indexing problem to foreign trade by suggesting that a higher gas price could be tied to French industrial imports. The French would also help at the LNG 2 facility at Arzew.[53] Claude Cheysson declared before the National Assembly that the price of Algerian LNG would not be linked to crude: "I have never envisaged any parity between natural gas and oil."[54] With talks conducted on a state-to-state basis, as Algeria preferred, GDF was kept out of the direct negotiation at this time (as the oil companies had been). On 22 December the respective foreign ministers, Cheysson and Benyahia, agreed on the "guiding principles" of an accord that would be based on an elevated price tied to financial cooperation.[55] Pierre Delaporte, director-general of GDF, and Mohamed Yousfi, SONATRACH's vice president for marketing, began to work on the technicalities, including pricing and retroactivity, while diplomats considered the cooperation dimension.

On 22 January the minister of planning, Michel Rocard, announced that a base price had been agreed by GDF and SONATRACH. Then on 26 January negotiations were interrupted as the Algerian delegation adjourned to Algiers for further instructions. The two questions needing resolution at this time were retroactivity and the type of development subsidy the French government planned.[56] Several possibilities had been suggested: (1) the Giraud tradeoff of gas for energy technology, (2) the exchange of gas for a development fund like the 1965 Accords' OCI (an option especially considered by the "sages" Jeanneney and Yala in their talks), and (3) simply a financial subsidy. Algeria, however, was more eager to publicize an over-$5.00/MMBtu agreed price because of ongoing negotiations with Italy, the receiving country of the Trans-Mediterranean gas pipeline, calling for the export of 12 billion m³. Algeria was very pleased that British Gas agreed to pay $6.10/MMBtu for a spot purchase of Algerian gas during this time, and contrasted it with "the 'neocolonial whims' of certain potential partners of Algeria."[57]

For its part, GDF emphasized that it was not prepared to pay more, since it wanted its product to be competitive with other domestic fuels in France. Like SONATRACH, the French national enterprise was in negotiations with other potential partners. It concurrently signed a twenty-five-year contract with the Soviet Union calling for the importation of 8 billion m³ annually at $4.60/MMBtu c.i.f. at the Czech border. Transport to France was expected to add only about $0.30 to the cost, compared with $0.70 or even $1.00 over an Algerian f.o.b. price.[58] By the Algerian formula, in February 1982 the gas price equivalent of crude oil would have been $6.61/MMBtu. It had reached $7.14/MMBtu. The Algerians faced, however, a softening oil market and strong competition from France's European partners and the Soviet Union. GDF was paying $3.70/MMBtu at the time, though it had paid more than $4.00 recently. In addition, Algerian efforts to establish an Organization of Gas Exporting Countries (OGEC) had failed, in part because of the USSR's aggressive entry into the market.[59] Nevertheless, after the decisive intervention of Foreign Ministers Cheysson and Benyahia, an accord was concluded on 3 February.

GDF agreed to a $5.11/MMBtu f.o.b. price, retroactive to January 1980, for the importation of 9.1 billion m³ of natural gas annually. The price would be based on a basket of eight crudes used in the Distrigaz contract, which would be reviewed quarterly. The French government would subsidize 13.5 percent of the price, justifying its involvement by pointing to anticipated contracts with Algeria. Thus Algeria would receive two payments: one from GDF and the other from the French government.[60] According to Jonathan Stern: "It cannot be claimed that France totally capitulated to Algerian demands; it has to be remembered that the final price was nearly $1 per [MMBtu] lower than the original demand."[61] An editorial in *Algérie informations* projected that "Algeria will be able to turn anew to French enterprises."[62] In a poll taken for GDF, 63 percent of those surveyed approved the gas accord.[63]

Cheysson and Benyahia's joint communiqué declared that the gas accord was signed in order "to promote policies favorable to the development of both countries and to give them their wish for security." It also

Table 6.1. French Trade with Algeria, 1980–1984 (in millions of FF)

	1980	1981	1982	1983	1984
French exports	11,077.6	12,815.4	13,990.7	18,565.8	23,583.7
French imports	7,431.4	12,993.7	25,815.4	23,372.8	24,900.6
Balance	3,646.2	-178.3	-11,824.7	-4,807.0	-1,316.9

Source: EIU, *QERs*.

proclaimed that the accord was made in the spirit of North-South relations.[64] Cheysson linked it to total cooperation with Algeria: "Many projects are being examined and we have decided to have a systematic cooperation, organized to cover all domains."[65] On 4 February on French radio, Cheysson said: "The Soviet contract is purely commercial. The [French] contract with Algeria is a commercial contract with a political connotation." Olivier Stirn wrote: "This contract justifies itself by political considerations."[66] As with the Algiers Accords of 1965, France aimed to project itself as a nation with particular Third World sensitivities while securing a privileged relationship with Algeria.

This ended the controversy of "neocolonialism." Cheysson termed the new direction "codevelopment." As Maurice Delarue commented: "There is no independence but in the organization of a diversification of dependences. The French-Algerian accord is destined to assure 'a reciprocal security'."[67] According to *El-Moudjahid,* the accord provided for "mutual advantages and for commercial equilibrium." The French market was secured and the principle of parity, while not fully recognized, was still respectfully considered and satisfactorily fulfilled. Most important, Algeria would receive higher revenues that would ensure development. The "battle of gas" was over.[68]

Michel Jobert reflected during this time that "if there is no formal link, there has always been an intellectual and a kind of political link between gas agreements and the growth of trade between the two countries."[69] The February LNG accord did have multiple effects upon the relationship, especially commercially. It was the catalyst of the *redressement* and its greatest symbol. The economic price seemed high but the monies spent were returned to France through contracts and restored a privileged French economic position in Algeria's development plans. Algeria's wish to reach a commercial advantage was soon realized. The political price underscored France's commitment to the Third World and especially its former territories overseas, while Algeria could justify its parity pricing principle. Furthermore, the LNG accord promoted more synergetic bilateral intiatives.

Other Codevelopment Accords

After reviewing sectoral opportunities for codevelopment (agriculture, hydraulics, industry, nuclear energy, and transportation, including the Algiers metro), Ministers of Planning Rocard and Brahimi initialed an accord on 14 June for the construction of 60,000 housing units. This agreement by itself was worth FF 10 billion.[70]

On 21 June, Cheysson and the new Algerian foreign minister, Ahmed Taleb Ibrahimi (succeeding Benyahia, who perished in an air crash trying to mediate the Iran-Iraq War, a terrible loss to Algeria), signed a convention of economic cooperation defining guiding principles, detailing specific types of sector participation, and establishing a joint commission to oversee cooperation. Taleb Ibrahimi affirmed: "We have found . . . an attentive interlocutor conscious of the stake that constitutes the restructuring of North-South relations. . . . Beyond the beneficial impact that this accord will have on our exchanges, it will permit our two countries to claim the [exemplary relationship] wished by both chiefs of state."[71] Cheysson declared: "We wish to inscribe our relations in a different philosophy. We have undertaken to weave our ties."[72] A Paris-Algiers-Paris circuit by ministers underscored French intentions.

Michel Jobert, the minister of external commerce, arrived in Algiers in September to attend the International Fair and to organize the first meeting of the joint commission that would convene in Paris. The first session met on 11–12 October with Jobert and Brahimi presiding. It aimed to "promote the original and exemplary forms of cooperation in line with the [summit communiqué]."[73] Surveying all major sectors, the commission reflected the scale of codevelopment. When Charles Fiterman, the minister of transportation, arrived in Algeria in November, he reaffirmed that "bilateral cooperation" was not merely a matter of "commercial relations but aims at codevelopment, to obtain for each the means to better assure its own development." This was underscored by a transportation convention that called for French involvement in the Algiers metro project, railway construction, the improvement of the Constantine airport, and the construction of a civil aviation school at the airport. The convention outlined contracts reaching almost FF 11 billion.[74] Edith Cresson, the minister of agriculture, concluded the last significant agreement in January 1983. This accord featured cooperation in agro-industry, forestry, and technology transfer.

There were other illustrations indicating the breadth of the redressed relationship. For the first time since independence, an Algerian parliamentary delegation officially visited Paris in November 1982.[75] Mitterrand proposed a "French school of development" to promote academic and scientific cooperation. French and Algerian specialists organized joint groups ranging from biotechnology to solar energy to explore "research and training (*formation*)."[76] This exemplified a new cooperation based on the training of Algerian cadres rather than the continuing substitution of French experts.[77]

Pestering and Festering Bilateral Problems

Despite these impressive achievements of political will, Mitterrand's "*vastes entreprises*" faced serious problems. The weakness of the franc and its subsequent devaluations jeopardized financial commitments. French private enterprises were also reluctant to transfer technology. Chronic bilateral problems concerning emigrant labor, the archives, and the transfer of colonial assets from Algeria to France qualified the "confident" relationship. In April 1982 *France-Soir* published a provocative report claiming that possibly one thousand Europeans and *pieds-noirs*, thought missing (*disparus*), were actually in detention outside Algiers.[78] Algerian authorities retorted that this was "ridiculous" and "madness."[79] The publicizing of Ahmed Ben Bella's political revival in the French media especially irritated the Algerian government. This contributed toward Mitterrand's stopover in May 1982 during his African tour "to reestablish trust."[80] Finally, the exit of men like Cot and Rocard from the cabinet affected the *tiersmondisme* of the government.[81]

Emigrant Labor: The September 1980 Agreement Shelved

Once elected, Mitterrand and the Socialists symbolically addressed illegal workers' fear of expulsion by expediting the "regularization" of their papers. This action benefited 14,600 Algerians.[82] On the other hand, Mitterrand's government became acutely vigilant of illegal entry and "clandestine immigration." Painstaking French practices impeded the visits of workers' relatives and led to a brief stopover in Paris by Benjedid in December 1982 to resolve the situation.[83] The expansion in 1983 of the Fonds d'Action Sociale's authority and the inauguration in 1984 of a National Council of Immigrant Populations illustrated, however, the French government's generally good intentions.

Ironically, Mitterrand's administration failed to appreciate fully how the September 1980 agreement represented a remarkable opportunity for codevelopment. From the Algerian perspective, the French abandoned a strict interpretation of the September agreement because of its cost.[84] In its effort to eliminate the threat of expulsion, France unwittingly undercut a dimension of cooperation that Algeria found unusually programmatic and pragmatic.[85] As Nicole Grimaud saw it, the "enforcement of the 1980 accord became less imperative."[86] The French government preferred to follow the spirit of the 1968 accord.[87] In 1984 the Socialists instituted a ten-year resident's card (*carte de résident*), but the emigrant had to demonstrate his financial ability to support himself and his family and profess his fidelity to the "public order." If he failed to follow these formalities, he could be deported. Max Silverman observed: "Discrimination was therefore built into the very fabric of the law."[88] The French also raised voluntary reinsertion payments from FF 90,000 to FF 130,000.[89] Of the thousands of emigrants who returned to Algeria annually, very few had training. Most were victims of unemployment.[90] For the first time since 1965, more Algerians left France in 1984 than arrived.

Western Sahara: Some Movement

The Socialist Party had close and sympathetic relations with Polisario. In August 1981 the Quai d'Orsay received a member of the Sahrawi organization for the first time. Cheysson also disclosed that France had influenced King Hassan's decision, announced during the Nairobi OAU summit, to permit a referendum in Western Sahara.[91] This encouraged Algiers while Rabat worried.

The Moroccan government acceded in principle to a "controlled referendum" in Western Sahara to mollify Mitterrand and the PS. In March 1982 the release of the imprisoned Moroccan socialist leader Abderrahim Bouabid underscored Rabat's desire to improve its bilateral relationship. Mitterrand perceived, however, the manifold strategic value of Morocco and exasperated the Polisario leadership by honoring military contracts. Furthermore, France abstained in UN votes on self-determination resolutions for Western Sahara. Mohamed Salem Ould Salek, a prominent member of Polisario and minister of the Sahrawi Arab Democratic Republic reacted: "We are very surprised to see a socialist goverment continuing a policy against which it campaigned."[92] Mohammed Ould Sidati, who represented the SADR at the opening of Polisario's Paris office on 29 March 1982, called the French attitude toward Western Sahara a year later "deceptive."[93] Mitterrand welcomed the 27 February 1983 summit between Benjedid and Hassan, though nothing substantial was accomplished toward resolving the conflict. Mitterrand had proposed a summit of western Mediterranean leaders while visiting Rabat, but an annoyed Algiers informed Cheysson of its reservations.

Chad: France Reluctantly Resumes Its Role

Chad also complicated the regional geopolitical situation. Paris promoted an "inter-African" force and solution for this chronically war-torn nation. Mitterrand tried to maintain a noninterventionist position, unlike de Gaulle and Giscard, in spite of internal and external political pressures. He also received Algeria's "discreet support" for this policy.[94] Libya's attempt to consolidate its control of the north forced a reluctant Paris to send logistical support in June 1983 and troops the following August. Mitterrand appeared to have slipped back to the policies of his predecessors. Sensitive to Algeria's wish of "noninterference," Mitterrand sent Prime Minister Pierre Mauroy to Algeria in September to explain Paris's military involvement.[95] Paris and Algiers had hoped to have the OAU resolve the Chadian conflict.

The Paris Summit and Its Consequences: From Promise to Disappointment

A month later and before Benjedid's state visit to France, Mauroy returned to Algiers to resolve lingering bilateral problems. He explained the selling of five Super-Etendard planes to Iraq. Algeria disapproved: its efforts to mediate a solution to the tragic and terrible Iran-Iraq conflict had cost the life of Foreign Minister Benyahia. On Western Sahara, Benjedid reiterated his position that France should play a more active role. The Algerian president wanted a French diplomatic "intervention" for peace. Mauroy's October visit also dealt with bilateral issues such as financial transfers by *pieds-noirs* who wished to return to France, the free circulation of *harkis,* clandestine emigrant worker traffic, French cemeteries in Algeria, and military service of the "second generation." All these issues were dealt with satisfactorily though not conclusively.[96]

Before his visit to France on 7–10 November 1983, President Benjedid told *Le Monde:* "We have turned the page to write a new one." With the sectoral agreements, codevelopment seemed well on its way. Benjedid clearly saw his visit as affirming a lasting cooperation, strong enough to transcend crises. He stated: "We now have a much clearer vision than in the past, for we have approached all difficulties in frank dialogue and have determined that they are not insurmountable." His visit did not symbolize "reconciliation"; Benjedid preferred "mutual trust." To *El-Moudjahid,* the visit was not a "turning point" but a "result" of the relationship.[97]

Benjedid in Paris

Benjedid's state visit was a remarkable event. While his presence did irritate some political figures and factions, Benjedid's conciliatory manner and statesmanship were impressive.[98] He laid a wreath on the tomb of the unknown soldier at the Arc de Triomphe, urged the *pieds-noirs* to visit, and assured the *harkis* that "Algeria is not vengeful." *Harki* children would be welcome, though Benjedid acknowledged that there could be security problems for adults.

Above all, Benjedid wanted to demonstrate that Algeria was prepared to "codevelop." During an interview with Antenne 2, he declared: "A new page in the domain of cooperation is open between the two countries." He later added: "It is a new page that the Algerian people inaugurate with the French people, in all sincerity, in all honesty." He associated "rancors" and "complexes" with the past.[99] As he told *Le Figaro,* Benjedid's objective, which he believed he shared with Mitterrand, was "to confer on Algerian-French cooperation an exemplary character."[100] Mitterrand's speech at the official dinner underscored the positive nature of the entire relationship. He reflected upon the difficult past ("We have endured") and encouraged the two countries "not only to dream for a harmonious future, but to build it."[101]

In a particularly poignant moment during his visit, Benjedid met with members of the emigrant community. He told them, "Your presence here . . . is provisional as much for you as for your sons."[102] The success of the summit showed that a serious and mature (*dépassionée*) relationship had supplanted those of the past. President Benjedid reiterated Mitterrand's wish that both countries should "leave the past to history; we are building the future."[103] The memory of this visit remained positive, though the following year demonstrated how future relations could be troubled by the past.

Codevelopment Declines

The Paris Summit illustrated that the bilateral relationship, while perhaps not at the same level of intensity as in 1981–82, was still vital and dynamic.[104] French contracts had been entered into (FF 15 billion in 1982 and 25 billion in 1983) which, as anticipated, balanced the commercial relationship. Algeria had taken a courageous risk predicated on a future of inelastic hydrocarbons prices. In the short term, this course was correct, though the parity formula was a double-edged sword. Jonathan Stern pointed out that indexing natural gas prices to crude oil "renders the exporter of both commodities doubly vulnerable to cyclical movements in the crude oil price."[105] On 1 January 1982 the c.i.f. price after GDF's regasification was $5.85/MMBtu, but two years later, with the change in the oil market, it dropped to $4.48.[106] This had a chilling effect upon the economic relationship which would be matched politically in 1984.

Recurrent problems such as the archives, the expulsion of emigrant workers without proper papers, the custody of children from broken mixed marriages, *harki* visitation rights, unfulfilled codevelopment, and *coopérant* complaints and restrictions all seemed resolvable as long as there was a political will. Each side appeared prepared to accommodate the other. Unfortunately, conflicting regional geopolitics again balked positive intentions and initiatives.

Chad Linked with Western Sahara

Paris's involvement in Chad escalated in early 1984 with the death of French military personnel. Mitterrand, perhaps fearing a Chadian quagmire like the one that had negatively affected Giscard, wanted to expedite French withdrawal for both political and ideological reasons. A linkage between Western Sahara and Chad soon appeared, as King Hassan and Colonel Muammar Qadhafi startled the region with their politically anomalous Treaty of Arab-African Union (or Treaty of Oujda) of 13 August 1984 by which Tripoli agreed to stop supporting Polisario. Rabat appeared as a natural intermediary between Paris and Tripoli concerning Libya's intervention in Chad.[107]

Subsequent events tested the French-Algerian relationship severely. Jean-Pierre Ferrier recounted how, in a clumsy effort to demonstrate friendship with Algeria, Foreign Minister Cheysson flew to Algiers to inform President Benjedid of the Moroccan-Libyan negotiation. Benjedid already knew about the negotiation and the treaty from press reports.[108] Aggravating France's differences with Algeria, President Mitterrand, in a remarkably insensitive and politically inept act, conspicuously "vacationed" in Ifrane, Morocco, while the treaty was ratified by the Moroccan people. This seemed to indicate French support for the treaty, tilting regional balance toward Morocco while alienating Algeria and further straining relations with the Polisario.

Claude Cheysson arrived in Libya the following month and it was announced that there would be a mutual withdrawal of troops. Mitterrand agreed to meet with Qadhafi in November. The agreement between Paris and Tripoli to withdraw all troops was fulfilled by France, but embarrassingly not by Libya. The Algerians' disappointment over Paris's new Chad policy (with its distressing ramifications for their Sahrawi revolutionary protégés) was the more deeply felt since Algeria was not even consulted as before. The glowing confidence of November 1983 dimmed. Mitterrand's "surprise visits" to Morocco heightened Algiers's concern over a Libyan-Moroccan axis. Algeria was "furious" and the word "neocolonialist" reappeared in the Algerian press.[109]

The relationship between the two presidents remained polite but was now distant. Algiers was disenchanted over the lack of codevelopment, especially in the transfer of technology. Cooperation, said *El-Moudjahid*, "demands constant attention."[110] Algiers also expressed concern over the French government's tightening controls on the emigrant community, especially with regard to familial dislocations and the rights of workers.[111] The emigrant community's insecurity was dramatically demonstrated by the highly publicized killing of an Algerian by French police.[112]

The deterioration of the bilateral relationship necessitated a brief visit by Mitterrand in October to "dissipate the malaise" and justify his recent actions in Maghribi affairs. Mitterrand tried to explain that nothing had been done against Algerian interests, but he underestimated Algerian sensibilities. Benjedid questioned Mitterrand's timing of his visit to Morocco to coincide with the ratification of the Treaty of Oujda. Both sides publicly affirmed that the summit was a "success." Taleb Ibrahimi reported: "The misunderstanding had been dissipated." Elysée spokesman Michel Vauzelle hoped the visit clarified the situation for "those who confused the *accessoire* with the essential."[113]

There was a price to pay for the "dissipation": a prominent French presence at the thirtieth anniversary of the outbreak of the War of Liberation. It was announced that Foreign Minister Cheysson would attend, but Mitterrand failed to gauge domestic reaction to having a high-ranking minister participate in the commemoration of a tumultuous and traumatic period in French history.

The 1 November 1984 Fiasco

In France, Mitterrand's decision outraged both political and public opinion. François Léotard called the decision a "malfeasance." Cheysson replied icily that the description was "juridically inexact." Edgar Faure, who had been premier during the War, stated that the "massacre" of French teachers should not be recognized. Jacques Chirac called Mitterrand's decision "a veritable transgression against memory." Jean-Marie Le Pen of the right-wing Front National (FN), whose increasingly popular Pouja-dist image was inherently anti-emigrant labor and by extension anti-Algerian, regarded Cheysson's presence in Algiers with "disgust and anger." The *pied-noir* group RECOURS considered the decision "a damaging blow delivered to the dignity and honor of France."[114] *Le Monde* questioned the timing of the announcement. It seemed an act of *marchandage* (bargaining), inappropriate at such a commemoration.[115]

The hostile French reaction to Mitterrand's decision astonished the Algerians. The uproar surprised even Benjedid, who responded in the course of an interview in *Le Point* (on the importance of France to Algeria economically: 30 percent of the country's imports) by recalling that he had merely questioned the timing of Mitterrand's visit to Morocco.[116]

Jean-Pierre Destrade, a spokesman for the PS, stated that "personal sensibilities" accounted for Mitterrand's actions. This might have been a most important reason. Mitterrand had intended the visit as another act symbolically purging France of its (and his own) painful past. He had genuinely hoped that positive relations would be "irreversible."[117] Instead of a catharsis, Mitterrand's decision conjured traumatic memories and illustrated how France was unable to "decolonize" mentalities. Though de Gaulle and Mitterrand tried to correlate grandeur and independence with new realities, these enduring French essentialist qualities remained also inextricably connected to the legacies of imperial glory and the infamous Algerian War.

The élan of codevelopment faded and the glowing confidence of the Paris Summit waned in memory and imagination. In December 1984 Algiers accused France of complicity in the fall of the pro-Polisario Mauritanian government.[118] The relationship began to slide toward another familiar yet impossible condition—"banality."

The Bilateral Relationship, 1984–1988: "Plus ça change"?

With the decline of codevelopment, the relationship seemed to enter one of those familiar estrangements reminiscent of the post-1975 period that usually lingered until the two countries reiterated or recast the unique strategic and historical bonds that linked them. But these post-codevelopment years would be profoundly different. For the first time since independence, Algeria faced severe and fearfully insoluble economic problems beginning with plummeting oil prices in 1986, which deepened the despair among the rising and increasingly restless younger generation.

The Resurgent, Retrogressive Past

The 1 November controversy lent weight to Benjamin Stora's persuasive thesis that the failure by both France and Algeria to recognize and report truthfully the history of colonialism and the War of Independence produced a festering, "gangrenous" condition chronically plaguing the post-colonial relationship.[119] Another controversy reinforcing Stora's thesis surrounded the ex-para Jean-Marie Le Pen who in 1972 had founded the nativist Front National. In April 1984 *Le Canard enchaîné* accused Le Pen of committing tortures while serving as an officer in Algeria.[120] Le Pen retorted that his honor had been called into question and sued for libel. *Libération* opened a second investigation in March 1985 after publishing interviews of Algerians claiming that Le Pen participated in atrocities. Le Pen's libel suit against *Le Canard* was dismissed in April 1985, but in a separate litigation *Libération* was chastised in January 1986 for the "partial" tone of its reporting.

Another grim and gruesome story surfaced with the commemoration of the Sétif-Guelma uprising of 1945 and conjured another historical nightmare. Algerian television broadcast a program in May 1985 featuring a dated accusation by a German legionnaire that claimed France used 150 Algerian prisoners as guinea pigs at the nuclear detonation at Reggane in 1960. Claude Cheysson, now serving as a European Union commissioner, termed the program "scandalous."

France drew more protests when in June, under the auspices of the Bonus Incentive Commodity Export Program (BICEP), the United States challenged the EC's (especially France's) subsidized agricultural sales by offering one million tons of wheat to Algeria. France's hostile reaction to this new American threat to its Maghribi markets provoked an article titled "Wheat and Nostalgia" in *El-Moudjahid* which criticized the ex-*métropole*'s commercial (read colonial) presumptions.[121]

Two weeks after Prime Minister Laurent Fabius's July visit to Algiers, which failed to revive confidence in the relationship, *Algérie Presse Service* (APS) condemned France for turning Algeria into a "concentration camp" during the War. France was also accused of "state terrorism." RECOURS retorted by threatening to publish a "white book" on Algerian atrocities. The Quai d'Orsay announced that it did not want "to carry on a polemic" with Algiers.[122]

The Front National's Popularity

Meanwhile, Le Pen was more than willing to continue polemics. Exploiting persistent economic problems such as deficits, inflation, and particularly unemployment, he blamed the emigrant presence. Le Pen couched his rhetoric in essentialist and racial terms: "We are today in the process of losing, through the blindness and cowardice of our leaders, our identity as a nation, as the French." According to one observer, the FN believed that "foreign blood . . . threatens to overwhelm the national essence."[123]

Le Pen specifically and speciously attacked emigrant workers as adversely affecting the balance of payments and their children (in part through the incorporation of Arabic in curricula) as slowing French students' development.[124] He assailed Georgina Dufoix, secretary of state for the family, the population, and emigrant workers, who stated on 13 November 1984 that "the housing of emigrant workers is my principal priority." Le Pen pointedly called into question her concern for French who also needed housing.[125] Because of the "Le Pen effect," the FN received 10.95 percent of the votes in the 1984 elections for the European Parliament.

The alarming popularity of the FN coincided with highly publicized assaults on emigrant workers and the emotional issue of estranged French wives whose Algerian husbands had taken children back to North Africa. Five mothers occupied the French embassy in Algiers in June 1985 and protested there until October, demanding to see their children or have them repatriated.

Parliamentary elections the following year brought more changes affecting the emigrant population. In April 1986 Jacques Chirac returned as prime minister and began an uncomfortable "cohabitation" with President Mitterrand. Chirac aimed to tighten controls over emigration and the Algerian community in France. After a series of bombings in September 1986, he instituted a visa policy beginning in October. The Pasqua Law of September 1986 (named after Minister of the Interior Charles Pasqua) expanded official power to deport emigrants for reasons ranging from adminstrative "irregularities" to criminal activities, especially among teenagers. Le Pen's ascendancy and the right's increasingly hard line on expulsion occurred ironically as the *beurs,* the emigrant community's second generation, emerged and began to assert growing cultural and political influence.

The *Beurs:* A Dislocated but Discovered Identity

The word *beur* is derived from a popular street-jargon form of *arabe.* The term refers to second-generation North Africans, who often find themselves suspended between Maghribi and French identities.[126] According to Driss Yazmani, editor of *Sans frontières:* "Many young Beurs feel alienated from both France and Algeria." Driss saw them "caught between two worlds, belonging truly to neither."[127] In an interview in April 1988, Akli Tadjer, a prominent writer of Algerian descent, addressed the torn *beur* identity as a "split . . . between two different parts of the self: one which identifies with the secular values of contemporary France, and one which, through the family home, remains engaged with the Islamic traditions of North Africa."[128] For obvious historical reasons, this existential if not ontological condition is particularly acute among Algerians. Though Algerians born in France since 1963 became automatic French citizens, older members of the community, including the children's parents, were denied this privilege. For example, Kaisa Titous, a Kabyle, directed the campaign of Pierre Juquin, but could not vote in the election.[129] The *beurs* demanded full integration into French society, especially the exercise of French citizenship. Ever sensitive to French racism, as dramatically demonstrated by the October 1983 March of the Beurs, they helped organize SOS-Racisme in 1984 with its defining slogan "Hands off my buddy" (*Touche pas à mon pote*). In June 1985 *beurs* also participated prominently in another highly publicized march which mobilized 300,000 protestors at the Place de la Concorde in Paris.[130]

The *beurs* may be suspended between identities, but they are not culturally inert. They have developed their own distinctive literature and media.[131] Azouz Begag recounts his childhood in Villeurbane, a suburb of Lyon, in his novel *Le Gone du Chaâba* (1986). In the autobiographical *La Marche* (1984), Bouzid Kara's "powerlessness" rages as a son of a *harki,* a community that he describes as "the Sioux of France." Yet as dislocated as he is, he ironically perceives his place: "The Algerian hills are beautiful, but they do not speak to me[;] the hills of Aix hold all my childhood." He finally finds dignity and solidarity during the March of the Beurs.[132] Sakinna Boukhedenna is also enraged by her wrenching existential predicament. She feels exiled in France but considers Algeria a neocolonial country. She assails patriarchy, avidly listens to alternative rockers Nico and Lou Reed, and sympathizes with the Baader-Meinhof gang. She remains defiant, irreconcilable, and dauntless.[133] Leila Sebbar is not a *beur* (she was born in Algeria to a French mother), but her novels reveal emigrant children's experiences. Her heroines rebel against patriarchy, try to escape it, and find themselves "on the road" experiencing a variety of existential searches for self.[134] Akli Tadjer sets his remarkable 1984 novel *Les Ani du "Tassili"* (Ani is short for *arabe non-identifié*) on the trans-Mediterranean Algerian ferry *Tassili,* an actual vessel. The protagonist is a *beur* who has failed in an attempt to live in Algeria and is returning "home." He finds himself associating with a variety of Algerians who serve as metaphors for the postcolonial period: the ALN veteran, the first-generation emigrant, the idealist. In a particular striking conversation, one traveler remains perplexed by the architectural symbolism of the recently completed Monument of the Martyr commemorating the resistance against colonialism and the Revolution. The *beur* protagonist concludes that he is more comfortable among his friends in France.

Beurs have also distinguished themselves in film. Mehdi Charef directed the acclaimed *Le Thé au harem d'Archimède* (1985), a film depicting a delinquent yet disarmingly sensitive *beur* youth. His second film, *Miss Mona* (1987), dealt with an illegal emigrant's relationship with a homosexual transvestite. The decadence and degradation of the situation served as a powerful social metaphor. Another admired *beur* director, Rachid Bouchareb, explored the social hybridity of an emerging transcultural generation in *Bâton rouge* (1985).[135] Isabelle Adjani, one of France's greatest cinema stars, is half Algerian.

Emigrant workers and *beurs* became increasingly activist in economic matters. When Talbot estimated in late 1983 that of 1,905 layoffs at its automobile plant 1,500 would be emigrant workers (mostly black and North Africans), an Algerian named Abderrazzak Dali declared: "For the first time the immigrants want their voice heard outside the framework of any labor union." Yazid Sabeg, a *beur* with a doctorate in economics and owner of a consulting firm, said: "Before, we did the dirty work. . . . now that we want the same jobs, we are rivals on the marketplace."[136]

The National Charter of 1986

The dissipation of the "confident" international "exemplar" influenced the reformulation of the National Charter of 1975. The conspicuous theme of Algeria's "enriched" National Charter of January 1986 was an appeal to "self-reliance." This document was yet another symbol of Algeria's existential disposition: the exigent need to define itself. The state was defined as "popular in essence, Islamic in religion, socialist in orientation, democratic in institutions, [and] modern in vocation."[137] Robert A. Mortimer concluded correctly that "the differences between 1976 and 1986 are more stylistic than substantive."[138] A new section titled "The Historical Foundations of Algerian Society" was added. Though it championed traditional historical "constants" such as the enduring heroic character of Algerian resistance dating back to Masinissa and Jugurtha, it also mentioned the efforts of the usually discredited Messali Hadj (d. 1974) and the recently rehabilitated Ferhat Abbas (d. 1985).[139] Paradoxically, the Charter's insistence on historicism failed to take into account Algeria's contemporary realities.

The Charter reaffirmed fundamental socialist principles and repeated platitudes while ignoring the significant social and economic institutional changes that had occurred in the 1980s. This reflected the intra-FLN difficulties Benjedid faced in implementing institutional reforms. In the first sector, Benjedid's creeping liberalism, highlighted by the return of land to private hands, effectively dismantled Boumedienne's inefficient Agrarian Revolution. His two five-year plans (1980–89) insisted on greater allocations for agriculture. In 1987 Algeria needed to import 60 percent of its food.[140] In the second sector, the state-building national companies, stoked as the engines of Boumedienne's development plans, were broken up into smaller "national enterprises." Soon after the promulgation of the Charter, the state companies and enterprises were further decentralized as "*entreprises publiques économiques*" to try to achieve financial efficiency and managerial autonomy.

The 19 August 1986 law liberalized the hydrocarbon sector in an effort to encourage foreign exploration and investment.[141] It allowed joint ventures and service- or production-sharing contracts, which appealed to Total (CFP). With the steep slump in oil prices, Algeria could not "afford" a socialist path. The ideology, like the economy, edged toward the brink of bankruptcy. The Charter now reads as a curious anachronism failing to take into account a very different Algeria from the one a decade earlier. What remained a constant was the latent insurrectionary character of the Algerian people, which soon catalyzed again as confrontation and finally conflict, not with foreign invaders, but tragically with their government and then later themselves.

Algeria's Increasing Political and Social Restlessness

Benjedid's economic liberalization and institutional reorganization sharpened intra-elite rivalries between his technocrats and longtime FLN apparatchiks. In December 1985 the personal and very public entente orchestrated between the "historic chiefs" (cofounders of the FLN) and longtime opponents Ahmed Ben Bella and Hocine Ait Ahmed and their respective political organizations, the Mouvement pour la Démocratie en Algérie (MDA, founded in 1984) and the Front des Forces Socialistes (FFS, first organized against Ben Bella in 1963), illustrated a mounting opposition to Benjedid and the FLN establishment. The most ominous opposition, however, was internal, and it not only posed a political threat but also had serious social and cultural ramifications. This was resurgent, and ultimately insurgent, Islamism.

Algerian postcolonial governments repeatedly affirmed their allegiance to Islam, especially for its existential service during the colonial period. According to one early official publication, Islam "preserved [Algeria's] personality."[142] Despite repeated efforts by postcolonial governments and their promulgated documents to emphasize the mutual compatibility of secularism, socialism, and Islam, Islamist groups such as al-Qiyam al-Islamiyya (Islamic Values) in the 1960s and al-Ahl al-Da'wa (People of the Call) in the 1970s questioned the official imagination and institutionalization of independent Algeria. The Cultural Revolution's emphasis on Arabization and national unity inevitably raised the existential question of identity and Islam. This was particularly displayed in the pages of the Ministry of Religious Affairs journal *al-Asala* (Authenticity), some of whose contributors, including Abbasi Madani, implicitly challenged Algerian secularism. The journal was stopped in 1981.

This period featured the growing influence of prominent Islamist intellectuals, foremost among them Malek Bennabi, or Malik Ibn Nabi (1905–73). This erudite scholar and teacher (and electrical engineer) cofounded and led al-Qiyam until its dissolution in 1966 and also wrote for *Révolution africaine*. He questioned Algerians' attachment to Western ideology, including Fanonism, as well as their willingness to ingest Muslim ideas imported from foreign sources like Egypt's Muslim Brotherhood. To Bennabi, Muslims must be modernist and moral; indeed, being a Muslim had to be rethought.[143] He invited Muslims to explore and liberate themselves—and their community; he advocated a Muslim commonwealth—by cherishing and upholding the "democratic" social values inherent in Islam. Algerians, he said, needed "exalting existential motivations" to rid themselves of *colonisabilité*.[144] He did not absolutely reject the West (he wrote both in French and Arabic), but he condemned its corrosive materialism and lack of spirituality. Bennabi's positions worried the authorities since they inherently challenged the political establishment. He attracted a coterie of students, as did the aged and venerable Shaykhs Abdellatif Soltani and Ahmed Sahnoun, who led al-Da'wa and preached against the government's secularism.

In 1982 a leftist student was killed by an Islamist militant during a period of intense confrontation at the University of Algiers's suburban Ben Aknoun campus. This resulted in a police crackdown and arrests, including the incarceration of Shaykhs Soltani and Sahnoun. Another prominent

person jailed was the popular professor of sociology Abbasi Madani. After a week the authorities released Soltani and Sahnoun to house arrest;
Madani remained imprisoned.

Benjedid's government continued its policy of both confrontation and
conciliation as many jailed "agitators" were exonerated and freed during
1983. It promoted the construction of mosques with the hope that the
imams employed by the Ministry of Religious Affairs would be able to
channel and monitor Islamist remonstrances. Nevertheless, in April 1984
at the funeral of Shaykh Soltani, hundreds of thousands of Islamists rallied
in what could be interpreted as a political protest against the government.
The passage later in 1984 of the conservative Family Code, which included traditional Muslim legal precepts from the Shari'a, was an effort
both to accommodate Islamists and to use them as a counterpoise against
Boumediennist elites.[145] Also in 1984, the opening of the Abdelkader Islamic University in Constantine to great fanfare was taken as another
opportunity to coopt Islamism. Though rioting in 1985 in Algiers's Casbah could be laid to the deplorable infrastructure, the widespread violence
that occurred at Constantine and Sétif in 1986 was incited by curricular
changes involving political and religious subjects at the *lycée* level. Protestors assaulted and pillaged official buildings, forcing a particularly severe
suppression by the authorities. Since December 1982 militant Islamists
and other opponents of the establishment had been organizing violent
operations, which eventually focused attention on an ALN veteran and
employee of the national electric power corporation named Mustapha
Bouyali, or Buyali.

After one of his brothers was killed by the police, Bouyali, a faithful
Muslim though hardly a fervent Islamist, mobilized and led a group that
repeatedly assaulted the police and public facilities. Bouyali's insurgency
and success in eluding capture gained him popular notoriety. According to
Rachid Benaissa: "He crystallized all the discontent. Everyone dreamed of
escaping from a regime which was stifling."[146] When he was finally cor-
nered and killed in 1987, Bouyali's resistance had been appropriated and
championed by a variety of Islamists, including radicals demanding the
repatriation of French *coopérants*.[147] Demonstrating his usual perspicacity, Michel Jobert had already commented in an interview that Algeria was
"most receptive to Islamic fundamentalism."[148] Few in Paris or Algiers
recognized this possibility.

Another event demonstrated the more overt opposition to the Algerian
political establishment. On 7 April 1987 André-Ali Mecili, a French lawyer of Kabyle descent and a close friend of Ait Ahmed, was gunned down

in Paris. The chief suspect, Amallou Abdelmalek, was deported soon after-wards, prompting many, including Ait Ahmed, to claim that the murder was the work of Algerian special services. Subsequent efforts to extradite Abdelmalek failed.[149]

The Bilateral Relationship Improves but Algeria's Economy Collapses

Bilateral relations slowly recovered, not only because of the traditional strategic axes and the human dimension, but because of immediacy. Plum-meting oil prices, woven intrinsically into those meticulously negotiated LNG price "baskets," plunged the Algerian economy inexorably into a deep recession, forcing unavoidable austerity and mounting debt. Algeria welcomed France's subsequent sensitivity and assistance, such as the ten-year renewal in March 1986 of the landmark Technical and Cultural Co-operation convention of 1966,[150] and especially Jacques Chirac's receptiv-ity during his "cohabitation" as prime minister (March 1986–May 1988).

Unlike Fabius's visit to Algiers in July 1985, Chirac's arrival in Septem-ber 1986 received substantial national media attention. He reviewed an array of problems ranging from mixed-marriage child custody to security and strategic issues (i.e., Western Sahara and Chad). Chirac also addressed GDF-SONATRACH negotiations, promoted Peugeot's proposal to build an automotive plant, and lobbied for Airbus contracts.[151] The Algerian government was concerned over the new visa policy and the harder line toward the emigrant community, but it felt confidence in Chirac's leader-ship—particularly his watchful monitoring of Ben Bella's MDA.[152]

The generally improving French relationship, marked by Algerian as-sistance in freeing French hostages in Lebanon, correlated with a series of positive regional events. Morocco abrogated the Treaty of Oujda with Libya in 1986, and Rabat and Algiers restored relations in 1988. This was the crucial step toward realizing the elusive ideal of Maghrib unity.[153] Regional reconciliation relieved Paris of the delicate policy of "equilib-rium" or political parity it had been forced to pursue with Maghribi con-testants over Western Sahara.[154]

Algeria's economic vulnerability emboldened its LNG clients.[155] Spain reduced imports after Algeria insisted that it comply with the "take or pay" stipulation in its 1985 contract. According to Italy, the plunging prices warranted a 40-percent price reduction.[156] Belgium refused to pay the posted high price for gas and began preparation to argue its case before the International Court of Justice. By March 1986 Algerian crude had plummeted to $12/barrel. (The USSR then briefly became France's chief LNG supplier.) Algeria's hydrocarbon revenues dropped 40 percent in

Table 6.2. French Trade with Algeria, 1985–1988 (in millions of French francs)

	1985	1986	1987	1988
French exports	21,806	15,858	11,759	9,444
French imports	20,752	11,457	8,542	8,282
Balance	1,054	4,401	3,217	1,162

Source: EIU, *CRs*.

1986 and its foreign debt soared to $17 billion in 1987. With a deepening recession, economic growth dropped to what heretofore had been unimaginable levels (-1.4 percent in 1987 and -2.7 percent in 1988).[157]

An interim agreement between GDF and SONATRACH in April 1986 eliminated the 1982 formula and established the price in reference to a basket of market, rather than OPEC, crude prices. The price was determined at $2.89/MMBtu, with no development subsidy. By November 1987 GDF reportedly paid an astonishing $1.97/MMBtu.[158] Concurrently, there were negotiations on a new price accord. In January 1988, Prime Minister Chirac "inscribed" the "technical problem" of pricing within "the framework of a policy of cooperation." In other words, a political dimension was infused once again into the pricing issue.[159] After President Mitterrand's reelection and the Socialists' return to power in May 1988, Foreign Minister Roland Dumas called for the "revitalization" of the relationship and clearly suggested that resolving the gas pricing question would achieve this objective.[160] In June while in Paris, Foreign Minister Ahmed Taleb Ibrahimi affirmed: "We are convinced . . . that gas will become again the driving force in the development of economic and commercial relations between Algeria and France."[161] With Algeria supplying 35 percent of France's natural gas in the first two months of 1988,[162] both sides trod again that tedious, tortuous path toward settlement; the psychodrama returned.[163]

Recognizing the decreasing bilateral trade as a sign of the relationship's decline, France, as Algeria's primary creditor, provided a welcome initiative in April 1987 by offering Algeria a credit line of FF 3 billion. This accord was to be linked to two other agreements: (1) settling lingering questions on blocked colonial assets and (2) assenting in principle to French participation (either Peugeot or Renault) in Algeria's second automobile plant.[164] The initiative concerning colonial property complemented Chirac's effort to resolve conclusively the painful and protracted *pied-noir* indemnity issue.[165] Algiers, however, balked at the loan conditions. COFACE's 50-percent guaranteed coverage was too low, and the interest rates offered by French banks were too high. Meanwhile, French businesses complained of lost contracts in the absence of financial and LNG accords.[166] France did recover from the United States' penetration of the grain market by negotiating the sale to Algeria of up to 500,000 tons of soft wheat in 1988, to be guaranteed by COFACE, though the Americans continued to be active, tendering an offer of one million tons under the Export Enhancement Program.[167]

Even with the problems posed by these two difficult negotiations, France and Algeria stepped again toward the threshold of a special relationship, including the obligatory ritual psychodrama. Both countries remained unaware of the coming epochal transformation of their relations as Algeria's incendiary economic, social, cultural, and political conditions ignited in what would rage as a national conflagration threatening to consume bilateral cooperation too.

7

Algeria's "Second Revolution" and France, 1988–1992

From the October Riots to the *Fitna*

> This working day . . . is more than a duty, [it is] a duty of friendship.
> **François Mitterrand, on his day-long summit with President Benjedid in Algeria, March 1989**

> Conscious of my historical responsibilities before this historic conjuncture being crossed by our nation, I consider that the only solution to the present crisis lies in the necessity of my retiring from the political scene.
> **Chadli Benjedid, announcing his resignation, January 1992**

After a series of strikes beginning in late September, general rioting broke out throughout Algeria in early October 1988, ravaging cities and shocking France and the world. Rapid democratic and constitutional reforms in November and February 1989 ended the FLN's monopoly of power and, with it, its conception of a state and national identity. Legislation in July 1989 officially inaugurated a multiparty system. Concurrently, Algeria's cultural florescence reaffirmed social and ethnic pluralism. An emerging and eager generation of authors and musicians, now freed from the politico-cultural constrictions of the past, engaged the existential task of defining or describing the nation.

The discrediting and disintegration of the FLN led to the astounding success of the FIS, the Front Islamique du Salut (Islamic Salvation Front) in local elections in June 1990 and in the first round of parliamentary elections in December 1991. Fearful of an Islamist takeover, military and civilian elites overthrew the Benjedid government in January 1992. Eventually, an Haut Comité d'Etat (HCE) took over, as Algeria inexorably confronted increasing Islamist violence and *fitna,* a "trial" of itself as a nation. Profoundly troubled by these unanticipated events, France responded by taking generally supportive yet often ambivalent and ambiguous positions toward Algeria as the bilateral relationship with its paradoxes and passions underwent a turbulent transformation.

The October 1988 Riots and the French-Algerian Relationship

On the surface, the riots stemmed from economic pressures, but they were deeply rooted in political, social, and cultural frustration. The deteriorating economic conditions since late 1985 — depressed oil prices, unemployment, food shortages, surging inflation — led to severe austerity measures. Above all, the entrenched leadership had suffocated the aspirations of the younger generation. More than half the population was under twenty-one. Clearly the socialist, revolutionary rhetoric articulated by the aging elite no longer provided coherence or credibility.[1] The younger generation rejected the hegemonic FLN-imposed mythology, a "closed myth of concern,"[2] and with it the illusion of the polity projected by its Constitutions and National Charters. The widening gap between the perception of an identity, the projection of the Algerian nation, as interpreted by the older "generation of 1 November" and experienced by the younger one of independence impelled the violence.[3] The youth who took to the streets in October 1988 were more than economic and social malcontents, they were existentially alienated from the kind of Algeria imagined by the FLN.[4] The riots represented "the irreparable fracture of polity and society."[5]

These "events" shocked the French government, leaving its officials either slack-jawed or tight-lipped. France's historical vision of Algeria as a reflection of French power and influence, whether through colonialism or cooperation, blurred; or, as one commentator simply put it: "The mirror shattered."[6] The *tiersmondiste* analytic championed especially by the left (Mitterrand, Rocard, Cheysson, Dumas) that applauded Algeria's socialist enterprises within the Third World was now called into question for its expedient, ideology-driven neglect of the repressive nature of Algeria's political system. The riots portended vexatious problems for the bilateral relationship and underscored France's difficulties with decolonizing or transcending its troubling Algerian past. The French essentialist and even sentimental posture, particularly reliant upon the Algerian relationship during both the colonial and postcolonial periods, was once again staggered by upheaval across the Mediterranean.

The October Riots and Subsequent Reforms

Destructive and deadly rioting broke out in Algiers on 4 October, convulsed Constantine and Sétif, and then burst forth in Oran and Mostaganem.[7] On 6 October the government proclaimed a "state of siege," and troops were deployed to restore order. On 9 October a communiqué from a mysterious Movement for Algerian Renewal called for the disbanding of the FLN, the ousting of the government, and the availability of cheaper food. There were also appeals for adherence to the *Shari'a*, signaling the startling appearance of Islamism as an ideological alternative. President Benjedid's meeting on 10 October with Islamist leaders including Shaykh Ahmed Sahnoun and Ali Belhadj (described as an amorphous "Islamic trend" group) constituted recognition not only of their cultural significance but also of their political legitimacy. Newspaper reports already disclosed the particular influence of the relatively unknown imam Ali Belhadj, who demanded political, economic, and social reforms and would later cofound the FIS.[8]

President Benjedid also addressed the nation on 10 October and asked for public confidence while promising a "complete program" of political reforms including revising the Constitution and making the government responsible to the National Popular Assembly. The most serious rioting was quelled by 11 October, and the government lifted the state of siege the following day. On 12 October Benjedid announced that a referendum would be held on 3 November on a reform package that would allow, too, "greater demonstration of political activity." The proposals articulated by the government on 23 October included separating the state from the FLN, permitting "mass organizations," and instituting free local and national elections. Though welcoming these initiatives or concessions, Algerians could not forget their bloody cost. The government claimed 176 citizens lost their lives, but unofficial sources reported at least five hundred killed, a thousand wounded, and three thousand incarcerated. Mohammed Harbi, the veteran Algeria watcher and past editor of *Révolution africaine,* viewed the violence as generational, another Sétif; it was "the end of an epoch."[9]

The historic 3 November referendum delivered a 92.27 percent "yes" vote, with 83 percent of the electorate participating. In a nod to the growing Islamist influence, the referendum was held on a Thursday rather than a Friday (*yawm al-Sabah,* the Muslim day of prayer) to avert imams' opposition. The rousing mandate for change, significantly, allowed Benjedid to draw away from the discredited FLN. At the Sixth FLN Congress (26–

27 November), Benjedid confirmed that there would be free expression and elections. Economically, state enterprises would be allowed to manage themselves and foreign investment would be invited, a jolting blow to the vaunted socialist option. On 22 December, Benjedid was reelected to the presidency with 81 percent of the vote.

France's Response to "The Events"

Mitterrand's government assumed a paradoxical profile, a muted "concern," during the October riots. It understood that Benjedid's government was acutely sensitive to French opinion. Prime Minister Rocard spoke obtusely of the "sympathy and solidarity of the French people."[10] On 12 October before the National Assembly he reaffirmed: "Our relations with Algeria do not have equivalence." He underscored that "the existence of an Algerian community in France and a French one in Algeria, the memory of seven years of war, create particular sensibilities." Claude Malhuret of the Parti Républicain responded: "When there is repression in Chile or in Haiti, the left demands economic sanctions, but when five hundred persons are killed in Algeria, one hears that one must accelerate cooperation."[11] Though Prime Minister Rocard spoke of the "weighty significance" of the government's silence, the "events" clearly unsettled Mitterrand's government. The French president would not criticize his counterpart, whom he genuinely liked. At a Council of Ministers meeting, Mitterrand expressed his frustration: "What are we going to do, call in the Algerian ambassador and tell him that if France were there now, order would be better kept?"[12] Foreign Minister Dumas ambiguously pronounced his "solidarity," but with whom? The Algerian government? Its people?[13] This signaled the beginning of an irresolute policy that would incapacitate French governments of the left and the right. Indeed, political immobilism threatened France's interests.

The French public and private hesitancy to protest the Algerian government's violent suppression of the October riots illustrated the particular power and influence of *tiersmondisme*. This stirred Franz-Olivier Giesbert, the new editor of *Le Figaro,* to question openly the "selective indignation" of the intellectuals on the left who were quick to condemn Pinochet, Jaruzelski, and "death squads" in Latin America, but remained silent over Algeria, a country he now considered a "flagrant *tiersmondiste* fiasco."[14] Ironically, even ex-president Giscard d'Estaing, with his anti-Algerian reputation, felt forced to keep silent.[15] Serge July added that France's position toward Algeria was curiously "neocolonialist," giving primacy to French interests over other considerations, "even the most fundamental with regard to the rights of people."[16] According to Patrick Rotman, who had studied the so-called *porteurs de valises* (French collaborators with the FLN during the War), the left viewed the socialist FLN in domestic terms as an "instrument of 'redemption,' the means to regenerate the French worker movement." Many of the French intellectuals who favored the FLN, however, were now appalled and embarrassed by the violence.[17] While Mitterrand, Rocard, and Dumas tempered their remarks, the Socialist Party intoned: "We condemn the brutality of the repression."[18]

Michel Rocard feared, too, that "any excessive commentary could incite [the emigrant community], even to fight among themselves on our own territory."[19] "Black October" evoked the pathological fear of a flood of refugees arriving on French shores fleeing destabilized Algeria. The emigrant community's response to the events varied, often mirroring attitudes in Algeria. Boumedienne's era was regarded with nostalgia by older Algerians upset with the destructive violence of the youth and with Benjedid's "capitalism for the privileged." Younger Algerians sympathized with the protesting youth. One said: "It is necessary to restore order in Algeria. To better redistribute wealth. If truth comes from Islam, then it is necessary to fight with Islam." Another man viewed France as responsible for "never leaving us alone."[20]

Indeed, in Algeria there was a general disgust for the amorphous yet insidious *hizb faransa* or the "party of France." This was a general belief that France had a particular sinister influence in high Algerian circles.[21] France became a scapegoat. During the October riots, an Air France office was targeted in Oran and burned. The Arabic daily *al-Chaab* (*al-Sha'ab*, or The People) published a communiqué issued by law students claiming that the killings were premeditated "with friends and interests in France."[22] Before the opening of the FLN party congress at the end of November, one member expressed dread that a multiparty system would "open the doors to traitors, to *harkis*, to the agents of France." Longtime FLN member Benaamar Benaouda contended that "the October riots were launched under orders from France."[23] The government had also tried to blame "foreign influences"[24] for the explosive "events." This was an obvious attempt to deflect hostility from its own incendiary policies.

During the discussion in the French National Assembly on 12 October, François Deniau said defensively: "I do not believe that anyone can say that what has happened in Algeria is the fault of France."[25] A day later, six thousand demonstrators marched in Paris denouncing "the complicity of the French government."[26] Was France responsible? Certainly, Paris's support since independence of repressive Algerian regimes charged France with guilt by association. Serge July said that the French relationship with Algeria was like U.S.–Latin American relations, including the "double-talk."[27] But how responsible could France be for postcolonial Algeria? How neocolonial had the relationship actually been throughout the postcolonial decolonizations? Was Algeria genuinely decolonized? The fundamental perception of Algeria as a nation needed reexamining—and France's own essentialist identity needed reimagining too.

Algeria Expresses Its Pluralism

On 5 February 1989 the text of a new constitution was published. It provided for freedom of expression and the right to strike. Article 40 called for a multiparty state ("associations of a political character"). Robert Mortimer observed that Algeria's new constitution "makes no reference . . . to the doctrinal text known as the National Charter."[28] Indeed, the FLN was not mentioned; the "irreversible" socialist course was over, which provoked sharp intra-elite criticisms. Political pluralism would now be promoted, terminating the FLN's political monopoly and the suddenly anachronistic positivity that a one-party state best served national interests. On 23 February the constitution was endorsed by 73.4 percent of the voters. Legislation concluded on 2 and 19 July reshaped electoral laws and provided criteria for newly organized parties to receive legal status. By the end of the year, three principal parties, besides the FLN, emerged from the many others: the FIS, organized by Abbasi Madani and Ali Belhadj; a secular Kabyle party, the Rassemblement pour la Culture et la Démocratie (RCD), led by Said Saadi, a psychiatrist; and Ait Ahmed's Kabylia-based FFS.[29] Ait Ahmed, the Kabyle "historic leader," returned to Algeria in December after twenty-four years in exile and was followed in October 1990 by Ben Bella, whose MDA also received legal status. Other significant parties included Shaykh Mahfoud Nahnah's moderate Islamist Movement for an Islamic Society (HAMAS) and Noureddine Boukrouh's modernist Islamic organization, the Parti du Renouveau algérien (PRA), or Algerian Renewal Party. According to Robert Mortimer, this would have been a decisive period for "a dialogue between secularists and Islamists about pluralism and basic liberties."[30] This window of opportunity would soon slowly but firmly close. Rémy Leveau referred to Algeria's new political pluralism as "more virtual than real."[31]

Algeria's Existential Engagement

Most observers accurately regard this period as one of uncertainty and instability. Yet the precious, propitious few years of civil and political rights before the coup against President Benjedid in January 1992 were among the most significant in postcolonial Algeria's history. For the first time, the country enjoyed freedom, no matter how flawed;[32] the country genuinely engaged and experienced itself, and explored the reality of its social, cultural, and historical pluralism. These were the years when the existential praxis was not only proposed from above but pursued and asserted from below by democrats, Islamists, socialists, secularists, francophones, arabophones, and berberophones. In many respects, it represented another cultural revolution, a more authentic one. Algeria's abundant creative energies and talents were unleashed.

A flourishing press developed with six national dailies in circulation in 1991, including *El-Watan, Le Matin,* and *Liberté.* Weekly publications such as *Le Nouvel Hebdo* sprang up, as well as independent publishing houses. One of the most popular periodicals was *Al Mounchar,* a cartoon weekly that featured the political artist Menouard Merabtene.[33] In all, about 150 new news publications appeared after the 1989 liberalization. Ironically, even with the rise of Islamism and Arabism, more Algerians were reading French than ever before and listening to French programs received by proliferating parabolic antennas.[34] Though its chief arabophone newspaper, *El-Mounquid,* included several pages of French, the FIS added a francophone publication, *El-Forkane,* in January 1991.

Algerian literature was also affected by the events of this turbulent period. Among the most prominent of a new generation of novelists were Rachid Mimouni and Tahar Djaout. In *The Honor of the Tribe (Honneur de la tribu,* 1989), Mimouni used the remote, "forgotten" fictional village of Zitouna as a metaphor for Algeria's modern history. The consequences of colonialism and the War of Liberation, emigration, the multiple problems of modernization with foreign technicians and consultants, and a corrupt Party and bureaucracy are all recounted by a tape-recorded narrator, who states resignedly: "Yes, our collective memory is tenacious. This is because our tribe has known so much misery."[35] This novel, as well as the nuanced ironies in his collection of short stories *The Ogre's Embrace (La Ceinture de l'Ogresse,* 1990), were appeals for Algerians to come to terms with themselves and their common history. Tahar Djaout in *Les Vigiles* (1991) presented the Kafkaesque experiences of an inventor, one Mahfoudh Lemdjad, who attempts to have his invention recognized by the state. He symbolically finds the state, itself a manufactured product, not wanting to be reinvented. The inventor is an individual, but individuality is interrogated and dispatched into the despair of a labyrinthine bureaucracy. One of Djaout's characters laments: "It is unanimity which makes me feel horrible."[36]

Rai music amplified the new freedom. Its creative, syncretic rhythms, blending traditional North African and Western musical genres, symbolized Algeria's modern historical identity. "Cheb" Hasni, "Cheb" Khaled (called the King of Rai), "Cheb" Mami (the Prince of Rai), and others expressed through their rhythms and rhymes the excitement of these changes, raising the eyebrows of the political establishment and also those of the Islamists.[37] The renowned Kabyle singer Lounès Matoub also found in this freer atmosphere an opportunity for the outspoken expression of his ideas concerning state and society.

Rachid Mimouni believed "the true Algerian Revolution is in the making."[38] He knew this meant that all factions would have to live together. He appealed for the Algerian government to create the conditions "to permit the coexistence of brother enemies." He wondered, would terror and civil war and tears be the price paid, "the necessary condition for the formation of a nation"?[39]

The Deconstruction of the Economy

These years witnessed the rapid demolition of the hitherto sacrosanct socialist edifice.[40] In 1989 the government permitted international banks to open branches (Société Générale, Banque Nationale de Paris) and welcomed an IMF standby credit. (The thought of IMF intervention would have been anathema to Boumedienne, a compromise of sovereignty.) In September, Benjedid replaced Premier Kasdi Merbah (who protested briefly, calling his dismissal unconstitutional) with Mouloud Hamrouche, indicating his impatience with the pace of reform and his preference for FLN technocrats. Hamrouche responded with accelerated reforms, such as the March 1990 money and credit law which promoted foreign investment and privatization. The strict Investment Codes of 1963 and 1966 were obliterated. Foreign trade was liberalized and private import-export ventures by local concessionaires were encouraged. This policy aimed to attract business from the flourishing black market (*trabendo*, French-Arabic slang). The reforming momentum was regarded approvingly by the IMF, which accorded Algeria another standby credit in 1991. Grants from the World Bank and the Arab Monetary Fund were also applied to buttress financial stability. Not surprisingly, French banks began playing crucial roles in refinancing short-term debt. The French state-owned Crédit Lyonnais expedited a $1.5 billion loan package from a number of international lenders. Still, reformers blamed French banks for not providing enough aid and for "torpedoing" their initiatives.[41]

Aid and reforms were both hampered by deteriorating economic conditions. The precipitate decline of the dinar (from 5.91/$ in 1988 to 18.47/$ in 1991) affected Algeria's balance of payments and debt service. Algeria could not pay its bills or adequately cover its credits. Air France, for example, cut its flights because of Algerian arrears.[42] Double-digit inflation (about 30 percent) compounded the financial situation, slashing consumer spending and confidence. The horrific fact was that 75 percent of Algerian government revenues were needed to service its spiraling national debt (approximately $20 billion). Also, liberalizing of the economy was not uniformly popular, after decades of accustomed subsidies. Rachid Mimouni, who was a trained economist, observed a fatal flaw in the reforming process: "They're trying to change the system with the same men. The state apparatus is resisting."[43] Finally, the deep political unrest, so misperceived or disbelieved by the FLN and Benjedid's technocrats, compounded by severe economic dislocation, undercut the reforms' efficacy, leaving little chance for amelioration in the life of distressed Algerian citizens or their deeply disoriented nation.

French-Algerian Ententes and Accords

The riots imparted a certain urgency to the French-Algerian relationship. Foreign Minister Dumas declared at the National Assembly on 12 October 1988 that France had to help. Growing worry over Algeria's domestic turmoil led to the conclusion of significant accords early in 1989. President Mitterrand during a short visit to Algeria in March termed the bilateral relationship *la vie en commun* (life in common), reiterating his sensitivity to Algeria's historical importance to France and, for that matter, to his personal political career.[44] According to the veteran specialist André Pautard, while Algeria was no longer viewed as the nation "opening . . . the doors to the Third World," it "remained the best field for the application of a North-South solidarity always wanted by François Mitterrand."[45] Intensified cooperation signaled France's endorsement of Algeria's dramatic political and economic reforms. President Benjedid particularly welcomed Mitterrand's support after the October 1988 destabilization. As Robert Mortimer pointed out: "France's stamp of approval was an important external guarantee."[46] Foreign Minister Boualem

Table 7.1. French Trade with Algeria, 1988–1991 (in millions of French francs)

	1988	1989	1990	1991
French exports	9,444	12,775	14,770	12,273
French imports	8,282	9,451	10,558	11,678
Balance	1,162	3,324	4,212	595

Source: EIU, *CRs*.

Bessaih said: "There exists a new vision in the bilateral relations based on mutual respect and reciprocal interest."[47]

Financial Accord

On 8 January negotiators signed an extraordinary financial accord. By this agreement FF 7 billion would be credited to Algeria. Two two-billion-franc tranches would be given, in 1989 and 1990, to be drawn equally from public and private agencies. The other FF 3 billion originated from the unused credit line of the 1987 agreement. The accord stipulated that 35 percent of this financial assistance be directed toward the commercial imbalance (at that time approximately FF 3 billion in France's favor). The French national credit agency COFACE now guaranteed an unprecedented 95 percent of the loans. Pierre Bérégovoy, the French minister of finance, said the accord would "permit the restoration of French-Algerian cooperation."[48]

The financial accords, and subsequent gas accords, increased bilateral trade significantly (see table 7.1). Furthermore, France had raised CCCE assistance to FF 369.3 million in 1988, from FF 236.1 million in 1987 and FF 39.5 million in 1986.[49] The signing of the financial accord reduced CCCE loans to FF 52 million in 1989.[50]

In July 1991 Bérégovoy arrived in Algeria to explore opportunities for private investment and to facilitate the refinancing of Algerian short-term debt by French and international banks. Soon to be France's largest medium- and long-term risk, Algeria's stability would be of particular concern and would have obvious political ramifications. Bérégovoy authorized the reactivation and the creation of credit lines of approximately FF 5 billion. Though ritually repeating that France "does not interfere in internal matters," he stressed "our attachment to democratic principles and pluralism."[51] These commercial credits, used to purchase such French durable goods as vehicles and machinery, assured France's position as Algeria's chief source of imports.

Hydrocarbons Accords

When Benjedid's government regained stability, natural gas negotiations resumed. The Algerians wanted to detach the financial arrangement from the LNG negotiations given the economic exigencies and restructurings. In other words, the 1965 and 1982 accords would no longer serve as cooperation templates. This in itself marked a different approach. On 12 January 1989, GDF and SONATRACH agreed on a price just under $2.30/MMBtu, and on arrears payments. France had been paying about a third less than what Algeria had calculated. It was reported that Algeria wanted $2.80/MMBtu. France would still pay a higher price than it did to its other providers of natural gas, the Netherlands and the USSR, though Algeria did charge France less than its other partners.[52] While there was a call at this time for a "realistic index," GDF president Francis Gutman claimed that the agreed price was not political but commercial. GDF also agreed to contribute to liquefaction costs, and to pursue joint projects with SONATRACH. Belkacem Nabi had previously remarked that "gas relations were the key to cooperation between Algiers and Paris."[53] Nevertheless, the gas negotiations had been facilitated by the politically significant financial accord.

El-Moudjahid, referring especially to the LNG agreement, saw "new perspectives of cooperation."[54] Indeed, Total (CFP), one of the first French enterprises to take advantage of Algeria's revised oil investment laws in 1986, undertook numerous ventures with SONATRACH and even regained operator control at some sites. A notable cooperation framework accord in January 1990 resulted in joint work groups to study production, technical and industrial projects, and marketing. Then in May 1991 the CFP agreed to purchase over a period of fourteen years approximately ten million tons of condensate and six million tons of liquefied petroleum gas, and to assist with the Algerian hydrocarbon infrastructure at El Hamra, 250 kilometers south of Hassi Messaoud.[55]

In July 1991 a joint natural gas company called Société Algéro-Française d'Ingéniérie et de Réalisations or SAFIR (36 percent SONATRACH, 15 percent Sonelgaz, 49 percent GDF) was organized to cooperate in liquefaction, production, transport, and distribution. In addition, GDF's Sofregaz was charged with modernizing GNL 3 at Arzew and, in September 1991, agreed to construct a compression facility to facilitate the oil flow at Mesdar, near Hassi Messaoud. France also expressed a strong investment interest in the projected trunkline through Morocco. Algeria continued to supply France with about one-third of its LNG.[56]

The law of 30 November 1991 added fourteen amendments to the 19 August 1986 legislation and further liberalized Algeria's hydrocarbons sector. Foreign companies were allowed equity interests in producing fields, and natural gas production would be handled in the same way as oil production, i.e., joint ventures, production sharing, or service contracts. Foreign partners were permitted to construct and operate trunklines, removing SONATRACH's monopoly in transport (a historically significant move, as the rationale for SONATRACH's creation was foreign concessionaires wanting to build a pipeline in 1963). Disputes would be handled by international arbitration.

The new legislation underscored Algeria's growing and even desperate need to attract foreign investment to develop its natural resources.[57] On the one hand, it assumed that foreign technical expertise would improve recovery rates and production assets from existing wells. On the other hand, the amendments particularly symbolized ideological rejection of the 24 February 1971 nationalization of the sector, as SONATRACH lost its monopoly in the production and transportation of petroleum, natural gas, and minerals.[58]

The amended hydrocarbons law suggested that Algeria needed to secure old clients, as well as attract new ones. GDF seized the opportunity and on 24 December 1991 concluded accords with SONATRACH extending its three LNG contracts for ten or fifteen years at a volume of 9.15 billion m^3 annually. A separate agreement called for delivery of a billion cubic meters of natural gas over six years when pipeline supply became available. The pricing for these deliveries was not made public. The two sides also declared their intention to cooperate closely on the Maghrib-European gas pipeline.[59] In the past, this event would have received extensive press coverage, including analyses of the accords' expected effect on the bilateral relationship. But with parliamentary elections set for 26 December, the 25 December El-Moudjahid, for example, merely printed a short APS dispatch (though still on the first page), which noted the obligatory "wish of both partners to intensify their relations and to sanction a long-term vision" in natural gas affairs.

Emigrant Workers, Harkis, and Integration

Concurrently, there was greater attention given to emigrant labor. On 31 December 1988 in Strasbourg, President Mitterrand expressed his repeated wish to improve the lot of the emigrant community in France, especially during the symbolic bicentennial year of the French Revolu-

tion.[60] Of course, his ideas on emigrant labor related to all the communities and not just the Algerian, but given its size (now about a million), it
obviously held special significance.

In January, Pierre Joxe, the minister of the interior (and son of the Evian
negotiator and former minister of the interior Louis Joxe), proposed
changing or "humanizing" the Pasqua Law of 9 September 1986 concerning "irregularities" that could trigger expulsion.[61] Often neglect of minor
administrative procedures would create naturalization problems, as when
emigrant youth had been uninformed of the eight-day filing period for a
temporary *carte de séjour* after their sixteenth birthday. The French government now aimed to establish grace periods for regularizing papers.[62]
According to France-Plus, an organization supporting emigrant integration, the Joxe Law would be more favorable than current bilateral agreements concerning entry and sojourn. Algerian officials favored a "revision" implicitly taking into account the Joxe initiative.[63] Joxe stated,
however, that he favored the Pasqua Law provisions on clandestine emigration, though not its intimidation.[64]

Debate over modification of the Pasqua Law, emigrants' right to vote in
local elections, naturalization processes, and France's divisive Code of
Nationality diverted attention from chronic problems of unemployment,
education, and housing.[65] Nevertheless, the Mitterrand government's proposals were also meant to blunt rising French racism, which was fiercely
anti-Algerian. This was highlighted in November 1989 by the furor over
North African girls wearing head scarves to school. A sartorial symbol of
Islam, the scarves seemed to contravene traditional French secular educational values. Eventually, the decision on the wearing of head scarves was
left to the discretion of the principal. This clothing issue acutely sharpened
the question of whether France could tolerate its multicultural social realities.

There was some reason for optimism. A poll by SOFRES for *Le Monde*
disclosed in January 1989 that Jean-Marie Le Pen's popularity had
dropped. Only 16 percent agreed with his positions, while 80 percent
disagreed.[66] Though Le Pen received a surprising 14.4 percent of the first-
round vote in the 1988 presidential elections, his Front National dropped
to 11.8 percent in the 1989 elections to the European Parliament. He still
boasted a receptive, if smaller, audience for code phrases such as "Each
people has a duty to preserve its own cultural identity."[67]

Despite the decline in popularity of Le Pen's ideas in 1989, by June
1991 Edith Cresson, the Socialist prime minister, talked of chartered
planes repatriating North Africans. Mitterrand talked of a "threshold of

tolerance," and Jacques Chirac spoke of the "noise and smells" of the emigrants.[68] The entire issue was heightened by Giscard d'Estaing's provocative statements in *Le Figaro Magazine,* where he proposed that French nationality be based on *sang* (blood) rather than *sol* (the ground underfoot).[69] Clearly, emigration was becoming immigration, as desperate migrant populations from North and sub-Sahara Africa sought to relocate permanently somewhere in Western Europe. This was no longer a French but a regional, continental problem.

The nationality question profoundly affected the marginalized *harkis.* These "Palestinians of France" continued to agitate for the full benefits of their citizenship, including opportunities for better housing, education, and employment.[70] By this time the "French Muslims" numbered 420,000, with two-thirds of their population under twenty-five. The summer of 1991 featured protests and the building of barricades at Narbonne, leading to one *harki* death. Their search for recognition continued to be a vain quest.

Islamism and Algerian Democracy

The emergence of the FIS and other Muslim parties was yet another reformulation of the existential praxis, the assertion of the authentic, undiluted Algerian self.[71] Indeed, according to many observers, Algeria's political Islamism was a recodified nationalism. It "filled the void" after the failures of pan-Arabism and single-party Arab nationalism, and engendered a "new fraternity" through its populism.[72] Most observers agree that the FLN "fathered the FIS" (an oft-used pun: *fils,* the word for "son," has a silent *l*), both by its emphasis on Arabization, which in the 1960s relied on Egyptian teachers, a significant number of whom had been influenced by the Muslim Brotherhood, and by its construction of mosques, which became convenient mobilization centers for antigovernment demonstrations. The FIS harked back not only to the Salafiyya movement and the Reformist Ulama of the recent past but to the mass movements associated with Messali Hadj.[73] Indeed, its attack against francophone Algerians recalled the conflicts between Messali Hadj and Ferhat Abbas. It became a potent force in Algeria in the wake of the FLN's political, economic, and moral bankruptcy. Couching its political populism in spiritual discourse, the FIS offered an attractive alternative to politically excluded and alienated Algerians.

The FIS perceived itself in a custodial role, perpetuating the legacy of the liberation struggle abandoned by a degenerate FLN. Linking piety to this political movement generated a powerful momentum. "Islamism was born," wrote Ahmed Rouadjia, "as an anti-FLN reaction."[74] To Benjamin Stora, the FIS's rejection of external ideologies, whether French or Arab, gave it a genuine autochthonous image and "posed itself thus as the genuine inheritors of an FLN disencumbered by all external ideology."[75] François Burgat viewed the Islamists as "inheritors" of Algerian nationalism even though they too, ironically, were a product of French colonialism. The FLN may have recovered the country physically, but not ideologically, spiritually.[76] Lahouari Addi also asserted that the FIS's popularity stemmed from its ability in "regenerating nationalism."[77] Nevertheless, as Arun Kapil wrote, the FIS contended with an Algeria "where Islam is deeply felt as an identity but not necessarily expressed through actual practice." Kapil noted that mosque attendance "was relatively low." And there was the attachment to Europe, reinforced by commerce, television, and personal relationships in the large emigrant Algerian community.[78] Nevertheless, the appeal of political Islamism, charged by a messianic nationalism, to the aggrieved youth of Algeria illustrated another refashioning of the existential praxis. Lahouari Addi concluded that Algerian Islamism was fundamentally a question of national identity.[79] To Abderrahim Lamchichi, Islamism was not only a product of social, economic, and political conditions but also "the resurgence of a new form of 'identity' and 'cultural' protest." It reformulated or "reread" Algeria's "cultural legacy in a context of identity crisis."[80]

Islamism Targets France: The Refashioned Existential Praxis

From the Islamist and particularly the FIS perspective, France corrupted Algeria with its secularism, modernism, republicanism, feminism, Marxism, and individualism. The idea that there could be two Frances, that of colonialism and that of cooperation, was rejected. From the Islamist perspective, Algerians who continued to permit French influence were "traitors" and "*harkis*." France had sought to "de-Islamicize" Algeria since the colonial period.[81] Abbasi Madani correlated "cultural aggression" with the Algerian educational system, which not only had perpetuated "French colonial policy" but had done so with greater "success [than] one and a half centuries of colonization."[82] Ali Belhadj wanted France "punished" for its colonial rule.[83] He vehemently vowed "with arms and faith, to ban [French oppression] intellectually and ideologically and to finish with its partisans who have suckled from its poisonous milk."[84]

To the FIS the War of Independence was "the affirmation of an Algerian personality forged by Islam."[85] But Islamists viewed decolonization as incomplete so long as the pervasive and reviled cultural influence of France persisted. Algerians needed to experience and live their genuine Muslim identity. According to one Islamist, the "war" between civilizations was "not finished yet."[86] Another contended that the Algerian personality cannot be free "without total cultural independence." This meant achieving "linguistic sovereignty," i.e., complete articulation in Arabic.[87] Another popular Islamist refrain was that France worked to discredit the FIS internationally while disseminating secular ideas within Algeria by its media transmissions and subversive agents.[88] France had "taken up the Cross" again as it crusaded against Muslim states, using, on the one hand, such cultural instruments as universities, associations, and religious organizations and, on the other hand, economic means such as the Paris Club of financial institutions.[89] As the FLN had done, the Islamists demonized France to reaffirm their own distinctive nationalist identity. The perceived French threat was cultural and political, as exemplified by the pervasive and perfidious influence of the *hizb faransa*. Ahmed Rouadjia pointed out, however, that this disgust with France did not prevent Islamists from visiting the ex-*métropole* to shop for video equipment and cassettes.[90]

Given the prominent role of Islamists in the riots, the French already feared, according to Dominique Moïsi, that "religious fundamentalists might take power."[91] Jacques Girardon, in an article entitled "Islamism: If Algeria Tilts," compared Islamist discourse with Le Pen's, labeling both "simplistic and effective."[92] The Islamists had correctly pointed out the French media's sensational spin to their movement in Algeria. For example, the 30 April 1990 issue of *Le Point* used the titles "Holy War Against the State" and "France: State of Emergency" (the latter on the threat of Islamism in the Muslim community in France). Ali Belhadj was referred to as "Savonarola." In 1989, two thousand apprehensive lawyers and jurists and doctors left Algeria for France, provoking French fear of surging waves of emigrating Algerians inundating their shores. The French also feared that Islamism would influence and provoke their Maghribi community, despite estimates that 90 percent of France's three million Muslims "do not actively practice their religion."[93]

The June 1990 Local Elections

French anxieties heightened with the Algerian local elections of 12 June 1990. Shocking many analysts, the Islamists scored a stunning success.[94] The FIS won 32 of 48 *wilayat* while obtaining 54 percent of the popular vote, and gained a majority in the city councils in all major Algerian cities. In all, the FIS took over 853 out of 1,535 councils. By comparison, the

FLN took 14 *wilayat* and 487 local councils with 28 percent of the vote. Several secular parties, notably the FFS, called for a boycott of these elections, which resulted in a lower registered-voter turnout (about 60 percent). The FIS's victory demonstrated the deep dissatisfaction of the public with the FLN, while illustrating, too, the appeal of FIS populism.

Alain Rollat canvassed French political opinion during this time. As he talked with three members of the Front National, one unsurprisingly conjured the specter of massive flight and asserted: "Immigration will end in invasion. . . . they want to make France Algerian." Former prime minister Michel Debré considered the Islamic movement "a menace for France." He feared that "Algiers may become the capital of an anti-French Maghrib." Meanwhile, Jacques Roseau of RECOURS urged French support for Benjedid "to combat sectarianism and dogmatism."[95]

The Arabization Law of December 1990

Though the Information Law of 1989 provided for a general Arabization of publications and public life, the rising pressures of political Islam led to the passage of a thirty-six-article law in December 1990 that aimed to complete the Arabization of the official administration by 5 July 1992 and of higher education by 1997. This law provoked protests, both in Algeria and in France, on the grounds of being unrealistic. About two-thirds of the new press publications in Algeria were in French. Ironically, the FIS began publishing its own francophone journal, *El-Forkane,* the very month after the new law was passed.

The linguistic issue also represented the generational shift in Algeria. Now, after Arabization, most of the young people spoke Arabic as their first language, while those forty and above were solidly French speakers. In 1989 the first completely Arabized class graduated from lycées. As Algeria's spoken dialect differed from the classical Arabic taught in the schools and used in publications and the media, this Arabization represented, in many ways, the imposition of a different language. Some believed that Algeria would be left in a linguistic limbo, with its people lacking proficiency in either language, a "bilingual illiteracy."[96] Although the French government called this an internal affair, it nonetheless was "attentive to everything that affects the use of French in the world."[97] The *beur* media were particularly upset over the law. Indeed, it exemplified how their community was alienated from both countries. Not surprisingly, the law received a hostile reception from SOS-Racisme and France-Plus. According to Georges Marion, "Arabization is above all a battle against French and its cultural references."[98] The law would obviously affect technical and cultural cooperation and technology transfers. Within Algeria, accelerated Arabization particularly threatened the Kabyles in two ways. First, many of them were francophone and, second, Arabization was an affront to their native Amazight languages, Kabyle (Tamazight) and Shawia (and the Tuareg's Tifinag).

The Gulf War

The crisis in the Gulf after President Saddam Hussein seized Kuwait in the summer of 1990 had serious repercussions for France and its relations with the Arab world, especially Algeria. Jean-Pierre Chevènement, the defense minister, worried about huge casualties (estimated at 100,000 on the two sides), while Mitterrand believed that Saddam Hussein had created "a logic for war." As the "architect" of the French-Iraqi special relationship in 1974, Jacques Chirac hesitated to take a firm position. His rivals on the right claimed that Saddam had provided him with large campaign contributions. Mitterrand was left to explain that France had supported Iraq against Iran in the Iran-Iraq War, even though Baghdad started the war, because he feared then that an Iraqi defeat might have opened the whole Arab world to Islamic fundamentalism. At one point during the Iran-Iraq War, France "loaned" Iraq five naval warplanes with deadly Exocet missiles so that the Iraqis could knock out Iran's main Gulf oil-loading station at Kharg Island. The value of the weapons France sold to Iraq was estimated at $30 billion. The reactor destroyed by Israeli bombers in 1981 was one sent by France.[99]

In 1990 France abandoned its support of Iraq. Mitterrand used an essentialist argument to defend France's participation in the United Nations' coalition. He claimed that France had to take an active role; otherwise "she would no longer be able to justify her permanent presence on the Security Council." He added, "She is one of the great powers of the world and must be worthy of her obligations."[100] Mitterrand's commitment to the coalition led by the United States was perceived as anti-Islamic, and fueled the FIS's political and cultural opposition to France. The Algerian government criticized the coalition's military buildup in Saudi Arabia, and President Benjedid eventually embarked on a shuttle diplomacy mission of his own to establish a dialogue between Baghdad and Riyadh.[101] There was talk of a combined French-Algerian peace initiative, a fruitless gesture reminiscent of better collaborative days in the past.[102]

French forces played an important role in the brief campaign against Iraq. Indeed, Mitterrand's approval rating reached 75 percent on his handling of the Gulf Crisis.[103] Nevertheless, Rémy Leveau believed that

France "lost much of its credibility" in the Arab world and the Maghrib because of its participation.[104] Not surprisingly, France was widely denounced in Algeria. Ben Bella reproached France's "crusading mentality."[105] Howard Lafranchi reported that Algeria "snubbed French overtures since the Gulf War's end: Algerians deride France as a once-independent nation that obediently followed the US into battle."[106]

According to correspondent William Echikson, France was experiencing an "existential crisis: given the reunification of Germany and the renaissance of US power in the Gulf." More accurately, France's crisis related to its essentialist self-perception. As Ghassan Salame of the Institut d'Etudes Politiques bluntly stated: "France's position in the world as an independent player is over."[107] During a visit to Algeria immediately before the 1991 parliamentary elections, Foreign Minister Dumas spoke of the need to "de-dramatize the past." Then in an honest and, in view of French essentialist pretensions, highly poignant statement, Dumas declared: "Obviously we cannot do everything in the modern world. France has commitments everywhere in the world, but France also has limited means, however successful its economy and its finances might be."[108]

As parliamentary elections approached, Prime Minister Mouloud Hamrouche reflected on France: "I have a feeling that on the other side of the Mediterranean a wait-and-see stance has been adopted." As for the repercussions of the Gulf conflict on the bilateral relationship, Hamrouche contended: "I think matters have not been going satisfactorily since 1988. The Gulf War had no effect on relations between France and Algeria."[109]

Though the Gulf War distracted Algeria, it did not deter the difficult democratic process. The *Economist* observed: "Algerians have inherited a French logic that induces them to carry things to a conclusion."[110] That conclusion would be convulsive.

The Parliamentary Elections of June 1991 and Their Consequence

The parliamentary elections scheduled for June 1991 were highly controversial. They were eventually postponed owing to violent Islamist protests over the electoral process, especially eleventh-hour gerrymandering measures passed in March and April by the FLN-controlled National Popular Assembly. The FIS called an indefinite nationwide strike beginning on 25 May to protest the electoral laws and the government's failure to schedule presidential elections. On 4 June police forces tried to dislodge Islamists who had occupied several squares in Algiers, which resulted in seventeen deaths by official count. On 5 June a state of siege was again declared and the elections postponed. Sid Ahmed Ghozali, who had been accused of mismanagement as head of SONATRACH but had distinguished himself as an ambassador when given that opportunity by Benjedid, replaced Hamrouche as prime minister. A curfew was imposed. As these events transpired, Mitterrand wistfully wished for "democracy, civil peace, and prosperity" for France's Algerian "neighbor" and "Mediterranean friend."[111]

Attempting to palliate political tempers, Ghozali gave assurances that there would be national legislative elections by the end of 1991. Nevertheless, on 25 June fighting resumed. Abbasi Madani threatened a "holy war" unless the state of siege was lifted. This provoked the government to arrest him and his deputy, Ali Belhadj, on 30 June for threatening state security. The national curfew was lifted on 17 July, but prohibitions on public demonstrations remained in force. In September the FIS leaders Madani and Belhadj insisted on being called political prisoners. This unsettling situation bolstered Robert Mortimer's contention that Algeria's transition to democracy from authoritarianism was "flawed" by the inability "to define the means by which to integrate an opposition force that threatened to subvert the very process of democratization itself."[112]

On 15 October Benjedid announced that the first round of national elections would take place in December. Former foreign minister Claude Cheysson expressed the hope of many in the French political elite who had a practically pathological fear of Islamism: "I am crossing my fingers hoping the fundamentalists won't get into power."[113] Relations between France and Algeria had become inert. In Prime Minister Ghozali's words, the "regard" of France projected an "unhealthy ambiguity." Ghozali correctly pointed out that "France lacks imagination toward Algeria." He also said that "preferential relations . . . are destructive terms which perpetuate ambiguity and which, in the final analysis, do not serve either of our two countries."[114] His anxieties as well as those of his colleagues intensified as the December elections approached.

Meanwhile the French television channel Antenne 2 broadcast the series *Annales Algériens,* a documentary history of the Algerian War (see chapter 10). Repressed memories were rekindled as France and Algeria revisited the brutality of a "war without a name."[115] Ironically, similar violence would soon sweep Algeria once more.

Elections of December 1991 and the Overthrow of Benjedid

With forty-nine parties participating, the first round of these elections gave the FIS an astounding 188 seats, just 28 short of a majority in the APN. The FFS won only 26 seats. Complaints of irregularities aside, the popular will (though only 47.5 percent of the voters) preferred the FIS over the FLN and other "secular parties." About 41 percent abstained. While some analysts contended that the abstention rate vitiated the legitimacy of Algeria's democratic voice, it was in itself a political act signaling dissatisfaction with all sides.[116] The runoff was scheduled for 16 January.

The press response in France to the elections was one of grave concern. *Le Figaro*'s front-page editorial claimed that the Algerians "have skipped from one revolution to another—from Lenin to . . . the ayatollah." *Le Monde* hoped that "sang-froid will prevail."[117]

In economic affairs, the FIS had intimated rather than elaborated a program. Indeed, Abdelkader Hachani, the acting FIS leader during the incarcerations of Abbasi Madani and Ali Belhadj, viewed the recent European Community loan of ECU 400 million as one "made by countries who are enemies of Islam." He also castigated the amended hydrocarbons law as a "transaction of shame."[118] Still, major French investors like Total (CFP), Peugeot, and Renault were reported to be quite calm about these potentially dislocating circumstances.[119]

As the second round approached, the French political elite articulated divided opinions. Charles Pasqua correlated an Islamist victory with a defeat for human rights which "would revise" bilateral cooperation. On the other hand, Jacques Delors envisioned cooperation between an Islamist Algeria and Europe. Bernard Kouchner pointed out that "all [Islamisms] are not the same" and that "Algeria is not Iran."[120] The Foreign Ministry was prudent and sanguine. A spokesman affirmed that France "supports democracy everywhere in the world" and was particularly pleased that "it was possible to hold a democratic vote for the first time since independence" for a parliament in Algeria. "Whatever the choice of the Algerian people, the relations which unite them with the French people are so strong in every area that they will persist."[121] It was generally agreed that Algeria was on the verge of a seminal event in its history. The impact could be dangerous and even devastating.

The emigrant community was not mobilized in the first round of voting. According to Azouz Begag, the FIS feared its secularism while the FLN government feared the strength of the community's Kabyle population, which could lend support to the opposition FFS and RCD. Amo Ferhati, president of the Association Espace Intégration de Lille and a prominent *beur*, worried that Algeria would not be able to progress without a secular democracy. He added: "If the Algerians renounce the French language, the flight of brains and capital is going to accelerate." Others couched this seminal change in existential terms. One student equated the

FIS's success to "the emergence of a generation that refuses to identify itself with materialist philosophy and values the principles decreed by the Prophet as highly as, if not more than, French Napoleonic or secular laws (*lois . . . à la française*)." Sadek Sallem, a prominent writer, had trouble understanding France's fear of an Islamist victory: "Algeria is not Iran and the FIS is itself very divided between pragmatic and extremist tendencies."[122] Nevertheless, Algeria's democratic odyssey left it "between Charybdis and Scylla," according to Jacques Girardon. To deny the Islamists victory would certainly mean "rioting."[123]

The expected FIS victory in the January 1992 second round provoked a coup against the administration of President Benjedid on 11 January by alarmed military and civilian elites. According to Robert Mortimer, "the military, one of the least 'Arabized' sectors of Algerian society, [with] many of its top officers having been trained in the French army," feared for its "institutional autonomy."[124] Benjedid, who was apparently prepared for a "cohabitation" with the FIS, was forced to resign.[125]

On Algerian television, a weary Benjedid described his "resignation" as "a sacrifice on my part in the interest of the stability of the nation."[126] The army was deployed in urban areas. The coup was conducted by an Haut Conseil de Sécurité (HCS), a constitutional but obscure organ. On 14 January an improvised Haut Comité d'Etat (HCE) took over Algeria. The selection of longtime exiled dissident Mohamed Boudiaf, one of the nine "historic chiefs" of the FLN, to be the HCE's collegial president linked the revolutionary past with what would increasingly be the revolutionary present.

France's Response to the Coup

The coup relieved the international community, especially France. But was France complicit in the coup? Many observers believed that it was. Ambassador Jean Audibert had urged President Benjedid to delay the elections. The first round was poorly administered. For example, not all the voting cards were issued, and a million were not even available. Audibert urged Paris to stop the election, but Mitterrand refused, hoping that Benjedid would survive the crisis. According to Julius Friend, Mitterrand "thought France would have little if any influence in Algeria or any right to a voice."[127]

French officials divided into three camps or "currents." One believed for ideological reasons that the democratic process should be continued, whatever the result. Another contended that a FIS government would be economically liberal compared with the more centralist "Jacobin-like"

FLN establishment. Another group feared that if the FIS did win, Islamism would proliferate politically in North Africa and spill across the Mediterranean to southern Europe.[128] What is certain is that France remained immobile. Foreign Minister Dumas referred publicly to Benjedid's resignation as "an important event of significant consequence." He also equivocally stated that "France reaffirms its solidarity with the Algerian people to which it has never ceased to give its support."[129]

On 12 January, Edouard Balladur of the opposition right commented that France should begin "reconsidering or adapting its cooperation," particularly "if things should evolve in a way contrary to our convictions and interests." Gérard Fuchs of the Socialist Party described France's dilemma concerning Algeria: "A victory of the FIS . . . would risk leading to changes that would be dangerous to society. But installation of a military regime, far from doing away with the dangers, would create an explosive situation."[130] Gérard Longuet of the Parti Républicain concluded that he preferred "democracy under the control of the army" in Algeria. A relieved Claude Cheysson concurred that the army "has decided to risk democracy (jouer la démocratie)." Jacques Roseau of RECOURS-France believed that the coup represented Algeria's chance "to save democracy" from "totalitarian" Islamism.

On the other hand, Jean-Marie Le Pen protested the end of the democratic process in Algeria and "formally opposed" welcoming political refugees to France. In a portentous assessment, Le Pen feared "troubles, confrontations, and perhaps a civil war" with the possibility of "repercussions in all of Europe and perhaps even in France." He thought that the FIS could have been amenable "to see returned to them the [emigrant] Algerians." Former President Giscard d'Estaing called the coup "antidemocratic" and "dangerous." He advised that France keep its "vigilance" toward Algeria and its new leaders. Jacques Chirac hoped that the new regime would "undertake as soon as possible the economic, political and social reforms that the Algerian people have waited too long for." He added: "It is obviously in France's interest that Algeria become as soon as possible a great modern democracy, endowed with a sound liberal economy."[131]

President Mitterrand responded on 14 January that "Algerian leaders must at the earliest possible moment pick up again the threads of democratic life." The takeover was "abnormal, to say the least."[132] To the London-based Saudi newspaper al-Hayat he reaffirmed that "France is profoundly attached to the maintenance and development of these relations, in keeping with its principles that it considers essential." This included "progress toward democracy and respect for human rights."[133] His statements stood starkly against the backdrop of arrests and detention camps being set up quickly in the Sahara. Mitterrand's comments were condemned in Algeria as "condescending" and "unacceptable." *Le Monde* reported that in Algerian circles the belief was that if the election had not been stopped, there would have been civil war. The Algerian press targeted French "alarmists and paternalists."[134]

Michel Rocard said that some of his Arab friends supported the coup. It was his belief that "we, with our culture of human rights, we think that an interruption of a democratic process is inevitably dangerous." Yet he also commented that Algeria had not reached "a certain democratic level" permitting democratic resolutions. He spoke of how his "friend" Abdelhamid Brahimi, the former prime minister, several months before the coup, attempted to persuade the FIS to "de-fanaticize" itself. Rocard did not view the FIS as "Khomeinist" and recognized that "many of the Islamists are francophone." Rocard also expressed his concern for women's rights. He said: "It is necessary to take into account the reality of Algeria's present government, even if the conditions of its seizing power were unacceptable." He viewed the FIS as a "momentary expression of an Algerian reality," a protest against "an inefficient regime, dominated by the military, and largely corrupt." He expected that between Ait Ahmed's FFS and the FIS "other ways will open."[135]

The Coup and France's Culpability

How responsible was France for the coup? There were certainly ties between the coup leaders and France. Many of the army's officers were French-trained and francophone. It was reported that the Algerian interior minister, General Larbi Belkheir, was at the Elysée Palace on 10 January and that there had been ongoing consultations with officials fearful of an Islamist takeover.[136] Moreover, France may have been worried about Algeria's nuclear weapon potential. *Libération* reported on 20 January that Paris had stepped up intelligence activities in the country.[137] Could this have contributed to French complicity in the coup?

Whether French involvement was direct or indirect, France, like Algeria, faced a no-win situation. An Islamist victory posed obvious threats to France's interests (including the stability of friendly Maghribi neighbors Morocco and Tunisia) and its cultural legacy, a particularly sensitive concern. The coup was an ideological repudiation of democracy and simply illegitimate, but it also may have stemmed a massive new *exode* by Algerians fearful of an Islamist victory. These dialectical rationales neutralized and immobilized French policy. Pierre Lafrance, the director of the North Africa–Middle East department of the Quai d'Orsay, was dispatched to Algeria to talk with the new leaders, but contacted the FIS as well. His activities symbolized France's quandary.

The sudden suspension of the electoral process catalyzed a conflict by polarizing political foes. A brutal, catastrophic violence, marked by barbarity and atrocity, devastated Algeria and even extended to France. This new "war without a name," yet another transformation of postcolonial relations, plunged the relationship into the fury of *fitna*.

8

The *Fitna*, 1992–1994

From the Annulment of the Parliamentary Elections to the Air France Hijacking

> Our big error in the past few years was that we decided we wanted de-
> mocracy, political pluralism, and a free press without specifying why
> we wanted them. Where is the society that we are building? We must
> agree on the basic attributes of such a society. If we disagree on the
> form of the society we want or we discuss establishing two different so-
> cieties, this will lead to civil war.
> **Lakhdar Brahimi, February 1992**

> This is madness and despair.
> **François Mitterrand, August 1994**

Like most Arabic words, *fitna* has multiple meanings depending on the
context. It can mean dissension, disorder, discord, temptation, trial, cap-
tivation, ordeal, or civil conflict. All of these definitions have been applicable in Algeria since President Benjedid's resignation and the cancellation
of national elections by the Haut Conseil de Sécurité (HCS) in January
1992. The agony of this "interminable nightmare" has wracked a profoundly suffering Algeria with unimaginable savageries and atrocities. It
has left France intermittently paralyzed, repeatedly shocked by the *fitna*'s
violence across the Mediterranean and, eventually, within its own shores
and cities. Memories of the War of Independence have haunted this period
with bizarre recastings of protagonists, antagonists, absurdities, nihilisms.
In many ways, this stage of the bilateral relationship, covered in this chapter and the next, illustrates how history may be not cyclical but "elliptical," not a replication but a reformulated recurrence impelled by unresolved historical questions. As the *fitna* raged, this became increasingly
obvious.

The Islamists wished to restore state and soul, mirroring the FLN's
proclaimed objective of 1 November 1954. From the perspectives of the
FIS and its offshoots, the generation of 1 November had failed to

decolonize completely. The FLN and the army were so deeply infused with foreign and particularly French values that they perpetuated an inauthentic culture antithetical to Algeria's fundamental Islamic values. That tainted legacy had to be purged and the existential praxis pursued at deeper levels of national identity to create a genuine *umma* (Islamic society/nation). The course of the *fitna* evoked the revolutionary past: large-scale military sweeps, fratricidal terror, torture, indiscriminate and brutal retaliation against communities for their "collective responsibility," vain searches for *interlocuteurs valables,* an unavailing policy of cease-fire before negotiation, elections to confer legitimacy, bombings in the ex-*métropole.*

Though France continued its vital direct and indirect economic assistance, political immobilism characterized its governments on the right and the left. The effort to insulate and isolate France from the *fitna* prevented it from playing a contributory, perhaps decisive, role in resolving the terrible conflict. When occasional French initiatives were presented, they were not well planned or pursued and usually succeeded only in alienating the contesting parties. The seemingly insolvable Algerian conflict produced less a passivity than a quiet despair, leaving French policy ambivalent and adrift.

The Ordering Frameworks and the *Fitna*

The *fitna* transformed the postcolonial era and its accustomed political discourses, practices, and strategies. It acted as a tumultuous, tortuous "trial" for Algeria and for France too, dismantling the familiar essentialist-existentialist framework of their relationship and disorienting the reception and perception of the other's knowledge, power, and identity. Thus the crisis was not only political, social, and economic but also epistemological. In Foucauldian terms, this meant an "epistemic shift" or, perhaps more applicable here, an epistemic drift. Complicating this historical discontinuity, this new transformation of relations, were concurrent geopolitical dislocations that had direct and indirect bilateral consequences.

France's Changing Essentialism and the *Fitna*

France's self-perceived unique national qualities of grandeur and independence, i.e., its essentialist identity as expressed in differing degrees by de Gaulle's globalism, Pompidou's Mediterranean policy, Giscard's *mondial-*

isme, and Mitterrand's "codevelopment," projected an important if over-rated international influence during relatively unchanging historical conditions. France presented itself as an unimpeded power able to act unilaterally. As Steven Philip Kramer pointed out, "Unlike the other nations of postwar Western Europe, France continued to conceive of itself almost entirely in traditional nation-state terms."[1] The rapid global, continental, and regional geopolitical changes of the late 1980s and early 1990s, including Algeria's destabilization, forced France to adapt its essentialism as well as reformulate its policies.

The sudden decline of Soviet will and power catalyzed the disintegration of the satellite system and subsequently permitted German reunification in 1991. Though President Mitterrand had strongly supported the Paris-Bonn alliance, initially established in 1963 by de Gaulle, his support for Germany's inevitable reintegration was tempered by the fear that a new Reich would dominate Europe and expose a now genuinely inferior France. This drew France closer to the protective federal European Community, soon to be the European Union. For example, French signing and support for the Maastricht Treaty (receiving unenthusiastic endorsement in a September 1992 referendum) was viewed as a strategic means to control Germany's potential by submerging the Deutschemark into a single European currency, introduced in January 1999 as the European Monetary Union's "euro." A more pronounced interdependence in an increasingly integrated Europe certainly threatened France's political and cultural identity. But changing historical realities necessitated policy shifts and, with them, a rethinking of French essentialism. Instead of "France alone," it would now be "France among" its continental neighbors, aspiring to play a leading role in the European Union. To be sure, this still involved pursuing unilateral traditional grandeur and certainly independence. Those values now had to be imagined and implemented through multilateral instruments.[2]

The disappearance of the Soviet Union also terminated France's vaunted but now anachronistic "third way," offered as an alternative course between the bipolar domination of the superpowers. The American success in the Cold War now provoked a new fear that this hegemon could overwhelm France, Europe, and the world by its political, economic, technological, and cultural predominance. France's participation in the Gulf War had symbolically reaffirmed its world power status. Its engagements in peacekeeping operations (admirable in Yugoslavia but disastrous in Rwanda) were also illustrations of the imperative to project a global presence. Even international protests over its atomic testing in 1995–96 could be endured if the result was to remind the world of France's presence and power.

Asia, as well as the United States, presented itself as a formidable economic competitor (even with its infectious recessions of the late 1990s). This too necessitated a multilateral European rather than a unilateral French response. To do its part, the French economy, plagued by double-digit unemployment and bloated state enterprises, needed to be transformed. Though the surprising strength of the labor movement, displayed in nationwide strikes in the mid-1990s, forced some tactical reappraisals, the decision to integrate the French economy with its European neighbors' necessitated budgetary reassessments, especially with regard to Africa.

It was announced in 1993 that the franc zone's monetary unit, the CFA (Communauté Financière Africaine), would no longer be subsidized by the French government at fixed parity with the franc, as it had been since 1948. This led in 1994 to the CFA's devaluation. Further, economies in the military sector cut French forces deployed in Africa. As France reduced its commitments in Africa, Hubert Védrine euphemistically called it "a modernization of our presence."[3] The benevolent paternalism of the post-colonial period seemed over, along with France's exclusive regional and arguably neocolonial privileges. Still, this was not total abandonment, since France, as it would do with Algeria, championed African financial assistance before international agencies.

The *fitna* forced France to confront the complexities of its colonial legacies and postcolonial policies in Algeria. No longer the country used to amplify French grandeur and independence before the Third World, it still provided opportunities for France to test its influence in a rapidly changing world. France had preferred unilateral or bilateral initiatives in its pre-1992 relations with Algeria. Now by using multilateral means—the IMF, the European Union, the Paris and London Clubs—France could have its interests served in North Africa (and among the ex–franc zone countries). Though its intimate historical relationship with Algeria posed severe political problems that limited its options and produced policy ambivalence, France still prided itself on being regarded internationally as best qualified to deal with the *fitna*. There was a certain prestige to be gained, despite the many risks, if the *fitna* could be resolved with decisive or recognizable French assistance.

Economically, Algeria's strategic importance, especially its hydrocarbons production and potential, remained a powerful incentive to maintain strong French links. Financial credits ensured market shares and profits for hundreds of French companies. Algerian liberalization of the secure hydrocarbons sector offered new opportunities. Total (CFP) and GDF were well placed to take advantage of them. At a time of economic global-ization, Algeria offered these companies opportunities to modernize and adapt their operations to the increasingly competitive environment.

The continuing support to Algeria cannot be explained simply as calcu-lated political and economic strategies. A deontological need persisted to perpetuate a presence in Algeria, even if circumscribed, as a matter of historical obligation as well as prestige. Algeria remained a bilateral means to a multilateral end. Instead of impressing the Third World, France could still portray itself internationally as an imaginative and influential power, as it redefined its role and its essentialist values in the face of new and challenging geopolitical realities. But that very direct or indirect French presence, whether intrusive or innocuous, posed existential prob-lems for a severely suffering Algeria.[4]

Algeria's Existentialism and the *Fitna*

The *fitna* represented a terrifying new chapter in Algeria's existential quest for national restoration and self-realization. Fundamentally, it was a result of the failure of political elites, dating back to the colonial period, to define and to institutionalize an inclusive, consensual national identity. The "vir-tual freedom" of the 1988–91 period vividly projected a vital multi-cultural society, but also revealed a society filled with potentially convul-sive dialectical contradictions and reformulated antagonisms—Islamist/secularist, arabophone/francophone, civilian/military, Berber/Arab, so-cialist/liberal, patriarchal men/"liberated" women. These apparently ir-reconcilable rivalries implicitly involved an imagination of independent Algeria. Democracy and pluralism threatened the corrupt, socially privi-leged, and anachronistic FLN establishment, tied historically to a political and social ideology now internationally recognized as failing—and threat-ened too the increasingly intolerant factions within the Islamist opposi-tion. The growth of desperation and extremism doomed an open, "trans-parent" democratic process.

As the *fitna* fomented its terror, Foreign Minister Lakhdar Brahimi, who had opposed parliamentary elections in December 1991, astutely commented: "I believe that one mistake we made was that we agreed to a democracy without specifying what type of democracy we were agreeing to. We did not agree on the identity of the society that we wanted to establish." He advised: "What we have to do now, and what we should have done before, is to build a single society. We might differ over some points but I assure you that we all agree on the general framework of the society that we want."[5] Nevertheless, in March the alienated but still powerful FIS was officially disbanded by the civilian-military leadership that had seized control of the government from President Benjedid. This terminated any viable opportunity to discuss and define that fundamentally existential question: a social-political "framework." Eventually, escalating assaults by both sides prevented genuine dialogue and widened political polarities.

Fouad Ajami correctly perceived the *fitna* as "a cultural war, cruel and ferocious[,] over the very soul and definition of Algeria."[6] The last Algerian government that genuinely understood the serious existential crisis of the country was the short-lived presidency of Mohamed Boudiaf. After that, factionalism and fanaticism swept the country up in a vortex of violence, suffering and sorrow. Surviving the *fitna* became more important than resolving it.

The Boudiaf Presidency, January–June 1992

As expected, the FIS (as well as the FLN and FFS) condemned the HCS's actions which deprived the Islamists of their expected electoral victory. Abdelkader Hachani, in charge of the FIS's Provisional Executive, warned soon after the coup and the cancellation of the elections that a battle was brewing between "the people, their religion and Algeria on one side, and colonialism and its lackeys on the other."[7] Clearly, the FIS viewed the HCE as a product of French influence. Hachani had warned FIS adherents to "prepare themselves for any eventuality" and called for "the Algerian people to arm themselves with vigilance and prudence."[8] A "dialectic of violence" was already posited with the organized attack at Guemmar near el Oued that killed three border guards on 29 November 1991.[9] The first killing after the coup occurred on 19 January and triggered a murderous momentum culminating in an unremitting civil war and the deaths of tens of thousands of Algerians. The HCE's intensive crackdown included the arrest of Hachani on 22 January. In early February, a group known as the Faithful to the Sermon declared a jihad and referred to the struggle as a continuation of the War of Independence.[10] What was at stake now was not only Algerian democracy but the very perception of the country's history. The *fitna* would reach profound existential levels.

The military and civilian elites who deposed Benjedid asked Mohamed Boudiaf, a "historic chief" of the FLN who had been in Moroccan exile since 1963, to head the HCE. Boudiaf agreed, but insisted that by no means would he be merely an anachronistic, symbolic presence linking the HCE with a purer revolutionary past. He ardently felt that it was his duty to lead Algeria on a different path, and repeatedly proclaimed that the HCS/HCE had saved the country.[11] He devoted considerable energy to this enormous endeavor, but encountered insurmountable obstacles that would cost him his life.

As the HCE secured its power, it rounded up thousands of Islamists and herded them into Saharan detention camps. Boudiaf reported six thousand detainees; Amnesty International put the figure at nine thousand. Concurrently, violence against the regime began its inexorable escalation. A series of university uprisings in February and March in Algiers and Blida, followed by Batna, Annaba and Sétif, underscored youth's continuing dissatisfaction. A year-long state of emergency was proclaimed on 9 February. The HCE suspended and dissolved the FIS and seized control of the organization's headquarters in Algiers. The party was banned on 4 March. Human rights activist Ali Yahia Abdenour called this "a serious mistake" that "could lead to all kinds of excesses."[12] By the end of the year the government had dissolved the popular communal assemblies and regional assemblies associated with the FIS's electoral successes in June 1990.

One of Boudiaf's chief preoccupations was the assertion of the HCE's credibility and legitimacy. On 16 February he announced a general economic program to stabilize the economy. This program consisted not of particulars but of general proposals—controlling liberalization, assistance to the poorest parts of the country, protection of state enterprises, and infrastructure development.[13] In its effort to project a positive image, the HCE appointed a sixty-member council, the Conseil Consultatif National (CCN) in April 1992 to advise the collective executive leadership. To his credit, Boudiaf recognized that Algeria's crisis was rooted in a failure to articulate an inclusive, unifying identity. At the installation of the CCN, he spoke of Algeria's existential predicament or "identity crisis." Algeria had been "suspended . . . between socialism and capitalism . . . between the East and the West, between the French and Arabic languages, between the Arab and the Berber, between tradition and modernity." He concluded: "The Algerian must stop imitating. We must break out from all complexes and be ourselves. . . . That is the principal meaning of 1 November [1954]: first be Algerian."[14] In May Boudiaf announced the formation of a new political party, the Rassemblement Patriotique National (RPN), to lend political backing and legitimacy to his initiatives. He also viewed the RPN as a means to coalesce national consensus as well as to confront political opposition.

Relations between the HCE and France were strained. Boudiaf praised the individual support of Raymond Barre, Jacques Delors, and Claude Cheysson, but he remained very dissatisfied with the official French reaction to his government.[15] Mitterrand emphasized that "France is deeply attached to the maintenance and development of relations," but he conditioned those relations on "progress toward democracy and respect for human rights."[16] The French governments of the left and the right of this period were understandably torn. While they were relieved that "secular" elites had thwarted an Islamist takeover, the illegitimacy of the regime and its annulment of a democratic process, even if flawed, presented an ideological and political dilemma. Whether France had played a direct or an indirect role in the events of early January, the consequences immobilized the existing French government and its successors.

Though France was politically ambivalent, it consistently provided Algeria with indispensable economic support. From Boudiaf's brief rule to this day, financial disaster was constantly averted by timely French intervention. For example, the French brokered the 4 March 1992 agreement with a consortium of banks led by the Crédit Lyonnais to "reprofile" Algeria's $25 billion debt, which gave the country some short-term financial relief ($1.45 billion) and "creditworthiness," and saved it from rescheduling.[17] Concurrently, Foreign Minister Lakhdar Brahimi arrived in Paris, though the Quai d'Orsay carefully noted that he came at his own request. Brahimi briefed the government and offered a "message of friendship and cooperation" from the HCE. He also optimistically declared: "There is no misunderstanding between France and Algeria."[18]

On 3 June the minister of agriculture and forests, Louis Mermaz, became the first member of the French government to visit Algeria after the cancellation of the January elections. Mermaz predicted that French-Algerian relations were "going to be more active than ever."[19] He was followed in July by Pierre Bérégovoy, the finance minister, who activated export credits that provided Algeria with FF 4 billion to succeed the original 1989 agreement. President Boudiaf was expected to visit Paris to negotiate a bilateral refinancing of the FF 33 billion COFACE export credits.[20]

Shocking Algeria and the international community, President Boudiaf was gunned down on 29 June, while delivering a speech in Annaba, by a security guard with apparent Islamist tendencies. To Martin Stone and other analysts, Boudiaf's death resulted from his assault on "government corruption rather than his opposition to the Islamists."[21] By the end of the year, Islamists were officially incriminated, but the evidence was incomplete and unconvincing. Indeed, Boudiaf was considered a threat to powerful military factions who had simply underestimated the independence and energy of the old "Ramses-like" revolutionary. In the popular view, Boudiaf was a political martyr, and annual commemorations are held on the date of his death. The assassination marked the beginning of anarchy and finally full-blown civil war. It also pointed up the intrinsic difficulty in interpreting Algerian affairs. Journalists and analysts increasingly dealt with dissimulation rather than information.

On 2 July Ali Kafi, a member of the HCE, succeeded Boudiaf as president. Kafi lacked Boudiaf's charisma, energy, and vision, and was more a figurehead and caretaker. Other governmental changes included the HCE's appointment on 8 July of Belaid Abdesselam, once the powerful minister of industry and energy under Boumedienne, to replace Ahmed Ghozali as prime minister. Ghozali was then appointed ambassador to France on 21 July.[22]

Though on 15 July the incarcerated FIS leaders Abbasi Madani and Ali Belhadj received relatively mild twelve-year prison sentences for conspiring against the state, the *fitna* continued its inexorable, explosive course. Indeed, their incarceration removed possible interlocutors and intensified the radicalization of the Islamist movement.[23] On 26 August a bomb exploded at Algiers's Boumedienne Airport near the Air France check-in, leaving nine dead and many wounded. A second bomb detonated at the Air France office in Algiers, while another device found at the Swissair office was defused. FIS sympathizers were blamed for the blasts. By the end of 1992, government security forces had suffered hundreds of deaths as a consequence of the Islamist insurgency.

As the violence relentlessly tormented the nation, the civil and political rights acquired by Algerian citizens between 1989 and 1991 eroded, with temporary suspension of freedom of the press, increasingly close monitoring of publications, and revocation of the right of appeal for acts of terror.[24] On 10 January 1993 the first executions for political crimes took place. Inevitably, the HCE announced on 7 February the extension of the state of emergency.

Greater French Attention toward Algeria

The rapid changess of 1992 created a rift in the bilateral relationship. The political and ideological dilemma posed by the coup produced estrangement, if not guilt, among French officials, especially those who had been resigned to the possibility of a FIS government. Indeed, there was a certain fatalism regarding the "ineluctability" of political Islamism. Algeria's future was hardly as "readable" as before. This attitude effected a listlessness in French policy.

From Algiers's perspective, Paris's passive view of the alarming violence signaled a suspicious lack of support. Bernard Kouchner, the minister of health, had bluntly commented in May 1992 that "the present [Algerian] government was born of a coup d'état."[25] France criticized Algeria for its "lack of democracy" but ignored the antidemocratic activities of its Maghribi neighbors, Morocco and Tunisia. Concerning Algeria's foreign debt, France preferred rescheduling rather than the Algerian-favored spreading out of repayments. As Algeria's largest creditor, holding loans calculated at about $6 billion out of a foreign debt of $25 billion, France, to protect its investments, wanted Algeria's financial burden to be shared and resolved by multilateral rather than bilateral negotiation and funding. This reflected how France's foreign policy was increasingly based on interdependence rather than independence.

Unmistakably significant was the snubbing of Ambassador Ghozali, the former prime minister, who had to wait months to present his credentials. Foreign Minister Lakhdar Brahimi stated the obvious: "Relations between Algeria and France have never been, and will not for a long time be, 'normal.'"[26]

Nevertheless, the fearful specter of Algeria's political and economic disintegration, with massive emigration like the exodus of the *pieds-noirs* in 1962, which could be exploited by the right in the upcoming March elections, impelled the Socialist government to reassess its inert Algerian policy.

Foreign Minister Roland Dumas arrived in Algeria on 8 January 1993 calling for the inauguration of "a new era" and the framing of a "partnership" with Algeria. He spoke of "old and deep bonds" and added: "As far as I am concerned, I will try to give fresh momentum to the consolidation of relations in all fields."[27] In a message handed by Dumas to President Ali Kafi in Algiers on 9 January, President Mitterrand called for "an open and confident political and economic dialogue."[28] Dumas gave an earnest of French intentions by announcing the opening of a FF 4–5 billion credit line and his resolve to solidify financial cooperation. He also invited Prime Minister Abdesselam to visit France in February.

Financial and Commercial Cooperation: The Sapin Template

On 13 February, several days before Abdesselam's expected arrival in Paris, Finance Minister Michel Sapin signed a financial protocol worth FF 6 billion in aid and trade credits for Algeria in 1993. One billion francs were earmarked for balance-of-payments aid and for the purchase of capital equipment. Five billion francs were in medium-term trade credits. France included another FF 100 million for joint projects in loans from the Caisse Française de Développement (CFD), the lending concessionary agency that succeeded the CCCE. Though there was no resolution of the debt burden through bilateral reprofiling, Sapin affirmed that France was "ready to accompany Algeria in its dialogue with international organizations so as to have Algerian specificities taken into account."[29] This publicly signaled that France would serve as Algeria's advocate before multilateral lending organizations. To Sapin, French financial help represented "a resumption of dialogue. . . . This difficulty in achieving democracy had at one time created a sort of interruption of dialogue between France and Algeria. That dialogue has resumed . . . and it has to resume in the economic field particularly."[30] The Sapin protocol served as a model for French financial cooperation during the *fitna,* with credits consistently set at the FF 5–6 billion level.

The package of financial cooperation tied to commercial credits also aimed to increase bilateral trade. Algeria's exports, especially the hydrocarbons that accounted for 96 percent of its exports to France, had declined by about 17 percent in the previous year. French exports had slipped by about FF 500 million.[31] The "aid" of commercial credits had particular advantages for France, since it secured Algerian markets for French exporters who were worried over Algeria's domestic upheaval as well as austerity plans to limit imports. But despite the mutual advantages, problems soon developed. By November the Algerian Ministry of the Economy protested: "Some of the [French] credits making up this six-

Table 8.1. French Trade with Algeria, 1991–1994 (in millions of French francs)

	1991	1992	1993	1994
French exports	12,273	11,780.5	11,896.6	13,355.5
French imports	11,678	9,961.4	7,784.1	8,283.7
Balance	595	1,819.1	4,112.5	5,071.8

Source: 1991 data—EIU, *CR*; 1992 data—*Maghreb Séléction*; 1993 and 1994 data—French Customs statistics and *Maghreb Séléction*.

billion-franc package are subject to very difficult conditions and procedures which makes them very slow [to activate]."[32] In many ways, French
credits seemed reminiscent of the *aide liée* of the 1960s. To Islamists, the
aid/credits sustained the battered Algerian economy and thereby fortified
the government they were trying to pull down.

Prime Minister Abdesselam in Paris

The financial cooperation agreement buoyed Abdesselam as he arrived in
Paris for a concentrated series of meetings. Where he had been effortlessly
self-assured during his much publicized visit in November 1974, Abdesselam now needed to make a good impression in order to secure political
support and convince his hosts of his wish to reestablish an "exemplary
cooperation."[33] He met with the leaders of the left and the right, the latter
expected to win the elections in March, as well as members of the French
patronat. *El-Moudjahid* noted with satisfaction that Prime Minister Abdesselam stayed in the same hotel as President George Bush: "The French
wish to prove already that the visit of an Algerian personality at this level
is not a commonplace event." Though it was hardly the inauguration of an
"era of partnership," as *El-Moudjahid* wistfully proclaimed, Dumas assured Abdesselam that "France wishes a strong and prosperous Algeria."[34] The Quai d'Orsay said, "This visit demonstrates that the misunderstandings between our two countries are a thing of the past, and is the
most tangible proof that political relations with Algeria have been resumed."[35] *El-Watan* spoke of "normalization," but wondered what kind
of normalized relations: those that are warmer "after a period of chill and
incomprehension [or] just simply normal."[36] Actually, relations became
neither warm and "comprehensible" nor normal; instead, they soon returned to their immobile, suspensive state. The prime minister's visit
ended by being symbolic rather than substantive, but it confirmed France's
recognition, even if reluctant, that it had to concern itself with Algeria's
worsening internal condition.

Algeria's Violence Intensifies

Abdesselam's failing austerity program, compounded by slumping hydrocarbons prices, steeply tilted Algeria's declining economy. Not surprisingly, given his Boumediennist past, Abdesselam adamantly refused to
negotiate with the IMF. His general ineffectiveness incited incessant criticism by the still legalized political parties, newspapers, and trade unions.
In acute opposition to the prime minister, the HCE declared its intention
in May to continue economic liberalization and the redemocratization of

Algeria through dialogue with acceptable political parties. A referendum was also planned for the end of the year. In June the HCE announced its plans for a presidential transition—its own dissolution through the establishment of a new executive, and eventually elections on all levels.

Meanwhile, sensational acts of violence rocked the nation. On 13 February the powerful and influential defense minister, Khaled Nezzar, narrowly escaped a bombing. Omar Belhoucet, the respected editor of *El-Watan,* was targeted but missed being assassinated on 17 May. On the other hand, Tahar Djaout, the esteemed novelist, poet, and cofounder of the popular weekly journal *Ruptures,* was mortally wounded on 26 May.[37] Other journalists were assassinated in July and August, including Abdelhammid Benmenni, editor of *Algérie Actualité.* Then on 21 August former prime minister Kasdi Merbah was ambushed and killed near Algiers along with one of his sons, his chauffeur, and a bodyguard. His death, like that of President Boudiaf, was initially blamed on Islamists, but Merbah had also alienated factions within the government or, as it was increasingly called, the Pouvoir (power establishment).[38] On 20 August the HCE removed Abdesselam and appointed the admired diplomat and Evian veteran Redha Malek, who had replaced the capable Lakhdar Brahimi as foreign minister on 3 February.

The Emergence of the GIA and the Targeting of French Citizens

In France, the right's landslide victory in March inaugurated the conservative government of Edouard Balladur and another political "cohabitation" with the Socialist president Mitterrand. Balladur's government would exemplify the torn and ambivalent French position of commitment to Algeria's welfare, but not necessarily to an HCE government unable to stabilize the domestic situation and restore the democratic process.

At first the Balladur government seemed amenable to closer relations with Algeria, especially in security matters. After discussions with Foreign Minister Redha Malek, his counterpart Alain Juppé pledged French support against "extremism and fundamentalism" on 18 June, the first time France evinced a willingness to help Algeria against the Islamists. Major-General Mohamed Touati, an influential politico-military figure, also conferred with French officials in mid-June in Paris.[39] But deteriorating conditions and a lack of redemocratization led to renewed criticism of Algiers's conduct. On 18 August Juppé declared, "The status quo is untenable," and called on the HCE to seek "political consultation with all democratic forces."[40] Adding to French inquietude was the increased radicalization of the Islamist insurgency, as there emerged in September a new organization known as the Groupe Islamique Armé (GIA). The adherents of this Armed Islamic Group included "Afghans," Algerians who had fought or trained with the *mujahidin* in war-ravaged Afghanistan. The GIA would be led by a variety of Islamists, eventually portraying themselves as caliphal "emirs," who viewed France as the chief enemy propping up an illegitimate, apostate regime.

Kidnappings and Crackdowns

A militant Algerian Islamist, denied his seat in the new National Assembly by the cancellation of the parliamentary elections, had warned in May 1993: "Let countries, like France, that continue to do business with this regime be warned that they must cut their ties. We are capable of carrying violence beyond our own borders, even to Paris."[41] This menace soon became a terrible reality.

On 21 September the bodies of two kidnapped French surveyors, apparent victims of Islamist extremists identified as the United Companions of the Jihad, were discovered near Sidi-Bel-Abbès.[42] Then on 24 October the GIA abducted three French diplomats, Jean-Claude and Michèle Thévenot and Alain Freissier, outside their consulate in Algiers. With the diplomats still missing, President Mitterrand during a television interview on 26 October considered aloud the repatriation of all French citizens. These numbered about five hundred diplomatic and cultural representatives, a thousand teachers and technicians (*coopérants*), five thousand other French nationals, and some seventy thousand dual citizenship holders. With the ominous revolutionary anniversary of 1 November looming, a French Foreign Ministry spokesman announced that "it would seem timely that families who so wish should return."[43] GDF announced a recall and offered employees scheduled for Algerian assignments the opportunity to change.[44] Giscard, now chairman of the National Assembly's Foreign Affairs Committee, stated that the killings and kidnappings of French citizens were "a testimony to the serious degradation of the internal situation in Algeria." He warned, however, that "each country handles its own affairs, and we should therefore not interfere in internal Algerian matters."[45] Though the diplomats were found and freed at the end of October, Madame Thévenot carried a communiqué from the GIA that described the recent killings of foreigners as "only a drop of water in the ocean of an armed jihad."[46] The GIA set 1 December as a deadline for the evacuation of foreigners from Algeria. It was a clear message for France and other nations to distance themselves from the Algerian government.[47]

Foreign Minister Juppé asserted that there would be "no compromise with those who use violence and terrorism, and who spread anti-French ideas," but he also restated dissatisfaction with the HCE and the Malek government: "We do not support such and such a government. We support the Algerian people, and we support stability in Algeria, because it is in our interests. . . . There must be reforms, there must be democratic dialogue."[48] The expanding violence in Algeria alarmed the French. Writing in *Le Quotidien de Paris* on 5 November, Philippe Marcovici feared that Algerian unrest and violence could "also threaten civil peace in France" since "history still links France and Algeria indissolubly."[49] Gérard Dupuy predicted in *Libération* on 10 November that "Franco-Algerian relations are fated to become increasingly explosive as the situation beyond the Mediterranean—in which civil war is, if not inevitable, at least likely—prolongs itself." He anticipated that "for a certain time, it is therefore necessary to become accustomed to the fact that France's 'Algeria' policy will be dictated, not by the search for the best solution, but for the least bad one."[50]

On 9 November the Balladur government responded to the consular kidnappings by detaining eighty-eight suspected members or sympathizers of the FIS living in France, including Moussa Kraouche, the head of the Fraternité Algérienne en France, an organization considered a front for the banned Islamist party. The brotherhood's newspapers, *Le Critère* and *Résistance,* were also suspended.[51] In response, a FIS communiqué to AFP on 15 November signed by Abdel Razak Redjam mentioned France not specifically but implicitly: "The government of a country that calls for the respect of human rights and then goes on to arrest dozens of . . . Algerians and provides material support to the fascists [in power] is the real party responsible for the death of its nationals."[52] Reflecting their own division, emigrant organizations such as the MRAP and FASTI protested the police crackdown, while France-Plus and Democratia praised it.

The combative interior minister, Charles Pasqua, warned members of the FIS not to "carry out political activities on our territory that run counter to the interests of the French government" and declared: "France will no longer tolerate in its territory the activities of any organization that are of a sort to damage the nation's interests or that violate its laws." When asked if the crackdown signaled support for the Algerian government, Pasqua responded: "There is no 'unreserved' support, as you put it. But what seems to me to be equally 'debatable' is the fate of the people, the intellectuals in particular, who are being assassinated by terrorists in Algeria." Illustrating the ambivalent position of the French government, Pasqua's perception of Algerian policy differed from that of Juppé: "We cannot but hope that the democratic process will be able to move ahead again. But the Algerian government cannot succeed in achieving that all by itself."[53] Pasqua was also not afraid to deal the "immigration card." He stated: "We won't give in to the pressure being put on us to withdraw from Algeria. . . . France has an interest in the economic development of these countries, because without economic development we shall be faced with problems of immigration that we will find hard to solve."[54]

Though Pasqua's hard line indicated support for the Algerian government, Juppé continued to express his dissatisfaction with the Pouvoir: "There is no question of giving a blank check to a policy that has ended up after so many years with the result we can all see, in other words a catastrophic failure in the economic, social, human, and political fields." When asked by the interviewer "Is the presence of French people in Algeria indispensable?" Juppé declared in a Gaullist tone: "The presence of French people is indispensable everywhere."[55] Endeavoring to extend French bilateral interests into multilateral policy, Juppé encouraged conversations between the IMF and Algeria, which "should make it possible for France to cease bearing the burden of economic aid to Algeria alone."[56] Juppé conditioned mulitilateral aid: "The position of the European Union and our partners is to say there is no point in helping Algeria if it does not reform its economy. . . . It has to get out of the socialism that belongs to another age."[57] Giscard called for a "dialogue" and called on the European nations to think about how to do this. The ex-president opined: "I do not believe that repression is a solution."[58] Mitterrand too reflected the ambiguous French policy by declaring that the French would be willing to "contribute" toward reconciliation but could not serve as "mediators."[59]

The fierce slaughter in Algeria intensified, claiming the lives of author Abderrahmane Chergou (28 September) and a number of magistrates, journalists, and teachers. The gruesome deaths of twelve technicians from Croatia and Bosnia, who were slain on 14–15 December, particularly "horrified" Prime Minister Redha Malek. The GIA claimed responsibility and announced that the killings were done "in response to the massacre of our Muslim coreligionists who were butchered in Bosnia."[60] The renowned poet Youssef Sebti was found with his throat slit in his home on 28 December. The GIA also reiterated its warning that "foreign crusaders" should depart Algeria.[61] By the end of the year 50 percent of French children had been repatriated.

Liamine Zeroual Appointed President

The HCE's failure to end the violence and earn political legitimacy quickened its demise and dissolution. The Pouvoir's factions jockeyed for position. Prime Minister Malek reportedly asked for French support in his failed bid for the new presidency.[62] On 25 January a National Consensus Council convened to replace the HCE with a president and a 178-member National Transitional Council, an unelected legislature to serve during the three-year presidency. Several minor parties participated, but Ait Ahmed quickly withdrew the FFS from the failing deliberations. The situation was aggravated by the Pouvoir's polarization between "eradicators" (of Islamists) and "conciliators." On 27 January the council adjourned without selecting a new president. On 30 January the HCE chose defense minister and former general Liamine Zeroual to be president for a three-year term. Zeroual had opposed President Benjedid and had been in retirement before accepting the defense portfolio in July 1993. He told the nation on 8 February, "We will regulate the crisis by dialogue."[63] During the rest of the year Zeroual pursued a moderate, conciliatory agenda. In late February he ordered the transfer of Abbasi Madani and Ali Belhadj from prison to a villa outside Algiers. This first initiative to create a dialogue with the FIS leadership failed. On 11 April, Prime Minister Malek resigned and Zeroual appointed Transport Minister Mokdad Sifi, a more conciliatory figure, as his replacement. Zeroual offered invitations on 8 August to eight small opposition parties, though not the FIS, to end their boycott of the government-named National Transition Council inaugurated in May and to take part in discussions to return Algeria to democracy.[64] On 21 August the FLN attended discussions along with the PRA, MDA, HAMAS, and others. This was approved by Juppé as a "good direction" and, though repeating this was an Algerian affair, he added: "To negotiate, it is necessary to cease killing."[65] This reflected Zeroual's negotiating position of securing a cease-fire before conducting discussions with the FIS. After a series of contacts, Zeroual released Madani and Belhadj to house arrest on 13 September, hoping that they would temper their views and finally persuade the Islamist insurgents to accept a truce. Juppé called this "an important step."[66] Nevertheless, by the end of October, Zeroual admitted that his effort to conceive and construct multiparty dialogues had failed. His attempt to press for dialogue while suppressing the Islamist insurgency recalled the past: the unsuccessful search by the French for *interlocuteurs valables* during the War of Independence. Like de Gaulle a generation before, Zeroual saw conciliatory initiatives chronically threatened by recalcitrant and resentful political factions, especially the "eradica-tors" within the Pouvoir. The past elliptically became the present.

The cruel violence continued, with assaults by Islamists and masked Ninja-like government forces, who resembled Latin American death squads. The *fitna* claimed another great literary figure, the playwright Abdelkader Alloula, who was shot and later died of his wounds on 14 March. On 12 March, about a thousand detainees escaped from the Tazult-Lambèse prison in southeast Algeria. This "inside job" demon-strated that the Algerian security forces were infiltrated by Islamists.[67] Women became increasingly targeted for not covering their heads; two female students were killed at a bus stop by a gunman on a motorbike.[68]

The *Fitna* Forces Greater French Involvement

As the ferocity of the *fitna* grew, President Mitterrand called it "the begin-nings of a civil war," Foreign Minister Juppé "a source of almost daily anguish."[69] On 15 January a Frenchwoman and a consular official were murdered, followed by a French television journalist two weeks later. Juppé confessed that he was "extraordinarily worried" by Algeria.[70] French companies were apprehensive about either staying or investing in Algeria as both security and the economy deteriorated.[71] On 23 March 1994 two French businessmen, a father and son, were murdered in front of their family. The Foreign Ministry advised again that French nationals "whose presence is not indispensable . . . take the necessary steps to return to France."[72] It was announced on 30 March 1994 that a number of French schools operating in several cities would not reopen after Easter because of "security concerns." All French cultural centers were also closed. According to Claude Pierre, a prominent member of the French community in Algiers, the decision to close these facilities "marks the end of a French presence."[73] With the departure of teachers and technicians, the *fitna* all but terminated decades-old cooperation.[74] A French monk and a nun were murdered while serving as librarians in Algiers on 9 May. These murders signaled the beginning of attacks against Christian clerics. Rabah Kebir, head of the FIS's Executive Abroad, denounced the killings, betraying deepening divisions within the Islamist movement.[75]

There was also increasing pressure on the French government to grant asylum to Algerians. The government resisted and particularly impeded freedom of movement and *mariages blancs* between French nationals and Algerians.[76] Pasqua, commenting in an 18 April interview with *Le Figaro* on the repatriation of French citizens from Algeria, said those with "dual nationality will have to justify their claim."[77] In the meantime, France heightened its antiterrorism efforts and found caches of arms and a logistical network for FIS.[78]

The French Internationalize Assistance to Algeria

French frustrations over Algeria and its government surfaced again in March 1994. Algerian economy minister Mourad Benachenou, while in Paris, was reportedly informed by his counterpart Edmond Alphandéry that France was reluctant to continue its volume of aid. According to one French correspondent, this pronouncement was "somewhat brusque."[79] France wanted its aid contingent on IMF rescheduling of the Algerian debt. By the end of the month Juppé, believing the Algerian situation was "deteriorating rapidly,"[80] was pressing the IMF to reach an accommodation with Algeria. This was a test of France's influence within the IMF and other international institutions.

The French strategy contributed to the signing on 10 April of a standby IMF loan which rescheduled about $5 billion of Algerian debt, conditioned on Algeria's raising interest rates and devaluing the dinar by about 40 percent.[81] The loan was engineered by Michel Camdessus, the managing director of the IMF and a Frenchman. Some circles questioned whether "the IMF is really just helping France throw money at the problem." The *Wall Street Journal* assessed: "The current state of chaos and bloodshed is untenable; no amount of foreign aid is going to lend Algeria's military regime the legitimacy it lacks or make the FIS go away."[82] Nevertheless, France effectively integrated its economic support of Algeria with a multilateral position.[83] This was done for two reasons: (1) to deflect Islamist criticism that France was the Algerian government's chief supporter, and (2) to mobilize others to share the inherent political, economic, and cultural risks.

By exercising its influence in multilateral organizations and circles, France disguised its extraordinary economic support to Algeria. On 1 June the Paris Club of major public creditors agreed to reschedule $5 billion in debt principal and interest, reducing interest charges by more than half and taking debt off the short-term market by spreading it over fifteen years with a four-year grace period. This was a great relief to Algeria, which now was reportedly spending more than 85 percent of its foreign revenues on debt payments.[84]

After the Paris Club agreement, on 11 July France committed new credits to Algeria, again reaching the FF 6 billion level. The new accord replaced the Bérégovoy revolving-credit system with specific allocations.

Three billion francs went to finance imports of French industrial goods, pharmaceuticals, and cereals, slightly more than a billion was earmarked to allow the Algerian government flexibility to relieve balance-of-payments pressures or initiate new projects, and the other two billion aimed to support private financing of projects guaranteed by COFACE. Though COFACE had previously guaranteed 95 percent of the financial credits, French banks wanted the remaining 5 percent risk covered too. There had also been problems with fulfilling the conditions for disbursal of the funds. These were addressed, satisfying consumers and creditors. The French government now directed its pressure toward private creditors, the so-called London Club where the Crédit Lyonnais, in particular, held heavy debt, though most French banks had sold down to Japanese banks on the secondary market.[85]

In May *al-Hayat* reported that France wanted to play a mediating role between the government and the FIS.[86] But Mitterrand in a television interview explained the difficulty of French intervention because of the need to exercise "extreme psychological precautions." Calling the *fitna* a "civil war," he contended that Algeria "needs to find the right slogans, its basic truths."[87] Algerian foreign minister Mohamed Salah Dembri found "great understanding of the Algerian situation on the part of French political circles."[88] Sensitive to French criticism of the lack of dialogue and democratization, Prime Minister Mokdad Sifi met with Juppé and later challenged: "I ask this of those who, far from the realities of the situation on the ground, advise us to negotiate: With whom? People tell us about the moderates all the time. . . . Let them declare themselves, and let them condemn violence and terrorism."[89] FFS chief Ait Ahmed condemned Paris's lack of political action, asserting that by "its silence, France encourages blind repression."[90] Yet Mitterrand believed that economic support could lead to political resolution: "The economic situation has contributed to swelling the numbers of supporters of extremist movements. In trying to help Algeria recover economically, we will also be helping future political reconstruction." He added: "We cannot go further, we are not the arbitrators between factions."[91] Yet France apparently had been "going further," as events soon proved.

August 1994

On 3 August five French citizens, three paramilitary policemen and two consular officials, were killed by the GIA at an embassy housing complex at Ain Allah, a suburb of Algiers. French government officials said the gunmen, dressed as police officers, had also planned to explode a car bomb. Mitterrand stated the victims' "mission was part of France's policy of cooperation and solidarity with Algeria," and added, "We must be forceful in telling Algerians, and especially those who have been perpetrating such acts, that they will not build in Algeria the abhorrence of everything foreign."[92] Foreign Minister Juppé and Defense Minister François Léotard hastily flew to Algeria to discuss better protection for the French population, which had dropped precipitously.[93] In reaction to the killings, it was announced that the French Lycée Descartes, a significant cultural symbol, would close. The Netherlands closed its embassy and Belgium advised its citizens to leave.[94] Juppé still insisted there had never been "unconditional support" for the Algerian regime, but the presence of French police and military advisers contradicted his position and indicated a deeper French involvement.[95]

France, Rabah Kebir claimed, "rejects the people's voice" by repudiating democracy while bestowing "maximum support" on the Pouvoir, a "flagrant provocation." Kebir repeated a familiar argument: "The notion in the minds of some French officials that 'Algeria is French' must be erased. . . . France should adhere to the principle of neutrality on the Algerian question." This was reinforced by Anouar Haddam, chairman of the FIS Parliamentary Delegation Abroad: "France considers itself a concerned party and it most insolently interferes in our internal affairs." The FIS contended that France had supported the cancellation of the elections and must take some responsibility for the tragedies in the country. The arrival of Juppé and especially Léotard in Algeria provoked these responses from Haddam: "a serious turning point" and "an irresponsible move by the French government."[96]

In the meantime, Pasqua called the possibility of a moderate Islamist government "wishful thinking" and criticized the United States and Germany for their failure to "neutralize" FIS operatives. He feared "hundreds of thousands of people fleeing Algeria. First of all, everyone at the management level, everyone in liberal professions."[97] In a rather unbelievable statement, Juppé claimed: "France has no responsibility whatsoever for what is happening in Algeria today. It is the task of Algeria alone, of the Algerian authorities, of the Algerian people to choose their own destiny."[98]

In the wake of the killings the French detained seventeen sympathizers of the FIS and terminated the printing and distribution of five Islamist publications. There were follow-up arrests of scores of suspects in France. French security forces also increased identification checks, eventually stopping tens of thousands. As one teenager, who held both French and

Algerian nationality, said: "If I'm asked where I'm from and I say Algeria, people immediately think I'm a fundamentalist."[99] By the end of the month twenty of the suspects, nineteen Algerians and a Moroccan, had been deported to Burkino Faso. Pasqua rationalized: "What should I do? Wait for the bombs to go off in our country and for people to be killed here, or . . . take action beforehand to break up the networks?"[100] The French crackdown on the FIS indicated that the Balladur government was now strongly supportive of the Pouvoir. Leila Aslaoui, the spokesperson for the Algerian government, suggested that these "anti-French events in Algeria should make people conscious of what the criminals would have done in Algeria if they had won the second round of the elections."[101] The French government's tilt toward the Pouvoir was a blow to the FIS as well as moderate Islamist parties and reinforced France's demonic image among the extremists.

The FIS promptly denounced the arrests as "a declaration of war." On 6 August its Armée Islamique du Salut (AIS) threatened reprisals and called for the "immediate liberation" of detained Islamists. It stated: "France must renounce its aggressive policy and immediately liberate our brothers, or take responsibility for what the mujahidin of the Islamic Salvation Army will make them suffer." The AIS claimed the French actions had been "incited by the junta."[102] Nevertheless, Shaykh Abdelbaki Sahraoui, a founder of the FIS, declared that neither the Islamist party nor the AIS "want to extend the conflict onto French territory." He reiterated: "The AIS is only opposed to the puppet government in Algiers and only hits the forces of oppression in Algeria."[103]

Within the space of a few weeks, a flurry of statements by French statesmen seemed to contradict each other and illustrated again a tortuous ambivalence. Defense Minister Léotard said, "Islamic nationalism in its terrorist version is as dangerous today as Nazism was in the past." He asked: "How can we be indifferent?"[104] Mitterrand reiterated: "We do not want to be dragged in toward one side."[105] Balladur spoke of being "equidistant from both sides," but Juppé suggested that there had been a dialogue between the government and the FIS.[106] "I have never said that the current Algerian government had to be supported," added Pasqua. "It is not up [to] us to intervene in Algeria's internal affairs."[107] This array of paradoxical discourse not only underscored the ambiguity of French policy but also ensured its immobilism. Mirroring Algeria, France appeared to have its own "eradicators" and "conciliators."

José Garçon analyzed French policy as "schizophrenic" in an article in

Libération on 4 August 1994.[108] *Le Monde* on 6 August 1994 called for "a courageous review" of the Algerian policy. It condemned as "clear interference" the French policy of supporting the unpopular Algerian government "at the taxpayer's expense."[109] Jacques Amalric in *Libération* on 8 August wrote that it was "a mistake to have approved, even reluctantly, of the suspension of the electoral process started at the end of 1991." He believed that France "stands to lose everything because . . . the crisis will be resolved at its expense sooner or later. The anti-French card will remain a trump card on the other side of the Mediterranean for a long time." Then he added: "It is no more possible to bail out a sinking society than a sinking ship."[110]

For its part, the GIA was threatening to "strike at French interests with force."[111] In a statement signed by the GIA leader, Chérif Gousmi, the extremist Islamist organization declared war on France economically by calling for a boycott "of all French products, in particular French cars and trucks made by Peugeot, Renault and Citroen." It warned that "all French products which enter Algeria from January 1, 1995, cars and other items, will be burnt and destroyed." A familiar cultural rationale repeated by Gousmi was that France was "continuing to seek to subject the Algerian Muslim people, and divert them from the Muslim religion."[112]

More Casualties, Contradictions, Crackdowns

The Pouvoir began a crackdown on the GIA, resulting in the deaths of Chérif Gousmi and the "throat-cutter" Abdessalam Djemaoune on 26 September 1994. Nevertheless, despite occasional successes against the Islamists, the fact was that the Algerian public impression of the Pouvoir was negative or numbed by the sheer terror unleashed by the *fitna*. As Francis Ghiles, the veteran North African observer for the *Financial Times,* related, the Pouvoir was referred to as the *hikkamat miki* (Mickey Mouse government).[113]

The unrelenting bloodshed claimed more celebrated Algerians. Shaykh Boudjara Soltani, a prominent HAMAS member and theologian, was shot dead on 17 September. Cheb Hasni, the popular rai singer, was killed in Oran at midday on 29 September, and the celebrated Kabyle singer Lounès Matoub was kidnapped in Tizi-Ouzou by Islamist extremists. He would later be released, only to be shot to death in June 1998. The rai singer Rachid was murdered on 15 February 1995. Farah Ziane, the editor of *Révolution africaine,* was assassinated on 21 October. While negotiating the surrender of Islamist gunmen in Algiers, the city's military commander, Colonel Djelloul Hadj Chérif, was gunned down on 2 November. Said Mekbal, the editor of *Le Matin,* died of gunshot wounds on 4 December.

France continued to be singled out for its support of the Pouvoir. The AIS joined the GIA in calling for a boycott of French commodities: "If France is stubborn enough not to abandon its colonial policies, we will take the necessary measures." The statement cited "the presence of police and French military experts" in Algeria and claimed that "the participation of the French air force in bombing raids in eastern Algerian mountains" amounted to "flagrant French interference."[114] In an interview with *al-Sharq al-Awsat,* Defense Minister Léotard referred to reports that 1,500 to 2,000 French police or armed forces were in service in Algeria as "prattle" and "nonsense." But he did assert that France had the right to protect its diplomatic installations.[115]

On 8 October a missing French citizen was found murdered, and on 10 October another French national was shot dead. Again the Foreign Ministry urged French citizens to return to France. A bilateral agreement signed on 11 October expedited French nationals' repatriation of their savings: under a simplified procedure, they could take whatever amount had been in their bank accounts on 31 July.[116] GDF announced its intention to repatriate most of its French staff after the killing of two European oil engineers. Other hydrocarbon corporations expressed their concern that *force majeure* would be declared, allowing commercial contracts to be breached.[117]

As the conflict worsened, worried French officials took more active and public positions to advocate dialogue among the contesting groups. In his interview with *al-Sharq al-Awsat* Léotard stressed the need for discussions between the government and "democratic forces" and feared that "Algeria is heading toward destruction."[118] The French denied a report in *al-Hayat* that Jean-Charles Marchiani, an aide to Interior Minister Pasqua, had met with Abbasi Madani and Ali Belhadj in order to get talks moving.[119] Rabah Kebir, who claimed he had talked to Marchiani, said France proposed to act as a mediator. The FIS leader termed the meeting "useful but stormy" and remarked that "it appears to us that France is running Algeria's affairs."[120] These comments and reports complicated the complex relations between Paris and the increasingly distressed Pouvoir.

On 3 November 1994 a French-Algerian agreement concerning entry and residence conditions was modified to facilitate the deportation of illegal Algerian emigrants and to restrict sojourns.[121] Algerian nationals now needed an "address certificate" upon arrival in France. A stay longer than three months required an "extended visa" obtained through a difficult administrative procedure. Algerian nationals staying less than three months had to have sufficient means of subsistence and a return ticket in their name. Basically, France was closing its borders to Algeria, the principle of "free circulation" now long forgotten. Juppé questioned the Evian Accords' validity; they had become outdated. Reminiscent of Giscard almost twenty years earlier, Juppé stated: "The real issue is whether, thirty-two years later and in view of the fact that generally speaking the reciprocity stipulated by the Evian agreements has not been effective, the time has come to consider a revision of these agreements."[122] This was another illustration of an end of an era and the transformation of the bilateral relationship.

Speaking in parliament on 7 November, Pasqua declared: "I will not allow people of foreign nationality living here to lead prayers, to become anti-French propagandists, to preach against the institutions of the republic and to advocate confrontation here or elsewhere."[123] His comments disclosed that the French-Algerian problem was cultural as well as political. The next day the French government conducted another sweep, detaining ninety-five suspects reportedly linked to the GIA.[124] Pasqua confirmed the "implantation" in France of a clandestine network of Muslim militants. Random identity checks again profiled Algerian emigrants and *beurs* as terrorists.[125] Pasqua also criticized the United States, Germany, and the United Kingdom for permitting the FIS to operate from within their borders. A FIS official, Abdelkarim Ould Edda in Belgium, accused Pasqua of acting "as though he had become Algeria's interior minister. His and France's attitudes reflect . . . the mentality of a spiteful crusader."[126]

The end of the year included controversies over the sale to Algeria of nine second-hand Ecureuil helicopters, the equipping with French night-fighting technology of Soviet-built Mi-24 helicopters, and the training of Algerian helicopter personnel at Le Luc, near Toulon. On 7 December *Le Canard enchaîné* termed France's involvement a "co-belligerency."[127]

The Hijacking Drama

On 24 December 1994 four members of the GIA ("Phalange of the Tigers in Blood"), dressed in Air Algérie uniforms, hijacked an Air France airliner preparing to leave Boumedienne Airport in Algiers with 271 passengers aboard.[128] The heavily armed gunmen killed two passengers, an Algerian policeman and a Vietnamese diplomat, soon after they took over the aircraft, and then released 63 Algerian passengers. It was reported that the hijackers demanded the liberation of Madani and Belhadj. Their chief demand was for France to stop supporting the Zeroual government. Urgency mounted when the gunmen murdered a French citizen, Yannick Beugnet, who worked as a cook in the French embassy in Algiers. Algerian authorities refused permission for the plane to leave Algiers, while France offered to send specially trained commandos to free the hostages.

Apparently applying heavy pressure on Zeroual, the Balladur government insisted that the Algerians let the plane fly to Marseille.[129] After landing there, the hijacked plane was soon seized on 26 December in an assault by French paramilitary commandos of the Intervention Group of the Gendarmerie Nationale. All four of the hijackers were killed. Thirteen passengers, three crew members, and nine policemen were wounded or injured, but the hostages were rescued. The French found twenty sticks of dynamite on board. According to Pasqua: "Their objective was a suicide operation over Paris with the plane."[130] Edouard Balladur praised the "exemplary courage and efficiency" of the commando operation, but the GIA retorted that the hijacking was in reprisal for France's "unconditional political, military and economic aid" to the Algerian government.[131]

There would be shocking retribution for the death of the hijackers. On 27 December in Tizi-Ouzou the GIA killed four Roman Catholic priests, White Fathers, three of them French and one Belgian. GIA leader Abou Abderrahmane Amin said the deaths of the four priests were in "retaliation for the death of four GIA members."[132] On 31 December, in its newsletter *El-Feth El-Moubine* (Crushing Victory), the AIS declared war on France: "The Algerian nation is today directly in conflict with France and all those who support it, including the Jews and Christians of the world." This tone was surprising, since the AIS was regarded as the least militant Islamist armed faction.[133]

The GIA had, however, succeeded in aggravating the bilateral relationship. On 26 December, France provisionally suspended air and sea links, exacerbating the difficulties in obtaining visas. Prime Minister Balladur stated that "France will inexorably fight terrorism and will not give in to blackmail wherever it comes from." According to Pasqua, Balladur had called Zeroual and used "decisive arguments" to insist that Algeria accede to the hijackers' demand to fly to France.[134] The French government now demanded that Algeria improve its security at airports and ports since, in Juppé's words, it "has not been effective." He then repeated the oblique argument "[French] aid is not to a government but aid to the Algerian people."[135] Meanwhile, the GIA reiterated its demand that Western governments close their embassies and warned that "all infidels will be killed in cold blood." Further, it stated, "Calling for war against France is a legitimate matter which we maintain in view of the fact that [France] has become a support to the oppressive regime, in addition to its military presence in Algeria."[136]

By the end of 1994 the *fitna* had claimed approximately thirty thousand Algerian lives. Nor, according to Rémy Leveau, could an end to the conflict be seen: "The FIS and the military are two opponents that can't destroy each other and can't find the basis for an acceptable compromise."[137] As for the bilateral relationship, the repatriation of French citizens and the savagery had all but ended French technical and cultural cooperation. Portentously, the conflict had crossed the Mediterranean when the fateful GIA-commandeered Airbus touched down at Marseille. The *fitna* soon clenched France within its frightful, terrible grip. France's "second Algerian War" was about to commence.

9

The *Fitna,* 1995–1998

From the Sant'Egidio Agreement

It is difficult to urge Algerian leaders to hold a dialogue when they do not want one. We shall not tire of saying that there can be no way out of the Algerian drama without dialogue.
Alain Juppé, February 1995

We have the means to surmount our crisis. The Algerian people have an extraordinary capacity and they have proved it throughout their history. And you are going to see elections take place normally and in a free and democratic manner. We have taken all necessary measures in that direction.
Liamine Zeroual, October 1995

The Airbus hijacking spectacularly demonstrated that France could not isolate itself from the *fitna*'s fury nor extract itself from its entangled, elliptical history with Algeria. As the "second Algerian War" raged among an increasingly disparate group of cruel antagonists, explosions were no longer confined to Algiers and the Casbah but soon echoed in Paris under the boulevard Saint-Michel among the caverns of the metro. France was now engaged in yet another Algerian "war without a name."

France's initial ambivalent policy toward Algeria during the *fitna* stemmed from its dilemma—in existential terms, "bad faith"—over the cancellation of the 1991 legislative elections. Though relieved that the FIS had not taken over the government, France could not ignore that the January 1992 coup had provoked the fierce *fitna*. The dilemma could be viewed philosophically as a political absurdity, but the violence was real, ruthless, and relentless. As the conflict transmuted into a nihilistic civil war, Paris reluctantly resigned itself to publicly supporting the unpopular Pouvoir, which was rebuilding the state institutionally through a closely controlled "redemocratization." The new Algerian democracy was far from inclusive, however, as major parties opposed its institutional constraints and conditions. The major opposition parties, too, were divided after bonding in the illusory and ephemeral unity of the Sant'Egidio Platform of January 1995. By the end of 1997 Algeria had held controversial presidential, legislative, and municipal elections. A tightly monitored multiparty political system was in place, but it failed to be enthusiastically embraced, and it did not terminate the *fitna*.

In some of the most gruesome killings, it was not clear who perpetrated the assaults. The Islamist movement was fractured by its own fratricidal factions and the Pouvoir was composed of competing "clans" vying for influence and advantage. In September 1998 President Zeroual announced that he would be retiring in early 1999, creating yet another unsettling situation for Algeria and, by extension, its relationship with France.

The Sant'Egidio Agreement and Its Consequences

Under the sponsorship of the Sant'Egidio Catholic Community in Rome, an organization that played an important role in the 1992 Mozambique peace talks, Algerian opposition parties deliberated in November 1994 and agreed to reconvene in January. Though twelve parties eventually took part in these discussions, the chief participants were the exiled FIS, the FLN, and the FFS, the parties that collectively polled 82 percent of the electorate in the curtailed December 1991 election. The presence of these major parties lent clout and legitimacy to the meetings. While the Airbus hijacking drama and its consequences captured world attention, the parties persevered to formulate a joint declaration. Foreign Minister Alain Juppé intimated French support during a radio broadcast: "I don't believe a solution can be reached by doing nothing. If we are faced with, on the one hand, the repression of the army and, on the other, the terrorist camp of the FIS, the violence will continue for years and years. . . . The way out is through a democratic process leading to real elections that allow united democratic powers to emerge in Algeria."[1]

On 13 January 1995, after days of difficult discussion and negotiation, the parties in Rome proclaimed a Platform for a Political and Peaceful Solution to the Algerian Crisis.[2] The Sant'Egidio Platform (sometimes called the National Contract or Compact) was another chapter in the enduring endeavor to define an Algerian nation. The first section, entitled "Framework: Values and Principles," recognized Algeria's lasting existential quest. It reiterated the Proclamation of 1 November 1954's appeal for the "restoration of the . . . Algerian state within the framework of Islamic principles" and specified that "the constituent elements of the Algerian personality are Islam, Arabism, and Amazighism (Berberism)." Concerning the Arab-Berber cultural conflict the Platform declared: "The culture and the two languages that contribute to the development of that personality should be accorded their stature and be promoted institutionally." Among other significant declarations, the Platform called for: (1) "the consecration of [political] pluralism," (2) the "annulment of the decision to dissolve the FIS," (3) "an urgent and unambiguous appeal for a cessation of hostilities," (4) a "commitment" to the Constitution of 23 February 1989, and (5) the convening of "a national conference bestowed with real powers" to organize "free and pluralist elections that permit the people the full exercise of their sovereignty." The Platform aimed to restore civil and political rights and to retire the army and resolutely consign it to "nonintervention in political affairs." This concerted action aimed to galvanize a national consensus and create an inclusive political climate and culture. John Entelis viewed the Platform as "a model of democratic governance and political reconciliation." The FIS agreed to these principles, signifying to Entelis that the Islamist party "was committing itself to a peaceful transition of political power."[3]

France's response to Sant'Egidio was initially positive. Juppé hoped this initiative would persuade the Pouvoir to revitalize the democratic process leading to elections. Yet he also understood that it was absolutely necessary to have extremist elements subscribe to the Sant'Egidio declarations and "leave their Kalashnikovs in the cloakroom." Abdennour Ali Yahya, the spokesman for the parties and the head of the LADDH (*Ligue Algérienne de Défense des Droits de l'Homme*, or Algerian League for the Defense of Human Rights), was pleased with the French reaction, as was Anouar Haddam of the FIS, a signatory, who was "very happy" with Juppé's response.[4]

The GIA pronounced itself ready to end its struggle with the Pouvoir upon the fulfillment of three conditions: (1) punishment of secularist Algerian generals, (2) prohibition of communist and atheist political parties, and (3) the liberation of Abdelhak Layada and Ahmen al-Oud from prison.[5] The rival AIS, however, called Sant'Egidio a "diversion" and claimed that the FIS representatives did not really represent them—a clear sign that fissures had widened within the FIS. Without the militants' adherence to the Platform, the proposal lost much of its momentum and promise.[6]

The Pouvoir reacted angrily. President Zeroual issued a "categorical rejection" of Sant'Egidio as an act of "outside interference" that "harms national sovereignty and invites foreign intervention in our internal affairs."[7] The Quai d'Orsay's advice of 16 January to engage the opposition parties and Juppé's appeal, made in Washington later that month, to initiate a "political dialogue" were ignored.[8] By refusing to liberate Islamist prisoners, notably Shaykhs Madani and Belhadj, the Pouvoir obliterated any hope of fulfilling the Platform's plank of establishing a national conference to resolve the *fitna*. Instead the Algerian government confirmed on 26 January, as Zeroual had declared in October 1994, that it would conduct its own regulated presidential elections later that year. Thus the regime repudiated the Platform's mapped democratization process.

The Platform might have been built on, with decisive action. The collaboration and shared vision of a new, pluralistic Algeria was an exciting prospect inviting national and international support. Even the FIS's volatile leader Ali Belhadj supported it in a letter smuggled out of Algiers, stating that Sant'Egidio "proved that the problem is not with the parties or the people, but between the legitimate parties and a regime that has lost legitimacy." Belhadj's apparent moderation and conciliation even included, according to his lawyer Ali Yahya Abdennour, a decision to study French! Though the Islamist armed wings rejected the Platform, Rabah Kebir believed that they would have become more accommodating if the FIS leaders had been liberated. In a slightly shaded reference to France, Kebir noted that "many parties, which I will not name, joined the regime in banking on the elimination of the FIS." He went on: "If all sides act to put pressure on the regime to accept the Rome document, we would be working together to save Algeria."[9]

A firm French policy insisting on dialogue, including implicit support for the National Platform with a strong endorsement of democratic pluralism, might have sustained progress toward a real accommodation. But France chose not to disturb the Algerian government's sensibilities about national sovereignty and its own legitimacy. French lack of determination at this crucial moment, combined with the defiance of the "eradicators" and exacerbated by the splintering of the opposition parties' solidarity, contributed to continuation of the *fitna*. Meanwhile, the violence still imperiled French citizens; in downtown Algiers on 22 January another businessman was murdered.

The *Fitna* Rages On

The initiative to construct a sober, conciliatory dialogue, whether by the Sant'Egidio group or the "conciliators" within the Pouvoir, contrasted dramatically with the devastation of the *fitna*. As Ramadan began, a car bomb killed 42 and wounded 256 in downtown Algiers on 30 January.

While the FIS contended that the regime was to blame for the tragedy—yet another illustration of the difficulty in assigning culpability for Algerian events—the GIA claimed responsibility and declared: "There is no peace, no truce and no compromise, because this holy month of Ramadan is a time for killing and fighting . . . and it is the duty of all fighters to intensify military work and religious struggle."[10] On 22 February, government troops stormed the Sekadji prison where inmates had attempted to seize control, resulting in about forty deaths. In late March, using artillery and helicopters, the Pouvoir mounted large-scale assaults, reminiscent of past French counterinsurgency tactics, on suspected Islamist strongholds.

Women continued to be targeted by extremists. On 15 February in Tizi-Ouzou, violence claimed the life of Nabila Djahnine, an architect and feminist, who led the Cry of Women group. Rashida Hammadi, a television reporter, was shot and her sister slain in an assault on 20 March; Hammadi succumbed from her wounds ten days later. A newspaper reporter, Malika Sabeur, was murdered on 21 May. The renowned Algerian singer Layla 'Amara and her husband were killed on 12 August. Algeria's great track star Hassiba Boulmerka, the victor in the 1500 meters at the Barcelona Olympics in 1992, was severely censured and repeatedly threatened by Islamists for showing her legs in her comparatively modest track uniform. She was forced to train overseas.[11] Abu Abdallah Ahmed, the GIA's new leader, issued an edict on 2 May threatening death to all women married to opponents of an Islamist state.[12]

In a telling irony, Abdelwahab Ben Boulaid, the son of Mostefa Ben Boulaid, one of the founding "historic leaders" of the FLN (d. 1956), was killed on 22 March while on his way to attend a ceremony commemorating the death of his father. Veterans of the War of Independence were particularly targeted by Islamists (122 died in 1994 alone), a symbolic repudiation of the FLN's revolutionary past, which to the Islamists was a failed liberation.

There were also increasing indications of fragmentation and antagonism within the armed Islamist movement. Madani Mezrag, the reputed chief of the AIS, offered negotiation on 30 March in a twenty-one-page open letter to President Zeroual. Mezrag's statement that "each day complicates the crisis" also referred to the fractured Islamist movement. It was generally known that Abbasi Madani opposed the assaults on intellectuals and women, while his associate Ali Belhadj encouraged a "holy war" and identified more with the GIA and the militant wing of the AIS.[13] By this time, there had been repeated intra-Islamist assaults between AIS and GIA cells.

Mitterrand Internationalizes the *Fitna*

In the immediate postcolonial period, Charles de Gaulle realized that Algeria could be a bilateral means serving France's multilateral ends. Now the situation was reversed. France attempted to use multilateral means to serve its bilateral Algerian interests. Taking advantage of its six-month presidency of the European Union, France tried to tie the EU to its own Algerian policy by proposing a commitment of emergency funds to the struggling Algerian government. This was opposed by several members, particularly the United Kingdom, which along with the United States favored dialogue among the parties.[14] Then on 3 February President Mitterrand floated an idea that the European Union host a conference "inspired by the different ideas raised in recent times, notably during the opposition conference in Rome," with Algeria's contending parties meeting to negotiate and terminate the fratricide. The former Algerian prime minister Abdelhamid Brahimi argued that the Mitterrand initiative had three objectives: (1) to gain Muslim votes for the Socialists in the upcoming presidential elections, (2) "to enhance the internal popularity of the [Pouvoir], because anyone who curses France in Algeria becomes more popular," and (3) to have France conform to international opinion, alleviating the risk of isolation. Brahimi concluded: "If the French government really wanted to stop the bloodletting in Algeria, it could have sufficed with telling its generals who rule Algeria to do this or do that. It is in possession of their files and knows what money they own in its banks." Brahimi identified the Pouvoir as "the party of France's generals" since many of the generals had fought in the French army during the Algerian War and were belated adherents of the revolutionary cause.[15]

In reaction to the French president's proposal, Algiers recalled its ambassador and the state media attacked Mitterrand for his "visceral hatred" of Algeria.[16] Algérie Presse Service (APS) saw Mitterrand's initiative as illustrating an alignment, if not collusion, with "American theories."[17] Implicitly, this was a condemnation of France's apparently subordinating its vaunted independence to the consistently conciliatory American position. *El-Watan* asked: "Are we heading for a new crisis between Algeria and France?"[18]

The Balladur government averted the crisis by owning it was uninformed and certainly unprepared for Mitterrand's suggestion. Juppé declared, "France does not have the immediate intention of launching a concrete initiative on Algeria," then hedged: "We'll see how this matures over the next few weeks." Charles Pasqua said: "I am not sure that we were associated with this move."[19] This public disarray was countered by the presidential spokesman, Jean Musitelli: "What the president said is perfectly in line with what has been French policy for months, that is, the call for a political dialogue." Juppé again weighed in: "France has always favored dialogue . . . but it is not for her to take the place of the Algerians to organize this dialogue."[20] Balladur defined his government's position and distanced himself from the EU conference idea: "It is up to the Algerians to settle their own problems." He added: "We think they will manage even better once they are able to meet among themselves to discuss their difficulties and reach a joint solution."[21] The lack of a clear and coordinated French policy in a cohabitation situation (called "dysfunctional" by *Libération* on 7 February 1995) sapped the initiative's moral as well as political strength. Meanwhile, the ferocity of the *fitna* forced France to close its consulates in Annaba and Oran on 23 February.

The Balladur government's efforts to separate France from the *fitna* failed to convince Algerians that the ex-*métropole* was not involved. On 9 March, Ahmed Ben Bella spoke to *al-Hayat* and pointed out that France's aid permitted the Pouvoir to purchase "arms and helicopters." He stated: "We condemn France's policy in this area. It is throwing oil on the fire. France should stop getting involved in our country." In words reminiscent of his discourse when he was Algeria's first president, he reiterated: "France has to recognize us as an independent country. We do not refuse cooperation, but there are conditions. Among these is a refusal to be under any form of trusteeship."[22]

News stories floated in April 1995 that France wanted to reduce its financial aid to Algeria from FF 6 billion to FF 5 billion. Though this signaled a "distancing," France continued to advocate and assert Algeria's case and cause with European banks, the IMF, and the Paris and London Clubs.[23] Under French pressure the IMF approved a three-year $1.8 billion extended credit facility on 22 May to replace the $1 billion standby credit of 1994. In a sense, this was in the spirit of Mitterrand's wish to internationalize the Algerian situation in a search for a solution. A spokesman for Balladur admitted, "We know some of what is earmarked for the people of Algeria will be used for weapons or wind up in Swiss bank accounts. But if we insist on looking into how the money is used, we will be accused of neocolonialism."[24] With French support the Paris Club rescheduled about $7 billion of debt in July 1995. In June 1996 the London Club followed suit with the conclusion of an agreement rescheduling $3.2 billion.

Jacques Chirac Confronts the *Fitna*

The presidential campaign to succeed the ailing François Mitterrand was distinguished by its lack of discussion of Algeria. As expected, only Jean-Marie Le Pen invoked Algeria's deepening civil war as a threat to France. Ironically, Le Pen's repeated appeals to seal borders and expel emigrants to North Africa had been adopted by governments on the left and right. Visa restrictions prevented easy access to France and "irregular" documents carried by emigrants led to deportation.[25] Other significant candidates distanced themselves from Algeria. Edouard Balladur stated: "No one, least of all France, can prescribe Algeria's own destiny."[26] Jacques Chirac wrote in *Le Monde* on 7 April: "There is no question of France's carrying out any form of interference by adopting a didactic stance. . . . There will be no solution to the Algerian crisis except through a reconciliation by means of genuinely democratic elections."[27] This was more in line with the Juppé-right rather than the Pasqua-right.[28] Yet in a campaign manifesto Chirac, who was very familiar with Arab and North African affairs, did adopt a didactic stance toward Algeria: "The destiny of this country cannot leave us indifferent. . . . The Algerian people must rediscover their identity today, mobilizing all their political and social forces in order to escape the vicious circle of violence that is inflicting terrible suffering on the population."[29]

The FIS's Anouar Haddam called on France to elect a president who would not support a "terrorist regime" in Algeria and called for "a cohabitation between our two civilizations." Haddam referred to the regime in Algeria as "secular fundamentalism." He pointed out that French trade with Algeria had increased 17 percent since 1988 and surmised: "This explains well why certain influential circles in Paris and the military security establishment of Algeria are adamantly against the principle of popular choice and the freedom of expression in Algeria." France, he said, "must stop its interference in Algerian affairs and its financial support."[30]

Chirac's victory and arrival in the Elysée on 17 May gave Juppé, the newly appointed prime minister, an opportunity to pursue an activist policy. Instead he announced a prudent but paradoxical stance of "non-indifference, non-interference" as France continued to provide annual aid, especially in the form of commercial credits, of FF 5–6 billion, roughly a billion dollars.[31] By avoiding active engagement, France hoped to preserve its interests and patiently wait out the *fitna*'s grim and inexorable course. Meanwhile on 7 June an elderly French couple were murdered in the El

Biar section in Algiers. Their deaths marked thirty French dead since the *fitna* fulminated.

Bombings in France

In a SOFRES survey before the French presidential election, 78 percent of those questioned felt that "Muslim fundamentalism is a very serious threat in our country which must be fought." Only 16 percent viewed fundamentalism as "not such a serious threat."[32] Of course, "fundamentalism" was implicitly equated with Algeria's troubles. Soon after the election, that fearful menace materialized, and the *fitna*'s terror spread throughout France.

As anti-French rhetoric by Islamists became increasingly virulent and the Pouvoir increasingly ineffective, the French government was forced to insist that Air Algérie operate from a more isolated and secure location at Charles de Gaulle International Airport at Roissy. This incensed the Algerian national carrier, which rejected being "quarantined" and announced the termination of its Paris service on 17 June. Its plan to add flights at alternate airports was blocked by the French government, which refused the carrier's requests for operations in Lille, Nice, and Toulon.[33] As relations again suffered, another French police sweep on 20 June resulted in sixty-seven people being charged with providing logistical support for suspected Islamist terrorists.

On 11 July, President Zeroual announced that his latest effort to create a productive dialogue with Abbasi Madani had failed. On that day Shaykh Abdelbaki Sahraoui, the eighty-five-year-old cofounder of the FIS, was shot dead along with a bodyguard in a mosque in northern Paris. Most believed that the GIA was to blame, since the venerable shaykh, a moderate who opposed assassinations of foreigners and favored dialogue, had been publicly targeted by the organization in May, but the FIS issued its habitual contention that Algerian government agents perpetrated the murders. The Algerian ambassador to France, Hocine Djoudi, retorted: "It is a ritual to accuse the Algerian services." He also said the assault aimed "to undermine relations between Algeria and France."[34] *France-Soir* commented: "Let us make no mistake, the gunshots which rang out in Paris . . . mark the prologue of a new chapter, this one French, of the civil war which is ravaging Algeria."[35]

The GIA then engineered a series of explosions in France beginning on 25 July. The first explosion rocked the rail station under the boulevard Saint-Michel, leaving seven dead and eighty-six wounded. On 17 August another device exploded near the Arc du Triomphe, wounding seventeen, including eleven tourists. French authorities discovered a large but defective bomb packed with explosives planted on a TGV (high-speed railroad) track north of Lyon on 26 August. Five days later French police in Paris and Lyon arrested twenty Muslims, including native Algerians and French converts. This was followed up by the arrests of thirty-one suspected Islamists in Lyon. Meanwhile Juppé warned in a Pasqua-esque tone: "We will not allow bases for terrorism in France."[36]

On 3 September a pressure cooker rigged as an explosive device detonated on the boulevard Richard-Lenoir near the Place de la Bastille, injuring four people. On that same day in Algiers, a French nun was killed. On 4 September a powerful bomb was found and defused in a public toilet near an outdoor market in the Fifteenth Arrondissement of Paris. The Algerian newspaper *La Tribune* claimed that five Algerian terrorists from the war in Afghanistan had journeyed from Bosnia to France.[37] On 7 September a car bomb injured fourteen outside a Jewish school in Lyon. This was condemned as "cowardly" by the National Council of French Muslims. At this time Chirac declared France's position "neither supporting the government nor the fundamentalists."[38] By the end of the month, suspected Islamist logistical depots had been discovered in southern France.

French authorities had lifted fingerprints off the device that failed to detonate on the TGV tracks and matched them to a twenty-four-year-old Muslim from Lyon named Khalid Kelkal. After a manhunt was mobilized on 27 September, Kelkal was slain in a police shootout two days later, provoking several days of protests and rioting. Kelkal perfectly fit the profile of an alienated member of the emigrant community, so feared by the French. He had been a bright student who had descended to delinquency. In a chance interview in 1992 with a German researcher, Kelkal described himself as "neither Arab nor French" but "Muslim."[39] According to Areski Dahmani, the founder and president of France-Plus, Kelkal was transformed into "a martyr, a Robin Hood who defied the state." He was also "the product of the twenty-year failure to integrate the races." Dahmani warned: "French society is not working. More and more people are excluded from participation. Unless there is dramatic change, we could fall into the abyss of civil war within a few years."[40]

The violence conjured up again the specter of an estranged Algerian youth of the second or third emigrant generation harboring resentment and possibly terrorist impulses. Again, North Africans were stopped and interrogated. One young woman stated the obvious: "I don't know why I was chosen, but I am sure they would not have stopped a blue-eyed blonde."[41]

Nevertheless, sociologist Djeloul Siddiki asserted, "I would say ninety-five percent of the Algerians living here want to live in peace and are very unlikely to be seduced by a militant fundamentalist call for any kind of action."[42] Though it had closely identified with the nationalist cause during the War of Independence, the Algerian community, for the most part, distanced itself from political Islamism.

On 6 October a gas canister stuffed with nails and bolts hidden in a trash can exploded near the Maison Blanche metro stop in southern Paris. The next day, the GIA faxed news agencies a statement dated 23 September from the GIA "emir" Abou Abderrahmane Amin. This statement claimed responsibility for the bombings and warned the French that the GIA planned "to leave you no happiness until Islam conquers France by prayer or by force." The GIA also disclosed that it had attempted to persuade President Chirac to convert to Islam ("Convert to Islam and you will live in peace"). The GIA concluded, however, that Chirac harbored "Crusader-like religious hatreds" and that this "explains his support for those apostate tyrants [in Algeria] despite the price his citizens pay and shows the lie of his claims to help the people of Algeria and not their government." The GIA vowed to continue its campaign "in the heart of France and its big cities."[43]

On the weekend of 15–16 October El-Ansar, an underground bulletin associated with the GIA, pictured an exploding Eiffel Tower superimposed on a map of Paris. The extremist Islamist organization asserted that "France's engagement in Algeria's moving sands verges on suicide." On 17 October another bombing on a Paris commuter train injured twenty-nine people between the Musée d'Orsay and Saint-Michel stations. This was the eighth bombing in three months. Prime Minister Juppé stated: "France will not allow itself to be intimidated, will not flinch under pressure and will not capitulate to barbarism." But he added ambiguously: "France has no intention of making the slightest interference in the internal affairs of Algeria."[44] A poll published on 23 October showed that 91 percent supported the government's antiterrorism policy and 61 percent wanted France to keep its policy toward Algeria unchanged to affirm its resistance to terrorist blackmail.[45]

The French government intensified its counterterrorist operations. In early September military personnel joined police forces to patrol vital areas, including tourist sites. Legionnaires were even stationed in the metro. On 2 November French authorities foiled a bombing planned for an outdoor market in Lille. Subsequently, as a result of wiretaps, Boualem Bensaid and several accomplices were arrested. Bensaid was described by

Interior Minister Jean-Louis Debré as a "pivotal figure" in the recent terrorist campaign. France also put more pressure on other European nations
harboring Islamists. Paris particularly continued to try to persuade Swe-
den to extradite a suspected figure in the bombings, Abdelkrim Deneche.[46]

In Algeria the violence continued to target the Christian religious community. Two nuns, one French and the other Maltese, were shot to death
in Algiers's Casbah on 3 September. A statement purportedly from the
GIA called their deaths part of a campaign to "eliminate Jews, Christians,
and wrongdoers from the Muslim soil of Algeria."[47] On 10 November a
French nun was killed, which brought the total to seven French religious
slain in Algeria since May 1994.

Many observers, including historian Benjamin Stora, questioned
whether the violence in France might be committed not only by Islamists
but also by factions within the Pouvoir hoping to bring France into closer
cooperation with the Algerian government.[48] These strong suspicions
deepened bilateral mistrust, as would be dramatically publicized in New
York City.

The Summit Fiasco

A presidential summit between Chirac and Zeroual had been planned in
New York to coincide with the fiftieth anniversary celebrations of the
United Nations in late October. Meeting in New York would relieve either
president, especially Chirac who had already been to Rabat and Tunis,
from visiting the other's capital. The likelihood of Zeroual visiting France
was minimal. Chirac was under pressure to postpone or call off the summit in view of the ongoing violence in France and the timing: the Algerian
presidential election was coming up on 16 November. Lionel Jospin called
it "inopportune" and Jean-Marie Le Pen attacked Chirac's "crazy policy
of moving closer to the Algerian dictatorship." Jean-Louis Arajol of the
General Police Union distinguished "a difference between fighting terrorism and provoking it. Chirac's handshake with Zeroual can only be seen
as a provocation."[49] Indeed, the summit would symbolize French official
support for Zeroual and the policies of his regime. Among Algerians, disapproval was not confined to extremist Islamists, who underscored it by
the 17 October blast in Paris; major opposition parties, participants and
nonparticipants in the November election, also viewed the planned summit negatively. Abdelhamid Mehri of the FLN said Chirac's support of the
"pseudoelections" and their legitimacy suggested that "France gives a certificate of good conduct to a regime for which democracy is purely a
façade." Foreshadowing the fiasco, the Algerian government itself was

upset over Chirac's repeated reminders to Zeroual to hold "credible and democratic" legislative elections.[50]

Chirac eventually declined to meet with Zeroual, contending that it would be only a photo opportunity benefiting Zeroual's image in the upcoming Algerian presidential election.[51] The Algerians, however, claimed that it was Zeroual who had canceled the summit on 22 October. A presidential spokesman condemned the "persistent unilateral attitudes" of French officials "that can be interpreted as an affront to the dignity and sovereignty of the Algerian people."[52] The Algerian press acclaimed the decision. *L'Authentique,* a pro-Pouvoir paper, proclaimed "Bravo Zeroual," *El Umma* called Zeroual's action "a slap in the face" of France, and *al-Salam* described it as "the end of provocation."[53] According to the Algerian press, Zeroual wanted "a review of bilateral relations based on mutual respect and equality of interests, a clarification of economic relations, and an end to 'equivocation on supposed aid from France'." The daily *Liberté* argued that French aid was only "credits which Algeria will have to pay back" and noted correctly that it benefited hundreds of French firms.[54] An unnamed Algerian minister commented: "If the French do not understand that we do not accept to be lectured by anyone, this means they have learned nothing from our history. Nothing infuriates Algerians more than the prospect of being dealt with on an unequal footing by the French."[55] The image of an Algerian government or forthright president repulsing repugnant French assaults upon national sovereignty was always popular and contributed to Zeroual's later electoral success.

French foreign minister Hervé de Charette referred to the cancellation as "a missed opportunity which ended up as a domestic Algerian electoral ploy." He noted that the French president "wanted genuine dialogue and not a parade in front of the television cameras." According to de Charette, "President Jacques Chirac's intention was for discussion and serious work and not an American-style media stunt." He said that "nothing of an insulting nature was ever said officially" about the Algerian government "except perhaps if talking about democracy is being insulting." The AFP concluded that the cancellation served both sides: "France can say the decision dispels the myth of unconditional support for Algiers and Algeria can say it is defending its 'dignity' and 'sovereignty'."[56]

Libération pointed out that "the cancellation . . . of the Chirac-Zeroual meeting illustrates the extreme difficulty for France to play a role, even as advisor, in Algeria, without being called into question by one side if not both." *Aujourd'hui* added: "In the end the meeting presented far more problems than it offered advantages. At the end of the day its cancellation will work out well for both sides." *France-Soir* observed that the "decision ... does not appear to have left either side unhappy." *InfoMatin* pointed out that President Zeroual "prefers saving face rather than being in France's debt. And since he could not win Chirac's support, he preferred to play the card of the man who is resisting France."[57]

Nevertheless, Chirac signaled significantly on 26 October that he was willing to shift his position on linking aid with Algerian democratization, claiming that it was "legitimate" to "link by proportion" aid to "the speed of the democratic process."[58] *El-Watan* responded: "By daring to interfere in such a direct manner in Algerian domestic affairs, Chirac has committed a sizable diplomatic blunder which risks provoking a very firm reaction from Algerian authorities." On the other hand, Rabah Kebir's office praised Chirac as having taken "a step ... which serves the interest of the Algerian people."[59]

On 27 October another FIS leader, Shaykh Abdel Kader Omar, told *al-Hayat*: "Algerian Moslem people expect nothing good to come out of France and its politicians. Yesterday France fought the Algerian people and today it is backing, financially and militarily, all those who persecute the people." Though he noted that "the French people have become the victim of their country's policies in Algeria," he condemned the GIA bombings in France as serving the interests of the Pouvoir, since they managed "to turn an internal political issue into international terrorism." Referring to the end of discussions in June between the Zeroual government and the FIS, he accused the Pouvoir of intransigence that impeded genuine dialogue with the opposition.[60]

Zeroual Begins "Redemocratization"

Although the major opposition parties boycotted it, the Pouvoir heralded the presidential election as an exercise in pluralist democracy, given the participation of several parties (even if they were marginalized, minor, or coopted). Indeed, a very impressive 75 percent of the electorate voted. In the Algerian community in France, there was also enthusiastic interest in the election. For the first time, approximately 630,000 registered Algerians had the opportunity to cast their ballots at ninety-four polling stations throughout France before the general election on 16 November.[61] The crowds were particularly intense at Lyon, where forty people fell ill. Though there were claims that Algerian diplomatic offices were meddling to influence the vote, Zeroual was clearly the candidate of choice for the emigrants in France and the electorate in Algeria. He received a mandate of 61 percent of the votes cast. As for the other candidates, Mahfoud Nahnah (HAMAS) garnered 25 percent, Said Saadi (RCD) 10 percent, and Noureddine Boukrouh (PRA) 3 percent of the votes. A *Christian Science Monitor* editorial mirrored other analyses by describing the vote as one "against turmoil" rather than a clear mandate for President Zeroual, as the earlier FIS victories had been protests against the FLN's political domination.[62] Nevertheless, after the relatively peaceful election, hope arose that Algeria finally was on its way toward an authentic redemocratization.

Prime Minister Juppé said the election was "an important stage. There must now be others."[63] In his analysis, I. William Zartman contended that Zeroual acquired a great opportunity: "It should enable him to open a long-awaited dialogue with the participating and the boycotting parties, which negotiated a common position in meetings hosted in Rome by the Sant'Egidio community."[64] When Zeroual was inaugurated on 27 November he pledged to produce "an authentic pluralistic democracy." Zeroual also directed his statements to the young: "I invite Algerian youth who are misled to look closely into the ruling passed by their people and to return to the correct path." He spoke of a new "national order."[65] While he did not mention the FIS, opposition parties concluded that the election, with its large turnout, was a legitimate expression of the will of the Algerian people. Rabah Kebir called for dialogue with Zeroual on 20 November, though rival FIS leader Anouar Haddam referred to the election as a "gimmick" and called for the continuation of the struggle.[66] It appeared that Zeroual's electoral success was a propitious opportunity to rally supporters and to reconcile the opposition. Michael Willis contended that "Algerians believed that by granting the President an electoral mandate, they could free him to embrace the solution proposed by the Rome Platform."[67] A determined, decisive initiative was undermined, however, by the eradicator/conciliator intra-Pouvoir rivalry, the disunity of the opposition, and the grim momentum of the *fitna*. Just a day after the inauguration, the head of Algeria's coast guard, General Mohammed Boutaghene, was shot and killed, and on 12 December a car bomb in Algiers claimed fifteen dead and more than forty wounded.

Despite the absence of the major opposition parties, the presidential election still impressed the French government. President Chirac called the vote "a first, decisive step toward establishing peace and democracy in Algeria." Chirac was asked on 3 December if he would be willing to meet with Zeroual and he responded: "President Zeroual is the legitimate president of Algeria and [a meeting] would pose no problem for me."[68] Still, the relationship had chilled considerably since the UN fiasco. In an interview with *Le Tribune,* Foreign Minister Salah Dembri called for a "sound assessment of the common interests in Algerian-French cooperation." He pointed out: "What is termed as assistance is in fact a process that benefits the French three times the amount granted to us and it is also connected with the marketing of French goods in the Algerian market."[69]

François Mitterrand's funeral in January 1996 offered an opportunity for Ahmed Attaf to meet his French counterpart Hervé de Charette and to "redress" the relationship and dissipate bilateral suspicions. After the meeting de Charette, using a most familiar discourse, commented, "We hope together to write a new page in our relations," while Attaf reported, "We both considered that the current course of our relations was not normal and that, on both sides, we could change this abnormal course." *Le Figaro* viewed the meeting as signaling a "new relationship." The Algerian daily *Al-Khabar* considered the meeting "the first step to an improvement in relations between Algeria and France."[70]

The *Fitna* Targets the Christian Presence

Ignoring a many-centuries-old presence distinguished especially by Algeria's native Church Father, Saint Augustine, Islamist extremists targeted the small Christian religious community. To Islamist extremists, Catholic orders collectively symbolized the "colonizing mission" of France. Beginning with the deaths of the priest and nun in the Casbah on 8 May 1994, the GIA had been conducting an assault against Christians, especially French priests and nuns, which intensified during this period. By the time seven Trappist monks were seized in March, eleven members of religious orders, seven French, had been murdered.[71]

The Abduction of the Trappist Monks

The Algerian government, which had referred to terrorism at this time as "vestigial," was particularly embarrassed by the abduction of seven French Trappist monks from their monastery of Tibéhirine near Médéa on 27 March. The GIA demanded the release of inmates from French and Algerian prisons in return for the lives of the monks. The French and Algerian governments refused. On 23 May the GIA released a grim communiqué signed by Abou Abderrahmane Amin, the alias used by Djamel Zitouni, the planner of the Airbus hijacking and bombings in France. It announced: "We cut the throats of the seven monks." The communiqué spoke of the need for the "re-Islamization" of Algeria and equated it with the elimination of "all the enemies of Islam." Foreign Minister Hervé de Charette, confirming the news, declared: "Those who first chose to kidnap them and then finished with them in cold blood bear a great responsibility." Rabah Kebir stated: "I strongly condemn this criminal act and I consider it absolutely opposed to the principles of Islam." According to President Chirac, the monks "incarnated tolerance, fraternity, and solidarity." Jean-Marie Le Pen, however, pointed out that during the Algerian War Christian clerics had "cared for the *fellahin* [ALN] and French soldiers. A different conception than ours of civic loyalty."[72]

It was soon reported that a French envoy had delivered a box of consecrated Communion wafers to the seven captured French monks.[73] This created more tension between the Algerian and French governments. Did the French go behind the Pouvoir's back and attempt to negotiate with the GIA? On 28 May de Charette admitted that they had had contact with the GIA when a messenger from the kidnappers brought an audio cassette to the French embassy on 30 April. De Charette insisted that the information was shared with the Algerian government, which had done "what it could" to find the monks.[74] Nevertheless, the kidnapping and the confusion over contacts with the monks and their abductors showed that bilateral trust was less than complete.

Several years before his martyrdom, one of the monks, Prior Christian de Chergé, anticipated the possibility of such a death. In a prescient statement he thanked his assassin, a "last-minute friend, who will not have known what you were doing," for permitting him "if God pleases, to look into His eyes." He also anticipated that people would "tie this death to so many equally violent deaths, which were anonymous and therefore did not affect people. My life has no higher price than any other, it has no lower price either."[75] Sadly, on 30 May, the same day that the monks' bodies were found, the venerable Cardinal Léon-Etienne Duval died at the age of ninety-two. The cardinal, who had courageously sympathized with Algerian independence aspirations and who had been mercilessly castigated by the advocates of *Algérie française* as "Mohamed ben Duval," symbolized and lived for Christian-Muslim toleration and accommodation in postcolonial Algeria.

Hervé de Charette's Visit and Bishop Claverie's Assassination

On 16 July the vehemently anti-French GIA leader Djamel Zitouni ("Abou Abderrahmane Amin"), who reputedly masterminded the Airbus hijacking and the kidnapping of the monks, was killed in an apparent intra-Islamist ambush. The day after Zitouni's death, it was announced that Foreign Minister Hervé de Charette would arrive on 31 July for a meeting with Algerian officials. The Algerian Press Service anticipated that the visit, the first by a French minister in three years, would "provide an opportunity to think about restoring relations in a serene climate in which the mutual and balanced interests of sovereign states are respected." *Le Figaro* believed that only a presidential visit would symbolize "true reconciliation."[76] Nonetheless, de Charette's visit promised to be an important event.

Upon arrival in Algiers, de Charette informed President Zeroual of "France's political will to take a new lead in Franco-Algerian relations, while observing the principles of mutual respect." A series of ministerial meetings were also planned, including a reciprocal visit by Foreign Minister Attaf to Paris. (The two ministers met again in Washington in September.) Specific issues such as easing visa restrictions and eliminating the ban on Air Algérie service to Paris were deferred to future sessions. There was substantial discussion about a new financial protocol to replace the 1994 agreement. De Charette pointed out: "We are sensitive to the Algerian concerns, but they must in turn be as attentive to French worries."[77] Because Algeria's stability, de Charette said, was essential for North Africa, the western Mediterranean, and specifically France with its complex historical relationship, "we must develop serene, extensive, and solid relations with Algeria."[78]

The French foreign minister also met with Christian clerics and prayed at the tomb of the seven martyred Trappist monks. One of the clerics he talked to was the bishop of Oran, a fourth-generation *pied-noir,* Pierre Claverie. The bishop was an outspoken opponent of Islamist violence and a popular figure in his city. He expected a successful sojourn by the French foreign minister, but he portentously warned on 30 July, while speaking on a Christian radio network in France, that "there could be a redoubling of violence or at least an attempt to carry out a spectacular attack to counter the positive effects of this visit." Hours after talking with de Charette on 1 August, Bishop Claverie was killed by a remote-controlled bomb. The French foreign minister described the bishop as "a man of faith, of justice, and of courage." He added that France "will not be deterred from its path" and that it "wants calm, friendly relations with Algeria" as, inspired by Bishop Claverie's engagement, France "takes up [his] message of . . . friendship and solidarity between the French and Algerian people." The archbishop of Paris, Cardinal Jean-Marie Lustiger, reflected upon Claverie's commitment to Algeria: "If he stayed, it wasn't because of a taste for danger but because he loved the hundreds of thousands of Algerians also suffering violence, injustice, and the threat of crime." To Cardinal Lustiger, Claverie remained in Algeria "to show that Christians and Muslims could live together by respecting each other and respecting human rights." A message of condolence from President Zeroual read: "This barbaric act shows a total indifference to human values, and to the harmony . . . which characterizes Islam and distinguishes the Algerian people." The FIS's Rabah Kebir condemned the attack, and Anouar Haddam feared that it would strengthen ties between Paris and Algiers.[79]

Among the economic consequences of Foreign Minister Hervé de Charette's visit to Algeria in 1996 was the decision to plan a new financial protocol. The Algerian government aimed to encourage French investment and security in the Algerian market, to unblock financial assistance valued at FF 1–2 million a year and medium-term COFACE credits of FF 3–4 million, and to secure a major credit line for SONATRACH.[80] By the end of the year, the new protocol remained unfinished. In part this reflected COFACE's reservations about risking more monies for Algeria, in part the availability of other sources of financial aid, a consequence of successful French lobbying within international agencies. This reduced France's self-perceived obligation and responsibility for maintaining Algeria's economic viability.[81]

French Frustration and the *Fitna*

On 3 December a bomb attack at the Port Royal station in Paris killed three people and injured about a hundred. No one claimed responsibility, but the design of the bomb, a gas canister filled with nails as shrapnel, was similar to past GIA devices, so it was assumed to be the work of Islamists.[82] On 24 December, President Chirac received a purported GIA letter which threatened to "destroy your country." It obliquely referred to the Port Royal bombing by noting that the GIA chose "the path of killings and massacres. We do what we say. The events of recent days prove this." The letter, signed by Antar Zouabri, the new GIA leader, inveighed that the French were "among the blasphemers, the most dangerous enemies of Muslims."[83] In another warning received on 5 January 1997, the usually more tempered AIS called for France to end its financial assistance to the "putschist" and "rotten regime." It stated: "The Algerian people sees with its own eyes that this aid is going towards the purchase of destructive and oppressive equipment which simply worsen the junta's crimes." The only aid considered legitimate was humanitarian. The AIS in this statement clearly separated itself from the GIA and denied "all responsibility for any act affecting the security of peoples who have nothing to do with the crimes committed by the putschist regime." In addition, the AIS asserted that the GIA letter to Chirac was a "manipulation" contrived by Algerian special services to draw Paris into a closer collaboration with Algiers.[84]

On 24 January 1997, in a televised speech, President Zeroual declared his government's "firm will to fight terrorist groups until their eradication."[85] At this time, much of the local pacification was by well-paid, well-armed, and "privatized" paramilitary groups rather than by the armed forces.[86] The proliferation of these "militias" and weapons intensified the violence and was poorly monitored by the apparently powerless government. This convoluted the conflict, since campaigns were obscured by vicious communal vendettas. Exasperated French authorities could ascribe neither responsibility nor reason for these vengeful operations as Algeria neared the threshold of anarchy.

French Frustrations Surface

In an interview with *Libération,* Lionel Jospin, the leader of the Socialist Party, candidly criticized French policy toward Algeria: "France must lift the taboo, it must not remain silent, or give the impression of unconditional support for the Algerian regime." Jospin regretted that civilian and military elites canceled the 1992 elections, "without doubt a mistake." He sharply criticized the Pouvoir's undemocratic nature: "All measures taken by the Algerian government to limit political openness, to demonize certain nonviolent political forces, to intimidate those who support them and to cut them off from international democratic and pacifist movements like the Socialist International [the FFS] are to be condemned. . . . No one is doing anything [about it] in Europe because France is not doing anything." He added that official reticence over the *fitna,* in fear of risking reprisal, was passé: "We have already been struck, the conflict is already with us." Jospin called for French support for genuine "democratic forces," asserting that "however feeble they are, they constitute a solution, a glimmer of hope." He also supported the Sant'Egidio Platform.[87]

De Charette acknowledged that "the situation is a very serious one." He pulled back from supporting involvement of Europe's Organization for Security and Cooperation (OSCE). Instead, he respected Algerian sensibilities since "Algeria is an independent country. And for the moment, we think it is the responsibility of the Algerian people [and] Algerian leaders to solve their problems."[88] De Charette appeared soon afterwards before the Foreign Affairs Committee of the National Assembly, chaired by

Valéry Giscard d'Estaing, to detail the deteriorating conditions in Algeria. He reported that between 150 and 200 people were being killed in Algeria weekly, a figure considerably higher than that officially acknowledged by its government. The assassination on 28 January of the powerful secretary-general of the Union Générale des Travailleurs Algériens (UGTA), Abdelhak Benhamouda, was another brutal reminder of the ceaseless violence.[89] De Charette explained the difficulty of the French position. He recounted how Algeria had asked France for help, but when help was offered, it was often condemned as interference. He also referred to Zeroual's 24 January televised speech in which the Algerian president related the violence in his country to "foreign political forces" and the "Sant'Egidio group." De Charette feared that the tone of the speech "put an end for all prospects for a political solution."[90]

After de Charette's report, Giscard, claiming "agreement with Monsieur de Charette on this general line," declared that "all Algerian political forces must be able to participate, to be present at the polls." With the exception of "people directly implicated in terrorist attacks, it is essential that all political tendencies, including the Islamists, participate in these elections." Though he stated "it is up to the Algerians to find a way out of this drama," Giscard sympathized with the "Algerians themselves who are caught in a trap between horrific and unjustifiable attacks and pitiless repression."[91]

Giscard's comments, along with those of de Charette and Jospin, provoked strong Algerian reactions. Ambassador Hocine Djoudi perceived "a certain feverishness in some French political circles." He stated that future elections would include "all parties, except those who have excluded themselves."[92] Foreign Minister Ahmed Attaf reiterated that France "should not get involved in [nor] interfere in the conduct of our national affairs." Disputing de Charette's statement, he said Algeria "has never asked for France's support" but rather "wanted France to keep as far away as possible from our internal affairs," a position he had reaffirmed to de Charette. Attaf also questioned Giscard's statement about the inclusion of Islamists in future elections: "This comment is . . . an unhealthy contribution to rehabilitate precisely those who are responsible for our country's tragedy."[93]

Though Anouar Haddam of the FIS seconded Giscard's implicit call for the FIS to participate in Algerian elections, the French ex-president specified on 1 February that he "did not pronounce the name of the FIS." He said that, given France's "special past with Algeria—although it is receding in time," there was and still is a need for a "special sensitivity." Yet now, with a legitimately elected president with a "mandate," it was time "to reopen a debate."[94] In an effort to deter that debate, Prime Minister Juppé echoed the Pouvoir's contention that "legal political groups should participate" in elections, and "as long as one uses bombs, booby-trapped cars, and knives, one is not a party which adheres to democratic values."[95] While repeating the usual policy line, Juppé referred to the *fitna* a month later as "a real headache" and urged that future elections "be as transparent as possible." The official response from Algiers was predictably sharp, claiming that Prime Minister Juppé "felt obliged, for the umpteenth time, to give his views on Algeria on a French television channel, and felt he was authorized to put forward the 'usual advice' to an independent state and sovereign people."[96]

Despite all this, there was some improvement. Air Algérie resumed flights to and from Paris-Roissy after a two-year suspension. British Airways particularly protested this French decision, since Air Algérie's check-in counter was viewed by the British carrier as a security hazard to its own airport operations. On 15 April de Charette and Attaf also met in Valetta, Malta, in an effort to revive the relationship.

Elections in Algeria and France

Algeria's "redemocratization" was another source of bilateral contention. On 28 November 1996 Algerians voted in a national referendum to revise the constitution. Ait Ahmed termed this process a "historically unprecedented masquerade."[97] The proposed changes included instituting a bicameral legislature and a supreme court, and limiting the presidency to two five-year terms. The prime minister could choose his own cabinet, but he was appointed or dismissed by the president rather than the parliament. The changes restricted parliament's right to pass legislation without the president's approval. Moreover, the president would appoint one-third of the upper house. Ironically, the expansion of the legislative branch actually extended executive privilege and power. The referendum also legitimized a revision of the July 1989 Law on Political Associations and the Electoral Law, prohibiting political parties based primarily upon religious, ethnic, lingual, or regional affiliations. Amid charges by opposition parties of irregularities, 85.5 percent of the 12.5 million voters supported the constitutional changes.

Algeria's legislative elections of 5 June 1997 resulted in President Zeroual's Rassemblement National Démocratique (RND) winning 155 of the 380 seats in the lower house. The FLN won 64 seats, and Mahfoud Nahnah's ex-HAMAS, since March 1997 called the Mouvement de la

Société pour la Paix (MSP), got 69. Surprisingly, the PRA of Noureddine Boukrouh, who had received more than 400,000 votes in the presidential election, did not get a seat, nor did the Alliance Nationale Républicaine of Redha Malek. There were many complaints of fraud, including those submitted by United Nations observers.[98] Officially 65.5 percent of the electorate voted but, according to critical observers, it was probably under 50 percent. The legislative elections aimed to confer legitimacy, but they failed to generate public enthusiasm in Algeria or the emigrant community in France.[99]

The local and regional elections of 23 October were likewise marked by tampering, which incited a thirty-thousand-strong protest march in Algiers on 30 October. Abdel Aziz Belaid, an FLN member of Parliament, reflected: "The extremism of the Islamic militants produced the extremism of the authorities, and this [vote rigging] will now, I think, produce another extremism."[100] The elections held on 25 December for the upper house, the Conseil d'Etat, gave the RND eighty seats, the FLN ten, the FFS four, and the MSP only two seats. This democracy was hardly "transparent," but institutions had been inaugurated and a new political system, no matter how "opaque," emerged.

Meanwhile in France, the Socialists regained power in the 1 June election, which created another political cohabitation. The new premier was the outspoken Lionel Jospin, who during the campaign argued that French policy must shift and "weigh heavily on Algeria in the direction of democracy."[101] *El-Watan* felt that Jospin's coming to power "does not bode well" for the bilateral relationship.[102] *La Tribune,* on the other hand, wrote: "In the face of the closeness of the Algerian-US cooperation in hydrocarbons, the new French Government knows that it will have difficulty in maintaining political tension with Algiers for too long, especially since, [with] the advance [in] legitimizing its institutions, the Algerian state is no longer in a position of political precariousness."[103]

When Foreign Minister Hubert Védrine arrived in Algiers in July to attend the fifth annual meeting of the Mediterranean Forum, he met and talked with his counterpart, Ahmed Attaf, about bilateral relations and especially an association agreement with the European Union.[104] Védrine was faced with a difficult situation; according to José Garçon of *Libération,* the new government was practicing "a balancing act." Jospin had said before being elected that he was against "supporting the Algerian Government whatever it does." He believed that "there is no solution to this tragedy through repressive policy alone, and that a political solution is necessary." Yet the strategic political, economic, and cultural imperatives so crucial in the bilateral relationship necessitated reconsideration. The Algerian newspaper *La Tribune* wrote: "This meeting will be an opportunity for France to reorient its strategy."[105]

In an interview in August, Védrine pointed out that Algeria had a pluralist parliament, and that political opponents such as Abbasi Madani had been released. In other words, progress had been made. He intoned the mantra "It is up to the Algerians to find themselves the solutions to their problems."[106] In September Jospin recognized that the Pouvoir was willing "to construct a compromise with a part of the Islamists that it does not call moderates but one can call, let's say, legalists."[107]

Jospin repeated in an interview with *Le Monde* that "a process of democratization is indispensable to Algeria."[108] Then two weeks later he conceded during a television interview that "the great difficulty is that we don't have much idea what is really going on in Algeria. . . . We can see appalling terrorism, the escalating violence against ordinary people, but [it] is extremely difficult to determine what is going on." He added: "It is not like Chile under Pinochet with democrats fighting a dictatorial regime. We are confronted with a fanatical and violent opposition fighting against a regime which . . . has recourse itself to violence and the power of the state, so we have to be careful."[109] A commission advising Jospin on human rights advised that the Algerian conflict be placed on the agenda of the United Nations. According to Foreign Minister Védrine, France was ready to take an active role in resolving the *fitna:* "All organizations, all countries that are deeply stirred by what is happening [in Algeria] cannot but express their availability to all sides—if they so wish and if they so ask." He carefully mentioned that this willingness was founded "not on a desire to interfere, but on humanity, friendship, and solidarity."[110] The aged though still active Ahmed Ben Bella commended "a moral intervention," but he contended that international political activism would be regarded by the vast majority of Algerians as interference. The only way to establish a political solution would be a negotiation between Islamists and the military.[111]

International Pressures and Pleas

From August 1997 to early 1998, Algeria suffered sustained slaughter. Unremittingly vicious attacks, from the burning of homes, incinerating those inside, to ritualistic mutilations featuring disembowelment, characterized the savagery. Algeria became a North African "killing fields." The perpetrators, however, could not be identified as a recognized party like Cambodia's Khmer Rouge, but were a variety of roiling, retributive groups—Islamists, secularists, local militias, "gangsters"—sharing only a taste for terror. The AIS attempted to distance itself from the bloodshed and, after calling for a truce in September, adopted a unilateral cease-fire on 1 October. Besides the inherent dangers of the *fitna,* national and international reporters faced stringent press censorship which prohibited independent reporting. Nevertheless, news still surfaced of such grisly events as the murder of eleven women teachers on 29 September. Algeria entered a Camusian nightmare matching nihilism with gangsterism and apostasy with absurdity.

There were increasing calls for international intervention. Amnesty International called for "independent investigations" and castigated the Algerian authorities for the human rights abuses of "security forces and state-armed militias . . . responsible for killings and abductions of individuals and groups of civilians which have been blamed by the authorities on 'terrorists.'"[112] On 10 November 1997 French humanitarian organizations, trade unions, and celebrities including Gérard Depardieu, Isabelle Adjani, Isabelle Huppert, Charles Aznavour, and Algeria's Khaled, the king of rai music, staged a "day of solidarity" with Algeria. The Algerian government "deplored" the tacit official approval of this demonstration.[113] In an interview with the French weekly *Evènement du Jeudi,* Jacques Attali, former president of the European Bank for Reconstruction and Development, suggested "the creation of international brigades" and added that "there would have to be another Algerian government. The current one is corrupt and bureaucratic."[114]

Nevertheless, the Socialist government signaled support of President Zeroual in early December. Foreign Minister Védrine stated: "Questions raised two or three years ago about the lifetime of the Algerian regime no longer apply today." He looked on the June parliamentary elections as indicative of Algerian support of a gradual political pluralism, "a fragile, complicated process." He urged that "Algerian authorities . . . complete this institutional process with a process of true democratization, by way of reform" and said that "one of the dimensions of our policy is to support and to encourage every day the solidarity of French society with Algerian society."[115] At the end of month Claude Cheysson, a strong supporter of Algeria's secular political culture, completed a visit there. He acknowledged that "religious fanaticism cannot be eradicated" and recognized, too, that "there is also pure and simple banditry in which, it is probably true, elements of the government take part." Cheysson judged that "there is poor coordination [among] the military police, the police, and the army. There is a certain disorder."[116]

Recurrent bloody rampages in villages, reminiscent of the FLN's terrorist tactics at Philippeville in 1955, ravaged Algeria in late 1997 and early 1998. It was estimated that during the first week of Ramadan, beginning 30 December 1997, a thousand people died.[117] These massacres impelled the French Foreign Ministry to issue an unprecedentedly provocative attack on the Algerian government: "French authorities condemn in the firmest fashion these terrorist crimes that can have no justification, especially not on religious grounds. . . . They issue a reminder of the Algerian population's right to be protected. The duty of any government is to enable its citizens to live in peace and security." It also urged that the Algerian government pursue an "authentic democratization," a thinly veiled rebuke of Algeria's recent institution-making. The statement also supported German foreign minister Klaus Kinkel's suggestion on 4 January that the European Union investigate the surging slaughter by dispatching a delegation to Algeria.

The fuming Algerian Foreign Ministry sternly retorted: "The French authorities have no right to remind the Algerian Government of its duties, and it is out of place that they suggest solutions while Algeria is carrying out is own approach to end the crisis." It declaimed that the French position "could only come from a lack of understanding or a deliberate willfulness to manipulate the facts" and "is unacceptable in every aspect."[118] Mohamed Ghoualmi, the offended Algerian ambassador to France, complained: "Instead of showing clear solidarity with Algeria . . . pressure is brought to bear exclusively on the state as if it were responsible for this situation." He cited the imputed indignity as "at the least unacceptable, that a sovereign state finds itself being summoned by another state to exercise its constitutional responsibilities to its own people."[119]

In an effort to cool the tempers across the Mediterranean, President Chirac affirmed France's "solidarity" with Algeria and called for "help and cooperation" with the troubled country.[120] Defense Minister Alain Richard deflected the growing clamor for international peacekeepers: "The view of the French government is that there are authorities in place in Algeria who, moreover, have made an effort toward some form of democracy." He added that France "does not see a reason to internationalize the conflict."[121] Foreign Minister Védrine acknowledged that "we do not have totally exact information," but said before a closed-door meeting of the French National Assembly that "no reliable source implicates the Algerian authorities."[122] Algeria's democracy was scripted, flawed, and conditioned, but it was a semblance of democracy, and that had to be appreciated. The formerly outspoken Jospin seemed resigned to the reality of the "redemocratization" of the Algerian government and its new institutions. Jospin's policy and that of his government became Pasqua-like, emphasizing the positive in Algeria rather than the negative. President Chirac, though in general agreement, still displayed shades of ambiguity like others on the right toward the Algerian situation.[123]

Nevertheless, former prime minister Abdelhamid Brahimi believed that France was deeply involved. According to Brahimi, it supported the cancellation of the 1992 elections and provided "advanced weapons" to the Pouvoir. Brahimi viewed three generals, Mohamed Lamari, chief of staff, Mohamed Mediene, head of military security, and Smain Lamari, head of special services, as having particularly strong affiliations with France if not memberships in the *hizb faransa:* "Today there is the Algerian people on the one hand and a French party—the three generals—on the other, representing a totalitarian and corrupt regime." He claimed that France held the "key to the crisis in its hand if it decided to pull out and to no longer keep Algeria as its exclusive hunting ground." He noted the historical recurrence: "Most Algerians consider the current conflict a continuation of the War [of 1954–62], nourished by the spirit of revenge."[124]

French Intellectuals and the *Fitna*

The Algerian War of Independence galvanized the engagement of Jean-Paul Sartre, Simone de Beauvoir, Francis Jeanson, François Mauriac. A generation later, the *fitna* numbed and muted their successors. Though many French intellectuals identified Islamism with obscurantism, they also assailed the oligarchic Pouvoir, which they deemed authoritarian and undemocratic. Their ambivalence reflected that of their government.

Foreign Minister Védrine, the architect of a more activist Algeria policy, decided to involve the intellectuals directly. He expedited a trip to Algeria by the influential (and Algeria-born) Bernard-Henri Lévy. Lévy subsequently wrote his impressions in an article in *Le Monde* which did not support the idea that the regime's military security arm was complicit in the terrible massacres. He found that contention neither warranted nor credible. As for Algeria's democratization, Lévy concluded that it would occur only when peasants were worth as much as petroleum.[125] André Glucksmann embarked on a similar trip. He praised Algeria's free press, blamed Islamists for the assaults, and berated the armed forces for not protecting the people.[126] In February 1998 the chairman of the Foreign Relations Committee of the National Assembly, Jack Lang, who had been minister of culture in the Mitterrand years, visited Algeria, received "good impressions" of the country, and concluded Algeria was becoming more democratic and pluralist.[127]

Taking a different view, François Gèze and Pierre Vidal-Naquet called on the Jospin government to support an international investigative group to provide objective truth about violations of human rights. They also called for scrutiny of French financial and commercial cooperation, given its "essential role in maintaining the dictators of Algeria in power."[128] Lévy in turn warned of the dangers of stereotyping the military as undemocratic, corrupt, and torturers. Though he recognized that some fit those descriptions, he knew others who were democratic and insisted on the rule of the law. To Lévy, the only option was "democracy" rather than "the policy of hate" because "there is no other choice in the struggle against the *Khmers verts.*"[129] Even so, a month later Lévy recognized that Algeria "is far from being a democratic state."[130]

International Investigations

Meanwhile, the Algerian government grudgingly acceded to the wishes of the international community for investigative inspections. It allowed the European Union to dispatch a low-level team known as the "troika" to visit the country on 19–20 January.[131] Their investigation, which was more of an orientation, had symbolic rather than substantive value—an indication of the EU's concern. The Europeans were careful not to question the legitimacy of the Algerian government or suggest an intervention. Foreign Minister Védrine acknowledged that there was "no reason to doubt" the official Algerian position and that he had not received "evidence" to think otherwise.[132]

From 22 July to 4 August 1998, a United Nations group led by Portugal's former president Mário Soares assessed the situation in Algeria. Though authorities restricted their freedom of movement in this "mission of information," the Soares team could recognize that government forces had committed human rights violations including torture, while still concluding that Islamists were most responsible for the killings in the country. Their report, published on 16 September, called for "political openness" and "a change of mentality in the judiciary, the institutions responsible for upholding human rights, in the police and the army; and in the Algerian body politic as a whole."[133] Amnesty International was unimpressed with the UN assessment and referred to its report as a "whitewash."[134]

The French National Assembly's Foreign Affairs Committee also sent a delegation to Algeria, on 21–23 July. The French delegation was not an investigative team but rather was interested in evaluating the bilateral relationship. Its report appeared on 21 October and reiterated the "extreme complexity" of the situation. It also detailed how Algeria had ignored France's political and economic "gestures." For example, instead of buying from the European Airbus consortium, Algeria chose America's Boeing to supply new planes for Air Algérie. Furthermore, though French businessmen had traveled to Algeria to make or extend contacts and contracts, Algerian counterparts did not follow up with return visits and shunned French suppliers for American ones. In order to improve France's position, the report urged that four "major dossiers" be addressed: (1) resumption of Air France flights to Algeria, (2) reclassification by COFACE to lower Algeria's risk and thereby improve the OECD's investment perspective, (3) ratification of the February 1993 reciprocal investments accord, and (4) France's assistance in negotiations with the European Union concerning Algeria's associateship (something already achieved by Morocco and Tunisia).[135] Those dossiers all were bound up with Algerian sensitivity to the symbolic significance of the bilateral economic relationship.

The Symbolic Death of Lounès Matoub

On 25 June 1998 Lounès Matoub, the Lion of Kabylia and one of Algeria's greatest musicians, was shot dead near Tizi-Ouzou. In many ways he incarnated an ideal of postcolonial Algeria. He was a fervent advocate of democracy, toleration, and pluralism; he also championed Kabyle rights and Tamazight. One of his most famous songs was "The Mute Algerian," alluding to those silenced by the Boumedienne regime, but the outspoken Matoub was hardly that. His music assaulted official corruption and oppression. During the October 1988 riots he was shot while urging a return to calm. Lounès had been kidnapped and held by the GIA from 25 September to 10 October 1994, which created an uproar in Kabylia, but after being condemned to death he was released. Lounès continued his protest music, assailing both Islamists and the Pouvoir. His death brought messages of grief from France, even a statement from President Chirac who felt "consternation with a great sadness." Jospin admired Matoub's "convictions" and termed his death "a victory for barbarity."[136] Kabyles were quick to blame the government.

Matoub wanted his latest compact disk to be released on 5 July, the date not only of Algerian independence but also of the implementation of the general Arabization law passed in 1990. This had been postponed by

President Boudiaf and later by Prime Minister Abdesselam owing to the pressing domestic situation. In December 1996, however, the National Transition Council mandated its implementation. The Algerian government then decided to accelerate the process, much to the chagrin of the Berbers, insisting that Arabic be institutionalized in July 1998. *El-Watan* regarded the whole idea as anachronistic and a grave affront to the Berbers. It was reminiscent of the FLN era of a single party and of "single thought." It was to be hoped, the paper suggested, that the events in restive Kabylia in the early 1980s and the October riots had proved that forced Arabization had to be abandoned.[137]

President Zeroual Decides to Leave Office

On 11 September, President Zeroual announced that he would be leaving office before the end of his term. *Le Monde* commented that Zeroual's leaving office was a setback for pluralism and democracy and seemed to indicate that the eradicator faction had become dominant in the Pouvoir.[138] The retirement surprised Algerian political circles, but soon parties and "clans" began advancing familiar names as candidates for the April 1999 elections: Mokdad Sifi, Abdelaziz Bouteflika, Mohamed Sahnoun, Mahfoud Nahnah, Mouloud Hamrouche, Hocine Ait Ahmed, Sid Ahmed Ghozali, Ahmed Taleb Ibrahimi. On 15 April, six presidential candidates charged massive fraud and withdrew from the election, leaving Bouteflika, the perceived candidate of the Pouvoir, as the only choice for president.[139] Bouteflika had proclaimed his intention to bring Algeria back to the "glory years" of the Boumedienne period. The presidential election was a blow to redemocratization and underscored the elliptical nature of Algeria's postcolonial history.

French-Algerian Economic Relations during the *Fitna*

For the most part, France and Algeria managed to isolate their political differences from their economic relations during the *fitna*. France remained Algeria's most important commercial partner, its share of Algeria's imports in 1994 ranking first at 27.4 percent, and its purchase of exports second at 15.4 percent. That year, France's export credit insurer, COFACE, covered contracts of FF 30 billion.[140] In 1996 France dominated Algeria's imports with almost 32 percent of the market; it received, however, only 13 percent of Algeria's exports. France's strong position, especially in the export of agricultural and pharmaceutical commodities, was enhanced by French commercial credits. France benefited from this arrangement. According to the French-Algerian Chamber of Commerce, about a thousand of the 9,500 exporting firms were almost solely dependent on the Algerian market.[141]

Algeria wanted to expand France's commercial relationship. Foreign Minister Attaf complained, in an interview with the Algerian daily *El Khabar*, that his country "cannot be satisfied with being a market for France in the absence of investment and partnership." Exchanges, he observed, "are limited to the commercial sphere," while France "is absent from anything resembling investment, partnership, and the reconstruction of our industrial fabric." This "troubled" the relationship.[142]

An often-raised point was that the trade deficit with France approximated the annual amount of commercial credits accorded to Algeria.[143] Nevertheless, French intervention in multilateral financial circles, even if self-serving given the size of its own loans, prevented Algeria's economy from suffering a meltdown and assisted in a slow but now more certain recovery. Since 1995 the growth of gross domestic product had increased by 3.5 percent, to about 5.5 percent in 1997. Concurrently inflation dropped from 32.2 percent in 1995 to approximately 23.5 percent in 1997, with 5.2 percent expected for 1998.[144] The considerable debt rose above $30 billion, but rescheduling, and an expanding hydrocarbons sector benefiting from the rise in petroleum prices in the mid-1990s, meant the country had money available and was no longer so dependent on France or the IMF.[145]

Algeria's economic expansion attracted greater French attention. Jean Audibert, ambassador from 1988 to 1992, led a delegation for "social solidarity" which included business leaders in December 1997. Foreign Minister Védrine's appeal for French businesses to "return to Algeria," was taken up in a highly publicized three-day visit by members of the *patronat* in March 1998. According to a spokesman for this group: "One of the purposes of this visit is to consolidate our role as Algeria's main partner . . . not just as a supplier but as an investment partner." He added: "We have confidence in the stability of this economy and in its development." The business leaders met with several Algerian ministers.[146] In May, Ingerop, part of the Suez Lyonnaise des Eaux, was awarded a contract for the construction of gas compression installations at Hassi Messaoud.[147] Another French business delegation arrived in November 1998. France's government and its businesses were worried about the United States' growing presence in the hydrocarbons sector. Indeed, Algeria not only could play its "America card" but had other clients who could serve as "trumps" neutralizing France's implicit economic interests, ambi-

Table 9.1. French Trade with Algeria, 1995–1997 (in millions of French francs)

	1995	1996	1997
French exports	14,238	13,123	13,357
French imports	7,539	9,439	12,642
Balance	6,699	3,684	715

Note: For the first half of 1998, exports to Algeria of FF 7,139 million and imports of FF 4,874 million were reported by *MEED*, 23 October 1998.
Source: Direction des Relations Economiques Extérieres, statistics bureau, Customs office, Paris.

tions, and particularly pretensions. Economic liberalization threatened the postcolonial notion of Algeria as a private French reserve.

The establishment of "exclusion zones" in 1995 insulated the hydrocarbons sector from the *fitna* and secured international confidence.[148] The sector's infrastructure, its oil and gas trunklines, were buried, protected from sabotage. In the 1990s the sector, catalyzed by liberalization legislation in 1986 and 1991, experienced great expansion. The volume of natural gas in the Transmed trunkline running from Algeria through Tunisia across the Mediterranean to Italy (and now Slovenia) was enhanced with more pipelines and compressors. The Gazoduc Maghreb-Europe (GME), begun in 1994, delivered its first gas to Spain in November 1996. The GME has a capacity of eight billion cubic meters, and with the added push of compression stations could easily be doubled, possibly reaching twenty billion. The trunkline is slated to link with France and possibly Germany. Algeria will continue to be the EU's largest supplier of natural gas well into the twenty-first century.[149]

France became a less sought-after partner than Anglo-American companies. The American Anadarko corporation has enjoyed repeated oil strikes in the Sahara. According to a spokesman for Anadarko: "We're increasing our investments and we're committed for the long term." He added: "We think Algeria makes sense for us."[150] Other American companies were also prominently involved in the sector's development. Bechtel played a leading role in the construction of the GME. In 1994 Atlantic Richfield (ARCO) signed a $1.3 billion production-sharing contract. And on 23 December 1995 British Petroleum (BP) entered a coveted partnership with SONATRACH to develop known gas fields south of In Salah. The commitment to spend $3.5 billion in Algeria, covering all stages from exploration to production to marketing, represented one of BP's greatest ventures. It was an important signal of faith in the Zeroual government, and stimulated new investments. With five thousand foreign hydrocarbons technicians in Algeria at this time, Nordine Ait Laoussine affirmed: "I think it is a clear expression of faith in the future development of the country by foreign oil companies in Algeria's biggest business, which is oil and gas."[151]

Though France was still Algeria's greatest single natural gas purchaser, one French official commented: "When the BP contract . . . was signed we felt we were being left with crumbs."[152] On 30 January 1996, Total (CFP) did sign a $950 million agreement with Spain's Repsol and SONATRACH to develop and produce natural gas reserves in the Tin Fouye Tabenkort in southeast Algeria.[153] But in August 1996, continued delays in GDF's planned renovation of the liquefaction facilities at Skikda forced SONATRACH to open bids for a new contractor. The American company M. W. Kellogg was conspicuously asked to bid for the work.[154] When Kellogg received the contract, GDF warned Algeria that it should review long-term contracts, as GDF had other producers available. SONATRACH tersely replied that it had other buyers.[155] Though the expanding "Anglo" domination of the sector has irritated the French, France's governments have realistically perceived, too, that a widely publicized major economic initiative or investment could endanger its nationals in Algeria and even its citizens at home.[156]

Algeria's expansion and enterprise have served as a metaphor for the changing global and regional realities in hydrocarbons. SONATRACH has undergone important structural changes to meet the demands of new clients both downstream and upstream.[157] Algeria has achieved its cherished diversification in the sector—ironically by liberal rather than socialist measures, and at a political cost: its relinquishing of absolute control over its natural resources. The hydrocarbons sector, now so isolated from the violence, has become internationalized. There are forty-four oil and gas companies operating in the country. Approximately 3.3 billion barrels of recoverable reserves have been discovered. About 10 percent of Algeria's petroleum production of 850,000 barrels per day is pumped by international firms.[158]

France's national hydrocarbon enterprises, especially in natural gas, have been unprepared or reluctant to adapt to the new global and regional conditions. Without a substantial reorganization of these enterprises, France will certainly not be able to keep up with international competitors in Algeria. It will lose its advantages of geographical proximity and language. The European Union's deregulation schedule has already affected GDF's protected and anachronistic monopoly status. GDF in particular needs its role redefined (which will involve a major political decision and substantial risk, given the power of French unions) and expanded downstream. Unlike other enterprises, GDF does not produce its own supplies.[159] The fields south of In Salah, now under BP control, would have been ideal for Total (CFP) and GDF to exploit mutually with SONATRACH. Elf Aquitaine has purposely stayed away from the Algerian fields, in part because of bitter memories of the 1971 nationalizations, and pursued profitable expansion elsewhere—the North Sea, West Africa, most recently Libya. Total has been particularly active in the Middle East, with controversial agreements with Iran and Iraq.[160]

France still wants to play an active role in Algeria for "sentimental" as well as profitable reasons. Indeed, Algeria also wants France as a partner, but on its terms. Their bilateral economic engagement remains qualified, however, by political conditions and historical memory.

Ending the *Fitna*

If the *fitna* genuinely illustrates an elliptical history, it would be only appropriate to anticipate the restaging of an event that occurred in August 1962. The brief fratricide that erupted between the ALN's internal and external groups, tainting the end of the Algerian Revolution, was ended by a mass protest in Algiers organized by the UGTA with demonstrators chanting "*saba'a sinine, barakat,*" or "seven years, enough of this." There is a pressing need for a similar swell of popular protest today. Perhaps the country has arrived at this point. Algerians are numbed and exhausted by the violence and its terrible toll. Amnesty International estimated that the *fitna* had claimed eighty thousand lives by the end of 1997, then qualified this statistic by reporting that "according to other sources, including Algerian political parties, health workers and journalists, the number of victims is considerably higher."[161]

Andrew J. Pierre and William B. Quandt outlined a plan to bring an end to the civil war. Since France was limited by its historical intimacy (though arguably not to the degree the two analysts contend), their plan featured a coordination of foreign financial assistance, to be linked with democratization and proctoring of elections by international observers. Yet Pierre and Quandt understood that "none of this will lead anywhere unless the vast majority of Algerians . . . are willing to raise their voices in support of a political solution." They argued: "An end to the Algerian civil war will happen sooner if those who support dialogue feel encouraged by the international community."[162]

Archbishop Teissier poignantly concluded that "as long as one does not hear those who cry" there will be no resolution of the *fitna*.[163] With the expectation of continuing redemocratization, despite the collapse of the April 1999 presidential election process, perhaps Algeria will be able "to get at the root of the problem," perceived by Robert Mortimer as "the need to forge a pact that would guarantee civil liberties while allowing the expression of the full range of views present in Algerian civil society."[164] Yahia Zoubir has expressed hope that "the completion of the 'democratisation from above' may break the status quo and allow democratic forces to emerge. Authoritarian rulers often dig their own political graves. They open breaches in the political system, which, if exploited astutely by democratic forces, could lead to genuine democratisation."[165]

Ahmed Taleb Ibrahimi, before withdrawing from the 1999 presidential election, said that Algeria had an opportunity once again to play an exemplary role: "Now after this trial of blood, with the winds of democracy blowing, we have a chance to achieve that. If we succeed, we will create a model for the rest of the Arab and Muslim world."[166] Taleb Ibrahimi's externalization of Algerian politics is typical of his generation. What has to happen is an internalization as well as institutionalization of the process. Claude Cheysson recognized this several years ago in an interview, when he saw elections as contributing toward the existential project of "fashioning an identity."[167] Yet the April 1999 setback proved how problematic Algeria's democratization remains.

Another enduring requirement of democratization was perceived by Salima Ghezali of *La Tribune:* "The day transparency prevails in the management of the economic questions, that will mean we are on the path to democracy."[168] This necessary step is a dangerous one, witness President Boudiaf's assassination, since it would threaten exposure of political and economic corruption. This embarrassment could also spill over into the French-Algerian relationship.

Le Monde asked in 1995: "Can France have an Algeria policy?" The debate considered whether France could morally insist on linking economic assistance to democratization, given its own bitter colonial history in Algeria.[169] France's ambivalence was burdened by its unresolved historical relationship with Algeria and, as chapter 10 will explore, by its lack of historicity. Policy inevitably drifted into inertia and immobilism. France waited to react rather than risk pressuring the Pouvoir toward democratization by tying aid to political progress complemented by an array of civil rights and freedoms. For all its fury, the *fitna* offered France an opportunity. A consistent French appeal for human rights and democracy, while honestly recognizing its past abuses in Algeria, would have contributed to purging its own colonial guilt and sublimating its traumatic decolonization of Algeria. France's fear of upsetting Algerian governments made it, too, captive of the *fitna*. This has been a very difficult period, as France questioned whether it was still a dynamic, influential power charged by timeless essentialist values, or a nation slipping into irrelevant and "decadent" decline.

Algeria's grievous suffering in the self-inflicted *fitna* has demonstrated repeatedly that the country needs to design and define a nation. History has shown that Algeria does not have one voice but many voices—and all need to be heard, including those that are francophone, through institutions that protect their rights. Any political resolution must take into account all parties ranging from the *hizb faransa* to extreme political Islamism. It also entails the withdrawal of the army from political affairs. Above all, Algeria cannot reject its own historical existence, an existence distinguished by a variety of cultural legacies. Rejection is no solution; resolution must accommodate historical and social realities. Once this is done, the existential praxis will resume and, in a free environment, finally restore state and self.

These two chapters have chronicled the bilateral conflict, cooperation, and complexity provoked by the *fitna*. They have attempted to provide an analysis despite the layers of dissimulation found in French and Algerian policies. What is certain is that the *fitna* demonstrated the paradoxes and the profundities of the relationship. It revealed that the bilateral history is an opaque, as well as an elliptical, reality—a relationship of mirrors and mirages, reflections and refractions, not merely surface representations but deeper ones, inscribed on epistemological, ontological levels.

10

Mirrors and Mirages, 1958–1998
Reflections, Refractions, and Representations

> A nation can have its *being* only at the price of being forever in search of itself, forever transforming itself in the direction of its logical development, always measuring itself against others and identifying itself with the best, the most essential part of its being.
> **Fernand Braudel,** *The Identity of France*

> Group feeling produces the ability to defend oneself, to offer opposition, to protect oneself, and to press one's claims. Whoever loses [his group feeling] is too weak to do any of these things.
> **Ibn Khaldun,** *Muqaddimah*

The history of the modern French-Algerian relationship is like a kaleidoscope, diffusing a wide spectrum of reflections, refractions, and representations. Appearance does not always equate with actuality; it is a relationship of mirrors and mirages which often deflect, distort, and disperse the reception and perception, the imagination and knowledge of the other. Yet this is what distinguishes this multifaceted relationship, its uniqueness, its singular perplexity and prominence among the world's most significant postcolonial relationships.

This chapter reviews the relationship through a variety of condensing, analytical optics. The lenses remain the essentialist/existentialist ordering frameworks that have provided this study with an interpretive depth of field rather than a reductive fixed aperture. During these years France's essentialist perspective and Algeria's existentialist praxis inevitably transformed or "refocused" to adapt to changing, even chimerical, historical conditions. The ongoing *fitna* has represented one of those "refocusings," compounded by all the variables and verities of the post–Cold War world. The relationship has now entered a period of new challenges necessitating a deeper and wider understanding of its past and present in order to transcend them and envision a promising future.

Bilateral Reflections and Refractions

This book's historical narrative has surveyed the paradoxes of the post-colonial relationship: confrontation yet cooperation, independence with dependence. While it can be argued that the relationship was adversarial and asymmetrical, a seemingly chronic conflict between contradictory identities and complex interests, there was a correlative "mirroring" in the relationship, a reflective-refractive measuring of one country's actions and ambitions vis-à-vis the other. This isomorphism, a mutual surveillance and narcissism, inherently characterized the paradoxical relationship and inevitably caused the two countries alternately to attract and repel each other. The way one country received and perceived the other transformed not only the relationship itself but concomitant bodies of knowledge, techniques of power and influence, and, crucially important, imagined identities. The intricate bilateral network of political, economic, social, cultural, epistemological, and even ontological relations were intrinsically reflexive dispositions.

France's Algerian Mirror

Thierry Fabre wrote that "Algeria is a pitiless prism [diffusing] France's failures, a reflector of its masks, and an unforgiving mirror of its misconduct."[1] Charles de Gaulle and, to a lesser degree, François Mitterrand attempted to replace that tainted reflective relationship with a new one radiating a polished and penitent France, the *coopérateur* rather than the colonialist, wedded not only to postcolonial realities but also to its changeless essentialist principles of grandeur and independence. Yet postcolonial France's vision, stubbornly atavistic, continued to "see an Algeria in its image."[2]

During the colonial period Algeria mirrored France's power and potential. Therefore, the loss of Algeria by decolonization was viewed as a reflection of decline and decadence. De Gaulle's masterful reformulation of grandeur and independence in the postcolonial period eased French anxiety. This necessitated a reimagination of Algeria which was begun with the Evian Accords. De Gaulle's generous and humanitarian cooperation, even if encrypted in enduring colonial atavisms, permitted France's passage through that strategic Algerian "doorway" to influence the Third World and reconcile the Arab one. Cooperation with Algeria also allowed France to amplify its strength by testing its *force de frappe* nuclear deterrent, the symbol of a world power. The innovative Algiers Accords of 1965 acted as a matrix for hydrocarbons contracts with Iraq and Iran and asserted

French independence from the hegemonic Anglo-American Cartel. Fundamental historical realities had changed, but the French-Algerian relationship, even if recodified, remained what Gaulle described as "organic."

Mitterrand, though ideologically antithetical to de Gaulle, also viewed the relationship as an opportunity to initiate a historic change, a reworking of discourse and practice. His government's proposal for "codevelopment" showcased France's progressive sensitivities toward the Third World by coordinating cooperation with an individual country's specific needs. The natural gas accord of 1982, the paramount example of codevelopment, resembled the Algiers Accords in strategic significance and served to reassure the developing nations that France had decisively renounced neocolonialism and desired to engage in real partnership.

For de Gaulle and Mitterrand the Algerian mirror acted as a prism too, no longer a "pitiless" one displaying a spectrum of colonial abuse but a refashioned lens projecting a positive French influence worldwide. During the 1970s, between the presidencies of de Gaulle and Mitterrand, the mirrored relationship became more refractive under presidents Georges Pompidou and Valéry Giscard d'Estaing who attempted to distance themselves from Algeria in order to achieve the unachievable, a bilateral "normalization."

Pompidou gauged that France's image in the world no longer needed to be reflected by the Algerian relationship. France had shown itself to be repentant and reconciliatory, and was now regenerated in a postcolonial context. Pompidou's distancing from Algeria, caused by the politically painful 1971 hydrocarbons nationalizations, focused a new perspective for cooperation, but hardly a "normalized" relationship. Algeria remained uniquely important to France because of the emigrant labor community and the availability of proximate petroleum and natural gas. Further, the international prestige Algeria gained from the 1971 nationalization lent it growing influence in a variety of forums such as the United Nations in 1974; this appealed to the ex-*métropole*. France and Algeria also shared political and military interests in the Mediterranean region. Above all, Algeria was determined to rekindle a warmer relationship with the ex-*métropole*. The continuation of French technical and cultural cooperation services and programs, at training institutes proliferating throughout the country, underscored that deontological as well as strategic reasons determined France's engagement in Algeria, which evolved into a bilateral *relancement* of relations.

Giscard particularly failed to perceive that France's postcolonial image remained a reflection, no matter how oblique, of its Algerian policy. He deflected the rising expectations of the *relancement* and sought a plain ("banal") rather than a privileged relationship with Algeria. As relations deteriorated, and his political support on the right eroded, as a consequence of the dismal Algiers Summit of 1975, the war in Western Sahara, problems over emigrant labor, and the pricing of natural gas, the reality again emerged that each nation needed the other. When Giscard finally realized this, it was too late to fulfill the promise of the *relancement*. Ironically, during the *fitna* Giscard would speak of the need for France's "special sensitivity" regarding Algeria; perhaps this also reflected a personal lesson learned.

The October 1988 riots cracked France's Algerian mirror and the *fitna* shattered it. Algeria's upheaval disoriented and dislocated France's vaunted Third Worldist (*tiersmondiste*) vision, mentality, and identity. *Tiersmondisme* conveniently ignored political abuses in Algeria, its ideologically favored country. According to Provost, France questioned whether Algeria had the ability to become democratic and whether liberalization would benefit French economic interests.[3] After decades of dealing with the FLN-military elite, repeating the customary practices, rehearsing the occasional psychodramas, reciting the obligatory discourses, and refusing to roil Algerian postcolonial sensibilities, France had to not only reassess the disrupted relationship but reperceive and rehistoricize it, a process that continues today (see below). The emergence of a hostile Islamist movement positing an alternative, antagonistic, and "authentic" Algerian identity was inimical not only to the French colonial legacy and postcolonial presence but also to France's projected image of a postcolonial Algeria. The FIS's electoral successes left France astonished and then finally anguished, torn between supporting a democratic process sure to elect the defiant, dangerous Islamists and favoring the familiar but authoritarian civilian-military elite. France's ambivalence concerning the 1991 election and the coup of January 1992, and its immobility in the face of the monstrously violent civil war, disclosed an inability to imagine or to adapt to a tumultuously transforming Algeria. The *fitna* diffracted Algeria's image and its fury dispersed relations. As the GIA had warned, Algeria's shifting sands were whipped into a sandstorm blurring then blinding France's perception of Algeria not only by obfuscating the relationship but by threatening its very obliteration. Algeria's deliberate and closely managed "redemocratization," with institutions vaguely resembling those of France (a bicameral legislature, a strong executive), has received increasing support from the French government. Relations are reconstituting; a new mirror is being pieced together. The question remains how reflective or faceted it will be.

Algeria's French Mirror

Algeria's postcolonial existential quest to define, develop, and direct a nation mirrored its relationship with France. Algeria's assertion of a postcolonial national identity was virtually configured with that of France; of course, the configuration was often commutative. Mohammed Harbi noted: "A coterie of Algerians, precisely those who had been the spokespersons and directors of Algerian nationalism, is strongly marked by French culture. This political francophone elite forged the idea of an Algerian nation, independent of any authentic historical reference, in symmetry with the idea of the French nation. At the same time and logically, it made France the exclusive source of its difficulties."[4] Said Saadi suggested that the "FLN was never very far from a mirror image [*l'effet miroir*]. It impressed on Algeria an image symmetrical to that of France."[5] This transnational narcissism should not be surprising. Benedict Anderson regarded "nationality" as a collection of "cultural artefacts" which "become 'modular,' capable of being transplanted, with varying degrees of self-consciousness, to a great variety of social terrains, to merge and be merged with a correspondingly wide variety of political and ideological constellations."[6] France's cultural power was immense and its imposition on colonial Algeria, as Frantz Fanon and Pierre Bourdieu among others demonstrated, was more than influential, it was inculcative. It was eventually even perceived as the perfidious postcolonial *hizb faransa*.

Algeria's focal plane aimed directly and indirectly on its French mirror. This optic constantly filtered Algeria's existential quest for self-identification. Sometimes the reflected image was flattened and virtual, at other times curved and oblique. Consider, for example, the Tripoli Program. It forcefully proclaimed the need to continue a postcolonial decolonization from France, particularly through the introversion of Algeria's colonial economy by nationalizations. Yet its "socialist option" imitated Marxist ideas admired also by the French left. Subsequent state plans were strategically similar to the *Perspectives décennales* and the Constantine Plan and inspired or blueprinted by French advisers like Gérard Destanne de Bernis. Cooperation, though theoretically a paramount example of neocolonialism, also ironically served to liberate Algerians from French academic and technical educational dependence (though not the French language). Its economic course since 1988, a mixed but increasingly liberalized economy, especially in the vital hydrocarbons sector, is again reminiscent of the French model.

The War of Independence from France and its continuing postcolonial decolonization from the ex-*métropole,* as ritualized by the monopolistic FLN, also produced, in Foucauldian terms, a "regime of truth," a practice of a variety of power formations/techniques, and a unifying discourse, an "archive," with its rhetorical "battles of oil and gas," as well as its edifying Industrial, Agrarian, and Cultural "Revolutions." Algeria's discourse and practice, while the opposite of France's, were still homologous, conceived and expressed in French, even earning Algerian diplomats plaudits from their counterparts for their "Cartesian" strategies.[7] Both sides practiced, to use Nicole Grimaud's term, "rules of the game" including noninterference in the other's internal affairs (Algerian emigrant labor plans excepted) and mutual respect for the other's independence.[8] France was the "partner of choice," but as Grimaud pointed out, there was initially little other choice. Great Britain and West Germany antagonized Algeria by their relations with Rhodesia and Israel respectively, and neither superpower had a strong interest. Geographic, strategic, and historical circumstances necessitated a close Algerian-French relationship. There were remarkable periods of exemplary creative cooperation (1963–65, 1974–75, 1981–84). Reminiscent of Sartre's thought was Boumedienne's statement that "France and Algeria are condemned to be on good terms and to cooperate."[9]

In addition, grandeur and independence were "transplanted" as Algerian policy. Presidents Ben Bella and Boumedienne pursued a "heroic" foreign policy equivalent to de Gaulle's *politique à tous azimuts,* aiming at championing the developing world and assisting liberation movements. Algeria also developed its own modest policy of cooperation. Boumedienne's highly centralized state was regarded as a virtual image of France. The ideologically imposed coalescence of socialism and Jacobinism (and, arguably, Boumedienne's "Bonapartism") with the incongruent claim that it all comported with Islam, was a multiple reflection of Algeria's French mirror.[10]

Collectively, the existential creeds defining postcolonial Algeria—the Tripoli Program, the Algiers Charter, and the National Charters of 1976 and 1986—were demystified by the transgressive October Riots 1988 and finally denied by the *fitna* itself. Not only was the government destabilized, but its revolutionary discourse and political legitimacy were discredited and discarded, and with them an official conception of the nation. From 1988 to 1991 a multiplicity of discourses appeared, shifting the existential praxis from the tightly controlled epistemological to the more introspective ontological. What was it to *be* Algerian? The variety of responses to this question, now that the debilitated government allowed freedom of expression including the will to democratize, was instructive and inspiring.

Unlike France's Algerian mirror, Algeria's French mirror clouded rather than broke. Despite the popularity of Islamism and its inherent hostility toward France, Algerian culture remained highly affected by the ex-*métropole*. During the *fitna*, France's ambivalence toward Algeria could not alter the Pouvoir's French proclivities.[11] Another bilateral mirrored image, one that was invisible but still present, was perceived by Omar Belhoucet, the renowned editor of *El-Watan*. Assessing the uproar over the failed Zeroual-Chirac summit in October 1995, he concluded that "this new crisis proves that relations between the two countries always obey the same passion, the same ardor."[12] It is that emotional equivalence, so deeply inscribed on both sides of the Mediterranean, that gives this relationship its particular historical significance.

Representations and Decolonization

The mirroring of the relationship, the surveillant similitude of the postcolonial gazes, the unresolved questions as a consequence of postcolonial transformation, strongly suggest that decolonization was incomplete—a mirage rather than a reality. Whether illusory or not, this is certain: decolonization is always a bilateral rather than a unilateral historical process. France as well as Algeria experienced postcolonial decolonization. This has particularly involved a mediation of reception, perception, and signification.

Recent contributions in postcolonial theory have emphasized the need to extend attention from traditional political and economic decolonization studies to include social and cultural representations. French-Algerian reflections and refractions offer an ideal opportunity to study a variety of differentiated representations that offer more interpretive and even convergent, stereoscoped optics such as hybridity and historicity.

Bilateral Mirages

A mirage is not only an optical illusion, it can also be a shimmering ideal. In 1962 Algeria knew that its cherished goal of independence remained incomplete and uncertain given the entrenched French postcolonial economic, social, and cultural presence. This forced the FLN to continue the liberation struggle in the postcolonial era. But decolonization was not only Algeria's affair, it was also France's. The ex-*métropole* had to adapt to new postcolonial realities on deeper epistemological levels than a simple reformulation of official political discourse and practice.

Postcolonial theory has featured an application of postmodern critical methodology and, in particular, a rereading of Frantz Fanon.[13] Thanks to Fanon's intimacy with the Algerian-French relationship, his writings offer an interpretive optic, a template, for assessing bilateral decolonization.

Fanon contended that colonialism was an all-embracing system. To graft Foucault to Fanon, it was a totalizing "discipline" dictating political, social, and cultural relations. Fanon defined "liberation" as "the total destruction of the colonial system, from the pre-eminence of the language of the oppressor and 'departmentalization,' to the customs union that in reality maintains the former colonized in the meshes of the culture, of the fashion, and of the images of the colonialist."[14] On the surface, Algeria seemed to accomplish this: it inaugurated Arabization, took over settler property, and left the franc zone. In reality, these changes were superficial rather than substantial.

Though its leaders spoke French fluently, the FLN judged that the post-colonial use of the French language was politically and culturally (though not economically) detrimental to the new polity. Fanon understood that language was an oppressive colonial instrument and contributed significantly to the "psychoexistential" problem in the Antilles. Language to Fanon (and, in postmodern thought, the neo-Freudian Jacques Lacan) often defined the subject or the reception of that subject. The definition was fraught, however, with psychological insecurity and cultural inauthenticity (whence the psychoexistential impact). Nevertheless, according to L. Adele Jinadu: "Fanon's analysis of the uses to which Algerian nationalists put the French language suggests that he is not opposed to the adoption of the colonizer's language as such. His condemnation, it seems, is directed at the manner of its imposition and particular psychopathological behavioral responses it generated among some of the colonized."[15] The FLN's mastery of the language and its profound familiarity with French culture was its greatest weapon against the colonialists and allowed it to maintain a competitive advantage during negotiations in the postcolonial period. In a way, the use of French as an ironic liberating instrument also freed it from its colonial past as a symbol of oppression.

Many disagreed. Abdellah Cheriet argued forcefully that the promotion of French in a bilingual educational system was ideologically unacceptable since it perpetuated, if not strengthened, the Algerian bourgeoisie.[16] To Islamists, who fervently favored Arabization, French correlated with secularism. Still the French language remains pervasive in Algeria's culture, especially in the media and in the government. Despite the passage and application of the most recent Arabization legislation (1996–98), Ahmed Ben Bella recognized this reality in an interview with London's *al-Wasat*: "Our relations with France are long-standing and the Algerians speak good French."[17] The numbers of francophones in Algeria is astonishing. The Haut Conseil de la Francophonie in Paris concluded that 30 percent of the population were *francophones réels* and another 30 percent occasionally spoke French. As for the educational attention given to French, despite Arabization, Algeria ranks as the world's second most francophone country.[18] In the mid-1990s, 1.2 million Algerian households, representing 64 percent of the viewing audience, had satellite dishes that enabled them to receive fifteen channels, including French transmissions.[19] It was no wonder that the installers and technicians of these parabolic antennas were targeted by extremists during the *fitna*. Rachid Boudjedra suggested that, though France lost its Algerian War, it reengaged culturally when the first parabolics were installed in the early 1980s.[20] "Why send troops to occupy a country," Boudjedra asked, "when one can send a satellite?"[21] Paul-Marie de la Gorce speculated on whether Algeria could ever erase the French presence, even with an Islamist victory: "[The Islamists] are of course going to try to cut all cultural ties with France and Europe, but how much can they do? Can they ban people from speaking French, which is what most Algerians speak? Can they remove satellite dishes hooked to practically every home? There is a limit."[22] Lucile Provost believed that the split between French and Arabic speakers "was often exaggerated by the French media."[23] Besides, the belief that a francophone Algerian is more inclined to be pro-French is just one more myth.

Arabization has proved to be not universally popular because of the resistance of the Berbers (who are particularly francophone) and simply because, as Karim Alrawi observed, "Algerians speak Arabic with the disconcerting correctness of a people who have learned their language from books and not at their mothers' laps."[24] The difference between Maghribi Arabic, with its Berber and colloquial influences, and the more classical Arabic of the Mashriq has already been alluded to in chapter 7. It should be remembered that Fanon's "pre-eminence" of a language did not mean the elimination of French or, for that matter, the Berbers' Tamazight. There also arises the question of how important language is to identity. Is language merely one expression or component of identity? Indeed, as

Maurice Merleau-Ponty and Roland Barthes have noted, there are crucial phenomenological differences between language, message, and perception of the other, between the seen, the signified, and the invisible.[25]

In *The Wretched of the Earth,* Fanon feared that a "national bourgeoisie" would undermine the revolutionary achievement by assuming the dominant social role previously held by colonialist counterparts. During the postcolonial period, Algerian governments attacked the "national bourgeoisie" ideologically, but in actuality it was tolerated and even palliated (with property appropriated from the colonists), since it posed the real possibility of political and economic opposition. This class was powerful enough to withstand any threats from the theoretically ambitious Agrarian Revolution of the early 1970s. Karen Pfeiffer contended that though this reform succeeded in "abolishing sharecropping and cancelling debts owed by small producers to landlords," its measures "did not eradicate exploitation in its capitalist form. For wage labor has by no means been abolished." There was "maintenance, even encouragement, of the private sector." Pfeiffer concluded that "Algeria in the 1970s seems to have completed the historic task begun by the French intruders in 1830."[26]

Algeria left the franc zone, but this shifted the country from a multilateral cooperation with the CFA African states (and competition for France's financial consideration) to a much more advantageous bilateral commercial relationship. Algeria was France's privileged overseas territory during the colonial period, and this continued after 1962. Throughout the postcolonial period, despite state-planned diversification, France retained commercial dominance in the Algerian economy. During the 1990s, as France reduced its support of its former West and Equatorial African colonies, Algeria continued to receive preferential treatment, though this was primarily motivated by the *fitna*'s exigencies and a growing Anglo penetration of the hydrocarbons sector.

Fanon appealed for "a program . . . for a government which really wants to free the people politically and socially" and insisted that an economic program include "a doctrine concerning the division of wealth." He emphasized that "there must be an idea of man and of the future of humanity; that is to say that no demagogic formula and no collusion with the former occupying power can take the place of a program."[27] Algerian governments fashioned dynamic state plans with detailed programs designed to stimulate domestic development, with the country's hydrocarbon resources fueling "industrializing industries." Critics called this publicized strategy "largely a myth" since Algeria's hydrocarbons exports were still vast compared with minuscule domestic consumption. Furthermore, the export of hydrocarbons for revenue and capital accumulation was hardly innovative. "Socialist" planning in the second sector was considered unsatisfactory because it was merely a reorganization of projects "inherited from the Constantine Plan."[28] Provost contended that Algeria was in "a schizophrenic mode." Championing the Third World internationally, it embarked on state plans and projects like the Agrarian and Industrial Revolutions that hardly took into account social and economic realities. Instead, a "false Algeria" was displayed, "a mirage for the [international] gallery."[29] On the other hand, Yves Lacoste wrote that it was wrong to criticize Algeria for everything it had done. The concept of "industrializing industries" was not Stalinist but came from the "counsels of the best specialists in Third World problems."[30] In social affairs, the large budget allocations to education (with French cooperation) cut illiteracy considerably and must rank as one of the great achievements of postcolonial Algeria.

The socialist option (an "idea of man") aimed to correct the division of wealth; unfortunately, it engendered a detrimental new class structure. The national bourgeoisie, which did not automatically ally itself with the ex-*métropole* as Fanon anticipated, transmuted, however, into a technocratic bureaucracy.[31] The colonial period's simple Manichaean dichotomy between colonialist and colonized was replaced by a postcolonial class system featuring a military-technocratic-bureaucratic power elite, a national bourgeoisie, a privileged proletariat, and ironically, after their suffering under the French, continued deprivation and neglect of the *fellahin* (peasantry). The reorientation toward agriculture in the 1980s did little to alleviate the sector's subordination to manufacturing. Indeed, Benjedid's liberalization strengthened the bourgeoisie.

Fanon justifiably feared that "collusion" with France qualified Algeria's independence. But cooperation also provided the means to continue postcolonial liberation. French aid policies were often ideologically compatible and well-intentioned partnerships, as spectacularly demonstrated by the Algiers Accords' OCI and ASCOOP in the 1960s and the codeveloped initiatives of the Mitterrand administration in the early 1980s. The "quiet cooperation" provided by French teachers and specialists in Algerian academic and technical programs was constantly present until the *fitna*.

Nationalism was a particular concern to Fanon. He warned: "If nationalism is not made explicit, if it is not enriched and deepened by a very rapid transformation into a consciousness of social and political needs, in other words into humanism, it leads up a blind alley."[32] Unfortunately, after independence from France, an exclusive, authoritarian apparatus imposed its power and mythology upon the country until the 1988 riots. The failure to create a freely expressed consensual national identity, reinforced by mobilizing social and economic programs, tempered the potential of independent Algeria and its completion of decolonization. The current "redemocratization" of the country, even if flawed, might still direct the country toward a light at the end of the "alley." Nevertheless, until Algeria frees itself from the *fitna,* which will take a veritable "transformation of consciousness" and the creation of a new civic humanism, the country will continue to suffer existential dislocation.

In an interpretation of Fanon, Homi Bhabha commented: "In the moment of liberatory struggle, the Algerian people destroy the continuities and constancies of the nationalist tradition which provided a safeguard against colonial cultural importations. They are now free to negotiate and translate their cultural identities in a discontinuous intertextual temporality of cultural difference."[33] It was this reinterpretation of difference that proved most problematic. It insisted on an inclusive negotiation and an implicit toleration of difference. Algeria's failure to achieve cultural negotiation and translation, a weaving of its society into an identifiable fabric, was a failure in the exercise of freedom, the fundamental prerequisite for the completion of decolonization and, with it, the definition of a postcolonial state. It created a mirage rather than a true mirror.

But how decolonized was France? De Gaulle managed with difficulty to persuade the French that decolonization did not equate with decadence. He prided himself on being wedded to the twentieth century and being able to replace colonialism with cooperation, satisfying essentialist imperatives.[34] Still, this master mythmaker (witness in his manipulation of the image of France's Resistance during the Second World War) could not alter the reality or purge the memory of France's defeat in Algeria.

Mirages more than memories still colonized the French national consciousness. Algeria's mirages may have been transient ideals, but France's were optical illusions. In many respects France failed to recognize the loss of Algeria and instead invented a colonial legacy, ignoring the consequences upon the colonized (as well as repatriated and displaced populations), while repeatedly reliving its Algerian War. Stora termed this affliction a "narcissistic scar."[35] It was a question of coming to terms with the reality and ramifications of Algerian independence and of its own history; but France has not been honest and the scar covers a festering wound.

In French popular culture, Algeria was romanticized in a kind of neo-Orientalism. Philip Dine examined the colonial and postcolonial literary and cinematic "ideological myths" that colored French perception of Algeria and especially the Algerian War. For example, the "leopard look" of their uniform, their "exclusivity and isolation, action and purity" represented the "basic givens of the *para* myth."[36] Jean Lartéguy's *Les Centurions* (1960) exemplified this mythology of men representing "true France," a recasting of Bertrand's ideas of a Latin North Africa (see chapter 1). Gilles Manceron and Hassan Remaoun have surveyed an eclectic group of French postcolonial novels on the War including notably Guy Croussy's *Ceux du djebel* (1967) and *Ne pleure pas, la guerre est bonne* (1975) which addressed the War's violence while attempting to provide realistic and balanced narratives.[37] In film, Gillo Pontecorvo's *The Battle of Algiers,* while remarkably balanced, drew French protests and was delayed in certification for distribution.[38] It is rarely shown in France today. *Fort Saganne* (1984) was another film that romanticized French military heroism in the Sahara.

During the postcolonial period, French society seemed anesthetized to the shared plight of the repatriated and displaced populations. The *pieds-noirs* were categorized as misfits, racists, and even fascists. The *harkis* were genuinely the "forgotten of France." As for the Algerian emigrants/ immigrants (a term explained below), they were stereotyped as incorrigibly criminal. The travails of these three communities were a result of France's inability to resolve, on social, cultural, even epistemological levels, the decolonization of Algeria. These populations have often been termed isolated and alienated. Ironically, they may be the agents able to dissipate France's postcolonial mirages and contribute to what would be less a resignation or even a resolution than a transcending historical reconciliation with Algeria, as well as with itself.

Ending Decolonization: Hybridity and Historicism

The powerful historical interaction between France and Algeria inevitably catalyzed an admixture of social and intellectual representations, i.e., hybridities of peoples and forms. These representations, a confluence of Algerian and French cultures, may be the means toward demythologizing the past by eliminating presumptions and preconceptions and subsequently delivering both countries from an unresolved decolonization.

If France and Algeria are to complete decolonization, the process must also involve an open and authentic account of their shared heritage. This means an honest appraisal of bilateral history with its glories and its miseries, and in particular its epistemologies and methodologies. A rigorous, determined engagement, intellectual as well as political, will finally decide decolonization and end a controversial chapter in this complex story.

Homi Bhabha emphasized "the need to think beyond narratives of originary and initial subjectivities and to focus on those moments or processes that are produced in the articulation of cultural differences. These 'in-between' spaces provide the terrain for elaborating strategies of selfhood—singular or communal—that initiate new signs of identity, and innovative sites of collaboration, and contestation."[39] The *pieds-noirs,* the *harkis,* and the emigrants/immigrants are strategically situated on "the interstices—the overlap and displacement of domains of difference [where] the intersubjective and collective experiences of *nationness,* community interest, or cultural value are negotiated."[40]

They represent "in-between" hybrid communities on the cultural crosscurrents of France and Algeria. With their inherent advantages they have great untapped potential to help Algeria and France resolve their decolonization and their postcolonial transformation of identities. Though they have been marginalized socially, and even spatially in the case of the *harkis* and the emigrant/immigrants, these hybrid communities, to their credit, have persisted in claiming an identity, becoming visible, with the hope that they would be recognized and integrated within the context of French culture. But before they can serve as cultural mediators, they must contend with their own hybridity, acknowledge it, and then have others recognize it. There are already encouraging signals that positive transformations are occurring.

The *pieds-noirs,* always a heterogeneous community of European peoples, have often been judged unfairly within France as a homogeneous bloc of unregenerate right-wing colonialists. Actually the *pieds-noirs* have exercised a strong degree of political independence, as when their disappointment with the right over the indemnity issue in the late 1970s led many to shift to the left. Paul Quilès, a *pied-noir,* was François Mitterrand's successful campaign manager in 1980–81. With the rise of Le Pen's popularity in the 1980s, the *pieds-noirs* were also mistakenly seen as practically unanimously supporting the Front National.[41] The French government's failure to resolve the indemnity issue until 1987 indicated the depth of metropolitan resentment against the ex–colonial settlers.

During the postcolonial period, the *pieds-noirs* and their organizations have exoticized their life in Algeria, especially when contrasted with their "welcome" in France during their painful repatriation. The nostalgia has been brought to the screen by *pied-noir* director Alexandre Arcady, as in

Le Coup de Sirocco (1979). This shared alienated, dislocative history has preserved a cultural identity, so historical memory is crucial to them. The Association Généologique d'Afrique du Nord and the Cercle Algérianiste, in particular, have reinforced this historicity and have promoted positive images of the *pied-noir* community's present and past. The Cercle's colorful historical journal, *L'Algérianiste,* may be nostalgic, but it also chronicles Algeria's colonial years in impressive detail, with emphasis on *pied-noir* cultural achievements.

When *pied-noir* associations rallied in Marseille in June 1997, their activities underscored "the obligation of memory" and the need to amplify "the cultural identity of the *pieds-noirs* today," a particularly worrisome issue to the "*exode* generation." Another concern was the symbolic and sacred historical presence of the *pied-noir* legacy in Algeria, "the preservation of desecrated cemeteries."[42] But undeniably many *pieds-noirs* have "knotted" memories, relentlessly rehashing de Gaulle's treasonous "I have understood you" and refusing to recognize Algeria's inevitable independence.[43] Closed memories can be dangerously obsessive. A case in point was the execution-murder in March 1993 of Jacques Roseau, cofounder and longtime spokesman for RECOURS, by *pied-noir* extremists who considered him too conciliatory.[44]

Pieds-noirs have spoken of the need to "exorcise" and rid themselves of a "bad conscience." Georges Morin, president of the Association Coup de Soleil, an organization promoting solidarity among *pieds-noirs, harkis,* and Jews, advised the expatriates: "Don't shoulder all the sins of colonialism." He added, however: "Do not falsify history on the theme: Ah, how good it was in French Algeria. Yes, let's say it, the conquest was a dirty war. And the Arabs were treated as second-class citizens."[45] Jacques Ferrandez, a *pied-noir* born in Algiers in 1955, produced a remarkable account of the French colonial presence in Algeria in the form of a multivolume epic comic series, *Carnets d'Orient* (1994–95), involving renowned historians Jules Roy and Benjamin Stora. It relates the history through the story of a loving mixed French-Algerian couple and explores (and supports) the legitimacy of French colonialism, but one styled on the ideal of a hybrid French-Algerian community.[46]

Addressing the *pieds-noirs* during decolonization, de Gaulle exhorted: "You, the French of Algeria, who for generations have done so much, if one page has been turned by the great wind of history, well, it is up to you to write another. Let there be a truce to vain bitterness, vain torments; take the future as it comes, and grapple with it."[47] The approximately 1.7 million *pieds-noirs* have indeed experienced bitterness and torment, but have "grappled" admirably with their future and have integrated very well in French society. This has helped especially to demythologize their colonialist image. Even with their legacy of spearheading French colonialism, President Benjedid recognized that they possess particular cultural sensibilities toward Algeria. It was not surprising that in a symbolic act of reconciliation during his summit in Paris in 1983 he cordially invited the *pieds-noirs* to visit Algeria.[48] But if the *pieds-noirs,* like the *harkis* and the emigrants/immigrants, are to contribute toward achieving decolonization, they must cease to see themselves as suffering victims of the past, and recognize that they are uniquely situated to negotiate and translate French and Algerian cultures and, by doing so, conciliate a shared history.

During the mid-1990s the *harkis* continued their recurrent agitation seeking recognition from the repressed and guilt-ridden French consciousness. In 1994 the French government passed the Romani Law, which aimed to give FF 110,000 to every *harki* family. This well-intentioned measure was bureaucratically flawed, especially regarding the disbursal of the money.[49] But it was a victory of recognition for the "forgotten of France."

Harkis were still occasional victims of racial attacks and beatings, including a terrible incident in August 1994 in which a *harki* youth was thrown from a cliff.[50] In November 1994 a violent police assault on *harkis* in Amiens was captured on videotape and forced an apology by the prefect.[51] Recalling *harki* protests in 1974, members of the *harki* second generation in late 1997 began well-publicized hunger strikes throughout France, including one at the Invalides in Paris.[52] There was a corresponding march in Paris by *harkis* on 15 November to protest the lack of recognition and integration of their community, as well as the decades of unfulfilled government promises.

The new generation no longer want to be called sons and daughters of *harkis.* They call themselves *passerelles,* "footbridges," implying that they are bridging from the culture of their parents.[53] This refashioning of themselves, both a recognition and a rejection of their victimization, is a very important step toward attaining the community's integration within French society and toward reconciling decolonization. They have also melded with the *beurs* and have contributed to a brilliant display of cultural hybridity in the arts. Mehdi Charef's novel *Le Harki de Meriem* (1989) deals with the racist killing of a brilliant *harki* student. Besides playing an increasingly important role in local politics, the younger generation have tried to merge fractious *harki* associations into more cohesive and effective organizations.[54]

Algerian workers and their families, those longtime expatriates, are another unresolved reminder of French colonialism in Algeria. The idea of repatriation (despite Le Pen's wishful rhetoric) and of reinsertion are fading dreams, given Algeria's social, economic, and political condition since 1988. Indeed, this community is no longer emigrant but *immigrant*, thus "emigrants/immigrants." Though the second-generation *beurs* continue to amplify their own culture, there is now a third generation emerging, who generally hold dual nationality and who remain divided between their parents' values and those of French society. Immigrant youth, like their counterparts in Algeria, have unemployed *hittistes*, "leaners on walls." Particularly since the *fitna* began, they are often stereotyped as terrorists or juvenile delinquents. Crime is indeed a serious problem among the community.[55] It is a Dantesque demimonde in the *banlieues* (outskirts) of Paris, Lyon, and Marseille where immigrants live with suspended identities and lives.[56] There are new and often undocumented arrivals from Algeria who have managed to squeeze through the net of French restrictions, sometimes after circuitous odysseys, even by way of Australia. They are always under scrutiny, their legal status tenuous. One such recent immigrant said wryly: "I have one foot here, and one over there [in Algeria], and both of them in shit."[57]

Algerian-descended immigrant youth, as well as *harkis*, now want to abandon ethnic affiliations. According to Séverine Labat's research in Algeria and France, these youth prefer calling themselves Muslim first.[58] They also prefer a type of Islam different from their parents', with its "mechanical" memorization of the Qur'an. But a more relevant Islamic ritual and reality remains to be defined.[59]

The French response to Islam has been predictably ambivalent. There is resentment that Muslims have resisted a full assimilation of French universalist values and the increasingly insistent republican ideal.[60] On the other hand, veteran analyst Bruno Etienne viewed Islam in France as a potential cultural and social "bridge" mediating between the North and South. He contended too that Islam could flourish within the context of French liberty and laity.[61] These ideas were shared by Areski Dahmani of France-Plus, who stated that his organization, dedicated to integration, "sees France as the laboratory for an experiment that can serve all Islam."[62] In an analysis in *Le Nouvel Observateur*, Jean Daniel observed that France could serve as a democratic model for Algeria and underscored how Islam was practiced freely within "the privileged context of French laicity."[63]

The French have endeavored to accommodate their Muslim community of four to five million adherents, easily the second largest religion in the nation, with now eight "cathedral-mosques." The official objective of integrating the Muslim population distinguishes France from more reluctant European neighbors like Germany, the United Kingdom, and Italy. Milton Viorst concluded: "France's Muslim community is probably the first in history that has contemplated integration into a Christian society."[64]

The *fitna* not only exacerbated the reflexive national fear that affiliated terrorism with Islam, it also forced France to reexamine its official relations with its Muslim community.[65] When the cathedral-mosque in Lyon was inaugurated in 1994, Charles Pasqua spoke of a "French Islam," implying, in Viorst's view, that "France . . . would not tolerate Islamic practices, religious or cultural, at odds with the character of French society."[66] In January 1995 the Ministry of the Interior, in collaboration with Paris's tightly monitored and Algerian-controlled Grand Mosque, proclaimed a Charter of the Muslim Faith in France. Pasqua and Shaykh Dalil Boubakeur, the Algerian-born imam of the Paris mosque, held a joint news conference introducing the charter. The minister of the interior affirmed: "The State recognizes French Islam. I have always wanted Islam in France to change from being a tolerated religion to one which is accepted by everyone, and which forms part of the French spiritual landscape."[67] The charter described a constricted role for Islam in French society and stipulated that the religion would be subject to French law (including oaths of loyalty by imams). The blatant political nature of the document, appearing as France became increasingly worried about infectious Islamism, discredited it, and it has been shelved. Still, the official recognition of Islam's importance and potential in French society was a progressive, if politically motivated, step.

There is growing willingness by Muslims to integrate into French society. A surprising 78 percent of Muslims polled in 1994 would accept the marriage of a non-Muslim with a son or brother, and an astonishing 67 percent with a daughter or sister.[68] Mixed marriages, however, involve difficult transcultural compromises ranging from religious allegiance to the naming of children. The intrinsic risks were dramatized by the abduction of children from their French mothers by their Algerian fathers, who returned to Algeria with them.[69] On the other hand, a Frenchwoman staged a forty-five-day hunger strike in May 1997 in order to marry an Algerian who was in hiding after receiving expulsion orders. The *fitna*, the difficulties in acquiring visas, and the 1993 revised French Code of Nationality have posed myriad problems especially for young people. It is not surprising that 75 percent of Muslims aged sixteen to twenty-five believed there was increasing racism in France, compared with 52 percent of those aged fifty and over.[70]

A strong challenge to French racism is offered by the cultural engagements and achievements of the immigrant second and third generations. In 1988 Sakinna Boukhedenna, the distinguished French-Algerian writer, declared that *beur* or *beurette* were neocolonialist terms since they ignored the person's actual ethnicity, Arab or Berber.[71] The words continue to be used, though, as the immigrant/minority presence, already considerable in the 1980s (see chapter 6), becomes ever more pervasive in French society. Writers keep writing novels, such as the prolific Azouz Begag with *Quand on est mort, c'est pour toute la vie* (1994), concerning the *fitna,* and the metaphorical *Les Chiens aussi* (1995). Farid Boudjellal, an Algerian *beur,* has emerged as a leading French cartoonist who has particularly addressed racism and *métissage,* ethnic mixing.[72]

Films regularly present the reality of Algerian-French hybridity.[73] Like literature, *beur* cinema appeals for cognition and recognition of the dignity of the immigrant and minority communities. The protagonists are often alienated young misfits who struggle against French discrimination and degradation while searching for an identity. Among the many significant films by Algerian *beur* directors in the 1990s were Rachid Bouchareb's *Cheb* (1991), Ahmed Bouchaala's *Krim* (1995), and Malik Chibane's *Hexagone* (1994) and *Douce France* (1995), the latter about a son of a *harki.* The renowned Algerian director Merzak Allouache filmed *Un amour à Paris* (1988), a love affair between an Algerian Jewish woman and a *beur.* Zaida Ghorab-Volta's *Souviens-toi de moi* (1996) was the first major film by a *beurette,* and explored the dynamics of an immigrant family. Yamina Benguigui, born in Lille to Kabyle parents, emerged also as an important woman director. Though *beurs* are still stereotyped in police films, there is no question that their presence is now part of the French cultural landscape. Indeed, Mattieu Kossovitz's *La Haine* (1995), which depicted the shared and tormented lives of three youths, a Jew, a *beur,* and a black, was honored at the Cannes Film Festival and the French César awards.

Minorities and especially Algerians have also appeared on television in such series as *Sixième gauche* (FR 3, 1990), *La Famille Ramdam,* (M6, 1990–91), and *Fruits et légumes* (F3, 1994). *La Famille Ramdam* was the creation of a *beurette* and a *beur* of Algerian descent. The images were intentionally positive to counterbalance stereotypes. In the 1990s the *banlieue* (ethnic suburb) culture was also portrayed in the television serials ("soaps") *Seconde B* and *C'est cool.* Smain, a popular Algerian-born comedian, is also a favorite of French television audiences.[74]

A salient example of cultural hybridity resonates throughout the world as rai music. This fusion of Algerian and Western pop styles began in the early 1980s and ranks as postcolonial Algeria's greatest cultural contribution. The popularity of the music, particularly in France, has made stars out of Cheb Khaled (the King of Rai) and Cheb Mami (the Prince of Rai). Rai music's criticism of both Islamism and the Pouvoir made it particularly appealing to the French. (It also made Cheb Hasni a martyr; see chapter 8). But as Chris Warne pointed out: "What was missing in this portrayal was an awareness that the people involved were rejecting not just monolithic Algerian or Arab identities, but also monolithic versions of French identity, or indeed any other monocultural tradition (including the liberal progressive one)."[75] Recently "techno-house-rai" has been introduced by Cheb Malik, a *beur*.

Kabyle music has always been popular in the immigrant community and in France generally, as reflected in the expressions of grief on Lounès Matoub's death in June 1998. Other important Kabyle singers with a devoted French-Algerian following are Malika Domrane and Samira and Hakima Benchikh. Rappers have particularly included Kabyles such as Kamel Houairi (K-Mel) of the group Alliance Ethnik, and Melaaz. Their music has enjoyed crossover popularity with French youth. Besides Radio Beur, there are also other stations that air Maghribi programs and music, such as Radio Soleil, Radio Gazelle, Radio Galère, Radio France-Maghreb.

The event that broadcast worldwide the hybridization of French society occurred in July 1998. Twenty-seven minutes into the 1998 soccer World Cup final between Brazil's favored team and France's, Zinedine Zidane, France's brilliant Kabyle-descended midfielder from Marseille's tough Castellane neighborhood, headed his first of two goals past the Brazilian goalkeeper. Shortly after the win, Zidane, known by the Frenchified pet name Zizou, brought out a book in which he wrote: "This victory also belongs to the thousands of Algerians of my generation who emigrated to France and who have not abandoned their own culture." His book was dedicated to his father who "always defended our origins." He said: "Our victory was the best reaction to intolerance."[76] Said one Algerian woman: "When Zizou is playing, I feel more French than the French."[77] Algerian newspapers celebrated the French victory at least as enthusiastically as those in France. *Demain de l'Algérie* ran the headline ZIDANE 3–BRAZIL 0.[78] *El-Watan* crowned ZIDANE, KING OF FRANCE.

After the World Cup success an ebullient Charles Pasqua, now out of office, urged the regularization of papers for illegal immigrants and said: "One cannot forget the part that Algerians, Moroccans, Tunisians, and

Africa took in the liberation of France." He added: "The *mondial* has shown to everyone's eyes that integration has succeeded in ninety percent of the country."[79] Jean-Marie Le Pen, who criticized the team for not singing the French national anthem, was compelled to admit that people of different races and backgrounds demonstrated that they shared "the love of the motherland [*la patrie*] and the will to serve it."[80] Richard Williams of the *Guardian* soberly reflected: "The existence of a team like this, with its implication that mankind has the potential to build a better society, is moving, humbling, and finally saddening because we know the dream it represents is no more than an illusion. Humanity cannot remake itself in the image of a successful football team, healing its divisions and unifying its objectives. All the more poignant, then, when such a team achieves such a feat."[81] Zidane concluded: "When we won the cup, everybody was on the street, white, black, brown, green. It was terrific that everybody could come together for something good. So why not the rest of the time?"[82] The French victory was a vision of an ideal, not the reality of one.

Harlem Désir of SOS-Racisme claimed that "multicultural youth is . . . the France of tomorrow."[83] Nevertheless, race and color remain impediments to accepting that future society infused with the cultural wealth of hybridity. As one Algerian teenager related: "I was born in Paris, but I feel Algerian. . . . Why? Because when the French look at me, they don't believe I'm French. They say, yes, but what's your origin?"[84] David A. McMurray finds the idea of a monocultural France antihistorical: "French culture has always been heterogeneous. The inspirational interconnections between the French and the Andalusian, Persian, Egyptian, and Levantine worlds, to name only a few, have always formed part of the French cultural bedrock."[85]

The present cultural confluence in France, and in Algeria too, may be convoluted, but it offers a variety of opportunities to understand each other's culture through this extraordinary hybridization.[86] If France and Algeria can negotiate and honestly recognize their internal and external cultural differentiations, this will significantly enhance both countries' ability to resolve lingering problems dating from political decolonization. Decades ago the Club Jean Moulin stated that "the page of colonization and decolonization" could not be completed until two objectives were met, (1) the establishment of new relations with Algeria and (2) the national integration of colonial compatriots.[87] As regards the latter, the page remains unfinished. Now there is no longer a binary relationship between an Algerian and a French culture, but a mixing of their cultures. Alain Juppé stated: "The French-Algerian past influences our present relationship, because that past has never been resolved on either side." He then returned to his familiar theme: "Algeria needs to find an identity compatible with the historical pluralism of its society. . . . It must provide itself with a real plan for society which will not be impaired by anybody either from inside or outside because it can only be the result of a dialogue among the different political and social components of the Algerian people."[88] Ironically, given the social transformations of his own country, he could have referred to France as well as Algeria.

The ability of France to adapt to its own pluralism, to restrain its patronizing neocolonial reflexes and refrain from practicing a cultural terrorism such as stereotyping Muslims or, worse, permitting blatant racism, will contribute significantly toward completing decolonization. Homi Bhabha suggests a strategy: "The challenge lies in conceiving of the time of political action and understanding as opening up a space that can accept and regulate the differential structure of the moment of intervention without rushing to produce a unity of social antagonism or contradiction."[89] This strategic area "is the 'inter'—the cutting edge of translation and negotiation, the *in-between* space—that carries the burden of the meaning of culture. It makes it possible to begin envisaging national, anti-nationalist histories of the 'people.' And by exploring this Third Space, we may elude the politics of polarity and emerge as the others of our selves."[90] This spacing is similar to Derrida's idea of *différance,* the area where truth can be discerned and negotiated. This space is inherently existential, epistemological, and historical.

Historicism

"The very question of identification only emerges *in-between* disavowal and designation," writes Homi Bhabha. "It is performed in the agonistic struggle between the epistemological, visual demand for a knowledge of the Other and its representation in the act of articulation and enunciation."[91] This "in-betweenness" and "representation" is also historical, or, to quote Lou Reed, the American rock and roll "proto-punk" and a favorite of *beur* literature, "Between thought and expression lies a lifetime."[92] That "lifetime" in all its complexity, its language and its silence, is history. Historicism has emerged as an essential epistemological and ontological agent in the quest to complete decolonization.

Benjamin Stora points out many examples in *La Gangrène et l'oubli* of how the Algerian War has respectively haunted the French and hallowed the Algerian consciousnesses, inspiring inventive mythologies.[93] Consider, for example, the statistics of war dead. Presidents Ben Bella and Boumedienne created 1.5 million martyrs in the cause of Algerian independence. Though Belkacem Krim estimated that 300,000 died during the War, Alistair Horne and David C. Gordon calculated that wartime conditions such as untreated wounded and population displacement added casualties that brought the number considerably higher.[94] On the other hand, Xavier Yacono, after a study of population growth and electoral statistics, argued that the official Algerian figure was inflated. He concluded that 140,000 to 150,000 nationalist fighters perished and another 29,674 Muslims were victims of other assaults.[95] According to William H. Lewis, 250,000 Algerians were killed and 500,000 wounded, compounded by two million homeless and 300,000 refugees.[96] Fraught with myth and memory, statistics provide neither consensus nor closure.

In November 1954, then-minister of the interior François Mitterrand reputedly said of Algeria that "the only negotiation is war." As the renowned historian Charles-André Julien pointed out, this statement was never proved to have been uttered by Mitterrand, but it was always associated with him.[97] Another prominent example of historical obfuscation was the concealment, until recently, of the actual dramatic and terrible details of the night of 17 October 1961, when emigrant workers were viciously assaulted by the police in what Jean Lacouture called a "police pogrom."[98] The Algerian War repeatedly undermined positive postcolonial relations with sensational reports—colonial *disparus* still imprisoned in remote locations in Algeria, native human guinea pigs used in French atomic testing. Indeed, the French called the Algerian War "the war without a name," and those who fought there did not receive the status of *anciens combattants*, veterans, until 1974.[99] In his 1992 book *La Guerre d'Algérie n'a pas eu lieu* (The war of Algeria did not take place), René Andrieu appealed for all parties to assume their responsibility for the tragic process of decolonization.[100] Lucile Provost wrote that French policy toward Algeria was similar to that of Pontius Pilate, trying to wash away the Algerian question.[101] Perhaps Lady Macbeth would be more appropriate, since France has had to deal with an enduring guilt. Jean-Pierre Rioux concluded that the Algerian War was simply "incompatible" with national identity and memory and that it was less a question of "amnesia" than of "ignorance," since it has not been honestly studied.[102]

It took thirty years for major documentaries on Algerian decolonization to appear on French television screens.[103] An English-produced film by Peter Batty, *The Algerian War,* was broadcast in August–September 1990. This was followed in September–October 1991 by the series *Les*

Années algériennes by Benjamin Stora. In February 1992 *La Guerre sans nom* by Bertrand Tavernier and Patrick Rotman examined the poignant memories of soldiers from Grenoble. A cable program in October 1994 by Philip Brooks and Alan Hayling dealt with the tragic Algerian emigrant worker march of 17 October 1961. Collectively, these programs contributed toward rekindling interest and memory and toward reconciling the past with the present.

The government has also became more historically conscious. Besides providing remunerations to the *pieds-noirs* and the *harkis,* President Jacques Chirac on 11 November 1996 formally dedicated a monument in the Nineteenth Arrondissement of Paris to the civilians and military of North Africa, 1952–1962. He paid homage to the repatriated populations "who have contributed to the grandeur of our country, incarnating the civilizing work of France," but he also spoke of the three million soldiers who served in Algeria, of whom 25,000 were lost "who had dreamed without doubt of a society more fraternal which would rest indissolubly linked to France, as these worried populations dreamt, menaced day and night by terrorism."[104] This too was an important measure toward recognizing their colonial sacrifice. Monuments and indemnity payments have signaled that it is time to move on.

There is an emerging problem concerning French reception and perception of the *fitna*. Youcef Hadj Ali detailed in a recent book how French analysts have stereotyped Algeria and have unfairly compared its unique situation with that of Somalia, Lebanon, and Iran.[105] He contests the idea that Islamism was purely the product of Algeria, but also places blame on the social restraints of French colonialism which inhibited "the emergence of a class of entrepreneurs, of cadres, of modernist Algerian elites."[106] Mitterrand is taken to task for his tolerance toward the FIS before the *fitna,* allowing them to establish a network in France, and his support of the Sant'Egidio Platform. Hadj Ali's portrait of Ait Ahmed, a favorite of the French media, is iconoclastic, tainting the Kabyle's image as a champion of democracy. He defends Algeria's democratization, which permitted thirty-nine parties to participate in the 1998 legislative elections, and compares Algeria's endeavors with de Gaulle's controversial practices during decolonization. Obviously, the *fitna* will also be a historicist challenge.

Algeria's historicism toward the War of Liberation had been closely controlled. A fixed and even coercive myth repeatedly circulated the idea that a fully armed and engaged People, rather than individuals, were the victorious heroes of the Revolution. History had to be "decolonized" (actually falsified), and this was a complementary objective of the Cultural Revolution (see chapter 5). It was only during President Benjedid's administration that tentative official efforts were made to acknowledge that a fuller history of Algeria's liberation existed.

Benjedid attempted to reconcile personalities of the past with the ruling establishment. He freed Ben Bella in 1980, and on the thirtieth anniversary of the beginning of the War of Independence, Benjedid proclaimed a presidential amnesty. Algeria also hosted an international commemorative conference of historians. Prominent nationalists, including Belkacem Krim and Ramdane Abane, were posthumously rehabilitated. The revised or "enriched" National Charter's historical section asserted the positive roles played by the former political pariahs Messali Hadj and Ferhat Abbas.

In 1982 Slimane Chikh, rector of the University of Algiers, courageously commented: "The study of the *harki* phenomenon remains taboo; it is time to lift the veil . . . and calmly approach the problem."[107] President Benjedid's tone toward the *harkis* during his official visit in 1983 was quite conciliatory. Discouragingly, when the French produced a commemorative stamp for the *harkis* in 1989, the Algerian government announced that it would not accept any mail from France bearing the new stamp. But children of *harkis* have been welcomed in the country. When the media were liberalized after the October 1988 riots, there were open discussions of the War of Liberation on television, with the participation of Ait Ahmed, one of the founders of the FLN.

During the *fitna,* however, the Pouvoir often portrayed France as an intrusive power, intractably attached to colonialist atavisms and interventions. In the wake of the presidential elections of November 1995, the official news agency APS assailed perceived French interference in Algerian affairs, explaining that "any attack against the sovereignty of their nation can only signify for Algerians an attempt to restore an order they have fought and defeated. . . . The colonial order has earned from the Algerian people neither forgiveness nor forgetting."[108] Clearly the War was viewed as a political instrument as well as a historical event.

Among the most effective Algerian advocates of historicism were not historians but writers. In 1963 the Union des Ecrivains boldly proclaimed in its charter that "our war was also an insurrection of the spirit. Our victory is that of the forces of progress against obscurantism and all forms of servitude."[109] The writers soon perceived the inauthenticity of revolutionary platitudes and mythmaking and expressed this in the dilemmas of their decolonized characters. The colonial existential trope was recodified to consider postcolonial realities. Kateb Yacine said in 1964: "The French having left, we no longer have the excuse to search for our faults outside of ourselves."[110] Ahmed Azeggagh in his *Chacun son métier* (1966) called for Algerians to "stop celebrating massacres / stop celebrating names / stop celebrating phantoms / stop celebrating dates."[111] Kateb's *Polygone étoilé* (1966) betrayed his disenchantment with Algeria's independence, as did Mourad Bourboune's *Le Muezzin* (1968) and Mohammed Dib's *Danse du roi* (1968). Mourad, the disconsolate veteran of the War of Independence in Mouloud Mammeri's *La Traversée* (1982) serves also as a symbol of disillusion and alienation. Tahar Djaout's wonderfully crafted *Les Chercheurs d'os* (1984) examines the changing values of Algeria, including the lack of respect for ancestral traditions and civility, in a coming-of-age novel about a youth searching for the skeletal remains of his older brother. In *L'Invention du désert* (1987), Djaout's plot involves a writer who is assigned to recount the history of the Almoravids. The writer begins his narrative while living in the cold climate of France and realizes that, to understand the Almoravids, he must imagine physical and metaphorical deserts. In a particularly interesting section, Ibn Toumart, the reformist spiritual leader of the rival Almohads, is imagined touring Paris commenting critically and observing its corrupt and corrosive sensuality and its random and racist metro graffiti.

Mohammed Dib's *Dieu en barbarie* (1970) specifically considers the French-Algerian relationship. The dedicated and idealistic *coopérant* Jean-Marie Aymard views cooperation as helping Algeria in its existential quest to find its destiny and history. This is seconded by his good friend Kamal Waed, a young technocrat, who parrots the official state-building discourse. The chief character is Hakim Madjar, who is married to a Frenchwoman, Marthe Deschamps. Hakim questions the positions of Aymard and Kamal. He views cooperation as serving primarily French interests and sees the importation of foreign (socialist) state-building ideology—and capital—as alien to Algerian customs. Using arguments reminiscent of those amplified by the Islamist Malek Bennabi, Hakim criticizes Western values and culture and urges a return to spirituality. Marthe admires the Algerian personality but senses "despair" within it, an important commentary on the incomplete existential quest for an authentic self. On the other hand, the loving relationship between Hakim and Marthe underscores a true "cooperation." The message is clear: Algerians must discover their true selves, their dignity (rather than mimicry), a constant theme in Dib's prodigious work. Dib stated that his writings aimed to show both Algerians and French "the essential . . . humanity we have in common."[112]

In *Malédiction* (1993) Rachid Mimouni particularly expresses the Camusian absurdities of the pre-*fitna* period where "the Party" and the Islamists have "taken God hostage." Set in 1991, the novel is an allegory of Algeria's seething existential crisis. Among its chief characters are a doctor, an alienated intellectual, a dissipated veteran of the War of Liberation, an innocent youth, and an opportunistic Islamist. The hospital where much of the action takes place is a metaphor for the country's unhealthy condition. Heroism is equated with the effort to preserve one's humanity in a malevolent and murderous milieu.[113] Mimouni's untimely death, of natural causes in February 1995 while in self-imposed exile first in Morocco and then in France, was a grievous loss to Algeria.

These agonistic general themes were also expressed in Arabic literature. Arabic poetry, such as that of Mohammed Lakhdar Abdelkader Saihi, criticized the Algerian bureaucracy.[114] Mohamed Zetili subtly decried the sterility and "silence" (*samt*) of postcolonial Algerian culture.[115] In Abdelhamid Benhadouga's novel about generational differences and oppressive patriarchy, *Le Vent du sud* (1971), the character Malek says, "The armed revolution delivered us from colonization, but it did not succeed in liberating us from myths. Another revolution remains to be undertaken."[116] Benhadouga's *La Fin d'hier* (1975) boldly addresses reconciling Algeria's history with social realities, such as the children of *harkis*. The protagonist Bachir reflects that "the Revolution is far from being completed."[117] Rachid Boudjedra's *Le Démantèlement* (1981) features a young woman, Selma, who searches history to find the causes of Algeria's troubles. She criticizes ancestors, usually officially praised for their resistance, who permitted France to establish a colonial presence. Selma voices Boudjedra's concern about the falsification of Algerian history, especially by those in power.[118] The novel represents an appeal to demystify the past.

Before deciding to write only in Arabic (only to return later to French), Boudjedra wrote a gripping novel entitled *La Répudiation* (1969) in which he assailed the perpetuated postcolonial mistreatment of women. Fettouma Touati's *Le Printemps désespéré* (1984) is another work celebrating the wisdom of several generations of Algerian women and their own diverse ambitions and dreams and struggle against patriarchal presumptions. Assia Djebar's works celebrate the "voices of women," as in her remarkable historical novel *L'Amour, la fantasia* (1985). In this work she explores the thoughts and expressions of women from the seizure of Algiers to the War of Liberation. In her collection of short stories *Femmes d'Alger dans leur appartement* (1980), she speaks of a common language of all women, a language of "feminine tones."[119] In a painful memoir, *Le Blanc d'Algérie* (1995), she reflects upon the tragic literary ellipse, the loss of great writers during the War of Independence and the *fitna*—Feraoun, Fanon, Djaout—leaving Algeria in a colorless void (*blanc*), the tragedy of a country "without writing." Women poets such as Salima Ait Mohamed, Myriam Ben, Aicha Bouabaci, Zineb Labidi, and Georgette Mecili have courageously composed works condemning the violence and dehumanization of the *fitna*.[120]

Among all the writers of the decolonizing and postcolonial era, Kateb Yacine (1929–89) epitomized the literary historicist. Profoundly historically conscious, he invoked ancestral resistance to colonizers in his plays *Le Cadavre encerclé* and *Les Ancêtres redoublent de férocité*. Kateb's most significant novel was *Nedjma* (1956), about a quest for a pure Algerian identity, symbolized by the Keblouti tribe and by Nedjma herself, who is significantly a cultural hybrid, half Algerian, half French Jewess. He constantly refers to Algeria's historical past in the novel—the Numidians, the Romans, the failed expedition of Charles V against Algiers. In an interview in 1987 he said: "*Nedjma* is Algeria, the quest for Algeria. Have we found it? In my opinion, no."[121] Kateb insisted that Algeria had to be understood in its totality. He asserted in 1962: "There is no Berber Algeria, there is no Arab Algeria, there is no French Algeria: there is *one* Algeria."[122] Sensitive to the plight of emigrant workers in France, he produced a play in 1971 composed in Maghribi Arabic entitled *Mohammed, prends ta valise*. As a guest on Radio Beur, Kateb pronounced that he was "not a Muslim nor an Arab, but an Algerian."[123] The unrest in Constantine in 1986 and especially the riots of October 1988 reminded him of those of Sétif in 1945 and provoked a bitter denunciation of Algerian authorities.

Kateb attempted to reconcile Algerian history and culture with the question of language and identity. In an interview with *Le Figaro littéraire* (26 January 1967), he contended: "It would be as absurd to cry out *Algérie arabe* or *Algérie kabyle* as *Algérie française*. We are trilingual. . . . We must therefore have a parallel development of these three cultures."[124] Professor Khaoula Ibrahimi has carried on this discourse by advocating the linkage of language to historicity. The Algerian quest for a homogeneous culture is in itself antihistorical, he says, as is the framing of binary relationships—Arabic/French, Arabic/Berber. Rather "it is necessary to accept the idea of a pluralist Algeria, as a wealth inherited from History. Algeria is Berber, Arab, Mediterranean, and African, also."[125] Djebar thought the insistence upon promoting "the national language" was a "sterilizing monolingualism."[126] Abdelhafid Hamdi Chérif viewed Arabophones and Francophones as incompatible. The overcommitment to Arabization in Algeria also marginalized the hybrid and francophone "cultural *métis*." Cooperation, when practiced as a neocolonialism, has ignored or "forgotten" Arabic.[127] Chérif stresses that there must be an accompanying cultural as well as historical accommodation.

Historicism can serve as a liberating agent. Indeed, Pierre Bourdieu argued during the *fitna* that colonial history could create an Algerian social consensus satisfying both modernists and traditionalists.[128] Stora saw the historical problem as a two-pronged one. For France, it was a matter of engaging the Algerian War truthfully for what it was, a "page of scant glory," and for the Algerians, it was necessary to "move on" from it (*en sortir*).[129] As for the *fitna,* Stora hoped for "the repossession of memory" along with individual rights.[130] Gilles Manceron and Hassan Remaoun point out that students on both sides of the Mediterranean receive little or skewed information in their textbooks about the War; the teaching of the War in France is understated and tangential to the general history of decolonization. They anticipate that as the years pass and new generations emerge, the War will be inscribed less in personal memory than in distant history, and that with the conscientious pursuit of that past will come objective truth.[131]

The current dominance of the War and memory in historiography particularly neglects the four decades of postcolonial history or examines these years through the optic of the War. Not everyone has had voluntary or involuntary historical amnesia. Though psychodramas often recurred in the postcolonial relationship, it must be remembered that there have been men and women who have endeavored to construct a new, albeit difficult, relationship through a willingness to recognize, repair, and reconcile the past. But this too is what is fascinating about the relationship: the personal transformations of leaders like de Gaulle, Mitterrand, and Boumedienne.[132] Certainly the de Gaulle of 1945 was different from that of 1962 despite (or because of) his profound essentialism, and the Mitterrand of 1955 from that of 1981, and the Boumedienne of 1962 from that of 1975. One can also point to the hard behind-the-scenes work of people like Mohamed Sahnoun, who was tortured during the War and who distinguished himself in the difficult emigrant-labor negotiations in 1980. He admired the diplomacy of his French counterparts like Ambassador Jean-Marie Mérillon and Foreign Minister Jean François-Poncet as they collectively worked on bilateral problems. Mohamed Benyahia ranks as another important individual sensitive to history but willing to move on with the relationship. All these writers and cultural contributors had a common view: though they were linked to the past for better or worse, they were more than willing to build a future.[133] Indeed, this could also be seen in the Evian negotiators and their memoirs, which share an eagerness to create a close postcolonial relationship despite the abhorrent violence of the War. Collectively, these individuals recognized that, as historical realities change, so must mentalities.

The eminent historian Charles-Robert Ageron has repeatedly declared that a history of the Algerian War can not be comprehensively undertaken until documentation is made fully available. He emphasized the positive: that the Evian Accords succeeded in ending a colonial war, prevented a civil war in France, and established, through an exemplary cooperation, a reconciliation. After decolonizing Algeria, France was regarded as a stronger power by the world.[134] Jacques Marseille stated: "It is necessary to lift the taboo and to say at what point the independence of Algeria was a good thing (*bonne affaire*) for France and at what point it was, perhaps, a bad thing for Algeria."[135] His work *Empire colonial et capitalisme français* argues that France was obliged to decolonize by a mistaken perception that the colonies dragged the consumer-driven, modernizing post–World War II French economy like a "ball and chain" (*boulet*).[136] Marseille's work established that, to the French imagination, the colonies' value still was not so much economic as political, reflecting the French essentialist values of grandeur and independence. The intangible was esteemed above the tangible benefits of colonialism. Furthermore, his research and others' indicated that France could afford the War while modernizing. The idea that it was a financial "burden" was a powerful misperception.[137] Fundamentally, French public opinion despised the War and regarded it as an unnecessary financial drain.[138]

Roland Barthes wrote in *Mythologies*, which appeared during the War of Liberation, that myth involves historical choice, the function of which "is to distort, not to make disappear."[139] But within myth, "history evaporates."[140] Certainly the French and the Algerians can be accused of myth-making and are both culpable of dissipating history. Their recent efforts to expunge myth from memory, to demystify the historical relationship, deserve acclaim. Nevertheless, Barthes reminded: "History never ensures the triumph pure and simple of something over its opposite: it unravels, while making itself, unimaginable solutions, unforeseeable syntheses."[141] Historicism demands constant inquiry and attention, and fortunately French and Algerian historians are increasingly willing to devote their combined energies to this restorative engagement. They seem to mirror Maurice Merleau-Ponty's statement that "human life and history in particular are compatible with truth *provided only that all its aspects are clarified.*"[142]

In a poignant reflection shortly before his death, Bishop Pierre Claverie of Oran observed: "We are confronted today by a historical reality which necessitates the taking into account of evolutions of society in all their complexity. It no longer suffices to recall myths. . . . It is thus necessary to recover history and to recast our existence together today upon the reality of our societies."[143] This was tantamount to the reclamation of humanity, so dear to the heart of Fanon, who penned: "It is through the effort to recapture the self and to scrutinize the self, it is through the lasting tension of their freedom that men will be able to create the ideal conditions of existence for a human world."[144]

Decolonization as a Transcendant Transformation

Another distinguishing aspect of the bilateral relationship's history has been a millennial significance attributed to decolonization. Decolonization equated with an epiphanic, transcendant transformation of men and women.

Ontologically, Fanon equated decolonization with a repersonalization, a new being. In a stirring moment in *The Wretched of the Earth* he wrote that decolonization "brings a natural rhythm into existence, introduced by new men, and with it a new language and a new humanity. Decolonization is the veritable creation of new men."[145] Despite the violent struggle, decolonization would be redemptive. These new men and women (as described in *A Dying Colonialism*), purged of the psychoexistential complex by the liberation struggle, would create a new humanism and implicitly new relations between peoples. Though Fanon wrote this in the context of Third World liberation, he clearly based it on his Algerian experience. The idea of a creation of a new consciousness, of a regenerated humanity, is a singular characteristic of the French-Algerian relationship. Composing in 1964, the great French-Algerian poet Jean Sénac (1926–73) wrote of the need for not only "new men" but also a "new vocabulary" and a "new language."[146] Ahmed Taleb Ibrahimi saw the role of the Cultural Revolution as "forming a new man within a new society" (see chapter 5). Malek Bennabi's collected writings have as a theme the creation of a new Muslim consciousness, though unlike Fanon he considered that the

"chaotic" West had little of value to offer the "post-Almohadian" be-
liever. Bennabi wrote: "In order to cease being colonized, it is necessary to
cease being colonizable, to cease 'making mythology'."[147] Kateb Yacine
had talked about the need for Algerians "to re-become Algerians."[148]

The "new humanity trope" also affected the French perspective on
decolonization. In November 1960 de Gaulle called France's contribution
to Algerian development "necessary to human progress."[149] The general
spoke of "the new Algeria associated with the new France."[150] He viewed
French-Algerian cooperation as a global catalyst as well as an exemplar:
"International life may be transformed by this."[151] As France recovered or
"renovated" from the trauma of decolonization, de Gaulle told Alain Peyrefitte on 23 April 1963: "The French are re-becoming themselves."[152]

The idea that decolonization would serve as some type of epiphany is
not as mystical or romantic as one might think. The idea of a new humanity recognizing the dignity of the other was shared by these, in Germaine
Tillion's words, "complementary enemies." Each side envisioned decolonization as profoundly transformative. It should be remembered that
Fanon, in particular, did not believe that these decolonized new men and
women would automatically appear as soon as the *tricolore* was lowered.
This was a gradual and fragile process, since the danger of the new country
becoming controlled by neocolonialist, "parasitical" comprador classes
had to be surmounted. Fanon urged the flourishing of a "national consciousness," which he defined as "an all-embracing crystallization of the
innermost hopes of the whole people."[153] Applying this definition to contemporary Algeria and France, this mandates an acceptance of pluralism.
Jacques de Barrin underscored Algeria's continuing existential dilemma in
an article aptly titled "A Country to Reinvent," pointing out that during
the *fitna* those who competed for power wanted to impose their vision on
Algeria rather than "taking into account [Algeria's] social realities."[154] But
this refashioning of a nation also applies to contemporary France.

The transformation that will end decolonization must be a reimagination (and relative deconstruction) of the postcolonial state. Julia Kristeva's analysis of French pluralism led her to advocate an idea of the baron
de Montesquieu (1689–1755), the idea of an *esprit général* or a "general
spirit" that recognized the "otherness" of "strangers" through a "thinking of the social body as a guaranteed hierarchy of *private rights*." She
urged: "Give a place to foreigners, in the 'nation' understood as *esprit
général*—such is, as I see it, the optimal version of integration and of the
nation today."[155] In her "Open Letter to Harlem Désir," she viewed the
idea of *esprit général* as reformulating the *national whole* as:

1. A *historical* identity
2. A layering of very concrete and very diverse causalities (climate, religions, past, laws, customs, manners)
3. A possibility of *going beyond* the political groups thus conceived as sharing an *esprit général* and into higher entities set forth by a spirit of concord and economic development.[156]

Kristeva's appeal for a reformulated, transcendent French nation-state, though still rooted in the universalist, tolerant, cosmopolitan (and essentialist) ideals of the Enlightenment, relates directly to another great philosopher of history who lived centuries ago across the Mediterranean.

Like Montesquieu, Ibn Khaldun (1332–1406) sought a logic to history or, from this book's perspective, an "ordering framework," and applied an extraordinarily "modernist" analytical approach. He concluded that *'asabiyya,* a "group feeling" or, as Muhsin Mahdi would refer to it, a "community of sentiment," is the determining historical agent in social development.[157] *'Asabiyya* was the source of the state; its solidarity led to strength and its disintegration to decline. Ibn Khaldun observed that state formation occurred when "a group feeling [emerged] that is stronger than all the other group feelings combined, that is superior to them all and makes them subservient, and in which all the diverse group feelings coalesce, as it were, to become one greater group feeling."[158] The only viable agent of a "superior group feeling" in Algeria today, with the power to cohere the country, is inclusive democracy. Ibn Khaldun and Montesquieu recognized that plurality, we may call it a hybrid "group spirit," must be integrated within a state. Their centuries-old prescriptions remain contemporary, convincing, and correlative to the French-Algerian relationship.

There is always an ambivalence in identities. Jacques Berque, a native of Algeria, reflected: "If he dares, and if he is permitted, to reach his goal, the erstwhile *colonisé,* having freed himself from the Other, will find the Other deep in himself."[159] Of course, the "othering" also refers to the inculcative effect of the ex-colonized upon the ex-colonialists. De Gaulle wrote that he "hoped to ensure that, in the sense in which France had always remained in some degree Roman ever since the days of Gaul, the Algeria of the future, by virtue of the impress which she had received and would wish to preserve, would in many respects remain French."[160] It seems, too, that "the France of the future," given its historical experience and impression, would inevitably remain in many ways attached to Algeria. Rachid Mimouni acknowledged that despite the cruelties of colonialism, the French presence in Algeria had a deep and even positive imprint upon the country ranging from the introduction of modern contractual relations to infrastructure to language and literature. He concluded that the French presence contributed "at least" toward a cultural "mutual comprehension" as exemplified by the teaching of Arabic courses at French cultural centers in Algeria.[161]

Roland Barthes's concluding appeal in *Mythologies* has a particular resonance to the history of the postcolonial relationship with its reflections, refractions, and representations: "This is what we must seek: a reconciliation between reality and men, between description and explanation, between object and knowledge."[162] If genuinely pursued, Barthes's conciliatory praxis would transform the relationship and finally end decolonization.

11

Conclusion

France and Algeria have experienced an unparalleled colonial and postcolonial history. Its complexity, marked by its multiplicity of relations, has produced extraordinary passions and paradoxes. Jean de Broglie said in 1964 that "with a country like Algeria there is no middle ground between amity and animosity."[1] Consider the range of emotions between the Augustinian "fraternal love" of Cardinal Léon-Etienne Duval and the racist nativism of Jean-Marie Le Pen or the acute literary sensibilities of Tahar Djaout, Abdelkader Alloula, Youcef Sebti, and others silenced by the *fitna*'s raging nihilism. Ten years after the signing of the Evian Accords, Louis Joxe wrote: "There exists between France and Algeria a certain specificity in their relations."[2] As the perspicacious Michel Jobert reflected during an interview published in 1975: "Relations between France and Algeria cannot be so simple or indifferent."[3]

Long before postmodernism and the *Annales* school of historiography, Ibn Khaldun spoke of two types of history, a history of "surface" events, primarily political surveys, and then another history of "inner meaning," which he described as "an attempt to get at the truth, subtle explanation of the causes and origins of existing things, and deep knowledge of the how and why of events."[4] He defined history as "a discipline that has a great number of [different] approaches." He believed that the writing of history "requires numerous sources and greatly varied knowledge."[5] This "modernist" methodology served the great scholar well in his inestimable studies of Islamic and Maghribi history. Appropriately, the Khaldunian pluralist approach remains particularly applicable toward understanding the modern French-Algerian bilateral relationship.

From 1962 to 1988 the two countries experienced a surface relationship, a relationship of bilateral and multilateral impressions, an *extroversion*. In 1962 both countries began projecting new postcolonial identities for external international audiences. Gaullist France featured a convincing conversion from colonialist to *coopérateur,* and nationalist Algeria continued its revolutionary engagement, shifting its struggle from the political to the economic and social neocolonial presence of France, notably its battles of oil and natural gas. Inevitably, France and Algeria manufactured exclusive mythologies to accord with their respective essentialist and existentialist dispositions. As the decades passed, the countries' extroverted identities became increasingly incongruent with changing external political and internal social and economic realities.

Algeria's convulsive political, economic, and social implosion in October 1988 reoriented each country toward the neglected "inner meaning" of the bilateral relationship. This represented an *introversion,* so vital to understand the events of this recent decade. The destabilization and dislocation of Algeria had serious repercussions not only for Algeria's self-conception but also for France's reception and perception of that nation as well as its own past and identity. Algeria's chronic instability followed by the calamitous *fitna* forced a reassessment of the relationship, a bilateral shift of each country's "signifying consciousness," a deeper consideration by both sides of the invisible along with the visible.

Through cooperation, France and Algeria once had a cohesive relationship; now there is need for greater coherence and comprehension. This will not occur until Algeria resolves its national identity, which must be defined as inclusive; the country has no other historical option. Redemocratization, even if constricted or contrived, has created a relentless expectation of pluralist democracy, no matter how deceptively latent or mute. The Pouvoir must recognize it or risk its being demanded from below.

These issues are Algeria's responsibilities, no matter how influential or insidious the perceived or imagined *hizb faransa.* Ammar Belheimer correctly perceived that "France has always worked with the strongest party in Algeria." He added: "This was the policy, and it will remain so."[6] Yet given its multiple ties, France remains Algeria's most important and problematic foreign relationship. This is why the Pouvoir has been quick to solicit France's support even while condemning France's enduring postcolonial presence and influence as interference and intrusion. France's consistent accommodation of the Pouvoir, and by extension the degradation or deprivation of Algerian democratization, is a symbolic rejection of its own democratic traditions and a betrayal of its cherished essentialism. This is a measure of the difficulty France has had, especially since 1992, in reconciling its ideals with its interests.

The author has argued that French essentialism and Algerian existentialism not only ordered and framed dispositions that regulated the decolonizing and postcolonial relationships, but also served as organizing strategies of power, perception, and identity. They cohered external relations and conceived internal impressions of the other. They created knowledge that disciplined the relationship and opened mutually accepted spaces of negotiation. The ordering frameworks produced policies, epistemologies, and ontologies. The frameworks, however, were not fixed but fluid during these years. This is why recurrent psychodramas and other less spectacular crises never ruptured the relationship, but instead revealed the astounding bilateral resilience characteristic of this elliptical, transformative history. The bilateral postcolonial relationship may have been rancorous, but it was never reckless. Each country discovered a synergy, a profound if reluctant need for the other, which affected each country's bilateral and multilateral relations.

As this study concludes, there is a growing conflation of the ordering frameworks. Ironically, France's growing awareness of its own pluralism has created an existential anguish, an identity crisis. Its own essentialist values traditionally identified with a dynamic nation-state are being adapted with difficulty to its multilateral position as one of Europe's leaders. Yet the exemplary, didactic France so loved by de Gaulle can still be instructive if it can resolve its own issues of hybridity and historicism. As for Algeria, the grueling events since 1988 have repeatedly forced it to recognize that its essential historical identity is pluralist and must take into account its social and political realities.

Several important events have recently occurred pointing up the elliptical nature of the relationship. In April 1999 the withdrawal of six candidates marred the election of Abdelaziz Bouteflika as president. Since then, Bouteflika has assiduously cultivated a variety of constituencies with charm and gestures. Though qualifying his remarks, he recognized the importance of Amazighism to the alienated, suspicious Kabyles. The president articulated carefully considered words concerning the Sant'Egidio initiative. His use of French has offended Arabists, including moderate supporters, but earned him international esteem. Thousands of Islamists have accepted his offer of full or limited amnesty. In an effort to end corruption (and to secure himself), he has replaced nearly half of the provincial (*wilayat*) governors. He has also praised the Jewish and Christian heritage in Algeria.

In an astute political stroke, he announced a referendum on the question: "Do you agree with the president's approach to restoring peace and civil concord?"[7] Bouteflika received a massive mandate on 16 September, when 97 percent voted affirmatively in what was actually a legitimizing plebiscite. Significantly, 85 percent of the electorate participated. Nevertheless, the military has resisted Bouteflika's efforts to form a more civilian-oriented government. Indeed, one commentator saw the situation as reminiscent of de Gaulle and the army in 1958.[8] If Algeria is to emerge from and resolve the *fitna,* the military must be depoliticized.

Meanwhile, Bouteflika's actions contributed to a vastly improved relationship with France. Given his long experience, he understood that, whether bad or good, "relations between Algeria and France are always important."[9] In late July 1999, Hubert Védrine arrived in Algiers. This was the first extended official visit of a French foreign minister to Algeria in three years. Védrine found President Bouteflika eager to reestablish a strong and positive bilateral relationship reinforced by a restoration of technical and cultural cooperation, and referred to the visit as a "refounding" of the relationship. Bouteflika also addressed acute French cultural sensibilities. He praised the French language and culture and asserted that French will play a significant role in Algerian education. Paris in turn announced its plans to reopen its consulates in Oran and Annaba and to open more visa application facilities. Indeed, France projected the delivery of 150,000 visas for 1999, compared with 50,000 in 1997 and 80,000 in 1998. France would also reactivate the Centre Culturel Français in Algiers as well as the centers at Oran, Tizi-Ouzou, Constantine, and Annaba. Bouteflika declared "a complete and total entente" concerning the mutual decision to set aside the misunderstandings in the relationship.[10] Reflecting on his visit during an interview with *Algeria-Magazine,* Védrine termed the situation in Algeria "entirely new." He declared: "We have decided to open new perspectives in our relations with Algeria. We hope to revive [*rénover*] bilateral cooperation between our two countries."[11]

On 21 September 1999 President Bouteflika and Prime Minister Lionel Jospin breakfasted together at the United Nations in New York. Jospin told the press that "relations between France and Algeria were exemplary in the past[;] they must become so again." The leaders discussed the reopening of the consulates and the liberalization of visa deliveries. Bouteflika reiterated his hope, expressed in July to Védrine, that Air France would resume flights to Algeria, and Jospin indicated that the French carrier would be accommodating. Reciprocal presidential visits to France and Algeria were discussed. Bouteflika concluded: "If the political will to settle problems exists at the highest level, then the problems will only have solutions." Jospin described the new bilateral climate as a "historic opportunity" now that Bouteflika was president.[12] *Le Monde* called for a new "serene" and "adult" relationship where France could not be accused of "paternalism" and Algeria would not resort to its "colonial past as an alibi."[13] It was as if the bilateral relationship had entered a time warp; the *relancement* of 1974–75 and the *redressement* of 1981–82 were being simultaneously relived.

The greatest symbol of France's current elliptical engagement with Algeria was economic. France remains the chief supplier of Algeria, providing 22 percent of Algeria's imports. It is the second client, behind Italy, buying 16.5 percent of Algeria's exports. With the violence of the *fitna* now isolated and intermittent, there is greater interest in investment. Bouteflika has urged that COFACE soften its assessment on risk insurance for investing companies. That decision has not been made yet, but more than two hundred French companies attended the International Fair of Algiers in October 1999; there were about a dozen in 1992. In another remarkable event, the takeover on 13 September 1999 of Elf Aquitaine by TotalFina—a merged company since that June composed of France's Total (ex-CFP) and Belgium's Pétrofina—resulted in an announcement the very next day that Elf (ex-ERAP) would be returning to the Sahara after nearly thirty years of absence. Elf then signed an accord with ARCO to co-develop the petroleum-rich Rhourde El Baguel fields. TotalFina and Elf Aquitaine combined represent the fourth largest oil company in the world and are poised to take advantage of Algeria's critical need to develop its hydrocarbons wealth.

As this book goes to press, the relationship appears to be entering a post-*fitna* phase and possibly a new era of privileged relations. Inevitably, Hervé de Charette recently repeated the time-honored and almost obligatory metaphor: "A page is turned after a long, tragic, [and] appalling period."[14] Nevertheless, this "new page" will be like the others in the history of the postcolonial relationship unless there is sustained bilateral political will and comprehension to fortify and fulfill the recent promising initiatives.

As a final ellipse, observations on decolonization offered forty years ago still correspond to contemporary bilateral conditions. Jean Amrouche recognized and emphasized that Algeria was "not only the symbol of a nationality in the juridical sense, but that of a historical and ontological identity."[15] He also viewed decolonization as an opportunity for France to "return to her self," the France emblematic of the universal mission of the Enlightenment, "the France of legend," and urged it "to incarnate its own myth."[16] Amrouche believed in an ultimately pluralist and tolerant Algeria and France. Germaine Tillion wrote: "We are what we are, the Algerians what they are, but it is with us that they will make peace, and with no one else. And we with them, and only with them."[17] That negotiation between France and Algeria over their mutual history of decolonization is not over. What is increasingly apparent is that the liberating transformation that will end this protracted decolonization will be a victory of the French and the Algerians no longer over the other, but over themselves.

Notes

Prologue

1. In its decolonization of its colonies, France preferred the phrase *transfert des compétences*. According to Keith Panter-Brick: "A *transfert des compétences* was usually made conditional on some powers being used for agreed purposes and in accordance with specified procedure. France thereby retained an interest and a voice in the exercise of these powers, even though they were attributes of a sovereignty that had been transferred." This certainly applies to Algeria. (Panter-Brick, "Independence, French Style," in Gifford and Louis, *Transfers of Power, 1960–1980*, 102).

2. de Gaulle, *Memoirs of Hope*, 3. This idea of essentialist identity relates to that of a True France. According to Herman Lebovics, True France was an unchanging national identity that was "profoundly static and ahistorical, indeed antihistorical, for despite all vicissitudes of history . . . a vital core persist[ed] to infuse everything and everyone with the undying if seriously threatened national character" (Lebovics, *True France*, 9). Roland Barthes analyzed how French history to Jules Michelet was a "continuity" and "relay" of equivalent and essentialist identities (Barthes, *Michelet*, 35–37).

3. Ministry of Information and Culture, *Algerian Revolution*, 193.

4. This philosophical dimension operates here similarly as Michel Foucault's concept of a *dispositif*, translated in various texts as an "apparatus," "analytic," "grid of intelligibility," or "disposition," which regulates rather than reduces discourses and practices. I have used "ordering framework," after conversing with Foucauldian scholar Hubert Dreyfus. Though the Foucauldian approach is useful as an organizing vehicle, Ibn Khaldun (1332–1406), that early "postmodernist" scholar, recognized the importance of multiple methodologies. Benedict Anderson studies the imagination of nationhood in *Imagined Communities*.

5. The term "postcolonial" is problematic, given the perpetuation of a pervasive French economic and cultural presence after Algerian independence. In this study, the term refers to the era after the transfer of government in 1962. Two important works in postcolonial theory deserve mention: Loomba's *Colonialism/Postcolonialism* and Bhabha's *Location of Culture*.

6. For example, see Manceron and Remaoun, *D'une rive à l'autre*, and Andrieu, *La Guerre d'Algérie*.

Chapter 1. French-Algerian Colonial Relations, 1830–1958

1. All citations from the Proclamation are from Mandouze, *Révolution*, 239–43.

2. Ahmed Tewfiq al-Madani provides a persuasive interpretation in his intro-

duction to *Al-Harb al-thalathami'a*, 5–11, and in *Hadhihi hia al-Jaza'ir*, 68–76. See also Wolf, *Barbary Coast*. French works during the seventeenth and eighteenth centuries referred to the *royaume d'Alger*. In the late eighteenth and early nineteenth centuries the discourse had become "condescending" and more "ideological" (Leimdorfer, *Discours*, 48–49). See Julien, *La Conquête*, 1–63; Julien, "Turkish Rule in Algeria and Tunisia, 1516–1830," in *History of North Africa*, 273–335; and Vatin, "L'Algérie en 1830: Essai d'interprétation des recherches historiques sous l'angle de la science politique," *RASJEP* 7 (December 1970): 927–1058.

3. Heggoy, *Historical Dictionary*, 7. See also Heggoy, *Conquest of Algiers*.

4. See Danzinger, *Abd al-Qadir*. Abd al-Qadir, a Qadiriyya leader, considered the struggle against the French a jihad. After his capitulation and incarceration, the French permitted the emir to live in exile first in Bursa (Turkey) and then Damascus, where in 1860 he saved many Christians during sectarian violence. Subsequently, Napoleon III honored and feted him in Paris.

5. Ageron, *De l'insurrection*, 429, 477–78.

6. See Bennoune, *Making*, 35–85. A convenient list of the principal measures of land confiscation is in Ministry of Information and Culture, *Faces od Algeria: The Agrarian Revolution* (1973), 13–14.

7. Bourdieu, *The Algerians*, 120.

8. The Ordinances of 1844 and 1846 called for the verification of titles. The Sénatus-Consulte ostensibly protected tribal and communal land, but still circumscribed it, thereby instituting the principles of property. Ageron relates that out of 168,000 hectares in the Algiers region, the Muslims maintained only 11,500 (*Algérie contemporaine [1830–1976]*, 21). More than one million hectares were transferred from 1863 to 1870. In addition, under the Warnier Law, the State appropriated 309,891 hectares out of 2,239,095 surveyed (Bennoune, "Algerian Peasants," 13–14; see also Lazreg, *Emergence of Classes*, 43–44). The Kabyles lost 574,000 hectares after the Revolt of 1871 (D. Gordon, *Passing*, 15). Muslims' pasturage and forestry were also limited (see Bennoune, *Making*, 43–50).

9. Bennoune, "Algerian Peasants," 13.

10. Amin, *L'Economie du Maghreb*, 1:39. In 1953, 471,878 hectares were devoted to viticulture (Ageron, *De l'insurrection*, 495). See also Isnard, *La Vigne en Algérie*.

11. About 73 percent of the arable Muslim land was parceled into ten-hectare farms. Moreover, the *pieds-noirs* held 42 percent of all industrial jobs, though they composed only 11 percent of the active working population (D. Gordon, *Passing*, 51). See also Charles Lainné, "Les Emigrants et les migrants de la faim," in Sécretariat social d'Alger, *Lutte des Algériens*, 135–52. Ageron provides similar data in *De l'insurrection*, 495.

12. Ageron, *Algérie contemporaine (1830–1976)*, 71. The Algerians replaced workers called to the Front. In addition, 173,000 native Algerians were recruited for military service (ibid.).

13. "L'Evolution économique. Deuxième partie. Questions sociales et culturelles," *ND,* no. 1963 (1954), 6. Algerian families began to settle in France after World War II. In 1953, about 5,000 emigrant families with 15,000 children lived in the *métropole* (Ageron, *De l'insurrection,* 529). The Statute of Algeria (1947) permitted free movement to France. Furthermore, postwar planners needed cheap labor to rebuild the economy. French industrial recovery particularly attracted labor to Paris, Lyon, Lille, Rouen, and Metz. In 1954, 32 percent of the Algerian emigrant work force labored in public works projects, 38 percent in construction, and 20 percent in mechanical and particularly automotive industry (Benjamin Stora, "Algériens, des bras pour la France," *LM,* 24 February 1997). Sustained metropolitan economic growth, compounded by the dislocation of the War of Independence, attracted tens of thousands of Algerians to France.

14. Fitzgerald, "Robinson Theory," 155–68.

15. D. Gordon, *Passing,* 51. According to Tillion, 94 percent of the women were illiterate and 25 percent of all Algerian children went to school. This meant, however, "only one Moslem boy in five was going to school and one Moslem girl in sixteen" (*Algeria: The Realities,* 58). Out of 4,914 students at the University of Algiers, only 442 were Muslims (*ND,* no. 1963 [1954], 21). There was, however, an important contingent of Algerian university students in France, many of whom would play significant roles during the Revolution. For an official Algerian account of colonial education see Ministry of Information, *Faces of Algeria: Education* (1970), 15–16, 18.

16. See "Réflexions sociologiques sur le nationalisme et la culture en Algérie," in Lacheraf, *L'Algérie: Nation et société,* 313–46. See also Pierre Bourdieu, "Le Choc des civilisations," in Secrétariat social d'Alger, *Sous-Développement,* 54.

17. Fanon, "Racism and Culture," in *Toward the African Revolution,* 34. French colonialism decisively influenced Fanon's life from his birth in the Antilles to his death (leukemia) while serving the cause of Algerian liberation. His writings provide a treasure of ideas and insights on colonialism, decolonization, and postcolonialism. See Zahar, *Frantz Fanon;* Lucas, *Sociologie de Frantz Fanon;* Hansen, *Frantz Fanon;* Jinadu, *Fanon;* Caute, *Frantz Fanon;* Bouvier, *Fanon;* Geismar, *Fanon;* and especially Gendzier, *Frantz Fanon.* A recent addition to Fanon studies is Gordon, Sharpley-Whiting, and White, *Fanon: A Critical Reader.*

18. Fanon, *Black Skin, White Masks,* 12. This book analyzes colonialism in the French Antilles. Fanon considered the "massive psychoexistential problem" to be a direct consequence of the "juxtaposition of the white and the black races." But it was more than a question of color. It related to the imposition and insistence of an alien culture. Hansen interprets correctly that "the notions of superordination and subordination" were rooted in colonialism (*Frantz Fanon,* 81). Later Fanon observed similar psychoexistential afflictions in the emigrant laborers in France ("North African Syndrome," in *Toward the African Revolution,* 3–16) as well as the colonized and colonialists in Algeria ("Colonial War and Mental Disorders," in *Wretched of the Earth,* 249–310).

19. *Black Skin, White Masks,* 139.

20. See Turin, *Affrontements culturels.* Resistance also took the form of rejecting the *mission civilisatrice.* Fanon's sensibilities toward the sociological consequences of colonialism are admired in Renée T. White, "Revolutionary Theory: Sociological Dimensions of Fanon's *Sociologie d'une révolution,*" in Gordon, Sharpley-Whiting, and White, *Fanon: A Critical Reader,* 100–109.

21. Architecture as a historical metaphor is a theme in Çeylik, *Urban Forms.* See also Prochaska, *Making Algeria French.*

22. Déjeux, *Littérature algérienne,* 60.

23. Ibid., 61. Amrouche hoped for a culturally pluralistic Algeria (see Arnaud, *Littérature maghrébine,* 1:129–59).

24. See Monego, *Maghrebian Literature,* 18–20. In *Etoile secrète* (1937), he regarded himself as an "orphan without a homeland (*patrie*)" (quoted in Amrouche, *Un Algérien s'adresse aux Français,* xxi).

25. D. Gordon, *North Africa's French Legacy,* 38.

26. D. Gordon, *Passing,* 171. Feraoun admired Camus's humanity and shared his abhorrence over the senseless violence during the War of Independence (*Journal, 1955–62,* 271).

27. Gordon, *North Africa's French Legacy,* 32.

28. al-Mili, *Tarikh al-jaza'ir,* 12.

29. Ibid., 7.

30. al-Madani, *Kitab al-Jaza'ir,* 2–4.

31. Harbi, *Archives,* 127, citing Archives Messali, excerpt of a letter from Messali to MNA (Mouvement Nationaliste Algérien) cadres, August 1956. In part, this was a result of the FLN's "different social forces—the liberalism of a weak new middle class, the reformist Islam of traditional urban and village elites, and the revolutionary nationalism of a proletariat that included . . . emigrants to France" (Clement H. Moore, "Political Parties in Independent North Africa," in Brown, *State and Society,* 25). Quandt, *Revolution and Political Leadership* remains the seminal work in English on colonial elite development. See also Kaddache, *Histoire du nationalisme algérien,* and Stora, *Sources du nationalisme algérien.*

32. See Stora, *Messali Hadj.*

33. Abbas's haunting statement confessed the *évolué's* existential despair in his search for an "Algerian nation." He wrote: "I looked to history, I questioned the living and the dead. . . . I visited cemeteries: no one mentioned it to me" (Heggoy, *Insurgency and Counterinsurgency,* 14, translated from Abbas's article in *L'Entente* [23 February 1936] as quoted in Le Tourneau, *Evolution politique*).

34. Harbi, *Archives,* 110 (cited from Nadir Ahmed, "Le mouvement réformiste algérien: son rôle dans la formation de l'idéologie," 3rd-cycle thesis, Paris, 1968).

35. See Carlier, *Entre nation et jihad.*

36. Camus, *The Rebel,* 10.

37. Ibid., 23.

38. See "L'Evolution de la société musulmane et l'expérience algérienne," *E-M,* no. 35 (1959).

39. This is the theme of Fanon's *A Dying Colonialism.*

40. Fanon, *Wretched of the Earth,* 94.

41. Chikh, *L'Algérie en armes,* 218. The FLN encouraged the development of a historical consciousness to refute the colonial argument that Algeria was the product of France and that it never had a significant heritage. Chikh wrote: "The history of Algeria occupied a large place in the program of the political commissars of the ALN (Armée de Libération Nationale)" (*Algérie en armes,* 321). See also Mohammed Bedjaoui's "legal history" of Algerian sovereignty (especially "Fondements juridiques de la restauration de l'état algérien," 18–39) in *Révolution algérienne et le droit.*

42. "Nous luttons pour notre dignité et notre droit," *E-M,* no. 17 (1958). Amrouche especially felt this pain. According to Gordon, "Amrouche laid emphasis on the psychological factor—the sense of dignity which colonialism, especially French colonialism, insults and suppresses" (*Passing,* 168).

43. Harbi, *Archives,* 126 (Messali excerpt to MNA, August 1956).

44. "Objectifs fondamentaux de notre révolution," *E-M,* no. 2 (1956).

45. Harbi, *Archives,* 297 (personal archives, 14 March 1960).

46. *E-M,* no. 2 (1956).

47. For example, the FLN contended: "Without a sovereign Algerian government that can direct the energy and enthusiasm of the popular masses, that can have the support of natural cadres of the country . . . no agrarian revolution is imaginable in Algeria" (*E-M,* no. 45 [1959]). On another occasion: "Only the independence of Algeria and the return of the people to power will permit the Algerian peasantry to recover its property" (*E-M,* no. 58 [1960]).

48. Algerian Office, "Requirements," 2.

49. *E-M* articles repeatedly attempted to relieve settler anxieties concerning Muslim retribution. See, for example, "La Question de la minorité européenne," no. 77 (1961).

50. Dahlab, *Mission accomplie,* 269, citing interview with the Tunisian journal *Afrique action,* no. 57 (1961).

51. de Bertier de Sauvigny, *La Restauration,* 602.

52. Cave, *The French in Algeria,* 49.

53. The debate over French colonization or withdrawal stimulated pamphleteering. (An example would be Montagne, *Avantages.*) Excited by imperialist emotions, writers often wildly speculated over Algeria's mineral wealth while others feared a colonial morass. The discovery of vast hydrocarbon resources in the 1950s during the War of Independence proved the validity of both positions.

54. *Procès-verbaux et rapports de la commission,* 61–64. The commission's report was a compilation of its members' observations. After an increase in its membership in December 1833, it became known as the African Commission. See also Julien, *La Conquête,* 108–14.

55. *Procès-verbaux et rapports de la commission,* 56.

56. Ibid., 64 and 61. The fear of national decline and decadence permeated colonial discourse (Girardet, *L'Idée coloniale,* 237). See also Smith, *French Stake,* 172–77.

57. *Procès-verbaux et rapports de la commission,* 60.

58. Ibid., 50.

59. Ibid., 56.

60. Ibid., 64.

61. The term *pied-noir* or "black foot" may have been coined by the Muslims in comment on the settlers' shoes. Later, *pied-noir* meant an urban settler while *colon* referred to a rural settler. Today, *pied-noir* implies all European settlers of French Algeria (and French North Africa). Significant studies of the settlers include Nora, *Français d'Algérie;* Lentin, *Dernier quart d'heure;* Leconte, *Pieds-noirs;* Baroli, *Algérie, terre d'espérances;* Mannoni, *Français d'Algérie;* and Etienne, *Problèmes juridiques.*

62. In 1954 there were 1,029,000 *pieds-noirs,* among them 196,000 rural settlers (Etienne, *Problèmes juridiques,* 34). There was always a strong non-French component (Italian, Spanish, Maltese) in the European settler community, as well as a small Jewish population (approximately 140,000 in 1954) which predated the Arab arrival during the seventh century.

63. Camus, "A Short Guide to Towns Without a Past," in *Lyrical and Critical Essays,* 145. John Phillips, a photo-reporter for *Life,* was born to British-American parents in Bouira. He returned to Algeria during the War of Independence and realized the inevitability of Algerian independence. Nevertheless, he reflected that if he had grown up in Algeria, despite his Anglo background, his *colon* identity would have probably placed him staunchly in support of the perpetuation of French Algeria (*Free Spirit,* 544).

64. Clegg, *Workers' Self-Management,* 26-27. See also Julien on the *pied-noir* mentality (*L'Afrique du Nord en marche,* 30-32, 41-44).

65. Plumyène and Lasierra, *Fascismes français,* 271.

66. Fanon, *Wretched of the Earth,* 51.

67. Fanon, "French Intellectuals and Democrats and the Algerian Revolution," in *Toward the African Revolution,* 85.

68. See Firestone, "Doctrine of Integration," 177-203.

69. David Prochaska discusses the creation of a settler identity in *Making Algeria French.* He also interprets the colonial cartoon caricature of Cagayous as a metaphor for *pied-noir* identity. Ignoring the native population and resenting the legal assimilation of Jews, the colonial settlers called themselves "Algerians" (Prochaska, "History as Literature," 705-6). The *pieds-noirs* also developed their own dialect, including Arabic words with their French, as explained and compiled by Duclos, *Dictionnaire du français d'Algérie.* They also have their own cuisine (Kasenty, *Cuisine pied-noir*).

70. Déjeux, *Littérature algérienne,* 21. Bertrand equated the French with the Romans in "We Latins" (Déjeux, *Littérature maghrébine,* 11). See also *RASJEP* 11 (March 1974) for studies on the colonial novel, and a succinct appraisal in Déjeux, "Regard sur la littérature algérienne de la langue française, 1re partie," *Grand Maghreb,* no. 27 (1983): 49-50.

71. Déjeux, *Littérature algérienne,* 39–43.

72. Alexis de Tocqueville perceived in 1841 how the *colon* attitude could lead toward "the ruin of the Europeans" (Gordon, *North Africa's French Legacy,* 24). See also Julien, *L'Afrique du Nord en marche,* 30–32, which includes particularly perceptive statements from General Georges Catroux.

73. Bourdieu, *The Algerians,* 131. Raymond Aron in the preface to this book stated that there was a "radical incompatibility" between the European and traditional cultures and "the Europeans did not understand and did not wish to understand the authentic nature of the traditional culture" (vi).

74. For a recent critique of Camus see Said, "Camus and the French Imperial Experience," in *Culture and Imperialism,* 169–85.

75. See particularly *Le Premier homme,* 178–80, and Jurt, "Albert Camus et l'Algérie," in *Algérie-France-Islam,* 97–109.

76. See appendix to *Le Premier homme,* 282.

77. See, for example, Guilhaume, *Les Mythes fondateurs;* Vatin, *L'Algérie politique,* 17–56; and Leimdorfer, *Discours.* Also involved here is the propagation of native stereotypes, specifically pro-Kabyle, anti-Arab prejudices; see Lorcin, *Imperial Identities.*

78. *De la domination,* 105.

79. Montagne, *Avantages,* 51.

80. *De la domination,* 91–92.

81. Fisquet, *Histoire de l'Algérie,* 11.

82. Rosenblum, *Mission to Civilize,* 146. Regarded as the man most responsible for the colonization of Algeria, Bugeaud nonetheless questioned if France's values could be transferred to such a different culture as Algeria's: "Must we proceed in Africa as in Europe, transporting to Africa our principles, our constitutions, our guarantees . . . ? No, one hundred times no" (Bugeaud, *De l'établissement de légions,* 25). Bugeaud reiterated that the army had a social as well as a military mission in a number of publications such as *L'Algérie: Des moyens de conserver et d'utiliser cette conquête.* Arthur Gobineau questioned French civilizing success: "Civilization is incommunicable, not only to savages, but also to more enlightened nations. This is shown by the efforts of French goodwill and conciliation in the ancient kingdom of Algiers at the present time" (*Inequality,* 171).

83. Ribourt, *Gouvernement de l'Algérie,* 92.

84. Mercier, *Centenaire de l'Algérie,* 1:290–91.

85. See Naylor, "Catholicism in Colonial and Postcolonial Algeria," paper presented at the American Catholic Historical Society on 7 April 1995, micropublished by TREN (Theological Research Exchange Network).

86. "L'Eglise Catholique en Algérie," *Maghreb,* no. 6 (1964), 35.

87. d'Ault-Dumesnil, *Relation de l'expédition,* 503. It should be noted that Marshal Bugeaud and other leading officers opposed proselytism. In addition, the settlers from their perspective preferred having the native Muslims remain in the

cultural inertia of Islam. The fear was that conversion would infuse values threatening the colonial position. See "Un Catholisme méditérranéen," in Baroli, *Vie quotidienne*, 221–35, concerning settler Catholicity.

88. O'Donnell, *Lavigerie in Tunisia*, 3, citing Xavier de Montclos, *Lavigerie, le Saint Siège et l'Eglise, 1846–1878* (Paris: Boccard, 1965), 332.

89. de Foucauld, *Inner Search*, 136. Father de Foucauld also condemned French toleration of slavery.

90. Talbott, *War Without a Name*, 121, 286.

91. See Julien, *La Conquête*, 256–64. Said briefly examines the Orientalist genre of nineteenth-century European painters in his widely influential *Orientalism*, 118–19.

92. Corporal de Gaulle penned a story entitled "Le Secret du spahi: La Fille de l'agha" wherein the hero officer kills himself to protect the woman he loves, the daughter of a fearsome ruler (Lacouture, *De Gaulle: The Rebel*, 17).

93. Viollette, *L'Algérie vivra-t-elle?* 472.

94. Lustick underscored that Algeria was cartographically color-coded differently from France during this time and that the "working perception of French political elites in the interwar period—that Algeria was *not* a part of metropolitan France—are also reflected in the substance of interwar proposals to streamline policies toward overseas France" (*Unsettled States*, 108).

95. See Lustick, *Unsettled States*, and Marshall, *French Colonial Myth*.

96. Giesbert, *François Mitterrand*, 120–21.

97. *Journal officiel* (National Assembly), 13 November 1954, 4967.

98. "L'Algérie française," *L'Opinion en 24 heures*, 31.

99. Ministère de l'Algérie, *Action du gouvernement*, 18.

100. Soustelle, *Drame algérien*, 69.

101. Smith, *French Stake*, 28.

102. *NYT*, 19 March 1962, 12. The imagination of True France was not limited to the Gaullist decolonizers and the partisans of *Algérie française* but extended to the active French opposition to the war and, of course, to French intellectuals' engagements. See the testimonies in Evans, *Memory of Resistance*, and Schalk's comparative study *War and the Ivory Tower*.

103. Gouvernement général, *Discours prononcée par M. Jacques Soustelle*, 16.

104. Ministère de l'Algérie, *Action du gouvernement*, 121.

105. *L'Algérie, terre franco-musulmane*, 49.

106. The social and economic programs of the Fourth and Fifth Republics are considered in greater depth in Naylor, "A Reconsideration."

107. Délégation générale, *Documents Algériens* (1958), 93; *L'Algérie, terre franco-musulmane*, 73; and "L'Autogestion agricole et la réforme agraire en Algérie," *Maghreb*, no. 7 (1965): 48. By this time the *colons*, insecure over their own future, had begun to sell their land. CAPER targeted the redistribution of about 1.5 million hectares by 1964 (Delegation General, *Algerian Documents 1960*, 97). Algerians accepting this land risked execution by the ALN.

108. Délégation générale, *Plan de Constantine,* 39. For other studies of the Constantine Plan see Gallagher, "New Economic Plans," 1–8; Delegation General, *Algeria's Development—1959;* Délégation générale, *Algérie, 1961; LMdipl,* March 1959, 1, 8–9; and Brandell, *Rapports franco-algériens,* 17–22.

109. There were 560 SAS units in 1958 (Délégation générale, *Documents Algériens* [1958], 51). See also Etienne Anthérieu, "Les SAS: Réponse au SOS de l'Algérie," *France outremer,* no. 318 (1956): 20–22. Though occasional tortures at SAS sites tainted their prestige and effectiveness, "they undoubtedly contributed toward saving . . . a French-Algerian friendship" (Droz and Lever, *Histoire de la guerre,* 139).

110. Philip, "Construire l'Algérie," 1289–90, 1292. The idea of communalism and even Algerian "kolkhozes" was posited before the Revolution by the French (Ageron, *De l'insurrection,* 499).

111. Gallagher, "Other Algeria," 6.

112. Ministère de l'Algérie, *Perspectives décennales,* 37.

113. The Saharan discoveries were covered extensively by French trade journals. See, for example, *MTM,* nos. 613–14 (1957): 1929–31. Cornet compared the promise of the oil discoveries with what the coal industry did for nineteenth-century Great Britain (*Du mirage au miracle,* 264–65). See also Soustelle, "Wealth of the Sahara," 626–36. Nazali correctly points out that the effect of the discovery was a "petroleum revolution" for France (*Al-'Alaqat,* 40).

114. Ministère d'Algérie, *Perspectives décennales,* 55. Gendarme criticized the *Perspectives* for ignoring how population growth, even if absorbed by the incipient industrial projects, would still leave an enormous underemployment problem in the agricultural sector as well as a need for professional training (*L'Economie,* 290–92).

115. Délégation générale, *Plan de Constantine,* 47.

116. See Délégation générale, *Industriels! Venez en Algérie.* For example, taxes on profits were 8.8 percent lower in Algeria than in France (35). See also Délégation générale, *Avantages,* and Daniel Lefeuvre, "L'Echec du Plan du Constantine," in Rioux, *Guerre d'Algérie,* 320–27.

117. Gallagher reported that 269 firms had invested in Algeria, 130 of them new investors. After nineteen months of the Constantine Plan's application, $500 million—or 2.5 billion of 1960's new francs: one *nouveau franc* equaled one hundred *anciens francs*—of private capital were repatriated. These repatriations did not have a significant effect upon official transfers generating economic activity ("Other Algeria," 3–4). Citing the *Plan de Constantine* (25), Bennoune contended that "the large French industrial firms had felt only the need to set up local subsidiaries in Algeria, mostly to facilitate the marketing of 'metropolitan' manufactured goods rather than to promote the industrialization of the country" (*Making,* 91). In general, the *patronat* was cool to the idea of investing in Algeria, with the exception of hydrocarbons firms. French industry was benefiting greatly from rapid modernization and preferred to invest in domestic projects. See Jacques

Marseille, "La Guerre a-t-elle eu lieu? Mythes et réalités du fardeau algérien," and Jean-Charles Asselain, "'Boulet colonial' et redressement économique (1958–1962)," in Rioux, *Guerre d'Algérie*, 281–303.

118. Secrétariat social d'Alger, *Construire la cité*, 74.

119. Délégation générale, *Documents Algériens* (1958), 37.

120. Institut d'étude du développement économique et social (IEDES), "La Politique scolaire en Algérie," in Perroux, *L'Algérie de demain*, 52.

121. Ministre résidant, *Algérie, quelques aspects*, 56, 58; Délégation générale, *Documents Algériens* (1958), 37. The vision of a "renaissance of the *bled*" projected the opening of 280 social centers to educate children and adults (Délégation générale, *Plan de Constantine*, 39).

122. D. Gordon, *Passing*, 60. For an excellent survey on educational policy during this period, see IEDES, "La Politique scolaire en Algérie," in Perroux, *L'Algérie de demain*, 24–54.

123. Ministre résidant, *Algérie, quelques aspects*, 43.

124. See Bourdieu and Sayad, *Déracinement*, and especially Descloitres, Reverdy, and Descloitres, *L'Algérie des bidonvilles*. In 1926, 608,000 Muslims lived in urban areas. This statistic inflated to 2,072,000 in 1959 (Amin, *L'Economie du Maghreb*, 1:27, citing *Tableaux de l'économie algérienne* 1960, 22). According to the FLN, some eight thousand villages were destroyed during the War of Liberation.

125. Maxine Champ, "The Problem of the Employment and Social Welfare of the Workers in Algeria," in *Survey of Algeria*, 44. French officials provided this extraordinary statistical information: "This transfer of money is great since it represents about 25 percent of wages paid in ALGERIA by trades and industries and nearly equals the total amount of wages paid in the agricultural field" (Délégation générale, *Documents Algériens* [1958], 45).

126. Michel Massenet, "Migration Algérienne et promotion humaine," in Perroux, *L'Algérie de demain*, 21. Though Massenet regarded this support as statistically exaggerated, it underscores how important the emigrant community was, especially during the tumultuous war years.

127. Belloula, *Les Algériens en France*, 70–72. See also Délégation générale, *Plan de Constantine*, 62–63; and Delegation General, *Algeria's Development—1959*, 62.

128. Smith, *French Stake*, 84.

129. *Major Addresses*, 117–18. De Gaulle reflected upon his rationale again in *Memoirs of Hope*, 112–13. Compare de Gaulle's ideals with those of a French officer in Jules Roy's *War in Algeria*: "We are fighting for a certain conception of man; to raise the standard of living of the people in these parts, to redistribute the land for their benefit, to keep them tied to us materially and spiritually so that our influence may remain" (quoted in Mansell, *Tragedy in Algeria*, 66).

130. Délégation générale, *Plan de Constantine*, 63.

131. Smith, *French Stake*, 179.

132. Délégation générale, *Plan de Constantine*, 6l. De Gaulle affirmed on 8 June 1962 that "the implementation of the Constantine Plan was making all Algeria realize how essential France's aid was for its life" (*NYT*, 9 June 1962). Ahmed Akkache related that the Constantine Plan projects were meant, in the words of Paul Delouvrier, "to fasten Algeria definitively to France" (*Capitaux étrangers*, 56).

133. *Major Addresses*, 4.

134. Ibid., 101.

135. Ibid., 145.

Chapter 2. The Political Decolonization of Algeria and the Evian Accords, 1958–1962

1. Rioux interpreted: "Having suffered a bitter civil war in 1950–5, France refused to be drawn into another one over Algeria. The overwhelming support for de Gaulle stemmed not from a sense of helpless resignation, but rather from a cautious but positive desire to see France at last endowed with a strong new Republican democracy" (*Fourth Republic*, 313). Tillion aptly described de Gaulle as "a statesman of liberal opinions and authoritarian character" (*Complementary Enemies*, 75).

2. De Gaulle called for "association" during his 30 June 1955 press conference (*Memoirs of Hope*, 45). See Naylor, "De Gaulle and Algeria." Bernard Tricot also succinctly reviews de Gaulle's decolonizing prescience (*Mémoires*, 101–2). To de Gaulle (and Tricot) integration was impossible, especially given the rising Algerian birthrates. De Gaulle quipped in March 1959 that if "all the Arabs and Berbers were considered French" eventually "my own village would no longer be called Colombey-les-Deux-Eglises, but Colombey-les-Deux-Mosquées" (Peyrefitte, *C'était de Gaulle*, 1:52). Furthermore, as Odile Rudelle asserted, de Gaulle's loyalties were to France rather than to republican institutions, particularly those of the Fourth Republic ("Gaullisme et crise d'identité républicaine," in Rioux, *Guerre d'Algérie*, 194–95). Nevertheless, he wanted to maintain an association with Algeria (Joxe, interview).

3. *Major Addresses*, 35.

4. By the end of the Fourth Republic, polls already disclosed that the French public no longer considered the preservation of the Algerian departments as vital (Lustick, *Unsettled States*, 119–20).

5. Maurice Couve de Murville reflected that de Gaulle had to educate France in order to decolonize Algeria (Interview).

6. Lustick, *Unsettled States*, 158.

7. *Major Addresses*, 55. Tony Smith asserted that "except for the offer of the possible alternative of secession, de Gaulle's proposal differed in no substantial way from Mollet's earlier triptych of cease-fire, elections, and negotiations (Smith, *French Stake*, 181).

8. *Major Addresses*, 115.

9. Redha Malek contended that de Gaulle viewed negotiating with the FLN as a "last resort" ("De Gaulle et la négociation avec le FLN," in Institut Charles de Gaulle, *De Gaulle et son siècle,* 6:86).

10. *Memoirs of Hope,* 115. Bernard Tricot, who accompanied Louis Joxe during the first Evian negotiations, recounted how de Gaulle especially wanted to learn how the FLN envisioned its future independent relationship with France. If the Algerian people chose "an association with France," implicitly the minority European population needed guaranteed protection and a voice in public affairs. De Gaulle regarded the Sahara as an "interior sea," a transnational area serving bordering countries (*Sentiers de la paix,* 225–26). See also the transcribed interview with Olivier Delorme in Tricot's *Mémoires* (75–185), which complements *Sentiers.*

11. Mandouze, *Revolution,* 243.

12. Horne, *Savage War,* 95–96.

13. See Malek, *L'Algérie à Evian,* for a detailed survey of this period from an Algerian perspective.

14. Hélie, *Accords d'Evian,* 25–29; Horne, *Savage War,* 157.

15. Malek, *L'Algérie à Evian,* 25–27.

16. Mollet (and Governor-General Robert Lacoste) "affirmed categorically to [Alistair Horne] their indignation at the order given" (*Savage War,* 159). Horne reasoned that Mollet "could have released Ben Bella and his colleagues, and have dealt with them, from a position of strength, as honoured negotiators" but that his "government possessed neither the will nor the power" (161). Indeed, Mollet feared correctly that his government would have collapsed (160). Mollet told Horne: "'Even if Ben Bella had not been sequestrated, I doubt whether things would have turned out very differently; because the F.L.N. never accepted our basic thesis that there should be, first of all, a cease-fire" (157).

17. Malek, "De Gaulle et la négociation avec le FLN," in Institut Charles de Gaulle, *De Gaulle et son siècle,* 6:86. Malek believed that de Gaulle finally decided to negotiate with the FLN after the December 1960 demonstrations in Algiers. Though the "Challe plan" was militarily effective, he realized that the urban Muslim population remained behind the GPRA (Malek, "La Place seconde des intérêts économiques," in Gallissot, *Accords d'Evian,* 14).

18. This premature negotiation took place outside Paris on 25–29 June 1960. It was not substantial, but the two sides established a tone of cordiality that continued throughout the tedious negotiations.

19. In an August 1959 GPRA report by Ahmed Boumendjel, he projected prenegotiation procedures to be held in a neutral country like Switzerland. The report also listed Algerian negotiating positions, most of which were actually pursued in 1961–62, underscoring the consistency in the FLN's positions (Harbi, *Archives,* 254, citing personal archives). At the secret negotiations, the Sahara already loomed as a problem (Roussel, *Georges Pompidou,* 118–19).

20. Hélie, *Accords d'Evian,* 84.

21. Joxe claimed there were no ulterior motives behind this statement. Describing the circumstances, he explained that he was harried by the press. Apparently he meant to emphasize the French government's willingness to talk with Algerian nationalists whoever they might be, as France wanted a negotiated solution (Interview). Hélie contended that Joxe's statement reflected the French position that there was a "plurality of Algerian voices" that had to be heard and that the MNA still held considerable influence in the emigrant community (Hélie, *Accords d'Evian*, 88). The FLN's hostile response illustrated its sensitivity to the question of France's recognition of its legitimacy—again the existential issue. Alistair Horne contended that this was "a last final attempt by France to resurrect the idea of a 'third force'" (*Savage War*, 467). Saad Dahlab, recognized as the FLN's most astute negotiator, thought the "maneuver" was "very gross" and contradicted the secret talks with Pompidou that recognized the FLN as "the only and sole representative of the Algerian people." Later, after the cease-fire, Dahlab claimed that the MNA in this case was a creation of French Special Services (*Mission accomplie*, 138–39). De Gaulle reconsidered the FLN's "legitimacy" during his 5 September 1961 press conference after the first Evian discussions.

22. *Major Addresses*, 117.

23. *E-M*, no. 4 (1956). The FLN questioned subtle French influences pervading independent Morocco and Tunisia which suggested that their independence involved "compromise" (Mandouze, *Revolution*, 83–84, citing *E-M*, April 1958). See also "Le Sahara algérien," *E-M*, no. 79 (1961).

24. *E-M*, no. 24 (1958).

25. Algerian Office, *Algeria: Questions and Answers*, citing *E-M*, 8 June 1959.

26. Mandouze, *Revolution*, 160–61, citing *E-M*, 20 February 1960.

27. Ibid., 173, citing *E-M*, 15 April 1961. Mandouze mentions (*Révolution*, 180) that *E-M*, no. 83, published on 19 July 1961 after the impasse at Evian and the beginning of the attempted Lugrin renewal of talks, had "the same doctrine." Again, this attested to the strength of the FLN's dedication to its principles. The Algerian position on the Sahara evolved from support for a "Maghribi union" to Algerian sovereignty by 1958; see *E-M*, nos. 27 and 28 (1958).

28. Algerian Office, "Franco-Algerian Negotiations," 2.

29. Interview.

30. Hélie, *Accords d'Evian*, 108. Ferhat Abbas would also refer to France's continued presence in postcolonial Algeria as stipulated by the Les Rousses negotiations as a form of "capitulations" (Malek, *L'Algérie à Evian*, 225).

31. *Sentiers de la Paix*, 241. Given his close association with de Gaulle and his friendship with Louis Joxe, Tricot's book remains the best work on the periods of negotiation despite his absence from the Les Rousses negotiations.

32. In January 1957 the French established the Organisation Commune des Régions Sahariennes (OCRS). It was a projected condominium aiming to share Saharan hydrocarbon wealth with surrounding independent states and French territories. By the time of the negotiation, Chad, Niger, and Tunisia were receiving

financial subventions or, in Tunisia's case, advances. See Malek, *L'Algérie à Evian*, 137–38.

33. Hélie, *Accords d'Evian*, 106–7.

34. Ibid., 113.

35. At Evian, the French broke off the talks. They were surprised when the Algerians did so at Lugrin (Malek, *L'Algérie à Evian*, 162).

36. Mandouze, *Revolution*, 196, citing *E-M*, no. 82 (1961).

37. Ibid.

38. Algerian Office, "French-Algerian talks," 1.

39. Ibid., 2. The FLN expected the continued presence of a large settler community. *El-Moudjahid* articles attempted to relieve anxieties about Muslim retribution, e.g., "La Question de la minorité européenne," no. 77 (1961). Lakhdar Ben Tobbal told Joxe that independent Algeria needed the expertise of the French of Algeria. The Algerians wanted certain French to stay (not the *gros colons*): "We demand it. Because they have the experience that we do not have" (Ben Tobbal, "Souvenirs du 'Chinois'," in Gallissot, *Accords d'Evian*, 22).

40. Algerian Office, "French-Algerian talks," 3.

41. Ibid.

42. See Horne, *Savage War*, 477.

43. Malek, *L'Algérie à Evian*, 171.

44. Joxe, interview. See also Joxe, "Evian et le jugement des peuples," *LM*, 17 March 1972. Bernard Tricot mirrored Joxe's observations (Tricot, interview).

45. The FLN feared a French settlement with Morocco of the enduring dispute over the western border. Ferhat Abbas's negotiation secured Moroccan diplomatic support (Hodges, *Western Sahara*, 91–92). Ever since the promulgation of the Proclamation of 1 November, the FLN had linked its liberation struggle with those of Algeria's Maghribi neighbors. There was also repeated FLN promotion of Maghrib unity or political integration—see, for example, *E-M*, no. 40 (1959)—besides the projected economic cooperation.

46. *Major Addresses*, 143.

47. Ibid., 145. C. L. Sulzberger perceived a French negotiating "wish list" including Algerian adherence to a Saharan "economic condominium" (*NYT*, 10 February 1962, 22). France was particularly concerned about protecting its oil concessions in the Sahara against international competitors after Algeria gained its independence. Saharan production in 1961 satisfied 94 percent of the national demand (Yergin, *The Prize*, 526). Philip M. Williams and Martin Harrison contended, concerning de Gaulle's change toward the Sahara, that "the act was typical of the Gaullist conception of negotiation by unilateral assertion or concession." Louis Joxe apparently discovered this change of position in the press. De Gaulle was also pressured by the Berlin Wall crisis and the possibility of a military confrontation (*Politics and Society*, 35).

48. *Major Addresses*, 144.

49. Ibid., 145.

50. In January 1957, Mohamed Lebjaoui was sent to France to organize the workers and ensure their adherence to the FLN's Fédération de France (FFFLN) rather than to the MNA. Though captured after only two months, he laid the groundwork for his successor Omar Boudaoud. FLN activists never reached the terrorist levels of the OAS. Their most successful operation was acquiring funds from the emigrant worker population. By the beginning of 1958, a total of 600 million *anciens francs* had been collected (Horne, *Savage War*, 236–37). The FFFLN and the MNA engaged in bloody fratricidal assaults.

51. *Année politique* 1961, 135–39; see also Belloula, *Les Algériens en France*, 89–102, and *E-M*, nos. 86 and 87 (1961). Accounts estimate 100–200 dead. The FFFLN contended that 200 died and 400 Algerians "disappeared" (Stora, *Ils venaient d'Algérie*, 308). Einaudi, with his extensive statistical research including records of inhumations, agreed with the figure of 200 dead (*Bataille de Paris*, 268). On 17 October 1997, Catherine Trautmann, the minister of culture, announced the French government's intention to open its archives concerning this tragedy "to clarify the tragic repression of that day." Einaudi then claimed that 300 Algerians perished (*NYT*, 18 October 1997; *LM*, 17 October 1997). A French government study released in May 1998 revealed in greater detail the scope of the repression, including the incarceration of 11,538 protesters (*NYT*, 5 May 1998). The recent interest in this episode stemmed from the trial of Maurice Papon for his criminal activities during Vichy; it was Papon who, as prefect of police in Paris, ordered the suppression of the worker demonstration.

52. *NYT*, 13 January 1962, 4.

53. Aron, "Dénouement provisoire," 5–6. On the OAS, see Delaure, *L'O.A.S. contre de Gaulle*; Bocca, *Secret Army*; Buchard, *Organisation armée secrète*; Joesten, *Red Hand*; Duranton-Crabo, *Le Temps de l'OAS*; sections in Horne, *Savage War*; and Courrière, *Guerre d'Algérie*.

54. *Le Journal de l'OAS*, *Demeurer Français sur une terre française*, no. 1 (1961).

55. *Appel de la France (Demeurer Français sur une terre française)*, no. 5 (1961).

56. See Camus, *The Rebel*, 282–86. Concerning Algeria, Camus contended that "aberrations, both on the Right and on the Left, merely define the nihilism of our epoch" (*Resistance, Rebellion, and Death*, 121). Plumyène and Lasierra (see *Fascismes français*, 267–69) consider Camus's character development of Meursault in *The Stranger* as having characteristics of an OAS member—the symbolic blinding of the Mediterranean sun, the objectification ("thingification" in Fanonist terms) of the Muslim, the senselessness of his murder. Conor Cruise O'Brien examines Meursault as a *pied-noir* metaphor (*Camus*, 11–31). Forsyth also describes the OAS mentality in the historical novel *The Day of the Jackal*.

57. See Bitterlin, *Histoire des "Barbouzes"*; Bitterlin, *Nous étions tous des térroristes*; and Hennissart, *Wolves in the City*.

58. Ben Khedda confided to Alistair Horne that the OAS also threatened the

FLN "because the union between the O.A.S. and dissident French army units was creating so much provocation, in its murders and indiscriminate massacres of Muslims, and was attempting to get the Muslims to demonstrate, out of control, in Algiers. Had they succeeded there would have been an appalling massacre" (*Savage War,* 507). See also Ben Khedda, *Accords d'Evian,* 27.

59. Ben Khedda related that he was most concerned about presenting a "united FLN" at this time. It would have been difficult, he explained, for the GPRA to address simultaneously negotiations and "Boumedienne's rebellion" (*Accords d'Evian,* 26).

60. Contacts had begun in August. In October, Mohamed Benyahia and Redha Malek listened to French proposals presented by Bruno de Leusse and Claude Chayet concerning particularly the Sahara, citizenship, the transition period and the provisional executive, the establishment of cooperation, and the postcolonial French military presence. At the second meeting at Basel on 9 November, the Algerians responded to the French proposals. Ben Khedda suggested that further progress would have been made except for Ben Bella's "unexpected" hunger strike. After Dahlab and Joxe met again on 23 December, a framework for an agreement definitely began to take shape (Ben Khedda, *Accords d'Evian,* 27–32; Dahlab, *Mission accomplie,* 154–56).

61. *Major Addresses,* 161.

62. *Memoirs of Hope,* 115. See also "From One Evian to Another" in Lacouture, *De Gaulle: The Ruler,* 287–300.

63. The Algerian team was composed of Krim, Dahlab, Malek, Lakhdar Ben Tobbal, M'hammed Yazid, Benyahia, and Seghir Mostefai. France's new team reassured the Algerians, since Buron represented the Mouvement Républicain Populaire (MRP) and de Broglie the Centre National des Indépendants (CNI), thereby illustrating de Gaulle's intention to broaden the political constituency and secure internal support for an accord (Malek, *L'Algérie à Evian*).

64. Buron, *Carnets politiques,* 187.

65. Mandouze, *Revolution,* 207, citing *E-M,* no. 89 (1962).

66. Joxe said cooperation was valued by the FLN as a means to construct the Algerian state. It was not forced upon the Algerians (Interview). According to Tricot, Joxe had informed the FLN earlier that the French would not impose aid but "were simply ready" to provide it (*Sentiers de la Paix,* 250). *E-M,* no. 86 (1961), stated that "it is vital, for a sound and fruitful cooperation between France and Algeria, that Algeria be liberated from neocolonialist contrivance" (Mandouze, *Revolution,* 234). See also Buron, *Carnets politiques,* 226. During this period, Ferhat Abbas anticipated a close postcolonial relationship (*Autopsie,* 313). Dahlab related that every issue was difficult, particularly the Sahara and the rights of the European minority. The idea of having French as the official language was resisted by the Algerians. Arabic was the logical choice, but few Algerians knew it well, except in its spoken Maghribi dialect. French would have a privileged "place of choice" (Dahlab, *Mission accomplie,* 157).

67. Buron, *Carnets politiques,* 193. See also Buron, *LM,* 17 March 1972.

68. Tricot, *Sentiers de la Paix,* 286; Joxe, interview; also Joxe, *LM,* 17 March 1972. In 1982 Joxe recalled being surprised that he had achieved so many safeguards for the *pieds-noirs* (*Le Figaro,* 19 March 1982).

69. Horne, *Savage War,* 519; Courrière, *Guerre d'Algérie,* 4:557–58; Dahlab, *Mission accomplie,* 166. Krim told Ferhat Abbas that if Ferhat had remained president of the GPRA, he would have had more negotiating strength (Abbas, *Autopsie,* 317). On the other hand, Dahlab believed that the GPRA under his friend Ben Khedda had strengthened the negotiating team.

70. Buron did not explain how this sudden turnabout occurred. It was a "voilà!" situation where agreement was suddenly attained. Malek is much more detailed concerning this negotiation and suggests the process was not unusual (*L'Algérie à Evian,* 231–46).

71. Courrière's interviews with Krim did not conclusively explain the GPRA delegation's behavior. According to Jackson: "The GPRA settlement at Evian seemed to indicate their strong desire to prevent further losses by terminating the war" (*FLN in Algeria,* 56). De Broglie reflected that at Evian the French negotiators faced "neither the team of Ben Bella nor that of Boumedienne" (*LM,* 17 March 1972). This in itself affected the Algerian compliance with the Accords. On the other hand, Redha Malek felt no elite pressure (*L'Algérie à Evian,* 231). Indeed, the Algerian delegation found it very strange that the French had hurried to complete the negotiation and suddenly slowed the process themselves. Years later, Joxe told Malek that the announcement of a cease-fire and an accord was to be timed with the liberation of the imprisoned FLN leaders. A concurrent negotiation with the Moroccans provided for France to release the cadres and fly them to Morocco (Malek, *L'Algérie à Evian,* 241–42).

72. Dahlab, *Mission accomplie,* 171.

73. *Memoirs of Hope,* 125. In his address to the nation on 18 March, he called the negotiation a "common-sense solution" (*Major Addresses,* 163).

74. Copies of the Evian Accords can be found in: *AAN* 1962; *Année politique* 1962; Ministre d'état, "Accords d'Evian"; *E-M,* no. 91 (1962); and (in translation, from the French Embassy) *Texts of Declarations.* See also *LM* during this period; *LMdipl,* April 1962; and *NYT,* 19 March 1962. A particularly interesting French perspective on the Accords, especially with regard to reassuring the European population of Algeria, is Ministre d'état, "L'Algérie à l'heure de la paix," 1–21. Mouhoubi provides a detailed analysis of the cooperation stipulations in *Politique de coopération,* 37–46.

75. Etienne, *Problèmes juridiques,* remains the finest analysis of the European minority and Evian. For an analysis of the Accords and their relationship to international legal precedents see Belkherroubi, *La Naissance et la reconnaissance,* 103–46.

76. *Journal Officiel* (Senate), 22 March 1962, 88.

77. Ibid., 89–92.

78. Ibid., 93. The lament over "lost opportunities" was repeated often. Consider Goutor's "almosts": "France *almost* made Algeria into a Western nation; she *almost* brought her into the modern world; she *almost* spared her the terrible pains which she must now endure. But it is this *almost* which makes France's failure in Algeria her most tragic failure" (*Algeria and France,* 74).

79. *Journal Officiel* (National Assembly), 21 March 1962, 474–75.

80. Ibid., 22 March 1962, 511–12.

81. Torti, "Evian: Défaillance," 30–31.

82. Maurice Allais, "Garantie des garanties," *LM,* 12 May 1962. Further arguments can be found in Allais's *Les Accords d'Evian* and *L'Algérie d'Evian.* See a similar interpretation by Pierre Fontaneau in "Les Garanties économiques," 3–6.

83. Grosser, *French Foreign Policy,* 47.

84. Jean-Pierre Gonon, "Les Accords d'Evian et la 'Révolution algérienne'," in Perroux, *L'Algérie de demain,* 134.

85. Daniel, "The Algerian Problem Begins," 609.

86. Camus had hoped for "federated settlements . . . linked to France" (*Resistance, Rebellion, and Death,* 124). He also believed that negotiations would mean "the eviction of 1,200,000 Europeans" (122). Jean Genet's brilliant and brutal play *The Screens* (1961) also depicts the atrocity and absurdity of the Algerian War and its effect upon the colonists and the colonized.

87. See Farès, *Cruelle vérité.* Farès's power was persuasive rather than political. His own police force was ineffective (Ottaway and Ottaway, *Politics,* 50–51). He tried to use his position to persuade both sides to abide by the Evian Accords and construct a new relationship in cooperation with the former *métropole.* He repeatedly used the popular metaphor "turning the page," a phrase that had particular significance during the postcolonial French-Algerian relationship. Nevertheless, during his brief administration ending 24 September, a series of skillfully timed agreements were signed (28 August, 7 and 23 September) that initiated and detailed formal cooperation with Algeria (*Cruelle vérité,* 130–32). He decreed on 7 September that abandoned settler property would be run by appointed managers, an ironic contribution to a climate that led to *autogestion* (see Ottaway and Ottaway, *Politics,* 51).

88. See Carréras, *L'Accord F.L.N.-O.A.S.* Farès struggled to reach conciliatory agreements between the OAS and the FLN as well as his own government (see Farès, *Cruelle vérité,* 117–30). Joxe warned the government in April that the OAS threatened the framework of the Evian agreements and worried that its terrorist operations psychologically impeded European and Muslim "adaptation" to the new social and political realities (Peyrefitte, *C'était de Gaulle,* 1:112).

89. *Année politique* 1962, 34–40.

90. Harbi, *Archives,* 317, citing personal archives.

91. Ben Khedda, *Accords d'Evian,* 9–10. The pragmatic Dahlab referred to the negotiations and agreements as compromises, the greatest diplomatic victory being the achievement of territorial integrity (*Mission accomplie,* 161). This was seconded by Redha Malek, who understood that compromises had to be made,

such as the assumption of colonial debts (abrogated by a subsequent 1966 accord); see Malek, "La Place seconde des intérêts économiques," in Gallissot, *Accords d'Evian,* 11–20).

92. Quandt, *Revolution and Political Leadership,* 164–65.

93. The Tripoli Program appears in *AAN* 1962, 683–704.

94. Gordon, *Passing,* 108–9.

95. This appeal signed by M'Hamed Chebouki appeared in the *Dépêche d'Algérie* on 22 August 1962. It was reproduced in *AAN* 1962, 712–13.

96. Etienne, *Algérie: Cultures et révolution,* 30.

97. See the chapter "Summer of Shame" in Humbaraci, *Revolution that Failed,* 69–80. See also D. Gordon, *Passing,* 71–76. Ben Bella discussed the fratricide with Robert Merle: "Two situations existed side by side in the Algerian Revolution. One, which was atrocious, was that of the fighters of the Intérieur and the frontier refugees. The other was the glittering and sumptuous life of certain ministers of the G.P.R.A., who were already living in the same fashion as some African régimes which I prefer not to mention by name. To sum up, it was clear that the Revolution would be replaced, immediately after independence, by a facile and corrupt régime which, installed with official blessings and amid widespread intrigue, would leave the people to struggle in their misery" (Merle, *Ben Bella,* 118–19).

98. *Major Addresses,* 109.

99. See *LM* throughout the spring and summer of 1962 for a chronicle of this traumatic time, e.g., Michel Goué, "Les Enlèvements d'Européens en Algérie," *LM,* 21 July 1962, 1, 7. Total European civilian casualties exceeded 10,000, with 2,788 killed including OAS victims. There were also 500 "disappearances" (Horne, *Savage War,* 538). Ferhat Abbas had hoped that the *pieds-noirs* would stay since they would have been "a link" to French technical expertise and civilization (*Autopsie,* 325). The massive settler flight was an ironic complement to the idea of "collective responsibility" which was applied against the Muslims during the War. The bitter consequences were also indiscriminate. Jean-Marcel Jeanneney, France's first ambassador to Algeria, questioned whether a "multicultural Algeria," with the French settlers still holding so much property (implying economic power), could have guided the new nation toward development. He called it "illusionary" (Jeanneney, "Recherche de la vision de l'époque," in Gallissot, *Accords d'Evian,* 28).

100. Interview, February 1978. All *pieds-noirs* interviewed by the author have been kept anonymous. Most of the interviews took place in Aix-en-Provence and environs.

101. Interview, March 1978.

102. Baroli, *Algérie, terre d'espérances,* 8.

103. Jacques Roseau, the prominent spokesman for RECOURS, a *pied-noir* organization founded in the mid-1970s, contended that *pieds-noirs* were unfairly represented as supporters of a settler "oligarchy." Their insecurity was caused not only by the OAS but by the FLN's own instability (*LM,* 27 November 1980). Maurice Calmein, president of the Cercle Algérianiste, also protested the negative

stereotype of the *pieds-noirs* which ignored their achievements in building up the country ("La Lettre du président," *L'Algérianiste*, no. 14 [1981]). See also chapter 10.

104. Interview, April 1978. This *pied-noir* had repatriated before the great *exode* and entertained General Salan in his home before he became the OAS's commander. He was interned at Saint-Maurice-l'Ardoise (Gard) in a "camp" which later became the "home" of the *harkis*. For more on the *pied-noir* internment see *Le Méridional*, 30 June and 1 July 1962. The author read old threats from the Républicains Français—an anticolonial and, by extension, anti-*pied-noir* group—addressed to the interviewee, who referred to this group's membership as *barbouzes*.

105. Bourdieu, *The Algerians*, 152. See also Angelelli, "Notes," 83–125.

106. Interview, April 1978.

107. Interview, March 1978.

108. French authorities estimated in December 1961 that 200,000 *pieds-noirs* would return, or possibly 300,000–400,000 in four years. Another estimate was 350,000 repatriates in four to five years (*LM*, 6 September 1962). A Club Jean Moulin study anticipated 400,000 returns in five years (*Deux pièces du dossier Algérie*, 17–62). In a pamphlet published immediately after the signing of the Evian Accords, the French government attempted to persuade the *pieds-noirs* to stay in Algeria and the Algerians to vote "yes" to independence in cooperation with France (*L'Algérie de demain*.) Marseille was prepared to handle a thousand refugees a day (*LM*, 17 May 1962; *NYT*, 11 January 1962). A month later, 338,000 *pieds-noirs* arrived in France, most of them coming through Marseille. The influx directly followed the signing of the OAS-FLN accord (June 1962). The OAS had tried to prevent the Europeans' flight to France when it was still actively fighting. When all seemed lost, the OAS exhorted the Europeans to leave despite captured General Salan's appeal to the settlers to stay. The OAS chief implored: "Keep your beautiful country in close cooperation with France" (*NYT*, 23 June 1962); see also *NYT*, 16 and 20 June 1962. Mayor Jacques Chevallier of Algiers anticipated 80 percent of the repatriated to return to Algeria (*AAN* 1962, 289); Gilbert Mathieu in *LMdipl*, April 1962, also expected the return of *pieds-noirs*. The French government had to reevaluate the entire repatriation project. See Maurice Denuzière, "A Marseille, où les services d'accueil ont été profondément réorganisées," *LM*, 22 June 1962. From January until September 1962, 580,000 left for France. Before 1962, 80,000 *pieds-noirs* and foreign residents had departed (*LM*, 6 September 1962). ANFANOMA, a repatriate organization composed primarily of former settlers to Morocco and Tunisia, also provided assistance for the *pieds-noirs*. De Gaulle believed that the *pieds-noirs* would stay in Algeria. He told Alain Peyrefitte in November 1961 that "the new Algeria will have need of them and they will need her" (Peyrefitte, *C'était de Gaulle*, 1:88). When the *exode* occurred, de Gaulle wanted to make sure that the *pieds-noirs* would return to France and not go to other countries. According to Peyrefitte, Joxe and Pompidou feared that the repatriation of the *pieds-noirs* "would inject fascism

into France" (ibid., 193). The FLN expected 600,000 to remain in Algeria (Ben Tobbal, "Souvenirs du 'Chinois'," in Gallissot, *Les Accords d'Evian*, 22).

109. Interview, April 1978. A Montpellier survey reported that only 10 percent of the repatriates felt that they were made very welcome in the *métropole* (*LM*, 11 November 1969). See also *NYT*, 19 August 1962, 16.

110. A representative article is Maurice Denuzière, "Les 'Pieds-noirs' parmi nous," *LM*, 6 and 7 September 1962. Denuzière reported on bureaucratic problems in *LM*, 27 December 1962. Alain Peyrefitte described the situation: "Everyone did his best to cope with the challenge; never were so many holes punched in administrative compartments, never did the administrative snail move so speedily. Yet everything seemed to stand still. Thousands of letters, of requests for help we could not provide, came to us daily. In those twelve weeks I became convinced that had France been just a little more bureaucratic than it is, the *pieds-noirs* would still be in their resettlement camps" (*The Trouble with France*, 61).

111. Lentin, "Situation," 29. Léo Palacio contended there were about 70,000 left in 1967 ("Avec le dernier carré des Français d'Algérie, *LM*, 6 May 1967). The total repatriation figure was put at 960,000 (*LM*, 30 May 1972). There were three stages of repatriation: 1962—insecurity; 1963—nationalizations; 1964–65—difficulties in adaptation. Lentin (29) contended that by 1967 the situation had stabilized at about 61,000. The French Embassy reported in March 1965 that there were about 60,000 French citizens left as permanent residents, one-third of them retired and elderly (Ottaway and Ottaway, *Politics*, 149). See also Baillet, "Rapatriés."

112. See Martin, *Israélites algériens*, and Chouraqui, *Between East and West*.

113. D. Gordon, *Passing*, 208. See also Julien, *L'Afrique du Nord en marche*, 32–33, 234–40.

114. Algerian Office, "Fate of Algerian Jews," 1.

115. Cohen, "Legacy of Empire," 101. *Le Nouvel Observateur* claimed 125,000 settled in France (19–25 June 1987, 88).

116. Michel Legris, "L'Exode des Israélites d'Algérie," *LM*, 19 November 1962. See also Eugène Mannoni, "D'Algérie en Israel," *LM*, 4 April 1962; Doris Bensimon, "La Guerre et l'évolution de la communauté juive," in Rioux, *Guerre d'Algérie*, 538–44; and *AAN* 1962, 558.

117. A few hundred were left about ten years after independence (Nyrop et al., *Area Handbook*, 139).

118. The FSJU provided an extraordinary service (*LM*, 19 September 1962). See also Ayoun and Cohen, *Les Juifs d'Algérie*, 190–204. The phrase "the Jewish family serves the Jew like an oasis in the desert" was quoted by Albert Memmi in *L'Express* (international), no. 1959 (1989): 33.

119. See Mandel, "France's Algerian Jews," 475–82. Other Jews wanted to return and thought that they could live in independent Algeria. See Daniel, "Jewish Future in Algeria," 198–203, and Himmelfarb, "Algerian Jews," 430–32.

120. Cohen, "Legacy of Empire," 101.

121. Baillet, "Rapatriés," 46–50. See also Ayoun, "En nouvel exode, les Juifs

d'Algérie au lendemain de l'indépendance," in Gallissot, *Accords d'Evian,* 107–19.

122. *Harakat* in Arabic means military enterprise. There were about 100,000 fighting with the French. This included 40,000 fighting with the regular French army, 20,000 Mokhazenis with the SAS as militialike self-defense units, 8,500 with the Ministry of the Interior in police activities, and 31,500 in paramilitary self-defense units (Baillet, "Rapatriés," 51). See also Saliha Abdellatif, "Algérie 62: 'Cessez-le-feu' et devenir des supplétifs musulmans," in Gallissot, *Accords d'Evian,* 121–31.

123. French officers ignored directives from Paris prohibiting *harki* repatriation. Colonel Bastien-Thiry's antigovernment operations were influenced by the plight of French Muslims (see Kaberseli, "Et les Français musulmans"). De Gaulle did not consider them, like the *pieds-noirs,* to be *rapatriés* (Peyrefitte, *C'était de Gaulle,* 1:196).

124. French figures accounted for 17,456 Muslim dead (including 5,966 killed "accidentally" and 892 officers killed in action), 64,985 wounded and injured, and a thousand missing, including deserters. Horne also details some of the atrocities committed against the *harkis* (*Savage War,* 537–38). See particularly "Le Massacre des harkis" in Méliani, *La France honteuse,* 56–109. Some believe as many as 65,000–100,000 Muslims loyal to France were executed (*LM,* 16 June 1997; Hamoumou, *Et ils son devenus harkis,* 46).

125. Georges Jasseron, director of the French Red Cross for the Rouen region, related that he had watched a television program documenting a Red Cross visit to an internment camp and that all the individuals appeared to be healthy. Later he was told by one of the *harkis* whom he was helping to relocate that the internment camp scene was staged (*Harkis en France,* 125–27; interview). Pierre Vidal-Naquet appealed for the protection of these loyal French citizens since they were selected and trained to become instruments of French military policy (*LM,* 11–12 November 1962).

126. See Baillet, "Rapatriés," 51–57, for a concise survey.

127. Jasseron's *Harkis en France* details gruesome accounts.

128. About 40,000 *harkis* and their families arrived after the war (Baillet, "Rapatriés," 51). With families reunited and a population explosion, their numbers have increased to more than 400,000. See Bernardi et al., *Dossiers noirs du racisme,* 161. Other figures account for only 20,000 arriving in France (*LM,* 16 November 1995).

129. I. William Zartman, "North African Foreign Policy," in Brown, *State and Society,* 60.

Chapter 3. Independence with Interdependence, 1962–1965

1. De Gaulle, *L'Appel,* 3.

2. *Major Addresses,* 244.

3. See Luethy, "De Gaulle: Pose and Policy." Luethy wrote: "It is the symbols that matter, not the facts: this is the summary of de Gaulle's wartime experience

and the essence of his policy" (569). Luethy contended that de Gaulle believed France needed a monarchical symbol, the "uncontested *chef*" (567). Grosser asserted: "Ordinary men live their own lives. General de Gaulle lives his biography" (*French Foreign Policy,* 26). When asked what he meant by his famous "certain idea of France" (found on the first page of *L'Appel*), de Gaulle equated it with his "reason for living" (*Discours et messages,* 4:413). Couve de Murville wrote: "De Gaulle was assuredly a man of an intransigent passion and his passion was France" (*Une politique étrangère,* 10). See also C. L. Sulzberger's analysis of de Gaulle's personal image and greatness, "The Pursuit of Grandeur," *NYT,* 3 February 1962; Hoffmann, "De Gaulle's Memoirs"; and particularly chapters in Hoffmann, *Decline or Renewal?* For example, Stanley and Inge Hoffmann observed: "De Gaulle succeeded in establishing that cycle of identifications—of France to himself and himself to France, of the people with him, of himself and France to higher causes" ("De Gaulle as Political Artist: The Will to Grandeur," in *Decline or Renewal?* 234). He was able "to make [his] personality the answer to historical crisis, to fill a collective identity vacuum with [his] own identity, and to erase a common humiliation through [his] acts" (ibid., 243). Similar ideas are discussed in Philip H. Gordon, *Certain Idea,* 14–22.

4. Kolodziej, *French International Policy,* 28.

5. French analysts tend to emphasize independence rather than grandeur as being the dynamic force in France's foreign policy. See de Carmoy, *Foreign Policies;* Grosser, *French Foreign Policy;* René de Saint-Legier, "La Conduite des affaires extérieures," in Tricot et al., *De Gaulle et le service de l'état;* and de la Gorce, "Idées-forcées." A more balanced view is that of Jean Lacouture in his analyses in *LMdipl* in January 1968, February 1970, and May 1971. An exception is Jean-Baptiste Duroselle, "Changes in French Foreign Policy Since 1945," in Hoffmann, *In Search of France,* 305–58. Duroselle perceived a continuing and complex conflict in French foreign policymaking between intangible/extroverted interests such as grandeur and tangible/introverted considerations which he terms "neo-realism." Non-French analysts tend to minimize the importance of independence in the determination of France's foreign policy. Indeed, Morse devotes his *Foreign Policy and Interdependence* entirely to discussing the contradictions between Gaullist independence and obvious French interdependencies. Kulski contends: "De Gaulle's revolt against the bipolar system is one aspect of his policy, but an independent formulation of policy must have an objective. De Gaulle's objective, the 'grandeur' of France, means a constant increase of French influence in the world" (*De Gaulle and the World,* 25). The significance that Kolodziej attributes to grandeur is illustrated in the subtitle of his survey: The Politics of Grandeur. Yet upon recent access, the website of the Ministry of Foreign Affairs, explaining the principles of French foreign policy, emphasized independence (diplomatie.fr/france/politiq/principe.html, 11 September 1999).

6. Press conference of 9 September 1965 (*Discours et messages,* 4:383).

7. Address of 11 December 1965. (*Discours et messages,* 4:410–11). On 5 February 1964 de Gaulle stated: "It is indispensable that France be independent to

sustain its own effort, but also to serve others" ("Les Grandes lignes de la politique extérieure française," *TN*, no. 76: 20).

8. Couve de Murville, "L'indépendance nationale," 157.

9. Lacouture, "La nation, réalité fondamentale dominant les idéologies," *LMdipl*, January 1968, 2.

10. Couve de Murville, *Une politique étrangère*, 446.

11. An excellent study is Kohl, *French Nuclear Diplomacy*. See also "Le Développement nucléaire français depuis 1945," *ND* no. 3246 (1965), and *France and the Atom*. Like so many policies and ideas that de Gaulle operated from, the *force de frappe* was a legacy of the Fourth Republic. But as Kohl explained: "The key difference is that the *force de frappe* was conceived by the Fourth Republic . . . to bolster France's security and political position within the Western alliance, and not independently of it as General de Gaulle later prescribed" (*French Nuclear Policy*, 357).

12. Daval, *Histoire des idées en France*, 120–21.

13. This was a continuing theme in Gaullist foreign policy. See Couve de Murville, *Une politique étrangère*, 447.

14. Hoffmann, "De Gaulle's Memoirs," 150–51. Cerney referred to "grandeur" as "the need to create a new and more profound sense of national consciousness, capable of transcending the traditional divisions which have characterized the French polity, thus allowing and reinforcing the development of a consensus supportive of a firmly established and active state pursuing the general interest, within a stable political system" (*Politics of Grandeur*, 4).

15. Kolodziej, *French International Policy*, 448.

16. Girardet, *L'Idée coloniale*, 292.

17. Robinson and Gallagher in their classic study of nineteenth-century British imperialism suggested that "inherited notions and biases of official thinking may have been a significant cause of this imperialism without impetus" (*Africa and the Victorians*, 25). Schumpeter, acknowledged by Robinson and Gallagher, contended that imperialism was "atavisitic in character." He explained that "it falls into that large group of surviving features from earlier ages that play such an important part in every concrete social situation. . . . It is an atavism in the social structure, individual, psychological habits of emotional reaction" (*Imperialism and Social Classes*, 65).

18. Brunschwig, *French Colonialism*, 104. Brunschwig wrote that there was a chauvinistic impulse (*poussée chauviniste*; Brown translates it as "chauvinism on the march") during the "new imperialism" era but that historically French colonial policy placed prestige over profits (*Mythes et réalités* 10–11).

19. Hessel, "Défense et illustration de la coopération," *Rencontres*, no. 3 (1967): 25–26.

20. Gallagher, "Co-operation," 2.

21. Ibid., 17.

22. I. William Zartman, "North African Foreign Policy," in Brown, *State and Society*, 61. See also Zartman, "Relations," 1105–6.

23. Grosser, *French Foreign Policy,* 49.

24. Hessel, "Mitterrand's France and the Third World," in Ross, Hoffmann, and Malzacher, *The Mitterrand Experiment,* 325.

25. Hartley, *Gaullism,* 15.

26. Couve de Murville, *Une politique étrangère,* 450; interview.

27. *Une politique étrangère,* 434.

28. Charles Flotte, "Un coopérant vous parle," *F-A,* no. 8 (1965–66): 9. Writing during the height of the French Empire, Albert Sarraut said simply that "the Frenchman is an altruist" (*Grandeur et servitude coloniale,* 79). Flotte and other *coopérants* shared that enduring ideal. In 1964, conceding that political and economic self-interest were present in French aid policy, Jeanneney contended in "Politique de coopération" (popularly called the Jeanneney Report) that the decisive determinant, reflecting France's essentialist nature, was a *besoin de rayonnement* (need to radiate influence): "France desires, more than any other nation, to diffuse far and wide its language and its culture" (62).

29. *Discours et messages,* 4:404. De Gaulle had expressed the same idea during Mexican president López Mateo's visit to France in March–April 1963 (Passeron, *De Gaulle parle,* 365). Raymond Triboulet perceived cooperation as "the *oeuvre* of a great nation which knows how to adapt itself to the modern world. It is the wish of an entire people" (Ministère de la Coopération, *10 réponses sur l'Afrique,* 3). During the colonial period, Algeria was regarded as an "organic" part of France. In another example of refashioned discourse, de Gaulle spoke in May 1962 of an "Algeria in the position of an independent State, cooperating organically with France." In June he looked forward to when "Algeria and France will be able to cooperate organically and regularly with each other" (*Major Addresses,* 182, 185).

30. Edouard E. Van Buu, "Evolution de la coopération franco-maghrébine," in Ruf et al., *Indépendance et interdépendances,* 79.

31. Grimaud, *Politique extérieure,* 40.

32. Robert Buron, "Il y a deux ans," *F-A,* no. 3 (1964): 2.

33. "L'Elaboration," 22.

34. *LM,* 10 July 1973. In his preface to Salah Mouhoubi's book on the bilateral relationship, Mohammed Bedjaoui, who served as Algerian ambassador to France, viewed cooperation "as a policy[, a] dialectic[, and] an ethic" (Mouhoubi, *Politique de coopération,* 10).

35. Redha Malek, "Al-Diblumasiyya al-jaza'iriyya (Algerian diplomacy)," *al-Mujahid al-thaqafi,* no. 1 (1967), 25. On the other hand, Rabah Bitat claimed that "there is neither alliance for progress nor sincere cooperation possible between imperialism and peoples recently liberated" (Grimaud, *Politique extérieure,* 44–45, quoting *RA,* no. 13 [1963]).

36. "Une page est tournée[,] irréversiblement tournée," *RA,* no. 581 (1975): 14.

37. Mustapha Sehimi, "Atouts et faiblesses," *RA,* no. 215 (1967): 26.

38. Aron, *France: Steadfast and Changing,* 147–48.

39. Marshall, *French Colonial Myth*, 11–12. Similarly, former governor-general Marcel-Edmond Naegelen, addressing a luncheon on 8 June 1956, spoke of France's unique ability to accommodate different peoples and called for a "fusion" of Islamic and Western values in Algeria ("L'Algérie française," 26–27). Georges Le Beau, another former governor-general, also speaking at the luncheon, shared these ideas. He hoped relations between France and Algeria would solidify, forming a "*bloc Afrique-Europe*" leading to "*une fraternité humaine*" (*L'Opinion*, 31).

40. Marshall, *French Colonial Myth*, 13.

41. *Major Addresses*, 26.

42. Ibid., 168.

43. Raymond Cartier, "Attention, la France dilapide son argent," *Paris-Match*, 29 February 1964, 105. Cartier began his "utilitarian" criticism of French colonial policy toward Africa in articles in *Paris-Match* in August–September 1956. He believed that the colonies were expensive and slowed French economic growth. For an assessment of Cartiérisme's effect on French decolonization in Algeria, see Nathalie Ruz, "La Force du 'Cartiérisme'," in Rioux, *Guerre d'Algérie*, 328–36.

44. Cartier, *Paris-Match*, 7 March 1964, 7. Robert Buron called for *coopérants'* usage of the language of the "*coopérés*" ("Aspects de la coopération," 15).

45. Cartier, *Paris-Match*, 29 February 1964, 105.

46. In a debate with Buron, Cartier again attacked Algeria over the indemnity issue. He also criticized President Boumedienne's absence during the de Gaulle memorial service at Notre Dame ("'A armes égales'," *F-A*, no. 34 [1971]: 22–25).

47. See Hayter, *French Aid;* Yves Berthelot, "French Aid Performance and Development Policy," in Dinwiddy, *European Development Policies*, 36–49; and Robarts, *French Development Assistance*, 29–44.

48. Georges Gorse, the second French ambassador to Algeria (Jeanneney was the first), was commissioned to conduct a study to update the Jeanneney Report. Its findings were embarrassing to the French government, especially concerning structural problems in the administration of aid. The criticisms of the Jeanneney Report remained valid. The reduction of French aid when compared to the Jeanneney period tainted the image of French generosity. The Gorse Report was never made public. The Abelin Report of 1975 called for a "new dimension" of cooperation that would be more regional and collaborative (Jean Poirier and Jean Touscoz, "Aid and Cooperation: French Official Attitudes as seen in the Jeanneney, Gorse and Abelin Reports," in Morris-Jones and Fischer, *Decolonisation and After*, 227–28).

49. Jeanneney, "Politique de coopération," 107.

50. Cartier, *Paris-Match*, 7 March 1964, 7.

51. de Carmoy, *Foreign Policies*, 239.

52. Fuchs, *La Coopération: Aide ou néo-colonialisme?* 127–28. See also René Gendarme, "Du colonialisme au néo-colonialisme," *LMdipl*, December 1970, 7.

53. Grosser, *French Foreign Policy*, 61.

54. Ibid., 61–62. Grosser also reflected: "The twentieth century requires that one no longer dominate, but cooperate — domination and cooperation both servic-

ing the cause of national ambition" (60). Grosser, de Carmoy, and even Cartier agreed that cooperation was admirable. Their criticisms were over means and methods. A future ambassador to Algeria, Jean Basdevant, suggested that France needed to examine and expand its resources—human, institutional, material—if Paris wanted to assert or preserve its cultural (educational) and technical influence internationally ("Politique culturelle"). In 1978 he said that with the exception of large lobbies, like the wine industry, opposition to cooperation with Algeria was individual, especially within the Quai d'Orsay, rather than systemic (Basdevant, interview).

55. Buron, "Il y a deux ans," *F-A*, no. 3 (1964): 2.

56. *Major Addresses*, 251. The ideals of self-liberation and of service to others, i.e., promoting their liberation in turn, relate also to the philosophy of *personnalisme*. Indeed, the personalist journal *Esprit* showed a particular interest in cooperation. See Mounier, *Le Personnalisme*.

57. *Major Addresses*, 251.

58. Kolodziej, *French International Policy*, 470.

59. Grosser, *French Foreign Policy*, 47.

60. Humbaraci, *Revolution that Failed*, 69–70. Humbaraci maintained that de Gaulle "chose" Ben Bella for his "malleability and his merits" (90).

61. Grimaud, *Politique extérieure*, 43.

62. *AAN* 1963, 349. Foreign Minister Mohamed Khemisti elaborated upon these anti-Evian remarks in Peter Braestrup, "Algeria Stresses Neutrality Policy," *NYT*, 25 November 1962, 9.

63. Etienne, *Problèmes juridiques*, 151.

64. Ben Bella, *Discours*, 26.

65. *Maghreb*, no. 1 (1964): 38, excerpted from a de Broglie interview in *La Nation*.

66. During the immediate postcolonial period the European community's experience was chronicled by the daily newspaper *Coopération* and its weekly cousin *Hebdo-Coopération* (1962–65). This publication approved of cooperation and gave support to the Ben Bella regime. It illuminated, too, the difficulties of the European community, especially the incompatibility of the *pieds-noirs'* interests with the socialist option. About five hundred French settlers decided to become Algerian citizens from 1962 to 1967 (Guy Pervillé, "Les Accords d'Evian et les relations franco-algériennes," in Rioux, *Guerre d'Algérie*, 489, citing Etienne, *Problèmes juridiques*, 292–300).

67. *Texts of Declarations*, 21.

68. See Clegg, *Workers' Self-Management*, and Maurice Parodi, "L'Autogestion des exploitations agricoles modernes en Algérie," *AAN* 1963, 61–84. See also Bennoune, *Making*, 104–8.

69. Merle, *Ben Bella*, 160.

70. Ministère de l'Orientation nationale, *Algérie an II*, 17. See also "Que fait l'Algérie pour se développer rapidement. Gestion et autogestion," *RA*, no. 94 (1964): 8. At first, the farms operated as independent, democratic cooperatives

receiving little direction from the government. Eventually, Algiers had to regulate their operation and production to meet market needs and improve efficiency. The exciting promise of *autogestion* as a viable economic alternative was eventually bureaucratized and subsequently stagnated.

71. Merle, *Ben Bella,* 160.

72. Brace and Brace, *Algerian Voices,* 223.

73. Merle, *Ben Bella,* 155.

74. "Communiqué relatif aux conversations ayant eu lieu à Paris du 28 au 30 janvier 1963 entre une délégation algérienne dirigée par M. Ouzegane et une délégation française dirigée par M. de Broglie sur l'ensemble des problèmes agraires," *AD* no. 0.1349 (1963), 1. See also Ben Bella's address of 28 September 1962 in *Discours,* 12.

75. The difference between the French and the Algerian concept of vacancy came down to "ownership" versus "occupation." Algerian nationalizations meant the takeover of 200,000 French properties (Ottaway and Ottaway, *Politics,* 151). In 1963, 2.3 million hectares were owned by 6,358 Europeans ("Seminaire 1963: Sur les problèmes économiques de l'Algérie indépendante," *RASJPES* 1 [January 1964]: 166).

76. Ottaway and Ottaway, *Politics,* 151.

77. "Communiqué lu à l'issue du conseil des Affaires algériennes par M. Jean de Broglie, secrétaire d'état chargé des Affaires algériennes" (Paris, 5 April 1963), *AD,* no. 0.1380 (1963): 1.

78. See Anselme-Rabinovitch, "Nationalisations," 331–36.

79. "Communiqué franco-algérien publié à l'issue des entretiens entre M. Ben Bella, président du Conseil algérien et M. Jean de Broglie, secrétaire d'état aux Affaires algériennes," *AD,* no. 0.1387 (1963): 1.

80. "Communiqué du Gouvernement français sur la nationalisation par le Gouvernement algérien des propriétés agricoles français (Paris, 2 October 1963)," *AD,* no. 0.1444 (1963): 4. In the National Assembly on 28 October 1963 de Broglie resignedly reflected: "The objectives of Evian have disappeared" (Grimaud, *Politique extérieure,* 54). Mallarde contended that de Gaulle's "indifference" expedited Ben Bella's actions (*L'Algérie depuis,* 153).

81. Peyrefitte, *C'était de Gaulle,* 2:439.

82. Kolodziej, *French International Policy,* 472. In *Qu'est-ce que le Gaullisme?* de Montalais wrote that "resistance" was an important characteristic of Gaullism (19). De Gaulle admired the Algerian resistance to colonialism and the pursuit of an independent, nonaligned foreign policy. Though not consciously aligned to Algerian *autogestion,* the Gaullist ideal of socioeconomic *participation* called for cooperative direction and effort among managers and workers (73–90). De Broglie called Algeria "a child of an old country which has a long experience in revolutionary matters" ("Quarante mois," 1835).

83. de Broglie, "Les Relations franco-algériennes," *Maghreb,* no. 1 (1964): 3. During this period Zartman contended: "France is negotiating in fact with itself" ("Relations," 1113). See also Ruzié, "Coopération franco-algérienne."

84. *Année politique* 1964, 326; *LM,* 7 November 1964.

85. Sékou Touré persuaded Guinea to vote *non* to the French Community in 1958 and receive complete independence. It was the only country in West and Equatorial Africa to repudiate de Gaulle, much to the general's chagrin.

86. See Club Jean Moulin, *Deux pièces;* "Les Perspectives de la coopération économique franco-algérienne," *TN,* no. 12 (1962): 1–12; and Daniel Vollereau, "Les Perspectives économiques de la coopération franco-algérienne," in Perroux, *L'Algérie de demain,* 171–91.

87. de Broglie, "Quarante mois," 1857.

88. The USSR honored Ben Bella as a Hero of the Soviet Union and offered general aid amounting to DA 1.1 billion ("La Visite du Président Ben Bella en U.R.S.S.," *Maghreb,* no. 4 [1964]: 5). The United States through charitable organizations distributed 300,000 tons of foodstuffs during the winter of 1962–63 and provided technical assistance in reforestation and rural development programs. American oil companies were active in the Sahara, though their presence and production were small. The United States received only 0.2 percent of Algeria's exports while accounting for 4.1 percent of the new country's imports ("Les Etats-Unis et le Maghreb," *Maghreb,* no. 8 [1965]: 48–49.)

89. *AAN* 1962, 685.

90. See *AAN* 1964, 543–74.

91. Ben Bella, *Discours,* 26. The first French atomic explosion occurred at Reggane on 13 September 1960. The French continued to test in the Sahara until May 1965. The contention over atomic testing is surveyed concisely in Nazali, *Al-'Alaqat,* 72–89. According to Alain Peyrefitte, de Broglie reported in May 1963 that Ben Bella was willing to accept secret testing (Peyrefitte, *C'était de Gaulle,* 2:436).

92. See Grimaud, *Politique extérieure,* 52.

93. Ottaway and Ottaway, *Politics,* 151.

94. *LM,* 18 June 1964.

95. Among the numerous studies on French financial aid during this time see Hayter, *French Aid,* 132–40; Gonon, "Mécanisme de l'aide financière"; Wolff, "Budget de l'Algérie"; de Broglie, "L'Aide liée"; and "L'Aide française à l'Algérie," *F-A,* no. 34 (1971): 6–7.

96. OECD, *Financial Flows,* 79.

97. Hayter, *French Aid,* 140.

98. Mustapha Sehimi, "Ou en est la coopération?" IV–V.

99. "Sur les problèmes économiques de l'Algérie indépendante," *RASJPES* 1 (January 1964): 241–42.

100. This was anticipated, given the "socialist option." See P. M., "Evolution de la Zone franc et coopération monétaire franco-algérienne," in Perroux, *L'Algérie de demain,* 146–47.

101. Ministère de l'Orientation nationale, *Politique économique,* 11. De Gaulle underscored Algeria's multiple dependence upon France when he made Boumaza the first Algerian minister to visit him, several months before the Algerian minister

of the economy spoke before his own country's National Assembly (Peyrefitte, *C'était de Gaulle*, 2:440).

102. Clegg, *Workers' Self-Management*, 72–73.

103. "Interview," *AD*, no. 30 (1964): 11–12.

104. Gérard Destanne de Bernis, "L'Economie algérienne depuis l'indépendance," in CRESM, *Economies maghrébines*, 27.

105. Evian's "Declaration of Principles" (*Texts of Declarations*, 28–33) provided general direction for cultural and technical cooperation. There followed a series of protocols defining a framework of cooperation until a formal accord could be negotiated. On 28 August 1962, protocols were signed that regulated *coopérant* recruitment, guarantees, and salaries. More protocols were needed to accommodate specific sectors such as infrastructure and tourism (24 September 1962), gas and electricity (17 December 1962), communication (23 January 1963), and the medical mission in the Sahara (19 April 1963); see "Accords passés entre la France et l'Algérie de juillet 1962 au 31 décembre 1963," *Recueils et monographies* (Documentation française), no. 49 (1964).

106. Ambassade de France en Algérie, "La Coopération culturelle et technique de juillet 1962 à juin 1965," n.d.: 2–3 (probable writer is Stéphane Hessel). David C. Gordon added: "Almost all the 1,800 trained European doctors left and Algeria was forced to depend heavily on forty-six doctors from Bulgaria" (*Passing*, 83, citing *E-M*, 1 February 1964). Ambassador Mohammed Sahnoun presented figures showing that Algeria lost 35,000 of its 50,000 teachers; see *AI*, no. 73 (1980): 20. Hessel complimented the commitment of "the generation of transition," those teachers who remained in Algeria and permitted a "miraculous" opening of the 1962 academic year ("Coopération franco-algérienne," 13). There were also colonial "*coopérants*": "Since 1892, contingents of school teachers recruited in France had served in Algeria following a one-year special course devoted to the aspects of the teaching profession peculiar to that country" (*Survey of Algeria*, 60). It should be noted, too, that Arab teachers arrived, especially from Egypt, many of whom were instilled with Islamist proclivities and placed particular pressure on Algerian authorities about the need to Arabize the public. Their influence on Algerian students contributed to the rise of political Islamism in the 1980s and the rage and violence of the 1990s.

107. See Adrien Sany-Marchal, "Les Coopérants militaires," *F-A*, no. 10 (1966): 6. Stéphane Hessel contended that the establishment of the VSNA owed much to the success of the American Peace Corps program ("De la décolonisation et la Coopération," *Esprit*, no. 394 [1970]: 9).

108. The most detailed report of French activities is "La Coopération culturelle et technique entre la France et l'Algérie" (July 1962–June 1965), *ND*, no. 3252 (1966).

109. Ibid., 3, 5–6. At this time, *coopérants* served for a variety of reasons ranging from ideological solidarity with revolutionary Algeria to simply financial profit; see "Trois professeurs français parlent de la Coopération culturelle et l'enseignement en Algérie," *RA*, no. 72 (1964): 6–8. As for the enormous problems

facing educators in Algeria, such as illiteracy, see J. P. Peroncel-Hugoz, "L'Enseignement en Algérie."

110. Merle, *Ben Bella*, 91. See also "French is Tongue of Modern Elite: Islamic Tradition is Weaker than in Neighboring North African Lands," *NYT*, 19 March 1962.

111. Ben Bella, *Discours*, 117. Ferhat Abbas reflected how Ben Bella ignored Algeria's Berber legacy (Abbas, *L'Indépendance confisquée*, 89).

112. See Mazouni, *Culture et enseignement*; Bruno Etienne, "Langue et élites au Maghreb," in CRESM, *Influences occidentales*, 65–94; and Noureddine Sraieg, "Enseignement, décolonisation et développement au Maghreb," and Christiane Souriau, "L'Arabisation en Algérie," in Ruf et al., *Introduction*, 131–53 and 375–97.

113. Etienne, *Algérie: Cultures et révolution*, 175.

114. Jeanneney, "Politique de Coopération," 62.

115. Bouveresse, "Phénomènes de dépendance," 66.

116. Merle, *Ben Bella*, 148.

117. Taleb Ibrahimi, *De la décolonisation*, 19.

118. An interesting article on a proposal to "Algerianize" French or to make it a "vehicle" leading to complete Arabization is "Algérianiser le français," *RA*, no. 241 (1967): 23–24.

119. Merle, *Ben Bella*, 148–49.

120. Ibid., 147.

121. The emigrant worker community has been the subject of many books and articles. Among the books see: Augarde, *La Migration algérienne*; Ath-Messaoud and Gillette, *L'Immigration algérienne en France*; Belloula, *Les Algériens en France*; Talha et al., *Maghrébins en France*; Benamrane, *L'Emigration algérienne en France*; and Cédétim, *Les Immigrés. Révolution africaine (RA)* and other Algerian publications have articles on the emigrant workers in practically every issue. In France, the same can be said of the publications of the Association France-Algérie, first *France-Algérie (F-A)* and then its successor *Algérie informations (AI)*, and of the Amicale des Algériens en Europe publication *L'Algérien en Europe*. *Hommes et migrations* provides general information on the emigrant population. See also Brian Fitzpatrick, "Immigrants," in Flower, *France Today*, 76–101; Bennoune, "Maghribin Workers in France"; and Stora, *Ils venaient d'Algérie*.

122. Haddad, *La Dernière impression*, 129–30. Other notable Algerian novels about the emigrant experience during decolonization and the early postcolonial period include Mouloud Feraoun, *La Terre et le sang* (1953), Kateb Yacine, *Le Polygone étoilé* (1966), and Mohammed Dib, *Habel* (1977).

123. Tillion, *Complementary Enemies*, 4.

124. Massenet, "Migration algérienne," in Perroux, *L'Algérie de demain*, 20–21.

125. *Texts of Declarations*, 10.

126. On 31 December 1962, there were 197,422 workers (as distinguished from a total Algerian population of about 400,000) in France (*AAN* 1963, 559). Their number rose to 232,690 by 31 March 1964 (*AAN* 1964, 188). Arguably,

there was a mini-*exode* concurrent with that of the *pieds-noirs*. See also René Gallissot, "La Guerre et l'immigration algérienne en France," in Rioux, *Guerre d'Algérie*, 337–47.

127. Miller, "Reluctant Partnership," 223. De Gaulle was very concerned about the numbers of Algerians entering France. He noted in May 1963 that the 40,000 workers who entered France in April equaled the number of French babies born that month, and said: "I would like more babies born in France and fewer emigrants coming here" (Peyrefitte, *C'était de Gaulle*, 2:436).

128. Production rose from 400,000 tons in 1958 to 20 million tons in 1962 (Balta and Rulleau, *L'Algérie des Algériens*, 120).

129. There are many works on the bilateral petroleum relationship. Most consider the sector from the Algerian perspective, since Algiers's policy was clearly articulated and applied, in contrast with those of the French government and oil companies. See, for example, "Les Hydrocarbures en Algérie," *RASJEP* 6 (March 1969): 161–294; Valberg, "Cinq ans après"; Jean-Pierre Séréni, "La Politique algérienne des hydrocarbures," *Maghreb*, no. 45 (1971): 31–49; *F-A*, no. 34 (1971); Destanne de Bernis, "Problèmes pétroliers"; Nouschi, "De la dépendance à l'indépendance?"; and especially Grimaud, "Conflit pétrolier." For general studies of French energy policy, see Vilain, *Politique de l'énergie*, and Oizon, *Evolution récente*. See also sections in Madelin, *Pétrole et politique*, and Chevalier, *The New Oil Stakes*. The "white books" published by Algeria's national hydrocarbons enterprise, SONATRACH, provide a comprehensive chronicle of the development of Algerian hydrocarbons policy from 1965 to 1971: *Background Information; Boumediène's Speeches; Events—Studies—Declarations*. Another important work which pays great attention to the Algerian-French oil relationship is Mazri, *Hydrocarbures*. Bouzana, *Contentieux*, examines Algerian oil policy through the perspective of arbitration stipulations. See also Brogini, "L'Exploitation des hydrocarbures." The French government, which negotiated for the companies, never published a complementary set of "white books" giving its interpretation of the events involving the nationalization. The relationship is also detailed in Naylor, "A Post-Colonial Decolonization."

130. Press conference of M'hammed Yazid, in Mandouze, *Révolution*, 79, citing *E-M*, no. 36 (1959).

131. Mandouze, *Révolution*, 73, citing *E-M*, no. 12 (1957).

132. France was in a state of "infeudation" to foreign oil interests before World War I (Madelin, *Pétrole et politique*, 104). Wartime exigencies forced governmental control of oil imports, which created a network of national refineries. After the war, Georges Clemenceau, Raymond Poincaré, and André Tardieu used their influence to promote the formulation of a national oil policy with the development of a national oil company to be its instrument. With the dissolution of the Turkish Petroleum Company, France received 23.75 percent of Iraqi oil, which led to the organization of the Compagnie Française des Pétroles. Though the CFP was a private company, the French government invested 35 percent of the capital and controlled 40 percent of the vote, assuring it a powerful minority status.

Gulbenkian's Red Line Agreement of 1928 seemed to promise French participation in oil prospecting and production in other potentially lucrative areas of the Middle East. But the dominant Anglo-American Cartel decreed the Red Line Agreement nullified by World War II. This set up the Cartel's expedient exclusion of France from the Saudi Arabian fields in 1948. France had to settle for allowed expansion in Iraq with Exxon assistance. In 1954 the CFP received a 6 percent share of the Iranian consortium, which again was dominated by the Cartel, but the Arabian exclusion remained a bitter memory. For a general survey of the French government's relations with the oil industry see sections in Mosley, *Power Play;* and Sampson, *The Seven Sisters.* For a specific work on the CFP see Rondot, *La Compagnie Française des Pétroles.* Sampson refers to the CFP as a "wayward eighth sister" (155). There was little expectation of significant hydrocarbon discoveries before the War of Independence (Gouvernement général de l'Algérie, *Algérie en 1953,* 40).

133. *AAN* 1962, 701.

134. *Maghreb,* no. 45 (1971): 39.

135. "La Situation économique de l'Algérie," *ND,* nos. 3406–3407 (1967): 55. See also "New Structure for Algerian Oil," *PPS* 31 (April 1964): 138–41; and "Algerian Oil Philosophy," *PPS* 31 (June 1964): 210.

136. "L'Algérie et les hydrocarbures," *AAN* 1965, 76–78; and "La Situation économique de l'Algérie," *ND,* nos. 3406–3407 (1967): 52–53.

137. *Maghreb,* no. 45 (1971): 35–36. For an inventory of Algeria's hydrocarbons infrastructure during this period see Pawera, *Algeria's Infrastructure.*

138. The speeches are reproduced in *RASPJES* 1 (December 1964): 82–103. See also "Regards sur le problème du pétrole," *RA,* no. 99 (1964): 6–7.

139. Bachir Boumaza recognized that there was a need for French cooperation in the hydrocarbons sector, but he also cited the need to transcend "anachronistic situations." He reaffirmed that "Algeria cannot remain the classic colonial market exporting raw materials" (Ministère de l'Orientation nationale, *Politique économique,* 23). As negotiations progressed, he spoke of how the two countries could produce "a model *(pilote)* experience in this matter" ("Conférence de presse du Ministre de l'Economie nationale, Bachir Boumaza (14 May)," *Actualité et documents,* no. 36 [1964]: 11). See also "Regards sur les problèmes du pétrole," *RA,* no. 99 (1964): 6–7.

140. Couve de Murville, *Une politique étrangère,* 440–41.

141. Peyrefitte, *C'était de Gaulle,* 2:445.

142. *AD,* no. 0.1512 (1964): 1. De Gaulle had been invited to Algiers, but told Georges Gorse: "It will become necessary that I go there but it will be painful for me" (Grimaud, *Politique extériere,* 46). The public opposition, even outrage, that Algerian decolonization still aroused was a consideration. In 1964 de Gaulle was not inclined to visit, given Algeria's domestic turmoil (Peyrefitte, *C'était de Gaulle,* 2:444). Four years later he expressed an interest in privately meeting Ben Bella's successor, Houari Boumedienne (Grimaud, *Politique extérieure,* 46).

143. "Après la rencontre entre le général de Gaulle et le président Ben Bella (13

March 1964)," *AD*, no. 0.1508 (1964): 4, extracted from *Le Peuple* (Algiers), 15 March 1964.

144. Duquesne, "La Rencontre de Gaulle–Ben Bella," 512.

145. Ben Bella, *Ben Bella . . . revient*, 58.

146. Grimaud, *Politique extérieure*, 46.

147. Joesten, *The New Algeria*, 100.

148. Humbaraci, *Revolution that Failed*, 195.

149. Ben Bella, *Discours*, 99.

150. Humbaraci, *Revolution that Failed*, 61. See "La Dénucléarisation de la Méditerranée," *El-Djeich*, no. 15 (1964): 12–13.

151. Ottaway and Ottaway, *Politics*, 148.

152. Ibid., 154.

153. "Que fait l'Algérie pour se développer rapidement. Comment industrialiser?" *RA*, no. 92 (1964): 16–17.

154. See "The Search for Political Authority," in Quandt, *Revolution and Political Leadership*, 204–35.

155. Ottaway and Ottaway, *Politics*, 176. Henry F. Jackson believed that Ben Bella did not have the time or the political milieu to construct a socialist society (*FLN in Algeria*, 208).

156. Bennoune, *Making*, 109.

157. Merle, *Ben Bella*, 8.

158. Of his political allegiance to Ben Bella, Boumedienne said on 15 May 1963, "Outside of the Tripoli Program, nothing links us together" (Francos and Séréni, *Un Algérien*, 130). See also Henry Tanner, "A Ben Bella Plot Reported Failed by His Removal," *NYT*, 25 June 1965, 1. Ben Bella's interest in a "people's militia" challenged the ANP. On the growing political role of the army, see I. William Zartman, "L'Armée dans la politique algérienne," *AAN* 1967, 265–78.

159. Tanner, *NYT*, 25 June 1965. Ironically, Ben Bella's decision to ally himself with the external ALN "paved the way for putschist elements . . . which carried out the military *coup*" (Bennoune, *Making*, 109). Fanon predicted that Boumedienne would take over the government and suggested that the colonel's "taste for power" was "pathological" (Abbas, *Autopsie*, 316–17).

160. At first, there were fears that Ben Bella had been executed. See Comité pour la défense d'Ahmed Ben Bella et des autres victimes de la répression en Algérie, *Qu'est devenu Ben Bella?* Actually, he was kept under solitary house arrest (though allowed to marry) until freed by President Chadli Benjedid in 1979. All restrictions on Ben Bella were lifted in 1980 and he left for France. He returned to Algeria in 1990.

161. "Excerpts from Statement by New Algiers Council," *NYT*, 20 June 1965, 2. The entire document is in *AAN* 1965 (627–29).

162. "Destitution pour trois années de gestion," *El-Djeich*, no. 27 (1965): 7.

163. Ferhat Abbas wrote that Abane Ramdane, another elite rival, called Ben Bella "without scruples" (*L'Indépendance confisquée*, 88). Entelis observed in the 1980s that "since his release, no one is certain about what exactly he stands for,

inasmuch as he has spanned the ideological spectrum from Islamic fundamentalism to liberal democracy, along with everything in between" (*Revolution Institutionalized,* 183).

164. Francos and Séréni, *Un Algérien,* 143.

165. Foreign Minister Bouteflika informed Ambassador Georges Gorse of the coup in a matter-of-fact manner (Gorse, interview). De Gaulle had expected Boumedienne to take over. Alain Peyrefitte recounts that in May 1963 de Gaulle displayed his political prescience by equating Ben Bella with Danton and Boumedienne with Robespierre: "First Danton, soon Robespierre, who in his turn is eliminated by the Thermidorians" (*C'était de Gaulle,* 2:437). De Gaulle saw nothing "anti-French" in the coup (ibid., 2:448).

Chapter 4. The Decline and Demise of Privileged Cooperation, 1965–1971

1. "La Destitution du président Ben Bella," *Maghreb,* no. 10 (1965): 21.

2. See Houari Boumediène, "La République algérienne face à ses responsabilités," *LMdipl,* special issue, October 1965, 1; Lewis, "Algeria Changes Course"; Herremann, "Du Socialisme passionel"; and Lewis, "Cycle of Reciprocal Fear."

3. Ministry of Information and Culture, *Faces of Algeria: The Socialist Organization of Enterprises* (1973), 10.

4. Grimaud, *Politique extérieure,* 22.

5. This model was developed and described by Sid Ahmed Ghozali, president of Algeria's national hydrocarbon enterprise SONATRACH, and Professor Gérard Destanne de Bernis, University of Grenoble, and published in *E-M* on 16 March 1968. It projected hydrocarbons as promoting the "introversion" rather than "extroversion" of the Algerian economy. The report was also published in SONATRACH, *Events—Studies—Declarations,* 1:209–39. See also Mazri, *Hydrocarbures,* and Martens, *Modèle algérien.*

6. Boumedienne believed that the Algerian Revolution in its postcolonial dimension rested on three revolutions: industrial, agricultural, and cultural (Mameri, *Citations,* 84).

7. Zartman, "The Algerian Army in Politics," in Zartman, *Man, State, and Society,* 211.

8. For analyses of the Accords see Valberg, "Cinq ans après"; "L'Accord franco-algérien"; Blardone, "Accords franco-algériens"; "L'Accord pétrolier franco-algérien du 29 juillet 1965," *Problèmes économiques,* no. 928 (1965): 5–7; Alain Murcier, "Les Accords franco-algériens sur les hydrocarbures décapitalisent l'activité pétrolière au Sahara," *LMdipl,* August 1965, 2; *RASJPES* 3 (March, June 1966); "Les Accords algéro-français: Une conception révolutionnaire et une portée internationale," *RA,* no. 132 (1965): 11; Byé, "Aide, commerce, ou co-production"; "Algeria's Bonanza," *PPS* 32 (September 1965): 324–27; "Algeria, Morocco, Tunisia," *QER,* no. 23 (1965), 7–8; *NYT,* 17 and 29 July 1965; and SONATRACH, *Events—Studies—Declarations,* 1:1–9.

9. "Quelques réactions de l'opinion internationale après la signature de l'accord franco-algérien," *Maghreb,* no. 12 (1965): 38–44.

10. Couve de Murville, *Une politique étrangère,* 441.

11. SONATRACH, *Events—Studies—Declarations,* 1:6. Algeria also admired France's independence from the Cartel. According to one observer, the Algiers agreement "constitutes a defeat for the great oil monopolies and . . . a defeat of global imperialism" ("Les Accords algéro-français: Une conception révolution-naire et une portée internationale," *RA,* no. 132 [1965]: 11). Later, Paris's appar-ent allegiance to the Cartel was used by Boumedienne as a rationale for national-ization.

12. Kolodziej, *French International Policy,* 474.

13. "French Assess Accord," *NYT,* 30 July 1965. The CFP regarded the Ac-cords as a "transition" (interview by author, Paris, May 1978). Eventually, nation-alization was seen as inevitable. The question would be the means and method.

14. SONATRACH, *Events—Studies—Declarations,* 1:7.

15. Ibid., 1:5–6.

16. Hayter, *French Aid,* 135. See "Décret no. 67-382 relatif aux attributions du secrétaire d'état aux Affaires étrangères, chargé de la coopération," *ND,* nos. 3428–30 (1967): 91. See also Cadenat, "La France et le Tiers Monde," Robarts, *French Development Assistance,* and *MTM,* no. 1625 (1976). However, Djamel Houhou headed the French desk at the Algerian foreign ministry for many years.

17. "L'Elaboration," 22.

18. Redha Malek, "Al-Diblumasiyya al-jaza'iriyya (Algerian diplomacy)," *al-Mujahid al-thaqafi,* no. 1 (1967): 25.

19. "L'Elaboration," 24.

20. Hayter, *French Aid,* 133–35, 137–38. By paying in francs, France saved approximately $280 million a year (Peter Braestrup, "Sahara Oil Accord," *NYT,* 17 July 1965, 28).

21. *AAN* 1968, 207.

22. OECD, *Resources for the Developing World,* 81–82.

23. OECD, *Development Cooperation* 1973, 216.

24. The CCCE also managed the Fonds d'Aide et de Coopération (FAC) for the Ministry of Cooperation and supplemented Fonds d'Action Sociale (FAS) funds for emigrant workers and foreign students living in France. On French financial organizations and their areas of responsibility, see the OECD/DAC series *Investing in Developing Countries.*

25. de Carmoy, *Foreign Policies,* 234. See also *NYT,* 10 December 1966.

26. Ministry of Information and Culture, *Algerian Revolution,* 68–72.

27. See *Industries et travaux d'outremer,* no. 267 (1976). The Algerian govern-ment also took seriously recent criticism by the International Monetary Fund (IMF) of its economic overreliance upon France (*QER,* no. 4 [1966]: 4).

28. "Le Vin," *F-A,* no. 34 (1971): 10–11. See also H. Isnard, "La Viticulture nord-africaine," *AAN* 1965, 37–48.

29. In the 1968 deal, the Soviets paid well below half what France had paid for

the same quality of wine ("Le Vin," *F-A,* no. 34 (1971): 11). The Soviet Union became the chief importer of Algerian wine in the 1970s (Benissad, *Economie du développement,* 188, 190).

30. "Les Principaux partenaires de l'Algérie," *Industries et travaux d'outremer,* no. 267 (1976): 118. This issue surveys the capitalization of Algeria since independence, including a comprehensive listing of contracts signed with its many trading partners.

31. *LM,* 28 June 1977.

32. Most notable was the Soviets' leading participation at the El-Hadjar steel complex at Annaba (*NYT,* 9 October 1971).

33. Ambassade de France en Algérie, "Introduction du Rapport trimestriel sur la Coopération technique et culturelle (15 October 1964–15 January 1965)," 1.

34. Ambassade de France en Algérie, *Rapport périodique,* 15 March 1966, 5.

35. *AAN* 1966, 276 (also 615–25 for text); Bruno Etienne, "La Coopération culturelle franco-maghrébine," in Debbasch, *Mutations culturelles,* 145; and "Pour une Coopération renouvelée," *F-A,* no. 32 (1970): 5. In 1973 a Convention of Scientific Cooperation was signed complementing the 1966 Technical and Cultural Cooperation Accord. In 1974 Algeria paid 70 percent of the *coopérant civil*'s salary.

36. Ambassade de France en Algérie, *Rapport périodique,* 1 June 1967, 3.

37. Ambassade de France en Algérie, *Rapport périodique,* 20 December 1967, 3.

38. See Hessel, "Coopération franco-Algérienne," 10–17. Hessel commended the *coopérants* of the "generation of transition" who enabled Algeria to continue educational services despite dislocations (13). He recommended in an embassy publication in 1969 that the number of cultural and technical *coopérants* be maintained for four to five years (*Rencontres,* no. 7 [1969]: 16). Though there was a drop in cultural *coopérants,* the technical *coopérants* more desired by Algiers were kept near the 1969 level (some 2,000 to 2,200) until 1975–76. Statistics are difficult to compile because *coopérants* were provided through different ministries and also through private cooperation, as in the hydrocarbons sector. In 1971 there were 7,865 official *coopérants;* of these 6,241 were *civils* and 1,624 were VSNA. The *civils* were divided, with 4,792 serving missions of cultural cooperation (education) and an additional 600 serving through the Office Universitaire et Culturel Français. The VSNA cultural cooperation component numbered 495. For technical cooperation there were 1,449 *civils* and 1,129 VSNA ("La Coopération technique et culturelle entre la France et l'Algérie," *F-A,* no. 24 [1971]: 4–5). In 1972 there were approximately 6,000 *coopérants* serving officially in Algeria ("Pour un renouveau des relations," 19). See also Maurice Flory, "Etats maghrébins et Coopération pour le développement" in Ruf, *Introduction,* 241–53.

39. See CCCE, *Annual Reports,* and tables. See also Marc Bonnefous, "L'Algérie n'est plus un cas à part"; Casas, "Cooperation for Agricultural Training"; and Gonon, "Adaptation de la formation." See also sections in Cadenat, "La France et le Tiers Monde."

40. CCCE, *Annual Report* 1970, 31.

41. "Journée régionale de la coopération," *Rencontres*, no. 4 (1968): 11.

42. According to one governmental source: "The role of these professors and teachers is at the same time to facilitate the training of an elite and to diffuse the French language[,] considered a means of communication between countries that learn it and other regions of the world" (Secrétariat d'état, *L'Enseignant français en Algérie*, 1). Stéphane Hessel reiterated that cooperation meant spreading not only the French language but also French techniques and methodologies (Editorial, *Rencontres*, no. 1 [1967]: 11).

43. Ambassade de France en Algérie, *Rapport périodique*, 1 June 1967, 2.

44. In 1967 there were 832 *boursiers* (scholarship holders) for technical, administrative, and higher academic education (Ministère des Affaires étrangères, *Relations culturelles, cooperation technique*, 78, 107), only 696 *boursiers* in 1968–69 (Ministère des Affaires étrangères, *Relations culturelles, scientifiques et techniques*, 109–10), and in 1977 there were 1,054 Algerian *boursiers* matriculating in France (statistic given the author at the Quai d'Orsay in 1978). In 1981–82 there were 9,957 Algerian students in French public universities and 10,535 in 1985–86 (André Lebon, "Les Etudiants étrangers en France," *Hommes et migrations*, no. 1108 [1987]: 14, citing Ministère de l'Education nationale statistics). Concerning military cooperation see Henri Menudier, "Des officiers algériens en Bretagne," *F-A*, no. 20 (1967): 14–15. Besides training cadets, the French operated a school for pilots at Bou Sfer, trained Algeria's internal security units at Sidi-Bel-Abbès, and sent military medical missions into the Sahara.

45. In 1967 there were five *centres culturels*. For a detailed account of cultural activities during this privileged period see Ministère des Affaires étrangères, Coopération, *Rapport d'activité* 1966 and 1967. See also Bouveresse, "Phénomènes de dépendance."

46. Ambassade de France en Algérie, *Rapport périodique*, 1 June 1967, 3.

47. Ambassade de France en Algérie, *Rapport périodique*, 20 December 1967, 1.

48. Miller, "Reluctant Partnership," 233. There was a growing Algerian push for a new accord. See Mustapha Sehimi, "Emigration et coopération," *RA*, no. 235 (1967): 22–23; and "Discours prononcé par le Ministre des Affaires étrangères à la Conférence des Présidents Assemblées populaires et communales (8 February 1968)," *Actualité et documents*, no. 94 (1968): 25–26.

49. See Schumann, "Politique française d'immigration," 938–39. The Algerian reaction was positive, owing to the number of workers allowed to emigrate and the multiyear provision of the Accord (Mustapha Sehimi, "Coopération et émigration," *Algérie- Actualité*, no. 169 [1969]: 6–7). André Philip feared that the Events of May would have an adverse effect upon the emigrant worker community's status; see "A propos des évènements de mai," *F-A*, no. 23 (1968): 3–4. Emigrants, says Miller, participated in demonstrations in solidarity with their French coworkers; see "Reluctant Partnership," 225, citing Narcisse Mayeta, "Les Organisations syndicales les plus représentatives face aux travailleurs immigrés," an unpublished University of Paris dissertation, 62; Léon Gani,

Syndicats et Travailleurs Immigrés (Paris: Editions Sociales, 1972), 141; and André Vieuguet, *Français et Immigrés* (Paris: Editions Sociales, 1975), 138–39.

50. In 1966, 42.8 percent of the emigrant workers lived in *bidonsvilles,* shantytowns constructed of corrugated metals. The *bidonsvilles* were subsequently demolished and better housing was provided, notably the HLMs, *habitations à loyer modéré.*

51. More accurately, the publicly known bases were transferred. It was revealed later that Algeria permitted France to lease a secret base at Beni Ouanif in the Sahara (lease renewed in 1967 and 1972) for chemical warfare testing until 1978 (AFP, 22 October 1997; *LM,* 23 October 1997; FBIS, *WEU/NES,* citing France-2 television program, 21 October 1997).

52. *Discours et messages,* 4:413–15 (from an interview, 13 December 1965).

53. Pierre Sudreau, a former Gaullist technocrat-minister, told John Ardagh: "Gaullism will die unless de Gaulle now makes some new reforms. The basic structures of France, over-centralised and too juridical, are rapidly being made obsolete by technical progress" (*New French Revolution,* 44). Ardagh's "Postscript, July 1968" in *New French Revolution* is an excellent analysis of the Events. Though there are many books on this "nonrevolution," a valuable retrospective review is provided by a series of articles in *LM* during the month of May 1978, especially 3–5 May. In applying the Orleanist comparison to de Gaulle, again, perhaps it was another period when "la France s'ennuie" (Duroselle, "Des réussites partielles et des échecs avérés," *LMdipl,* December 1970, 2).

54. John L. Hess, "Bidault Assails Gaullist Regime," *NYT,* 10 June 1968, 1, 13.

55. *Sondages,* nos. 1–2 (1971): 161.

56. Basdevant, a former chief of the Quai d'Orsay's technical and cultural cooperation section, was instructed by de Gaulle to remember that Algeria was building a state. The French president remained sensitive to Algerian affairs and showed his desire to continue a privileged cooperation, as Basdevant's remarks in Algiers would confirm (interview).

57. "Jean Basdevant, nouvel Ambassadeur de France en Algérie, soumis 17 décembre, ses lettres de créances au Président Boumedienne," *F-A,* no. 25 (1969): 3–4.

58. Pompidou, *Entretiens et discours,* 1:26. Soon after entering the Elysée Palace, Pompidou told a friend: "Now I must find my own style. It won't be easy." Alexandre wrote: "Pompidou inherited a France that was not really his own; and yet he could not change it suddenly, lest he be accused of betrayal" (*The Duel,* 335).

59. Pompidou, *Entretiens et discours,* 1:28. In this interview on 12 February 1970, Pompidou indicated that he would follow the general course (*grandes lignes*) outlined by de Gaulle, but that there would be a change in "methods." Nevertheless, Pompidou once remarked: "De Gaulle leaves, Gaullism must remain. And that's my responsibility" (Alexandre, *The Duel,* 300).

60. Kolodziej saw in the Mediterranean Policy "as much an admission as a

330 I Notes to Pages 87–90

genuine attempt to stem the erosion of its position there" (*French International Policy*, 543). Overall, it indicated a "weakness." Couve de Murville was skeptical of a Mediterranean strategy since each nation "possesses its particular problem" (*Une politique étrangère*, 467). Pompidou's politics and diplomacy involved trade-offs of global policies for regional ones that were determined by the immediate needs of France (Kolodziej, *French International Policy*, 594). For a succinct analysis of the Mediterranean strategy, see Jean Lacouture, "Plutôt de réactions en chaîne qu'une véritable stratégie," *LMdipl*, February 1970, 3–4.

61. See *LM*, 6 May 1971, 1, 6. An institutional and ideological similarity between Libya and Algeria can be seen in the former's Constitutional Proclamation. See *Maghreb*, no. 38 (1970): 44–47.

62. Lacouture, "Plutôt de réactions,' *LMdipl*, February 1970, 4. France had just begun to penetrate the Libyan hydrocarbon fields before the coup. Paris wanted to protect its investment and initiate others. The Libyan sale impressed Boumediènne, according to Lacouture, who perceived it also as a means for France to restore some of its prestige in the face of Willy Brandt's dynamism on the continent.

63. Jean-Jacques Bérreby, "Paris cherche à exploiter à son avantage les atouts pétroliers du monde arabe," *LMdipl*, February 1970, 5.

64. Kolodziej, *French International Policy*, 548.

65. Roussel, *Georges Pompidou*, 119–20, citing M. Bromberger, *Le Destin secret de Georges Pompidou* (Paris: Fayard, 1965), 184–85. Eric Roussel interviewed important figures of this period and explored Pompidou's feelings toward Algeria. Soustelle found Pompidou "very skeptical on this question." Michel de Saint-Pierre contended that Pompidou "strongly misunderstood the colonial problem in general and the Algerian situation in particular." During a luncheon with Raymond Arasse, Pompidou said: "I do not want to go there [Algeria], because, if I made the trip, I know that I would return from it with Soustelle's ideas." (Roussel, 120). Nevertheless, Pompidou supported de Gaulle's stance and was particularly attached to the notion of cooperation with the Third World. He appreciated the imperative of cooperation, given France's colonial past, economic markets, and political competition with the superpowers. "Finally and above all," Pompidou spoke of "moral and humane reasons" (*Journal Officiel* [National Assembly], 11 June 1964, 1782).

66. *NYT*, 15 October 1965.

67. SONATRACH, *Events—Studies—Declarations*, 1:392–95.

68. Francos and Séréni, *Un Algérien*, 225.

69. See Nyssen, *L'Algérie en 1970*, and Viratelle, *L'Algérie algérienne*.

70. SONATRACH, *Events—Studies—Declarations*, 1:155–61.

71. See "SONATRACH Buys BP Interests," *PPS* 34 (February 1967): 65.

72. See "Algerian Moves," *PPS* 34 (July 1967): 250–51. This had little effect on their oil supplies.

73. *Maghreb*, no. 45: 41, and "Selective Nationalization," *PPS* 34 (September 1967): 346. These nationalizations were of distribution monopolies (Mobil and Esso) within the country. See also "La Nationalisation des pétroles: Une voie à

suivre," *RA,* no. 239 (1967): 22–23. In June 1970 all foreign oil companies except the French were nationalized.

74. The Getty Accord is analyzed in most surveys on Algerian-French hydrocarbon relations. See *RASJEP* 6 (March 1969): 161–294. For a succinct analysis see "Getty-SONATRACH Accord," *PPS* 35 (November 1968): 423–24. A mixed association was formed, with SONATRACH obtaining 51 percent of the interest. Thus the Algerian national enterprise became the operator. Getty agreed to finance exploration for five years, which was expected to cost $16 million including an outright advance of $2.25 million. If a discovery should be made, Getty could amortize some of its prospecting costs. If natural gas were discovered, Getty would cede all rights to its Algerian partner. There were new fiscal arrangements. Getty would post $2.36/barrel f.o.b. Bougie, but the American company would be taxed on the $2.19/barrel fixed Bougie price. Taxes on profits would be 54 percent for the fiscal year of 1968 and 55 percent thereafter. Getty was obliged to repatriate 75 percent of its earnings back into Algeria. Disputes would be handled by an arbitration court, but the Algerian Supreme Court would have appellate authority. Algeria's objective of placing disputes under national law was achieved. See also Bouzana, *Contentieux,* and Chevalier, "Contrat." Though this agreement would serve as a model for post-nationalization relations with French oil companies, the author was told that SONATRACH did not have this in mind at the time (Interview, Algiers, March 1978). An Algerian publication, however, reflected that the Getty Accord did underscore "the inadequacy of the agreements signed with France" (Ministry of Information and Culture, *Algerian Revolution,* 54).

75. Mallarde, *L'Algérie depuis,* 142, 239. See also "Two In—One Out," *PPS* 36 (June 1969): 228, and "Présence américaine en Algérie," *Moniteur du commerce international,* no. 1017 (1971): 11.

76. "La Politique pétrolière française," *TN,* no. 247 (1968): 4–5. See also "Policy Spelled Out," *PPS* 34 (December 1967): 471; "Re-shaping French Energy Policy," *PPS* 31 (July 1964): 244–47; Vilain, *Politique de l'énergie,* 89–106; sections in Madelin, *Pétrole et politique,* 103–23; and "La Création de l'E.R.A.P."

77. "The French as NIOC Contractors," *PPS* 33 (September 1966): 324–26; "A Contract Compared," *PPS* 34 (February 1967): 59–62; "ERAP's Expanding Interests," *PPS* 34 (June 1967): 219–23; "The INOC/ERAP Contract," *PPS* 35 (March 1968): 104–5; "Lypian[*sic*]-French Partnership," *PPS* 35 (May 1968): 183–84; and "ERAP Develops Its Inheritance," *PPS* 37 (February 1970): 54–57.

78. For a survey of the "positive roles" of each corporation during this period, see Feigenbaum, *Politics of Public Enterprise,* 63–71.

79. There had been some important changes from 1962 to 1969 in the Algerian market. Though French companies still lifted 70 percent of the crude, Algeria increased its production from 10 to 18 percent. In refining, the French companies' percentage dropped from 32 to 20 percent while Algeria's rose from 10 to 56 percent. By 1969, Algeria controlled 100 percent of the distribution facilities, up from 0 percent (*LM,* 20 March 1969).

80. Algeria, feeling that OPEC was not politically dynamic or unified, had

delayed its application for membership; see "Regards sur les problèmes," *RA,* no. 99 (1964): 6–7.

81. Jobert, *L'Autre regard,* 143.

82. Ibid., 143–44.

83. "Proposal Made by the French Government After 8 Months of Discussions for the Settlement of the Fiscal Provisions (June 1970)," in SONATRACH, *Background Information,* A3-3–A3-5. The earlier scale-back proposal was not unsound economically, given oil price fluctuations, it was just psychologically disastrous.

84. Grimaud, "Conflit pétrolier," 2391.

85. SONATRACH, *Events—Studies—Declarations,* 2:61.

86. Grimaud, "Conflit pétrolier," 1291–92.

87. "Pour une coopération renouvelée," *F-A,* no. 32 (1970): 5, 11.

88. Basdevant, interview. See *E-M* and other Paris press in January and February 1971.

89. Grimaud, "Conflit pétrolier," 1295–96.

90. Ibid., 1297. To Jean-Paul Pigasse, Algerian oil was neither an assured source of supply (given Middle East politics) nor the only nearby source (since the North Sea discoveries), and after Algeria's selling of francs in 1968, the *pétrole franc* was no longer financially attractive ("La France prisonnière," 133). Pigasse's reasoning is compelling, but it minimizes Algeria's special position in French policymaking. This negotiation was not only over oil, but also over the changing nature of the political relationship. This was well demonstrated by Ortoli's proposals.

91. Grimaud, "Conflit pétrolier," 1297. See also "France at the Crossroads," *PPS* 37 (December 1970): 459. The proposed accord was also discussed by Maurice Schumann before the Senate on 27 April 1971.

92. Grimaud, *Politique extérieure,* 77–78.

93. "M. Bedjaoui présente ses lettres de créances au Président Georges Pompidou," *F-A,* no. 33 (1970): 13.

94. The taxes amounted to FF 675 million. When the French government forced this remuneration upon the companies, their reaction was bitter, as was that of the French press (Grimaud, "Conflit pétrolier," 1299). This was another indication of how polarized the French government and the oil companies were. See also "France's Algerian Dilemma," *PPS* 38 (March 1971): 85–88.

95. Pigasse, "La France prisonnière," 135; Grimaud, "Conflit pétrolier," 1299. Grimaud observed that Arab solidarity did not crystallize in spite of Algerian pressures.

96. SONATRACH, *Boumediène's Speeches,* 136.

97. Ibid., 149.

98. SONATRACH, *Events—Studies—Declarations,* 2:295–96; the interview was also published in *E-M,* 2 March 1971.

99. SONATRACH, *Background Information,* A7-3–A7-4.

100. Alphand, *L'Etonnement d'être,* 549.

101. Ibid., 550.

102. Grimaud, "Conflit pétrolier," 1302. During the tense summer of 1970, Algeria signaled its intent to preserve cultural and technical cooperation by announcing that it would assume 60 percent of the wages and salaries of the *coopérants*. According to Pigasse, Ortoli felt at this time that Algeria wanted to strengthen bilateral ties ("La France prisonnière," 137).

103. "Communiqué from the Quai d'Orsay, Released after the Council of Ministers Meeting of April 14, 1971," in SONATRACH, *Background Information*, A10-3.

104. See "Algeria Without the French," *PPS* 38 (June 1971): 203–6. In 1965, French companies were responsible for approximately 80 percent of Algeria's total oil production. This dropped only to 69 percent in 1970 despite ASCOOP and Algerian capitalization (*F-A*, no. 34 [1971]). France still had a profound influence in the sector. According to Philippe Manin, the French oil companies reacted to Algerian nationalization as the Anglo-Iranian Oil Company did to nationalization by Muhammad Mosaddeq (Mossadegh). The French companies pressured the Export-Import Bank and the World Bank's International Bank of Reconstruction and Development to stop loans to Algeria (see "Le Différend franco-algérien relatif aux hydrocarbures," *Annuaire française du Droit international* 1971, 147–69).

105. See SONATRACH, *Hydrocarbons in Algeria*. The CFP and SONATRACH reached an accord in June. The CFP received an indemnity of DA 300 million ($61 million) for its interests. This indemnity would be paid off in seven annual installments beginning in May 1972. Tax arrears (about $25 million) were settled satisfactorily. The CFP's new Algerian subsidiary, Total-Algérie, became a minority partner of SONATRACH. The CFP agreed to help finance exploration projects. While losing operating control, the private company was allowed to lift 7 million tons of crude. The CFP settled on a $2.75/barrel repatriation price. The SONATRACH-ERAP Accord was signed in December. ERAP had a greater investment and enormous tax arrears ($79.6 million), while its assessed indemnity was DA 183.5 million ($37.4 million). To make up the difference, ERAP transferred non-nationalized interests. ERAP consented to lift 5.5 million tons in 1971, rising to 6.5 million by 1975. The French state-owned enterprise accepted a $2.46/barrel repatriation price, equivalent to the CFP's since transport costs beyond Algeria's border (through the Tunisian pipeline owned by ERAP) were not included. See also "CFP-Sonatrach Agreement," *PPS* 38 (August 1971): 304–5; "Algeria," *QER*, no. 4 (1971): 7–8; "Old and New Friends," *PPS* 39 (January 1972): 23–24; and Desprairies, "L'Evolution de la crise pétrolière de 1970–71: le problème de la dépendance," 738–57. The CFP had better relations than ERAP with SONATRACH. The private company's investment in Algeria, however, involved less infrastructure and production. The CFP's agreement with SONATRACH pressured ERAP to conclude its mutually satisfactory accord (Interviews by author, Paris, May–June 1978).

106. *PEF* (1er 1971), 153.

107. According to the Quai d'Orsay's 14 April 1971 communiqué, France was willing "to continue to participate in the industrial development of Algeria within the framework of international competition on certain specific projects" (SONATRACH, *Background Information*, A10-3).

108. Kolodziej, *French International Policy*, 505 (table), 537–38.

109. *Entretiens et discours*, 2:192–93. See also *PEF* (1er 1971), 151.

110. *CSM*, 8 May 1971.

111. Ibid.

112. *Journal Officiel* (National Assembly), 29 October 1963, 5747.

113. *PEF* (1er 1971), 153 (20 April 1971).

114. Ibid., 202–5 (1 June 1971). See also *PEF* (1er 1971), 151.

115. Mouhoubi, *Politique de coopération*, citing *LM*, 6 July 1972.

116. Roussel, *Georges Pompidou*, 450. It seems strange that Pompidou did not appreciate the gravity of the petroleum situation. According to Philippe Alexandre, Pompidou's "experience at the Rothschild Bank had taught him to value the oil of the Sahara" (*The Duel*, 49). In an interview with *Time* magazine (23 February 1970), Pompidou declared: "I would like to extend the French presence" (*Entretiens et discours*, 1:111). However, his equivocation risked this presence in Algeria.

117. Balta and Roulleau, *L'Algérie des Algériens*, 208.

118. *Sondages*, nos. 1–2 (1971): 160–61. Reflecting the desultory diplomatic situation, another poll taken in April–May 1972 asked if granting Algeria independence was a good choice on the part of France: 38 percent agreed that it was, while 30 percent did not (*Sondages*, no. 4 [1972]: 28).

119. Kolodziej, *French International Policy*, 471.

120. Grimaud, *Politique extérieure*, 41.

121. Lacouture, *LMdipl*, February 1970, 4.

122. Sanson, "L'Après-coopération," in Ruf et al., *Indépendance et interdépendances*, 47–58. The inability of Paris and Algiers to reorient their relationship and accept new realities led to miscomprehension and crises for the rest of the decade.

Chapter 5. Turning the Page, 1972–1980

1. SONATRACH, *Boumediène's Speeches*, 199; see also *LM*, 26 February 1972.

2. SONATRACH, *Boumediène's Speeches*, 233. This was underscored in Boumedienne's response to Ambassador Jean-Marie Soutou's presentation of letters; see *F-A*, no. 38 (1972): 5.

3. Bennoune viewed France as being hostile to Algerian industrialization and a supporter of *comprador* interests. His contention is overstated, however, that "French academics of all persuasions tried to discredit Algeria's model of development in general, and its mode of industrialisation in particular" (see *Making*, 130 ff.). Provost reported, however, that during the period 1967–78, 50 percent of the contracts for equipping Algeria's infrastructure and industry were from several

French firms including Creusot-Loire, Krebs, Technip, Berliet, and Chantiers de l'Atlantique (*Seconde Guerre,* 38–39).

4. Ruedy, *Modern Algeria,* 219.

5. Consider ratios of production in 1962–65 as compared with 1977–81 for the following grains: hard wheat, 0.75; soft wheat, 1.60; barley, 1.95; oats, 1.23. Note that the population of Algeria doubled during this period, from 9 to 18 million. Though meat production matched population growth, it too could not satisfy demand (Ruedy, *Modern Algeria,* 223). For assessments of the Agrarian Revolution see Pfeiffer, *Agrarian Reform,* and Bedrani, *L'Agriculture algérienne.*

6. Complementing the Agrarian Revolution was the physical elimination of a colonial legacy, the removal of vineyards and their replacement with food crops. By 1972 the number of hectares devoted to viticulture had been reduced from more than 400,000 to 238,500 (Marc Olliver, "La Nouvelle politique agricole de l'Algérie," *Problèmes économiques,* no. 1326 [1973]: 22, citing *Algérie actualités,* no. 364 [1972]). There were efforts to reforest the land and, in particular, to create in the south a *barrage vert* (green barrier) of trees and vegetation to stem the encroaching Sahara.

7. René van Malder, "Un bilan de la reforme agraire en Algérie," *Problèmes économiques,* no. 1471 (1975): 16. See also *Maghreb-Machrek,* no. 77 (1977): 31–48.

8. Nico Kielstra, "The Agrarian Revolution & Algerian Socialism," *MERIP,* no. 67 (1978): 11.

9. Mameri, *Citations,* 84.

10. Taleb Ibrahimi, *De la décolonisation,* 218–19. In 1974–75 allocations for education were DA 3 billion, which amounted to one-third of the budget.

11. "Hadha al-majalla (This journal)," *al-Thaqafa,* no. 1 (1971): 3–7. *Al-Thaqafa* constantly equated the Revolution with an assertion of national culture. See, for example, Muhammad al-Arabi Walid Khalifa, "Thawra noufambr qimma al-thaqafa (The November revolution, the crowning of culture)," *al-Thaqafa,* no. 62 (1981): 5–16. Khalifa contended that the Revolution confirmed that Algerian culture had managed to sustain itself during colonialism. He also related the Revolution's influence to postcolonial decisions concerning nationalizations (9).

12. Boghli, *Aspects of Algerian Cultural Policy,* 17.

13. See Vatin, *L'Algérie politique,* 307, 311 ff.; D. Gordon, *Passing,* 184–90; Sahli, *Décoloniser l'histoire;* Cubertafond, *La République algérienne,* 58–94; and Rouadjia, *Grandeur et décadence,* 35–82.

14. *Majallat al-tarikh* (Algiers: Centre national d'Etudes historiques, 1974), 12. The Ordinance of 5 August 1971 called for the creation of a National Center of Historical Studies.

15. Gordon, *Passing,* 190.

16. The renowned author Rachid Boudjedra related Martin Heidegger's belief that "language is the house of being" (*FIS de la haine,* 25).

17. Taleb Ibrahimi, *De la décolonisation,* 16–17. Nicole Grimaud stated that the acclamation "We are Arabs!" was an "existential" as well as a "spontaneous

cry." She reiterated: "Algeria feels the need to affirm [its Arabism,] for it constitutes an essential component of its personality" (*Politique extérieure*, 187–88).

18. Ben Bella, *Discours*, 117.

19. Mameri, *Citations*, 71.

20. P. J. Vatikiotis, "Tradition and Politial Leadership," in Zartman, *Man,
State, and Society*, 312. Boumedienne referred to opponents of Arabization as
members of the "party of France" (*hizb faransa*); see chapter 7.

21. Cheriet, *Opinion*, 62.

22. Grandguillaume, *Arabisation*, 96.

23. At this time, 99 percent of the Arabized primary teachers were Algerians
(80 percent in middle schools and 45 percent at the secondary level). About a third
of the university students studied in Arabic, up from only 8 percent in 1970
(Heggoy, *Historical Dictionary*, 104).

24. Taleb Ibrahimi, *De la décolonisation*, 36.

25. Ibid., 222.

26. Lacheraf, "L'Avenir de la culture algérienne," 745.

27. Grandguillaume, *Arabisation*, 103. France also contributed to the Arabization movement by providing Arabic classes for emigrant children in French
public schools.

28. Deheuvels, *Islam et pensée contemporaine*, 141, citing Yahya BuʿAziz,
"Waqiʿa wa mustaqbal harakat al-taʿrib fi al-jazaʾir (The situation and future of
Arabization in Algeria)," *al-Asala*, nos. 17–18 (1973–74): 126. BuʿAziz is particu-
larly critical of the lack of commitment of higher education to Arabization (129).

29. Thirty-two Algerians were killed during the first nine months of 1973
(Cohen, "Legacy of Empire," 112). For a survey of recurrent violence against the
emigrant community, see Gaudice, *Arabicides: Une chronique française*. The situation was also abusive and murderous in Paris and environs, which incited the
publicized protests and engagements of Jean-Paul Sartre, Claude Mauriac, and
Michel Foucault (Macey, *Lives of Michel Foucault*, 305–13).

30. According to Ammour, Leucate, and Moulin, this was a political rather
than an economic decision. In addition, the quota for the year had already been
met (*La Voie algérienne*, 103).

31. *AAN* 1973, 490.

32. The Amicale recognized in reintegration not only economic problems but
promising potential ("Pour une prochaine réinsertion," *Algérien en Europe*, no.
198 [1974]: 15–16). The developing Algerian economy needed skilled, qualified
labor, and the emigrant workers were a possible source. The vast majority of the
jobs they held in France, however, were unskilled positions in construction, industry, and mining. It was estimated that only 35,000 workers had the specific skills
needed by the Algerian economy (Gildas Simon, "Industrialisation, émigration et
réinsertion de la main-d'oeuvre qualifiée au Maghreb: Le Cas de la Tunisie et de
l'Algérie," *Hommes et migrations*, no. 902 [1976]: 11). Education and *formation*
in France were projected as ways to expedite reinsertion ("La Recherche des voies

d'une migration-coopération," *Hommes et migrations,* no. 884 [1975]: 15–17).

33. Boumediène, *Discours,* 5:85.

34. *PEF* (2ᶜ 1973), 123 (Pompidou press conference, 27 September 1973).

35. Brian Fitzpatrick, "Immigrants," in Flower, *France Today,* 85. In 1973 the Pierre Messmer cabinet promulgated the Fontanet and Marcellin circulars which "revealed that the government intended to subordinate immigration to short-term fluctuations in the labour market." The Conseil d'Etat overruled the circulars as possibly splitting families and repudiating accords with individual countries. Of course, labor unions also challenged the circulars (87).

36. The suspension of familial emigration would be lifted by the Dijoud circulars of 1974 and 1975. Even with restrictions, the Algerian population in France kept rising; it was 884,320 at the end of 1975 (Stora, *Ils venaient d'Algérie,* 402).

37. While attending Algeria's ten-year celebration of independence, Hervé Alphand invited Foreign Minister Abdelaziz Bouteflika for an official visit to Paris (*L'Etonnement d'être,* 580).

38. Commission Française de Justice et Paix and l'Association France-Algérie, "Pour de nouvelles relations," 19–20.

39. See *LM,* 10–12 July 1973. During the *relancement,* there was talk of a Boumedienne visit to Paris. Bouteflika responded that Boumedienne would not want to enter France "by the small door. He likes big doors" (*LM,* 12 January 1974). This suggested the fanfare of a state visit.

40. *LM,* 10–12 July 1973. See also Philippe Herremann, "La France et le Maghreb: Un nouveau dialogue pour élargir la coopération," *LMdipl,* August 1973, 13, and Nicole Grimaud, "Visite officielle de M. Bouteflika à Paris et les relations franco-algériennes (9–11 juillet)," *Maghreb-Machrek,* no. 59 (1973): 14–16.

41. "Communiqué commun publié au terme de la visite de M. Michel Jobert, ministre des Affaires étrangères (Alger, 23 mars 1974)," *Document d'actualité internationale* (Documentation française), no. 15 (1974): 301–2. According to *Le Monde,* a Paris-Algiers axis was "indispensable" for France and its European partners vis-à-vis the Arab world. Furthermore, closer relations with Algiers could limit the growing American influence (24–25 March 1974).

42. *LM,* 24–25 March 1974, 1. See also "France-Algérie: La Relance," *Regards sur l'actualité* (Documentation française), no. 6 (1974): 29.

43. *LM,* 18 April 1974.

44. Balta and Rulleau, *L'Algérie des Algériens,* 213. Ironically, an editorial in *RA,* no. 219 (1967): 5, foresaw a "normal" and "banal" cooperation.

45. Frears, *Giscard Presidency,* 125.

46. Ibid., 96.

47. F. R. Willis, *French Paradox,* 11 (citing *L'Express,* 17 May 1980, 46). Frears wrote: "The neo-imperial role in Africa is in the pure Gaullian tradition, the policy of rapprochement with Germany was begun by de Gaulle in 1963 and the idea of

a directorate for Europe (not just Franco-German) was floated by de Gaulle in 1968, while the prestigious notion of Germany and France in a leadership class of their own is pure Gaullism" (*Giscard Presidency,* 125). Gaullists criticized Giscard's new nuclear defense policy of a *sanctuarisation élargie,* but Frears argued that this "was both absurd and in direct contradiction to any ambitions to play a leading role in Europe" (125). Frears suggested that Giscard was more "Gaullian" than Pompidou: "In defence the nuclear deterrent plays to the full the symbolic role it played under de Gaulle and conventional forces have been greatly strengthened. Gaullian themes like the independence of France from the two superpowers predominate. In accepting the invitation to meet Brezhnev in Warsaw in May 1980, Giscard was pursuing the characteristically Gaullian obsession that France was to be considered a front-rank power in any East-West dialogue" (124). His defense policy, coupled with Paris's collaborative relationship with Bonn, was Gaullist. As Willis put it: "The much debated defense policy that Giscard implemented in 1976 was far from being a break with Gaullist policy, which the more intransigent members of the Gaullist party suggested" (*French Paradox,* 12). On the other hand, Giscard did support European Parliament elections by universal suffrage in 1979 and was more prone to multilateral than unilateral actions.

48. Alan Clark, "Foreign Policy," in Flower, *France Today,* 112.

49. Willis, *French Paradox,* 59. For example, France actively endorsed and encouraged the completion of the Lomé Convention, which gave Third World states in Africa, the Caribbean, and the Pacific favored relationships with the EEC.

50. *LM,* 23 November 1974.

51. See Charles Zorgbibe, "La Diplomatie giscardienne ou les contradictions du 'mondialisme'," *LMdipl,* March 1978, 3.

52. *LM,* 31 August 1974.

53. Ibid., 30 November 1974. See also M. Chabbi, "Algérie-France: Une franche coopération," *RA,* no. 561 (1974): 16–18.

54. *LM,* 6 December 1974.

55. Ibid.

56. *LM,* 2–3 March 1975.

57. *Année politique* 1975, 190–91.

58. See "'La Population algérienne est intimement mêlée à notre effort de production' affirme le président de la République française lors d'une émission télévisée," *Algérien en Europe,* no. 193 (1974): 3–4.

59. Interviews by author, Paris and Algiers, 1978.

60. *LM,* 10 April 1975 (quoting from *F-A*).

61. Boumediène, *Discours,* 6:87. See also coverage in *RA,* no. 581 (1975).

62. Boumediène, *Discours,* 6:87.

63. Ibid., 6:89.

64. *Le Monde* and *El-Moudjahid* detailed the presidential voyage (10–12 April). See also *PEF* (1er 1975), 126–28.

65. *LM,* 9 April 1975.

66. Grimaud, *Politique extérieure,* 93, citing Paul Balta, "L'Epineux dossier des rapports franco-algériens," *Revue d'études politiques méditerranéennes,* no. 15 (1976): 14–28.

67. Ibid., 94. The author acknowledges Professor Grimaud's kindness in sending him a copy of "L'Introuvable équilibre maghrébin," her paper detailing reasons for the disappointing consequences of the summit.

68. *Discours,* 6:89. According to Francos and Séréni, Boumedienne "was convinced" of France's potential role as an intermediary between the North and South states (*Un Algérien,* 311). Even when relations had deteriorated after the hydrocarbon nationalization, Boumedienne stated: "For our part, we have a higher conception of the role that France can play in the world" (*CSM,* 8 May 1971). Bennoune recounted "a revelation by a former member of the US government" that "the French secret service suggested to the CIA in 1975 the possibility of assassinating Boumedienne in an attempt to neutralise Algeria's influence in world affairs and to put an end to its internal development" (*Making,* 134). While an anti-Algerian prejudice would be likely among members of the French intelligence community, it is highly unlikely that France would have wanted Algeria destabilized, especially during the *relancement,* which would have risked the chief objective of cooperation: maintaining a French postcolonial presence, albeit by this time a reduced one.

69. See *LM,* 18 June 1975.

70. *LM,* 29 May 1975.

71. *LM,* 31 May 1975.

72. *LM,* 3 February 1976.

73. See Pautard, "Dix ans de relations franco-maghrébines."

74. *Année politique* 1975, 133.

75. Among the numerous works on the Western Sahara see Hodges, *Western Sahara;* Assidon, *Sahara occidental;* Barbier, *Conflit;* Damis, *Conflict;* Hinz, *Le Droit à l'autodétermination;* Lawless and Monahan, *War and Refugees;* and Miské, *Front Polisaire.* Timely articles include Raoul Weexsteen, "La Stratégie du Front Polisario face à ses adversaires directs et à leurs protecteurs," *LMdipl,* August 1977, 4–5; "The Struggle for Sahara," *MERIP,* no. 45 (1976); André Dessens, "Le Litige du Sahara occidental," *Maghreb-Machrek,* no. 71 (1976): 28–46; "Le Problème du Sahara occidental trois ans après le départ des Espagnols," *Maghreb-Machrek,* no. 83 (1979): 73–86; numerous articles in *Africa Report* 23 (March–April 1978); Brian Weinstein, "The Western Sahara"; and "Western Sahara: Africa's Forgotten War," *Africa Today* 34, no. 3 (1987). See also U.S. House Committee on Foreign Affairs, *Hearings Before the Subcommittees on Africa and on International Organizations,* 96th Cong., 1st sess., 23–24 July 1979. The Saharan Peoples Support Committee and the Western Sahara Campaign, U.S.A., for Human Rights and Humanitarian Relief provided information and literature. For example, see Anne Lippert, "The Struggle in Western Sahara and Foreign Intervention," distributed by the Support Committee. Sipe, *Western Sahara: A Comprehensive Bibliography* is a valuable research aid, as is Pazzanita and Hodges, *Historical Dictionary.*

76. The "Marrakesh plan" involved military agreements by which France undertook to supply Morocco with armaments and matériel. (Pazzanita and Hodges, *Historical Dictionary,* 222–23, citing *Le Nouvel Observateur,* no. 591 [1976]; Damis, *Conflict,* 115–16; and Barbier, *Conflit,* 248). France supplemented this military cooperation with $168 million in development credits (July 1975) and $200 million in government loans and commercial credits. Premier Raymond Barre's visit in January 1981 led to agreements in the energy and industrial sectors and earmarked $4.5 billion support (Damis, *Conflict,* 115–16). See also Assidon, *Sahara occidental,* 143–48, for a sector listing of economic assistance.

77. See Lucienne Hubert-Rodien, "Avec la France des relations politiques et économiques priviligiées," *Europe outremer,* no. 552 (1976): 14–15.

78. On 15 June 1972 two conventions were signed between Algeria and Morocco that seemed to resolve their political and economic frontier disputes. The agreements called for a recognition of present borders and the mutual exploitation of the iron deposits at Gara Djebilet. Though Morocco refrained, Algeria ratified them in 1973.

79. Francos and Séréni, *Un Algérien,* 321. According to Goytisolo, Boumedienne had a "Bismarckian obsession to make [Algeria] the dominant power of the Maghrib by its external prestige and its status as leader of the non-aligned movement" (*L'Algérie dans la tourmente,* 11). This was one of the reasons why Western Sahara's decolonization was such a crucial issue to Boumedienne.

80. See Balta, "Politique africaine"; Fessard de Foucault, "La Question du Sahara espagnol"; and Colin, "Réflexions sur l'avenir." The Western Sahara received constant coverage in *E-M, RA,* and *El-Djeich.*

81. According to Francos and Séréni, Boumedienne contended that France influenced Spain on behalf of the United States (*Un Algérien,* 334).

82. Balta and Rulleau, *L'Algérie des algériens,* 211–12. Boumedienne, in his effort to cultivate stronger relations with France, had even given Giscard credit for the Algerian idea of an economic *"triologue."*

83. Francos and Séréni, *Un Algérien,* 343. The Western Sahara War represented a multiple foreign policy failure: the collapse of *relancement,* the establishment of a privileged relationship between France and Morocco, and the deterioration of commercial cooperation.

84. *E-M,* 29 October 1977. The media on both sides of the Mediterranean were accusatory.

85. T. Belghide, "Une 'neutralité' démentie par les faits," *E-M,* 29 October 1977.

86. Youcef Bournine, "L'Objectif de la France coloniale," *E-M,* 6 November 1977.

87. See Balta and Rulleau, *La Stratégie de Boumediène,* 249–53, citing speech of 14 November 1977; see also *LM,* 16 and 19 November 1977.

88. See *RA,* nos. 724 and 742 (1978).

89. During this period, the author, who apparently fit the profile of a suspected

illegal emigrant, was asked for his *"papiers"* by gendarmes in a subway tunnel at the Concorde metro station.

90. Brian Fitzpatrick, "Immigrants," in Flower, *France Today,* 88–89.

91. Ibid., 89; *AAN* 1977, 645. Between 1977 and the end of 1981, only 3,515 Algerians (workers and family members) took advantage of financial incentives to repatriate (R.-E. Verhaeren, "L'Immigration algérienne et la crise économique en France," in Talha, *Maghrébins en France,* 121, citing an OCDE-SOPEMI report of July 1982). According to some, Giscard had a "secret policy" aiming to repatriate 500,000 Algerians (*LM,* 16 November 1995).

92. See *AI,* no. 50 (1978): 21.

93. *E-M,* 2–3 December 1977.

94. See Stern, "Algeria," in *International Gas Trade,* 72–104.

95. Cornet, *Du mirage au miracle,* 250–271. See also Nouschi, "Histoire des hydrocarbures gazeux."

96. Destanne de Bernis, "Problèmes pétroliers," 601.

97. See SONATRACH, *Events—Studies—Declarations,* 1:84–104, citing *E-M,* 15 April 1967.

98. Destanne de Bernis, "Problèmes pétroliers," 601. France's own natural gas resources at Lacq were close to depletion.

99. *LM,* 15 April 1976, quoting APS.

100. "Gaz: À propos de la commercialisation du gaz algérien sur le marché français," *LM,* 17 April 1976.

101. *LM,* 4 April 1976.

102. *LM,* 28 February 1978.

103. *LM,* 16 April 1976.

104. See Stern, *International Gas Trade,* 73–74, citing VALHYD. Arthur D. Little also played an active consulting role concerning production and marketing. It projected large volumes of Algerian LNG exported to the U.S.

105. Giscard's comments received scant attention in *El-Moudjahid.*

106. *LM,* 4 April 1978.

107. *E-M,* 30 April 1978.

108. *LM,* 6 May 1978.

109. *LM,* 14 July 1978.

110. *LM,* 16 July 1978.

111. Boumediène, *Discours,* 8:124.

112. *CSM,* 8 May 1971.

113. "La Charte Nationale Algérienne (27 juin 1976)," with an introduction by Nicole Grimaud, *ND,* nos. 4349–4350 (1976): 29. See Nellis, *Algerian National Charter.* A referendum on 27 June 1976 resulted in a 98.5 percent approval of the National Charter. In December Boumedienne received 95.23 percent of the presidential vote, in which Algeria's second constitution, adopted on 22 November 1976, was also implemented.

114. On the other hand, Bennoune contended that the succession "resulted in

unexpected disruptive changes. . . . In less than two years the strategy of development, the model of growth, the priorities, the overall objectives of industrialisation, the social policy and the political ideology of the state were revised" (*Making,* 262).

115. See Entelis, *Revolution Institutionalized,* for an analysis of the political culture of Benjedid's Algeria. See also R. Mortimer, "Algeria's New Sultan" and "Politics of Reassurance," and Ghiles, "Chadli's Pragmatic Economics." Before his April 1985 visit to the United States, President Benjedid said: "My policy is based on pragmatism rather than dogmatism. I want to be close to the needs of our people, their basic aspirations" (Nelson, *Algeria,* xxvi).

116. Benjedid, *Discours,* 3:154, cited in *E-M,* 27–28 November 1981.

117. Ibid., 5:159.

118. Quandt, *Revolution and Political Leadership,* 276.

119. *AI,* no. 53 (1979): 7.

120. On 15 February 1979, Benjedid informed Giscard of his wish for "sincere dialogue and loyal concertation" (*LM,* 24–25 June 1979).

121. *AI,* no. 62 (1979): 11.

122. *LM,* 21–22 January 1979.

123. *Le Figaro,* 25 June 1979.

124. *LM,* 26 June 1979.

125. *E-M,* 18–19 January 1980.

126. Ibid.

127. Ibid.

128. *E-M,* 21 January 1980.

129. *E-M,* 20 January 1980.

130. "L'Esprit de compréhension et de dialogue a prévalu," *E-M,* 20 January 1980.

131. *AI,* no. 73 (1980): 19. The team of Benyahia, Sahnoun, François-Poncet, and Ambassador Jean-Marie Mérillon in Algiers worked well together and substantially repaired the relationship by restoring and arguably realizing the *relancement.*

132. See *AI,* no. 62, supplement (1979). If this legislation had been implemented, approximately 150,000 unskilled workers would have been deported (Findlay, Findlay, and Lawless, "Algeria: Emigration," 85).

133. *AI,* no. 55 (1979): 25.

134. "Communiqué de l'Association France-Algérie du 27 novembre 1979," *AI,* no. 62 (1979): 30. The Association focused particular attention on the worker legislation. See, for example, "Les Projets de loi concernant l'immigration," supplemented to *AI,* nos. 58–59 (1979), and "Informations sur les textes Bonnet-Stoléru," supplemented to *AI,* no. 62 (1979). See also Grimaud, "A la recherche d'un accord," *Maghreb-Machrek,* no. 88 (1980): 25–43. Cardinal Duval also argued that repatriation of emigrant workers would not solve French unemployment. He believed their expulsion would cause problems for the economy. He appealed on moral grounds as well: "An emigrant is a man. A man is subject to

law. Otherwise, he is not a man" (*AI,* no. 55 [1979]: 23–24, citing APS, 6 April 1979).

135. *AI,* no. 73 (1980): 5–14, details the emigrant worker agreement. See also "L'Accord franco-algérien: Une étape vers la détente," *Regards sur l'actualité,* no. 65 (1980): 3–11, which places the emigrant worker agreement in context with the other important concurrent negotiations. The Algerians saw themselves as negotiating for all emigrant workers irrespective of nationality (Sahnoun, interview).

136. East Germany had also concluded such an arrangement with Algeria. Georges Gorse, the former ambassador and minister of labor, believed that France should follow that innovative direction. See "Georges Gorse: 'S'inspirer des accords Algérie-RDA'," *Algérien en Europe,* no. 198 (1974): 9–10. More than a decade earlier Michel Massent related that emigrant labor not only contributed to Algeria's finances but could also provide a qualified and skilled workforce to assist in Algeria's industrialization ("Migration algérienne," in Perroux, *L'Algérie de demain,* 19).

137. Sahnoun, interview.

138. Stern, *International Gas Trade,* 74. On the one hand, the VALHYD plan underestimated the cost of investments in the sector. Instead of the anticipated $34.4 billion, these would cost $83.5 billion. On the other hand, the plan overestimated revenues (see Brahimi, *Stratégies de développement,* 119–20).

139. Stern, *International Gas Trade,* 75, citing Nordine Ait Laoussine, "LNG Exports—A Contribution to World Energy Supplies in the Decades to Come," *OPEC Review* 1, no. 7 (1977): 21–35.

140. Ibid., 75, reference to Ait Laoussine from "The Development of the International Gas Trade," *OPEC Review* 2, no. 3 (1978): 15–21.

141. See Bruno Dethomas, "L'Algérie n'entend pas céder sur le principe d'un alignement du prix du gaz sur celui du pétrole," *LM,* 12 April 1980.

142. Stern, *International Gas Trade,* 78. Ait Laoussine's departure was particularly regrettable (78). The Boumedienne technocrats saw the parity of petroleum to gas as a "medium to long-term aspiration" (79).

143. Ibid., 80, citing Nabi interview in *OAPEC Bulletin* 11, no. 18 (1980).

144. *LM,* 15 and 21 March 1980. The SNEA *Bulletin mensuel d'information du groupe Elf,* no. 3, of March 1980, called the correlation of gas and oil prices "irresistible" and suggested that it, too, might be forced to elevate the price of its nationally produced gas, given the "law of the market." Bruno Dethomas found this position uncalled-for in view of the "delicate commercial conjuncture" that GDF faced. Less delicately, he called it a "kick in the ass" ("L'Anarchie du marché pétrolier est un obstacle à l'alignement du prix du gaz sur celui du brut," *LM,* 6 May 1980). This was another example of an uncoordinated French energy position, this time by two national enteprises. Actually, the editorial was in press before the GDF negotiations. Albin Chalandon, the president of Elf Aquitaine, declared that this was not the intention of the SNEA (*LM,* 12 May 1980).

145. Gabriel Farkas, "Gaz: Epreuve de force entre Paris et Alger," *France-Soir,* 14 April 1980.

146. *LM,* 1 November 1980.

147. *LM,* 31 January–1 February 1982.

148. See Daniel Junqua, "Rupture des négociations sur le prix du gaz entre l'Algérie et les Etats-Unis," *LM,* 20 February 1981.

149. *LM,* 23 December 1980.

150. *LM,* 10 April 1981.

151. See *NYT,* 18 April 1962 and 22 March 1964.

152. See Palacio, *Les Pieds-noirs dans le monde.*

153. See Cohen, "Legacy of Empire," 100.

154. The arrival of 12,000 *pieds-noirs* in Corsica stemmed a population decline. A *pied-noir* declared: "Very simply, it is necessary to colonize it" (*LM,* 25–26 November 1962).

155. This was reinforced in practically every interview or casual conversation that the author engaged in with *pieds-noirs* in France and Algeria in 1978. For example, when a *pied-noir* decided to marry a metropolitan French person, the question arose in repatriate circles whether the partner-to-be was "too French."

156. See Routier, *Derrière eux, le soleil.* In March 1978 the author interviewed a *pied-noir* grande dame from Oran. Though knowing better, this astute woman felt she was "on vacation" and explained that the sun shone differently in southern France than "*là-bas.*"

157. Consider this brief list of representative books: Dessaigne, *Déracinés;* Bailac, *Les Absinthes sauvages;* Bérard, *Bel-Abbès: Ne jamais oublier;* Conesa, *Bab-el-Oued: Notre paradis perdu;* and Santini, *Les Sacrifiés.* The "Africa Nostra" press provided a forum for *pied-noir* intellectuals, writers, poets, and artists, while the Cercle Algérianiste and its journal, *L'Algérianiste,* were most concerned with integration and the preservation of a *pied-noir* identity.

158. *Pied-noir* organizations computed a loss of nearly FF 50 billion, while the French government contended that it was approximately half that figure (Baillet, "Rapatriés," 42).

159. The law created a formulating framework that significantly undervalued patrimonies. For example, real estate was assessed at 50 percent below its real 1962 value, commercial enterprises at 15 percent, and agriculture at 60 to 70 percent. Furthermore, the maximum payment was FF 80,000. The legislation hoped to satisfy smaller claims and relieve *pied-noir* debts incurred by their sudden repatriation (Blanquer, "Le Feuilleton," 175). A claim of FF 20,000 would receive 100 percent remuneration, while another of FF 500,000 received merely 5 percent (Baillet, "Les Rapatriés," 41).

160. Grimaud, *Politique extérieure,* 40. The previous year, 33,000 dossiers had been resolved, but some 150,000 still were outstanding (*LM,* 8 April 1975).

161. Blanquer, "Le Feuilleton," 176–77. By the 1975 law, a patrimony of FF 500,000 could receive FF 106,000. This was raised in 1978 to FF 394,000. *France-horizon: Le Cri du rapatrié,* no. 190 (1978), published by the Association Nationale des Français d'Afrique du Nord (ANFANOMA), provides a compara-

tive analysis of the 1970 and 1978 laws. On 8 July 1975 *pieds-noirs* engaged in a bloody skirmish at Paris's Cour des Comptes, demanding indemnification.

162. RECOURS was founded on 18 December 1976 and immediately rejected the strategy of cultivating "*amis*" or political "friends" to lobby on behalf of *pied-noir* interests. RECOURS's strategy was to mobilize the power of voting. From its beginning, it criticized the right's inaction and soon voted for the left (*Le Matin*, 2 December 1977).

163. The *harki* housing situation was especially onerous. Thirteen years after their repatriation, hundreds of *harkis* still lived in repatriation camps such as Bias (Lot-et-Garonne) and Saint-Maurice-l'Ardoise, which was built originally for refugees of the Spanish Civil War and then successively inhabited by German prisoners of war, Algerian nationalists, and OAS members and sympathizers (*LM*, 3–6 July 1974).

164. *LM*, 1 June 1972.

165. *LM*, 21 September 1976.

166. Interview. The author was invited to attend the Bachaga's elevation to the rank of *grand officier* of the Legion of Honor (26 February 1978). The subsequent lamb feast attended by *pieds-noirs, harkis,* French politicians, and the Foreign Legion band created a "temporal displacement," as one seemed transported to colonial Algeria. A guest reminded the author that he should not regard the apparent "*fraternisation*" as truly genuine.

167. *LM*, 31 October 1974.

168. *LM*, 21 and 22 June 1975.

169. Bernardi et al., *Dossiers noirs du racisme*, 163.

170. Conversations with *coopérants*, Algiers, March–April 1978; the author was also allowed to examine *coopérant* reports at the Institut Supérieur Technique d'Outre-Mer in Le Havre which described their service and experiences in Algeria.

171. Domenach, "Enquête auprès des coopérants," 94–95.

172. Ibid., 66.

173. *E-M*, 5 December 1977.

174. *AI*, no. 73 (1980), 20.

175. *AAN* 1973, 53. John Entelis observed in the mid-1980s: "Even the psychocultural benefits that are supposed to accrue through increased Arabization may be undermined by the inadequacy of language training in literary Arabic, theoretically the only effective means by which enlightened cultural values, national symbols, and political ideology can be communicated" (*Revolution Institutionalized,* 97).

176. It should be noted that the younger generation was also divided by privilege. The *tchitchis* enjoyed the latest fashions and social amenities, while the *bouhis* were the social opposites, giving rise to the cliché that "the *tchitchi* change their jeans daily, the *bouhi* once a month." The term *hittistes,* or those "of the wall," eventually referred to youth with nothing to do, no jobs, no prospects, who just leaned on walls during the day. With 75 percent of the country's population (at

that time twenty-four million) under thirty, this situation provided kindling for what would be a national conflagration (*LM*, 2 July 1987).

177. This was highlighted by a colloquium organized by the renowned Kabyle author and poet Mouloud Mammeri. Mammeri reflects on these events in *Culture savante, culture vécue*, 133–35. Philologists believe that the Berber language, Tamazight, is related to ancient Egyptian.

178. This is discussed in Pierre Rondot, "Pluralité des cultures dans l'unité nationale," *MTM*, no. 2262 (1989): 712–13.

179. "La Culture en question," *RA*, nos. 899–904 (1981). See also Boucebci, *Psychiatrie sociale et développement*.

Chapter 6. Redressing the Relationship, 1981–1988

1. "Dernière minute," *AI*, nos. 77–78 (1981). For this period in the relationship, see also Naylor, "French-Algerian Relations," in Entelis and Naylor, *State and Society*, 217–40.

2. Sahnoun, interview.

3. Mitterrand, *Politique 2*, 324. This is reminiscent of Pompidou's position. Note, however, that Mitterrand declared in a National Assembly debate during the Algerian War that "the Mediterranean has become the axis of our security and thus of our foreign policy" (Grosser, *Western Alliance*, 149).

4. Mitterrand, *Politique 2*, 314.

5. See Daniel Junqua, "France-Algérie: Enfin l'entente cordial?"

6. François Mitterrand, *Politique*, 57. For more of Mitterrand's colonial ideas see *Politique 2*, 11–12. Desjardins wrote that Mitterrand, like de Gaulle, believed in defending the empire while tempering French authority with reforms (*François Mitterrand*, 100–101, 149).

7. Mitterrand, *Politique*, 54.

8. Giesbert, *François Mitterrand*, 120–21.

9. Ibid., 125.

10. Ibid., 127.

11. Mendès-France, *Choisir*, 81.

12. MacShane, *François Mitterrand*, 61. Desjardins contended that Mitterrand's comments must be placed in political context (*François Mitterrand*, 101). Mitterrand recalled that he was convinced that the old colonial system had to be replaced (*Politique 2*, 7).

13. Giesbert, *François Mitterrand*, 136.

14. MacShane, *François Mitterrand*, 63. Mitterrand's Algerian legacy was brought up when his Socialist Party leadership was challenged by Michel Rocard in 1978–79. At one point Rocard asked, "Who was it who was a minister during the Algerian war, and who was a student being pursued by the police?" (Bell and Criddle, *French Socialist Party*, 105, citing *L'Express*, 31 March 1979).

15. Mitterrand, *Politique*, 122. See also his *Présence française et abandon*, 237.

16. Robert Pesquet, a former Poujadist deputy, warned Mitterrand that he was

targeted for assassination. During the night of 15–16 October, Mitterrand was followed and fired upon. A few days later Pesquet declared that the attack had been staged in collaboration with the "victim." Mitterrand saw this elaborate plan as a means to neutralize him politically. It did, in the short term (*Politique*, 387–409).

17. Willis, *French Paradox*, 13–14.

18. See Serfaty, *Foreign Policies*. Charles Zorgbibe perceived Mitterrand's foreign policy as "incoherent" and related it metaphorically to a "disassociated" cubist painting ("La Diplomatie éclatée de François Mitterrand," in Joyau and Wajsman, *Pour une nouvelle politique étrangère*, 92).

19. Mitterrand, *The Wheat and the Chaff*, 269. See also his *Politique 2*, 13.

20. William Styron, introduction to *The Wheat and the Chaff*, x. Styron added: "Mitterrand's love of France is as passionate as [the General's], though mercifully shorn of its mysticism."

21. Mitterrand, *The Wheat and the Chaff*, 9.

22. Ibid., 18.

23. Desjardins, *François Mitterrand*, 289. Desjardins also wrote that Mitterrand was "obsessed by an idée fixe" which was "to serve France" (291). See also Hoffmann, "Gaullism by Any Other Name." Mitterrand's "Gaullism" was particularly evident during the "cohabitation" after the right's electoral success in 1986. See, for example, *NYT*, 19 March 1986, and *LM*, 29 May 1986 (concerning French defense and national independence). Mitterrand's confidant Roland Dumas claimed: "François Mitterrand sincerely wants to be the incarnation of France like de Gaulle was" (*WSJ*, 9 March 1988).

24. Moïsi, "French Foreign Policy," 162.

25. Willis, *French Paradox*, 14.

26. Rondos, "Mitterrand's Two-Year Record," 10.

27. Ronald Teirsky, "The French Left and the Third World," in Serfaty, *Foreign Policies*, 68. The Common Program "urged an end to colonial and neocolonial domination, and in particular recognized that France faces special responsibilities in its former colonial realm, first of all in Africa" (68–69). African leaders perceived Mitterrand's election as a real "break" in French African policy (Bayart, *Politique africaine*, 21–23).

28. Whitman, "President Mitterrand and Africa," 330.

29. Willis, *French Paradox*, 14–15.

30. Manceron and Pingaud, *François Mitterrand*, 147.

31. Codevelopment projected assistance through state-to-state private modalities to targeted sectors (Bayart, *Politique africaine*, 89). Jean-Pierre Cot as minister of cooperation (May 1981–December 1982) particularly popularized this idea. Through a new cooperation, inappropriate projects, termed *mal-développement*, would be replaced by "self-centered development" aiming at such sectors as health, *formation* (training), energy, and particular industrial needs (Cot, "What Change?" 13). The idea of Paris imposing its type of cooperation upon other

countries was regarded by some African states as neocolonialist (Bayart, *Politique africaine*, 33). Algeria was not integrated within a total codevelopment program with Africa. Instead, it received a traditional privileged relationship.

32. *The Wheat and the Chaff*, 34.

33. *LM*, 26 February 1976.

34. *LM*, 29 February 1976.

35. Interviews from French and Algerian perspectives underscored that Mitterrand's personal past with Algeria influenced his policy. See also Cot, *A l'épreuve du pouvoir*, 70.

36. *LM*, 17 July 1981.

37. *LM*, 11 August 1981. Paris projected Algeria, along with Mexico, Brazil, and India, as strategic axes with the Third World (*LM*, 17 July 1981).

38. *LM*, 21 October 1981.

39. Ibid.

40. *E-M*, 22 October 1981.

41. *LM*, 29 November 1981.

42. Ibid.

43. Quoted by *E-M*, 27–28 November 1981.

44. *E-M*, 29 November 1981.

45. *LM*, 1 December 1981.

46. Mitterrand, *Réflexions sur la politique extérieure*, 322, 325, 330.

47. *LM*, 3 December 1981.

48. *E-M* enthusiastically publicized Mitterrand's visit (30 November–1 December 1981). But it also printed a concurrent series on the plight of the second-generation emigrant worker in France.

49. *LM*, 24 December 1981.

50. *LM*, 28 August 1981.

51. *LM*, 10 September 1981.

52. *LM*, 29 September 1981.

53. *LM*, 4 December 1982.

54. *WSJ*, 14 December 1981; *LM*, 15 December 1981.

55. *LM*, 24 December 1981, 28 January 1982.

56. *LM*, 28 January 1982.

57. *LM*, 31 January-1 February 1982.

58. *PE*, 49 (March 1982): 105.

59. Davis, *Blue Gold*, 264.

60. See *PE* 49 (March 1982): 105; *FT*, 4 February 1982; *LM*, 4 February 1982; *E-M*, 4 and 5–6 February 1982; *Maghreb-Machrek*, no. 97 (1982): 87–91; and *AI*, no. 88 (1982). By the time the accord was reached, FF 12 billion of contracts had already been signed (*LM*, 21 January 1988).

61. Stern, *International Gas Trade*, 87.

62. *AI*, no. 88 (1982): n.p.

63. Ibid.

64. *LM*, 4 February 1982.

65. *E-M,* 4 February 1982.

66. *AI,* no. 88 (1982): 20–21.

67. *LM,* 4 February 1982. According to the *WSJ:* "The French . . . were anxious to reach an agreement in order to start deliveries under the third LNG supply contract, signed in 1976. This contract . . . will more than double France's intake of Algerian LNG and contribute to the diversification of its sources" (*WSJ,* 4 February 1982). In addition, with supplies secure from Algeria, "Gaz de France need no longer plan on speculative future supplies of LNG from Nigeria's Bonny project, in which Elf still has a stake" (*PE* 49 [March 1982]: 105). With Mitterrand wanting to promote North-South political and economic cooperation, French leaders of public industry such as GDF and the Société Nationale Elf Aquitaine worried about the effect of a privileged French-Algerian relationship on other Third World clients. According to Albin Chalandon of the SNEA, other gas-producing states (e.g., Nigeria and Cameroon) "will search to obtain the same advantages" (*LM,* 2 February 1982). Nevertheless, France's other Third World interests seemed to understand the special nature and nurture devoted to the Algerian relationship.

68. *E-M,* 4 February 1982.

69. *MEED,* special report (May 1982): 7.

70. *LM,* 19 June 1982. Hodges surveys this period in "François Mitterrand, Master Strategist." See also Grimaud, "Nouvelles orientations"; Grimaud, "Algeria and Socialist France"; and Giraud, "France-Algérie."

71. *LM,* 23 June 1982.

72. Ibid.

73. "Procès-verbal de la première session." See also *AI,* nos. 96–97 (1982): 17–21.

74. *LM,* 4 November 1982.

75. *LM,* 5 November 1982.

76. *LM,* 11 November 1982.

77. Christian Nucci, who headed the cooperation and development subministry at the Quai d'Orsay, stated before the National Assembly on 27 February 1984 that codevelopment was characterized by *concertation* as particularly seen in the creation of "mixed organs" (joint commissions), the housing, transport, and agricultural accords, and the addition of a "supplementary title" to the 1966 Technical and Cultural Cooperation Accord (*AI,* no. 111 [1984], 10).

78. *France Soir,* 19 April 1982; *LM,* 18–19, 20 April 1982.

79. *LM,* 20 April 1982; see also *E-M,* 23–24 April 1982.

80. *LM,* 20 May 1982.

81. Cooperation's direction received orientation from too many sources: the Ministries of Cooperation and Foreign Affairs (though Cooperation was placed under the Quai d'Orsay in May 1981), the Elysée, and the Socialist Party. This produced contentions and rivalries between "realists" and "idealists." Cot resigned under ambiguous circumstances. Mitterrand began to pursue a more traditional African policy based on "personal relations" (Bayart, *Politique africaine,*

35, 46, 56). See also Rondos, "Mitterrand's Two-Year Record," and Whitman, "President Mitterrand and Africa," 334–43.

82. Grimaud, "Algeria and Socialist France," 258.

83. *AI*, no. 98 (1982): 32–33.

84. Sahnoun, interview.

85. *E-M* (28 October 1979) had asserted that reinsertion could not be realized without a "minutely elaborated process" (*AI*, no. 61 [1979]: n.p.); Sahnoun, interview.

86. Grimaud, "Algeria and Socialist France," 257.

87. For the Mitterrand government's position, see Georgina Dufoix, interview in *La Semaine de l'émigration*, no. 62 (1983), reprinted in *AI*, no. 107 (1983): 19–22.

88. Max Silverman, "*Travailleurs Immigrés* and International Relations," in Aldrich and Connell, *France in World Politics*, 90.

89. Grimaud, "Algeria and Socialist France," 264.

90. Efforts to create a policy of training for reinsertion (with CCCE aid) did not appeal to the workers. Algeria has also tried to create its own corps of training cadres supplementing French efforts (*AI*, no. 90 [1982]: 47–48). A report by the Cour des Comptes found French social services for the workers to be poorly organized and managed (*LM*, 14 July 1981). In 1983 an Algerian could repatriate with some training and FF 15,000 in his pocket (*AI*, no. 107 [1983]: 21, citing Georgina Dufoix in *La Semaine de l'émigration*, no. 62 [1983]). M. E. Benissad argued that there was an "importation of unemployment" during the 1930s and this applied again to France in the late 1970s and 1980s (*L'Economie algérienne contemporaine*, 10); in 1930–31, 15,340 returned to Algeria, 3,341 in 1934, and 10,259 in 1938–39 (9). These economic contingencies make it difficult to assess statistics and the reinsertion program. *E-M* reported that five thousand dossiers from the Paris region were under consideration for reinsertion in 1981 (*AI*, nos. 77–78 [1981]: 33–35, citing *E-M*, 25 March 1981).

91. *LM*, 11 August 1981.

92. Hodges, "François Mitterrand, Master Strategist," 20.

93. *LM*, 16 March 1983. A disillusioned Polisario official told the author that there was "no difference between Giscard and Mitterrand" (conversation, Aix-en-Provence, 1984).

94. Bayart, *Politique africaine*, 32.

95. *LM*, 11–13 September 1983.

96. *LM*, 10 October 1983; *Le Matin*, 12 October 1983.

97. *E-M*, 7 November 1983.

98. The pomp and circumstance was thought to be excessive by Edmond Jouhaud, the former general and OAS leader.

99. *AI*, hors série (December 1983): 62, 66.

100. *Le Figaro*, 7 November 1983. Salah Mouhoubi contended that Benjedid wanted to place cooperation in a "much larger context" to secure the relationship (*Politique de la coopération*, 91).

101. *AI,* special issue (December 1982): 9–18.

102. *E-M,* 9 November 1983.

103. *LM,* 10 November 1983.

104. In December the joint commission met in Algiers to explore the possibility of creating French-Algerian companies (*LM,* 7 December 1983). France also was willing to help the Algerian military with naval training and matériel (*LM,* 22 February 1984). It should be remembered that France faced economic problems during this time. Mitterrand's initial expansionist fiscal policies led to deficits and a declining balance of payments. Jacques Delors, the finance minister, advocated major shifts in economic policy, including the devaluation of the franc (5.75/$ in June 1982) and austerity. Mitterrand accepted these changes.

105. Stern, *International Gas Trade,* 154. Stern also refers to P. J. Lehmann, *Economic Principles for Gas Consumer Pricing,* paper presented at the Forum on the Economics of Natural Gas Transportation, Norwegian Petroleum Society, 8–9 February 1983.

106. *AI,* no. 111 (1984): 20, citing Grimaud, "Nouvelles orientations."

107. Hassan stated: "Morocco did not play a role of negotiator. It only transmitted messages" (Grimaud, "Algeria and Socialist France," quoting *LM,* 10 November 1984). The *CSM* reported that "Morocco agreed to mediate a mutual withdrawal of French and Libyan troops from Chad" (19 November 1984).

108. Jean-Pierre Ferrier, "Maghreb: Les Vertus de l'audace," in Joyau and Wajsman, *Pour une nouvelle politique étrangère,* 322–23.

109. William Echikson, "French and Algerians Mystified by Mitterrand's Trips to Morocco and Portugal," *CSM,* 6 September 1984.

110. *E-M,* 19 October 1984.

111. *E-M,* 12–13 October 1984.

112. *E-M,* 17 October 1984.

113. AFP, *Sahara,* no. 693 (1984): 15, 23–24. See *E-M,* 29 October 1984, reproducing Benjedid interview in *Le Point.* This was certainly more than a "minor misunderstanding," given Algeria's favored codevelopment status.

114. AFP, *Sahara,* no. 693 (1984): 26.

115. See *LM,* 23 and 31 October 1984, for prominent reactions.

116. Sahnoun, interview; see also *E-M,* 29 October 1984, reprint of *Le Point* article. *E-M* listed the French delegation last among the dignitaries (1 November 1984). While in Algiers on 2 November, the Catholic remembrance day, Cheysson joined Cardinal Léon-Etienne Duval at a European cemetery to commemorate the French of Algeria who died for France.

117. *E-M,* 7 November 1983.

118. Balta, "French Policy," 248; *QER,* no. 3 (1985): 10.

119. This is the theme of Stora, *La Gangrène et l'oubli.*

120. See Simmons, *French National Front,* 38–39.

121. *QER,* no. 3 (1985): 26–28.

122. AFP, *Sahara,* no. 713 (1985): 33–35. See *RA* during this period for representative articles castigating France and the use of torture during the War.

123. Richard Bernstein, "Fanning French Fears," *NYT Magazine,* 4 October 1987, 50. Another analyst contended that the FN is rooted in xenophobia and in the appealing "penchant [to] take refuge in abstraction, the unrealizable, negation, derision or absurdity" (Roussel, *Le Cas Le Pen,* 172). See also Simmons, "On National Identity and Racism," in *French National Front,* 161–63.

124. Le Pen, *La France est de retour,* 233.

125. Ibid., 243.

126. There are many works on the "second generation." Those covering this period include Malewska-Peyre et al., *Crise d'identité et déviance;* Chaker, *Jeunesse algérienne en France;* and chapters in Talha, *Maghrébins en France.*

127. *NYT,* 13 March 1986.

128. Hargreaves, *Voices,* 20.

129. *LM,* 25 February 1988.

130. *Grand Maghreb,* in its short publication life, often featured articles on the *beurs,* for example, Thierry Leclère, "Les Beurs entrent en scène," no. 27 (1983): 52–54. *Beurs* call bigoted French racists *beaufs,* slang for *beau-frère* (brother-in-law) and the name of a featured character in a popular satiric comic book (Rosenblum, *Mission to Civilize,* 265).

131. See Hargreaves, *La Littérature beur,* and Renaud Revel, "Les Radios immigrés," *Grand Maghreb* no. 22 (1983): 57–59.

132. Bouzid, *La Marche,* 10, 32, 36.

133. See Boukhedenna, *Journal: Nationalité: Immigrée.*

134. For example, Dalila in *Fatima, ou les Algériennes au square* (1981) and Shérazade in *Shérazade, frisée, les yeux verts* (1982) and *Les Carnets de Shérazade* (1985). A concise description of Sebbar's literature is in M. Mortimer, *Journeys,* 177–94. Shérazade, the beautiful *beur* runaway, refuses to be exoticized by a French boyfriend steeped in "orientalist" studies, a form of patriarchy.

135. For a detailed account of *beur* and minority filmmaking, see Carrie Tarr, "French Cinema and Post-Colonial Minorities," in Hargreaves and McKinney, *Post-Colonial Cultures,* 59–83.

136. *WSJ,* 24 June 1988.

137. The Charter was published in special inserts of *E-M,* 7–9 January 1986. See also *LM,* 9–11 January 1986.

138. R. Mortimer, "Development and Autonomy," 45.

139. Benjedid's government was greatly interested in history and especially in collecting the oral histories of war veterans (*mujahidin*). Benjedid regarded the understanding of "the historical continuity of our society" as an imperative (Balta and Rulleau, *L'Algérie des Algériens,* 187, citing *E-M,* "Rapport sur la politique culturelle," 15–23 July 1981). This was underscored by Algeria's first international conference (November 1984) on the history of the War of Liberation. Alistair Horne attended and remarked: "That it should have been held at all, given the pain of memories only so recently in the past, was a remarkable—and courageous—feat on the part of the Algerians" (*Savage War,* 19); see also chapter 10.

140. *LM*, 2 July 1987.

141. See OECD, *North Africa Oil and Gas*, 18.

142. Ministère de l'Orientation nationale, *Algérie: An II*, 196.

143. See Bennabi, *Vocation de l'Islam*.

144. Bennabi, *Les Grands thèmes*, 12. In Bennabi's Arabic text, he uses the word *qabiliyya*, which can mean in this context "disposition" or "liability" or "tendency"; *qabiliyya lil-isti'amar* would be "tendency toward colonialism." The Arabic title, *Afaq jaza'iriyya* (Algerian horizons), is much more existentially descriptive than the French.

145. Women protested their uncomfortable new social and legal subordination. An earlier Family Code had been proposed in 1981 but shelved because of the protests of prominent women of the Revolution (see Knauss, *The Persistence of Patriarchy*, 125–40).

146. Benaissa interview in Burgat and Dowell, *The Islamic Movement in North Africa*, 266.

147. Ibid., 267.

148. "Tunis West Sahara Peace Bid Stalled," *Arabia: The Islamic World Review* 4, no. 43 (1985): 29. Even the casual observer could notice the increase of traditional Muslim clothing among the young during this time.

149. See *LM*, 8 January 1991. Mohammed Harbi and others believed that the French aided Algerian special services at the request of the Algerian government: the operation against Mecili was an act of cooperation between security forces (*LM*, 20 August 1994).

150. See *AI*, no. 147 (1987), 10–11. By this agreement French aid to *coopérants* would be FF 300 million. The CCCE would also lend 300 million (*CR*, no. 2 [1986]: 24). Ironically, Stéphane Hessel, who once equated cooperation with giving Algeria its modern identity, thought cooperation in general in Africa was "largely . . . a neocolonial type of cultural and technical assistance" and needed to be reformed ("Mitterrand's France and the Third World," in Ross, Hoffmann, and Malzacher, *The Mitterrand Experiment*, 336). He supported the Socialist government's intention of linking human rights and democracy (e.g., the La Baule Conference of 1990) with cooperation. In addition, he affirmed that cooperation must take into account stated African needs and desires. One can still detect the French deontological need to assist Africa. See Stéphane Hessel, "Socialist France and Developing Countries," 130–40.

151. *CR*, no. 4 (1986): 7–8.

152. In December 1986 Ben Bella's newspaper *El-Badil* was banned from circulation for its negative effect on "diplomatic interests." Other Ben Bellist publications interdicted include *Alternative démocratique* (March 1987) and *Le Changement* (July 1987). By this time the MDA was headquartered in Switzerland.

153. See Deeb, "Inter-Maghribi Relations," and Naylor, "Maghrib Unity," 305–15. On 17 February 1989 the long-aspired Union du Maghreb Arabe (UMA) was officially inaugurated.

154. See Naylor, "Spain and France and the Western Sahara," in Zoubir and Volman, *International Dimensions of the Western Saharan Conflict*, 17–51.

155. See Naylor, "French-Algerian Relations," in Entelis and Naylor, *State and Society*, 234.

156. *LM*, 3 June 1986.

157. *LM*, 10 March 1989. The collapse of oil prices meant a 15-percent reduction of Algeria's GNP in 1985 alone (*WSJ*, 3 November 1988).

158. *CR*, no. 4 (1987): 15–16. In 1988, GDF was apparently still paying this low price but was being invoiced at $2.70/MMBtu (*CR*, no. 3 [1988]: 14).

159. AFP, *Sahara*, no. 778 (1988): 42.

160. AFP, *Sahara*, no. 795 (1988): 28–29.

161. AFP, *Sahara*, no. 791 (1988): 39.

162. *CR*, no. 2 (1988): 11. Algeria supplied France with 31.4 percent of its gas needs in 1987 (*CR*, no. 1 [1988]: 19).

163. Michel Jobert applied this term concerning the 1982 LNG Accord. See especially Bruno Dethomas, "Un psychodrame franco-algérien," *LM*, 11 March 1988, and Jean Guéneau, "Gaz algérien: L'Enjeu," *MTM*, no. 2202 (1988): 169–74.

164. *LM*, 25 April 1987; *CR*, no. 2 (1987): 25.

165. Chirac announced a budget of FF 30 billion to be allocated over fifteen years beginning in 1989, which would resolve the indemnity question by 2004. According to Roland Blanquer, the repatriated would have been satisfied if these monies could be distributed in half the time ("Le Feuilleton," 178–79). *LM* reported that the state had already paid FF 25 billion toward indemnification (25 June 1987). The payments would be prorated according to age (see *LM*, 23 July 1987). Chirac should be credited for his substantial, if inevitably (from the *pied-noir* and French-Algerian viewpoints) inadequate, tackling of this painful issue. *Pied-noir* households could expect a possible million-franc indemnity. A *harki*—or, if deceased, his wife or children—could receive sixty thousand francs in three installments (1989–91). According to a contemporary poll, 49 percent of the French felt "indifference" toward the *pieds-noirs*. For example, 32 percent believed that France owed them a debt and 49 percent disagreed (*Nouvel observateur*, 19–25 June 1987, 81). The indemnification law was officially registered on 19 July 1987.

166. *CR*, no. 2 (1988): 7.

167. *CR*, no. 4 (1988): 19.

Chapter 7. Algeria's "Second Revolution" and France, 1988–1992: From the October Riots to the *Fitna*

1. One woman remarked: "The young people of Algeria have nothing" (*BG*, 10 October 1988). A young man affirmed: "This country is run by *des grosses têtes* (swelled heads). . . . They have kept power for themselves and left us with nothing. That's what socialism and revolution mean here" (*CSM*, 4 November 1988).

2. According to Northrop Frye: "A society with a closed myth of concern

makes it compulsory for all its citizens to say that they support it, or at least will not overtly oppose it" (*The Critical Path,* 106). Frye also wrote: "Every myth of concern is religious, in the sense of establishing a *religio* or common body of acts and beliefs for the community" (106). The author thanks Professor Lewis Livesay of St. Peter's College (Jersey City, New Jersey) for access to his manuscript "Critique of Structuralism." In Foucauldian terms, Algeria's rejection of a "regime of truth" would have vast social consequences, restructuring power and perception relations (see chapter 10).

3. See *WSJ,* 23 January 1992, for an excellent overview of the generation gap.

4. Consider these astute observations before the "events." John Entelis observed that "neither the secular ideology—socialism—nor the state-sponsored religion—official Islam—provided the kind of psychological palliative necessary for a people to overcome the stressful and dislocating consequences of rapid social change" (*Revolution Institutionalized,* 83–84). Almost a decade earlier, P. J. Vatikiotis perceived that "the Algerian . . . finds himself on the horns of a dilemma between the Scylla of the Islamic ethic and the Charybdis of the industrial-technological revolution—the latter being the characteristic achievement of nineteenth and twentieth century Europe" ("Tradition and Political Leadership," in Zartman, *Man, State, and Society,* 316). See also Jean-Claude Vatin, "Popular Puritanism versus State Reformism: Islam in Algeria," in Piscatori, *Islam in the Political Process,* 98–121. Compounding this situation were the demographic changes in the country. In the 1980s almost 50 percent of the population lived in the congested cities, compared with only 30 percent at independence (Provost, *Seconde Guerre,* 68).

5. Tahi, "Algeria's Presidential Election," 282.

6. Yves Cuau, "Le Miroir brisé," *L'Express* (international), 29 June 1990. The author presents a different interpretation of this metaphor in chapter 10.

7. French newspapers like *LM, Libération,* and *Le Figaro* ran many articles on the riots during 4–17 October.

8. The rapid rise of Ali Belhadj is illustrated by the comment of one Western diplomat: "We know nothing about him" (*NYT,* 19 October 1988). His name is sometimes given as Benhadj, but it consistently appeared as Belhadj at this time in French and English and in *al-Sharq al-Awsat,* the Arab international daily. Eventually *al-Sharq al-Awsat* referred to him as Bin Hajj.

9. *Libération,* 12 October 1988.

10. *Libération,* 10 October 1988.

11. *Le Figaro,* 13 October 1988.

12. Friend, *The Long Presidency,* citing Pierre Favier and Michel Martin-Rolland, *La Décennie Mitterrand* (Paris: Editions du Seuil, 1996), 3:386–87, quoting minutes of the council meeting.

13. *NYT,* 18 October 1988.

14. *Le Figaro,* 11 and 13 October 1988. *Libération* wrote: "Algeria was and remains a case apart. A massacre in Algiers or in Oran remains an 'internal affair' when the same massacre in any other part of the world would insult human rights

and draw from our rulers, on the right as well as on the left, automatic condemnation" (*NYT,* 18 October 1988). In a work produced by the Groupe de Recherches sur le Maghreb et le Monde musulman at the University of Paris VII (Jussieu), Claude Liauzu studied Algeria, *tiersmondisme,* and French intellectuals, especially of the left. The "romanticism" of *tiersmondisme,* created in part by the writings of Fanon and others, was jolted during the 1980s by institutionalized authoritarianism and the failures of socialist ideologies and programs. Of intellectuals and Algeria, Liauzu related Edgar Morin's reluctance to get caught up in a revolutionary romanticism during the War of Independence. Prophetically, he feared that "the struggle for national liberation" could turn to one of "liberation of peoples oppressed by their nation" (Liauzu, "Les Intellectuels français," 166, citing *Arguments,* November 1958).

15. *Libération,* 12 October 1988.

16. Ibid.

17. Patrick Rotman, "L'indignation désenchantée des anciens porteurs de valises," *Libération,* 17 October, 23–24. See also *Libération,* 12 October 1988, and *Le Figaro,* 13 October 1988.

18. *Le Figaro,* 13 October 1988.

19. *NYT,* 18 October 1988.

20. *Libération,* 12 October 1988. On *beur* youth, see *Libération,* 11 October 1988.

21. See Charef, *L'Algérie: Le Grand dérapage,* 91–99; Monique Gadant, "*Hiz' farança,* le parti de la France," in Reporters sans Frontières, *Le Drame algérien,* 83–84; Provost, *Seconde Guerre,* 31–32; and Rashid Messaoudi, "Algerian-French Relations: 1830–1991 (A Clash of Civilizations)," in Shah-Kazemi, *Algeria: Revolution Revisited,* 6–46. Boumedienne used the term pejoratively to assail those who opposed Arabization (see *LM,* 20 August 1994). M. S. Tahi claimed that the powerful Sécurité Militaire was behind "the slogan 3F+F (FIS, FFS, FLN + France) in order to discredit them. FIS was thus a French 'creation,' or at least 'supported' by France, which also 'supported' Ait Ahmed of the FFS and the former single political party, the FLN!" ("Algeria's Presidential Election," 291).

22. *LM,* 5 November 1994.

23. *Le Figaro,* 26–27 November 1988. These comments were published originally in *al-Chaab.*

24. Clearly, the French card was being played among others. Unsubstantiated reports circulated that the riots had been staged initially by the government in order to persuade intransigent members of the FLN to follow Benjedid's liberalizing course.

25. *Le Figaro,* 13 October 1988.

26. See *Libération,* 14 October 1988.

27. "Les Embarras français," *Libération,* 12 October 1988, 3.

28. R. Mortimer, "Maghreb Matters," 170.

29. The Berber population was, of course, Algeria's largest minority, 17 percent of Algeria's 27.9 million people in 1994 (*NYT,* 5 March 1995).

30. R. Mortimer, "Islamists, Soldiers, and Democrats," 19.

31. Leveau, *Le Sabre et le turban,* 12.

32. See Mohammed Harbi, "La Fausse 'démocratie' de l'après-88," in Reporters sans Frontières, *Le Drame algérien,* 134–36.

33. See *NYT,* 19 March 1995.

34. The last bilingual *baccalauréat* was awarded in 1988.

35. Mimouni, *The Honor of the Tribe,* 28.

36. Djaout, *Les Vigiles,* 72.

37. *CSM,* 20 September 1989. Rai's roots are also Andalusian, according to Nour-Luc Chaulet, "Le Chaâbi, musique des racines," in Reporters sans Frontières, *Le Drame algérien,* 41–43. *Cheb* (m.) or *cheba* (f.) means "young one." The word is derived from the Arabic *sha'ab* or "people," suggesting their music is the voice of the people.

38. Mimouni, *De la barbarie,* 167.

39. Ibid., 166–67.

40. For an economic assessment of this period, see Brahimi, *Stratégies de développement,* 336ff. Brahimi's analysis is colored by his intimate participation in Benjedid's governments during the 1980s. Nevertheless, it is a valuable comparative analysis. See also Charef, *L'Algérie: Le Grand dérapage,* 21–27.

41. Akram Belkaid, "L'Echec de Hamrouche et des réformateurs," in Reporters sans Frontières, *Le Drame algérien,* 106.

42. *Economist,* 4 August 1990, 32.

43. *CSM,* 12 June 1990. Illustrating the divisions within the increasingly fractured FLN, Belaid Abdesselam called for a "war economy," a philosophical rejection of liberalism (AFP, *Sahara,* no. 877 [1991]: 48).

44. See *Le Figaro,* 11–12 March 1989; *LM,* 11 March 1989.

45. André Pautard, "Les Compteurs remis à l'heure," *L'Express* (international), no. 1959 (1989): 17.

46. Robert Mortimer, "Algerian Foreign Policy in Transition," in Entelis and Naylor, *State and Society,* 257.

47. *Le Figaro,* 10–11 March 1989.

48. AFP, *Sahara,* no. 805 (1989): 26; *LM,* 11 January 1989. It was hoped in Algiers that the recent devaluations of the DA (30 percent in 1986–87 and another 20 percent in 1988) would encourage commerce. Peugeot signed an industrial cooperation agreement to plan the construction of a second automobile factory (*CR,* no. 3 [1989]: 13).

49. *CR,* no. 2 (1989): 21.

50. *CR,* no. 4 (1990): 24.

51. AFP, *Sahara,* no. 871 (1991): 25.

52. *LM,* 13 and 14 January 1989; *CR,* no. 1 (1989): 17.

53. *LM,* 14 January 1989.

54. *E-M*, 13–14 January 1989.

55. AFP, *Sahara*, no. 865 (1991): 47. Algerian authorities also tried to interest Elf Aquitaine in participating (AFP, *Sahara*, no. 871 [1991]: 24).

56. Naylor, "French-Algerian Relations, 1980–1990," in Entelis and Naylor, *State and Society in Algeria*, 236. SAFIR was also charged to rework GNL 4. The implementation of the joint company was very slow. By the final quarter of 1992, only eight GDF technicians were working in Arzew (*Africa Energy & Mining*, no. 103 [1993], on lexis-nexis.com).

57. The need to increase revenues pressured Ghozali, who had appointed his former associate Nordine Ait Laoussine minister of energy. Ait Laoussine stated the obvious: "It is not possible for a country like Algeria to content itself with a recovery level of 22 per cent when you compare that with the levels achieved elsewhere in the world" (Reuters Textline, *African Economic Digest*, 16 December 1991, on lexis-nexis.com). With the approach of the Gulf War, speculation in oil caused Algeria's crude to skyrocket to $42/barrel, immediately assisting its economy in the short term (*L'Express* [international], 12 October 1990, 17).

58. OECD, *North Africa Oil and Gas*, 18; *LM*, 3 December 1991; *NYT*, 1 December 1991. Foreign companies would be allowed a 49 percent stake in hydrocarbons projects.

59. Reuters, 24 December 1991; BBC Summary of World Events, 7 January 1992; *African Economic Digest*, 13 January 1992, on lexis-nexis.com. The 1962 accord for 500 million m³ was to have expired in 1992, the 1971 accord for 3.6 billion m³ in 1998, and the 1976 accord for 5.3 billion m³ in 2003. The last contract would run until 2013.

60. *LM*, 3 January 1989.

61. In 1985, 7,435 emigrants were "accompanied" to the border, 12,354 in 1986, 15,837 in 1987, and 9,522 from January to July 1988 (*LM*, 3 January 1989).

62. See *LM*, 3, 4, and 6 January for discussion of the Socialist initiative and political reaction. The Socialists felt political pressure from SOS-Racisme, the Ligue des Droits de l'Homme, and other organizations.

63. AFP, *Sahara*, no. 817 (1989): 36.

64. *LM*, 11 February 1989.

65. See Robert Solé, "Les Zigzags socialistes," *LM*, 3 January 1989.

66. *LM*, 6 January 1989.

67. *CSM*, 12 December 1990.

68. Ibid.

69. See *LM*, 21 and 23 September 1991. Algerian-descended children born in France received French nationality, if at least one parent was born in Algeria before 1963.

70. AFP, *Sahara*, no. 869 (1991): 24; Méliani, *La France honteuse*, 176, 200–202. This period sadly included the death of Ali Boualam, the son of the Bachaga Boualam and a *harki* activist; he died, according to the *Guardian*, from "stress

during the . . . nationwide protests against French ingratitude to the thousands of Algerians who fought for France" (*Guardian*, 23 July 1991, on lexis-nexis.com).

71. Francis Jeanson, Jean-Paul Sartre's longtime friend and FLN collaborator during the War of Liberation, viewed Islamism as an existential phenomenon, a "self-affirmation." When Jeanson asked Abassi Madani about Algeria's identity crisis, the Islamist leader denied that there was one. Algeria's authentic, changeless personality ("the soul is not modifiable") was based upon the truth of the Qur'an and the Sunna. It was the Islamist task "to impose the Absolute" (Jeanson, *Algéries: De retour en retour,* 93, 83–84). Juan Goytisolo viewed Islamism as "the identifying common denominator of all the marginalized" in Algeria's society (*L'Algérie dans la tourmente,* 30).

72. Stora, *Histoire de l'Algérie,* 87; see also Addi, *L'Impasse du populisme,* 15–16, and Khellad, *Algérie: Les Islamistes face au pouvoir,* 13. Rémy Leveau added that the FIS was a "product of the decomposition of the FLN," especially in social matters ("L'Algérie en état de siège," *Maghreb-Machrek,* no. 133 [1991]: 93).

73. See Carlier, *Entre nation et jihad,* and Stora, *La Gangrène et l'oubli,* 312–13. Stora referred to political Islam as a "neo-nationalism" (313).

74. Ahmed Rouadjia, "Du Nationalisme du FLN à l'islamisme du FIS," *Les Temps modernes* 50, no. 580 (1995): 133. The entire issue of *Les Temps modernes* is devoted to the *fitna* ("Algérie: La Guerre des frères"). According to Provost, the Algerian regime since 1962 had "in fact slipped into the skins of the former *colons*" (regarding the expropriation of French property) and had "interdicted the definition of an Algerian identity" (*Seconde Guerre,* 12).

75. Stora, *Histoire de l'Algérie,* 93.

76. "Les Héritiers islamistes," *Libération,* 17 October 1988, 6.

77. Addi, *L'Algérie et la démocratie,* 209.

78. Kapil, "Algeria's Elections Show Islamist Strength," 36.

79. Addi, *L'Algérie et la démocratie,* 202–6.

80. Lamchichi, *L'Islamisme en Algérie,* 56–57.

81. Burgat, "La Mobilisation," 21. Western ideas imported by French colonialism such as the Enlightenment contributed to a refashioned *jahiliyya,* i.e., the period of "ignorance" before the revelation of Islam. The Islamists viewed themselves as spiritual (and political) liberators (see Lamchichi, *L'Islamisme en Algérie,* 54–55).

82. Khellad, *Algérie: Les Islamistes face au pouvoir,* 107, quoting an interview between Madani and Abdellali Rezagui in *Les partis politiques en Algérie* (ONAC, 1990).

83. *Economist,* 4 August 1990, 32. Hassan Tourabi of Sudan argued in an interview with *El País* that "Islamism represents the liberation of societies that had been subjected to Western colonialism" (*LM,* 2 August 1994).

84. Addi, *L'Algérie et la démocratie,* 203, citing an interview in *Politique internationale,* no. 49 (1990): 156.

85. Stora, *Histoire de l'Algérie,* 91.

86. al-Ahnaf and Frégosi, *L'Algérie par ses islamistes*, 274 (Fayçal Tlilani in *El-Mounquid*, no. 5). The FIS's own program perceived the party's mission as protective against the cultural "intrigues of hostile civilizations" (Lamchichi, *L'Islamisme en Algérie*, 33).

87. al-Ahnaf and Frégosi, *L'Algérie par ses islamistes*, 275 (Dr. Ahmad Ben No'man in *El-Mounquid*, no. 9).

88. Ibid., 278 (Fouad Benabdelhalim in *El-Mounquid*, no. 9).

89. Ibid., 279 (from *al-Irchad*, no. 4).

90. Rouadjia, *Les Frères et la mosquée*, 24.

91. *NYT*, 18 October 1988.

92. *L'Express* (international), 9 February 1990, 26.

93. *CSM*, 13 November 1989.

94. See Kapil, "Algeria's Elections Show Islamist Strength," and *LM*, 22 June 1990.

95. *LM*, 20 September 1990.

96. *L'Express* (international), 10 January 1991, 10–11.

97. AFP, *Sahara*, no. 856 (1991): 29.

98. *LM*, 31 December 1990.

99. Ronald Koven, "France's Ambivalent Line in the Sand Against Iraq," *BG*, 7 October 1990.

100. *LM*, 11 January 1991. Among the harshest critics of Mitterrand's Gulf War policy were Le Pen on the right and, ironically, members of his own Socialist Party.

101. *CSM*, 14 December 1990. According to APS, Benjedid intended "to pursue his consultations with them and continue the efforts of Algeria for the good of all peoples in the region as well as for the superior interests of the Arab nation" (*BG*, 11 December 1990).

102. This was mentioned, too, in Mitterrand's 9 January 1991 press conference (*LM*, 11 January 1991).

103. *LM*, 15 March 1991.

104. *LM*, 1 February 1991. Concerning France's involvement in the War see P. Gordon, *Certain Idea*, 178–83.

105. AFP, *Sahara*, no. 858 (1991): 44.

106. *CSM*, 7 May 1991.

107. *CSM*, 22 February 1991.

108. FBIS, *NES*, 28 May 1991, 4. Ait Ahmed criticized the European Community and especially France for paying more attention to and doing more for Eastern Europe than Algeria. He called France's lack of economic assistance to Algeria a "political stranglehold" (*LM*, 21 May 1991).

109. FBIS, *NES*, 20 May 1991, 3. See also *LM*, 17 May 1991.

110. *Economist*, 9 June 1991, 43.

111. *LM*, 8 June 1991.

112. R. Mortimer, "Islamists, Soldiers, and Democrats," 19. Abdelhamid

Brahimi, the former Algerian prime minister, claimed that General Larbi Belkheir met with French officials at the Elysée Palace in June 1991 when the decision was made to jail Madani and Belhadj ("Algeria's Rulers").

113. *NYT,* 21 October 1991.

114. *LM,* 1 November 1991.

115. French memory was also stirred by the documentary *La Guerre sans nom* by Bertrand Tavernier and Patrick Rotman, which was screened in February 1992 (see chapter 10).

116. In comparison with the 1990 elections, the FIS lost more than a million votes. It really received only 24 percent of the vote cast by registered citizens (see *Maghreb-Machrek* 135 [January–March 1992]: 154–65, and R. Mortimer, "Islamists, Soldiers, and Democrats," 25–26).

117. *BG,* 29 December 1991.

118. *Financial Times,* 8 January 1992.

119. *E-M,* 9 January 1992.

120. *LM,* 7 January 1992.

121. AFP, 28 December 1991.

122. *LM,* 30 December 1991. The FIS had already disclosed dangerous fissures between moderate and more radical factions within its ruling Majlis Shura. After Madani's arrest, Shaykh Mohammad Iman of the FIS claimed that Madani had created a "personality cult" (*CSM,* 1 July 1991). John Entelis, one of the few analysts who forecast turmoil if elections were suspended, presents a more sympathetic view of FIS moderation as compared with other international Islamist organizations in "Islam, Democracy, and the State: The Reemergence of Authoritarian Politics in Algeria," in Ruedy, *Islamism and Secularism,* 219–51. Leveau compared the FIS's rhetoric with that of the Third Republic's Radical-Socialists, and said the FIS understood its "limits" in Algeria's political environment (*Le Sabre et le turban,* 135).

123. *L'Express* (international), 17 January 1992, 20.

124. R. Mortimer, "Islamists, Soldiers, and Democrats," 20. Mortimer points out that "certain of its officers enjoyed lucrative import licenses or access to tidy commissions on state contracts" (ibid.). This was a far cry from the ALN in the *bled* in the 1950s. Khaled Nezzar and Abdelmalek Guenaizia, two of the leading generals, began their careers in the French army (22). Rémy Leveau wrote: "The army . . . remains one of the most Frenchified [*francisés*] sections in the Algerian system" (*Le Sabre et le turban,* 146).

125. Rémy Leveau wrote that there had been "discreet" discussions between the FIS and the president (*Le Sabre et le turban,* 148).

126. *NYT,* 12 January 1992; see also *LM,* 14 January 1992.

127. Friend, *The Long Presidency,* 245, citing his interview with Jean Audibert, 17 May 1996; Védrine, *Les Mondes de François Mitterrand,* 685–86.

128. Daguzan, "Rapports franco-algériens," 893–94.

129. FBIS, *WEU,* 13 January 1992, 8.

130. AFP, 12 January 1992.

131. *LM,* 15 January 1992.

132. See *BG,* 15 January 1992; *NYT,* 15 January 1992; *LM,* 14–15 January 1992; AFP, 26 January 1992. *LM* printed the Benjedid statement on 14 January. Ex-prime minister Abdelhamid Brahimi declared that "Mitterrand is not innocent of what happened since the early 1990s and the January coup itself" ("Algeria's Rulers").

133. *LM,* 28 January 1992.

134. *CSM,* 21 January 1992; *LM,* 21 January 1998. This provoked the recall of Algeria's ambassador to France, Smail Hamdani, for consultations.

135. *LM,* 22–23 March 1992.

136. Rashid Messaoudi, "Algerian-French Relations: 1830–1991," in Shah-Kazemi, *Algeria: Revolution Revisited,* 32, citing Moussa Ait-Embarek, *L'Algérie en murmure: Un cahier sur la torture en Algérie* (Plan-les-Ouates, Switzerland: Hoggar, 1996), 121.

137. *BG,* 21 January 1992. Algeria had received nuclear technology, too, from Argentina (*CSM,* 8 June 1989).

Chapter 8. The *Fitna,* 1992–1994: From the Annulment of the Parliamentary Elections to the Air France Hijacking

1. Kramer, *Does France Still Count?* 26. After the Cold War, Kramer states, France perceived it "had to trade sovereignty for influence," and he acknowledges that this was "one of the major accomplishments of the rethinking of French policy" (101).

2. According to one former French foreign minister, Europe could be "a means" serving French interests (Stanley Hoffmann, "French Dilemmas and Strategies in the New Europe," in Keohane, Nye, and Hoffmann, *After the Cold War,* 129).

3. *LM,* 29 August 1997.

4. This is a theme in Provost, *Seconde Guerre.*

5. FBIS, *NES,* 19 February 1992, 14. Brahimi articulated these ideas on 7 February 1992.

6. "France's Poisoned Chalice," *U.S. News & World Report,* 9 January 1995, on proquest.umi.com.

7. *LM,* 15 January 1992. A few days later, Hachani declared prophetically: "If this junta goes too far, it will be impossible for us to keep the people under control" (*NYT,* 20 January 1992). According to one report, the FIS had reassured France that its interests would be safeguarded in the event of a FIS election victory (FBIS, *NES,* 22 January 1992, 13). Another interpretation was that the establishment of the HCE illustrated that France "no longer has any influence in the political arena" (FBIS, *NES,* 22 January 1992, 11).

8. *LM,* 15 January 1992.

9. See R. Mortimer, "Algeria: The Dialectic."

10. *BG,* 9 February 1992.

11. See his press conference of 16 February (*E-M*, 17 February 1992). In an interview with a French journal, Boudiaf expressed his belief that Algeria had "escaped from an Islamist dictatorship" (*E-M*, 28–29 February 1992).

12. *BG*, 5 March 1992.

13. See *E-M*, 17 February 1992. In June the government eliminated price controls, in part to attract IMF support. Inefficient state companies and foreign debt particularly affected the national budget. Subsidies had already been lifted, though there would still be some government price support for bread, milk, and semolina (couscous) (AFP, 22 June 1992, on lexis-nexis.com).

14. *E-M*, 23 April 1992.

15. FBIS, *NES*, 18 February 1992, 13. For example, after the FIS was banned, France provided a haven for its leaders and adherents, including Shaykh Abdelbaki Sahraoui, an FIS founder.

16. *LM*, 28 January 1992.

17. AFP, 27 February, 5 March 1992; French finance minister Pierre Bérégovoy and foreign minister Roland Dumas were particularly active in official circles with their American counterparts, Nicholas Brady and James Baker, to help persuade American banks to support refinancing (*MEED*, 13 March 1992, 9). At this time, Algeria allotted 75 percent of its hard-currency earnings to servicing the debt. Abdelhamid Brahimi, the former prime minister, claimed that the debt equated with the amount embezzled by Algerian officials since 1962 (see Provost, *Seconde Guerre*, 41).

18. FBIS, *WEU*, 5 March 1992, 16; AFP, 5 March 1992.

19. *LM*, 9 June 1992.

20. *CR*, no. 3 (1992): 23. COFACE had "virtually frozen all commitments to Algerian contracts" (*Le Figaro*, 3 January 1992).

21. Stone, *The Agony of Algeria*, 108. Boudiaf's speech of 22 April underscored his intention to end corruption in the country. Subsequently, the anniversary of his death saw commemorative demonstrations that protested the continuing violence and received considerable regional and international attention (see *al-Sharq al-Awsat*, 29 and June 1993). According to many observers, the Islamist insurgency was used to mask intra-elite murders. Fatiha Boudiaf, the widow of the assassinated president, blamed a "political-financial mafia" for his death and was "absolutely certain that it did not involve Islamists" (*LM*, 19 July 1998).

22. This appointment left Ghozali on the periphery of Algerian politics. Several months later he commented that 90 percent of the Algerian people disapproved of the regime. Not surprisingly, he was removed from office in December (BBC Summary of World Broadcasts, 4 December 1993, on lexis-nexis.com).

23. Goytisolo, *L'Algérie dans la tourmente*, 45,

24. On 9 August, the offices of *Le Matin, La Nation*, and *al-Djezair al-youm* (Algeria Today) were temporarily closed (until 7 October).

25. See *LM*, 12 and 14 January 1993.

26. Reuters Library Report, 8 January 1993, on lexis-nexis.com.

27. *LM,* 10–11 January 1993; FBIS, *NES,* 11 January 1993, 9.

28. *LM,* 12 January 1993. Mitterrand also informed Kafi that "in the delicate transition phase it is going through, Algeria can count on the support of France and the French" (AFP, 16 February 1993).

29. The financial arrangements are detailed in *LM,* 16 February 1993, and *MEED,* 26 February 1993, 19. The *MEED* also reported that Algeria sought to persuade COFACE to raise its credit ceiling. The French official insurance agency dropped it from FF 2 billion in 1992 to 1 billion in 1993, a telling assessment of Algeria's domestic situation (*MEED,* 12 February 1993, 17). On the other hand, the CFD awarded FF 160 million in loan commitments, primarily to Algerian industry, during 1992, the first year the CFD had account autonomy. Before that, the CCCE/CFD's chief responsibility was providing, supervising, and monitoring technical cooperation projects and treasury loans for the Ministry of Foreign Affairs (*MEED,* 26 March 1993, 19). The *MEED* calculated the debt to France at $4.2 billion on 22 January 1993 (*MEED,* 12 February 1993, 17).

30. FBIS, *WEU,* 19 February 1993, 28.

31. The chief categories of French exports in 1992 were capital goods (FF 3 billion), agro-industrial products (FF 2 billion), consumer goods (FF 2 billion), and automobiles and parts (FF 2.1 billion) (*MEED,* 9 April 1995, 15).

32. *MEED,* 15 November 1993.

33. *LM,* 21–22 February 1993.

34. *E-M,* 19–20 February 1993.

35. Daniel Martinez, "Relations with Algeria Back to Normal Says French Official," Inter Press Service, 18 February 1993, on lexis-nexis.com.

36. *El-Watan,* 21 February 1993.

37. Djaout penned and lived the poem "Silence is death / and you, if you silence yourself / you die / and if you speak / you die / so speak and die," referred to in numerous works; see Goytisolo, *L'Algérie dan la tourmente,* 100.

38. Culpability for this murderous operation remains uncertain even after claims of responsibility by Islamist extremists of the GIA; see, for example, *El-Watan,* 28 October 1993. Merbah had acquired many enemies over the decades through his activities in domestic intelligence. Indeed, Pouvoir agents reportedly infiltrated Islamist groups.

39. *LM,* 21 June 1993; *MEED,* 2 July 1993, 25.

40. *LM,* 19 August 1993. In another interview, Juppé explained that he meant the economic "status quo" needed to be changed and reformed (*LM,* 2 September 1993).

41. *NYT,* 12 May 1993.

42. This began a harrowing cycle of violence against foreigners. On 16 October two Russian military instructors were killed in Laghaout. Subsequently three engineers working for the Italian company Sadelmi were kidnapped in Tiaret and discovered thirty miles away with their throats slit.

43. AFP, 26 October 1993. AFP reported on 5 November that a thousand civil servants, including four hundred teachers, were told to repatriate their families.

44. *NYT*, 27 October 1993; FBIS, *WEU*, 5 November 1993, 39. Foreign hydro-carbon firms, including ENI, Total (CFP), BP, Occidental Petroleum, and Anadarko repatriated personnel. Employees of other European firms like Siemens and Mercedes-Benz left as well (AFP, 25 October 1993). On 2 November Redha Malek stated: "It is not normal for a great state to change its diplomacy when some of its nationals have been attacked" (*MEED*, 8 November 1993).

45. United Press International, 28 October 1993, on lexis-nexis.com).

46. FBIS, *WEU*, 5 November 1993, 38. A raid by Algerian security forces rescued the men and resulted in six deaths. Indeed, the effectiveness of the opera-tion itself was called in question. French and British media asked if the French government had in some way intervened. The hostages did not recount their expe-riences and Monsieur Thévenot was perceived as a "military man" (*Times* [Lon-don], 3 November 1993). AFP reported that the two Frenchmen were found in a prayer hall at Oued Koreiche, near the Defense Ministry, and Madame Thévenot was left twenty-four hours later by her kidnappers near the French embassy. She called the ambassador and was picked up (AFP, 1 November 1993). AFP reported the note's contents as: "Leave the country. We give you one month. Anybody remaining after that date will be to blame for their own sudden death. There will be no kidnapping and it will be more violent than in Egypt" (AFP, 3 November 1993).

47. On 19 November the GIA also threatened other Islamist parties who pur-sued dialogues with the Pouvoir. The GIA receives insightful interpretation in Martinez, *La Guerre civile*.

48. FBIS, *WEU*, 8 November 1993, 41.

49. FBIS, *WEU*, 24 November 1993, 30. Violence in Tourcoing, near Lille, between North African youth and the police after the shooting death of an Alge-rian youth in April illustrated the pent-up frustration of the Maghribi community (*al-Sharq al-Awsat*, 11 April 1993).

50. FBIS, *WEU*, 24 November 1993, 30.

51. *NYT*, 10 November 1993. The next day eight-five of the detainees were released.

52. FBIS, *NES*, 16 November 1993, 14.

53. FBIS, *WEU*, 7 December 1993, 22–24, from interview in *LM*, 17 Novem-ber 1993. Pasqua was reported to have close dealings with the Algerian secret services (Provost, *Seconde Guerre*, 41).

54. FBIS, *WEU*, 9 December 1993, 34–35.

55. FBIS, *WEU*, 6 December 1993, 48.

56. FBIS, *WEU*, 17 December 1993, 38.

57. FBIS, *WEU*, 20 December 1993, 29.

58. *LM*, 24 December 1993.

59. FBIS, *WEU*, 22 November 1993, 31.

60. *NYT*, 16 December 1993.

61. *Milwaukee Journal*, 19 December 1993.

62. *Mideast Mirror* 7, no. 224 (1993), citing *al-Hayat*. Secret trips to Paris by

Redha Malek and his interior minister Salim Saadi were also reported in *al-Sharq al-Awsat,* 16 November 1993.

63. *El-Watan,* 8 February 1994. With the GIA using tactics reminiscent of the ALN, such as attacking infrastructure and schools, Abdenour Ali Yahya, a human rights activist, pointed out the elliptical nature of the *fitna:* "The regime will have to retreat, to release the FIS leaders, to talk—just as the French did in the end" (*Guardian Weekly,* 6 February 1994).

64. *NYT,* 10 August 1994. Eight parties were officially invited: the FLN, MDA, PRA, FFS, RCD, the communists' Mouvement Ettahaddi, HAMAS, and MRI (Mouvement pour la Renaissance Islamique)-Ennahda. The FIS was not invited. Indeed, at this time Ali Belhadj was providing moral support for Islamist forces calling for the boycott of French products and schools (*LM,* 23 August 1994). HAMAS eventually took five seats in the two-hundred-member council.

65. *LM,* 6 September 1994.

66. *LM,* 16 September 1994.

67. One analyst suggested that twenty thousand members of the Algerian army had joined the Islamist cause (*CSM,* 26 April 1994). Another prison revolt occurred in November at the Berouaghia jail south of Algiers.

68. *NYT,* 31 March 1994.

69. *Reuters,* 6 January 1994.

70. *El-Watan,* 28 February 1994.

71. *al-Sharq al-Awsat,* 4 February 1994.

72. AFP, 23 March 1994.

73. The three-hundred-pupil Lycée Descartes in Algiers would remain open. Closures included one school in Annaba, two in Oran, and three in Algiers. These schools served only foreign students, since Algerians were not allowed to enroll after 1988 (Reuters, 31 March 1994).

74. There were also problems about pensions for *coopérants* who had worked under Algerian auspices (*LM,* 14 January 1995).

75. AFP, 9 May 1994. The FIS would organize veterans of the Mouvement Islamique Armé of the Bouyali years into a FIS military organization known as the Islamic Salvation Army (Armée Islamique du Salut, or AIS) in July. The GIA favored attacks against foreigners, while the AIS did not. The AIS also supported dialogue. Their disputes led to intra-Islamist violence (M. Willis, *The Islamist Challenge,* 350–53).

76. See *NYT,* 14 February 1994. Danielle Mitterrand, France's activist first lady, announced her resignation from the National Consultative Commission on Human Rights on 10 March in protest of the commission's passivity before the increasingly hard position and restrictive legislation taken by the Balladur government against the immigrants.

77. FBIS, *WEU,* 20 April 1994, 30.

78. *NYT,* 7 April 1994.

79. FBIS, *WEU,* 7 March 1994, 23.

80. FBIS, *WEU*, 25 March 1994, 19.

81. *LM*, 12 April 1994. The dinar was rapidly losing value, from 8.90/$ in 1990 to 35.06/$ in 1994.

82. *WSJ*, 12 January 1995. At this time Algeria was having great difficulties, in part because of depressed oil prices and delayed repayments. France held 18 percent of the debt (*African Economic Digest,* 14 March 1994, 16).

83. See *al-Sharq al-Awsat,* 9 April and 5 July 1994.

84. AFP, 2 June 1994.

85. *MEED*, 18 July 1994; Jon Marks, "The View from Paris," *MEED*, 27 June 1994.

86. FBIS, *NES*, 4 May 1994, 26. *Al-Hayat* (London) even reported a quadrilateral secret discussion in June among France, the United States, the Algerian government, and the FIS in an effort to end the violence and construct the conditions for a possible coalition government (Compass Newswire, 14 June 1994, on lexis-nexis.com).

87. FBIS, *WEU*, 11 May 1994, 16.

88. FBIS, *NES*, 24 May 1994, 15.

89. FBIS, *WEU*, 29 June 1994, 27.

90. *LM*, 8 July 1994.

91. AFP, 14 July 1994; *LM*, 16 July 1994.

92. FBIS, *WEU*, 4 August 1994, 4; see also *LM*, 5 August 1994. Apparently, to reinforce the anti-France campaign, Yasmina Drici, a teacher of French, was killed by extremists several weeks before in Rouiba.

93. From 500 in November, there were now about 200 teachers, diplomats, and consular officials. "Short-term expatriates" fell from 8,000 to 1,000 (AFP, 24 August 1994). This did not include 75,000 Algerians who also had French citizenship dating from independence. A French national who had opted for Algerian citizenship, René Bouhanna, a Jew, was shot and killed on 25 August.

94. Italy had already reduced its diplomatic staff after the gruesome deaths on 6–7 July of seven Italian sailors who slept aboard their ship at Djedjen, east of Algiers, and a shoot-out in front of the embassy on 12 July.

95. AFP, 11 August 1994.

96. FBIS, *NES*, 5 August 1994, 7–8. While praising American "realism" contrasted with French policy, Haddam still asserted: "Yes, we do want to establish an Islamic state, but not at the expense of good neighborly relations with France" (*Mideast Mirror* 8, no. 153 [1994]).

97. FBIS, *WEU*, 5 August 1994, 17. The United States's position toward the *fitna* was a consistent call for dialogue among the parties, including the FIS. This had created friction between Paris and Washington. The French were also worried about a greater American influence in Algeria, especially in the hydrocarbons sector. Besides the United States and Germany, the United Kingdom was also singled out (*LM*, 13 August 1994).

98. FBIS, *WEU*, 12 August 1994, 9.

99. *NYT,* 10 August 1994. Though *LM* reported that the majority of Muslims in France were moderates, a concurrent headline read "French Islam Is Radicalizing" (12 August 1994).

100. AFP, 1 September 1994; *LM,* 2 September 1994.

101. *El-Watan,* 11 August 1994. Aslaoui's husband would be stabbed to death by intruders in October.

102. AFP, 6 August 1994.

103. AFP, 9 August 1994.

104. FBIS, *WEU,* 15 August 1994, 18–19.

105. FBIS, *WEU,* 1 September 1994, 23.

106. FBIS, *WEU,* 12 September 1994, 28.

107. FBIS, *WEU,* 19 September 1994, 22.

108. FBIS, *WEU,* 8 August 1994, 26.

109. FBIS, *NES,* 9 August 1994, 17.

110. FBIS, *WEU,* 9 August 1994, 37.

111. AFP, 12 August 1994.

112. AFP, 27 August 1994.

113. *NYT,* 1 October 1994.

114. AFP, 3 October 1994.

115. *al-Sharq al-Awsat,* 10 October 1994.

116. AFP, 11 October 1994. It was estimated that by 1 October twelve thousand French citizens were left in the country, of whom ten thousand held dual nationality.

117. *MEED,* 14 November 1994.

118. *al-Sharq al-Awsat,* 10 October 1994.

119. AFP, 25 October 1994; *LM,* 15 OCtober 1994. Benjamin Stora saw France's tough exterior while seeking a negotiated resolution as reminiscent of de Gaulle's decolonizing policy. Pasqua regarded de Gaulle as a political mentor (Reuters, 11 August 1994).

120. AFP, 11 December 1994.

121. After discussions beginning in December 1993, an agreement was signed in April 1994. Pasqua explained its terms in a memo to police prefects that was circulated in July.

122. FBIS, *WEU,* 7 November 1994, 21–22. The number of visas issued to Algerians had dropped drastically, leaving many students and workers stranded in Algeria. The French consulate in Algiers had issued 800 visas daily, but by the end of March the consulates in Oran, Annaba, and Algiers collectively distributed only 400 (*LM,* 8 April 1994). In August the Quai d'Orsay announced that decisions on visa applications would be centralized in Nantes. Benjamin Stora related that Algerians regarded this as the "closing . . . of [France's] Mediterranean border" (*L'Algérie en 1995,* 97). In all of 1994 only about 100,000 visas were issued, compared with 800,000 in 1989. (*LM,* 5 June 1996).

123. *NYT,* 9 November 1994. In an interview Pasqua had expressed frustra-

tion: "Where does the FIS stop, the AIS or GIA begin?" (*LM*, 15 October 1994).

124. Included was Mohamed Chalabi, a thirty-nine-year-old Algerian who was a senior figure in the pro-GIA network.

125. A poll among Muslims in France found two-thirds opposing the FIS. When differentiated by nationality, Algerians expressed a corresponding anti-FIS position (*LM*, 13 October 1994).

126. FBIS, *NES*, 28 November 1996, 17, citing *al-Hayat*, 24 November 1994.

127. FBIS, *WEU*, 16 December 1994, 19; *MEED*, 2 December 1994, 26). According to *MEED*, COFACE was now reluctant to provide insurance coverage for French personnel in Algeria.

128. On 13–14 November, an Air Algérie flight had been hijacked to Majorca, Spain. There were no injuries.

129. France was chiefly interested in having the hostages released. The Algerian government seemed to be preparing some type of assault, in part to demonstrate its political and military will against the Islamist insurgency. Bilateral cooperation was missing, leaving Juppé "irritated" (*LM*, 27 December 1994).

130. *NYT*, 26 December 1994. See also *LM*, 27 December 1994.

131. *NYT*, 27 December 1994.

132. AFP, 29 December 1994.

133. AFP, 31 December 1994.

134. *NYT*, 28 December 1994. See also *LM*, 27 December 1994.

135. AFP, 4 January 1995. The French were very critical of Algerian airport security, especially how easy it was for the GIA to mount their operation (*LM*, 29 December 1994).

136. FBIS, *WEU*, 3 January 1995, 28; *NYT*, 5 January 1998; *MEED*, 13 January 1995, citing GIA statement of 3 January 1995.

137. *WSJ*, 31 October 1994.

Chapter 9. The *Fitna*, 1995–1998: From the Sant'Egidio Agreement

1. AFP, 4 January 1995.

2. A translation (from *Mideast Mirror*) is provided in Pierre and Quandt, *The Algerian Crisis*, 59–63. The Platform also appeared in *LMdipl*, March 1995, and *AAN* 1995, 553–55.

3. John P. Entelis, "Political Islam in the Maghreb: The Nonviolent Dimension," in Entelis, *Islam, Democracy, and the State in North Africa*, 68–69.

4. AFP, 13 January 1995. Writing in the London-based *al-'Arab*, Ali Aouhida contended that Interior Minister Charles Pasqua had been "isolated" within the cabinet as the French government appeared to head toward dialogue rather than confrontation with Islamists (*Mideast Mirror* 9, no. 17 [1995]).

5. *NYT*, 16 January 1995.

6. *NYT*, 23 January 1995. By the end of the year, the FIS and the GIA would be feuding. The GIA began assaults on ex-FIS leaders, including the execution of Muhammad Sa'id and Abdel Razak Redjam on 17 December 1995.

7. FBIS, *NES,* 9 January 1995, cited in Migdalovitz, "Algeria: Four Years of Crisis," 6.

8. AFP, 26 January 1995. For a timely article on the internal politics of the Pouvoir and the political "invisibility" but real influence of the military, see the Information Access Company, IAC Newsletter Database, Arab Press Service Organization, *APS Diplomat Operations In Oil Diplomacy* 29, no. 1 (1995), on lexis-nexis.com. This includes analyses of key generals in and out of the Algerian government. Among the most important at this time were Lieutenant-General Mohammed Lamari, a fervent eradicationist, and retired general Mohammed Betchine, who shared President Zeroual's more conciliatory views. Both generals reportedly met with Madani and Belhadj in the failed effort to create a genuine dialogue.

9. *Mideast Mirror* 9, no. 17 (1995), citing *al-Sharq al-Awsat,* 25 January 1995.

10. *NYT,* 6 February 1995.

11. See *NYT,* 2 February 1995; *CSM,* 24 March 1995.

12. *NYT,* 4 May 1995. On violence against women, see also *NYT,* 15 March 1995.

13. *NYT,* 31 March 1995.

14. *Times* (London), 23 January 1995. One French official tried to explain the French attitude toward Algeria in comparative terms: How would the United States react if Mexico became communist, threatening an anxious California with mass immigration? (*International Herald Tribune,* 24 January 1995).

15. Brahimi, "Algeria's Rulers."

16. AFP, 4 February 1995. The FIS's Anouar Haddam supported the proposal as "a good sign."

17. AFP, 5 February 1995. France was shifting toward an American position. Frustrated and fearful over the Algerian situation, French military personnel shared contingency plans for evacuation of foreign populations and security strategies concerning the vital oil and gas fields (*San Francisco Examiner,* 22 March 1995). Former president Jimmy Carter expressed interest in going to Algeria (*al-Sharq al-Awsat,* 25 March 1995).

18. AFP, 4 February 1995.

19. AFP, 6 February 1995.

20. AFP, 7 February 1995.

21. AFP, 13 February 1995.

22. AFP, 9 March 1998. The French Foreign Ministry had stated that French "supplies are very modest, and mainly consist of protection and communication equipment." This included "a certain number" of civilian helicopters (ibid.).

23. *NYT,* 29 April, 1998. This was part of France's general retrenchment in Africa, e.g., the floating of the CFA. France also championed francophone African states before international financial bodies. The paring of French aid was, of course, in preparation for monetary union in Europe.

24. *CSM,* 21 April 1995.

25. For example, only 103,000 tourist visas (for three-month sojourns) were issued to Algerians in 1994, down from 572,000 in 1987 (*LM*, 5 April 1996); see also chapter 8. More than 200,000 Algerians sought to enter France as political refugees, but only sixteen received permission (*LM*, 5 June 1996). Also, the Pasqua Law of 1993 had broadened the power to expel emigrants who had committed crimes, including emigrant parents of French children and spouses of French citizens who committed crimes punishable by five years in prison. Amnesty International criticized the French policy of expulsions to Algeria and asked for a moratorium (*LM*, 29 October 1998).

26. *Guardian*, 19 April 1995.

27. FBIS, *WEU*, 11 April 1995, 25.

28. *NYT*, 21 October 1995.

29. *NYT*, 31 October 1995.

30. AFP, 26 April 1995.

31. *CSM*, 28 June 1995.

32. *CSM*, 13 April 1995.

33. AFP, 20 June 1995. Air Algérie continued to provide service at Marseille, Lyon, and Toulouse.

34. AFP, 12 July 1995; *LM*, 13 July 1995. Shaykh Sahraoui was also admired by Charles Pasqua for his moderation. Moussa Kraouche, the head of the FAF (associated with the FIS), was placed under close police surveillance owing to perceived threats against him.

35. AFP, 11 July 1995.

36. AFP, 30 August 1995. Also in late August, the Ministry of the Interior banned the distribution of a Swiss-published work entitled *A Report on Repression in Algeria (1991–1994)* which gave the Islamist position on the *fitna* (AFP, 13 September 1995). The Juppé government also implemented the Vigipirate Plan, used during the Gulf War of 1991, to deploy French troops at strategic centers.

37. *NYT*, 5 September 1995.

38. *LM*, 12 September 1995.

39. Viorst, "Muslims of France," 90. See also *LM*, 13 September and 3 and 13 October 1995.

40. Viorst, "Muslims of France," 91.

41. *NYT*, 7 September 1995.

42. Ibid.

43. AFP, 7 and 17 October 1995.

44. *NYT*, 18 October 1995.

45. *LM*, 24 October 1995.

46. *Milwaukee Journal Sentinel*, 3 November 1995.

47. AFP, 4 September 1995.

48. *Mideast Mirror* 9, no. 201 (1995); see also *LM*, 19 October and 11 November 1997. The GIA publication *al-Jama'a* catalogued the organization's violent operations in France. Curiously, the GIA did not claim some of the bombings,

notably the suspected Kelkal operation against the TGV and the bombings of 3, 4, and 7 September, while it assumed responsibility for some events that authorities had not associated with political Islamism (*LM*, 19 April 1997).

49. *Mideast Mirror* 9, no. 201 (1995); *San Francisco Chronicle*, 19 October 1995, on proquest.umi.com.

50. FBIS, *NES*, 30 October 1995, 28.

51. See *LM*, 28 October 1995. Chirac would have preferred a "working session."

52. AFP, 22 October 1995; *LM*, 24 October 1995.

53. AFP, 23 October 1995. The *Independent* reported an Algerian woman's reaction: "When Zeroual gave a slap to Jacques Chirac[,] it was like Dey Hussein slapping the face of the French consul in 1827" (*Independent* [London], 20 November 1995). The exasperated dey had slapped the consul with a fly whisk.

54. AFP, 24 October 1995. *El-Watan* quoted "sources close to official circles" as saying "French aid never existed" since it was allocated for specific purchases benefiting French interests (24 October 1995).

55. *Mideast Mirror* 9, no. 205 (1995), citing *al-Sharq al-Awsat*, 24 October 1995.

56. AFP, 23 October 1995. There was also contention over who had wanted the summit. De Charette said that Algeria had requested the summit on 28 August. But President Zeroual's spokesman, the veteran diplomat Mihoubi el-Mihoub, said de Charette suggested in July to Mohamed Saleh Dembri, the Algerian foreign minister, that the two presidents confer (*Mideast Mirror* 9, no. 205; *LM*, 24 October 1995).

57. AFP, 23 October 1995. For other French political reaction, see *LM*, 24 October 1995. For example, Claude Cheysson thought the summit was from the start poorly planned.

58. AFP, 26 October 1995; *LM*, 28 October 1995. Concerning the Algerian presidential candidates, Chirac stated that "our preference" was Algeria's progress toward democracy (*LM*, 28 October 1995).

59. AFP, 28 October 1995; *LM*, 28 October 1995.

60. AFP, 27 October 1995.

61. *LM*, 13 and 14 November 1995.

62. *CSM*, 4 December 1995, 30 January 1996.

63. FBIS, *WEU*, 20 November 1995, 17.

64. *CSM*, 28 December 1995.

65. *NYT*, 28 November 1995. HAMAS and the PRA were given a voice in the new government. A dissident ex-FIS member, Ahmed Merrani, was appointed minister of religious affairs.

66. FBIS, *NES*, 20 November 1995, 23.

67. M. Willis, *The Islamist Challenge*, 364.

68. AFP, 3 December 1995. The *Independent* noted paradoxes in the bilateral relationship. The summit fiasco had considerably chilled relations, but General Christian Quesnot, a classmate and friend of Zeroual's in the mid-1970s when

both pursued military studies in Paris, was a military adviser to Chirac; also, Charles Pasqua, a political opponent of Chirac within the right, was again "a welcome visitor at the Elysée Palace" (*Independent* [London], 20 November 1995). The bombings in France forced closer cooperation between the two countries' intelligence agencies including "a highly discreet trip to France" by General Mediene, head of Algeria's Département de Recherche et Sécurité. Algeria also was interested in the "surveillance potential" of France's Helios-1 military satellite, launched in July 1995 (*Intelligence Newsletter,* 21 December 1995, on lexis-nexis.com). Messages were passed between the presidents in December. Philippe Séguin, president of the National Assembly, delivered Chirac's in an unexpected visit to Algiers. Séguin said after meeting with Zeroual that "Algeria and France must cooperate, listen, and talk to each other" (*LM,* 22 December 1995; Compass Media, 12 January 1996, on lexis-nexis.com).

69. FBIS, *NES,* 11 December 1995, 14.

70. AFP, 13 January 1996; Reuters, 11 January 1996. In February Denis Bauchard of the Foreign Ministry also paid a visit, according to *al-Sharq al-Awsat* (Compass Media, 16 February 1996).

71. At this time there were 23,000 Catholics in Algeria, including 136 priests and 210 nuns (*Washington Times,* 7 August 1996).

72. AFP, 24 March 1994; *LM,* 25 and 27 May 1996. *Al-Hayat* ran a story suggesting that the monks were victims of intra-Islamist rivalries. According to one report, they had supported the AIS against the GIA. The GIA was also torn concerning the prisoner exchange. "Emir" Zitouni regarded the monks as "foreign agents and spies" (FBIS, *NES,* 30 May 1996, 14). *El-Watan* reported an intra-GIA fratricide on 2 May. M. Basil Pennington recounted that the GIA had asked for the monks' cooperation during a visit on Christmas Eve 1993. They refused to take sides or accept protection from the Algerian authorities (Pennington, "Cistercian Martyrs," 605–606).

73. AFP, 26 May 1996.

74. AFP, 28 May 1996. Another GIA-related report was that an emissary from Djamel Zitouni was met at the French Embassy and later dropped off in downtown Algiers (in the Hussein Dey section, a stronghold of Islamists). The GIA claimed that "the monks were killed because of the French betrayal." The French denied there was a negotiation (Reuters, 20–21 June 1996).

75. Reuters, 29 May 1996; see also *LM,* 27, 29, and 30 May and 8 and 10 June 1996, for more on the monks' lives and martyrdom. *Le Monde* was particularly critical. While acknowledging that non-negotiation was the standard procedure in terrorist kidnappings, it also asked whether France was too tentative in this case in order not to upset Algerian sensibilities. The editorial cited this tragedy as another situation which "conceals a mélange of a bad conscience and a powerlessness toward Algeria which all French governments have shared since independence" (*LM,* 29 May 1996). Father Christian's Testament is published in its entirety in Pennington, "Cistercian Martyrs," 607–608.

76. AFP, 31 July 1996.

77. AFP, 1 August 1996; see also Attaf's interview with *al-Sharq al-Awsat,* as cited by FBIS, *NES,* 4 October 1996, on wnc.fedworld.gov.

78. *CSM,* 5 August 1996.

79. AFP, 2 August 1996. Pope John Paul II also paid tribute to Bishop Claverie and said Algeria "more than ever needs acts of peace and fraternity" (AFP, 5 August 1996).

80. *MEED,* 12 August 1996. COFACE was particularly anxious about further investments and risks in Algeria. In a published report it called Algeria's civil war "a social, economic, and political catastrophe" and warned of serious risks in the medium term. It recognized that, while divisions within "the terrorist camp" did not threaten to overturn the Algerian government, they still posed a security threat that would continue. It also worried about divisions within the government (*LM,* 19 January 1998).

81. *LM,* 26 December 1996.

82. *LM,* 5 December 1996. Rabah Kebir denounced it as a "criminal act, which we reject because it is an act against innocent people" (FBIS, *WEU,* citing France-2 television program, 4 December 1996). Meanwhile in the United States, Anouar Haddam was arrested on 11 December for violating American immigration laws after his request for political asylum was rejected.

83. AFP, 24 December 1996; *LM,* 25 and 26 December 1996. The GIA also reportedly called for the release of prisoners notably including Abdelhak Layada, a former GIA leader and founder who was arrested in Morocco in March 1993 and extradited to Algeria. The Pouvoir had hoped Layada could mediate the Air France hijacking in December while the Airbus was still in Algiers. In March 1995 he failed to mediate a prison uprising where he was being held; security forces subsequently killed a hundred inmates (*Mideast Mirror* 10, no. 243 [1996], citing *al-Sharq al-Awsat,* 12 December 1996).

84. AFP, 5 January 1997; *LM,* 7 January 1997.

85. *LM,* 27–28 January 1997. Zeroual's strong tone seemed to suggest that, for the moment, the eradicators had displaced the conciliators within the Pouvoir. This could also have signaled Zeroual's own frustration after repeated efforts, albeit on the Pouvoir's terms, to establish a dialogue with the Islamists.

86. *LM,* 23 January 1997.

87. AFP, 26 and 31 January 1997; *LM,* 28 January 1997. The Jospin interview appeared in *Libération* on 27 January 1997. At the Socialist Party convention Jospin criticized the French government's "complaisance" with regard to Algeria (*LM,* 10 February 1997).

88. AFP, 27 January 1997. The EU conditioned its transfer of all of its $280 million of allocated aid upon Algerian democratization (*al-Sharq al-Awsat,* 10 February 1997).

89. While Islamists were blamed, the "word on the street" in Algiers was that Benhamouda may have been a victim of one of the Pouvoir's clans (*LM,* 31 January 1997). Francis Ghiles, the veteran *Financial Times* reporter, assessed: "No one who has observed Algeria over the years believes that General Bettagane and Gen-

eral Saidi, both political allies of . . . Zeroual, were murdered by the fundamental-ists. Nor were the head of the trade unions, Abdelhak Benhamouda, or the secre-tary of state for planning, Ali Hamdi, killed by such groups" (*Times Literary Supplement,* 6 February 1998, 36). Benhamouda had agreed to become head of a new presidential party.

90. AFP, 31 January 1997; *LM,* 1 February 1997.

91. AFP, 30 January 1997; *LM,* 1 February 1997.

92. AFP, 30 January 1997; *LM,* 1 February 1997.

93. AFP, 31 January 1997; *El-Watan,* 31 January–1 February 1997; *LM,* 1 February 1997. In an interview with *al-Sharq al-Awsat,* Attaf reiterated that the "conspicuous problem between us and France concerns the efforts to interfere in our internal affairs" (29 March 1997).

94. FBIS, *WEU,* citing Europe No. 1 (Paris) radio interview, 1 February 1997. Giscard's comments about "sensitivity" must have been particularly ironic to Al-gerian political circles, given his 1975 snubbing of Boumedienne's offer of a special bilateral relationship.

95. AFP, 3 February 1997.

96. AFP, 16 March 1997.

97. R. Mortimer, "Algeria: The Dialectic," 234.

98. *LM,* 9 June 1997. The RCD and FFS each received nineteen seats and the Islamist party MRI-Ennahda got thirty-four.

99. Four seats in the new legislature were reserved for the emigrant community (see *LM,* 6 June 1997).

100. *Economist,* 1 November 1997, 46.

101. *MEED,* 9 June 1997.

102. *CSM,* 4 June 1997; *LM,* 3 June 1997. Members of the FIS sent Jospin a congratulatory note (*LM,* 7 June 1997).

103. FBIS, *WEU,* 14 July 1997, citing *Libération,* 12 July 1997.

104. *LM,* 14 July 1997; AFP, 12 July 1997.

105. FBIS, *WEU,* 14 July 1997, citing *Libération,* 12 July 1997.

106. *LM,* 29 August 1997.

107. *LM,* 11 September 1997.

108. *LM,* 16 September 1997.

109. AFP, 30 September 1997.

110. AFP, 2 October 1997.

111. AFP, 3 October 1997.

112. Amnesty International, *Algeria: Civilian Population Caught,* 3.

113. *LM,* 11 November 1997.

114. AFP, 26 November 1997.

115. AFP, 7 December 1997.

116. AFP, 23 December 1997. The horrific violence included repeated atroci-ties in the *wilaya* (province) of Relizane claiming more than five hundred victims within ten days, including many women and children.

117. *NYT,* 8 January 1998.

118. *NYT*, 7 January 1998; *LM*, 7 January 1998; AFP, 5 January 1998.

119. AFP, 6 January 1998. Ambassador Ghoualmi also lamented: "There is an international pressure, unfortunately not on the terrorists but on the Algerian state" (*LM*, 8 January 1998).

120. AFP, 7 January 1998.

121. AFP, 12 January 1998. The United States, the UN High Commissariat for Human Rights, and the European Union called for external intervention.

122. AFP, 16 January 1998.

123. According to Randa Takieddin of *al-Hayat*, Jospin's critical attitude was moderated by the particular influence of Foreign Minster Hubert Védrine and Interior Minister Jean-Pierre Chevènement. Védrine, who had lived in Morocco, argued that though the legislative elections were not completely democratic they still represented an important step. For example, parliamentary debates took place which were often critical of the government. Chevènement, married to an Egyptian, was also well aware of Muslim fundamentalism (*LM*, 19 January 1998; *Mideast Mirror*, 29 April 1998).

124. AFP, 6 February 1998.

125. *LM*, 8 and 9 January 1998. This comment was another example of the historical ellipse. Germaine Tillion wrote during the throes of decolonization: "Many people in France believed (as I did) that throughout this horrible and stupid war the life of a little Algerian shepherd was worth more than all the oil to be found in the Sahara." She then added: "Concerning the extremely conditional value of the oil, the Algerians are still better informed than we are" (*Complementary Enemies*, 180–81).

126. *El-Watan*, 20 January, 30–31 January 1998.

127. *LM*, 6 April 1998. Lang was interviewed by the Algerian newspaper *Saout el Ahrar*.

128. *LM*, 4 February 1998.

129. *LM*, 12 February 1998.

130. *LM*, 20 March 1998.

131. Its membership was composed of Derek Fatchete from the United Kingdom's foreign office, George Wohlfart of Luxembourg, and Benita Ferrero-Waldner of Austria. Manuel Marín, an EU commissioner, also attended. The European Parliament had passed resolutions in April 1995, December 1996, and September 1997 which appealed for "political dialogue and condemnation of terrorism" (Amnesty International, *Algeria: Civilian Population Caught*, 33).

132. *LM*, 19 January 1998. NATO was increasingly concerned with Algeria; Secretary-General Willy Claes claimed Islamism was "at least as dangerous as communism" for the West (*CSM*, 24 February 1998).

133. *LM*, 17 September 1998; see also Reuters, 15 September 1998, and www.waac.org/rep98/UN_mission_report9–16.html. The team was not allowed to talk with Abassi Madani and Ali Belhadj.

134. *NYT*, 17 September 1998.

135. *LM*, 12 November 1998. The reciprocal investments agreement was ratified by the end of the year.

136. World Algeria Action Coalition (WAAC), "Articles and Reports: Lounès Matoub," *North Africa Journal*, on waac.org/rep98/NAJ_matoub.html; *LM*, 27 June 1998.

137. *El-Watan*, 6 July 1998.

138. *LM*, 11 September 1998.

139. The candidates were Ait Ahmed, Hamrouche, Youcef el-Khatib (who had managed Zeroual's campaign in 1995), Taleb Ibrahimi, Sifi, and Abdallah Djaballah. See *Libération*, 15 April 1999.

140. *MEED*, 1 May 1995.

141. *Manchester Guardian Weekly*, citing *Le Monde* section, 22 October 1995.

142. FBIS, *NES*, 3 May 1997, citing AFP, 3 May 1997.

143. See *El-Watan*, 24 October 1995.

144. *CR*, no. 4 (1998): 9.

145. *LM*, 1 February 1997. Algeria's debt-service ratio in 1993 was 80.3 percent. With rescheduling it fell in 1998 to 45.0 percent. The sag in petroleum prices in 1998 and early 1999 slowed but did not stop Algeria's economic recovery.

146. AFP, 30 March 1998; *LM*, 27 March 1998.

147. *European Information Service: Europe Report*, 13 May 1998, on lexis-nexis.com.

148. This was after a May attack on oil company personnel by the GIA resulting in six deaths, including two French. In July petroleum infrastructure was targeted in Blida with no casualties.

149. According to Arthur D. Little, Europe's gas consumption could increase by 55 percent by 2010, placing Algeria in a strategically advantageous position (see *WSJ*, 23 March 1993).

150. *Austin American Statesman*, 19 January 1997, on proquest.umi.com. The United States also approved export credits in August 1996 and rescheduled its Algerian debt of more than a billion dollars in March (*LM*, 23 October 1997).

151. *NYT*, 21 December 1995.

152. *MEED*, "France and the Middle East," 25 October 1996.

153. www.total.com. Production by Total (CFP) in Algeria increased from 5,900 barrels per day in 1991 to 8,600 in 1995. The Algerian fields are rather insignificant compared with the CFP's in Colombia and the North Sea. According to the International Energy Agency: "Tin Fouye Tabenkort is one of the largest undeveloped hydrocarbon fields in Algeria, with recoverable natural gas and liquids estimated at 1 billion barrels equivalent" (OECD, *North Africa Oil and Gas*, 65).

154. *MEED*, 19 August 1996. Kellogg did take over to complete the project begun by the French. The French revamped two of the six liquefaction trains (*MEED*, 19 May 1997).

155. *Maghreb Confidentiel*, 29 October 1998.

156. French "anglophobia" was intensified by the remarkable American-Algerian naval maneuvers. This would have been unthinkable in the pre-*fitna* period (see *LM,* 14 November 1998).

157. In 1996 SONATRACH created three new subsidiaries, specializing in sector strategy, drilling, and infrastructure.

158. *Aberdeen Press and Journal,* 4 May 1998.

159. GDF has developed some partnerships with the national French producers, Total and Elf (privatized in 1994). It does hire out its own highly regarded expertise and has been approached by Russia's Gazprom to take a more active role downstream. See *Oil and Gas Journal,* 30 November 1992, on ovid.com, and *PE,* March and May 1997, from the Dow Jones *News/Retrieval* database.

160. Hydrocarbons are an arena where France still asserts its independence. France has been critical of a "unilateral world" dominated by the United States. It has ignored American protests and concluded several provocative hydrocarbons contracts, such as the $2 billion agreement between Total (CFP) and Iran's National Iranian Oil Company (NIOC) for the production of two billion cubic feet of natural gas from the South Pars field. With gas slated to flow in 2001, the contract also called for Total and its partners to cede control to NIOC in 2002 for compensation in oil. France also announced on 29 September 1997 that it would exploit the Nahr Umar oil field in Iraq when the UN lifted its embargo against Iraq. These French hydrocarbons actions conflicted with the American policy of a "dual containment" of these two nations. Sensitive to criticism, Thierry Desmarest, president of Total, said, "These stories about financing terrorism are absurd." The United States threatened it would invoke the Iran-Libya sanctions act which authorized the president to impose sanctions on any company investing more than $40 million in either country on grounds of abetting terrorism (*NYT,* 30 September 1997).

161. Amnesty International, *Algeria: Civilian Population Caught,* 1. Martin Stone estimated that from 1992 to 1997, 120,000 Algerians perished (*The Agony of Algeria,* 1).

162. *International Herald Tribune,* 24 January 1995. See also their book *The Algerian Crisis: Policy Options for the West.*

163. *El-Watan,* 15 February 1994.

164. R. Mortimer, "Algeria: The Dialectic," 234.

165. Zoubir, "The Algerian Political Crisis," 97.

166. *NYT,* 7 March 1999.

167. *al-Sharq al-Awsat,* 21 April 1995. Cheysson also observed that a "large section" of the population opposed "extremists," the government, and the army. This correlates to the political environment in Algeria today.

168. *CSM,* 21 April 1995.

169. *LM,* 6 September 1995.

Chapter 10. Mirrors and Mirages, 1958–1998: Reflections, Refractions, and Representations

1. Thierry Fabre, "France-Algérie: Questions de mémoire," *AAN* 1990, 353.

2. Provost, *Seconde Guerre,* 107. Provost also applies a mirror metaphor, especially in the context of the *fitna* (107–11). The author's use of it in this chapter considers wider epistemological, ontological, and historical perspectives.

3. Ibid., 192.

4. *LM,* 20 August 1994. Lucile Provost calls Algerian anti-French sentiments the country's "only political culture" (*Seconde Guerre,* 16).

5. "Algérie: trente ans de dérive . . ." *L'Express,* 10 January 1992, 40.

6. Anderson, *Imagined Communities,* 4.

7. Buron considered the Algerians more "Cartesian" than their French counterparts during the Evian discussions ("Aspects de la coopération," 17).

8. See Grimaud, *Politique extérieure,* 42–47. Indeed, a corollary Algerian objective was "to win the esteem of its French partner" (44).

9. Balta and Rulleau, *L'Algérie des Algériens,* 203.

10. The FLN claimed that its revolution was influenced by others, including the French Revolution (Ministère de l'Information, *Qu'est-ce que le Programme de Tripoli?*). According to Tlemcani, there was a "re-activation" of colonial administrative institutions "with only minor changes" (*State and Revolution,* 89–91). Bennoune criticized: "The maintenance of the colonial administrative structures, personnel, laws, regulations and even practices turned out to be detrimental to the development of a public administration at the service of the citizens and the economy" (*Making,* 109–10). Bennoune thought Boumedienne's "construction of a pyramidal and highly centralised state" to be "in the Jacobin tradition" (111). See also Ilya Aboutaki, "Héritage et innovation dans l'administration locale en Algérie: Aliénation, intériorisation, pragmatisme," in Ruf, *Indépendance et interdépendances,* 323–39, and sections in Borham Atallah, "L'Acculturation juridique dans le nord de l'Afrique: Le Cas de l'Algérie et de la Libye," *Indépendance et interdépendances,* 162–200. To underscore the "reflective" revolutionary perspective, Ahmed Rouadjia used the French Revolution as an interpretive model in his analysis *Grandeur et décadence de l'état algérien.*

11. Gilbert Grandguillaume argued that for genuine bilateral relations to exist "it is necessary to help Algeria do without France" ("Introduction: Comment a-t-on pu en arriver là?" in Benrabah et al., *Les Violences en Algérie,* 58).

12. *El-Watan,* 23 October 1995.

13. See Said, *Orientalism,* Bhabha, *Location of Culture,* and Loomba, *Colonialism/Postcolonialism.* The degree of Fanon's influence in postcolonial Algeria has been debated. While discussing the nature of Algerian culture (in *RA,* 7 December 1963: 18–19 and 19 December 1963: 22–23), Mostefa Lacheraf perceived Fanon as a European and used such words as "romantic" and "sentimental" to characterize the ideologue (D. Gordon, *Passing,* 131). Though Ian Clegg and Gérard Chaliand were critical of Fanon's perceptions, Irene Gendzier and

Mohammed Harbi maintained that his influence was significant, especially on the ideological bent of the Tripoli Program. Boumedienne read Fanon (Gendzier, *Fanon*, 2d ed., xiv; see also Leca and Vatin, *Algérie*, 250). Fanon was a frequent subject in the journal *al-Thaqafa*. See, for example, Muhammad al-Mili, "Al-Thawrat al-jaza'iriyyat wa Fanun (The Algerian revolution and Fanon)," *al-Thaqafa*, no. 2 (1971): 40–54, comparing Fanon's conclusions in *Black Skin, White Masks* with those written during the Algerian Revolution. An application of Fanon to Algeria is also discussed by Olufemi Taiwo in "On the Misadventures of National Consciousness: A Retrospect on Frantz Fanon's Gift of Prophecy," in Gordon, Sharpley-Whiting, and White, *Fanon: A Critical Reader*, 255–270. Abdelkader Djeghoul considered Fanon a "theoretician" rather than a system maker ("Vingt ans après . . . relire Fanon," *Grand Maghreb*, no. 19 [1983]: 41).

14. "Decolonization and Independence," in *Toward the African Revolution*, 186.

15. Jinadu, *Fanon*, 64.

16. Cheriet, *Opinion*, 59.

17. FBIS, *NES*, 13 August 1997, citing *al-Wasat* (London), 11–17 August 1997.

18. Ahmed Moatassime, "Islam, Arabisation, et Francophonie," in Jurt, *Algérie-France-Islam*, 68, citing the 1993 *Etat de la francophonie dans le monde* (Paris: Documentation Française), 435, and the 1994 *Etat*, 87 ff. Moatassime considers Algerians to be in actuality *"francarabisée"* (67). *Al-Sharq al-Awsat* ran a series in February 1998 on *francophonie* in the Arab World and featured Algeria in its editions of February 26 (especially the emigrant/immigrant community) and 27 (francophone literature).

19. Tewfik Hakem, "La Télévision, arme du pouvoir," in Reporters sans Frontières, *Le Drame algérien*, 37.

20. Boudjedra, *FIS de la haine*, 28.

21. Ibid., 22.

22. *NYT*, 12 March 1995.

23. Provost, *Seconde Guerre*, 16. Nevertheless, France has remained an important postcolonial politico-cultural symbol. Provost contended that the "illegitimate regime" of the FLN followed by the Pouvoir took the place of the French in postcolonial Algeria. When officials criticized France, ironically, the "influence of the ex-metropolitan power grew in the eyes of the population" (16–17).

24. *Vancouver Sun*, 9 January 1998.

25. In his working notes to his incomplete *The Visible and the Invisible*, Merleau-Ponty writes: "There is . . . this difference between perception and language, that I *see* the perceived things and that the significations on the contrary are invisible." Later he states: "The perceived world (like painting) is the ensemble of my body's routes and not a multitude of spatio-temporal individuals" (Merleau-Ponty, *The Visible and the Invisible*, 214, 247). Barthes distinguishes between the signifier, the signified, and the sign in "Myth Today," in his *Mythologies*, 109–17.

Barthes's work was originally published in 1957 during the era of French decolonization. See also Lavers, *Roland Barthes*, 105–6.

26. Pfeiffer, *Agrarian Reform*, 80–81.

27. Fanon, *Wretched of the Earth*, 203–4.

28. Ammour, Leucate, and Moulin, *La Voie algérienne*, 108. There is an important literature, usually Marxist, that criticized Algerian development. See, for example, Chaliand's *L'Algérie est-elle socialiste?* and *Revolution in the Third World*. See also Nellis, "Algerian Socialism and Its Critics."

29. Provost, *Seconde Guerre*, 66.

30. Yves Lacoste, "L'Algérie en danger," *Libération*, 17 October 1988, 5.

31. Beckett contended that Fanon "underestimated" the threat of a "technical elite" ("Algeria vs. Fanon"). Besides the "comprador" class, Mahfoud Bennoune related that "a new breed of *affairistes* started to become local representatives of multinational firms in Algeria. As middlemen, specialising in import-export activities, they came to play an important role in the country up to 1978, when the state monopoly on external commerce attempted, in vain, to put an end to their services and deals" (*Making*, 96–97). Daniel Guérin observed immediately after independence that the new Algeria was threatened by "statism and bureaucratization" (Guérin, *L'Algérie qui se cherche*, 31–32).

32. *Wretched of the Earth*, 204.

33. Bhabha, *Location of Culture*, 38.

34. De Gaulle stated during decolonization (5 September 1961 press conference): "Our conception for Algeria is completely different from that which we have held . . . because all the conditions . . . have themselves completely changed" (*Major Addresses*, 143).

35. Stora, *La Gangrène et l'oubli*, 320.

36. Dine, *Images*, 34.

37. See Manceron and Remaoun, *D'une rive à l'autre*, 75–78.

38. Dine, *Images*, 227. See also Manceron and Remaoun, *D'une rive à l'autre*, 79–81.

39. Bhabha, *Location of Culture*, 1–2.

40. Ibid., 2. See Joëlle Hureau, "Associations et souvenir chez les Français rapatriés d'Algérie," in Rioux, *Guerre d'Algérie*, 517–25.

41. See Alain Rollat, "Les *Pieds-noirs* et l'effet Le Pen: L'Expérience d'un désarroi," *Grand Maghreb*, nos. 33–34 (1984): 64–65.

42. *LM*, 17 June 1997. José Sanchez provided this definition of the settler repatriate: "The *pied-noir* is he who does not forget" ("Mort et survie des pieds-noirs," *Itinéraires*, no. 264 [1982]: 262).

43. Thierry Fabre, "France-Algérie: Questions de mémoire," *AAN* 1990, 356.

44. Roseau aligned RECOURS with the political party that served the repatriated populations best. There was a rumor that Roseau had shaken the hand of Yacef Saadi, an ALN mastermind of the Battle of Algiers. The anti-Roseau rumors stemmed primarily from a rival and more extremist organization, USDIFRA

(Union Syndicale de Défense des Intérêts des Français Rapatriés d'Algérie) (*LM*, 16 December 1996).

45. Jean-Paul Mari, "Le Pouvoir des pieds-noirs," *Le Nouvel Observateur*, 19–25 June 1987, 79–80.

46. Mark McKinney, "*Métissage* in Post-Colonial Comics," in Hargreaves and McKinney, *Post-Colonial Cultures*, 172–74. ANFANOMA publicized the indemnity issue through the use of the comic character Fanfan, who befriends Baba, a Muslim and Moïse, a Jew. The comic is *Fanfan la ficelle*, text by Cortez and drawings by Camault (Paris: Editions BdB, 1977).

47. *Major Addresses*, 65 (10 November 1959).

48. The author came upon a *pied-noir* group visiting Oran in the spring of 1978. One of them said that he felt he was home ("chez moi") when he returned to Algeria and that he had always been welcomed back by Algerians. Unlike the *métropolitains*, the *pieds-noirs* have often initiated conversations with emigrant workers to talk about *là-bas* (over there, Algeria).

49. See *LM*, 27 October 1997.

50. See *LM*, 5 December 1994.

51. *LM*, 17 November 1994.

52. Others were at Pertuis (Vaucluse), Peyrolles-en-Provence, and Fameck (Moselle).

53. *LM*, 28 November 1994.

54. See Catherine Wihtol de Wenden, "The *Harkis:* A Community in the Making?" in Hargreaves and Heffernan, *French and Algerian Identities*, 199.

55. See *Los Angeles Times*, 27 February 1997, concerning immigrant youths.

56. See Creamean, "Membership of Foreigners," 49–67.

57. *LM*, 2 September 1997.

58. *LM*, 13 October 1995.

59. See *LM*, 1 January 1998.

60. See David Blatt, "Immigrant Politics in a Republican Nation," in Hargreaves and McKinney, *Post-Colonial Cultures*, 40–55.

61. Bruno Etienne, preface to Kaltenbach and Kaltenbach, *La France: Une chance pour l'Islam*, 20.

62. Viorst, "Muslims in France," 92.

63. FBIS, *WEU*, 17 January 1995, citing *Le Nouvel Observateur*, 28 December 1994–4 January 1995.

64. Viorst, "Muslims in France," 80.

65. A poll at this time reported that two-thirds of the French "associate Islam with religious fanaticism" (ibid.).

66. Ibid., 81.

67. Information Access Company, vol. 42, no. 2 (14 January 1995), on lexis-nexis.com.

68. *LM*, 13 October 1994. Those polled also indicated a greater acceptance, if the occasion arose, of having a Muslim as their mayor.

69. See *LM,* 29 July 1992, concerning a publicized case between a mixed couple where a French mother finally received custody of her children.

70. *LM,* 13 October 1994. Unquestionably, the behavior of French security forces monitoring immigrant youth during the *fitna* influenced the staggering response of those polled.

71. Hargreaves and McKinney, *Post-Colonial Cultures,* 20.

72. See Mark McKinney, "*Métissage* in Post-Colonial Comics," in Hargreaves and McKinney, *Post-Colonial Cultures,* 180–84.

73. See Carrie Tarr's very helpful survey "French Cinema and Post-Colonial Minorities" in Hargreaves and McKinney, *Post-Colonial Cultures,* 59–83.

74. Alec G. Hargreaves, "Television Gatekeepers and Gateways," in Hargreaves and McKinney, *Post-Colonial Cultures,* 90–93.

75. Chris Warne, "The Impact of World Music in France," in Hargreaves and McKinney, *Post-Colonial Cultures,* 143, referring in this section to Marie Virolle, *Le Chanson raï* (Paris: Karthala, 1995). Warne's entire article is very informative.

76. Africa News Service, Panafrican News Agency, 5 November 1998, on lexis-nexis.com. As Rachid Boudjedra noted, half of France's national team was Algerian during the War of Independence (David A. McMurray, "La France arabe," in Hargreaves and McKinney, *Post-Colonial Cultures,* 29, citing Boudjedra, *Lettres algériennes* [Paris: Grasset, 1995], 190–91).

77. *International Herald Tribune,* 4 July 1998.

78. The *Irish Times* gave particular attention to the Algerian press (14 July 1998).

79. *LM,* 17 July 1998.

80. *El-Watan,* 13 July 1998.

81. *Guardian,* 13 July 1998.

82. *NYT Magazine,* 14 March 1999, 35.

83. *LM,* 18 January 1990.

84. *NYT,* 5 December 1993.

85. David A. McMurray, "La France arabe," in Hargreaves and McKinney, *Post-Colonial Cultures,* 34.

86. Ahmed Moatassime views the bilingual and trilingual speakers of Algeria as strategically placed to conduct a "cultural interface" and an "indispensable mediation" within that country (Moatassime, "Islam, Arabisation, et Francophonie," in Jurt, *Algérie-France-Islam,* 74–75).

87. Club Jean Moulin, *Deux pièces,* 61–62.

88. FBIS, *WEU,* 6 February 1995, 14.

89. Bhabha, *Location of Culture,* 25.

90. Ibid., 39.

91. Ibid., 50.

92. "Some Kinda Love," in Reed, *Between Thought and Expression,* 20.

93. See Stora, *La Gangrène et l'oubli,* 275–76.

94. Horne, *Savage War,* 538; and D. Gordon, *Passing,* 83–84.

95. Yacono, *Les Etapes de la décolonisation française,* 118.

96. Lewis, "Algeria Changes Course," 11.

97. Stora, *La Gangrène et l'oubli,* 14–16.

98. Ibid., 93–100; see also chapter 2. The official opening of archives concerning this tragic event was announced on 5 May 1999 (*NYT,* 6 May 1999).

99. See Claude Liauzu, "Le Contingent entre silence et discours ancien combattant," in Rioux, *Guerre d'Algérie,* 509–16. French veterans have been expressing themselves. See Fauchon, *Journal de marche,* for a rare view of the Algerian War from the perspective of a citizen-soldier.

100. See Andrieu, *La Guerre d'Algérie.*

101. Provost, *Seconde Guerre,* 20.

102. Jean-Pierre Rioux, "La Flamme et les bûchers," in *Guerre d'Algérie,* 503, 508.

103. There were a few programs on the war, such as Denis Chegaray's exceptional *Moeurs en direct. Guerre d'Algérie. Mémoire enfouie d'une génération* (1982). See Evelyne Desbois, "Des images en quarantaine," in Rioux, *Guerre d'Algérie,* 560–71.

104. *LM,* 12, 13 November 1996.

105. Hadj Ali, *Lettre ouverte aux Français,* 11. In an interview, Mahfoud Nahnah warned about Algeria becoming a "second Lebanon" (*al-Sharq al-Awsat,* 25 March 1997).

106. Hadj Ali, *Lettre ouverte aux Français,* 66.

107. Hamoumou, *Et ils sont devenus harkis,* 18.

108. FBIS, *NES,* 22 November 1995.

109. Maschino and M'rabet, *L'Algérie des illusions,* 231.

110. Déjeux, *Littérature algérienne,* 84. The author wishes to acknowledge the late Jean Déjeux, who was kind enough to spend time conversing and educating him about Algerian literature (Algiers, 8–9 April 1978). For more examples of writers' historicism, see Manceron and Remaoun, *D'une rive à l'autre,* 69–71.

111. Déjeux, *Littérature algérienne,* 83.

112. Déjeux, *Mohammed Dib: Ecrivain algérien,* 11, citing interview by Claudine Acs, *L'Afrique littéraire et artistique,* no. 18 (1971).

113. Mimouni's characters just wanted to endure the absurdities that they faced. This was mirrored in the letters of an Algerian teacher of French, addressed to a colleague in France, expressing her concern about mere survival and her mission to educate. Indeed, her fear amid the violence surrounding her, reminiscent of Primo Levi's in his works, is of self-"dehumanization" (*LM,* 18 November 1997).

114. Déjeux, *Littérature algérienne,* 106.

115. See Zetili's poem "Eclaircie"/"Al-Sahwu" (1979) in Lanasri, *Anthologie,* 135–38, 236–40. The Arabic title is suggestive of recovery or regaining consciousness. To Zetili, this equated with being able to write what one thought. From 1966 to 1985 the official Algerian press (SNED/ENAL) produced 996 books in Arabic

and 523 in French. Some years were particularly meager: only 24 in 1977 (François Burgat, "Le Livre au Maghreb," *AAN* 1984, 319).

116. Benhadouga, *Le Vent du sud,* 138.

117. Benhadouga, *La Fin d'hier,* 106.

118. See Gafaiti, *Boudjedra,* 36–37.

119. Djebar, "Overture," in *Women of Algiers in Their Apartment,* 1.

120. See the collection compiled by Salima Ait Mohamed, *Ecrits d'Algérie* (Marseille: Editions Autres Temps, 1996). This book also includes contributions by the venerable Noureddine Aba and the renowned Nabile Farès.

121. Yacine, *Le Poète comme un boxeur,* 101.

122. Ibid., 52.

123. *LM,* 31 October 1989.

124. Maschino and M'Rabet, *L'Algérie,* 243.

125. *LM,* 5–6 July 1998. Ibrahimi feared that the imposition of a language creating an "exclusivity" threatened Algeria's authentic cultural heritage ("Algérie: L'Arabisation, lieu de conflits multiples," *Monde Arabe: Maghreb-Machrek,* no. 150 [1995]: 70).

126. Djebar, *Le Blanc de l'Algérie,* 274.

127. Abdelhafid Hamdi Chérif, "Identité et coopération," in Verlet, *Coopérer avec l'Algérie,* 139–40.

128. *El-Watan,* 1 November 1993.

129. Stora, *La Gangrène et l'oubli,* 321.

130. *El-Watan,* 5 October 1998.

131. See Manceron and Remaoun, *D'une rive à l'autre,* 225–55. Professor Khaoula Ibrahimi spoke of a need for a cultural "cohabitation" in Algeria, to be reinforced by an educational system that does not "deny reality," i.e., of a pluralist culture and history (*LM,* 5–6 July 1998).

132. A distressed and frustrated Houari Boumedienne stated: "We have made efforts; we have wanted to reconcile ourselves with the French people. But it is impossible; there is perhaps no possible reconciliation between the generations of the war" (Francos and Séréni, *Un Algérien,* 333). Nevertheless, Boumedienne continued on both national and personal levels to conciliate Algeria with France.

133. Pierre Bourdieu has played a particularly important role. He has spearheaded the establishment of the Comité International de Soutien aux Intellectuels Algériens (CISIA) and the publication of a new journal entitled *Alternatives algériennes,* which was dedicated to promoting discussion among the French and the Algerians. In late 1995 *Alger Info,* a new publication edited by Rabah Mahiout, who ran *Journal des Algériens en Europe,* targeted a French as well as an Algerian readership. A salient example would be the architect Fernand Pouillon, who remained active designing for postcolonial Algeria. One can also add the commitment of those affiliated with the Association France-Algérie and private cooperation groups.

134. Charles-Robert Ageron, "La Signification politique des Accords d'Evian," in Gallissot, *Accords d'Evian,* 218–19.

135. Gallissot, "Les Accords d'Evian dans la longue durée," in *Accords d'Evian*, 242.

136. Marseille, *Empire colonial et capitalisme français*, 372.

137. See Jacques Marseille, "La Guerre a-t-elle eu lieu? Mythes et réalités du fardeau algérien," and Jean-Charles Asselain, "'Boulet colonial' et redressement économique (1958–1962)," in Rioux, *Guerre d'Algérie*, 281–303.

138. Despite these sentiments, two-thirds of those surveyed in a poll in 1961 believed that France still had a responsibility to help Algeria develop through financial aid (Charles-Robert Ageron, "L'Opinion française à travers les sondages," in Rioux, *Guerre d'Algérie*, 44).

139. Barthes, *Mythologies*, 121.

140. Ibid., 151.

141. Ibid., 157.

142. Merleau-Ponty, *Humanism and Terror*, 185.

143. *AAN* 1995, 599.

144. Fanon, *Black Skin, White Masks*, 231.

145. Fanon, *Wretched of the Earth*, 36.

146. Déjeux, *Les Tendances depuis 1962*, 33. Déjeux also explores other examples of "new men" in the writings of Mourad Bourboune, Abdellatif Laâbi, and Nabile Farès (32–35).

147. Bennabi, *Vocation de l'Islam*, 75.

148. *El-Watan*, 9 November 1993.

149. *Major Addresses*, 101.

150. Ibid., 117 (11 April 1961).

151. Ibid., 167–68 (21 March 1962).

152. Peyrefitte, *C'était de Gaulle*, 1:284. On the other hand, Jean-Marie Le Pen viewed decolonization and the failure to defend *Algérie française* as a lost opportunity: "We could have made a national revolution to forge new, different men." Harvey Simmons interprets this as "echoing one of the major themes of orthodox fascism" (Simmons, *French National Front*, 40, citing Serge Dumont et al., *Le Système Le Pen*, 48).

153. Fanon, *Wretched of the Earth*, 148.

154. *LM*, 14 October 1994.

155. Kristeva, *Nations without Nationalism*, 31.

156. Ibid., 55.

157. See Mahdi, *Ibn Khaldûn's Philosophy of History*, 204–209.

158. Ibn Khaldun, *Muqaddimah*, 1:284–85.

159. D. Gordon, *Passing*, citing Berque, *Dépossession du monde*, 170.

160. de Gaulle, *Memoirs of Hope*, 46.

161. Mimouni, "L'Algérie sans la France," in Ageron, *L'Algérie des Français*, 335–41.

162. Barthes, *Mythologies*, 159.

Chapter 11. Conclusion

1. Grimaud, *Politique extérieure*, 39, citing de Broglie before the Senate, *Journal Officiel* (Senate), 25 November 1964.

2. *LM*, 17 March 1972.

3. *F-A*, no. 44 (1975): 3.

4. Ibn Khaldun, *Muqadddimah*, 1:6.

5. Ibid., 15.

6. *NYT*, 12 March 1995.

7. APS, 17 September 1999.

8. *LM*, 31 July 1999.

9. *NYT*, 24 September 1999.

10. *LM*, 1–2 August 1999; *Liberte* 30–31 July 1999.

11. "France-Algerie: Entretien du ministre des Affaires étrangères, M. Hubert Védrine, avec l'hebdomadaire algérien 'Algeria-Magazine'," on www.france.diplomatie.fr/actual/ nouvelles/communiques/fralger.html, accessed 14 September 1999. Védrine told the *Journal du Dimanche:* "We are in a radically different situation. The climate has changed. An atmosphere of freedom has returned to Algiers. The French people I met in Algeria . . . told me, 'In recent months, we are no longer afraid'" (*NYT*, 5 August 1999).

12. *Libération*, 22 September 1999.

13. *LM*, 1–2 August 1999.

14. AFP, 17 September 1999.

15. Amrouche, *Un Algérien s'addresse aux Français*, 94, citing *La Nef*, January 1959.

16. Ibid., 64, citing *LM*, 11 January 1958.

17. Tillion, *Complementary Enemies*, 183.

Selected Bibliography

Note: Arabic names with the article *al-* are alphabetized according to the principal element (look for al-Madani under *M*). French names with the particle *de* are under *D*. Spelling of authors' names, especially transliterations of Arabic ones, may vary from work to work owing to language of publication and publishers' caprice. Likewise, names of government agencies and such may alter over time, occasioning multiple entries.

Abbreviations are listed in the front of the book.

Some important works do not appear in this bibliography but nonetheless were studied extensively over many years. They include: *Actualité et documents* (Ministry of Information, Algiers); *Africa Report; Africa Research Bulletin; Algérie actualité; Algérie agricole; Articles et documents (AD); Document d'actualité internationale; El-Djeich* (Algerian army journal); *France-Algérie (F-A)/Algérie informations (AI); Grand Maghreb; Jeune Afrique; Journal Officiel* (French National Assembly and Senate); *La Documentation française illustrée; L'Algérianiste; Les Cahiers français; Maghreb/Maghreb-Machrek; Middle East Economic Digest (MEED); Moniteur du Commerce internationale; Notes et études documentaires (ND); Politique étrangère de la France (PEF); Problèmes économiques; Recueils et monographies; Regards sur l'actualité; Rencontres* (French embassy in Algeria); *Révolution africaine (RA); Revue algérienne des sciences juridiques, économiques et politiques (RASJEP)/Revue algérienne des sciences juridiques, politiques, économiques et sociales (RASJPES); Sondages; Textes et notes (TN);* and *al-Thaqafa.*

Abbas, Ferhat. *Autopsie d'une guerre.* Paris: Editions Garnier Frères, 1980.

———. *L'Indépendance confisquée, 1962–1968.* Paris: Flammarion, 1984.

———. *La Nuit coloniale.* Paris: Julliard, 1962.

Abou-Chahla, Michel, et al. *Algérie.* Paris: Publications Economiques Internationales, 1986.

Abu-Lughod, Ibrahim, and Baha Abu-Laban, eds. *Settler Regimes in Africa and the Arab World: The Illusion of Endurance.* Wilmette, Ill.: Medina University Press International, 1974.

"L'Accord franco-algérien sur les hydrocarbures." *Revue française de l'énergie,* no. 176 (1966): 230–36.

Achour, Christiane. *Anthologie de la littérature algérienne de langue française.* Paris: ENAP-BORDAS, 1990.

Addi, Lahouari. *L'Algérie et la démocratie: Pouvoir et crise du politique dans l'Algérie contemporaine.* Paris: La Découverte, 1995.

———. *L'Impasse du populisme: L'Algérie, collectivité politique et état en construction.* Algiers: ENAL, 1990.

Ageron, Charles-Robert. *"Algérie algérienne" de Napoléon III à de Gaulle.* Paris: Sindbad, 1980.

———. *Les Algériens musulmans et la France (1871–1919).* 2 vols. Paris: PUF, 1968.

———. "Ferhat Abbas et l'évolution politique de l'Algérie musulmane pendant la deuxième guerre mondiale." *Revue d'histoire maghrébine,* no. 4 (1975): 125–44.

———. *De l'insurrection de 1871 au déclenchement de la guerre de Libération (1954).* Vol. 2 of *Histoire de l'Algérie contemporaine.* Paris: PUF, 1979.

———. *Histoire de l'Algérie contemporaine (1830–1976).* 6th ed. Paris: PUF, 1977.

———, ed. *L'Algérie des Français.* Paris: Editions du Seuil, 1993.

al-Ahnaf, M., and F. Frégosi, eds. *L'Algérie par ses islamistes.* Paris: Karthala, 1991.

Ait Mohamed, Salima, ed. *Ecrits d'Algérie.* Marseille: Editions Autres Temps, 1996.

Akkache, Ahmed. *Capitaux étrangers et Libération économique: L'Expérience algérienne.* Paris: François Maspéro, 1971.

Aldrich, Robert, and John Connell, eds. *France in World Politics.* London: Routledge, 1989.

Alexandre, Philippe. *The Duel: De Gaulle and Pompidou.* Translated by Elaine P. Halperin. Boston: Houghton Mifflin, 1972.

Algerian Delegation. *What Is Algeria? The Algerian Problem in Outline.* Cairo, 1955.

Algerian Office (FLN). *Algeria: Questions and Answers.* New York: Algerian Office, 1976.

———. "Blackmail or Partition." Translation of an article by A.-P. Lentin in *Cahiers internationaux* (July–August 1961). Doc. 61-36-E, 1.

———. "The Franco-Algerian Negotiations (Evian, 20 May 1961)." Doc. 61-17-E.

———. "Report on the French-Algerian talks held at Evian (May 10–June 13, 1961)." Doc. 61-20-E.

———. "The Requirements of Our Economic Development." Doc. 62-1-E. (Originally published in *E-M,* no. 88 [1961]).

———. "Statement on Situation and Fate of Algerian Jews." Doc. 61-46.

———. "Text of the Appeal Addressed to the Algerian People by Premier Benyoussef Benkhedda, Tunis, September 15, 1961." Doc. 61-31-E.

"L'Algérie." *Autrement,* no. 38 (1982).

"Algérie." *Les Temps modernes* 39 (July–August 1982).

L'Algérie de demain: Voici tout ce que vous devez savoir après le cessez-le-feu. Paris: Imprimerie spéciale de la SNEP, 1962.

"L'Algérie française." *L'Opinion en 24 heures* (Paris: Centre de Documentation générale), 1956.

"Algérie: La Guerre des frères." *Les Temps modernes* 50 (January–February 1995).

L'Algérie, terre franco-musulmane. Paris: Commissariat de l'Algérie à l'Exposition universelle et internationale de Bruxelles en 1958, 1958.

L'Algérien en Europe. Amicale des Algériens en Europe.

Allais, Maurice. *Les Accords d'Evian: Le Référendum et la résistance algérienne*. Paris: Plon, 1962.

———. *L'Algérie d'Evian*. Paris: L'Esprit Nouveau, 1962.

Alleg, Henri, et al. *La Guerre d'Algérie*. 3 vols. Paris: Temps Actuel, 1981.

———. *The Question*. New York: George Braziller, 1958.

Alphand, Hervé. *L'Etonnement d'être: Journal, 1939–1973*. Paris: Fayard, 1977.

Alwan, Mohamed. *Algeria Before the United Nations*. New York: Robert Speller, 1959.

Amari, Malek. *Le Père et le FIS*. Paris: Maisonneuve, 1996.

Ambassade de France en Algérie, Service de la Coopération culturelle et technique. *Rapports périodiques*. 1965–67.

Ambler, John S. *The French Army in Politics, 1945–1962*. Columbus: Ohio State University Press, 1966.

Amicale des Algériens en Europe. *Nouvelles perspectives pour l'émigration algérienne*. Paris: Amicale des Algériens en Europe (Imprimerie ETC), 1977.

Amin, Samir. *L'Economie du Maghreb*. 2 vols. Paris: Editions de Minuit, 1966.

———. *The Maghreb in the Modern World: Algeria, Tunisia, Morocco*. Translated by Michael Perl. London: Penguin, 1970.

Ammour, Kader, Christian Leucate, and Jean-Jacques Moulin. *La Voie algérienne: Les Contradictions d'un développement national*. Paris: François Maspéro, 1974.

Amnesty International. *Algeria: Civilian Population Caught in a Spiral of Violence* (MDE 28/23/97). New York: Amnesty International USA, 1997.

Amrouche, Jean–El Mouhoub. *Un Algérien s'adresse aux Français, ou l'histoire d'Algérie par les textes (1943–1961)*. Edited by Tassadit Yacine. Paris: Awal/L'Harmattan, 1994.

Anderson, Benedict. *Imagined Communities: Reflections on the Origin and Spread of Nationalism*. Revised edition. London: Verso, 1991.

Andrews, William G. *French Politics and Algeria: The Process of Policy Formation, 1954–1962*. New York: Appleton-Century-Crofts, 1962.

Andrieu, René. *La Guerre d'Algérie n'a pas eu lieu: 8 ans et 600,000 morts*. Paris: Messidor, 1992.

Angelelli, Jean-Paul. "Notes sur l'Algérie et l'opinion française, 1972–1982." *Itinéraires*, no. 264 (1982): 83–125.

Anglade, Jean. *La Vie quotidienne des immigrés en France de 1919 à nos jours*. Paris: Hachette, 1976.

Anselme-Rabinovitch, L. "Les Nationalisations d'Algérie devant les tribunaux français." *Banque*, no. 239 (1966): 331–36.

Ardagh, John. *The New France: A Society in Transition.* New York: Penguin, 1978.

———. *The New French Revolution.* New York: Harper & Row, 1969.

Argoud, Antoine. *La Décadence, l'imposture et la tragédie.* Paris: Fayard, 1974.

Arnaud, Jacqueline. *La Littérature maghrébine de langue française.* Vol. 1, *Origines et perspectives.* Vol. 2, *Le Cas de Kateb Yacine.* Paris and Algiers: Publisud, 1986.

Aron, Raymond. *L'Algérie et la République.* Paris: Plon, 1958.

———. "Dénouement provisoire." *Preuves,* no. 136 (1962): 3–11.

———. *Dimensions de la conscience historique.* Paris: Agora, 1964.

———. *France: Steadfast and Changing.* Translated by J. Irwin and Luigi Einaudi. Cambridge: Harvard University Press, 1960.

———. *La Tragédie algérienne.* Paris: Plon, 1957.

Aron, Robert. *An Explanation of de Gaulle.* Translated by Marianne Sinclair. New York: Harper & Row, 1966.

———. *Les Origines de la Guerre d'Algérie.* Paris: Fayard, 1962.

Assidon, Elsa. *Sahara occidental: Un enjeu pour le Nord-ouest africain.* Paris: François Maspéro, 1978.

Ath-Messaoud, Malek, and Alain Gillette. *L'Immigration algérienne en France.* Paris: Editions Entente, 1976.

Augarde, Jacques. *La Migration algérienne.* Paris: Hommes et Migrations, 1970.

Ayoun, Richard, and Bernard Cohen. *Les Juifs d'Algérie: Deux mille ans d'histoire.* Paris: Jean-Claude Lattès, 1982.

Bachaga Said. *See* Boualam.

Bailac, Geneviève. *Les Absinthes sauvages: Témoignages pour le peuple pieds-noirs.* Paris: Fayard, 1972.

Baillet, Pierre. "Les Rapatriés d'Algérie en France," *ND,* nos. 4275–4276 (1976).

Balta, Paul. "French Policy in North Africa." *MEJ* 40 (spring 1986): 238–51.

———. "La Politique africaine de l'Algérie." *RFEPA,* no. 132 (1976): 54–73.

Balta, Paul, and Claudine Rulleau. *L'Algérie des Algériens: Vingt ans après.* Paris: Editions Ouvrières, 1981.

———. *La Stratégie de Boumediène.* Paris: Sindbad, 1978.

Barakat, Halim, ed. *Contemporary North Africa: Issues of Development and Integration.* Washington: Center for Contemporary Arab Studies, 1985.

Barbier, Maurice. *Le Conflit du Sahara occidental.* Paris: L'Harmattan, 1982.

Baroli, Marc. *Algérie, terre d'espérances: Colons et immigrants (1830–1914).* 2d ed. Paris: L'Harmattan, 1992.

———. *La Vie quotidienne des Français en Algérie, 1830–1914.* Paris: Hachette, 1967.

Barthes, Roland. *Michelet.* Translated by Richard Howard. New York: Hill and Wang, 1987.

———. *Mythologies.* Translated by Annette Lavers. New York: Hill and Wang, 1972.

Barzini, Luigi. *The Europeans*. New York: Penguin, 1983.

Basdevant, Jean. Interview by author. Paris, 9 May 1978.

————. "La Politique culturelle de la France." *RDN* 18 (February 1962): 211–25.

Bayart, Jean-François. *La Politique africaine de François Mitterrand*. Paris: Karthala, 1984.

Beckett, Paul A. "Algeria vs. Fanon: The Theory of Revolutionary Decolonization and the Algerian Experience." *Western Political Quarterly* 26 (March 1973): 5–27.

Bedjaoui, Mohammed. *La Révolution algérienne et le droit*. Brussels: Editions de l'Association Internationale des Juristes Démocrates, 1961.

Bedrani, Slimane. *L'Agriculture algérienne depuis 1966: Etatisation ou privatisation?* Algiers: Office des Publications Universitaires, 1981.

Belkherroubi, Abdelmadjid. *La Naissance et la reconnaissance de la République algérienne*. Algiers: SNED, 1982.

Bell, David Scott, and Byron Criddle. *The French Socialist Party: The Emergence of a Party of Government*, 2d ed. Oxford: Clarendon Press, 1988.

Belloula, Tayeb. *Les Algériens en France*. Algiers: Editions Nationales Algériennes, 1965.

Benachenhou, A. *L'Expérience algérienne de planification et de développement, 1962–1982*. Algiers: Office des Publications Universitaires, n.d.

Benamrane, Djilali. *L'Emigration algérienne en France: Passé, présent, devenir*. Algiers: SNED, 1983.

Ben Bella, Ahmed. *Ben Bella . . . revient*. Paris: Editions Jean Picollec, 1982.

————. *Les Discours du président Ben Bella (1962–1er trimestre 1964)*. Algiers: Ministère de l'Orientation nationale, 1964.

Bendeddouche, Jacqueline. *Notion de nationalité et nationalité algérienne*. Algiers: SNED, 1982.

Benhadouga, Abdelhamid. *La Fin d'hier*. Translated by Marcel Bois. Algiers: SNED, 1977.

————. *Le Vent du sud*. Translated by Marcel Bois. Algiers: SNED, 1974.

Benissad, M. E. *L'Economie algérienne contemporaine*. Paris: PUF, 1980.

————. *Economie du développement de l'Algérie: Sous-développement et socialisme, 1962–1982*. 2d ed. Paris: Economica, 1982.

Benjedid, Chadli. *Discours du président Chadli Benjedid*. 5 vols. Algiers: Ministère de l'Information, 1980–83.

Ben Khedda, Benyoucef. *Les Accords d'Evian*. Paris and Algiers: Publisud-OPU, 1986.

Bennabi, Malek. *Les Grands thèmes*. Algiers: Omar Benaissa, 1976.

————. *Vocation de l'Islam*. Tipaza, Algeria: Société d'Edition et de Communication, 1991.

Bennoune, Mahfoud. "Algerian Peasants and National Politics." *MERIP*, no. 48 (1976): 13–14.

————. "Impact of Colonialism and Migration of an Algerian Peasant Community: A Study of Socio-economic Change." Ph.D. dissertation, University of Michigan, 1976.

———. "Maghribin Workers in France." *MERIP*, no. 34 (1975): 1–12, 30.

———. *The Making of Contemporary Algeria, 1830–1987: Colonial Upheavals and Post-independence Development*. Cambridge: Cambridge University Press, 1988.

Benrabah, Mohamed, et al., *Les Violences en Algérie*. Paris: Odile Jacob, 1998.

Bérard, Joseph. *Bel-Abbès: Ne jamais oublier*. Paris: Pensée universelle, 1971.

Berliet, Paul. "L'Industrie automobile en Afrique." *CT*, nos. 49–50 (1967): 37–38.

Bernardi, François-Noël, et al. *Les Dossiers noirs du racisme dans le Midi de la France*. Paris: Editions du Seuil, 1976.

Berque, Jacques. *French North Africa: The Maghrib Between Two World Wars*. Translated by Jean Stewart. New York: Praeger, 1967.

Bhabha, Homi K. *The Location of Culture*. London: Routledge, 1997.

Bitterlin, Lucien. "De Gaulle et la décolonisation de l'Algérie." *Etudes gaulliennes* 6, no. 22 (April–July 1978): 91–101.

———. *Histoire des "Barbouzes."* Paris: Palais Royal, 1972.

———. *Nous étions tous des térroristes*. Paris: Témoignage Chrétien, 1983.

Blair, John M. *The Control of Oil*. New York: Vintage, 1978.

Blanchard, Jean. *Le Problème algérien: Réalités et perspectives*. Paris: PUF, 1955.

Blanquer, Roland. "Le Feuilleton de l'indemnisation." *Historia*, no. 484 (1987): 175–79.

Blardone, G. "Les Accords franco-algériens sur les hydrocarbures: Une Révolution dans la politique de coopération." *Croissance des jeunes nations*, no. 47 (1965): 4–11.

Bocca, Geoffrey. *The Secret Army*. Englewood Cliffs, N.J.: Prentice-Hall, 1968.

Boghli, Sid-Ahmed. *Aspects of Algerian Cultural Policy*. Paris: UNESCO, 1978.

Bonn, Charles. *Le Roman algérien de langue française: Vers un espace de communication littéraire décolonisé?* Paris: L'Harmattan, 1985.

Bonnefous, Marc. "L'Algérie n'est plus un cas à part." *CT*, nos. 49–50 (1967): 16–23.

Bothorel, Jean. *Histoire du septennat giscardien, 19 mai 1974–22 mars 1978*. Paris: Grasset, 1983.

Boualam, [Bachaga] Said. *Les Harkis au service de la France*. Paris: France-Empire, 1963.

———. *Les Harkis sans la France*. Paris: France-Empire, 1964.

———. Interview by author. Le Mas Thibert, 18 February 1978.

———. *Mon pays . . . la France!* Paris: France-Empire, 1962.

Boucebci, Mahoud. *Psychiatrie sociale et développement (Algérie)*. Algiers: SNED, 1982.

Boudjedra, Rachid. *Le Démantèlement*. Paris: Denoël, 1992.

———. *FIS de la haine*. Paris: Denoël, 1992.

———. *La Répudiation*. Paris: Denoël, 1969.

Boukhedenna, Sakinna. *Journal: Nationalité: Immigrée*. Paris: L'Harmattan, 1987.

Boumediene, Houari. *Discours du président Boumèdiene*. 8 vols. Algiers: Ministère de l'Information et de la Culture, 1966–79.

Bourdieu, Pierre. *The Algerians*. Translated by Alan C. Rosa. Boston: Beacon Press, 1962.

———. *Sociologie de l'Algérie*. Paris: PUF, 1974.

Bourdieu, Pierre, and Abdelmalek Sayad. *Le Déracinement: La Crise de l'agriculture traditionelle en Algérie*. Paris: Editions de Minuit, 1964.

Bouveresse, Marie-Odile. "Les Phénomènes de dépendance dans la coopération culturelle franco-algérienne. Mémoire." Thesis, Université d'Aix-Marseille III, 1976.

Bouvier, Pierre. *Fanon*. Paris: Editions universitaires, 1971.

Bouzana, Belkacem. *Le Contentieux des hydrocarbures entre l'Algérie et les sociétés étrangères*. Algiers: Office des Publications Universitaires, 1985.

Bouzid Kara. *La Marche: Traversée de la France profonde*. Paris: Sindbad, 1984.

Brace, Richard M. *Morocco, Algeria, Tunisia*. Englewood Cliffs, N.J.: Prentice-Hall, 1964.

———. *Ordeal in Algeria*. New York: D. Van Nostrand, 1960.

Brace, Richard, and Joan Brace. *Algerian Voices*. New York: D. Van Nostrand, 1965.

Brahimi, Abdelhamid. "Algeria's Rulers Remain 'France's Generals'." *Mideast Mirror* 9, no. 31 (1995).

———. *Stratégies de développement pour l'Algérie: Défis et enjeux*. Paris: Economica, 1991.

Brandell, Inga. *Les Rapports franco-algériens depuis 1962: Du pétrole et des hommes*. Paris: L'Harmattan, 1981.

Braudel, Fernand. *The Identity of France*. Vol. 1, *History and Environment*. Translated by Siân Reynolds. New York: Harper & Row, 1988.

Brogini, Maurice. "L'Exploitation des hydrocarbures en Algérie de 1956 à 1971." 3ᵉ cycle thesis, Université de Nice, 1973.

Brown, Leon Carl, ed. *State and Society in Independent North Africa*. Washington: Middle East Institute, 1966.

Brunschwig, Henri. *French Colonialism, 1871–1914: Myths and Realities*. Translated by William Granville Brown. London: Pall Mall, 1966.

———. *Mythes et réalités de l'impérialisme colonial français*. Paris: Armand Colin, 1960.

Buchard, Roger. *Organisation armée secrète*. 2 vols. Paris: Albin Michel, 1963.

Bugeaud, Thomas-Robert. *L'Algérie: Des moyens de conserver et d'utiliser cette conquête*. Paris: Chez Dentu, 1842.

———. *De la colonisation de l'Algérie*. Paris: A. Guyot, 1847.

———. *De l'établissement de légions de colons militaires dans les possessions français*. Paris: Firmin Didot Frères, 1838.

Burgat, François. "La Mobilisation islamiste et les élections algériennes du 12 juin 1990." *Maghreb-Machrek,* no. 129 (1990): 5–22.

Burgat, François, and William Dowell. *The Islamic Movement in North Africa.* 2d ed. Austin: Center for Middle Eastern Studies, University of Texas, 1997.

Buron, Robert. "Aspects de la coopération entre les pays ex-colonisateurs et nations ex-colonisés." *Développement et civilisations,* no. 11 (1962): 14–18.

———. *Carnets politiques de la guerre de l'Algérie: Par un signataire des accords d'Evian.* Paris: Plon, 1965.

Byé, Maurice. "Aide, commerce, ou co-production." *Développement et civilisations,* no. 24 (1965): 39–47.

Cadenat, Patrick. "La France et le Tiers Monde: Vingt ans de coopération bilatérale." *ND,* nos. 4701–4702 (1983).

Caisse Algérien de Développement. *Rapport 1964.* Algiers, 1965.

Caisse Centrale de Coopération Economique (CCCE). "Bilan des programmes de formation et de Coopération technique en Algérie (1968–1980)." Stenciled report. CCCE, 1981.

———. "Les Interventions de la Caisse Centrale de Coopération Economique en Algérie." Stenciled report. CCCE, 1982.

———. *Rapport d'activité* (Annual reports). Paris: CCCE, 1967–87.

Camus, Albert. *Actuelles III: Chronique algérienne (1939–1958).* Paris: Gallimard, 1958.

———. *L'Exil et le royaume.* Edited for English readers by B. F. Bart. New York: Charles Scribner's Sons, 1965.

———. *Lyrical and Critical Essays.* Edited by Philip Thody. Translated by Ellen Conroy Kennedy. New York: Vintage, 1970.

———. *Le Premier homme.* Paris: Gallimard, 1994.

———. *The Rebel: An Essay on Man in Revolt.* Translated by Anthony Bower. New York: Vintage, 1956.

———. *Resistance, Rebellion, and Death.* Translated by Justin O'Brien. New York: Knopf, 1961.

Carlier, Omar. *Entre nation et jihad: Histoire sociale des radicalismes algériens.* Paris: Presses de la Fondation Nationale des Sciences Politiques, 1995.

Carréras, Fernand. *L'Accord F.L.N.-O.A.S.: Des négociations secrètes au cessez-le-feu.* Paris: Robert Laffont, 1967.

Casas, Joseph. "French-Algerian Cooperation for Agricultural Training." *CT,* no. 68 (1972): 34.

Caute, David. *Frantz Fanon.* New York: Viking, 1970.

Cave, Laurence Trent. *The French in Algeria.* London: Charles J. Skeet, 1859.

Cédétim. *Les Immigrés: Contribution à l'histoire politique de l'immigration en France.* Paris: Stock, 1975.

Centre de Recherches et d'Etudes sur les Sociétés Méditerranéennes (CRESM). *Annuaire de l'Afrique du Nord (AAN).* Aix-en-Provence, 1962–.

———. *Les Economies maghrébines.* Paris: CNRS, 1971.

————. *Les Influences occidentales dans les villes maghrébines à l'époque contemporaine.* Aix-en-Provence: Editions de l'Université de Provence, 1974.

Cerney, Philip G. *The Politics of Grandeur: Ideological Aspects of de Gaulle's Foreign Policy.* London: Cambridge University Press, 1980.

Çeylik, Zeynep. *Urban Forms and Colonial Confrontations: Algiers under French Rule.* Berkeley and Los Angeles: University of California Press, 1997.

Chaker, Abdelkader. *La Jeunesse algérienne en France: Eléments d'étude de l'émigration familiale.* Algiers: SNED, 1977.

Chaliand, Gérard. *L'Algérie est-elle socialiste?* Paris: François Maspéro, 1964.

————. *Revolution in the Third World.* Translated by Diana Johnstone. New York: Penguin, 1978.

Chaliand, Gérard, and Juliette Minces. *L'Algérie indépendante (bilan d'une révolution nationale).* Paris: François Maspéro, 1972.

Challe, Maurice. *Notre révolte.* Paris: Presses de la Cité, 1968.

Charef, Abed. *L'Algérie: Le Grand dérapage.* Paris: Editions de l'Aube, 1995.

Charpentier, Pierre. "Les Immigrés maghrébins de France." *L'Afrique et l'Asie modernes,* no. 135 (1982): 33–48.

Charras, Marie-Ange. *Bidonvilles.* Paris: François Maspéro, 1971.

La Charte d'Alger—Ensemble des textes adoptés par le premier Congrès du Parti du Front de Liberation Nationale du 16 au 21 Avril 1964. Algiers: Imprimerie Nationale Algérienne, 1964.

Cheriet, Abdellah. *Opinion sur la politique de l'enseignement et de l'arabisation.* Algiers: SNED, 1983.

Chevalier, Jean-Marie. *The New Oil Stakes.* Translated by Ian Rock. London: Allen Lane, 1975.

Chevalier, Philippe. "Le Contrat passé le 19 octobre entre l'Algérie et le Getty Petroleum Cie." Doctoral dissertation, Université de Dijon, 1972.

Chikh, Slimane. *L'Algérie en armes, ou le temps des certitudes.* Paris: Economica, 1981.

Chirac, Jacques. *La Lueur de l'espérance: Réflexion du soir pour le matin.* Paris: Table Ronde, 1978.

Chouraqui, André. *Between East and West: A History of the Jews in North Africa.* Translated by Michael M. Bernet. New York: Atheneum, 1973.

Ciment, James. *Algeria: The Fundamentalist Challenge.* New York: Facts on File, 1997.

Claude, H. "Les Accords d'Evian." *Economie et politique,* no. 93 (1962): 2–8.

Clegg, Ian. *Workers' Self-Management in Algeria.* New York: Monthly Review Press, 1971.

Club Jean Moulin. *Deux pièces du dossier Algérie: Pour une politique du rapatriement; La Solidarité économique franco-algérienne.* Paris: Editions du Seuil, 1962.

Codding, George A., Jr., and William Safran. *Ideology and Politics: The Socialist Party of France.* Boulder, Colo.: Westview Press, 1979.

Cohen, William B. "Legacy of Empire: The Algerian Connection." *Journal of Contemporary History* 15, no. 1 (1980): 97–123.

Colin, Jean-Pierre. "Réflexions sur l'avenir du Sahara occidental." *RFEPA*, nos. 152–53 (1978): 80–92.

Collot, Claude, and Jean-Robert Henry, eds. *Le Mouvement national algérien: Textes, 1912–54.* Paris: L'Harmattan, 1978.

Colquhoun, Robert. *Raymond Aron.* Vol. 2, *The Sociologist in Society, 1955–1983.* Beverly Hills: Sage Publications, 1986.

Comité pour la défense d'Ahmed Ben Bella et des autres victimes de la répréssion en Algérie. *Qu'est devenu Ben Bella? (19 juin 1965–19 juin 1967).* Paris: François Maspéro, 1967.

Commission Française de Justice et Paix and l'Association France-Algérie. "Pour de nouvelles relations entre la France et l'Algérie." *F-A,* hors série (January 1974).

Conesa, Gabriel. *Bab-el-Oued: Notre paradis perdu.* Paris: Robert Laffont, 1970.

Confer, Vincent. *France and Algeria: The Problem of Civil and Political Reform, 1870–1920.* Syracuse, N.Y.: Syracuse University Press, 1966.

Cook, Don. *Charles de Gaulle: A Biography.* New York: G. P. Putnam's Sons, 1983.

Cooke, James J. "Eugene Etienne and the Failure of Assimilation in Algeria." *Africa Quarterly* 9 (January–March 1972): 285–96.

Cornaton, Michel. *Les Regroupements de la décolonisation en Algérie.* Paris: Editions Ouvrières, 1967.

Cornet, Pierre. *Du Mirage au miracle: Pétrole saharien.* Paris: Nouvelles Editions Latines, 1960.

Cot, Jean-Pierre. *A l'épreuve du pouvoir: Le Tiers-mondisme pour quoi faire?* Paris: Editions du Seuil, 1984.

———. "What Change?" *Africa Report* 28, no. 3 (May–June 1983): 12–16.

Cotteret, Jean-Marie, and René Moreau. *Recherches sur le vocabulaire du général de Gaulle: Analyse statistique des allocutions radio-diffusées, 1958–1965.* Paris: Armand Colin, 1969.

Courrière, Yves. *La Guerre de l'Algérie.* 4 vols. Paris: Fayard, 1968–71.

Couve de Murville, Maurice. "L'indépendance nationale." *Etudes gaulliennes,* nos. 3–4 (1973): 154–62.

———. Interview by author. Paris, 20 May 1978.

———. *Une politique étrangère, 1958–1969.* Paris: Plon, 1971.

Creamean, Letitia. "Membership of Foreigners: Algerians in France." *Arab Studies Quarterly* 18, no. 1 (winter 1996): 49–67.

"La Création de l'E.R.A.P.: Révolution ou évolution." *Revue française de l'énergie,* no. 176 (1966): 237–38.

Crosbie, Sylvia K. *A Tacit Alliance: France and Israel from Suez to the Six Day War.* Princeton: Princeton University Press, 1974.

Crozier, Brian. *De Gaulle.* New York: Charles Scribner's Sons, 1973.

Cubertafond, Bernard. *L'Algérie contemporaine*. Paris: PUF, 1981.

———. *La République algérienne*. Paris: PUF, 1979.

Daguzan, Jean-François. "Les Rapports franco-algériens, 1962–1992: Réconciliation ou conciliation permanente?" *Politique étrangère* 58, no. 3 (1993–94): 885–95.

Dahlab, Saad. *Mission accomplie*. Algiers: Editions Dahlab, 1990.

Dahmani, Mohamed. *Algérie: Légitimité historique et continuité politique*. Paris: Sycomore, 1979.

Damis, John. *Conflict in Northwest Africa: The Western Sahara Dispute*. Stanford: Hoover Institution, 1983.

Daniel, Jean. "The Algerian Problem Begins." *Foreign Affairs* 40 (July 1962): 605–11.

———. "The Jewish Future in Algeria: A Dissenting View." *Commentary* 34 (September 1962): 198–203.

Danzinger, Raphael. *Abd al-Qadir and the Algerians: Resistance to the French and Internal Consolidation*. New York: Holmes & Meier, 1977.

d'Arcy, François, Annie Krieger, and Alain Marill. *Essais sur l'économie de l'Algérie nouvelle*. Paris: PUF, 1965.

d'Ault-Dumesnil, Edouard. *Relation de l'expédition d'Afrique en 1830 et de la conquête d'Alger*. Paris: Victor Palme, 1868.

Daval, Roger. *Histoire des idées en France*. Paris: PUF, 1973.

Davis, J. D. *Blue Gold: The Political Economy of Natural Gas*. London: George Allen & Unwin, 1984.

Debbasch, Charles, et al. *Les Economies maghrébines: L'indépendance à l'épreuve du développement économique*. Paris: CNRS, 1971.

———. *Mutations culturelles et coopération au Maghreb*. Paris: CNRS, 1969.

de Bertier de Sauvigny, Guillaume. *La Restauration*. Paris: Flammarion, 1955.

de Broglie, Jean. "L'aide liée." *Dialogues*, no. 4 (1963): 4–7.

———. "Quarante mois de rapports franco-algériennes." *RDN* 21 (December 1965): 1833–57.

de Carmoy, Guy. *The Foreign Policies of France, 1944–1968*. Translated by Elaine P. Halperin. Chicago: University of Chicago Press, 1970.

Deeb, Mary-Jane. "Inter-Maghribi Relations since 1969: A Study of the Modalities of Unions and Mergers." *MEJ* 43 (winter 1989): 20–34.

de Foucauld, Charles. *Inner Search: Letters (1889–1916)*. Translated by Barbara Lucas. Maryknoll, N.Y.: Orbis Books, 1979.

de Gaulle, Charles. *Discours et messages*. 4 vols. Paris: Plon, 1970.

———. *The Edge of the Sword*. Translated by Gerard Hopkins. New York: Criterion, 1960.

———. *Major Addresses, Statements, and Press Conferences, May 19, 1958–January 31, 1964*. New York: French Embassy, Press and Information Division, 1964.

———. *Mémoires de Guerre*. Vol. 1, *L'Appel, 1940–1942*. Paris: Plon, 1971.

————. *Memoirs of Hope: Renewal and Endeavor.* Translated by Terence Kilmartin. London: Weidenfeld and Nicolson, 1971.

Deheuvels, Luc-Willy. *Islam et pensée contemporaine en Algérie: La Revue al-Asâla (1971–1981).* Paris: CNRS, 1991.

Déjeux, Jean. "Bibliographie algérienne." *RASJEP* 5 (March 1968): 171–84.

————. *Dictionnaire des auteurs maghrébins de langue française.* Paris: Karthala, 1984.

————. *La Littérature algérienne contemporaine.* Paris: PUF, 1975.

————. *La Littérature maghrébine d'expression française.* Algiers: Centre Culturel Français, 1970.

————. *Mohammed Dib: Ecrivain algérien.* Sherbrooke, Quebec: Editions Naaman, 1977.

————. *Situation de la littérature maghrébine de langue française.* Algiers: Office des Publications Universitaires, 1982.

————. *Les Tendances depuis 1962 dans la littérature maghrébine de langue française.* Algiers: Centre Culturel Français, 1973.

————, ed. *Jeunes poètes algériens.* Paris: Editions Saint-Germain-des-Prés, 1981.

De la domination française en Afrique, et des principales questions qui fait naître l'occupation de ces pays. Paris: Dondey-Dupré père et fils, 1832.

de la Fournière, Xavier. *Giscard d'Estaing et nous.* Paris: Plon, 1976.

————. *La Zone franc.* Paris: PUF, 1971.

de la Gorce, Pierre-Marie. "Les Idées-forcées du Général de Gaulle," *La Nef,* no. 33 (1968): 9–52.

de Launay, Jacques. *De Gaulle and His France: A Psychopolitical and Historical Portrait.* Translated by Dorothy Albertyn. New York: Julian Press, 1968.

Delaure, Jacques. *L'O.A.S. contre de Gaulle.* Paris: Fayard, 1981.

Delegation General [of the French Government in Algeria]. *Algerian Documents 1960.* Algiers: Delegation General, 1960.

————. *Algeria's Development—1959.* Paris: Information Services of the Delegation General, 1959.

Délégation générale [du gouvernement en Algérie]. *L'Algérie, 1961.* Paris: Direction de l'information de la Délégation générale, 1961.

————. *Les Avantages consentis en faveur de l'industrialisation de l'Algérie.* Algiers: Imprimerie officielle, 1960.

————. *Documents Algériens* (General Progress Report). Paris: Editions Arts et Métiers géographiques, 1958.

————. *Industriels! Venez en Algérie.* Paris: Imprimerie Georges Long, n.d.

————. Direction du Plan et des Etudes économiques. *Plan de Constantine, 1959–1963, rapport général.* Algiers: Imprimerie officielle, 1960.

Deleuze, Gilles. *Foucault.* Translated by edited by Seán Hand. Minneapolis: University of Minnesota Press, 1988.

de Montalais, Jacques. *Qu'est-ce que le Gaullisme?* Paris: Mame, 1969.

De Porte, Anton. *De Gaulle's Foreign Policy, 1944–46.* Cambridge: Harvard University Press, l968.

Dersa (pseud.). *L'Algérie en débat*. Paris: François Maspero, 1981.

Descloitres, Robert, Jean-Claude Reverdy, and Claudine Descloitres. *L'Algérie des bidonvilles: Le Tiers Monde dans la cité*. Paris: Mouton, 1961.

Desjardins, Thierry. *François Mitterrand: Un Socialiste gaullien*. Paris: Hachette, 1978.

Desprairies, Pierre. "L'Evolution de la crise pétrolière de 1970–71: Le Problème de la dépendance." *RDN* 28 (May 1972): 738–57.

Dessaigne, Francine. *Déracinés*. Nanteuil, à Meaux: Fuseau, 1964.

Destanne de Bernis, Gérard. "Les Problèmes pétroliers algériens." *Etudes internationales* 2 (December 1971): 575–609.

Devèze, Jean-Claude. "View of Junior Technical Assistants Working in Algerian Agricultural Sectors." *CT*, no. 75 (1975): 15.

Dib, Mohammed. *Dieu en barbarie*. Paris: Editions du Seuil, 1970.

Dijoud, Paul. "La France et les immigrés." *RDN* 32 (May 1976): 11–18.

Dine, Philip. *Images of the Algerian War: French Fiction and Film, 1954–1992*. Oxford: Clarendon Press, 1994.

Dinwiddy, Bruce, ed. *European Development Policies*. New York: Praeger, 1973.

Dirlik, André. "Abd al-Hamid ibn Badis (1889–1940): Ideologist of Islamic Reformism and Leader of Algerian Nationalism." Ph.D. dissertation, McGill University, 1971.

Djaout, Tahar. *Les Chercheurs d'os*. Paris: Editions du Seuil, 1984.

———. *L'Invention du désert*. Paris, Editions du Seuil, 1987.

———. *Les Vigiles*. Paris: Editions du Seuil, 1991.

Djebar, Assia. *Le Blanc de l'Algérie*. Paris: Albin Michel, 1995.

———. *Women of Algiers in Their Apartment*. Translated by Marjolijn de Jager. Charlottesville: University of Virginia Press, 1992.

Domenach, Jean-Marie. "Enquête auprès des coopérants." *Esprit*, no. 394 (1970), 45–130.

Doucy, Arthur, and Francis Monheim. *Les Révolutions algériennes*. Paris: Fayard, 1971.

Dreyfus, Hubert L., and Paul Rabinow. *Michel Foucault: Beyond Structuralism and Hermeneutics*. 2d ed. Chicago: University of Chicago Press, 1983.

Droz, Bernard, and Evelyne Lever. *Histoire de la guerre d'Algérie, 1954–1962*. Paris: Editions du Seuil, 1982.

Droz, Jacques. *Histoire des doctrines politiques en France*. Paris: PUF, 1975.

Duchemin, Jacques C. *Histoire du F.L.N.* Paris: Table Ronde, 1962.

Duchoc, René, et al. *Les Immigrés du Maghreb: Etudes sur l'adaptation en milieu urbain*. Paris: PUF, 1977.

Duclos, Jeanne. *Dictionnaire du français d'Algérie*. Paris: Editions Bonneton, 1992.

Dupuy, Marie-Thérèse, comp. *Fors l'honneur*. Paris: SERP, 1963.

Duquesne, Jacques. "La Rencontre de Gaulle–Ben Bella." *Confluent*, no. 41 (1964): 511–16.

Duranton-Crabo, Anne-Marie. *Le Temps de l'OAS*. Paris: Editions Complexe, 1995.

Economist Intelligence Unit (EIU). *QER and CR*, 1964–.

Einaudi, Jean-Luc. *La Bataille de Paris, 17 octobre 1961*. Paris: Editions du Seuil, 1991.

"L'Elaboration de la coopération ou la vertu du dialogue: Une interview de M. Bouteflika, Ministre des Affairs étrangères." *RA*, no. 204 (1967): 22–24.

El-Djeich. Algiers.

Entelis, John P. "Algeria in World Politics: Foreign Policy Orientation and the New International Economic Order." *American-Arab Affairs* 6 (fall 1983): 70–78.

———. *Algeria: The Revolution Institutionalized*. Boulder, Colo.: Westview Press, 1986.

———. "Elite Political Culture and Socialization in Algeria: Tensions and Discontinuities." *MEJ* 35 (spring 1981): 191–208.

———, ed. *Islam, Democracy, and the State in North Africa*. Bloomington: Indiana University Press, 1997.

Entelis, John P., and Phillip C. Naylor, eds. *State and Society in Algeria*. Boulder, Colo.: Westview Press, 1992.

Esprit, no. 394 (1970). (On Cooperation.)

Etienne, Bruno. *Algérie: Cultures et révolution*. Paris: Editions du Seuil, 1977.

———. *Les Problèmes juridiques des minorités européennes au Maghreb*. Paris: CNRS, 1968.

Evans, Martin. *The Memory of Resistance: French Opposition to the Algerian War*. Oxford: Berg, 1997.

Facélina, Raymond. *Théologie en situation: Une communauté chrétienne dans le Tiers-Monde (Algérie 1962–1974)*. Strasbourg: Cerdic Publications, 1974.

Fanon, Frantz. *Black Skin, White Masks*. Translated by Charles Lam Markmann. New York: Grove Press, 1967.

———. *A Dying Colonialism*. Translated by Haakon Chevalier. New York: Grove Press, 1967.

———. *Toward the African Revolution (Political Essays)*. Translated by Haakon Chevalier. New York: Grove Press, 1969.

———. *The Wretched of the Earth*. Translated by Constance Farrington. New York: Grove Press, 1968.

Farès, Louis Abderrahmane. *La Cruelle vérité: L'Algérie de 1945 à l'indépendance*. Paris: Plon, 1982.

Farsoun, Karen. "State Capitalism in Algeria." *MERIP*, no. 35 (1975): 3–30.

Fauchon, Paul. *Journal de marche du Sergent Paul Fauchon (Kabylie, juillet 1956–mars 1957)*. Edited by Jean-Charles Jauffret. Montpellier: Université Paul-Valéry, 1997.

Fauvet, Jacques, and Jean Planchais. *La Fronde des généraux*. Paris: Arthaud, 1961.

Favrod, Charles-Henri. *Le F.L.N. et l'Algérie*. Paris: Plon, 1962.

Feigenbaum, Harvey B. *The Politics of Public Enterprise: Oil and the French State*. Princeton: Princeton University Press, 1985.

Feraoun, Mouloud. *Journal, 1955–1962*. Paris: Editins du Seuil, 1962.

Fessard de Foucault, Bertrand. "La Question du Sahara espagnol." *RFEPA*, no. 119 (1975), 73–106; no. 120 (1975), 71–105.

Findlay, Allan, Anne Findlay, and Richard Lawless. "Algeria: Emigration from a Centrally Planned Economy." *Maghreb Review* 4 (May–June 1979): 82–85.

Firestone, Ya'akov. "The Doctrine of Integration with France among the Europeans of Algeria, 1955–1960." *Comparative Political Studies* 4 (July 1971): 177–203.

Fisquet, M. H. *Histoire de l'Algérie: Depuis les temps anciens jusqu'à nos jours*. Paris: Direction Rue de Seine, 1841.

Fitzgerald, E. Peter. "An Application of the Robinson Theory of Collaboration to Colonial Algeria after the Post-War Reforms: The *Instituteur indigène* and French Dominance in the 1920s." In *Proceedings of the French Colonial Historical Society* (Milwaukee, 1976), 155–68.

Flower, J. E., ed. *France Today*. 4th ed. London: Methuen, 1980.

Fontaine, Pierre. *Alerte au pétrole franco-saharien*. Paris: Sept Couleurs, 1961.

———. *Bataille pour le pétrole français*. Paris: Editions 'Je Sens,' 1957.

Fontaneau, Pierre. "Les Garanties économiques des accords d'Evian." *Développement africain* 2 (April 1962): 3–6.

Foreign Broadcast Information Services (FBIS). *Western Europe Series (WEU)* and *Near East Series (NES)*.

Forsyth, Frederick. *The Day of the Jackal*. New York: Viking, 1971.

Foucault, Michel. *The Archaeology of Knowledge*. Translated by A. M. Sheridan Smith. New York: Pantheon, 1972.

———. *Discipline and Punishment: The Birth of the Prison*. Translated by Alan Sheridan. New York: Vintage, 1979.

———. *History of Sexuality*. Vol. 1, *Introduction*. Translated by Robert Hurley. New York: Vintage, 1980.

———. *The Order of Things: An Archaeology of the Human Sciences*. New York: Vintage, 1973.

France: Aid and Cooperation. New York: French Embassy in the United States, Service de presse et d'information, 1962.

France and the Atom. New York: Ambassade de France, Service de presse et d'information, 1962.

La France doit-elle conserver Alger? Paris: Béthune et Plon, 1835.

France outremer; Europe-France-outremer; Europe outremer. 1958–73.

Francos, Ania, and Jean-Pierre Séréni. *Un Algérien nommé Boumediène*. Paris: Stock, 1976.

Frears, John R. *France in the Giscard Presidency*. London: George Allen & Unwin, 1981.

The Freedom Fighter. Special Issue. New York: Algerian Resistance (FLN), 1956.

Friend, Julius W. *The Long Presidency: France in the Mitterrand Years, 1981–1995*. Boulder, Colo.: Westview Press, 1998.

Frye, Northrop. *The Critical Path: An Essay on the Social Context of Literary Criticism*. Bloomington: Indiana University Press, 1971.

Fuller, Graham E. *Algeria: The Next Fundamentalist State?* Santa Monica: Rand, 1996.

Furniss, Edgar S. *De Gaulle and the French Army*. New York: Twentieth Century Fund, 1964.

Fuchs, Yves. *La Coopération: Aide ou néo-colonialisme?* Paris: Editions sociales, 1973.

Gafaiti, Hafid. *Boudjedra ou la passion de la modernité*. Paris: Denoël, 1987.

Gallagher, Charles F. "Co-operation: The New French Revolution." *AUFS: NAS* 9 (October 1963): 1–25.

———. "New Economic Plans for Algeria." *AUFS: NAS* 4 (October 1958): 1–8.

———. "The Other Algeria: Notes on a Developing Economy." *AUFS: NAS* 6 (October 1960): 1–8.

———. "What Price Algeria?" *AUFS: NAS* 3 (November 1957): 1–7.

Gallissot, René, ed. *Les Accords d'Evian: En conjoncture et en longue durée*. Paris: Karthala, 1997.

Gardinier, David E. "French Colonial Rule in Africa: A Bibliographical Essay." In *France and Britain in Africa: Imperial Rivalry and Colonial Rule,* edited by Prosser Gifford and William Roger Louis, 787–902. New Haven: Yale University Press, 1971.

———. "Decolonization in French, Belgian, and Portuguese Africa: A Bibliographical Essay." In *The Transfer of Power in Africa: Decolonization, 1940–1960,* edited by Prosser Gifford and William Roger Louis, 515–66. New Haven: Yale University Press, 1982.

———. "Decolonization in French, Belgian, Portuguese, and Italian Africa: Bibliography." In *Decolonization and African Independence: The Transfers of Power, 1960–1980,* edited by Prosser Gifford and William Roger Louis, 573–635. New Haven: Yale University Press, 1988.

Gaudice, Fausto. *Arabicides: Une chronique française*. Paris: La Découverte, 1992.

Gauthier, Yves, and Joel Kermarec. *Naissance et croissance de la République Algérienne Démocratique et Populaire*. Paris: Edition Marketing, 1978.

Gautier, Théophile. *Voyage en Algérie*. Paris: La Boîte à Documents, 1989.

Geismar, Peter. *Fanon*. New York: Dial Press, 1971.

Gendarme, René. *L'Economie de l'Algérie: Sous-Développement et politique de croissance*. Paris: Armand Colin, 1959.

Gendzier, Irene. *Frantz Fanon: A Critical Study*. New York: Pantheon, 1973; 2d ed., Grove Press, 1985.

Genet, Jean. *The Screens*. Translated by Bernard Frechtman. New York: Grove Press, 1962.

Germidis, Dimitri. *Le Maghreb, la France, et l'enjeu technologique.* Paris: Cujas, 1976.

Ghiles, Francis. "Chadli's Pragmatic Economics." *Africa Report* 29 (November–December 1984): 10–13.

Giesbert, Franz-Olivier. *François Mitterrand, ou la tentation de l'histoire.* Paris: Editions du Seuil, 1977.

Gifford, Prosser, and William Roger Louis, eds. *Decolonization and African Independence: The Transfers of Power, 1960–1980.* New Haven: Yale University Press, 1988.

Girardet, Raoul. *L'Idée coloniale en France de 1871 à 1962.* Paris: Table Ronde, 1972.

Giraud, Jacqueline. "France-Algérie: La Voie de l'intérêt mutuel." *Actuel et développement,* no. 52 (1983): 31–32.

Gobineau, Arthur. *The Inequality of Human Races.* Translated by Adrian Collins. New York: Howard Fertig, 1967.

Gonon, Jean-Pierre. "Adaptation de la formation à l'emploi en Algérie: Un exemple de coopération positive." *CT,* no. 71 (1973): 17–26.

———. "Mécanisme de l'aide financière française à l'Algérie." *CT,* nos. 44–45 (1966): 60–68.

Gordon, David C. *North Africa's French Legacy: 1954–1962.* Cambridge: Harvard University Press, 1962.

———. *The Passing of French Algeria.* London: Oxford University Press, 1966.

Gordon, Lewis R., T. Denean Sharpley-Whiting, and Renée T. White, eds. *Fanon: A Critical Reader.* Oxford: Blackwell, 1996.

Gordon, Philip H. *A Certain Idea of France: French Security Policy and the Gaullist Legacy.* Princeton: Princeton University Press, 1993.

Gorse, Georges. Interview by author. Paris, 19 May 1978.

Goumeziane, Smail. *Le Mal algérien: Economie, politique d'une transition inachevée, 1962–1994.* Paris: Fayard, 1994.

Goutor, Jacques. *Algeria and France, 1830–1963.* Muncie, Ind.: Ball State University, 1965.

Gouvernement général de l'Algérie. *Algérie en 1953.* Algiers: Service d'Information et de Documentation, 1953.

———. *Discours prononcé par M. Jacques Soustelle Gouverneur général de l'Algérie à la séance solennelle de l'Assemblée algérienne, le 23 février 1955.* Algiers: Imprimerie officielle, 1955.

———. *15 mois d'action en Algérie.* Paris: Imprimerie nouvelle, 1957.

Goytisolo, Juan. *L'Algérie dans la tourmente.* Translated by Mohamed Saad' el Yamani. Strasbourg: La Nuée Bleue, 1994.

Grandguillaume, Gilbert. *Arabisation et politique linguistique au Maghreb.* Paris: Editions G.-P. Maisonneuve et Larose, 1983.

Grimaud, Nicole. "Algeria and Socialist France." *MEJ* 40 (spring 1986): 252–66.

———. "Le Conflit pétrolier franco-algérien." *Revue française de science politique* 22 (December 1972): 1276–1307.

———. "L'Introuvable equilibre maghrébin." Paper presented at a colloquium, "La Politique extérieure de Valéry Giscard d'Estaing," Paris, 26–27 May 1983.

———. "Nouvelles orientations des relations entre la France et l'Algérie." *Maghreb-Machrek*, no. 103 (1984): 96–106.

———. *La Politique extérieure de l'Algérie*. Paris: Karthala, 1984.

Grosser, Alfred. *French Foreign Policy under de Gaulle*. Translated by Lois Ames Pattison. Boston: Little, Brown, 1965.

———. *La IVᵉ République et sa politique extérieure*. Paris: Armand Colin, 1967.

———. *The Western Alliance: European-American Relations Since 1945*. Translated by Michael Shaw. New York: Vintage, 1982.

Groussard, Serge. *L'Algérie des adieux*. Paris: Plon, 1972.

Guérin, Daniel. *L'Algérie caporalisée?* Paris: Colombes, 1965.

———. *L'Algérie qui se cherche*. Paris: Editions Présence Africaine, 1964.

Guilhaume, Jean-François. *Les Mythes fondateurs de l'Algérie française*. Paris: L'Harmattan, 1992.

Guillaumat, Pierre. "L'Industrie du pétrole à l'horizon 80." *RDN* 26 (October 1970): 1415–34.

Haddad, Malek. *La Dernière impression*. Paris: Julliard, 1958.

———. "La Langue française est mon exil." *Dialogues*, no. 7 (1963–64): 26–27.

Hadj Ali, Youcef. *Lettre ouverte aux Français qui ne comprennent décidément rien à l'Algérie*. Paris: Albin Michel, 1998.

Hamel, Benaouda. *Système productif algérien et indépendance nationale*. 2 vols. Algiers: Office des Publications Universitaires, 1983.

Hamilton, Paul. *Historicism*. London: Routledge, 1996.

Hamon, Hervé, and Patrick Rotman. *Les Porteurs de valises: La Résistance française à la guerre d'Algérie*. Paris: Albin Michel, 1979.

Hamoumou, Mohand. *Et ils son devenus harkis*. Paris: Fayard, 1993.

Hansen, Emmanuel. *Frantz Fanon: Social and Political Thought*. Columbus: Ohio State University Press, 1977.

Harbi, Mohammed. *Le FLN, mirages et réalités: Des Origines à la prise du pouvoir (1945–1962)*. Paris: Editions Jeune Afrique, 1980.

———, ed. *Les Archives de la Révolution algérienne*. Paris: Editions Jeune Afrique, 1981.

Hargreaves, Alec G. *Immigration and Identity in Beur Fiction: Voices from the North African Immigrant Community in France*. Rev. ed. Oxford: Berg, 1997.

———. *La Littérature beur: Un guide bio-bibliographique*. New Orleans: Celfan Edition Monographs, Tulane University, 1992.

———. *Voices from the North African Immigrant Community in France: Immigration and Identity in Beur Fiction*. New York: Berg, 1991.

Hargreaves, Alec G., and Michael J. Heffernan, eds. *French and Algerian Identities from Colonial Times to the Present*. Lewiston, N.Y.: Edwin Mellen Press, 1993.

Hargreaves, Alec G., and Mark McKinney, eds. *Post-Colonial Cultures in France*. London: Routledge, 1997.

Hartley, Anthony. *Gaullism: The Rise and Fall of a Political Movement*. New York: Outerbridge & Dienstfrey, 1971.

Hayter, Teresa. *French Aid*. London: Overseas Development Institute, 1966.

Heggoy, Alf Andrew. "Books on the Algerian Revolution in English: Translations and Anglo-American Contributions." *African Historical Studies* 3, pt. 1 (1970): 163–68.

———. "Development or Control: French Policies in Colonial and Revolutionary Algeria." *Journal of African Studies* 5 (1978–79): 427–43.

———. *The French Conquest of Algiers, 1830: An Algerian Oral Tradition*. Athens, Ohio: Ohio University for International Studies, 1986.

———. *Insurgency and Counterinsurgency in Algeria*. Bloomington: Indiana University Press, 1972.

———. "The Two Societies of French Algeria and the Failure of Coexistence." *African Quarterly* 13 (April–June 1973): 32–.

———, ed. *Through Foreign Eyes: Western Attitudes Toward North Africa*. Washington: University Press of America, 1982.

Heggoy, Alf Andrew, with Robert R. Crout. *Historical Dictionary of Algeria*. Metuchen, N.J.: Scarecrow Press, 1981.

Hélie, Jérôme. *Les Accords d'Evian: Histoire de la paix ratée en Algérie*. Paris: Olivier Orban, 1992.

Hennissart, Paul. *Wolves in the City: The Death of French Algeria*. New York: Simon and Schuster, 1970.

Hernandez, Philippe. "Ceux qui étaient les 'Pieds-noirs'." *La Nef*, nos. 12–13 (1962–63): 33–46.

Herremann, Philippe. "Du Socialisme passionel de Ben Bella au socialisme 'tempéré' de Boumediène." *RFEPA*, no. 11 (1966): 56–66.

Hessel, Stéphane. "La Coopération franco-algérienne en 1966." *Coopération et Développement*, no. 11 (1966): 10–17.

———. Editorial. *Rencontres*, no. 1 (1967): 5–11.

———. "Socialist France and Developing Countries." *French Politics & Society* 9, nos. 3–4 (summer-fall 1991): 130–40.

Himmelfarb, Milton. "Algeria's Jews and Other Matters." *Commentary* 33 (May 1962): 430–32.

Hincker, M. "Aspects économiques des accords d'Evian." *Economie et politique*, no. 95 (1962): 32–39.

Hinz, Manfred O. *Le Droit à l'autodétermination du Sahara occidental: Le Chemin difficile du peuple sahraoui*. Bonn: Progress dritte Welt Verlag, 1978.

Historia, no. 486 (1987).

Hodges, Tony. "François Mitterrand, Master Strategist of the Maghreb." *Africa Report* 28, no. 3 (May–June 1983): 17–21.

———. *Historical Dictionary of Western Sahara*. Metuchen, N.J.: Scarecrow Press, 1982.

———. *Western Sahara: The Roots of a Desert War.* Westport, Conn.: Lawrence Hill, 1983.

Hoffmann, Stanley. "De Gaulle's Memoirs: The Hero of History." *World Politics* 13 (October 1960): 140–55.

———. "Gaullism by Any Other Name." *Foreign Policy,* no. 58 (1984–85): 38–52.

———, ed. *Decline or Renewal? France Since the 1930s.* New York: Viking, 1974.

———. *In Search of France.* Cambridge: Harvard University Press, 1963.

Hommes et migrations.

Horne, Alistair. *A Savage War of Peace.* 2d ed. New York: Penguin, 1987.

Houart, Pierre. *L'Attitude de l'Eglise dans la guerre d'Algérie, 1954–1960.* Brussels: Le Livre Africain, 1960.

Huguenin-Gonon, Nicole. "Compte rendu de l'enquête sur l'alphabétisation des Algériens en France." *CT,* no. 63 (1970): 24–33.

Humbaraci, Arslan. *Algeria: A Revolution that Failed.* London: Pall Mall, 1966.

Hutchinson, Martha Crenshaw. *Revolutionary Terrorism: The FLN in Algeria, 1954–1962.* Stanford: Hoover Institution, 1978.

Ibn Khaldun. *The Muqaddimah: An Introduction to History.* 3 vols. Translated by Franz Rosenthal. Princeton: Princeton University Press, 1967.

Ibrahimi, Ahmed Taleb. *See* Taleb Ibrahimi, Ahmed.

"L'Immigration maghrébine en France: Les Faits et les mythes." *Les Temps modernes* 40 (March-April-May 1984).

"Immigrés: Le Retour est-il possible?" *L'Express,* 18–24 May 1984.

Industries et travaux d'outremer, no. 267 (1976).

Institut Charles de Gaulle. *De Gaulle et le Tiers Monde.* Paris: Editions A. Pedone, 1984.

———. *De Gaulle et son siècle.* Vol. 6, *Liberté et dignité des peuples.* Paris: Documentation française, 1992.

Isnard, Hildebart. *La Vigne en Algérie: Etude géographique.* Paris: CNRS, 1951.

Israel, Gérard. *Le Dernier jour de l'Algérie française, 1er juillet 1962.* Paris: Robert Laffont, 1972.

Itinéraires, no. 264 (1982). (On repatriated populations.)

Iseman, Frederick. "The War in the Sahara." *Harper's,* September 1980, 41–56.

Jackson, Henry F. *The FLN in Algeria: Party Development in a Revolutionary Society.* Westport, Conn.: Greenwood Press, 1977.

Jansen, G. H. *Militant Islam.* New York: Harper & Row, 1979.

Jasseron, Georges. Interview by author. Rouen, 25 January 1978.

———. *Les Harkis en France: Scènes et témoignages.* Paris: Editions du Fuseau, 1965.

Jeanneney, Jean-Marcel. "La Politique de coopération avec les pays en voie de développement" (Jeanneney Report). *Documentation française illustrée,* no. 201 (1964).

Jeanson, Francis. *Algéries: De retour en retour.* Paris: Editions du Seuil, 1991.

————. *La Révolution algérienne: Problèmes et perspectives*. Milan: Feltrinelli, 1962.

Jinadu, L. Adele. *Fanon: In Search of the African Revolution*. London: KPI, 1986.

Jobert, Michel. *L'Autre regard*. Paris: Bernard Grasset, 1976.

Joesten, Joachim. *The New Algeria*. Chicago: Follett, 1964.

————. *The Red Hand: The Sinister Account of the Terrorist Arm of the French Right-Wing "Ultras"—in Algeria and on the Continent*. New York: Abelard Schuman, 1962.

Joffé, George, ed. *North Africa: Nation, State, and Region*. London: Routledge, 1993.

Johnson, Douglas. "Algeria: Some Problems of Modern History." *Journal of African History* 5, no. 2 (1964): 221–42.

Jouhaud, Edmond. *Ce que je n'ai pas dit*. Paris: Fayard, 1977.

Joxe, Louis. Interview by author. Paris, 22 May 1978.

Joyau, François, and Patrick Wajsman, eds. *Pour une nouvelle politique étrangère*. Paris: Hachette, 1986.

Judet, Pierre. "L'Evolution des relations et des échanges entre l'Algérie et la France en fonction des perspectives de l'économie algérienne et en particulier son industrialisation (Horizon 80)." Commissariat général du Plan, et Ministère des Affaires étrangères. Grenoble: Centre de recherche sur l'industrialisation et le développement, 1976.

Julien, Charles-André. *L'Afrique du Nord en marche: Nationalismes musulmans et souveraineté française*. 3d ed. Paris: Julliard, 1972.

————. *La Conquête et les débuts de la colonisation (1827–1871)*. Vol. 1 of *Histoire de l'Algérie contemporaine*. Paris: PUF, 1964.

————. *History of North Africa: Tunisia, Algeria, Morocco*. Translated by John Petrie. London: Routledge & Kegan Paul, 1970.

Junqua, Daniel. "France-Algérie: Enfin l'entente cordial?" *Croissance des jeunes nations*, no. 230 (1981): 9–11.

Jurt, Joseph, ed. *Algérie-France-Islam*. Paris: L'Harmattan, 1997.

Kaberseli, Ahmed. "Et les Français musulmans." *Itinéraires*, no. 264 (1982): 34–48.

Kaddache, Mahfoud. *Histoire du nationalisme algérien: Question nationale et politique algérienne, 1919–1951*. 2 vols. Algiers: SNED, 1981.

Kadra-Hadjadji, Houaria, and Hamdan Hadjadji. *Méthode d'arabe moderne*. Algiers: Office des Publications Universitaires, 1983.

Kaid, Ahmed. *Aspects essentiels de la révolution culturelle*. Algiers: Département Orientation et Information du Parti, 1971.

Kaltenbach, Jeanne-Hélène, and Pierre-Patrick Kaltenbach. *La France: Une chance pour l'Islam*. Paris: Editions du Félin, 1991.

Kapil, Arun. "Algeria's Elections Show Islamist Strength." *Middle East Report* 20 (September–October 1990): 31–36.

Kara, Bouzid. *See* Bouzid Kara.

Kasenty, I. and L. *La Cuisine pied-noir.* Paris: Denoël, 1979.

Keohane, Robert O., Joseph S. Nye, and Stanley Hoffmann, eds. *After the Cold War: International Institutions and State Strategies in Europe, 1989–1991.* Cambridge: Harvard University Press, 1993.

Khellad, Aissa. *Algérie: Les Islamistes face au pouvoir.* Algiers: Alfa, 1992.

Knauss, Peter R. "Algeria's 'Agrarian Revolution': Peasant Control or Control of Peasants?" *African Studies Review* 20 (December 1977): 65–78.

———. *The Persistence of Patriarchy: Class, Gender, and Ideology in Twentieth Century Algeria.* New York: Praeger, 1987.

Knight, M. M. "The Algerian Revolt: Some Underlying Factors." *MEJ* 10 (autumn 1956): 355–67.

Kohl, Wilfred L. *French Nuclear Diplomacy.* Princeton: Princeton University Press, 1971.

Kolodziej, Edward. *French International Policy under de Gaulle and Pompidou: The Politics of Grandeur.* Ithaca, N.Y.: Cornell University Press, 1974.

Kraft, Joseph. "Settler Politics in Algeria." *Foreign Affairs* 39 (July 1961): 591–600.

Kramer, Steven Philip. *Does France Still Count? The French Role in the New Europe.* Washington: Center for Strategic and International Studies, 1994.

Kristeva, Julia. *Nations without Nationalism.* Translated by Leon S. Roudiez. New York: Columbia University Press, 1993.

Kulski, W. W. *De Gaulle and the World: The Foreign Policy of the Fifth Republic.* Syracuse, N.Y.: Syracuse University Press, 1966.

Lacheraf, Mostefa. *L'Algérie: Nation et société.* 2d ed. Algiers: SNED, 1978.

———. "L'Avenir de la culture algérienne." *Les Temps modernes* 19, no. 204 (1963): 720–45.

Lacouture, Jean. *De Gaulle.* Translated by Francis K. Price. London: Hutchinson, 1970.

———. *De Gaulle: The Rebel.* Translated by Patrick O'Brian. New York: Norton, 1990.

———. *De Gaulle: The Ruler.* Translated by Alan Sheridan. New York: Norton, 1992.

———. *Pierre Mendès-France.* Translated by George Holoch. New York: Holmes & Meier, 1984.

Lakehal, Mokhtar, ed. *Algérie: De l'indépendance à l'état d'urgence.* Paris: L'Harmattan, 1992.

Lamchichi, Abderrahim. *L'Islamisme en Algérie.* Paris: L'Harmattan, 1992.

Lanasri, Ahmed, ed. *Anthologie de la poésie algérienne de langue arabe.* Paris: Publisud, 1994.

Lassassi, Assassi. *Non-Alignment and Algerian Foreign Policy.* Aldershot, England: Avebury, 1988.

Lauprêtre, Claude. "L'Evolution des rapports de coopération franco-algérien." Thesis, Université de Bordeaux, 1974–75.

Lavers, Annette. *Roland Barthes: Structuralism and After*. Cambridge: Harvard University Press, 1982.

Lawless, Richard I., comp. *Algeria: Volume 19*. Oxford: Clio Press, 1980.

———. *Algerian Bibliography: English Language Publications, 1830–1973*. London: Bowker, with Center for Middle Eastern and Islamic Studies, University of Durham, 1976.

———. *A Bibliography of Works on Algeria Published in English Since 1954*. Durham, England: University of Durham, Center for Middle Eastern and Islamic Studies, 1972.

Lawless, Richard, and Laila Monahan, eds. *War and Refugees: The Western Sahara Conflict*. London: Pinter, 1987.

Lazreg, Marnia. *The Emergence of Classes in Algeria: A Study of Colonialism and Socio-Political Change*. Boulder, Colo.: Westview Press, 1976.

Lebovics, Herman. *True France: The Wars over Cultural Identity*. Ithaca, N.Y.: Cornell University Press, 1992.

Leca, Jean, and Jean-Claude Vatin. *Algérie: Politique, institutions et régime*. Paris: Presses de la Fondation Nationale des Sciences Politiques, 1975.

Leclair, Marc-Louis. *Disparus en Algérie: 3,000 Français en possibilité de survie*. Paris: Jacques Grancher, 1986.

Leconte, Daniel. *Les Pieds-noirs: Histoire et portrait d'une communauté*. Paris: Editions du Seuil, 1980.

Ledwidge, Bernard. *De Gaulle*. New York: St. Martin's Press, 1982.

Leimdorfer, François. *Discours académique et colonisation: Thèmes de recherche sur l'Algérie pendant la période coloniale*. Paris: Publisud, 1992.

Lentin, Albert-Paul. *L'Algérie entre deux mondes*. Vol. 1, *Le Dernier quart d'heure*. Paris: Julliard, 1963.

———. "La Situation de la minorité européenne en Algérie." *RFEPA*, no. 12 (1966): 22–49.

Le Pen, Jean-Marie. *La France est de retour*. Paris: Editions Carrère/Michel Lafon, 1985.

Leriche, Joseph. *Les Algériens parmi nous: Essai psycho-sociologique*. Paris: Editions sociales français, 1959.

Le Tourneau, Roger. *Evolution politique de l'Afrique du Nord musulmane, 1920–1961*. Paris: Armand Colin, 1962.

Le Tourneau, Roger, et al. *L'Unité maghrébine: Dimensions et perspectives*. Paris: CNRS, 1972.

Leulliette, Pierre. *St. Michael and the Dragon: A Paratrooper in the Algerian War*. Translated by Tony White. London: Heinemann, 1964.

Leveau, Rémy. *Le Sabre et le turban: L'Avenir du Maghreb*. Paris: Editions François Bourin, 1993.

Lewis, William H. "Algeria Against Itself." *Africa Report* 12 (December 1967): 9–15.

———. "Algeria Changes Course." *Africa Report* 10 (November 1965): 537–62.

———. "Algeria: The Cycle of Reciprocal Fear." *African Studies Bulletin* 12 (December 1969): 323–37.

———. "Algeria: The Plight of the Victor." *Current History* 44 (January 1963): 22–28.

———. "The Decline of Algeria's FLN." *MEJ* 20 (spring 1966): 161–72.

Liauzu, Claude. "Les Intellectuels français au miroir de la guerre de l'Algérie." *Cahiers de la Méditerranée* (Groupe de recherches sur le Maghreb et le monde musulman, Université de Paris VII-Jussieu), no. 3 (1984).

Lippert, Anne. "The Struggle in the Western Sahara and Foreign Intervention." Paper distributed by the Saharan Peoples Support Committee, 1980.

Livesay, Lewis. "A Critique of Structuralism and the Metaphysical Systematizing of Lévi-Strauss." Unpublished manuscript.

Loomba, Ania. *Colonialism/Postcolonialism*. London: Routledge, 1998.

Lorcin, Patricia M. E. *Imperial Identities: Stereotyping, Prejudice and Race in Colonial Algeria*. London: I. B. Tauris, 1995.

Lottman, Herbert R. *Albert Camus: A Biography*. Garden City, N.Y.: Doubleday, 1979.

Lucas, Philippe. *Sociologie de Frantz Fanon: Contribution à une anthropologie de la Libération*. Algiers: SNED, 1971.

Luchaire, François. *L'Aide aux pays sous-développés*. Paris: PUF, 1977.

Luethy, Herbert. "De Gaulle: Pose and Policy." *Foreign Affairs* 43 (July 1965): 561–73.

———. *France Against Herself: A Perceptive Study of France's Past, Her Politics, and Her Unending Crises*. Translated by Eric Mosbacher. New York: Praeger, 1955.

Lustick, Ian S. *Unsettled States, Disputed Lands: Britain and Ireland, France and Algeria, Israel and the West Bank–Gaza*. Ithaca, N.Y.: Cornell University Press, 1993.

Macey, David. *The Lives of Michel Foucault: A Biography*. New York: Pantheon, 1994.

MacShane, Denis. *François Mitterrand: A Political Odyssey*. New York: Universe, 1983.

al-Madani, Ahmed Tewfiq. *Hadhihi hia al-Jaza'ir* (This is Algeria). Cairo: Maktaba al-nahda al-misriyya, 1959.

———. *Al-Harb al-thalathami'a bayna al-Jaza'ir wa Isbana, 1492–1792* (The three-hundred-year war between Algeria and Spain, 1492–1792). Algiers: SNED, 1968.

———. *Kitab al-Jaza'ir.* (Book of Algeria). Algiers: al-Mu'assassa al-wataniyya, 1984.

Madelain, Jacques. *L'Errance et l'itinéraire: Lecture du roman maghrébin de langue française*. Paris: Sindbad, 1983.

Madelin, Henri. *Pétrole et politique en Méditerranée occidentale*. Paris: Armand Colin, 1973.

Mahdi, Muhsin. *Ibn Khaldûn's Philosophy of History: A Study in the Philosophic Foundation of the Science of Culture.* Chicago: University of Chicago Press, 1971.

Mahsas, Ahmed. *Le Mouvement Révolutionnaire en Algérie: De la 1re Guerre mondiale à 1954.* Paris: L'Harmattan, 1979.

Mahiout, Rabah. *Le Pétrole algérien.* Algiers: En.A.P., 1974.

Malek, Redha. *L'Algérie à Evian: Histoire des négociations secrètes, 1956–1962.* Paris: Editions du Seuil, 1995.

Malewska-Peyre, Hanna, et al. *Crise d'identité et déviance des jeunes immigrés.* Paris: Ministère de Justice (Documentation française), 1982.

Mallarde, Etienne. *L'Algérie depuis.* Paris: Table Ronde, 1975.

Malley, Robert. *The Call from Algeria: Third Worldism, Revolution, and the Turn to Islam.* Berkeley and Los Angeles: University of California Press, 1996.

Malraux, André. *Felled Oaks: Conversation with de Gaulle.* Translated by Irene Clephane and Linda Asher. New York: Holt, Rinehart, and Winston, 1971.

Mameri, Khalfa, ed. *Citations du Président Boumediène.* 3d. ed. Algiers: SNED, 1977.

Mammeri, Mouloud. *Culture savante, culture vécue: Etudes, 1938–1989.* Algiers: Association Culturelle et Scientifique (TALA), 1991.

———. *La Traversée.* Paris: Plon, 1982.

Manceron, Claude, and Bernard Pingaud. *François Mitterrand: L'Homme—les idées—le programme.* Paris: Flammarion, 1981.

Manceron, Gilles, and Hassan Remaoun. *D'une rive à l'autre: La Guerre d'Algérie de la mémoire à l'histoire.* Paris: Syros, 1993.

Mandel, Arnold. "France's Algerian Jews." *Commentary* 35 (June 1963): 475–82.

Mandouze, André, ed. *La Révolution algérienne par les textes.* 3d ed. Paris: François Maspéro, 1962.

Mannoni, Pierre. *Les Français d'Algérie: Vie, moeurs, mentalité: De la conquête des Territoires du Sud à l'indépendance.* Paris: L'Harmattan, 1993.

Mansell, Gerard. *Tragedy in Algeria.* London: Oxford University Press, 1961.

Marchés tropicaux du monde, to 1958; *Marchés tropicaux et méditerranéens (MTM),* after 1958.

Marie, René. "Algérie: Terre de dialogue?" *RDN* 19 (August–September 1963): 1318–40.

Marrou, Henri-Irénée. *The Meaning of History.* Translated by Robert J. Olsen. Baltimore: Helicon, 1966.

Marseille, Jacques. *Empire colonial et capitalisme français: Histoire d'un divorce.* Paris: Albin Michel, 1984.

Marshall, D. Bruce. *The French Colonial Myth and Constitution-Making in the Fourth Republic.* New Haven: Yale University Press, 1973.

Martens, Jean-Claude. *Le Modèle algérien de développement: Bilan d'une décennie (1962–1972).* Algiers: SNED, 1973.

Martin, Claude. *Les Israélites algériens de 1830 à 1902.* Paris: Herakles, 1932.

Martinez, Luis. *La Guerre civile en Algérie, 1990–1998*. Paris, Karthala, 1998.

Maschino, T. M., and Fadéla M'rabet. *L'Algérie des illusions: La Révolution confisquée*. Paris: Robert Laffont, 1972.

Massu, Jacques. *La Vraie Bataille d'Alger*. Paris: Plon, 1971.

Mazouni, Abdallah. *Culture et enseignement en Algérie et au Maghreb*. Paris: François Maspéro, 1969.

Mazri, Hamid. *Les Hydrocarbures dans l'économie algérienne*. Algiers: SNED, 1975.

Meducin, Denis Y. "Le Modèle algérien de coopération pour le développement." Doctoral dissertation, Université d'Aix-Marseille, 1974.

Méliani, Abd-El-Aziz. *La France honteuse: Le Drame des harkis*. Paris: Perrin, 1993.

Memmi, Albert. *Anthologie des érivains maghrébins d'expression française*. Paris: Présence africain, 1964.

Mendès-France, Pierre. *Choisir: Conversations avec Jean Bothorel*. Paris: Stock, 1974.

Mercier, Gustave, ed. *Le Centenaire de l'Algérie, exposé d'ensemble*. 2 vols. Algiers: P. G. Soubiron, 1931.

Merle, Robert, comp. *Ahmed Ben Bella*. Translated by Camilla Sykes. New York: Walker, 1967.

Merleau-Ponty, Maurice. *Humanism and Terror: An Essay on the Communist Problem*. Translated by John O'Neill. Boston: Beacon Press, 1969.

———. *The Visible and the Invisible*. Edited by Claude Lefort. Translated by Alphonso Lingis. Evanston, Illinois: Northwestern University Press, 1968.

Messaoudi, Khalida. *Unbowed: An Algerian Woman Confronts Islamic Fundamentalism*. Interviews with Elisabeth Schemla. Translated by Anne C. Vila. Philadelphia: University of Pennsylvania Press, 1998.

Meynier, Gilbert. "Les Algériens en France, 1914–1918." *Revue d'histoire maghrébine*, no. 5 (1971): 47–58.

Micaud, Charles A. "Bilingualism in North Africa: Cultural and Sociopolitical Implications." *Western Political Quarterly* 27 (March 1974): 92–103.

Michel, Andrée. *The Modernization of North African Families in the Paris Area*. The Hague: Mouton & Company, 1974.

———. *Les Travailleurs algériens en France*. Paris: CNRS, 1956.

Migdalovitz, Carol. "Algeria: Four Years of Crisis." Report for Congress. Washington: Congressional Research Service, 1996.

al-Mili, Muhammad. *Tarikh al-Jaza'ir fi al-qadim wa al-hadith* (The history of Algeria in the past and present.) 1931. Reprint, Algiers: SNED, 1976.

Miller, Mark J. "Reluctant Partnership: Foreign Workers in Franco-Algerian Relations, 1962–1979." *Journal of International Affairs* 33 (fall-winter 1979): 219–37.

Mimouni, Rachid. *De la barbarie en général et de l'intégrisme en particulier*. Paris: Belfond, Le Pré aux Clercs, 1992.

——. *The Honor of the Tribe.* Translated by Joachim Neugroschel. New York: William Morrow, 1992.

——. *La Malédiction.* Paris: Stock, 1993.

——. *The Ogre's Embrace.* Translated by Shirley Eber. London: Quartet, 1993.

Minces, Juliette. *Les Travailleurs étrangers en France.* Paris: Editions du Seuil, 1973.

Ministère de la Coopération. *10 réponses sur l'Afrique: Opinions sur la coopération entre l'Afrique et la France.* Paris: Ministère de la Coopération, 1963.

Ministère de l'Algérie. *Action du gouvernement en Algérie: Mesures de pacification et réformes.* Algiers: Service de l'Information du Cabinet du Ministère de l'Algérie, 1957.

——. *Perspectives décennales de développement économique de l'Algérie.* Algiers: Ministère de l'Algérie, 1958.

Ministère de l'information. *Qu'est-ce que le Programme de Tripoli?* Algiers: Direction de la documentation et des publications, 1962.

Ministère de l'information et de la culture. *Textes fondamentaux du Front de Libération Nationale (1954–1962).* Dossiers documentaires, no. 24. Algiers: Direction de la lecture publique et de la documentation, 1976.

Ministère de l'orientation nationale. *Alger: Capitale de la solidarité afro-asiatique.* VIᵉ Session du Conseil de la Solidarité Afro-Asiatique, Algiers, 22–26 March 1964. Algiers: Direction de la documentation et des publications, 1964.

——. *Algérie, an II: 1962–1964.* Algiers: Direction de la documentation et des publications, 1963.

——. *De Bamako à Addis-Abéba.* Algiers: Direction de la documentation et des publications, 1964.

——. *Politique économique du gouvernement: Exposé de Bachir Boumaza devant l'Assemblée nationale (30 December 1963).* Algiers: Direction de la documentation et des publications, 1964.

Ministère des affaires étrangères. *Relations culturelles, coopération technique: Rapport d'activité.* Paris: Direction générale des Relations culturelles et Direction de la Coopération technique, 1967–70.

——. *Relations culturelles, scientifiques et techniques (1968–69).* Paris: Direction générale des Affaires culturelles et techniques, 1969.

Ministre d'état chargé des affaires algériennes. "Les Accords d'Evian: Textes et commentaires." *Recueils et monographies* (Documentation française), no. 40 (1962).

——. "L'Algérie à l'heure de la paix." *TN,* no. 10 (1962): 1–21.

Ministre résident en Algérie. *Algérie, quelques aspects des problèmes économiques et sociaux.* Algiers: Imprimerie Baconnier, 1957.

Ministry of Information. *Aspects of Algeria.* Algiers: Documents and Publications Department, 1967.

Ministry of Information and Culture. *The Algerian Revolution: Facts and Pros-*

pects (10th Anniversary of Independence). Algiers: Documents and Publications Department; Madrid: Altamira, 1972.

———. *The Faces of Algeria*. Algiers; Madrid: Altamira, 1970–77. (The Ministry of Information and then the Ministry of Information and Culture published this series, which described the activities of different sectors—public works, self-management, youth and sports, agricultural development, the Agrarian Revolution, trade policy, the socialist organization of enterprises, education, hydrocarbons, and the Four-Year Plan.)

Miské, Ahmed-Baba. *Front Polisaire: L'Ame d'un peuple*. Paris: Editions Rupture, 1978.

Mitterrand, François. *Politique*. Paris: Fayard, 1977.

———. *Politique 2 (1977–1981)*. Paris: Fayard, 1981.

———. *Présence française et abandon*. Paris: Plon, 1957.

———. *Réflexions sur la politique extérieure de la France: Introduction à vingt-cinq discours (1981–1985)*. Paris: Fayard, 1986.

———. *The Wheat and the Chaff*. Translated by Helen R. Lane and Concilia Hayter. New York: Seaver/Lattès, 1982.

Moïsi, Dominique. "French Foreign Policy: The Challenge of Adaptation." *Foreign Affairs* 67 (fall 1988): 151–64.

Monego, Joan Phyllis. "Algerian Man in Search of Himself: A Study of the Recent Novels of Mohamed Dib." Ph.D. dissertation, Case Western Reserve University, 1975.

———. *Maghrebian Literature in French*. Boston: Twayne, 1984.

Monnerville, Gaston. *Vingt-deux ans de présidence*. Paris: Plon, 1980.

Montagne, D. J. *Avantages pour la France de coloniser la Régence d'Alger, avec indication d'une mode de colonisation; réfutation d'une brochure intitulée: Considérations sur la difficulté de coloniser la Régence d'Alger, et sur les résultats probables de cette colonisation, par M. A. [Maurice Allard]*. Paris: Delaunage; Ch. Vimont, 1831.

Moore, Clement Henry. "The Maghrib." In *History of Africa: Africa from c. 1940 to c. 1975*, vol. 8 of *The Cambridge History of Africa*, ed. Michael Crowder, 564–610. Cambridge: Cambridge University Press, 1984.

———. *Politics in North Africa: Algeria, Morocco, and Tunisia*. Boston: Little, Brown, 1970.

Morris-Jones, W. H., and Georges Fischer, eds. *Decolonisation and After: The British and French Experiences*. London: Frank Cass, 1980.

Morse, Edward A. *Foreign Policy and Interdependence in Gaullist France*. Princeton: Princeton University Press, 1973.

Mortimer, Mildred Palmer. "The Algerian Novel in French." Ph.D. dissertation, Columbia University, 1969.

———. *Journeys through the French African Novel*. Portsmouth, N.H.: Heinemann, 1990.

Mortimer, Robert A. "Algeria: The Dialectic of Elections and Violence." *Current History* 96 (May 1997): 231–35.

———. "Algeria and the Politics of International Economic Reform." *Orbis* 22 (fall 1977): 671–700.

———. "The Algerian Revolution in Search of an African Revolution." *Journal of Modern African Studies* 8, no. 3 (1970): 363–87.

———. "Algeria's New Sultan." *Current History* 80 (December 1981): 418–21.

———. "Development and Autonomy: The Algerian Approach." *TransAfrica Forum* 4, no. 2 (1987): 35–48.

———. "Foreign Policy and Its Role in Nation-Building in Algeria." Ph.D. dissertation, Columbia University, 1968.

———. "Islamists, Soldiers, and Democrats: The Second Algerian War." *MEJ* 50, no. 1 (winter 1996): 18–39.

———. "Maghreb Matters." *Foreign Policy,* no. 76 (1989): 160–175.

———. "The Politics of Reassurance in Algeria." *Current History* 84 (May 1985): 201–204, 228–29.

Mosley, Leonard. *Power Play: Oil in the Middle East.* New York: Random House, 1973.

Mouhoubi, Salah. *La Politique de coopération algéro-française: Bilan et perspectives.* Paris and Algiers: Publisud, 1986.

Mounier, Emmanuel. *Le Personnalisme.* Paris: PUF, 1971.

M'rabet, Fadéla. *Les Algériennes.* Paris: François Maspéro, 1967.

———. *La Femme algérienne.* Paris: François Maspéro, 1964.

Murcier, Alain. "L'Algérie condamnée au gaz!" *L'Expansion,* no. 126 (1979): 31, 34.

Naylor, Phillip C[hiviges]. "Algeria and France: The Post-Colonial Relationship." In *Proceedings of the Fifth Meeting of the French Colonial Historical Society* (Atlantic Beach, Fla., 1979), 58–69.

———. "Conflict and *Coopération:* French-Algerian Relations, 1962–78." Ph.D. dissertation, Marquette University, 1980.

———. "De Gaulle and Algeria: Historiography and the Decision of Decolonization." In *Proceedings of the Twentieth Meeting of the French Colonial Historical Society* (Cleveland, 1994), 136–47.

———. "France and the Western Sahara: Colonial and Postcolonial Intentions and Interventions." In *Proceedings of the Eleventh Meeting of the French Colonial Historical Society* (Quebec, 1985), 203–15.

——— (Phillip J.). "Frantz Fanon and French Colonialism." Master's essay, Marquette University, 1972.

———. "Maghrib Unity: Illusive or Elusive?" *Africana Journal* 15 (1990): 305–15.

———. "A Post-Colonial Decolonization: French-Algerian Hydrocarbon Relations, 1962–71." In *Proceedings of the Eighth Annual Meeting of the French Colonial Historical Society* (Evanston, Ill., 1982), 179–90.

————. "A Reconsideration of the Fourth Republic's Legacy and Algerian Decolonization." In *Proceedings of the Twenty-fourth Meeting of the French Colonial Historical Society* (Monterey, Cal., 1998), in press.

————. "Spain and France and the Decolonization of Western Sahara." *Africa Today* 34, no. 3 (1987): 7–16.

Naylor, Phillip C[hiviges], and Alf Andrew Heggoy. *Historical Dictionary of Algeria.* 2d ed. Metuchen, N.J.: Scarecrow Press, 1994.

Nazali, Ahmad. *Al-ʿAlaqat bayna al-Jazaʾir wa Faransa min ittifaqiyat I(v)ian ila taʾmim al-bitrul* (Relations between Algeria and France from the Evian Accords to the petroleum nationalization.) Cairo: al-Haiʾat al-misriyyat al-ʿammat lil-kitab, 1978.

Nellis, John R. *The Algerian National Charter of 1976: Content, Public Reaction, and Significance.* Papers in Contemporary Arab Studies. Washington: Georgetown University Press, 1980.

————. "Algerian Socialism and its Critics." *Canadian Journal of Political Science* 13 (September 1980): 481–507.

————. "Socialist Management in Algeria." *Journal of Modern African Studies* 15, no. 4 (1977): 529–54.

Nelson, Harold D., ed. *Algeria: A Country Study.* DA Pam 550-44. 3d and 4th eds. Washington: GPO, 1979, 1986.

"1962–1982." *Algérie informations,* hors série (July 1982).

Nora, Pierre. *Les Français d'Algérie.* Paris: Julliard, 1961.

Nouschi, André. "De la dépendance à l'indépendance? La France, le pétrole et les Algériens de 1956 à 1965." *Les Cahiers de Tunisie* 29, nos. 3–4 (1981): 345–66.

————. "Histoire des hydrocarbures gazeux." Paper presented at the "Journées d'études sur les Hydrocarbures gazeux et le Développement des pays producteurs," Université de Dijon, Institut des Relations internationales, 1973.

————. *La Naissance du nationalisme algérien.* Paris: Editions de Minuit, 1962.

Nyrop, Richard F., et al. *Area Handbook for Algeria.* DA Pam 550-44. 2d ed. Washington: GPO, 1972.

Nyssen, Hubert. *L'Algérie en 1970: Telle que je l'ai vue.* Paris: Arthaud, 1970.

O'Brien, Conor Cruise. *Albert Camus of Europe and Africa.* New York: Viking, 1970.

Odell, Peter R. *Oil and World Power.* New York: Penguin, 1979.

O'Donnell, J. Dean. *Lavigerie in Tunisia: The Interplay of Imperialist and Missionary.* Athens: University of Georgia Press, 1979.

Offredo, Jean. *Algérie: Avec ou sans la France.* Paris: Editions du Cerf, 1973.

Oizon, René. *L'Evolution récente de la production énergétique française.* Paris: Larousse, 1973.

"On les appelait les pieds-noirs." *L'Express* international edition, no. 1619 (1982).

Organization for Economic Cooperation and Development (OECD). *Develop-*

ment Co-operation: Efforts and Policies of the Members of the Development Assistance Committee. Paris: OECD, 1970–85.

————. *The Financial Flows to Less-developed Countries.* Paris: OECD, 1964.

————. *Investing in Developing Countries: OECD/DAC Member Countries' Policies and Facilities with Regard to Foreign Direct Investment in Developing Countries.* 5th ed. Paris: OECD, 1985.

————. *North Africa Oil and Gas.* Paris: OECD, 1997.

————. *Resources for the Developing World: The Flow of Financial Resources to Less-developed countries, 1962–1968.* Paris: OECD, 1970.

Ottaway, David, and Marina Ottaway. *Algeria: The Politics of a Socialist Revolution.* Berkeley and Los Angeles: University of California Press, 1970.

Ourabah, Mahmoud. *Les Transformations économiques de l'Algérie au 20ᵉ anniversaire de l'indépendance.* Paris: Publisud, 1982.

Palacio, Léo. *Les Pieds-noirs dans le monde.* Editions John Didier, 1968.

Parker, Richard B. "Appointment in Oujda." *Foreign Affairs* 63 (summer 1985): 1095–1110.

————. *North Africa: Regional Tensions and Strategic Concerns.* 2nd ed. New York: Praeger, 1987.

Passeron, André, ed. *De Gaulle parle, 1962–66.* Paris: Fayard, 1966.

Paul, Jim, and Nico Kielstra. "Algeria's Agrarian Revolution." *MERIP*, no. 67 (1978): 3–11.

Pautard, André. "Dix ans de relations franco-maghrébines." *RFEPA*, no. 63 (1971): 36–54.

————. *Valéry Giscard d'Estaing.* Paris: Editions Edipa, 1974.

Pauwels, Jean-Pierre. *Réflexions sur les nouvelles orientations économiques et énergétiques du Plan Quinquennal (1980–1984) et sur l'organisation de l'économie algérienne.* Algiers: ENAL, 1983.

Pazzanita, Anthony G., and Tony Hodges. *Historical Dictionary of Western Sahara.* 2d ed. Metuchen, N.J.: Scarecrow Press, 1994.

Pawera, John C. *Algeria's Infrastructure: An Economic Survey of Transportation, Communication, and Energy Resources.* New York: Praeger, 1964.

Péju, Paulette. *Les Harkis à Paris.* Paris: François Maspéro, 1961.

Peneff, Jean. *Industriels Algériens.* Paris: CNRS, 1981.

Pennington, M. Basil. "The Cistercian Martyrs of Algeria, 1996." *Review for Religious* 55, no. 6 (1996): 601–12.

Perkins, Kenneth J. "The Bureaux Arabes and the Colons." In *Proceedings of the French Colonial Historical Society* (Athens, Ga., 1975), 96–105.

Peroncel-Hugoz, J. P. "L'Enseignement en Algérie." *RFEPA*, no. 52 (1970): 21–34.

Perroux, François, comp. *L'Algérie de demain.* Paris: PUF, 1962.

Peyrefitte, Alain. *C'était de Gaulle.* 2 vols. Paris: Fayard, 1994, 1997.

————. *The Trouble with France.* Translated by William R. Byron. New York: Knopf, 1981.

Pfeiffer, Karen. *Agrarian Reform Under State Capitalism in Algeria*. Boulder, Colo.: Westview Press, 1985.

Philip, André. "Construire l'Algérie, à partir de la commune, comme il a été fait en Yougoslavie." *MTM*, no. 603 (1957): 1289–90, 1292.

Phillips, John. *Free Spirit in a Troubled World*. Zurich: Scolo, 1996.

Pickles, Dorothy M. *Algeria and France: From Colonialism to Cooperation*. New York: Praeger, 1963.

Pierre, Andrew J., and William B. Quandt. *The Algerian Crisis: Policy Options for the West*. Washington: Carnegie Endowment for International Peace, 1996.

Pigasse, Jean-Paul. "La France prisonnière du pétrole algérien?" *Entreprise*, no. 784 (1970): 130–37.

Piscatori, James P., ed. *Islam in the Political Process*. Cambridge: Cambridge University Press, 1983.

Plumyène, Jean, and Raymond Lasierra. *Les Fascismes français, 1923–1963*. Paris: Editions du Seuil, 1963.

Pompidou, Georges. *Entretiens et discours, 1968–1974*. 2 vols. Paris: Plon, 1975.

———. *Le Noeud gordien*. Paris: Plon, 1974.

"Pour un renouveau des relations entre la France et l'Algérie." *Parole et société* 85, no. 1 (1977).

Popular Front for the Liberation of Saguia el Hamra and Rio de Oro (Polisario). *Statement Intended to the President of the Twenty Four Members Committee on the Occasion of the Thirty First Session United Nations—1976*.

Pradier, Jean-Boisson. *L'Eglise et l'Algérie*. Paris: Etudes et Recherches historiques [1965?].

Price, David Lynn. *63: Western Sahara*. Georgetown Center for Strategic and International Studies. Beverly Hills: Sage Publications, 1979.

"Procès-verbal de la première session de la Commission mixte de coopération économique franco-algérienne." Stenciled report. CCCE, 1982.

Procès-verbaux et rapports de la commission nommée par le roi, le 7 juillet 1833, pour aller recueillir en Afrique tous les faits propres à éclairer le gouvernement sur l'état du pays et sur les mesures que réclame son avenir. Paris: Imprimerie royale, 1834.

Prochaska, David. "History as Literature, Literature as History: Cagayous of Algiers." *American Historical Review* 101, no. 3 (1996): 670–711.

———. *Making Algeria French: Colonialism in Bône, 1870–1920*. Cambridge: Cambridge University Press, 1990.

Provost, Lucile [pseud.]. *La Seconde Guerre d'Algérie: Le Quiproquo franco-algérien*. Paris: Flammarion, 1996.

Qaddash, Mahfuz. *Al-'Amir 'Abd al-Qadir fi thaqafat*. Algiers: Ministry of Information, 1982.

Quandt, William B. *Revolution and Political Leadership: Algeria, 1954–1968*. Cambridge: M.I.T. Press, 1969.

Rabinow, Paul, ed. *The Foucault Reader*. New York: Pantheon, 1984.

Raffinot, Marc, and Pierre Jacquemot. *Le Capitalisme d'état algérien*. Paris: François Maspéro, 1977.

Ramdani, Mohamed. "Les Relations franco-algériennes de 1965 à 1975 à travers le journal *Le Monde*." Master's thesis, Université de Lille III, 1980.

Rammal, Hussein. "L'Expérience algérienne de huit années d'aide étrangère: 1962–1970." Thesis, Université de Rennes, 1970.

Ray, Marie-Christine, comp. *Le Cardinal Duval: "Evêque en Algérie."* Paris: Centurion, 1984.

Recueils des traités et accords de la France. Paris: Imprimerie nationale, 1962–.

Reed, Lou. *Between Thought and Expression: Selected Lyrics of Lou Reed*. New York: Hyperion, 1991.

Reporters sans Frontières. *Le Drame algérien: Un peuple en otage*. Paris: La Découverte, 1995.

Revel, Jean-François. *The French*. Translated by Paula Spurlin. New York: George Braziller, 1966.

Ribourt, Colonel. *Le Gouvernement de l'Algérie de 1852 à 1858*. Paris: E. Panckoucke, 1859.

Rioux, Jean-Pierre. *The Fourth Republic, 1944–1958*. Translated by Godfrey Rogers. London: Cambridge University Press, 1987.

———, ed. *La Guerre d'Algérie et les Français*. Paris: Fayard, 1990.

Robarts, Richard. *French Development Assistance: A Study in Policy and Administration*. Beverly Hills: Sage Publications, 1974.

Robinson, Ronald, and John Gallagher. *Africa and the Victorians: The Official Mind of Imperialism*. London: Macmillan, 1961.

Romanet-Abdurahman, Nicole, and Christiane Lanz. "Le Français en Algérie: Situation actuelle et enseignement dans les lycées." Master's thesis, Université de Besançon, 1978.

Rondos, Alex. "Mitterrand's Two-Year Record." *Africa Report* 28, no. 3 (May–June 1983): 8–11.

Rondot, Jean. *La Compagnie Française des Pétroles: Du franc-or au pétrole franc*. Paris: Plon, 1962. Reprint, New York: Arno Press, 1977.

Ronsanvallon, A. "Les Aspects économiques de l'émigration algérienne." Thesis, Université de Grenoble, 1974.

Rorty, Richard. *Philosophy and the Mirror of Nature*. Princeton: Princeton University Press, 1980.

Rosenblum, Mort. *Mission to Civilize: The French Way*. New York: Harcourt Brace Jovanovich, 1987.

Ross, George, Stanley Hoffmann, and Sylvia Malzacher, eds. *The Mitterrand Experiment: Continuity and Change in Modern France*. New York: Oxford University Press, 1987.

Rouadjia, Ahmed. *Les Frères et la mosquée: Enquête sur le mouvement islamiste en Algérie*. Paris: Karthala, 1990.

———. *Grandeur et décadence de l'état algérien*. Paris: Karthala, 1994.

Roussel, Eric. *Le Cas Le Pen: Les Nouvelles Droites en France.* Paris: Jean-Claude Lattès, 1985.

———. *Georges Pompidou.* Paris: Jean-Claude Lattès, 1984.

Routier, Marcelle. *Derrière eux, le soleil.* Paris: Stock, 1974.

Roy, Jules. *The War in Algeria.* Translated by Richard Howard. Westport, Conn.: Greenwood Press, 1975.

Ruedy, John. *Modern Algeria: The Origins and Development of a Nation.* Bloomington: Indiana University Press, 1992.

———, ed. *Islamism and Secularism in North Africa.* New York: St. Martin's Press, 1994.

Ruf, Werner K., et al. *Indépendance et interdépendances au Maghreb.* Paris: CNRS, 1974.

———. *Introduction à l'Afrique du Nord contemporaine.* Paris: CNRS, 1975.

Ruzié, David. "La Coopération franco-algérienne." *Annuaire française du Droit international* 1963, 906–33.

Saadallah, Belkacem. "The Algerian Ulemas, 1919–1931." *Revue d'histoire maghrébine,* no. 2 (1974): 138–50.

———. (Aboul-Kassem). *La Montée du nationalisme en Algérie.* Translated by Nevine Fawzy-Hemiry. Algiers: ENAL, 1983.

———. "The Rise of the Algerian Elite, 1900–1914." *Journal of Modern African Studies* 5 (May 1967): 69–77.

———. "The Rise of Algerian Nationalism, 1900–1930." Ph.D. dissertation, University of Minnesota, 1965.

Sahli, Mohamed C. *Décoloniser l'histoire: Introduction à l'histoire du Maghreb.* Paris: François Maspéro, 1965.

Sahnoun, Mohamed. Interview by author. Washington, D.C., 9 January 1985.

Said, Edward W. *Culture and Imperialism.* New York: Knopf, 1993.

———. *Orientalism.* New York: Vintage, 1979.

Sampson, Anthony. *The Seven Sisters: The Great Oil Companies and the World They Shaped.* New York: Bantam Books, 1980.

Sanson, Henri. *Laicité islamique en Algérie.* Paris: CNRS, 1983.

Santini, Lucie. *Les Sacrifiés.* Salon-de-Provence: Imprimerie Isoard, 1973.

Sarraut, Albert. *Grandeur et servitude coloniale.* Paris: Editions du Sagittaire, 1931.

Schalk, David L. *War and the Ivory Tower: Algeria and Vietnam.* New York: Oxford University Press, 1991.

Schnetzler, Jacques. *Le Développement algérien.* Paris: Masson, 1981.

Schumann, Maurice. "La Politique française d'immigration." *RDN* 25 (June 1969): 933–40.

Schumpeter, Joseph A. *Imperialism and Social Classes.* Translated by Heinz Norden. New York: Meridian, 1960.

Sebbar, Leila. *Sherazade Missing: Aged 17, Dark Curly Hair, Green Eyes.* Translated by Dorothy S. Blair. London: Quartet, 1991.

Sécretariat d'état auprès du premier ministre chargé des Affaires algériennes, and Ministère de l'Education nationale. *L'Enseignant français en Algérie.* 1963.

Secrétariat social d'Alger. *Construire la cité: l'Algérie et sa jeunesse.* Algiers: Editions du Secrétariat social d'Alger, 1957.

————. *La Lutte des Algériens contre la faim.* Algiers: Editions du Secrétariat social d'Alger, 1955.

————. *Recherches d'identité: Essai sur la quête de soi en Algérie.* Algiers: SNED, 1972.

————. *Le Sous-Développement en Algérie.* Algiers: Secrétariat social d'Alger, 1959.

Sehimi, Mustapha. "Où en est la coopération algéro-française?" *RA,* no. 351 (1970): 1–16.

Serfaty, Simon, ed. *The Foreign Policies of the French Left.* Boulder, Colo.: Westview Press, 1979.

Shah-Kazemi, Reza, ed. *Algeria: Revolution Revisited.* London: Islamic World Report, 1997.

Shepard, William E. "Islam and Ideology: Towards a Typology." *International Journal of Middle East Studies* 19 (August 1987): 307–36.

Siblot, Paul. "Retours à 'l'Algérie heureuse,' ou les mille et un détours de la nostalgie." *Revue de l'Occident musulman et méditerranéen,* no. 37 (1984): 151–64.

Siegfreid, André. *France: A Study in Nationality.* New Haven: Yale University Press, 1930.

Simmons, Harvey G. *The French National Front: The Extremist Challenge to Democracy.* Boulder, Colo.: Westview Press, 1996.

Sipe, Lynn. *Western Sahara: A Comprehensive Bibliography.* New York: Garland, 1982.

Smith, Tony. *The French Stake in Algeria, 1945–1962.* Ithaca, New York: Cornell University Press, 1978.

————. "The Political and Economic Ambitions of Algerian Land Reform, 1962–1974." *MEJ* 29 (summer 1975): 259–78.

Société nationale pour la recherche, la production, le transport, la transformation et la commercialisation des hydrocarbures (SONATRACH). *The Algerian Oil Policy: Events—Studies—Declarations, 1965–1972.* 2 vols. Algiers: SONATRACH, 1972.

————. *The Algerian Oil Policy: President Houari Boumediene's Speeches (1965–1972).* Algiers: SONATRACH, 1972.

————. *Background Information on the Relationship Between Algeria and the French Oil Companies.* Algiers: SONATRACH, 1971.

————. *Hydrocarbons in Algeria: The 1971 Agreements.* Algiers: SONATRACH, 1972.

Solinas, PierNico, ed. *Gillo Pontecorvo's "The Battle of Algiers," A Film Written by Franco Solinas.* New York: Charles Scribner's Sons, 1973.

Soustelle, Jacques. *Aimée et souffrante Algérie*. Paris: Plon, 1956.

——. *Le Drame algérien et la décadence française: Réponse à Raymond Aron*. Paris: Plon, 1957.

——. "The Wealth of the Sahara." *Foreign Affairs* 37 (July 1959): 626–36.

Stern, Jonathan P. *International Gas Trade in Europe: The Policies of Exporting and Importing Countries*. London: Heinemann, 1984.

Stobaugh, Robert B. "The Oil Companies in the Crisis." *Daedelus* 104 (fall 1975): 171–202.

Stone, Martin. *The Agony of Algeria*. New York: Columbia University Press, 1997.

Stora, Benjamin. *L'Algérie en 1995: La Guerre, l'histoire, la politique*. Paris: Editions Michalon, 1995.

——. *La Gangrène et l'oubli: La Mémoire de la guerre de l'Algérie*. Paris: La Découverte, 1992.

——. *L'Histoire de l'Algérie depuis l'Indépendance*. Paris: La Découverte, 1994.

——. *Ils venaient d'Algérie: L'Immigration algérienne en France, 1912–1992*. Paris: Fayard, 1992.

——. *Messali Hadj, 1898–1974*. Paris: Sycomore, 1982.

——. *Les Sources du nationalisme algérien: Parcours idéologiques; origines des acteurs*. Paris: L'Harmattan, 1989.

Stora, Fernande. *L'Algérie pour mémoire*. Paris: Guy Authier, 1978.

Stork, Joe. *Middle East Oil and the Energy Crisis*. New York: Monthly Review Press, 1975.

"The Struggle for the Sahara." *MERIP*, no. 45 (1976).

Sulzberger, C. L. *The Test: De Gaulle and Algeria*. New York: Harcourt, Brace & World, 1962.

Suret-Canale, Jean. "L'Algérie d'aujourd'hui: Le Développement d'une nation indépendante." *Cahiers d'histoire de l'Institut Maurice Thorez*, nos. 12–13 (1975): 58–65.

A Survey of Algeria. Paris: Service de propagande, d'édition et d'information, 1956.

Tadjer, Akli. *Les ANI du "Tassili"*. Paris: Editions du Seuil, 1984.

Tahi, Mohand Sahi. "Algeria's Presidential Election: The Rejection of Compromise." *Journal of North African Studies* 1, no. 3 (winter 1996): 279–305.

Talbott, John. *The War Without a Name: France in Algeria, 1954–1962*. New York: Knopf, 1980.

Taleb Ibrahimi, Ahmed. *De la décolonisation à la révolution culturelle (1962–1972)*. Algiers: SNED, 1973.

Talha, Larbi, et al. *Maghrébins en France: Emigrés ou immigrés?* Paris: CNRS, 1983.

——. *Les stratégies des matières premières au Maghreb*. Paris: CNRS, 1976.

Tamba, Said. *Kateb Yacine*. Paris: Seghers, 1992.

Tcheho, Isaac Celestin. "The Novel and Identity in Algeria: A Study of the Works of Mohammed Dib, Mouloud Feraoun and Kateb Yacine (1950–1966)." Master's thesis, University of Yaoundé, 1980.

Temmar, Hamid. *Structures et modèle de développement de l'économie de l'Algérie.* Algiers: SNED, 1974.

Terrenoire, Louis. *De Gaulle et l'Algérie: Témoignage pour l'histoire.* Paris: Fayard, 1964.

Texts of Declarations Drawn up in Common Agreement at Evian, March 18, 1962, by the Delegations of the Government of the French Republic and the Algerian National Liberation Front. New York: Ambassade de France, Service de presse et d'information, n.d. [1962?].

Tiano, André. *Le Maghreb entre les mythes: L'Economie nord-africaine depuis l'indépendance.* Paris: PUF, 1967.

Tillion, Germaine. *Algeria: The Realities.* Translated by Ronald Matthews. New York: Knopf, 1958.

———. *France and Algeria: Complementary Enemies.* Translated by Richard Howard. New York: Knopf, 1961.

Tivec, André. *Bab el Oued, mon quartier: Figé dans sa mort.* Paris: Pensée universelle, 1975.

Tlemcani, Rachid. *State and Revolution in Algeria.* Boulder, Colo.: Westview Press, 1986.

Torti, Marcel. "Evian: Défaillance de la contrepartie." *Revue politique et parlementaire,* no. 734 (1963): 30–42.

Touati, Fettouma. *Le Printemps désespéré: Vies d'Algériennes.* Paris: L'Harmattan, 1984.

Trebous, Madeleine. *Vie et travail des Algériens en France.* Paris: Editions du Jour, 1974.

Tricot, Bernard. Interview by author. Paris, 6 June 1984.

———. *Mémoires.* Paris: Quai Voltaire, 1994.

———. *Les Sentiers de la paix: Algérie, 1958–1962.* Paris: Plon, 1972.

Tricot, Bernard, et al. *De Gaulle et le service de l'état.* Paris: Plon, 1977.

Turin, Yvonne. *Affrontements culturels dans l'Algérie coloniale: Ecoles, médecines, religion, 1830–1880.* Paris: François Maspéro, 1971.

Valberg, Pascal. "Cinq ans après: Bilan des accords franco-algériens de coopération industrielle et pétrolière du 29 juillet 1965." *AAN* 1969, 55–91.

Vatin, Jean-Claude. *L'Algérie politique: Histoire et société.* Paris: Presses de la Fondation Nationale des Sciences Politiques, 1983.

———, ed. "Eléments pour une bibliographie d'ensemble sur l'Algérie d'aujourd'hui." *RASJEP* 5 (March 1968): 167–278.

Védrine, Hubert. *Les Mondes de François Mitterrand: A l'Elysée, 1981–1995.* Paris: Fayard, 1996.

Verlet, Martin, ed. *Coopérer avec l'Algérie: Convergences et solidarités.* Paris: Publisud, 1995.

Veyne, Paul. *Comment on écrit l'histoire[;] Foucault révolutionne l'histoire.* Paris: Editions du Seuil, 1978.

Viansson-Ponté, Pierre. *Histoire de la République gaullienne.* 3 vols. Paris: Fayard, 1971.

Vilain, Michel. *La Politique de l'énergie en France.* Paris: Cujas, 1969.

"Vingt ans d'indépendance: L'Espace d'une génération." *Afrique-Asie,* no. 270 (1982).

Viollette, Maurice. *L'Algérie vivra-t-elle? Notes d'un ancien gouverneur général.* Paris: Félix Alcan, 1931.

Viorst, Milton. "The Muslims of France." *Foreign Affairs* 75 (September–October 1996): 78–96.

Viratelle, Gérard. *L'Algérie algérienne.* Paris: Editions économie et humanisme, 1973.

Wansbrough, John. "The Decolonization of North African History." *Journal of African History* 9 (winter 1968): 643–50.

Weinstein, Brian. "The Western Sahara." *Current History* 79 (March 1980): 110–14, 136–37.

Werth, Alexander. *The Strange History of Pierre Mendès-France and the Great Conflict over French North Africa.* London: Barrie Books, 1957.

Whitman, Kaye. "President Mitterrand and Africa." *African Affairs* 82 (July 1983): 329–43.

Williams, Philip M., and Martin Harrison. *Politics and Society in de Gaulle's Republic.* Garden City, N.Y.: Doubleday, 1972.

Willis, F. Roy. *The French Paradox: Understanding Contemporary France.* Stanford: Hoover Institution, 1982.

Willis, Michael. *The Islamist Challenge in Algeria.* New York: New York University Press, 1996.

Wolf, John B. *The Barbary Coast: Algiers under the Turks, 1500–1830.* New York: Norton, 1979.

Wolff, J. "Le Budget de l'Algérie de 1959 à 1965." *Revue de science financière,* no. 2 (1967): 209–46.

Wright, Robin. *Sacred Rage: The Wrath of Militant Islam.* New York: Simon & Schuster, 1986.

Yacine, Kateb. *Le Cercle des représailles.* Paris: Editions du Seuil, 1959.

———. *Nedjma.* Paris: Editions du Seuil, 1956.

———. *Le Poète comme un boxeur: Entretiens 1958–1989.* Compiled by Gilles Carpentier. Paris: Editions du Seuil, 1994.

Yacono, Xavier. *Les Etapes de la décolonisation française.* Paris: PUF, 1975.

———. *Histoire de la colonisation française.* Paris: PUF, 1973.

Yergin, Daniel. *The Prize: The Epic Quest for Oil, Money, and Power.* New York: Simon & Schuster, 1991.

Zagoria, Janet D. "The Rise and Fall of the Movement of Messali Hadj in Algeria, 1924–54." Ph.D. dissertation, Columbia University, 1973.

Zahar, Renate. *Frantz Fanon, Colonialism and Alienation: Concerning Frantz Fanon's Political Theory.* Translated by Willfried F. Feuser. New York: Monthly Review Press, 1974.

Zaimeche, Salah E., and Keith Sutton. "Persistent Strong Population Growth, Environmental Degradation, and Declining Food Self-Sufficiency in a Rentier Oil State: Algeria." *Journal of North African Studies* 3, no. 1 (spring 1998): 57–73.

Zartman, I. William. "Les Relations entre la France et l'Algérie depuis les accords d'Evian." *Revue française de science politique* 6 (December 1964): 1087–1113.

———, ed. *Man, State, and Society in the Contemporary Maghreb.* New York: Praeger, 1973.

Zehraoui, Ahsène. *Les Travailleurs algériens en France: Etude sociologique de quelques aspects de la vie familiale.* Paris: François Maspéro, 1971.

Zeldin, Theodore. *The French.* New York: Vintage, 1984.

Zeller, Adrien. "Le Problème du vin: Une solution de coopération algéro-française." *Développement et civilisations,* no. 33 (1968): 26–41.

Zoubir, Yahia H. "The Algerian Political Crisis: Origins and Prospects for the Future of Democracy." *Journal of North African Studies* 3, no. 1 (spring 1998): 74–100.

Zoubir, Yahia, and Daniel Volman, eds. *International Dimensions of the Western Saharan Conflict.* Westport, Conn.: Praeger, 1992.

Index

Armée de Libération Nationale (ALN), 41,
54, 72, 232, 249, 295n.41, 298n.107,
324n.159, 361n.124, 366n.63, 381n.44.
See also Front de Libération Nationale
(FLN)
Armée Islamique du Salut (AIS), 210, 212,
220, 234–35, 366n.75, 369n.123; decla-
ration of war on France, 214; on
Sant'Egidio, 218; truce and cease-fire of,
240. *See also fitna*; Front Islamique du
Salut (FIS); Groupe Islamique Armé
(GIA)
Armée Nationale Populaire (ANP), 72,
324n.158
Aron, Raymond, 52, 110, 297n.73
Arthur D. Little, 90, 341n.104
al-Asala (Authenticity), 105–6, 159
Aslaoui, Leïla, 210, 368n.101
association, between Algeria and France,
21–22, 24–25, 31, 33–34
Association Coopérative (ASCOOP), 76,
92, 262, 333n.104. *See also* Algiers Ac-
cords; SONATRACH
Association Coup de Soleil, 266
Association Espace Intégration de Lille,
184
Association France-Algérie, 127, 342n.134,
385n.133
Association Généologique d'Afrique du
Nord, 266
Association Nationale des Français
d'Afrique du Nord (ANFANOMA),
310n.108, 344–45n.161, 382n.46
Association of Reformist Ulama, 9–10, 177
Atlantic Richfield. *See* ARCO
Attaf, Ahmed, 231, 233, 236–38, 375n.93;
on French economic relationship, 246
Attali, Jacques, 240
Audibert, Jean, 185, 246
Augustine, Saint, 231
autogestion, 20, 71, 76, 318nn.75, 82; imple-
mentation of, 56–57, 317–18n.70; French
reaction to, 57. *See also* agriculture
Awlad Sidi Shaykh Rebellion (1864), 6
Azeggagh, Ahmed, 277
Aznavour, Charles, 240

Baker, James, 363n.17
Baldwin, Hanson, 19
Balladur, Edouard, 186, 203, 210, 366n.76;
becomes prime minister, 201; and Air
France hijacking, 214; on Mitterrand's
European Union proposal, 222; presiden-
tial campaign of, 223
Balta, Paul, 113
Balzac, Honoré de, 17
Bandung Conference, 27, 72
Banque Algérien de Development (BAD), 80
Banque Nationale de Paris, 171
barbouzes, 33
Baréty, Leon, 16
barrage vert, 335n.6
Barre, Raymond, 139, 196, 340n.76; on
emigrant repatriations, 117
Barricades Week (January 1960), 25
Barthes, Roland, 261, 281, 285, 291n.2,
380–81n.25
Basdevant, Jean, 86, 317n.54, 329n.56
Bastien-Thiry, (Colonel) Jean-Marie,
312n.123
Battle of Algiers (1956–1957). *See* Algiers;
War of Independence
Battle of Gas. *See* hydrocarbons
Battle of Petroleum. *See* hydrocarbons
Batty, Peter, 274
Bauchard, Denis, 373n.70
Bechtel, 121, 247
Beck, Djaafer, 23
Beckett, Paul A., 381n.31
Bedjaoui, Mohammed, 96, 124; on coopera-
tion, 315n.34
Begag, Azouz, 156, 270; on December 1991
elections and emigrant community, 184
Belaid, Abdel Aziz, 238
Belhadj (Benhadj), Ali, 166, 184, 212–13,
220, 355n.8, 366n.64, 370n.8, 376n.133;
and formation of FIS, 169; on France,
178; French impression of, 179; arrest
(June 1990) of, 183; sentencing of, 197;
transfer to house arrest of, 205; on
Sant'Egidio, 219. *See also* Front
Islamique du Salut (FIS)
Belheimer, Ammar, 287

Phillip C. Naylor is an associate professor of history at Marquette University and the director of the Western Civilization Program. He coedited, with John P. Entelis, *State and Society in Algeria* (1992) and coauthored, with Alf Andrew Heggoy, the second edition of *The Historical Dictionary of Algeria* (1994).